INTERPRETATION OF COMMERCIAL CONTRACTS
IN EUROPEAN PRIVATE LAW

This book is sponsored by Banca Intesa Sanpaolo.

INTERPRETATION OF COMMERCIAL CONTRACTS IN EUROPEAN PRIVATE LAW

Edited by
Jaap Baaij
David Cabrelli
Laura Macgregor

INTERSENTIA
Cambridge – Antwerp – Chicago

Intersentia Ltd
8 Wellington Mews
Wellington Street | Cambridge
CB1 1HW | United Kingdom
Tel: +44 1223 736 170
Email: mail@intersentia.co.uk
www.intersentia.com | www.intersentia.co.uk

Distribution for the UK and
Rest of the World (incl. Eastern Europe)
NBN International
1 Deltic Avenue, Rooksley
Milton Keynes MK13 8LD
United Kingdom
Tel: +44 1752 202 301 | Fax: +44 1752 202 331
Email: orders@nbninternational.com

Distribution for Europe
Lefebvre Sarrut Belgium NV
Hoogstraat 139/6
1000 Brussels
Belgium
Tel: +32 (0)800 39 067
Email: mail@intersentia.be

Distribution for the USA and Canada
Independent Publishers Group
Order Department
814 North Franklin Street
Chicago, IL 60610
USA
Tel: +1 800 888 4741 (toll free) | Fax: +1 312 337 5985
Email: orders@ipgbook.com

Interpretation of Commercial Contracts in European Private Law

ISBN 978-1-78068-959-3
D/2020/7849/69
NUR 822

British Library Cataloguing in Publication Data. A catalogue record for this book is available from the British Library.

GENERAL EDITORS' PREFACE

It is a special pleasure to welcome the 18th book in the series The Common Core of European Private Law, the first published by Intersentia. This book is edited by three scholars, who together represent two different legal cultures: the Dutch and the Scottish. Their works are already renowned and appreciated well beyond the 'Common Core' circles.

The Common Core project was launched in 1993 at the University of Trento under the auspices of the late Professor Rudolf B. Schlesinger. The methodology used in the Common Core project, then novel, is now a classic. By making use of case studies, it goes beyond mere description to detailed inquiry into how most European Union legal systems resolve specific legal questions in practice, and to thorough comparisons between those systems. It is our hope that these volumes will provide scholars with a valuable tool for research in comparative law and in their own national legal systems. The collection of materials that the Common Core project is offering to the scholarly community is already quite extensive and will become even more so as more volumes are published. The availability of materials attempting a genuine analysis of how things seem to be is, in our opinion, a prerequisite for an intelligent and critical discussion on how they should be. Perhaps in the future European private law will be authoritatively restated or even codified. As of today, the Common Core project is the longest-running scholarly enterprise in the field. The analytical work carried out by the more than 300 scholars that have so far joined us in the Common Core project is also a precious asset of knowledge and legitimisation for any such a normative enterprise.

We must thank the editors and contributors for their work. With a sense of deep gratitude, we also wish to recall our late Honorary Editor, Professor Rudolf B. Schlesinger. We are sad that we have not been able to present him with the results of a project in which he believed so firmly.

No scholarly project can survive without committed sponsors. The International University College of Turin allows us to organise the General Meetings together with the Centro Studi di Diritto Comparato of Trieste. The European Commission has partially sponsored some of our past General Meetings, having included them in their High Level Conferences Program. The Italian Ministry of Scientific Research, the University of Turin, the University of Trieste, the University of Salento, the University of Gothenburg, the Fromm Chair in International and Comparative Law at the University of California and the Hastings College of Law, the University of Trento, the Collegio Carlo Alberto and the Consiglio Nazionale del Notariato all contributed to, or are still contributing to, the funding of this Project. Last but not least, we must thank all those involved in our ongoing Common Core projects in contract law, property, tort and other areas, whose results will be the subject of future published volumes.

Our website home page can be found at www.common-core.org. There you can follow our progress in mapping the common core of European private law.

General Editors

Mauro Bussani, University of Trieste – University of Macao
Ugo Mattei, University of Turin – University of California, Hastings College of Law

Honorary Editor

Rudolfo Sacco, Emeritus, University of Turin

Late Honorary Editor

Rudolf B. Schlesinger, Cornell University – University of California, Hastings College of Law

ACKNOWLEDGEMENTS

The editors would like to thank a number of people without whose efforts this book would not have been possible. Our thanks go to the national reporters for all their hard work, including engaging in discussions with the editors to design the scenarios, and for producing such thoughtful and well-referenced reports. We are grateful to Professor Aurelia Colombi Ciacchi, Head of the Contract Group within The Common Core of European Private Law, for providing us with support and encouragement. Her cheerful attitude and willingness to help supported us throughout the process. We would also like to thank all at Intersentia, particularly Ann-Christin Maak-Scherpe and Rebecca Moffat. Their meticulous attention to detail and useful suggestions have significantly enhanced our work. As the Common Core Project passes its 25th anniversary, we provide all good wishes for the future.

Jaap Baaij
David Cabrelli
Laura Macgregor

CONTENTS

LIST OF CASES

CROATIA

ENGLAND AND WALES

FINLAND

FRANCE

GERMANY

GREECE

ITALY

PORTUGAL

SCOTLAND

SOUTH AFRICA

SPAIN[1]

[1] Every decision of the Supreme Court comes from the 'Sala Primera' (First Section), i.e. the Civil Section.

SWEDEN

OTHER

AUSTRALIA

EUROPEAN UNION

LIST OF LEGISLATION

INTERNATIONAL SOURCES OF LAW

EUROPEAN UNION SOURCES OF LAW

CROATIA

ENGLAND AND WALES

FINLAND

FRANCE

GERMANY

GREECE

ITALY

NETHERLANDS

POLAND

PORTUGAL

SCOTLAND

SPAIN

SWEDEN

LIST OF ABBREVIATIONS

A	Appellate Division
AC	Appeal Cases (UK)
AC (HL)	Appeal Cases, House of Lords (UK)
AD	Appellate Division (1910–1946)
AJA	Acting Judge of Appeal
All ER	All England Law Reports (England and Wales)
All SA	All South African Law Reports
AP	Άρειος Πάγος (Greek Supreme Court)
ArchNom	Archeion Nomologias (Αρχείο Νομολογίας; Greek law journal)
Arm	Armenopoulos (Αρμενόπουλος; Greek law journal)
Art(s).	article(s)
B & Ad	Barnewall & Adolphus (England and Wales)
B2B	Business-to-business
B2C	Business-to-consumer
BGB	Bürgerliches Gesetzbuch [Civil Code] (Germany)
BLR	Building Law Reports (UK)
Bpk	Beperk [Limited]
Bull. civ.	Bulletin civil
BW	Burgerlijk Wetboek (Netherlands)
C	Cape Provincial Division (South Africa)
CA	Cour d'appel [Court of Appeal] (France)
CA	Appellate Court [Εφετείο] (Greece)
CAO	Collectieve arbiedsovereenkomst [collective employment contract]
CC	Civil Code (Greece, Portugal, Spain)
CC	Close Corporation (South Africa)
c.c.	Codice civile [Civil Code] (Italy)
cca.	Circa (approximately; about)
Cciv	Code civil [Civil Code] (France)
Ccom	Code de commerce [Commercial Code] (France)
CCom	Código de Comercio [Code of Commerce] (Spain)
CESL	Common European Sales Law

Ch D	Law Reports, Chancery Division (England and Wales)
Ch. réun.	Chambres réunies de la Cour de cassation (France)
ChrID	Chronika Idiotikou Dikaiou (Χρονικά Ιδιωτικού Δικαίου; Greek law journal) (Greece)
CISG	United Nations Convention on Contracts for the International Sale of Goods
Civ.	Chambre civile de la Cour de cassation (France)
CJ	Colectânea de Jurisprudência (Portugal)
CK	Sign indicating division of court (Poland)
CLR	Commonwealth Law Reports
COA	Civil Obligations Act (Croatia)
COJ	Code de l'organisation judicaire [Code of the Judicial Organisation] (France)
Com.	Chambre commerciale de la Cour de cassation (France)
CPC	Code of Civil Procedure (Greece)
CSIH	Court of Session – Inner House (Scotland)
CSK	Sign indicating division of court (Poland)
CSOH	Court of Session – Outer House (Scotland)
CZP	Sign indicating division of court (Poland)
D.	Recueil Dalloz (France)
DCFR	Draft Common Frame of Reference
DEE	Dikaio Epiheiriseon kai Etairion (Δίκαιο Επιχειρήσεων και Εταιριών; Greek law journal)
Dike	Dike (Δίκη; Greek law journal)
DP	Deputy President (of the Supreme Court of Appeal)
ed(s).	Editor(s)
edn	Edition
EDPol	Epitheorisi Dikaiou Polykatoikias (Επιθεώρηση Δικαίου Πολυκατοικίας; Greek law journal)
EEmpD	Epitheorisi Emporikou Dikaiou (Επιθεώρηση Εμπορικού Δικαίου; Greek law journal)
EEN	Efimeris Ellinon Nomikon (Εφημερίς Ελλήνων Νομικών; Greek law journal)
EllD	Elliniki Dikeosyni (Ελληνική Δικαιοσύνη; Greek law journal)
EPolD	Epitheorisi Politikis Dikonomias (Επιθεώρηση Πολιτικής Δικονομίας; Greek law journal)
ER	English Reports
EU	European Union
EWCA Civ	England and Wales Court of Appeal, Civil Cases
EWHC (Ch)	England and Wales High Court, Chancery Division Cases
EWHC (Comm)	England and Wales High Court, Commercial Cases

EWHC (Pat)	England and Wales High Court, Patent Cases
EWHC (QB)	England and Wales High Court, Queen's Bench Division Cases
F	Fraser's Session Cases (Scotland)
Fasc.	Fascicule [booklet] (France)
GAJC	Les grands arrêts de la jurisprudence civile (France)
GGI	Government Gazette Issue (Φύλλο Εφημερίδας Κυβερνήσεως) (Greece)
GP	Gazette du Palais (France)
GSJ	South Gauteng High Court, Johannesburg
GTC	General Terms and Conditions
GWD	Green's Weekly Digest
HGB	Handelsgesetzbuch [German Commercial Code] (Germany)
HL	House of Lords (UK)
Hous LR	Housing Law Review (UK)
IA	International Agreements
Inc.	Incorporated
Isocrates	Law database of the Athens Bar Association
JA	Judge of Appeal
JAR	Jurisprudentie arbiedsrecht (Netherlands)
JCl. Civil Code	Juris-classeur Civil Code (France)
JCP G	Juris-Classeur périodique (Semaine juridique), édition générale (France)
JDI	Journal du droit international (France)
JOR	Jurisprudentie ondernemingsrecht (Netherlands)
KB	Law Reports, King's Bench Division Cases (England and Wales)
KC	Kodeks Cywilny [Polish Civil Code]
KKO	Korkein oikeus (Supreme Court of Finland)
KM	Komitean mietintö (committee report) (Finland)
KZP	KwaZulu-Natal High Court, Pietermaritzburg (South Africa)
LEC	Ley de Enjuiciamiento Civil [Civil Procedure Act] (Spain)
LGCGC	Ley General de Condiciones, Generales de la Contratación [Standard Contracts Act] (Spain)
Lloyd's Law Rep	Lloyd's Law Reports (England and Wales)
Lloyd's Law Rep (CA)	Lloyd's Law Reports, Court of Appeal Cases (England and Wales)
LR Eq	Law Reports, Equity Cases (England and Wales)
m.n.	Margin number
n(n).	(foot)note(s)

N	Natal Provincial Division (South Africa)
NJ	Nederlandse Jurisprudentie (Netherlands)
NJA	Nytt juridiskt arkiv I (Sweden)
NN	Narodne novine (Croatia)
NO/NNO	nomine officio/nomine officii [in the name of office] (South Africa)
no(s).	number(s)
NOMOS	Greek law database
NoV	Nomiko Vima (Νομικό Βήμα; Greek law journal)
NSWCA	New South Wales Court of Appeal (Australia)
NSWLR	New South Wales Law Reports (Australia)
OG	Official Gazette
OJ	Official Journal
para(s).	Paragraph(s)
PC	Privy Council (Commonwealth and UK Overseas Territories)
PD	Presidential Decree (Προεδρικό Διάταγμα) (Greece)
PD	Law Reports, Probate, Divorce and Admiralty Division (Scotland)
PECL	Principles of European Contract Law
PPH	Przegląd Prawa Handlowego [Commercial Law Review] (Poland)
PS	Privredni sud [Commercial Court] (prior to 1991) (Croatia)
(Pty) Ltd	(Proprietary) Limited
QBD	Law Reports, Queen's Bench Division Cases (England and Wales)
R	Rettie's Session Cases (Scotland)
R (HL)	Rettie's Reports, House of Lords (Scotland)
RCb	Tribunal da Relação de Coimbra (Portugal)
RCR	Rechtspraak contractenrecht (Netherlands)
RDC	Revue des contrats (France)
Req.	Chambre des requêtes de la Cour de cassation (France)
rev.	Revised
RH	Republic of Croatia
RJ	Repertorio Jurisprudencia Aranzadi (Spain)
RLx	Tribunal da Relação de Lisboa (Portugal)
RTDCiv	Revue trimestrielle de droit civil (France)
Rv	Wetboek van Burgerlijk Rechstvordering (Netherlands)
RvdW	Rechtspraak van de Week (Netherlands)
S.	Recueil Sirey (France)
SA	South African Law Reports
SC	Session Cases (Scotland)

SC (HL)	Session Cases, House of Lords (Scotland)
SC (UKSC)	Session Cases, United Kingdom Supreme Court (Scotland)
SCA	Supreme Court of Appeal (South Africa)
(S)CFI	(Single-member) Court of First Instance ((Μονομελές) Πρωτοδικείο) (Greece)
SCLR	Scottish Civil Law Reports
SE	South Eastern Cape Local Division (South Africa)
SFRY	Socialistic Federative Republic of Yugoslavia
SLT	Scots Law Times
SLT (Notes)	Scots Law Times, Notes of Decisions
SN	Sąd Najwyższy [Supreme Court of Poland]
SOU	Statens offentliga utredningar (Sweden)
STJ	Supremo Tribunal de Justiça [Supreme Civil Court] (Portugal)
STS	Sentencia del Tribunal Supremo [Supreme Court Decision] (Spain)
T/TPD	Transvaal Provincial Division
t/a	trading as
TS	Trgovački sud [Commercial Court] (Croatia)
TS	Tribunal Supremo [Supreme Court] (Spain)
UKSC	United Kingdom Supreme Court
US	Upravni sud [Administrative Court] (Croatia)
USRH	Ustavni sud Republike Hrvatske [Constitutional Court of the Republic of Croatia]
vol.	Volume
VSRH	Vrhovni sud Republike Hrvatske [Supreme Court of the Republic of Croatia]
VTSRH	Visoki trgovački sud Republike Hrvatske [High Commercial Court of the Republic of Croatia]
W	Witwatersrand Local Division
W & S	Wilson & Shaw, House of Lords, Appeal Cases (Scotland)
WCC	Western Cape High Court, Cape Town (South Africa)
WLD	Witwatersrand (Transvaal) Local Division (South Africa)
WLR	Weekly Law Reports (England and Wales)
WLR (HL)	Weekly Law Reports, House of Lords Cases (England and Wales)
WLR (PC)	Weekly Law Reports, Privy Council (Commonwealth and UK Overseas Territories)
ZASCA	South Africa: Supreme Court of Appeal (judgmentsonline)
ZPO	Zivilprozessordnung [Code of Civil Procedure] (Germany)

LIST OF CONTRIBUTORS*

C.J.W. (Jaap) Baaij
Jaap Baaij is Assistant Professor at Leiden Law School. In 2018, Jaap obtained a doctorate degree at Yale Law School on contract law and commercial arbitration and a PhD degree, cum laude, at Amsterdam Law School on linguistic diversity and legal harmonisation in the European Union. Previously, he was Assistant Professor of Private Law at Amsterdam Law School and Visiting Scholar at Columbia Law School and the National University of Singapore Faculty of Law. He was also a guest lecturer at various universities in Europe and the United States, including London School of Economics, Yale Law School, and Princeton University. Jaap's publications include, among others, articles in the *Harvard International Law Journal* and *King's Law Journal*, and books with Oxford University Press and Kluwer Law International.

David Cabrelli (Scotland)
David Cabrelli is Professor of Labour Law at the Law School, University of Edinburgh, with teaching and research interests which lie in the fields of labour law and employment law, as well as commercial law, company law and private law. David has published a number of books and papers in a number of academic journals in the field of labour law, for example a leading textbook on employment law (now in its fourth edition), as well as a book on comparative company law (now in its second edition). His articles have been cited with approval by Lords Hope, Wilson and Sumption in the UK Supreme Court, and various other articles published by David have been cited by the Federal Court of Australia, the Supreme Court of South Australia, the Hong Kong High Court, the Law Commission of England and Wales and the Scottish Law Commission.

Laura Macgregor (Scotland)
Laura Macgregor is Professor of Scots Law at the Law School, University of Edinburgh. A qualified solicitor, she spent five years practising law with a large commercial firm in Edinburgh before joining academia. Her interests lie broadly in the area of commercial contract law, and specifically agency and partnership contracts. She is particularly interested in comparative law. She is the author of *The Law of Agency in Scotland* (2013) and, most recently, 'Empire, Trade and the Use of Agents in the Nineteenth Century: the "Reception" of the Undisclosed

* The country reported on is shown in brackets after the contributor's name.

Principal Rule in the law of Louisiana and Scotland' (2019) *Louisiana Law Review* 985. She is currently working on a book on partnership law for the Scottish Universities Law Institute Series.

Katharina Erler (Germany)
Katharina Erler Dipl.-Jur. is Research and Teaching Fellow at the University of Bayreuth, where she also serves as the General Manager of the Research Centre for Consumer Law. Katharina is a doctoral candidate, whose thesis is supervised by Professor Dr Martin Schmidt-Kessel (Chair for German and European Consumer Law, Private Law and Comparative Law). Katharina was a non-residential fellow of the Stanford-Vienna Transatlantic Technology Law Forum at Stanford Law School from 2017–2019, where she was invited to conduct her research during February 2018. In 2015, Katharina passed her First State Examination (J.D. equivalent). Prior to commencing her doctoral studies, Katharina studied law at the University of Bayreuth, specialising in international law, European law and international private law. As a student assistant, she worked for the German Society of Comparative Law.

Nicole Kornet (Netherlands)
Dr Nicole Kornet is Senior Lecturer at the Faculty of Law of Maastricht University. She holds degrees from the University of Otago (BA, LL.B. (Hons)) and Maastricht University (LL.M., PhD). In her doctoral dissertation, entitled 'Contract Interpretation and Gap Filling: Comparative and Theoretical Perspectives', Nicole made a comparative and theoretical study of the approaches to contract interpretation and gap-filling in the Netherlands, Germany and England. She has published on international commercial law, European and comparative contract law, and legal education. Nicole is responsible for courses on comparative contract law and international commercial law in the Master's and Bachelor's programmes at Maastricht University, and is the current coordinator of the European Law School's Bachelor's programme.

Adam Kramer (England and Wales)
Adam Kramer is a commercial barrister at 3 Verulam Buildings in London, UK, and the author of practitioner text *The Law of Contract Damages* (Hart Publishing, currently in its second edition). He previously lectured at the University of Durham.

Ivana Kunda (Croatia)
Ivana Kunda is Professor and the Head of the Department of International and European Private Law at the Faculty of Law of the University of Rijeka and a Vice-Dean for Science. She was awarded the University of Rijeka Foundation Award for 2008. She has been granted international scholarships, including the Fulbright Research Fellow scholarship in 2010 for research at the Columbia University, the Gewerblicher Rechtsschutz und Urheberrecht scholarships in 2007, 2008 and 2014 for research at the Max Planck Institute for Innovation

and Competition, and the Deutsche Stiftung für internationale rechtliche Zusammenarbeit scholarship in 2002 for research at the Max Planck Institute for Comparative and International Private Law and the University of Hamburg. She has been a Visiting Professor at the University of Navarra, the IULM, the University of Antwerp, the University of Ljubljana, the WIPO Summer School and the MSU Croatia Summer Institute. She is a member of the International Law Association and the Deputy President of the Croatian Comparative Law Association.

Antonio Las Casas (Italy)
Antonio Las Casas is an Associate Professor at the University of Catania (Department of Law), where he teaches comparative private law and European contract law. He holds a PhD (Dottorato di Ricerca) in '*Profili della Cittadinanza nella Costruzione dell'Europa*' [Issues of citizenship in the development of Europe] from the University of Catania. He was a visiting researcher at the University of California Berkeley School of Law. His research interests include the law of contracts and torts in comparative perspective, with special attention on the relationship between the common law and civil law traditions.

Joasia Luzak (Poland)
Joasia Luzak is an Associate Professor and Director of the Centre for European Legal Studies at the Law School of the University of Exeter, UK. She is also a Visiting Associate Professor at the Centre for the Study of European Contract Law at the University of Amsterdam, the Netherlands. She has over 10 years of experience with research in the area of European consumer law and its implementation in Poland, the Netherlands, the UK and Germany. In her research she often includes insights from consumer behaviour science. Her PhD research, conducted at the University of Amsterdam, examined the influence and scope of duties to warn in the area of consumer construction law. Since 2016 she has been leading an international, interdisciplinary research project assessing requirements for compliance with the principle of transparency in online consumer contracts: *The ABC of Online Disclosure Duties: Towards a More Uniform Assessment of the Transparency of Consumer Information in Europe* (Open Research Area funding).

Kalle Mäenpää (Finland)
Kalle Mäenpää is a District Judge at the District Court of Helsinki and a doctoral student of law of obligations at the University of Helsinki. He is writing his doctoral thesis on pre-contractual liability under Finnish law.

Adelaide Menezes Leitão (Portugal)
Adelaide Menezes Leitão holds a Bachelor of Laws (1993), Master's in Law (1998) and PhD in Law (2008) from the Law Faculty of Lisbon University, and has been an Associated Teacher there since 2017. She was an attorney from 1994 to 2003, Legal Assistant to the Prime Minister (2003–2004) and Legal Assistant to the

Minister of Culture, acting as Deputy Chief of Staff (2004–2005), and has been a legal consultant and arbiter since 2007. She has spoken at dozens of conferences in the areas of civil liability, bankruptcy law, industrial law and consumer law. She is the author of books in the area of civil liability and bankruptcy law and numerous published articles in the areas of unfair competition, copyright law, industrial property law, consumer law and civil liability. She was the Portuguese participant in the *Common Core of European Private Law: The Enforcement of Competition Law in Europe* and *Immaterial Damages in European Contract Law*.

Emilia Mišćenić (Croatia)
Emilia Mišćenić is an Associate Professor at the Department of International and European Private Law at the Faculty of Law of the University of Rijeka. She obtained her Master's degree at the scientific study programme of the Europa-Institut Universität des Saarlandes, and her doctoral degree at the scientific study programme of the Rechtswissenschaftliche Fakultät Karl-Franzens Universität Graz. She authored a book on consumer loan agreements, entitled *Gegenwart und Zukunft der Verbraucherkreditverträge in der EU und in Kroatien*, that was cited by AG Trstenjak in the CJEU case *Pereničová et Perenič*. She was part of the Croatian negotiation team during accession to the EU. She was awarded the National Science Award granted by the Croatian Parliament in 2011, and the University of Rijeka Foundation Award in 2012. In 2013, the Ministry of Science, Education and Sports selected her as one of 20 research assistants in the country fulfilling criteria of scientific excellence.

Anastasios Moraitis (Greece)
Anastasios Moraitis is a dually qualified attorney in Greece and New York working with the Global Transactions practice of Freshfields Bruckhaus Deringer LLP in Munich, Germany. He studied law at the universities of Athens, Greece (LL.B., LL.M. civ.), Hannover, Germany (M.L.E.) and Harvard Law School (LL.M.). From 2006 to 2009, Anastasios worked for the Study Group on a European Civil Code, a research project under the auspices of the European Commission on harmonising European private law, and he contributed to the volume on *Acquisition and Loss of Ownership of Goods* (Sellier 2011). From 2009 until 2013 he was a university assistant at the University of Graz, Austria, conducting research on comparative and European law issues; at the same time, he acted as national reporter for various groups of the Common Core of European Private Law, including the present volume. Anastasios is a Greek native speaker, fluent in English and German and proficient in French and Spanish.

Franziska Myburgh (South Africa)
Franziska Myburgh, LL.D., is a Senior Lecturer in the Department of Private Law, Faculty of Law, at Stellenbosch University. She specialises in contract and consumer law, and her current research interests lie in contractual interpretation,

the provision of credit and the implications of imposing formal requirements for the conclusion of valid contracts.

Ville Pönkä (Finland)
Ville Pönkä LL.D. is a Full Professor of Nordic law and the Director of the Master's Degree Program in International Business Law, teaching contract and commercial law as well as law and economics at the University of Helsinki's Faculty of Law. Ville's main fields of research include Nordic company law, cooperative law, contract law and commercial dispute resolution. Currently, Ville is leading an Academy of Finland funded research project called the 'Challenges and Prospects of Cooperatives in a Globalizing World'. He is a member of several international scholarly communities such as the European Corporate Governance Institute, the European Consortium for Political Research and the Nordic Company Law Network. He is also a member of the board of directors of the Finnish Arbitration Institute.

Lorna Richardson
Lorna Richardson is a Lecturer in Commercial Law at the University of Edinburgh Law School. Her research interests are principally in the area of contract law, in particular interpretation of contract, breach and remedies. She also works in the area of special contracts, principally sale and lease. Lorna has published a number of papers on contract law, often in a historical or comparative context. She is co-author of a leading text on commercial law in Scotland, and a book on the law of commercial leases in Scotland. Prior to joining the University of Edinburgh, Lorna practised as a solicitor in commercial and property litigation for eight years. During her time in practice, Lorna was involved in a number of cases which resulted in significant developments to Scots contract law. Lorna's time in practice influences her research agenda. She focuses her research on areas of the law that are unclear, but which often arise in contract disputes.

Isabelle Rueda (France)
Dr Isabelle Rueda is a Senior Lecturer in Law (Education and Research). She joined Exeter Law School in January 2016. She previously held positions as a Lecturer at the University of Sheffield (2012–2015) and as a postdoctoral researcher in European private law at the University of Luxembourg (2009–2012). She studied law at the University of Toulouse (France) before working as a Lecturer at the same university until the completion of her PhD on European contract law (2008). She was a visiting researcher at UNIDROIT (Rome) in 2000, 2002 and 2016.

Joel Samuelsson (Sweden)
Joel Samuelsson, Dr. iur., is Professor of Private Law at the Faculty of Law of Uppsala University. He specialises in the methods of interpretation of commercial

contracts but his research and teaching interests also include general issues in the law of obligations, European private law, jurisprudence and legal hermeneutics.

Martin Schmidt-Kessel (Germany)
Professor Dr iur. Martin Schmidt-Kessel studied law in Freiburg im Breisgau, Munich and Cologne and again Freiburg where he was awarded his doctorate in 2001 and his habilitation in 2003. From 2004 to 2010, he worked as Full Professor for Comparative Law at the European Legal Studies Institute at the University of Osnabrück. Since 2010, he has been a Full Professor of German and European Consumer Law, Private Law and Comparative Law and Director of the Centre for Consumer Law at the University of Bayreuth. In 2014, he became Associate Member to the International Academy of Comparative Law. Since 2015, he has worked as speaker of the Joint Doctorate Verona-Bayreuth in European Legal Studies and in 2017 he became a member of the PhD Committee in European and International Legal Sciences within the PhD School of Law and Economics of the University of Verona.

Gema Tomás (Spain)
Gema Tomás holds a PhD in law from the University of Deusto (1999) and has been a Full Professor of Civil Law since 2015. Her teaching and research interests are focused on civil law, comparative law and Roman law. She publishes regularly in these areas: European contract law, civil responsibility, Roman law and gender studies focused on private law. She served as a Magistrate in the Regional Court (1999–2002) and has occupied several academic positions in Deusto Law School since 1999 (Director of Private Law Department, Director of Legal Practice School and currently Dean since 2015). She often lectures at law schools abroad (Chile, Germany) and she belongs to the European Law Institute and the Société de Histoire et Droits de la Antiquité. She is evaluator for journals such as the *Journal of Civil Law* and the *Journal of Human Rights*, and is a member of the Editorial Board of the journal *Education and Law Review*.

Vesna Tomljenović (Croatia)
Vesna Tomljenović is the first Croatian Judge at the General Court of the European Union, elected in 2013. She is a Full Professor at the Department of International and European Private Law at the Faculty of Law of the University of Rijeka, as well as the Head of the Institute of European and Comparative Law at the same Faculty. She is the organiser of a number of international and domestic conferences, author of many papers and author or editor of several books. She is also one of the founders and the director of the postgraduate programme 'Law of European Integrations' at the Faculty of Law in Rijeka. During the negotiations for the Croatian accession to the EU, she was appointed the Head of the Negotiating Team Working Group for Consumer Protection and

Health. She is a long-term active member of the International Law Association and since 2006 she has been the President of the Croatian Comparative Law Association.

Remus Valsan

Dr Remus Valsan is Senior Lecturer in Corporate Law and Programme Director of the LL.M. in Corporate Law at Edinburgh Law School. His teaching and research interests include corporate law and governance, law and economics, fiduciary duties and trusts.

Aneta Wiewiórowska-Domagalska (Poland)

Aneta Wiewiórowska-Domagalska has been a Senior Researcher at Osnabrück University (the European Legal Studies Institute) since January 2015. She holds a law degree from Warsaw University and a PhD from Utrecht University. She participated as a researcher in the work of the Study Group on a European Civil Code (she is a co-author of the Principles of European Law on Sales). From 2008 to 2014, she worked as a chief specialist for the Polish Ministry of Justice, where she was involved in preparing and conducting legislative proposals in the area of private law as well as negotiating private law instruments in the European Council. Aneta chaired the CELS working group during the Polish Presidency. Between 2007 and 2015, she was a member of various working groups of the Polish Civil Law Codification Commission. She is one of the reporters of the ELI's Model Rules on Online Intermediary Platforms project.

PART I

INTRODUCTORY MATTERS

INTRODUCTION

Jaap BAAIJ, David CABRELLI and Laura MACGREGOR

1. THE SIGNIFICANCE OF COMPARING THE INTERPRETATION OF CONTRACTS

Questions of interpretation are an integral feature of the law. This holds true in relation to the principles, rules, standards and conventions that coalesce to form discrete legal disciplines such as contract law. The observation is equally valid in the case of express contractual terms which are drawn up by contracting parties in written contracts.[1]

Questions of contract interpretation will arise by dint of the fact that – as economists have shown – written contracts are naturally incomplete by design, in the sense that no matter how conscientious the contracting parties are in terms of negotiating and fixing the necessary detail in drafting its provisions, there inevitably will be gaps in the instrument.[2] A written contract will lack coverage of all the contingencies and eventualities which may arise during the course of the contract, due to the limited foreseeability of such contingencies at the point of formation. Party autonomy also implies the interpretation of contractual language. The judicial enforcement of contracts cannot avoid interpretation of the language expressed by the parties in their contract.[3] In fact, few contractual disputes would not also include questions of the meaning, import or legal effect of contractual terms.[4]

From time to time, the idea of including a project on the interpretation of contracts had been brought up during the 'Common Core' Project's annual plenary meetings. This recurring interest is a testament to the significance of

---

1 N. MacCormick, *Rhetoric and the Rule of Law: A Theory of Legal Reasoning* (Oxford: Oxford University Press, 2005) 122.

2 See O. Hart and J. Moore, 'Foundations of Incomplete Contracts' (1999) 66 *Review of Economic Studies* 115, 134–135 and O.E. Williamson, 'Transaction Cost Economics: The Governance of Contractual Relations' (1979) 22 *Journal of Law and Economics* 233.

3 A. Schwartz and R.E. Scott, 'Contract Theory and the Limits of Contract Law' (2003) 113 *Yale Law Journal* 541, 547.

4 A. Schwartz and R.E. Scott, 'Contract Interpretation Redux' (2010) 119 *Yale Law Journal* 926, 928, 932, n. 17.

interpretation in the field of contract law. The authors believed that a project on contractual interpretation would be an ideal addition to the numerous comparative studies and books published to date under the banner of the Common Core Project.[5] The Common Core website and further books provide explanations and reflections on the distinctive 'Common Core' method.[6] In essence, the Common Core comparative methodology involves a number of steps. First, carefully crafted hypothetical cases on a given topic are produced. Second, national reporters are asked to describe how the various questions posed in these cases would be approached (rather than resolved) in their legal system. The reason that country experts were asked not to solve or resolve the conceptual and doctrinal questions of law arising from the hypothetical cases is that the editors of the project were particularly interested in (1) the manner in which different elements of statutory law, case law and scholarly writings interact with and potentially contradict each other in particular legal systems, and (2) how policy considerations, values, economic and social factors, and the structure of legal processes may affect the approach of the courts to the case.[7] The project in hand adhered to this methodology, selecting 10 cases and 14 jurisdictions in total.[8]

Notwithstanding the value of adding a comparative study on contract interpretation, for well over 10 years the Common Core meetings concluded that the Common Core method would not be well suited for such a study. This trepidation is understandable. On its surface, a comparative survey of contract interpretation appears difficult to undertake within the Common Core approach.

For one, as discussed in more detail below, the Common Core approach tells national reporters to inform the editors of how courts in their respective jurisdictions would resolve a legal dispute. In contrast, typically, interpretation issues are preliminary issues. Unless the claimant asked for a declaratory judgment, resolving an interpretative issue does not represent the resolution of the legal dispute itself. The determination of the meaning of the contractual terms is part of the court's reasoning. It provides the court with one of the possibly many reasons for resolving the legal dispute in one way or another.

Furthermore, the contractual language is specific to an individual contractual relationship. Unless the interpretation question involves widely used standard

5 See the list at https://www.cambridge.org/core/series/common-core-of-european-private-law/9A1F0195629A3C0607233F14029C3A25.

6 See common-core.org, as well as M. Bussani and U. Mattei (eds.), *Opening Up European Law, The Common Core Project* (Bern: Staempfli, 2007).

7 On legal formants, see also R. Sacco, 'Legal Formants: A Dynamic Approach to Comparative Law' (1991) 39 *American Journal of Comparative Law* 1–34 and 343–401.

8 See the description of the 10 cases and the choice of jurisdictions below in section 3.2 of this Introduction and the various methodological challenges and editorial choices in this Contract Interpretation project in the Chapter 'Designing a Method to Compare Interpretation Methods' below.

terms, predicting which meaning a court would attribute to the specific wording of a particular clause would produce little information about the legal system in question.

Notwithstanding these seemingly compelling reasons to refrain from a Common Core study on contract interpretation, the editors of this volume were convinced that there would be a way to accommodate the Common Core approach. This chapter explicates the methodological choices and challenges the editors subsequently faced.

2. THREE UNIVERSAL ISSUES OF CONTRACT INTERPRETATION

2.1. INTRODUCTION: A LIMITED SCOPE

The editors aim to gain a greater understanding of the ways courts deal with the interpretation of written contracts in general. The scope of this study, therefore, should exclude the interpretation of legal documents governed by special legal regimes. Hence, this study does not include the interpretation or construction of unilateral private legal documents such as wills, or consumer, employment or arbitration agreements, or agreements for the transfer of real property. Oral agreements are excluded as well, even though this does not prevent national reports from indicating that courts would consider oral statements by the contracting parties while interpreting a written contract. In brief, the scope of this study is limited to written commercial agreements between professionals 'at arm's length'.

This study is further limited to ascertaining the meaning of contractual language rather than the determination of contractual terms. That is to say, some authors have made a distinction between the 'interpretation' and 'construction' of contracts.[9] Interpretation in this sense involves ascertaining the meaning and thus legal effects of the terms of the contract; construction is determining which terms are part of this agreement and which are not. Expressed in terms of this distinction, this comparative study concentrates solely on the interpretation and not the construction of contracts. However, throughout the book, the terms 'interpretation' and 'construction' will be used interchangeably. Hence, both terms are to be understood to refer to the ascertainment of the meaning of the contractual language.[10]

9 See e.g. A. Schwartz and R.E. Scott, 'Contract Interpretation Redux' (2010) 119 *The Yale Law Journal* 926.

10 It is worth noting that the interpretation of an express term can further be contrasted with the process of interpretation *stricto sensu*. The latter process is confined to a literal translation whereas construction entails the ascription of meaning to words or terms from

Within this limited scope, the editors wish to concentrate on interpretation problems that relate to or originate from three presumably universal issues that courts across legal systems and legal cultures may face, which are set out below.

2.2. THE FIRST ISSUE: THE NATURE OF INTERPRETATIVE UNCERTAINTY

A variety of possible meanings may be ascribed to the import of a word or words in a legally binding contract. It is also in the nature of contracts and their terms that they cannot be applied or enforced in the absence of action on the part of some actors or authorities.[11] Therefore, to the extent that a dispute arises between the contracting parties about the meaning of a contractual provision, this will invariably involve them in advancing competing propositions. An impartial adjudicator in the guise of a court of law or some other adjudicative agency[12] ultimately will be called upon to exercise its judgment as to the 'true meaning' of that provision. As the Scottish jurist and institutional writer Bell observed:

> But in bargains there is so much taken for granted, so loose a confidence, so vague an adoption of usage, so great uncertainty as to the ordinary understanding in such cases, and so much ambiguity and imperfection of language, even where the identity of the words is not disputed; that courts of justice are frequently compelled to make an election between different meanings, and sometimes to admit the evidence of usage to qualify the whole.[13]

Sometimes, the issue to be resolved will involve an interpretation of the facts and whether the interpretation arrived at falls within the compass of the words of the contract. In other circumstances, the interpretative process will be confined to the proper construction of the words at a generic level, rather than the facts. It is also possible that the court's or adjudicator's task will involve the interpretation of an express contractual term and an enquiry into whether the facts are within the scope of that term, i.e. a mixed interpretation of fact and law.

---

the spirit of the text. See E. Farnsworth, '"Meaning" in the Law of Contracts' (1967) 76 *Yale Law Journal* 939, 939–940. This study aims to examine interpretation in the latter meaning. It also excludes consideration of techniques adopted in certain jurisdictions subsequent to the interpretation of the terms of a contract where the conclusion has been drawn that a gap remains in the meaning of the contract that must be plugged.

11 MacCormick makes the point generally in relation to law and legal rules, but it is equally valid in the case of contracts and contractual terms, see N. MacCormick, *Institutions of Law: An Essay in Legal Theory* (Oxford: Oxford University Press, 2006) 258–259.

12 For example, the parties may refer the dispute resolution process to an arbitrator.

13 G.J. Bell, *Principles of the Law of Scotland* (4th edn, Edinburgh: Thomas Clark Bookseller, 1839) §524.

Thus, the courts will become involved in a process which can be conceptualised as 'gap-filling'. Where there is some form of ambiguity or vagueness in words employed, some meaning must be attributed to that provision. It is this role of construction in the context of express terms in written contracts which is the focus of this book.

Attributing a construction will be relevant where it is unclear whether the words which feature in the contract include or exclude certain circumstances, examples, factors or matters within their scope of application. Farnsworth has referred to this 'scope' factor as an example of what is referred to as 'vagueness' which is distinct from 'ambiguity'.[14] Words are 'ambiguous' where the words are capable of more than one meaning or connotation, for example whether the verb 'cast' means 'throw out'[15] or 'appoint'.[16] Furthermore, as the Scottish Law Commission has pointed out, the word 'ambiguous' is also used to describe an 'expression [which] is unclear or uncertain'.[17]

2.3. THE SECOND ISSUE: THE NATURE OF THE INTERPRETATIVE TASK

The work of the Roman jurists undoubtedly has had a significant influence on the development of the contract law rules governing the interpretation of words in contracts in the vast majority of European jurisdictions. Most of the rules on the interpretation of contracts that are considered in this book relate to European countries (with the exception of South Africa, although in that country too Roman law has been highly influential). For that reason, the Roman law approach to the construction of expressions in written contracts is of paramount importance. It provides an essential background to the discussion of the rules in each of the European legal systems covered in this book.

When subjecting the position of Roman law on contractual interpretation to scrutiny, it is instructive to adopt a division between the classical Roman period (during the Roman Republic and early Roman Empire) and its post-classical period around the time of Justinian. Turning to the classical period, one might query the extent to which Roman law prioritised the literal meaning of a written declaration in a contract (the *verba*) over a contextual approach which instead seeks to understand the import of the expressions in the contract by reference

14 E. Farnsworth, '"Meaning" in the Law of Contracts' (1967) 76 *Yale Law Journal* 939, 953. See also A. Schwartz and R.E. Scott, 'Contract Theory and the Limits of Contract Law' (2003) 113 *Yale Law Journal* 541, 570–572.

15 As in 'cast a net'.

16 As in 'Noel Coward cast Edward Woodward to play the part of …'.

17 *Report on Interpretation in Private Law* (Scot Law Com No. 160, 1997) para. 2.12 at p. 12.

to circumstances surrounding its conclusion.[18] This, of course, is an allusion to the classic *literal versus contextual* dichotomy, which is a distinction to which we will return many times in this book. One might also conjecture whether the approach to contractual interpretation in the classical Roman period was characterised by an objective search for the true meaning of the words deployed. Alternatively, did it emphasise a search for the subjective intentions of the parties (the *animus* or *voluntas*)? This is sometimes referred to as the *objective versus subjective* distinction. At the very least, it can perhaps be said that the position fluctuated over the course of the classical Roman period, but on balance, as time progressed, there would appear to have been a gradual drift towards a subjective approach, the search for the 'will' of the parties and a hint of the abandonment of formalism in interpretation.[19]

However, a note of caution ought to be struck. As Zimmermann has argued, a process which seeks to identify the nature of the interpretative task which applied in the classical period of Roman law along such lines of enquiry is a particularly fraught endeavour.[20] Modes of analysis in terms of diametrically opposed categorisations such as (1) *subjectivity versus objectivity* and (2) *literal/formalistic versus contextual* do not quite capture the way in which Roman jurists thought about the task of interpretation. Indeed, there is a danger that such a process is superficial, since it entails the conduct of an enquiry in accordance with rival conceptualisations representing modes of thought developed in modern times, which were not wholly endemic at the time.

However, by the time of the post-classical period of Roman law, it is fairly clear that a radical form of subjectivism had taken hold, i.e. precedence was afforded to the search for the subjective intention of the parties.[21] The general trend amongst the Roman jurists of this time was to engage in a search for *animus* and to be less concerned about the literal construction of the written words. The desire to discover the 'true meaning' of an expression in accordance with the *animus* of the parties is perhaps the product of a philosophy which perceives it to be morally sound to give effect to what the parties actually intended, rather than imposing an alien interpretation upon the parties from outside. Although admirable, such a sentiment is perhaps naïve, given that the interpretative process is to some extent necessarily an impressionistic endeavour.

Once we reach the *ius commune* period in the civilian world, it is abundantly clear that the process was primarily motivated by a desire to ascertain the

---

18 R. Zimmermann, *The Law of Obligations: Roman Foundations of the Civilian Tradition* (Cape Town: Juta, 1990) 622–623.

19 Ibid., 634; F. Pringsheim, '*Animus* in Roman Law' (1933) 49 *Law Quarterly Review* 43, 48.

20 R. Zimmermann, *The Law of Obligations: Roman Foundations of the Civilian Tradition* (Cape Town: Juta, 1990) 626.

21 F. Pringsheim, '*Animus* in Roman Law' (1933) 49 *Law Quarterly Review* 43, 47–48.

subjective common intention of the parties.[22] This chimes happily with the 'will theory' of contract law associated with Savigny[23] and the Pandectist scholars which became prevalent in later times.[24] The will theory entails that a contract was an expression of the will of the parties, and so a court of law or an adjudicator should do everything in his/her/its power to interpret that instrument in accordance with the actual will and intention of the parties. Another feature of the texts of the *ius commune* period is a predilection for resorting to canons of interpretation, articulated in Latin; for example, the *plus valeat quam pereat* and *contra proferentem* canons are freely cited.[25]

Constructing the indicators and hallmarks of the aforementioned polar opposites of (1) *subjectivity versus objectivity* and (2) *literal/formalistic versus contextual* is useful inasmuch as it enables a spectrum to be drawn, against which the approaches of European (and other) legal systems can be plotted. To that extent, it is submitted that a purely subjective assessment would enjoin a court to consider what the parties individually or collectively intended to say in complete ignorance of the terms or words deployed: this is consistent with the extreme form of anti-formalism adopted by the Byzantines in the late Roman period. By definition, a search for the former would be undertaken in isolation from the other contracting parties' intentions, which is particularly unsound.

A distinction can be drawn between an approach which is entirely subjective and one which is the polar opposite, i.e. wholly objective. In the case of the latter, the court would have the luxury of deciding itself on what the parties had intended by the words contained in their contract. This could legitimately involve the court replacing or substituting its own judgment for that of the parties. The licence given to the court in such a case would be extraordinary. That is to say that the court would have the power to overlook the meaning that the parties themselves had ascribed to the words that they had used. The difficulty with such an emphatic incarnation of an objective approach is that it completely dispenses with the intention and consent of the parties, which jars quite forcefully against the consensual roots of contract law that are grounded on the principle of party autonomy.

As for the distinction between literalism and contextualism, whilst related to the dichotomy between subjective and objective interpretative assessments, they are not the same thing. A literal adherence to the words employed by the parties in the contract could equally be eschewed by the court on the application of a subjective or objective examination, for example where the court decides to

---

22 R. Zimmermann, *The Law of Obligations: Roman Foundations of the Civilian Tradition* (Cape Town: Juta, 1990) 625 and 636.

23 F. Karl von Savigny, *System des Heutige Romanes Rechts* (vol. 3, 1840) §130.

24 B. Windscheid, *Lehrbuch des Pandektenrechts* (vol. I, 6th edn, 1887) §69 at 187–188.

25 R. Zimmermann, *The Law of Obligations: Roman Foundations of the Civilian Tradition* (Cape Town: Juta, 1990) 637–638.

examine the genuine and honest beliefs and intentions of the parties in isolation from the plain meaning of the text (subjective) or instead identifies what it believes is the true meaning of the terms in the contract without resort to the ordinary meaning of the text (objective). Alternatively, a literal interpretation could just as much entail clinging to either a subjective or objective determination of the parties' intentions. Exactly the same point can be made about contextual interpretations, i.e. that such a mode of construction of contractual terms cannot be equated to either of the subjective or objective approaches. In the final analysis, although there is a sliding scale from the literal to the contextual forms of interpretation and another sliding scale from the subjective to objective, they are not necessarily aligned along parallel lines.

2.4. THE THIRD ISSUE: CULTURAL DIFFERENCES BETWEEN COMMON LAW AND CIVIL LAW

One might presuppose that a particular approach to interpretation is civilian in outlook, whereas the opposite rival stance is symptomatic of the common law method. This caricature posits that civilian legal systems in Europe whose rules of interpretation derive from Roman law are predominantly wedded to a subjective methodology. The orthodox argument runs that this can be contrasted with common law systems such as English law, where the norms governing interpretation cleave to a complex amalgam of a contextual and objective approach. Indeed, it is common to think of the search for the subjective intention of the parties in accordance with the parties' will as the prevalent method in civilian systems and a more objective and contextual endeavour to be characteristic of the process adopted in the common law world.

However, as Eric Clive has argued, the reality is likely more complex.[26] What may be perceived to be a civilian mode of analysis of contract terms may, in fact, turn out to be one grounded in the common law or vice versa. For example, it is somewhat artificial to talk of legal systems as having a 100% subjective or objective measure of scrutiny. Ultimately, it may be more accurate to claim that lazy stereotypes underplay the subtlety of the interpretative approaches adopted in legal systems grounded in the civilian and common law traditions. In this vein, if there is a difference between the two traditions, the question is whether it may be 'smoothing itself out', although 'one continues to find … differences of emphasis'.[27]

---

26 See E. Clive, 'Interpretation' in K. Reid and R. Zimmermann (eds.), *A History of Private Law in Scotland* (vol. 2, Oxford: Oxford University Press, 2000) 47. See also *Report on Interpretation in Private Law* (Scot Law Com No. 160, 1997) paras. 1.17–1.20 at p. 5.

27 J.H. Herbots, 'Interpretation of Contracts' in J.M. Smits (ed.), *Elgar Encyclopaedia of Comparative Law*, (2nd edn, Cheltenham: Edward Elgar, 2012) 421 at 422 and 426.

The civilian/common law distinction also fails to take into account those so-called 'mixed legal systems' which have been influenced by *both* legal traditions.[28] Whether such a category exists is controversial: some argue that every legal system has been shaped by different influences.[29] Even those who suggest that such a category exists concede that it is 'far from clear'.[30] Mixed legal system scholarship has asserted that mixed legal systems, in the commercial law area, assimilate entirely over time with the common law.[31] The approach to interpretation in the mixed system may mirror the 'dominant' influence (whether civilian or common law) or it may be a hybrid of both.

Perhaps '[m]ost modern contract law regimes hover between [a] subjective and objective [approach].'[32] This project, of course, is an excellent opportunity to test the accuracy of these competing claims and to reach definitive conclusions on the similarity or otherwise of civilian, common law and mixed legal systems. In that way, an open mind is maintained at this stage, with the lessons to be drawn from the case studies set out in the concluding chapter.

3. STRUCTURE OF THE BOOK

3.1. EXPLORATORY CHAPTERS

Before presenting the 10 hypothetical problems and the solutions the national reports offer, the book will first both introduce the subject matter of contract

28 On mixed legal systems generally see J. du Plessis, 'Comparative Law and the Study of Mixed Legal Systems' in M. Reimann and R. Zimmermann (eds.), *Oxford Handbook of Comparative Law* (2nd edn, Oxford: Oxford University Press, 2019) 474 at 476–478; and J.M. Smits (ed.), *Elgar Encyclopaedia of Comparative Law* (2nd edn, Cheltenham: Edward Elgar, 2012) ch. 48, 'Mixed Jurisdictions' by V.V. Palmer.

29 This is, essentially, the starting point of E. Örücü et al. (eds.), *Studies in Legal Systems: Mixed and Mixing* (The Hague: Kluwer Law International, 1996).

30 R. Zimmermann, D. Visser and K. Reid, 'Introduction' in R. Zimmermann, D. Visser and K. Reid (eds.), *Mixed Legal Systems in Comparative Perspective: Property and Obligations in Scotland and South Africa* (Oxford: Oxford University Press, 2004) 3.

31 See V.V. Palmer, 'Mixed Jurisdictions' in J.M. Smits (ed.), *Elgar Encyclopaedia of Comparative Law* (2nd edn, Cheltenham: Edward Elgar, 2012), who states at 597: 'At their founding, the mixed jurisdictions, Israel excepted, had a civilian-based commercial law. However over time common law commercial rules were fully assimilated. The reasons for this were based upon the requirements of commerce, perceptions of economic self-interest and the belief that civil law differences would be a hindrance to trade and should be eliminated'. This contention is discussed in greater detail in L. Macgregor, 'Empire, Trade and the Use of Agents in the Nineteenth Century: The "Reception" of the Undisclosed Principal Rule in Louisiana Law and Scots Law' (2019) 79 *Louisiana Law Review* 895.

32 H. Beale, B. Fauvarque-Cosson, J. Rutgers and S. Vogenauer, *Cases, Materials and Texts on Contract Law,* (3rd edn, Oxford: Hart, 2019) 722 and B. Großfeld, *Core Questions of Comparative Law*, trans. V. Grosswald Curran (Durham, NC: Carolina Academic Press, 2005).

interpretation in a broader perspective. The first of four introductory chapters explores the challenges and choices of subjecting methods of contract interpretation to a comparative study. Any comparison of jurisdictions that use different general language necessarily entails translation. As all national reports are drafted in English, most reporters translated their respective national legal concepts and idiom into English. The editorial instructions therefore included directions aimed to minimise the chance of translation distorting the fluency of this book's cross-legal discourse.

In the second chapter, the legal rules of contractual interpretation are placed under the magnifying glass of economic theory. In particular, economic analysis is applied to one of the classic choices faced by a legal system: should it adopt a literal or contextual approach to interpretation? The objective of this chapter is to assess whether it is possible to design an optimal interpretative regime in economic terms in the abstract: in the absence of any context or particular case studies, is there an interpretative approach that is consistently the most efficient economic choice?

If we turn first to a choice that prioritises contextualism, the primary factor in its favour is the saving in transaction costs. By deferring the task to a court (at a much later date) of ascribing meaning to contractual terms, the parties can save up-front bargaining, negotiation and drafting costs. On the negative side, however, is the costs borne by the parties in handling the unpredictability of understanding the contractual provisions and the ex post litigation costs necessary to attribute meaning to them. Likewise, the economic inefficiencies associated with a literal approach mirror those in play as the advantages and disadvantages of contextualism. For example, although greater certainty is secured by selecting a textualist rule of interpretation, the parties must invest greater time and effort in ensuring their terms are framed as accurately as possible, which invariably entails expense. Meanwhile, the certainty associated with a literalist approach and the comparatively fewer litigation costs operate in its favour. The chapter concludes by suggesting that it is impossible to draw up an efficient choice of rule outside of context and that the likelihood for the courts to take a wrong turn – whichever rule of interpretation they opt for – is too great. The end result is that private ordering by the parties themselves is superior to any legal rule that the courts may devise to give meaning to their contract. This speaks to an approach that does not see literalism and contextualism as in conceptual opposition, but rather one in which both techniques are seen as complementing each other in search of the most efficient choice for the parties in their particular case.

The third chapter considers interpretation of contract in two European harmonisation measures: the Principles of European Contract Law, the Draft Common Frame of Reference and the Common European Sales Law. Given that the Draft Common Frame of Reference is more recent in date, the author has been able to identify ways in which thinking on interpretation has developed in recent times. Both measures adopt, as a primary rule, the common intention of the parties, even if that differs from the literal interpretation. In both, this rule seeks to combine the subjective and objective approaches to interpretation. The author's themed approach permits a focus on many of the issues brought to the fore by the questionnaire used in this book, for example the relevance to the interpretative process of prior negotiations, post-contractual conduct, usages or good faith and fair dealing.

The fourth introductory chapter presents the opening remarks by all reporters introducing the law pertaining to contract interpretation in their respective jurisdictions. Any legal comparison seeks to associate different jurisdictions in an intelligible manner. After all, elements of the law need to be made sufficiently similar to be comparable. A side effect of this unavoidable aspect of the comparative legal research is the risks of concealing significant yet subtle idiosyncrasies of the jurisdictions in questions. This is why the editors have asked the national reporters to write opening remarks, that is to say, a general introduction to contract interpretation in their legal system. That space permits the reporter to highlight any features that they deem important for the reader to be aware of before reading their answers to the editors' questions.

3.2. NATIONAL REPORTS

3.2.1. The Choice of Jurisdictions

The remainder of the book will consist of the aforementioned 10 hypothetical cases, the questions the editors asked about the fact patterns in question, and the answers that each national report offers on the basis of the jurisdictions under comparison.

There are 14 national reports, covering the law of Croatia, England and Wales, Finland, France, Germany, Greece, Italy, the Netherlands, Poland, Portugal, Scotland, South Africa, Spain and Sweden. We sought to include jurisdictions from the north, east, south and west of Europe.[33] While it was not possible to recruit a reporter from each Member State of the European Union, the 14 reports cover jurisdictions from all corners of Europe, including common law, civil law and mixed legal systems, and thus provide both a comprehensive and illustrative cross-section of Member States.

All national reports discuss the law of a European country, except for the South African report. South Africa was included because the editors considered it helpful to include a *second* mixed legal system (the decision had already been made to include Scotland, a mixed legal system within Europe). The questions

33 All national reports were updated last between December 2018 and May 2019, except for the Portuguese report, which was updated last in September 2013.

raised above (in section 2.4) can be considered in the light of the national reports from the two mixed systems. Is there evidence that the mixed legal system has followed a 'dominant' tradition? Is there evidence of the adoption of a hybrid approach?

Reporters were recruited by invitation by the editors mainly from the participants who attended Common Core meetings from year to year. Certain reporters were recruited by the editors from outside the Common Core Project. It was, for example, considered important to include the French legal system, as an influential European legal system. Given the lack of French participants in the Contract Group of the Common Core Project, a reporter who was an expert on French law was explicitly invited to participate.

3.2.2. Selecting the Cases and Issues Addressed

Each of the remaining 10 chapters are dedicated to a single case. In every chapter we firstly set out the case and pose questions to the national reporters. These are followed by the relevant answer from each national report, in alphabetical order. The editors conclude each chapter with a Comparative Analysis for the case in question, synthesising the national answers and identifying common trends, differences, and themes.

The editors tailored the 10, hypothetical fact patterns to address 10 distinct interpretation problems. These specific problems follow from the three universal issues of contract interpretation discussed above. The editors did not design the cases in a vacuum. At various stages, drafts were discussed with national reporters at annual meetings of the Common Core Project. All participants in the Common Core Project who attended the meetings, therefore, had the opportunity to influence the drafting of each case.

For each case, the editors drew up an overview of the problems that they wished to address with each case. To avoid indoctrinating the national reporters, the editors did not share these background considerations with them. The only information the editors shared consisted of the cases, the accompanying questions, and the Instructions that are included in this book as an appendix. The background considerations have now been incorporated into the discussion of the individual cases in Part II of this book, under the heading 'Key Issues'.

3.2.3. Editorial Comparative Observations

Each chapter dedicated to a case will be concluded with the comparative observations by the general editors. In addition, in the conclusion to the book as a whole, the editors offer their overall conclusions and findings. The editors' comparisons offer the reader an overview and analysis of the similarities, differences and other results that the editors draw from the national reports. These observations are not intended to provide a full summary of the national reports, nor to record any and every possible comparative inference. The readers should not allow these comparisons to prevent them from discerning or underscoring additional valuable comparisons. Ultimately, the national reports speak for themselves.

DESIGNING A METHOD TO COMPARE INTERPRETATION METHODS

Jaap Baaij

1. THE CHOICE OF COMPARATIVE METHODOLOGY

1.1. THE FACTUAL APPROACH OF THE COMMON CORE PROJECT

As with any study in the Common Core Project, the methodology designed by the editors of this volume rests on the fundamentals of the general approach developed by Mauro Bussani and Ugo Mattei. The Common Core Project employs a factual approach to comparative law in two related respects.[1]

First, in a Common Core comparison, both the '*comparanda*'[2] and the *tertium comparationis* are of a factual nature. Rather than contrasting the legal rules applicable to a common legal concept, the Common Core comparatist seeks to measure how courts in different legal systems would solve a common factual problem of societal life.[3] This strategy takes inspiration from the method that Rudolf Schlesinger developed in the 1960s.[4] By this method, a comparatist develops a questionnaire that asks legal scholars from different jurisdictions to explain how a set of hypothetical problems would likely be resolved in their respective legal systems. Because a Common Core comparatist, therefore,

---

1 M. Bussani and U. Mattei, 'The Common Core Approach to European Private Law' (1997) 12 *Columbia Journal of European Law* 344, 346.

2 Örücü uses the term '*comparanda*' to refer to the objects of comparison: A.E. Örücü, 'Methodology of Comparative Law' in J.M. Smits (ed.), *Elgar Encyclopedia of Comparative Law* (2nd edn, Cheltenham: Edward Elgar) 560.

3 K. Zweigert and H. Kötz, *An Introduction to Comparative Law*, trans. T. Weir (3rd edn. Oxford: Oxford University Press, 1998) 32, 34.

4 M. Bussani and U. Mattei, 'The Common Core Approach to European Private Law' (1997) 12 *Columbia Journal of European Law* 344, 343–344. See R.B. Schlesinger (ed.), *Formation of Contracts: A Study of the Common Core of Legal Systems* (Dobbs Ferry, New York: Oceana, 1968).

compares not the rules of law, but the *application* of them, the objects of comparisons are not conceptual content but predictions of factual events.[5]

Second, the data on which the Common Core comparatist relies is factual in nature. Rather than looking to the content of legal rules and concepts to predict how a court would resolve a given problem, the comparatist studies both legal and non-legal predictors. Put differently, it concentrates on how a court, *in fact*, would apply the law. Here, the Common Core Project builds on Rodolfo Sacco's theory of 'legal formants'.[6] Sacco called these the 'many different elements' that the 'living law' contains, ranging from statutory rules to scholarly commentary, to other elements that might influence a judge's thinking not contained in the *ratio decidendi* of the court's opinion.[7] Here, therefore, formal legal rules may provide the comparatist with an answer to its question, but not because the law itself is encapsulated in the logical structure of its semantic content. Rather, as judges tend to be susceptible to arguments deduced from formal legal sources, a legal rule is simply a significant indicator of a judge's decision in a given case.[8] The rules derived from legal sources are only 'legal formants' among other equally formative circumstances possibly affecting the ways courts apply the law.[9] Non-legal formants may include 'policy considerations, economic and/or social facts, social context and values'.[10]

1.2. ADAPTING THE GENERAL METHOD TO THE INTERPRETATION OF CONTRACTS

The general methodological approach of the Common Core Project required further fine-tuning to adapt it specifically to a comparative study on the

5 M. Bussani and U. Mattei, 'The Common Core Approach to European Private Law' (1997) 12 *Columbia Journal of European Law* 344, 344, suggesting Common Core comparatists must predict what courts will do in a particular case by writing, 'we must not only know how courts have acted but we must also consider the influences to which the judges may be subject.'

6 M. Bussani and U. Mattei, 'The Common Core Approach to European Private Law' (1997) 12 *Columbia Journal of European Law* 344, 343–6.

7 See R. Sacco, 'Legal Formants: A Dynamic Approach to Comparative Law (Installment I of II)' (1991) 39(1) *The American Journal of Comparative Law* 1, 22. These formants must necessarily point harmoniously in the direction of a single outcome to legal questions, see R. Sacco, 'Legal Formants: A Dynamic Approach to Comparative Law (Installment II of II)' (1991) 39(2) *The American Journal of Comparative Law* 343, 343. Like Bussani and Mattei, Sacco, too, took Schlesinger's philosophy as guidance, see R. Sacco, ibid., 'Installment I of II', 27.

8 The value of formal rules of law in predicting what 'officials are going to … do about disputes' is recognised by American Legal Realists like Karl Llewellyn (K.N. Llewellyn, *The Bramble Bush: The Classic Lectures on the Law and Law School* (Oxford: Oxford University Press, 1960) 6–7).

9 M. Bussani and U. Mattei, 'The Common Core Approach to European Private Law' (1997) 12 *Columbia Journal of European Law* 344, 352.

10 Ibid., 355.

interpretation of contract. First, the purpose of the study is not to ask scholars to compare the *meanings* courts will attribute to the language of a contract. To put it differently, the wording of the contract in question is not the *tertium comparationis*. After all, the comparative study involves the adoption of a single language, i.e. English. The hypothetical contractual language in the questionnaire's cases is, therefore, also drafted in English. We do not wish to compare the meaning that, for example, Croatian, Dutch, English and Spanish courts would ascribe to a contract drafted in English. It would disrupt the comparability of the results because the English, Scottish, and South African reporters will be reporting on the interpretation of contracts drafted in the language of their legal system, while all non-English-speaking reporters would describe how courts would interpret a foreign-language contract. Instead, we wish to compare how courts interpret contracts generally. Therefore, the editors of this study chose to examine *how* courts ascertain the meaning of contractual language. That is to say, it compares the judicial *methods* of interpretation. In this respect, this study's methodology follows the general Common Core approach, as it concentrates on the ways in which courts solve practical problems.

Second, a choice needed to be made regarding the features or aspects of the interpretative exercise this study would compare. We decided to focus on 'interpretation factors', that is to say, the factors a court may find relevant in deciding how to interpret a contract. These factors include the contractual language itself as well as circumstantial data, such as written or oral statements of the parties or their conduct before, during or after the closing of the agreement. Other factors may be the agreement's preamble, and practices or conventions in the particular business or industry in which the parties are operating.

Third, given the role of legal formants in the Common Core approach, reporters were asked to report on a host of legal formants affecting a court's choice of interpretation methods. These may include formal rules in a jurisdiction's civil code, solely case law, or a combination thereof. These may be rules of private law or rather rules of evidence or other procedural rules, or 'unwritten law' or legal principles.

However, in this respect, the rules of the law are not the sole source of the reporter's answer. The law is merely one of multiple possible formants. The reporter should likewise indicate whether the reason for her or his answer lies outside positive law altogether, namely in legal doctrine or scholarly writings, maxims or canons of interpretation, or any other relevant legal or extra-legal formants. We specifically wished to know whether there exists a doctrinal order or hierarchy of interpretation factors the court would adhere to, whether the interpretive question is a question of law or rather of fact, and whether a court seeks to find the common intent of the parties, the linguistic meaning of the contract at hand, or the most 'reasonable' construction of the agreement. The current comparative method invited reporters to report on all these idiosyncrasies.

1.3. BALANCING SAMENESS AND DIFFERENCE

Comparative legal research intrinsically entails a fundamental dilemma. The comparatist requires a critical degree of 'sameness' to render the comparative data comparable. A reliable output of any comparative analysis relies on the comparability of the *comparanda*, the data under comparison.[11] At the same time, the comparatist will want to avoid overlooking meaningful differences, especially those easily concealed behind superficial similarities. The challenge of securing a minimum degree of sameness while maximising the capacity of registering difference multiplies when a dozen different teams of legal scholars from different legal cultures speaking different languages provide the raw data.

First, to increase the comparability of the data on the various national legal systems, it was deemed crucial that all participants followed a single set of instructions meticulously. These instructions are included as Appendix I. The national reporters were asked to avoid answering the questionnaire by predicting *what* a court in their respective jurisdictions would derive from the parties' statements, conduct or other interpretation factors. As explained above, that would amount to attributing meaning to the contract rather than ascertaining *how* a court would attribute that meaning. Therefore, the cases and questions in the questionnaire presumed certain semantic 'facts' that all national reporters had to accept. A question might, for example, invite the reporter to assume that a text is ambiguous or whether a statement or act confirms one of the parties' readings of the contract.

Second, reporters were instructed not to add events or characters to the case, to avoid giving answers that were incomparable with those in other reports. However, if reporters felt that their answer to the question would be more precise if they contrasted it with their response if the facts were different, adding a hypothetical was considered helpful. The reporter could simply explain this by starting a sentence with, for example, 'This would have been different if … (and so on).'

For the same reason, reporters also avoided adding information about their legal systems that were irrelevant to their response to the question at hand. Here, too, the reporter was free to include the passage in a footnote or in the opening remarks, if they found the addition nonetheless to be informative. More generally, reporters were advised to inform the reader, in a footnote, if the facts of the cases or the focus of the question did not sit comfortably with their legal system. This occurred when, for example, the assumptions underlying the case or question would appear odd in the context of their jurisdiction.

---

11 See for terminology, A.E. Örücü, 'Methodology of Comparative Law' in J.M. Smits (ed.), *Elgar Encyclopedia of Comparative Law* (2nd edn, Cheltenham: Edward Elgar) 560.

Finally, the editors provided the reporters with an opportunity to inform the reader of the particularities of their respective legal systems without being confined by the parameters of questions and cases. To this end, reporters were asked to include opening remarks and discuss more general matters relating to contract interpretation that they believed the reader should know about their legal system in advance. Starting off with a country-specific introduction helps the reader to understand the answers to the questions better. It also compensates for the reporter's experience that the inescapable presumptions of the questionnaire are too restrictive of her or his answers. Relatedly, allowing the reporters to clarify matters that the questionnaire would otherwise prevent them from doing advances the reliability of the output of the comparative analysis. Again, one of the comparatist's most likely pitfalls is the need for comparability and comprehensibility accidentally covering up the subtler differences and peculiarities.

2. DEVISING A METHOD OF TRANSLATION

2.1. COMPARATIVE LAW AND THE INEVITABILITY OF TRANSLATION

The most elementary but generally disregarded challenge of comparative law is language. Every time a comparative legal analysis involves jurisdictions that use different general languages, law and language are inherently entwined. For the sake of accuracy and reliability, each participant in a Common Core study carries the earnest task of making every effort to choose their language with the utmost care and diligence.

The intimate connection between law and language is twofold. On the one hand, at some point in the comparative process, someone will have to translate a legal source or commentary from one language to another. This necessary act of translation does not comprise merely the rendition of foreign legal terminology. It includes grammar, syntax, terminology, phraseology, idiom, and so on. One only needs to imagine a text drafted in a language utterly unknown to the reader to appreciate the necessity and scope of legal translation involved in comparative law.

On the other hand, translating legal sources and commentary will entail some degree of comparative legal analysis to produce a translation that is sufficiently equivalent to the source text. We turn to the questions about *what* degree of comparative analysis it is that legal translation requires, and *what* counts as a 'sufficiently equivalent' translation. At this point it is sufficient to say that like *any* translation in *any* field or discipline, translating the artefacts of the law requires some comprehension and preferably significant expertise in the subject matter at hand, i.e. the foreign legal system.

When a single bilingual comparatist carries out a comparative analysis, the translation step may go unnoticed as submerged in the comparative analysis itself. In fact, it might be difficult to distinguish the challenges of translation from challenges of comparisons. In contrast, a team of scholars may divide tasks such that some of them carry out the legal translation and the others the comparative legal analysis. In those instances, it becomes – or should become – clear that legal translation and comparative legal analysis are qualitatively distinct steps, and that both are unavoidably involved in any comparative law project – at least when jurisdictions that use different general languages are involved.

The studies of the Common Core Project present the kind of group project implementing the following division of labour: the national reporters are the translators, and the editors the comparatists. The reporters report on their jurisdiction by answering the editors' questionnaire. The reporters are the experts in their respective jurisdictions. The editors are not. In contrast, the editors are comparatists. They tailor the questionnaire in a manner that will allow them to compare as meaningfully as possible the reporters' answers and draw conclusions as to the nature and degree of similarities and differences. This division of labour is crucial to maintain the reliability of the study's output.

2.2. THE PHILOSOPHICAL UNDERPINNINGS OF THE FACTUAL APPROACH

The division of labour between the reporter-translator and editor-comparatist calls for a careful methodology that integrates legal translation and comparative legal analysis. The philosophical underpinnings of the Common Core approach inform the development of such integrated method. Its factual approach ties the Common Core Project to certain philosophical commitments regarding the tripartite relationship between the nature of the law, the possibility of cross-cultural knowledge of the law, and the facilitative role of language in attaining such knowledge.

As to the first prong of this tripartite relationship, the Common Core comparatist makes the most intuitive yet philosophically controversial presumption: that people share a single factual reality. This supposition necessarily follows from the factual features of the method described above, namely the assumptions that a *tertium comparationis* is available, factual *comparanda* are comparable, and factual data are reliable legal formants.

The second prong of the tripartite relationship involves the presumption of a shared factual world. This is part of the Common Core Project's optimism regarding the possibility of cross-cultural legal knowledge. It shares this optimism with the functional approach to comparative law as famously developed by Konrad Zweigert and Hein Kötz in the 1980s. Zweigert and Kötz believe that the comparatist is capable of attaining reliable comparative legal knowledge because the law is presumptively addressing similar factual problems across societies, legal systems or legal cultures.[12] While legal language and legal concepts are particular to distinct legal systems and therefore difficult or impossible to compare, they argue that analysing the law in its factual manifestation permits the comparison in 'neutral terms'.[13]

Third, the Common Core Project's factual approach implicitly claims that the role of language occupies key territory in facilitating comparative legal knowledge. As with all comparative analyses that involve jurisdictions using different general languages, the Common Core comparatist compares the various legal systems within a single language. To date, this language has been English. Even if a comparative study were to result in a book that uses more than one language, any individual comparative analysis itself will unavoidably be articulated in a single language that either belongs to one of the legal systems under comparison or a third language. Consequently, the Common Core Project commits to a concept of language that permits the comparatist to describe and communicate knowledge of a shared factual world across different languages. Put differently, it presumes the cross-lingual transferability of legal knowledge. It commits to the possibility that the comparatist translates information about a given legal system from one general language into another without corrupting the content of that information. Whether comparative knowledge can be transmitted from one language to another perfectly or imperfectly, the Project assumes issues of translation will not radically obstruct the possibility of comparative legal knowledge.

2.3. REFUTING THE RELATIVIST CRITICISM

Its philosophical underpinnings show that the Common Core Project enjoys a certain optimism as to the feasibility of translation facilitating the comparison of legal formants in distinct legal systems or cultures. This type of methodological optimism, originating from the factual understanding of law, knowledge and translation, has been the subject of harsh criticism: adherents to philosophical relativism contend that a shared factual world is lacking, and comparative legal knowledge is therefore precluded in a radical way. This criticism fails to convince, however, and refuting the inconsistency of its philosophical implications signposts the method of translation most appropriate for this book's comparative study.

---

12 K. Zweigert and H. Kötz, *An Introduction to Comparative Law*, trans. T. Weir (3rd edn. Oxford: Oxford University Press, 1998) 32, 38, 43, 45.

13 Ibid., 10–11.

Legal relativism holds that distinct legal cultures, especially the common law and civil law cultures, are incommensurable because our experience with, and perception of, reality itself is conditioned and confined by the culture in which we find ourselves.[14] Without a meta-cultural vantage point, and thus without a shared experience of a factual reality across legal cultures, comparative knowledge is flawed at best and fictional at worst, the critique goes.[15] Any similarity between legal rules, concepts or other artefacts of legal culture, let alone a 'common core', is the product of an idealised similarity, unavoidably caused by the comparatist's inherent predispositions.[16]

Linguistic relativism entails, similarly, that our experience with the world in which we find ourselves originates from and is confined to the language with which we learned to experience the world to begin with.[17] In this respect, language embodies a grid or framework of intelligibility, a conceptual filter through which we experience reality.[18] As languages provide the categories through which the world presents itself, languages are incommensurable.[19] Hence, as speakers of different languages fail to share a single factual universe, a comparatist is radically barred from communicating legal knowledge from one language into another.[20] Put differently, legal translation stands in the way of a comparatist producing reliable comparative legal knowledge.

---

14 P. Legrand, 'The Same and the Different' in P. Legrand and R. Munday (eds.), *Comparative Legal Studies: Traditions and Transitions* (Cambridge: Cambridge University Press 2003) 265–268.

15 Ibid., 252–253, 281–282, 284; P. Legrand, '"Il n'y a pas de hors-texte": Intimations of Jacques Derrida as Comparatist-at-Law' in P. Goodrich, F. Hoffmann, M. Rosenfeld and C. Vismann (eds.), *Derrida and Legal Philosophy* (London: Palgrave Macmillan, 2008) 138; P. Legrand, 'European Legal Systems Are Not Converging' (1996) 45(1) *International and Comparative Law Quarterly* 52, 59, 75; P. Legrand, 'Econocentrism' (2009) 59(2) *University of Toronto Law Journal* 215, 215.

16 P. Legrand, 'The Same and the Different' in P. Legrand and R. Munday (eds), *Comparative Legal Studies: Traditions and Transitions* (Cambridge: Cambridge University Press, 2003) 240, 284.

17 J.E. Joseph, 'Indeterminacy, Translation and the Law' in M. Morris (ed.), *Translation and the Law* (Philadelphia: Benjamins, 1995) 17.

18 S. Fish, *Doing What Comes Naturally: Change, Rhetoric, and the Practice of Theory in Literary and Legal Studies* (Durham, NC: Duke University Press, 1989) 394–396, 563 n. 31; D. Patterson, *Law and Truth* (Oxford: Oxford University Press, 1996) 101; R. Phillipson, *English-Only Europe? Challenging Language Policy* (New York: Routledge 2003) 108.

19 For example, J. Ainsworth, 'Lost in Translation? Linguistic Diversity and the Elusive Quest for Plain Meaning in the Law' in L. Cheng, K.-K. Sin and A. Wagner (eds.), *The Ashgate Handbook of Legal Translation* (Farnham: Ashgate 2014) 44; J. Boyd White, 'Law as Rhetoric, Rhetoric as Law: The Arts of Cultural and Communal Life' (1985) 52 *The University of Chicago Law Review* 684, 690, 696; J. Boyd White, 'Thinking About Our Language' (1987) 96 *The Yale Law Journal* 1960, 1962.

20 J. Boyd White, 'Thinking About Our Language' (1987) 96 *The Yale Law Journal* 1960, 1962–1964; B. Großfeld, *Core Questions of Comparative Law*, trans. V. Grosswald Curran (Durham, NC: Carolina Academic Press, 2005) 46.

reports containing comparative analyses disturb or compromise the eventual comparison of the national reports. Hence, any elements that they find to be characteristic of their legal system should be explained without reference to foreign law. If the reporter thought particular comparative legal findings were relevant to the project, they were asked to share these insights with the editors in a separate communication.

Likewise, the translations the reporters offered contained as little comparative analysis as possible. While comparative legal analysis is impossible without translation if the jurisdictions involved use different language, legal translation can in fact take place without comparative legal analysis even if imperfectly. When a comparative study includes jurisdictions using different languages, there is no comparing legal texts whatsoever without translation. Imagine a comparatist who cannot read the language of the foreign legal system. She or he might on its face recognise the text as text, that is to say, a document with words and syntax having meaning and conveying a message rather than a piece of paper with randomly dispersed ink. Yet, beyond this, the comparatist would not be able to have any idea of what the document conveys about the foreign legal system – or whether it narrates anything related to law altogether.

Conversely, for the national reporters to translate the information about their legal systems into English, strictly speaking, no comparative analysis is needed. An individual may carry out a legal translation without having any comparative legal knowledge. The eventual translation might turn out to be seriously deficient, missing specific legal context and overlooking the many subtle legal niceties. Yet a genuinely flawed legal translation is still a legal translation. Hence, while comparative legal analysis cannot even get off the ground without an antecedent translation, legal translation does not necessitate a precedent comparative legal analysis, even if resulting in a poor translation.

The translations offered by the national reporters are essential for the editor's comparative analyses. Given the division of labour between reporter-translators and editor-comparatists, it was vital, therefore, that all national reports stayed as close to the language and expression of the language of their legal system while maintaining intelligibility in English, the language of the comparative project. The reporter-translator is therefore advised to follow the following four steps in conveying the meaning of legal concepts and institutions.

3.1. STEP 1: USING INVERTED COMMAS

The first step is to signpost to the reader that a particular word is a legal term or legal phrase referring to a domestic legal concept or institution. The word is best placed within single inverted commas. This applies to all national reports, regardless of whether the language of the reporter's legal system is English or not.

3.2. STEP 2: USING ORIGINAL LANGUAGE FOR DOMESTIC LEGAL CONCEPTS

The second step is to list the legal terms in the original language of the legal system in question. Hence, if the language of a reporter's legal system is not English, the legal term or word naming a domestic legal concept or legal institution should be in the language of the reporter's legal system. Even if the editor-comparatist and the eventual reader cannot understand the term, it will be apparent to all that the term is foreign to the English language or legal system. In a Dutch report, this method might result in a sentence like this:

> Courts tend to solve this problem by appealing to the concept of 'aanvullende werking van de redelijkheid en billijkheid'.

The reporter might be tempted to use the English legal term 'good faith' to refer to this domestic legal concept. This should be avoided, however, because the report risks slipping into a covert comparative analysis suggesting that 'de aanvullende werking van de redelijkheid en billijkheid' is the same or similar to the English concept of good faith, and thus tainting the editor's comparative analysis. The reporter might indeed believe these concepts are the same or at least similar enough to be translated as such. The editor might come to this conclusion as well. Nevertheless, the editor's conclusion should follow from a comparative analysis of 'clean' data provided in the national reports. To this end, the national report should use language that is as free as possible from hidden, antecedent comparisons.

3.3. STEP 3: ADDING A (LITERAL) ENGLISH TRANSLATION

The third step is for the national reporter to add an English translation directly following the domestic legal term, placed in square brackets. This step helps to inform the editor-comparatist and the eventual readership of the semantic meaning of that domestic legal concept in the English language. After all, using a domestic legal term in the original language may convey the concept's foreignness, but it might also prevent the reader from understanding its conceptual meaning or role as a legal formant, and thus prohibits a meaningful comparison.

By adding an English translation, the sentence in the Dutch language version in our example would be expanded as follows:

> Courts tend to solve this problem by appealing to the concept of 'aanvullende werking van de redelijkheid en billijkheid' [the complementary effect of reasonableness and fairness].

To avoid slipping into a covert comparison after all, the English translation should be as *literal* as possible.[27] In fact, the reporter should not shun odd or absurd results. Here, it is better to convey the foreignness of the domestic legal concept within the English language than to use familiar language and inadvertently suggest that the domestic concept is similar to or the same as the English legal concept. Again, the national reporter might deem the concepts alike, but here she or he is acting as a national reporter, not as comparatist.

3.4. STEP 4: ADDING AN EXPLANATION OR DESCRIPTION

The fourth step entails the reporter adding an explanation or description of the domestic concept in the English language. This should follow the English translation directly, hence it also features in the body of the text. This step is geared toward clarifying the possibly odd-looking English translation. Again, for the reasons stated above, the subsequent explanation should under all circumstances avoid referencing English or other foreign legal concepts or institutions that the reporter may consider to be equivalent or near-equivalent terms. Instead, the explanation should be in layman's terms, that is, without further domestic legal terminology. Eventually, the Dutch rendition of a domestic legal term in the English language in our example would look like this:

> Courts tend to solve this problem by appealing to the concept of 'aanvullende werking van de redelijkheid en billijkheid' [the complementary effect of reasonableness and fairness]. This concept entails that … (and so on).

Naturally, while a literal translation between square brackets will not be required if the language of the national legal system is English, further description or explanation should still be provided in the text directly after the use of the term. This would read, for example:

> Reference is often made to the 'four-corner rule'. This rule entails that … (and so on).

---

27 See for a more elaborate defence of literal legal translation for the purpose of comparative legal research, C.J.W. Baaij, 'Legal Translation and the "Contamination" of Comparative Legal Research' in S. Glanert (ed.), *Comparative Law: Engaging Translation* (New York: Routledge, 2014) 112–118. In legal scholarship, literal legal translation does not find broad support. The last notable defenders of literal translation in legal scholarship were Boyd White (*Justice as Translation* (Chicago: University of Chicago Press, 1990) 200, 252–253). Today, Lawrence Venuti is the most vocal proponent of literal over freer methods of translation in general and literary translation studies, see e.g. L. Venuti, *The Translator's Invisibility: A History of Translation* (2nd edn, London: Routledge, 1995/2008).

Furthermore, the method for introducing legal terms in the English language by national reporters from non-English-speaking jurisdictions applies also to citations from, for example, court opinions, authoritative texts and textbooks. The quotation in the body of the text should use the original language of one's jurisdiction, and subsequently add a translation of the quote in the footnote when the original language is not English. Here, too, the translation should be as literal as possible, without using any legal terms that the reporter deems the legal equivalent in the English language. As with using domestic legal terms, the reporter best explains the significance of the quote in the body of the text. Again, the explanation should occur in layman's terms and avoid further domestic legal terminology as much as possible.

4. CONCLUDING REMARKS

The methodology that the editors have chosen to manage the challenges intrinsic to comparative analyses, translation and language in general is not a guarantee of perfect cross-legal and cross-lingual communication. The reason is not because this method falls short of achieving full precision and flawlessness. Rather, it is because there is no such thing as 'perfection' in communication. Assuming that there is implies a bird's-eye view of an 'un-interpreted world' that Donald Davidson has shown to be an inconsistent construct. That is to say, there is no extra-lingual standard by which anyone would be capable of claiming a point of unobstructed communication. Hence, those engaged in cross-lingual comparative legal analysis should not aim to achieve purity of content. Consequently, the methodology chosen in this book is geared toward minimising the risk of implicit inferences in one person's observations 'contaminating' the observations of others. The editors seek to increase the reliability of the findings of the book procedurally by advancing a division of labour between reporters and comparatists.

THE LAW AND ECONOMICS OF CONTRACT INTERPRETATION

Remus VALSAN

1. INTRODUCTION

In the economic analysis of contract law, a complete contingent contract is a hypothetical contract that anticipates every possible circumstance relevant to contract performance and specifies in complete detail all rights and duties of each party in response to these circumstances.[1] A complete contingent contract requires no interpretation, and the court's role is limited to enforcing it according to its terms. No real contract ever achieves this level of completeness, however. In the real world of high transaction costs and bounded rationality, ambiguous or incomplete contracts are a frequent source of litigation.

In the law and economics literature, contract interpretation is usually defined as the undertaking by a court to determine what the terms of a contract are, or should be understood to be.[2] In law, interpretation of express terms is often distinguished from construction, the process of identification of implied terms.[3] In law and economics, the tasks of identifying the contract terms and clarifying their meaning are often analysed together.[4] The focus is on the parties' preferences

---

1 S. Shavell, 'Damage Measures for Breach of Contract' (1980) 11 *Bell Journal of Economics* 466, 468.

2 R.A. Posner, 'The Law and Economics of Contract Interpretation' (2005) 83 *Texas Law Review* 1581, 1582. It should be noted that in common law the process of interpretation is objective – the courts aim to identify what reasonable contractual parties in similar circumstances would have agreed to. In contrast, civil law jurisdictions tend to focus on the subjective intentions of contracting parties (G. McMeel, *The Construction of Contracts: Interpretation, Implication and Rectification* (2nd edn, Oxford: Oxford University Press, 2011) 111). This chapter reviews the economic literature on contract interpretation and does not engage with the legal issues arising in particular legal traditions or jurisdictions.

3 J. Morgan, *Great Debates in Contract Law* (2nd edn, Basingstoke: Palgrave Macmillan, 2015) 114–119; E. Patterson, 'The Interpretation and Construction of Contracts' (1964) 64 *Columbia Law Review* 833.

4 G.M. Cohen, 'Implied Terms and Interpretation in Contract Law' in B. Bouckaert and G. De Geest (eds.), *Encyclopedia of Law and Economics* (vol. III, Cheltenham: Edward Elgar, 2000) 78; R.A. Posner, above n. 2, 1586 (stating that, although gap filling and disambiguation may place different demands on courts, both are interpretive issues in the sense that they

for a certain interpretive regime, and on the effect that the interpretive norms have on the parties' ex ante and ex post costs and behaviour. It is generally agreed that the process of determining the content and meaning of contractual terms should be goal neutral: a court resolving an interpretive dispute should aim to recover the parties' intentions, whatever those intentions were at the moment of contract formation.[5] Goal neutrality is often justified as an extension of the principle of freedom of contract. If parties are allowed to create their own contract, the interpreter's role should be restricted to determining the parties' intentions prospectively and objectively.[6] In determining the parties' intentions, an interpreter should pay attention to the parties' contractual ends (the shared objectives pursued by the parties in entering the contract) as well as to the means they chose to determine those ends (their preferred interpretive method).[7]

A related justification for a goal-neutral interpretive framework is economic efficiency. Parties enter commercial contracts in order to maximise their joint gain. This entails agreeing to terms that maximise their joint surplus and agreeing on a division of the surplus via the contract price.[8] Parties rarely bargain ex ante on every possible contingency that may affect performance over the life of the contract. When the transaction costs of negotiating, drafting and monitoring a complete contract are higher than the expected benefits of completeness, parties leave gaps in their contracts. They invest in contract writing only to the extent needed for courts to find the correct answer, on average, and rely on courts to fill in the remaining gaps. Courts reduce the parties' transaction costs and maximise the utility of their relation by interpolating the terms the parties themselves would have agreed to, had they bargained over that matter.[9] In determining these terms, courts often use majoritarian defaults, which are the terms that most parties in similar circumstances would choose if contracting were costless. For example, courts will sometimes read into a contract a best-efforts clause, except when the parties expressly excluded such a clause, or will excuse non-performance based on impossibility, impracticability or frustration, unless the contract expressly

are efforts to determine how the parties would have resolved the issue had they foreseen it); E.A. Posner, 'The Parol Evidence Rule, the Plain Meaning Rule, and the Principles of Contractual Interpretation' (1998) 146 *University of Pennsylvania Law Review* 533, 559–560 (arguing that there is no theoretical justification for adopting different regimes with respect to incompleteness and ambiguity).

5 A. Schwartz and R.E. Scott, 'Contract Interpretation Redux' (2010) 119 *Yale Law Journal* 962, 964.

6 See e.g. J.S. Kraus, 'Philosophy of Contract Law' in J. Coleman et al. (eds.), *The Oxford Handbook of Jurisprudence and Philosophy of Law* (Oxford: Oxford University Press, 2004) 687; A. Schwartz and R.E. Scott, above n. 5, 937.

7 A.W. Katz, 'The Economics of Form and Substance in Contract Interpretation' (2004) 104 *Columbia Law Review* 496, 521.

8 A. Schwartz and J. Watson, 'Conceptualizing Contractual Interpretation' (2013) 42 *The Journal of Legal Studies* 1, 2.

9 A. Schwartz and R.E. Scott, above n. 5, 945.

precludes this possibility.[10] When the population of similarly situated parties is narrow, the majoritarian default becomes a tailored default that follows more closely the particular characteristics of the contractors.[11] Thus, in determining the missing terms by reference to the parties' hypothetical bargain, the courts further the parties' objective of maximising their contractual surplus. This process of interpolation decreases the parties' ex ante costs and the risks of ex post interpretation error.[12] Nonetheless, majoritarian or tailored defaults are not always efficient gap-fillers. In certain cases, courts respond to contractual incompleteness by providing penalty defaults (such as the *contra proferentem* rule, or the rule that only foreseeable damages will be awarded). Penalty defaults induce contracting parties to invest more in the ex ante transaction costs by disclosing private information or bargaining explicitly with regard to a particular matter, in order to avoid the less favourable default.[13]

A significant part of the law and economics literature on contract interpretation focuses on the most appropriate method the courts should use to retrieve the parties' intention: the textualist (or formalist) interpretation, which emphasises the primacy of ex ante contract design, and the contextualist (or purposive) interpretation, which focuses on ex post adjudication by courts. An emerging strand of research seeks to move beyond the relative merits of textualism and contextualism as universal interpretive regimes, and emphasises the importance of interpreting contracts using the methodology that best suits the circumstances of each contract. With limited exceptions, the methodology that meets this requirement is the one chosen by the parties, or, failing that, the one that reasonable parties in their circumstances would have preferred.[14]

---

10 R.A. Posner, above n. 2, 1585.

11 C. Goetz and R.E. Scott, 'The Limits of Expanded Choice: An Analysis of the Interactions between Express and Implied Contract Terms' (1985) 73 *California Law Review* 261; D. Charny, 'Hypothetical Bargains: The Normative Structure of Contract Interpretation' (1991) 89 *Michigan Law Review* 1815. For a discussion of the difficulties associated with identifying and implementing majoritarian, tailored and penalty defaults see I. Ayres, 'Default Rules for Incomplete Contracts' in P. Newman (ed.), *The New Palgrave Dictionary of Economics and the Law* (vol. I, New York: Stockton Press, 1998) 585; J. Johnson, 'Strategic Bargaining and the Economic Theory of Contract Default Rules' (1990) 100 *Yale Law Journal* 615; E.A. Posner, 'Economic Analysis of Contract Law after Three Decades: Success or Failure?' (2003) 112 *Yale Law Journal* 829.

12 A. Schwartz and R.E. Scott, 'Contract Theory and the Limits of Contract Law' (2003) 113 *Yale Law Journal* 541, 544; C. Goetz and R.E. Scott, above n. 11, 262.

13 I. Ayres and R. Gertner, 'Filling Gaps in Incomplete Contracts: An Economic Theory of Default Rules' (1989) 99 *Yale Law Journal* 87; L. Bebchuk and S. Shavell, 'Information and the Scope of Liability for Breach of Contract: The Rule of *Hadley v. Baxendale*' (1991) 7 *Journal of Law Economics and Organization* 284; I. Ayres, 'Ya-Huh: There Are and Should be Penalty Defaults' (2006) 33 *Florida State University Law Review* 589.

14 S. Bayern, 'Contract Meta-Interpretation' (2016) 49 *The University of California, Davis Law Review* 1097, 1101. Respecting the parties' choice of interpretive regime does not mean that all aspects of the interpretive regime should be fully under their control. Rules such as

Contractual parties' preferences over interpretive rules are heterogeneous, and are influenced by factors such as the expected ex ante and ex post transaction costs, their degree of sophistication, the nature and duration of their relationship, the novelty and riskiness of their project, the need to leave a complete and accurate record of their bargain, the need to deter opportunism, or the need to reduce the risk of court error. Thus, in this view, the desirability of an interpretive regime depends on the parties' rational preferences and the attributes of the underlying transaction, and not solely on the independent merits of textual or contextual interpretation.

The need for flexibility in the application of interpretive methods is a normative insight of the emerging law and economics literature on contract interpretation. In many jurisdictions, the applicable interpretation rules are unitary and mandatory, in the sense that a given legal or judicial choice for a textualist or contextualist method applies across all types of contracts, and contracting parties cannot instruct courts to apply a different method.[15] To advance the principle of goal neutrality in interpretation and to respect the parties' freedom to choose their contractual means and ends, it is submitted that, from an economic theory perspective, courts should adjust their methodology to reflect the parties' intentions either to regard their contract as complete (entire agreement clause), or to regard it as incomplete and rely ex post on relevant context to fill in the contractual gaps. The remaining part of this chapter is structured as follows. Section 2 summarises the main features of textualism and contextualism. Section 3 is an in-depth analysis of the relations between ex ante or ex post transaction costs and the optimal interpretive regime. Section 4 concludes.

2. INTERPRETIVE METHODOLOGIES: TEXTUALISM AND CONTEXTUALISM

Legal commentators have long debated over the relative merits of the textual and contextual methods of interpretation.[16] In the textualist interpretation method,

contra proferentem, the formal requirements for enforceability of promises, or mandatory rules regarding evidence should not be under the parties' control (ibid., 1139–1142).

15 Parties can choose indirectly among interpretive regimes by choosing the jurisdiction to govern their contract or by choosing between courts and private arbitration (A.W. Katz, above n. 7, 508–509).

16 The debate between the two schools of thought has deep historical roots. See P. Stein, 'The Two Schools of Jurists in the Early Roman Principate' (1972) 31 *Cambridge Law Review* 8, 17–18 (discussing an analogous debate on interpretation in Roman law between the Sabinian and Proculian schools of jurists). For a detailed discussion of the development and main critiques of the two interpretive methods see A. Barak, *Purposive Interpretation in Law* (Princeton: Princeton University Press, 2011) chs. 10 and 11.

the contract is regarded as the primary evidence of the parties' understanding. The contract is presumed to be complete if it appears final and complete on its face. More ambiguous extrinsic evidence, such as previous understandings or industry norms and customs, is excluded.[17] Textualist jurisdictions give a presumptively conclusive effect to merger or integration clauses and, in their absence, presume that the contract is fully integrated if it appears to be complete (the 'hard' parol evidence rule).[18] Textualism is often associated with literalism, which gives contractual terms a plain-language meaning that cannot be contradicted at the adjudication stage by contextual evidence supporting a different meaning.[19] Thus, textualism rejects the relevance of the social aspect of contracting, and requires 'separation of law from life, of the meaning of the text from its context.'[20] In its moderate form, textualism does not reject entirely the importance of context.[21] Instead, context is embedded in contract design by giving the parties, not the court, the power to decide the extent to which a court can consider context at the enforcement stage.[22]

Traditionally, textualism has been defended on grounds of freedom of contract and autonomy of contractual parties. By setting clear and predictable rules, textualism operates as a safeguard against the state infringing on individual choice.[23] The interpretive regime is thus a mechanism for allocating decision-making powers among various groups and institutions.[24] Formalism restricts the courts' discretion and prompts them to uphold the bargain of the parties instead of creating a new one.[25] It inculcates the view that sometimes it

---

17 C. Mitchell, *Interpretation of Contracts* (London: Routledge, 2007) 123. See also J. Steyn, 'Does Formalism Hold Sway in England' (1996) 49 *Current Legal Problems* 43, 44; M. Stone, 'Formalism' in J. Coleman et al. (eds.), *The Oxford Handbook of Jurisprudence and Philosophy of Law* (Oxford: Oxford University Press, 2004) 173; A.W. Katz, 'Contract Theory – Who Needs It?' (2014) 81 *University of Chicago Law Review* 2043.

18 R. Gilson, C. Sabel and R.E. Scott, 'Text and Context: Contract Interpretation as Contract Design' (2014) 100 *Cornell Law Review* 23, 43.

19 C. Mitchell, above n. 17, 93.

20 O. Ben-Shahar, 'The Tentative Case against Flexibility in Commercial Law' (1999) 66 *University of Chicago Law Review* 781, 781. Parties are encouraged or constrained to write complete contracts by the use of penalty defaults (G.M. Cohen, above n. 4, 82).

21 See C. Sunstein 'Must Formalism Be Defended Empirically?' (1999) 66 *University of Chicago Law Review* 636, 645 (stating that formalism is 'a doomed enterprise if it is an effort to give meaning to terms apart from cultural understandings and context.').

22 R. Gilson, C. Sabel and R.E. Scott, above n. 18, 43.

23 A.W. Katz, above n. 7, 514. See also N. MacCormick, *Rhetoric and the Rule of Law: A Theory of Legal Reasoning* (Oxford: Oxford University Press, 2005) 127; M.J. Trebilcock, *The Limits of Freedom of Contract* (Cambridge, Mass: Harvard University Press, 1997) 55; R.E. Barnett, 'A Consent Theory of Contract' (1986) 86 *Columbia Law Review* 269, 291–319; R.E. Barnett, 'The Sound of Silence: Default Rules and Contractual Consent' (1992) 78 *Virginia Law Review* 821, 857–860.

24 C. Sunstein, *Legal Reasoning and Political Conflict* (Oxford: Oxford University Press, 1998) 168–169.

25 C. Mitchell, above n. 17, 101.

is appropriate for judicial decision makers to recognise their lack of jurisdiction and to defer to private ordering, even when they believe that their own judgement is preferable.[26] Thus, the fundamental question in relation to interpretation is determining whether the parties have withdrawn from the court the opportunity to give a contextual interpretation of their agreement.[27]

The traditional formalist view engaged with difficult normative issues of legitimacy and decision-making authority. In recent years, the formalist argument has been recast in economic terms. This new trend is often referred to as neoformalism or anti-anti-formalism.[28] Neoformalism argues that a default textualist regime is better suited to promote economic and practical goals such as efficiency, procedural fairness or public accountability. This recent wave of economically influenced scholarship analyses the relative merits of textualism and contextualism using economic tools and concepts, such as rational behaviour, transaction costs, opportunism or information asymmetry.[29] An important strand of neoformalist research aims to justify textualism on empirical grounds, rather than on grounds of theory or principle.[30] By moving away from difficult arguments about legitimacy, neoformalism refocuses the debate on the pragmatic considerations underpinning why contracting parties favour a formal interpretative regime over a substantive one. For this reason, many neoformalists do not regard their position as the antithesis of contextualism. Their concern is with economic incentives and choices, rather than with contract as a social institution. The issue is not which interpretive rules yield more accuracy, but which interpretive defaults best reflect the parties' preferred trade-offs among accuracy in interpretation, contract-writing costs and contract enforcement costs.[31]

Contextualism holds that the goal-neutral objective of recovering the parties' intentions is best achieved if courts are allowed to access a broad evidentiary base.[32] Contextualism views contracts primarily as social phenomena, and

---

26 F. Schauer, 'Formalism' (1988) 97 *Yale Law Journal* 509, 543–544.

27 W. Woodward, 'Neoformalism in a Real World of Forms' (2001) *Wisconsin Law Review* 971, 975.

28 D. Charny, 'The New Formalism in Contract' (1999) 66 *University of Chicago Law Review* 842; R.E. Scott, 'The Death of Contract Law' (2004) 54 *University of Toronto Law Journal* 370; R.E. Scott, 'The Case for Formalism in Relational Contract' (2000) 94 *Northwestern University Law Review* 847; J. Murray 'Contract Theories and the Rise of Neoformalism' (2002) 71 *Fordham Law Review* 869; T.C. Grey, 'The New Formalism', Stanford Law School, Public Law and Legal Series Working Paper No. 4, 1999, available at http://ssrn.com/ abstract=200732; C. Mitchell, above n. 17, 99.

29 A.W. Katz, above n. 7, 499; C. Mitchell, above n. 17, 102.

30 C. Sunstein, above n. 21, 642. See also L. Kaplow, 'Rules versus Standards: An Economic Analysis' (1992) 42 *Duke Law Journal* 557, 563 (arguing that the choice between rules and standards in legal regulation depends on the interplay of various factors that can only be verified empirically).

31 C. Mitchell, above n. 17, 101; A.W. Katz, above n. 7, 520; C. Sunstein, above n. 21, 641–642; A. Schwartz and R.E. Scott, above n. 5, 964; A.W. Katz, above n. 7, 497.

32 A. Schwartz and R.E. Scott, above n. 5, 938.

contract incompleteness as unavoidable and desirable. Courts recover the reasonable expectations of the contracting parties by taking into consideration elements of the social and commercial context of the agreement, such as the parties' past practices, their course of performance, or the conduct of similarly situated parties (trade customs).[33] In contextualist regimes, a contract that appears final and complete on its face, or an express merger clause declaring the contract to be integrated, are usually regarded as raising only a rebuttable presumption of integration, which can be overridden by extrinsic evidence that the parties lacked any such intent (the 'soft' parol evidence rule).[34] Courts can also override the prima facie plain meaning of contractual terms, by considering contextual evidence that realigns the parties' written contract with its true meaning. Contextualism thus serves as a kind of judicial insurance policy that facilitates replacement or clarification of contract terms that, viewed in what the court believes to be the proper context, do not accurately reflect the parties' intentions.[35]

A variant of the contextualist theory argues that contextualism should be used primarily to determine the parties' choice of interpretive method. In line with the freedom of contract and party autonomy principles, courts faced with an interpretive dispute should first determine whether the parties opted for a more or less formal approach to interpreting their contract.[36] This inquiry, however, should be contextual. A broader range of evidence is preferable, in order to allow courts to determine with accuracy the parties' preferred interpretative method.[37]

In their pure forms, the two interpretive regimes are the extremes of a continuum of approaches. Pure textualism would mean that contracts are self-sufficient, and words have acontextual, indisputable meanings that require no interpretation. Pure contextualism would mean the opposite – the interpreter would be free to discard the contract altogether and recover the parties' intentions from extrinsic evidence.[38] The preferable view is to regard textualism and contextualism as complements rather than opposites. This view shifts refocuses the debate on the relative weight that text and context should bear in the interpretation process, and on how far toward the formal or contextual ends of the spectrum the interpretation exercise should go. Interpretation

---

33 C. Mitchell, above n. 17, 105.

34 R. Gilson, C. Sabel and R.E. Scott, above n. 18, 36–37.

35 R.E. Scott, 'Text versus Context: The Failure of the Unitary Law of Contract Interpretation' in F.H. Buckley (ed.), *The American Illness: Essays on the Rule of Law* (New Haven, Connecticut: Yale University Press, 2013) 313; J.S. Kraus and R.E. Scott, 'Contract Design and the Structure of Contractual Intent' (2009) 84 *New York University Law Review* 1023, 1025.

36 W. Woodward, above n. 27, 977.

37 C. Mitchell, above n. 17, 104.

38 J. Morgan, above n. 3, 94.

thus becomes 'a composite exercise, neither uncompromisingly literal, nor unswervingly purposive.'[39]

3. TRANSACTION COSTS AND THE OPTIMAL INTERPRETIVE METHOD

The goal of contract interpretation is to determine the parties' understanding of the content and meaning of the terms in their contract. Accuracy in interpretation is highly desirable, but it comes at a cost to all parties involved in the interpretive process. The economic view of contract interpretation emphasises the need to take into account the various ex ante and ex post transaction costs relevant to contract formation and interpretation, and the need to trade off interpretive accuracy against these costs. Contracting parties often have more detailed and accurate information about the relevant costs and benefits, and thus have a comparative advantage over courts or legislators in choosing the interpretive rules that achieve an efficient trade-off.[40]

In general terms, where the costs of negotiating and writing a contract are low, parties can draft relatively complete contracts. Other things being equal, they will have a strong preference for formal contract interpretation, which is best suited to ensure the interpretation of these contracts in accordance with their express terms. When the ex ante costs of negotiating and drafting an agreement are high, due to factors such as the duration and complexity of the transaction or the parties' level of sophistication, complete contracts are more difficult to write. In these cases, the ex ante decision of how much to invest in filling contractual gaps is a key determinant of the interpretive regime that a given set of contracting parties is likely to prefer.[41]

Some contracting parties may prefer to incur low ex ante negotiating and drafting costs and undertake the risk of high ex post enforcement costs, which are

---

39 Lord Bingham, 'A New Thing under the Sun? The Interpretation of Contracts and the ICS Decision' (2008) 12 *Edinburgh Law Review* 374, 376. See also J. Steyn, 'The Intractable Problem of the Interpretation of Legal Texts' (2003) 25 *Sydney Law Review* 5, 8 (stating that interpretation 'is not a science [but] an art. … Educated intuition may play a larger role than the examination of niceties of textual analysis'); J.H. Wigmore, *Wigmore on Evidence* (vol. 9, 9th edn, Boston: Little, Brown and Company, 1981) para. 2461 ('The history of the law of interpretation is the history of a progress from a stiff and superstitious formalism to a flexible rationalism').

40 A. Schwartz and R.E. Scott, above n. 5, 944.

41 A.B. Badawi, 'The Attributes of Transactions and Interpretive Preferences: The Limits and Borders of Contractual Formalism', Bepress Working Paper, 2007, available at http://works.bepress.com/adam.bbadawi/3 at 1–3. See also G.G. Triantis, 'The Efficiency of Vague Contract Terms: A Response to the Schwartz-Scott Theory of U.CC. Article 2' (2002) 62 *Louisiana Law Review* 1065 (discussing economic justifications of contractual gaps other than high ex ante transaction costs).

future and uncertain.[42] Such parties will rely on courts to fill in the contractual gaps through the process of contract interpretation. An efficient interpretation regime in this case would allow courts to use contextual evidence indicating the parties' understanding of their obligations under the contract.[43] When parties rely on courts to fill in the contractual gaps, the more expansive the courts' interpretative approach, the less specific the parties have to be in the written terms of their agreement.[44] Nevertheless, if litigation occurs and significant judicial gap filling is required, a contextual interpretation regime may increase significantly the overall transaction costs. This is because the relevant context must be established drawing on a broader evidentiary base, which increases the costs of litigation and the possibility of court error.[45]

When the ex ante transaction costs are high, a contextual interpretive regime allows parties the flexibility to shift costs from the front-end of the contracting process to the back-end litigation stage.[46] The price for this flexibility is the risk of high ex post costs, such as litigation costs, court error or opportunism. In some instances, such as long-term or repeat contracts, parties may decide that it is more efficient to incur the high ex ante costs and draft more complete contracts. Where parties voluntarily incur higher ex ante transaction costs, an interpretive regime that aims to maximise their expected joint surplus will aim to decrease the litigation-stage costs (the parties' own litigation costs, the cost of litigation to the judiciary, and judicial error costs). In other words, the more time the parties spend negotiating and drafting the contract, the more restrictive the court's approach to implied terms and interpretation should be.[47] A more formalist approach to interpretation is also desirable where courts are not better suited than parties to fill in contractual gaps. When the court's costs (the cost of determining the efficient implied term and the probability of error) are significantly higher than the parties' ex ante costs, an efficient regime will place the obligation to supply the missing term with the contractual parties, via penalty defaults that create incentives for further negotiations and information disclosure.[48] In other instances, where the contractual incompleteness could be an indication that the parties' negotiations have not reached the stage of actual agreement (such as lack of price or quantity), the court will refuse to fill in the gap.

---

42 A. Schwartz and R.E. Scott, above n. 12, 585. For discussion of the reasons for incompleteness, see for example O. Hart and B. Holmstrom, 'The Theory of Contracts' in T. Bewley (ed.), *Advances in Economic Theory* (Cambridge: Cambridge University Press, 1987) 71; O. Hart and J. Moore, 'Foundations of Incomplete Contracts' (1999) 66 *Review of Economic Studies* 115; and J. Tirole, 'Incomplete Contracts: Where Do We Stand?' (1999) 67 *Econometrica* 741.

43 A.B. Badawi, above n. 41, 1.

44 C. Mitchell, above n. 17, 109.

45 Ibid., 110; A. Vermeule, 'Three Strategies of Interpretation' (2005) 42 *San Diego Law Review* 607, 614.

46 R.E. Scott, above n. 35, 317.

47 G.M. Cohen, above n. 4, 88.

48 I. Ayres and R. Gertner, above n. 13, 87.

Otherwise, judicial interpolation would amount to writing the contract on behalf of the parties, rather than enforcing a pre-existing agreement.[49]

In yet other cases, contractual parties may decide to structure their transaction in ways that by-pass the high ex ante transaction costs. Techniques of avoiding or reducing such costs include agreeing to renegotiate potentially controversial matters, using catchall clauses such as best efforts or good faith as gap plugs, entering a series of shorter-term contracts that reduce the costs arising from imperfect foresight, or substituting vertical integration for contracting.[50] The selection of the optimal interpretive regime in these cases should be dynamic, in line with the structure that the parties have chosen for their transaction. As the remaining part of this section will show, there are a variety of reasons and factors that compel some parties to incur higher ex ante transaction costs, with a view to minimising the expected ex post litigation costs, while other parties leave broader gaps in their contracts that can be filled in ex post by courts.

3.1. EX ANTE TRANSACTION COSTS AND CONTRACT INTERPRETATION

As mentioned in the previous section, a simplified approach to understanding the parties' choice of interpretive regime links high ex ante transaction costs for the parties with a preference for contextualism, and low ex ante costs for the parties with formalism. This section discusses several scenarios where these correlations do not hold. In certain cases, rational economic actors prefer a formalist interpretation regime despite high ex ante transaction costs.

One instance of high ex ante costs is where the contract is negotiated and entered into by agents, especially where the principal is a company.[51] In this case, the principal may insist on greater formality and completeness of the documents in order to ensure that it will be bound only by the terms of the agreement, to the exclusion of negotiation statements, and to ensure that the contract can be used in the future by persons who had little or no involvement in its negotiation and drafting.[52] A principal may have incentives to invest in the ex ante drafting costs and select a formal interpretive regime in order to minimise the risk of

---

49 R.A. Posner, above n. 2, 1587–1588.

50 G.M. Cohen, above n. 4, 80; R.A. Posner, above n. 2, 1584; O. Hart and J. Moore, 'Agreeing Now to Agree Later: Contracts that Rule Out but do not Rule In', NBER Working Paper No. 10397, 2004, available at http://www.nber.org/papers/w10397; J. Kraus and S. Walt, 'In Defense of the Incorporation Strategy' in J. Kraus and S. Walt (eds.), *The Jurisprudential Foundations of Corporate and Commercial Law* (Cambridge: Cambridge University Press, 2000) 193, 211–212. On vertical integration see O.E. Williamson, *The Economic Institutions of Capitalism* (New York: Free Press, 1985) 60–61; H. Collins, *Regulating Contracts* (Oxford: Oxford University Press, 1999) 163.

51 C. Mitchell, above n. 17, 113–114.

52 A. Berg, 'Thrashing through the Undergrowth' (2006) 122 *Law Quarterly Review* 354, 359.

loss resulting from agency costs. Agency costs arise due to the misalignment between the interests of the principal and those of the agent. Because agents are rational actors that seek to maximise their own utility, they have incentives to shirk or promote their own interest, while only satisfying the interests of the principal.[53] An insurance agent, for instance, may misrepresent the extent of the policy coverage or the applicant's insurability in order to earn a commission. A manager charged with supervising a supplier's obligations may shirk by failing to object to defective performance, thus jeopardising the principal's claims against the supplier.[54] In such contexts, principals can use formalism to disable agents from binding them in contracts that maximise the agent's private interests. For example, entire agreement clauses, anti-waiver clauses or clauses negating reliance on statements during negotiations can reduce the principal's loss from shirking or self-serving oral representations made by agents dealing with third parties.[55] A similar situation arises when third parties, such as banks or insurance companies, acquire an interest in the contract. Such third parties are more likely to demand detailed contractual provisions and are more likely to seek the enforcement of the legal rights according to the terms of the agreement.[56] More generally, contracts whose value depends significantly on the participation of third parties will have higher value when interpreted under a relatively formalistic regime, other things being equal.[57]

Another instance where parties may incur higher ex ante costs is the case of new repeat contractors between whom trust has not yet been established. Such contractors are encouraged to incur higher initial transaction costs, due to the expectation of using their detailed contractual framework multiple times in the future, with the same or different contracting partners.[58] This is even more likely to happen when the contract is in an emerging field with high rates of failure, where parties enter an unusual venture with high litigation risks, or where parties have wide access to legal counselling.[59]

---

53 M.C. Jensen and W.H. Meckling, 'Theory of the Firm: Managerial Behavior, Agency Costs and Ownership Structure' (1976) 3 *Journal of Financial Economics* 305. In economics, 'satisficing' (a mix between satisfying and suffice) is used to denote the fact that agents pursue a goal until they reach a satisfactory level, rather than strive for the best result (see C. Doucouliagos, 'A Note on the Evolution of Homo Economicus' (1994) 28 *Journal of Economic Issues* 877, 879).

54 A.W. Katz, above n. 7.

55 Ibid., 533; see also E.A. Posner, above n. 4, 563–564; K. Davis, 'Licensing Lies: Merger Clauses, the Parol Evidence Rule and Pre-contractual Misrepresentations' (1999) 33 *Valparaiso University Law Review* 485, 534.

56 C. Mitchell, above n. 17, 119.

57 A.W. Katz, above n. 7, 534–535.

58 C. Mitchell, above n. 17, 110; D. Charny, 'Non-Legal Sanctions in Commercial Relationships' (1990) 104 *Harvard Law Review* 375, 436–437.

59 L. Cunningham, 'Toward a Prudential and Credibility-Centered Parol Evidence Rule' (2000) 68 *University of Cincinnati Law Review* 269, 274; H. Beale and T. Dugdale, 'Contracts between Businessmen: Planning and Use of Contractual Remedies' (1975) 2 *British Journal of Law and Society* 45, 48; A.W. Katz, above n. 7, 536.

A similar scenario arises in high-frequency transactions.[60] High-frequency transactions create the potential for economies of scale.[61] Contractual parties capitalise on the opportunity to save transaction costs by choosing vertical integration of their businesses or by investing in drafting and negotiation costs. Contracts in high-frequency transactions tend to have a higher degree of completeness for several reasons. First, rational parties will incur a large upfront cost in drafting the initial contract, with a view to saving ex ante costs in future similar transactions. As a transaction becomes more frequent, the marginal cost of drafting a governing contract will decrease. Second, as the transaction repeats, contracting parties have renewed opportunities to learn about the gaps in their contracts and how to plug them. Rational parties that are able to draft nearly complete contracts would prefer more formal types of interpretation. Because contracts contain fewer gaps, there is little need for extrinsic evidence.[62] If repeated over a significant period of time, high-frequency transactions generate a body of industry norms and customs that parties could incorporate ex ante or rely on ex post to plug the gaps in their contracts.[63] In such cases, parties will lose their incentives to incur the high ex ante costs, and will prefer instead a contextualist interpretation that allows the norms and customs to be incorporated into their agreement. Not all industry norms, however, are economically efficient. Inefficient norms may arise and persist for a number of reasons, including information asymmetries, strategic behaviour, negative externalities, high renegotiation costs or status-quo bias.[64]

In contrast, parties to infrequent and highly complex relations prefer to rely on courts to complete their contract through ex post contextual interpretation. In such relations, a large number of low-probability contingencies that could affect the value of contractual performance exist, but the efficient responses to those

60 Frequency refers to the number of times a firm or individual carries out a particular type of transaction. See A.B. Badawi, above n. 41, 3.

61 For examples of high-frequency transactions and the related interpretive regime see Bernstein's studies of the diamond, grain and cotton trades (L. Bernstein, 'Merchant Law in a Merchant Court: Rethinking the Code's Search for Immanent Business Norms' (1996) 144 *University of Pennsylvania Law Review* 1765; L. Bernstein, 'The Questionable Empirical Basis of Article 2's Incorporation Strategy: A Preliminary Study' (1999) 66 *University of Chicago Law Review* 710; L. Bernstein, 'Private Commercial Law in the Cotton Industry: Creating Co-operation through Rules, Norms and Institutions' (2001) 99 *Michigan Law Review* 1724).

62 A.B. Badawi, above n. 41, 7–8. See also S.J. Choi, M. Gulati and E.A. Posner, 'The Dynamics of Contract Evolution' (2013) 88 *New York University Law Review* 1.

63 See R.D. Cooter, 'Decentralized Law for a Complex Economy: The Structural Approach to Adjudicating the New Law Merchant' (1996) 144 *University of Pennsylvania Law Review* 1643, 1646.

64 R.A. Posner, 'Let Us Never Blame a Contract Breaker' in O. Ben-Shahar and A. Porat (eds.), *Fault in American Contract Law* (Cambridge: Cambridge University Press, 2010) 3, 17; E.A. Posner, 'Law, Economics, and Inefficient Norms' (1996) 144 *University of Pennsylvania Law Review* 1697, 1713–1723.

contingencies cannot easily be specified in advance.[65] Mergers, for instance, are complex idiosyncratic transactions that involve high time constraints and uncertainty. The acute time pressure specific to merger transactions leaves parties to such transactions little scope for drafting nearly complete contracts. Even when time constraints are not severe, the particularities of each deal prevent parties from applying previously negotiated or standard clauses to the same extent possible in high-certainty commodities transactions.[66] Construction contracts are another example of low-frequency, high-uncertainty deals that lead to a preference for contextual interpretation. Similar to mergers, construction agreements require bargaining over a high number of contingencies during a narrow time window. Rather than incurring the high ex ante negotiation and drafting costs, parties to such contracts often use standard form contracts supplied by the construction industry. These boilerplate agreements often mandate that any disputes be resolved through compulsory arbitration or other forms of alternative dispute resolution machinery, with an ensuing preference for contextualism.[67]

Uncertainty is another variable that affects the parties' drafting costs and their preference for a particular interpretive regime. Uncertainty in contractual relations arises due to the limits of the human capacity to receive, store, retrieve and process information without error, as well as due to the limitations of language to convey meaning.[68] These limits of the human cognition and language, referred to as bounded rationality,[69] affect the way in which economic agents structure their transactions. When the number and type of contingencies associated with a given transaction are unknown, it is impossible or prohibitively costly for parties to describe the substance of their agreement and to specify the contract terms to govern it. If parties envisage long-term or high-frequency relations and the predictive and linguistic uncertainties are acute, they may rely on internal organisational mechanisms such as vertical integration to structure their relation and attenuate the risk of opportunism.[70] Alternatively, they may

---

65 G.M. Cohen, above n. 4, 81; G.K. Hadfield, 'Judicial Competence and the Interpretation of Incomplete Contracts' (1994) 23 *Journal of Legal Studies* 159, 165.

66 A.B. Badawi, above n. 41, 40–42. For empirical evidence showing that parties to merger transactions prefer jurisdictions that have a contextualist approach to interpretation see G. Miller, 'Bargaining on the Red-eye: New Light on Contract Theory', New York University Law and Economics Working Papers, 2008, available at http://lsr.nellco.org/cgi/viewcontent.cgi?article=1135&context=nyu_lewp.

67 A.B. Badawi, above n. 41, 46 (discussing standard form contracts provided by the American Association of Architects).

68 O.E. Williamson, *Antitrust Economics: Mergers, Contracting, and Strategic Behaviour* (New York: Basil Blackwell, 1987) 74–78.

69 H.A. Simon, 'Theories of Bounded Rationality' in C.B. McGuire and R. Radner (eds.), *Decision and Organization* (Amsterdam: North-Holland, 1972) 161–176.

70 A.B. Badawi, above n. 41, 10.

choose to leave gaps in contracts and rely on courts to fill the gaps through contextual interpretation.

Behavioural insights about contracting and contract as a social institution may also explain why some parties prefer to rely on a contextual interpretation regime and shift high front-end transactions to the back-end enforcement stage of the contracting process. In relational contracts, trust and confidence between parties is essential to the creation and survival of the relationship.[71] In such contracts, a narrow focus on negotiating detailed terms may create an adversarial atmosphere by making the parties conscious of the risk of litigation and opportunism.[72] Incurring high ex ante transaction costs may cause parties to lose sight of the values necessary for the preservation of their relations, such as performance planning or the building of mutual trust.[73] Another behavioural reason for contractual gaps is that parties may rely on alternative governance mechanisms to regulate their behaviour, such as social norms or commercial reputation. These mechanisms are particularly suitable for commitments that have low stakes relative to litigation costs, or complex relations characterised by a high degree of mutual trust and good faith. The flexible and conciliatory nature of alternative governance mechanisms helps to preserve ongoing commercial relations. In these relations, leaving contractual gaps and relying on a contextual interpretive regime may provide stronger incentives for parties to adhere in good faith to the relevant norms, lest evidence to the contrary be admitted in a dispute.[74]

At the same time, there are arguments which favour a more formalist approach to interpretation of relational contracts. In markets where a high level of mutual trust is necessary to preserve a contractual relation and to encourage cooperation with regard to performance of non-verifiable aspects of the contract, the prospect of extended litigation can undermine this trust and cooperation. Consequently, parties would prefer that disputes be kept short and straightforward through textualist adjudication.[75] This argument is supported by empirical research showing that parties who are members of trade associations and who thus rely on social norms as well as third-party enforcement mechanisms, prefer formal interpretive rules and avoid contextualised jurisdictions.[76]

---

71 D. Campbell (ed.), *The Relational Theory of Contract: Selected Works of Ian Macneil* (London: Sweet and Maxwell, 2001) 154, 161.

72 D. Charny, above n. 58, 407.

73 C. Mitchell, above n. 17, 111; W. Whitford, 'Relational Contracts and the New Formalism' (2004) *Wisconsin Law Review* 631, 637.

74 C. Mitchell, above n. 17, 119–120; R.A. Posner, above n. 2, 1584; G.M. Cohen, above n. 4, 81–82; D. Charny, above n. 58, 408–409; A. Badawi, 'Interpretive Preferences and the Limits of the New Formalism' (2009) 6 *Berkeley Business Law Journal* 1, 34.

75 A.W. Katz, above n. 7, 525; See e.g. L. Bernstein, 'Opting Out of the Legal System: Extralegal Contractual Relations in the Diamond Industry' (1992) 21 *Journal of Legal Studies* 115, 119–130 (describing relations of trust and dispute resolution mechanisms in the diamond market).

76 A. Schwartz and R.E. Scott, above n. 5, 955.

Another important current of thought in the law and economics literature on contract interpretation focuses on the link between the degree of sophistication of contractual parties and the optimal interpretive regime applicable to their contract. When both parties are legally unsophisticated or are commercial entities that choose not to invest in ex ante contract design, and such parties do business in fields where legal norms blend with social and commercial norms, the optimal interpretation regime allows courts to determine the details of the contract by reference to a broader evidentiary base. An interpretive regime that prevents courts from accessing contextual information bearing on the parties' real relationship may result in an interpretation that is in opposition to the parties' actual intentions and may frustrate these parties' efforts to govern their transactions efficiently.[77]

Contextualist interpretation is also desirable when legally unsophisticated individuals enter into written contracts with sophisticated parties who supply the written contract terms, such as consumer contracts. In these types of contract, the more sophisticated party has scope for abuse of its position by providing written contract terms that alter previous understandings.[78] Conversely, the passive parties are at risk of exploitation through adhesion to formal contract terms that do not reflect their real intentions.[79] The non-drafting parties will generally not have the economic incentives or the ability to examine the standard terms with the care required to reveal the self-serving provisions. These parties will either enter into contracts that do not fully reflect their intentions or will assume that the self-serving terms have been included and discount the price they are willing to pay accordingly.[80] The role of lawyers in drafting such contracts is another factor that unsettles the balance of bargaining power between parties. Most standard commercial contracts are drafted by lawyers, whose compensation structure provides them with incentives to draft terms that are inefficiently favourable to their corporate client. Transactional lawyers are more likely to be punished for omitting a term that could lead in some remote contingency to a loss for their client firm, than they are to be rewarded for the time saved by the omission of unnecessary terms. Consequently, lawyers will

---

77 R. Gilson, C. Sabel and R.E. Scott, above n. 18, 27. For a discussion of the scholarship supporting this view, see S.J. Burton, 'A Lesson on Some Limits of Economic Analysis: Schwartz and Scott on Contract Interpretation' (2013) 88 *Indiana Law Journal* 339; S. Bayern, 'Rational Ignorance, Rational Closed-Mindedness, and Modern Economic Formalism in Contract Law' (2009) 97 *California Law Review* 943; J.W. Bowers, 'Murphy's Law and the Elementary Theory of Contract Interpretation: A Response to Schwartz and Scott' (2005) 57 *Rutgers Law Review* 587.

78 A.W. Katz, 'Your Terms or Mine? The Duty to Read the Fine Print in Contracts' (1990) 21 *Rand Journal of Economics* 518, 533.

79 R. Gilson, C. Sabel and R.E. Scott, above n. 18, 27.

80 A.W. Katz, above n. 7, 531.

tend to overdraft the contract, and include terms that place on the customer risks and duties that can be cheaply borne by the company.[81]

The inequality of bargaining power and expertise that characterises these contracts contradicts the assumptions of individualised contract design that are associated with the textualist argument. Formal interpretive rules that exclude certain categories of extrinsic evidence would deprive courts of potentially relevant information, thus distorting their ability to determine the real terms of the agreement.[82] Allowing the courts to examine ex post the context of these transactions helps them to identify any disparity between the terms of the bargain and the written contract terms, thereby protecting unsophisticated parties from hidden forms of exploitation.[83] Even when abuse of bargaining power is not a concern, a contextualist regime of interpretation could be justified by the notion that both individual consumers and commercially sophisticated firms would prefer courts to take advantage of hindsight in assisting them to achieve their contractual objectives.[84] Moreover, an interpretive regime that de-emphasises the text of the agreement in favour of evidence that is harder to manipulate, such as market expectations, could serve as a bonding cost that allows the dominant party to commit to abstaining from such self-serving behaviour.[85]

While these concerns are valid reasons for applying a contextualist interpretation regime to consumer contracts, they are less persuasive for negotiated contracts between commercially sophisticated firms.[86] The prototypical sophisticated parties are profit-maximising risk-neutral firms, which have access to legal counsel.[87] Sophisticated risk-neutral firms prefer to limit their drafting and enforcement costs to the level where a court has enough information to make an accurate interpretation of the contract on average. Although a high degree of interpretive accuracy is desirable, judicial accuracy comes at a cost to contractual parties. When parties are sophisticated and risk-neutral, they have no incentives to expend further resources to shrink the variance around the correct mean.[88] Under a textual interpretation

---

81 Ibid., 533.

82 R.E. Scott, above n. 35, 317.

83 R. Gilson, C. Sabel and R.E. Scott, above n. 18, 38.

84 R.E. Scott, above n. 35, 314.

85 A.W. Katz, above n. 7, 531.

86 A. Schwartz and R.E. Scott, above n. 12, 541.

87 R. Gilson, C. Sabel and R.E. Scott, above n. 18, 26. Sophisticated firms include corporations with five or more employees, limited partnerships and professional partnerships such as law and accounting firms (A. Schwartz and R.E. Scott, above n. 12, 544–545). See also S. Bayern, above n. 14, 1104–1118 (rejecting Schwartz and Scott's assumption that all sophisticated firms are risk-neutral profit maximisers).

88 A. Schwartz and R.E. Scott, above n. 5, 931–933. For empirical evidence supporting the view that sophisticated parties would prefer a regime that excludes contextual evidence, see G. Miller, above n. 66.

regime, a hard parol evidence rule coupled with a plain meaning rule allows such parties to balance their ex ante drafting costs and ex post enforcement costs in a manner that reflects their preference for interpretation accuracy on average. Parties are able to retain control over the relevant context via a merger clause that integrates their entire understanding, including relevant context, into the written contract, and excludes particular categories of evidence, such as the parties' practice under prior contracts between them or their course of performance.[89] Thus, legally sophisticated parties are likely to reject a court's efforts to supplement or circumvent their original design by its own contextual investigation.[90] A contextual meaning rule would limit the parties' freedom to narrow the interpretive context, even when doing so is necessary to maximise the expected value of their contract.[91]

3.2. CONTRACT INTERPRETATION AND EX POST TRANSACTION COSTS: OPPORTUNISM AND JUDICIAL ERROR

Contract interpretation is often regarded as a means for courts to reduce the problem of opportunism in contractual relations. Economic opportunism means 'self-interest seeking with guile'.[92] Opportunistic behaviour results in an unbargained-for redistribution of wealth that runs counter to the parties' agreement, or the relevant contractual or moral norms.[93]

The threat of opportunism induces parties to spend additional resources to protect themselves against this eventuality, thus raising their overall transaction costs.[94] In many instances, ex ante contractual protection is impossible or prohibitively costly. In complex contracts, for instance, the parties must anticipate not only potential changes in the relevant economic variables but also the risk of opportunistic behaviour by the other party in every possible contingency. Even when contractual protection is possible, opportunism can be difficult to detect when it has the appearance of legitimate conduct.[95] When the risk of opportunism is high and the costs of preventing or detecting it are prohibitive,

[89] A. Schwartz and R.E. Scott, above n. 5, 584–588; R. Gilson, C. Sabel and R.E. Scott, above n. 18, 316; see also R.E. Scott and G.G. Triantis, 'Anticipating Litigation in Contract Design' (2006) 115 *Yale Law Journal* 814.

[90] R. Gilson, C. Sabel and R.E. Scott, above n. 18, 319.

[91] A. Schwartz and R.E. Scott, above n. 5, 963.

[92] O.E. Williamson, *The Economic Institutions of Capitalism* (New York: Free Press, 1985) 47.

[93] G.M. Cohen, 'The Negligence-Opportunism Tradeoff in Contract Law' (1992) 20 *Hofstra Law Review* 941, 957; T.J. Muris, 'Opportunistic Behavior and the Law of Contracts' (1981) 65 *Minnesota Law Review* 521, 523.

[94] T.J. Muris, above n. 93, 524.

[95] Ibid., 525.

contractual relations may fail to form. Courts can reduce transaction costs and prevent market failures by adopting an interpretive regime that minimises the risk of opportunism. No single interpretive regime, however, can achieve this goal across all types of contract and all forms of opportunism. Contextualism and textualism have their relative advantages in deterring opportunism, depending on whether this is a more significant problem ex ante or ex post, or whether it is more likely to arise in relation to the contractual text or context.[96]

Opportunism can arise ex ante, during the negotiation and drafting stage. For instance, a party may be tempted to fill the negotiating record with self-serving proposals and offers, in the hope that it can later convince a court applying a contextual interpretation that these statements were in fact part of the contract. The risk of such opportunism explains why, even in a contextual regime, courts are more sceptical of evidence that can be easily manipulated, such as pre-contractual negotiations,[97] As such, here, the courts will protect contracting parties from 'unfair surprise' and their reasonable reliance interests as well those whose rights, duties and liabilities may be affected by the behaviour of opportunist parties.[98] In a textualist regime, an opportunist party may be tempted to sneak self-serving terms into the text of the contract, with a view to invoking them subsequently at the interpretation stage.[99] The contextual regime is arguably more conducive to ex ante opportunism, given the range of evidence that it is possible to adduce.[100]

More often, opportunism arises ex post. When contract terms are susceptible to several meanings, some reflecting the original bargain and others deviating from it in a way that serves the interests of one party, this party may be able to exploit this ambiguity and claim that his performance is compliant, or the other party is in breach. Alternatively, an opportunistic party may use court interpretation to his advantage by seeking a term interpreted according to its common or plain meaning, when that meaning fails to reflect the original bargain.[101] Ex post opportunism can also arise from a contractual gap. When parties have not formulated an intention with regard to a particular contingency, due to lack of foresight or to deliberate use of vague or broad terms, a party may use the relevant context to seek an unbargained-for advantage. Because incentives to act opportunistically can arise under both textualism and contextualism, the

---

96 A.W. Katz, above n. 7, 531; G.M. Cohen, above n. 4, 92–93.

97 See E.A. Posner, above n. 4, 564–565 (arguing that the risk of opportunism is a possible reason in favour of a formalistic parol evidence rule); G.M. Cohen, above n. 4, 92.

98 *Report on Interpretation in Private Law* (Scot Law Com No. 160, 1997) para. 2.6 at pp. 9–10.

99 A.W. Katz, above n. 7, 531; A. Schwartz and R.E. Scott, above n. 12, 585–586.

100 C. Mitchell, above n. 17, 113.

101 J.P. Kostritsky, 'Plain Meaning vs. Broad Interpretation: How the Risk of Opportunism Defeats a Unitary Default Rule for Interpretation' (2008) 96 *Kentucky Law Journal* 43, 49; G.M. Cohen, above n. 4, 91.

aim of preventing or reducing this form of abuse cannot be taken to call for a specific interpretive approach.[102]

The holdup problem is another example of ex post opportunism. When sellers must make private sunk-cost investments in order to produce goods or services for particular buyers, they expose themselves to the risk of ex post opportunistic renegotiation or termination of the relationship by the buyer. When the sunk costs are low, the risk of opportunism is low. In a thick market for substitute performance, a seller can recoup the sunk costs simply by switching to a new contracting partner.[103] When asset specificity is high, rational sellers tend to under-invest in the sunk costs, for fear of losing some or all of their value in an ex post holdup.[104] In such cases, a high degree of interpretive accuracy is needed to induce sellers to invest efficiently. To the degree that a contextual regime is able to reduce the difference between the interpretive outcomes ex post and the parties' agreement at the time when the sunk costs are made, contextualism could help minimise the holdup problem.[105] When the parties are able to negotiate a contractual solution that decreases the risk of holdup, such as drafting a complex contract or giving the seller control over the quantity of goods to be delivered, they will have less need for interpretive accuracy and will prefer a more formalist regime.[106]

Chiselling behaviour is another instance of ex post opportunistic deviation from an agreement. Chiselling occurs when a party supplies less than the performance required under the contract, but claims that the performance is compliant and entitles him to the full price.[107] In one view, parties have fewer incentives to chisel in a contextualist regime.[108] A party's incentive to chisel is directly proportional to the likelihood that his chiselling behaviour will be protected by an erroneous contract interpretation.[109] When a party is willing

---

102 J.P. Kostritsky, above n. 101, 48–49; C. Mitchell, above n. 17, 113. See also D. Campbell, 'The Relational Constitution of Contract and the Limits of "Economics": Kenneth Arrow on the Social Background of Markets' in S. Deakin and J. Michie (eds.), *Contracts, Co-operation and Competition: Studies in Economics, Management and Law* (Oxford: Oxford University Press, 1997) 307, 312–313.

103 C. Goetz and R.E. Scott, above n. 11, 262; G.M. Cohen, above n. 4, 92. For an in-depth discussion of sunk costs and asset specificity, see D. Baird and E. Morrison, 'Serial Entrepreneurs and Small Business Bankruptcies' (2005) 105 *Columbia Law Review* 2310.

104 A.W. Katz, above n. 7, 529.

105 Ibid., 530.

106 E. Maskin and J. Tirole, 'Unforeseen Contingencies and Incomplete Contracts' (1999) 66 *The Review of Economic Studies* 83; O. Hart and J. Moore, 'Contracts as Reference Points' (2008) 123 *The Quarterly Journal of Economics* 1; G. Noldeke and K. Schmidt, 'Option Contracts and Renegotiation: A Solution to the Hold-up Problem' (1995) 26 *The Rand Journal of Economics* 163; A.W. Katz, above n. 7, 530.

107 A. Schwartz and R.E. Scott, above n. 5, 948.

108 S. Bayern, above n. 77, 943.

109 J.W. Bowers, 'Murphy's Law and the Elementary Theory of Contract Interpretation: A Response to Schwartz and Scott' (2005) 57 *Rutgers Law Review* 587, 601.

to chisel and gamble on an erroneous (but favourable to him) interpretation from the court, a rule that allows the maximal evidentiary base counteracts such incentives by increasing interpretive accuracy and shrinking the variance of the court's expected result.[110] Nonetheless, there are arguments which favour literalism as a means to deter chiselling and opportunistic litigation. The chiselling party only benefits when the court erroneously finds that the contract requires only the performance that he tendered. He will stand to lose, however, if the court correctly finds that the contract required a conforming performance, or if it erroneously finds that the contract requires a greater performance than what the parties actually agreed on. In other words, the chiselling party benefits from errors on the low side but stands to lose both from a correct interpretation and from errors on the high side. Since the textualist regime relies on less evidence, the variance of the court's expected result is higher, which means a higher probability that the chiselling party will lose. In this view, parties would select a textualist interpretation regime in order to reduce the incentives to chisel.[111]

In conclusion, no single optimal interpretation regime that is able to address all forms of opportunism can be identified. Contextualism has the advantage of a higher likelihood that the interpretive result corresponds to the parties' real bargain. Its downside is that parties are tempted to invest substantial resources in manipulating the context or engaging in opportunist litigation in order to maximise the chance of obtaining an unbargained-for favourable outcome. Formalism, in contrast, limits the scope for ex post interpretive disputes, thus reducing the marginal productivity of opportunist litigation and decreasing this component of transaction costs.[112]

The possibility of the court erring in its interpretation of a contract is another ex post contingency that parties have to take into account under both textualism and contextualism. When courts are accurate and competent, the parties' litigation costs are minimised because they have fewer incentives to raise spurious interpretive issues, and because the judges need less help from the lawyers to reach the correct result. This would encourage parties to write more contracts, which in turn might lead to an increase in the litigation rate. Litigation might increase also because parties might prefer the highly competent judicial dispute resolution to arbitration. This would result in an increase in the governmental costs with the judiciary, but such costs would presumably be offset by the social benefits of correct interpretive outcomes and additional contracts.[113] Real courts, however, are prone to errors. A judicial error occurs when the outcome at the litigation

110 S. Bayern, above n. 77, 970.

111 For a numerical example illustrating the effect of textualism on chiselling incentives see A. Schwartz and R.E. Scott, above n. 5, 949–951.

112 A.W. Katz, above n. 7, 531.

113 R.A. Posner, above n. 2, 1592.

stage is different than what the parties would have agreed to at the formation stage. This may occur, for instance, where the court interprets a contract term in a way that runs counter to the parties' real intentions. When the court must fill in a contractual gap, under both contextual and formal interpretation techniques, it may have to make a decision on a matter that the parties had not considered and over which they had not expressed any intention. This makes it difficult to determine whether a judicial error occurred or not.[114]

Determining the optimal interpretation regime applicable to a particular transaction involves determining which methodology has the lowest rate of court error, and at what cost.[115] One way of minimising the decision and error costs is requiring courts to ascribe to contractual terms their objective meaning, without investigating what the parties would have chosen had they made explicit provision on the point.[116] Taking into account the principle of goal neutrality in interpretation, however, this solution is unlikely to yield optimal results. The better view is that the question of which regime is less prone to judicial error cannot be answered in the abstract. Courts and parties should have the option of selecting a more textual or contextual approach to interpretation, depending on the circumstances of each case. In a textualist regime, when transaction costs are low, parties can minimise the risk of court error by drafting more detailed and complete contract terms.

Textualist courts will interpret a detailed contract more accurately than contextualist courts, which will sometimes erroneously rely on contextual evidence in addition to the written text.[117] At the same time, low drafting costs do not necessarily eliminate the risk of interpretive error. The more detailed the contracts are, the higher the risk that such contracts contain ambiguous or contradictory terms. Textualist courts that must interpret longer and more complex contracts are more likely to misconstrue a term to cover a particular contingency the parties did not intend to cover.[118]

When ex ante costs are high, contextualism has the advantage of decreasing these costs by allowing courts to fill in the contractual gaps. The decreasing costs argument in favour of the contextual approach only holds if the parties trust that the interpretive result reflects what they would have bargained for ex ante.[119] Contextualism increases the risk of judicial error by increasing the amount of information that is relevant to the interpretation exercise.[120] Courts may err in

---

114 C. Mitchell, above n. 17, 114.

115 G.M. Cohen, above n. 4, 97.

116 C. Sunstein, above n. 21, 648; E.A. Posner, 'A Theory of Contract Law under Conditions of Radical Judicial Error' (2000) 94 *Northwestern University Law Review* 749.

117 R.A. Posner, above n. 2, 545–546.

118 G.M. Cohen, above n. 4, 95.

119 C. Mitchell, above n. 17, 109; D. Charny, above n. 58, 405.

120 See J. Gava and J. Grene, 'Do We need a Hybrid Law of Contract? Why Hugh Collins Is Wrong and Why It Matters' (2004) 63 *Cambridge Law Journal* 605, 616–620.

determining the parties' reasonable expectations or by adopting an inaccurate view of what the parties consider an unreasonable or absurd result.[121]

Parties that doubt a court's ability to provide a correct interpretation may prefer the occasional incorrect or absurd result associated with textualism to a regime where ineffectual judges are empowered to search for purpose or absurdity. The broad interpretive powers that courts have in the latter case present a risk of error or variance of decision that is more harmful than the risk of an absurd result arising in the former case.[122] The costs of using an incompetent or corrupt court to determine the parties' intentions or to find the most efficient resolution of the interpretive question might be prohibitive. When these ex ante costs are lower than the expected savings resulting from fewer court errors, textualism becomes the efficient regime.[123] When the costs are higher than the expected benefits, the parties may be forced to over-invest in negotiation, drafting and monitoring costs, or may avoid the courts altogether by choosing arbitration or vertical integration.[124]

From the courts' perspective, conventional wisdom suggests that limited judicial discretion is preferable when courts are unsure about their analytical abilities. A court that feels unsure of how to identify and process the information necessary to retrieve the parties' intention may prefer a textualist regime composed mainly of straightforward bright-line rules. Courts that feel more confident in their abilities, in contrast, may prefer a more cautious and nuanced approach to interpretation and liability.[125] Nevertheless, the high risk of error associated with ineffectual or corrupt courts does not necessarily create a preference for a textualist method that limits the court's interpretive role. Some parties may respond to this risk by simply adjusting the price of the contract to reflect their estimated likelihood of court error.[126] Moreover, arguments exist to support the rather counter-intuitive view that, when the court effectiveness is low, a contextual regime that allows for the use of standards rather than bright-line rules of interpretation is preferable.[127] Bright-line rules require courts to determine whether a party's performance falls short of a fixed level, whereas standards instruct the court to attempt to determine whether the performance meets a certain minimum value, given the information available to the court.[128] When courts have a low degree of competence, a contextual

121 C. Mitchell, above n. 17, 115–117.

122 F. Schauer, *Playing by the Rules: A Philosophical Examination of Rule-Based Decision-Making in Law and in Life* (Oxford: Oxford University Press, 1991) 214.

123 R.A. Posner, above n. 2, 542–544.

124 Ibid., 1539; G.M. Cohen, above n. 4, 94.

125 See R. Posner, *The Problems of Jurisprudence* (Harvard University Press, 1990) 94, 319.

126 G.M. Cohen, above n. 4, 94.

127 G.K. Hadfield 'Judicial Competence and the Interpretation of Incomplete Contracts' (1994) 23 *Journal of Legal Studies* 159.

128 Ibid., 175–176.

regime may require them to devote more effort to understanding the contextual details necessary to determine if performance is compliant. Contractual parties, in turn, are likely to realise that their marginal liability can be reduced through increases in cooperative efforts that the court can observe. Thus, parties are encouraged to take steps in the direction of optimal behaviour. In contrast, when low-competence courts apply bright-line rules, parties are likely either to ignore the rule and make no adjustments in behaviour, or to adopt the safe harbours chosen by the courts, which may deviate significantly from an optimal outcome for different types of defendants.[129]

A similar problem arises with regard to a court's determination of the interpretive methodology that the parties chose, a process sometimes referred as meta-interpretation.[130] In one view, the risk of error in meta-interpretation is reduced when the courts use all available information to determine the agreement that the parties had, or the agreement that reasonable parties would have had, about their preferred mode of interpretation. As with the interpretation of the substance of a contract, the diversity and complexity of contractual relations makes it difficult to derive from theoretical principles an optimal meta-interpretive regime. The appropriate resolution of meta-interpretive questions should parallel the resolution of interpretive questions, and relevant features of context should be taken into account when they are necessary to determine the parties' preferences in individual cases.[131] When contracting parties formulate an express preference for textualism through, for example, merger clauses/entire agreement clauses, a textual meta-interpretation that lowers the parties' costs of accurately expressing their methodological intentions is preferable, from an economic perspective.[132] But, once again, if courts make errors in determining the parties' intentions, they may also err in determining their methodological preference and choose contextualism too often.[133] In some cases, error in meta-interpretation may be irrelevant. Contractual parties may be indifferent to the court's error in identifying their preferred interpretation method, provided that the court is likely to reach a correct substantive interpretation outcome using the wrong interpretive methodology.[134]

---

129 Ibid., 180–183. See also A. Schwartz and R.E. Scott, 'The Common Law of Contract and the Default Rule Project' (2016) 102 *Virginia Law Review* 1523 (discussing the use of rules and standards by courts in the filling of contractual gaps).

130 S. Bayern, above n. 14, 1102.

131 Ibid., 1145.

132 G.M. Cohen, above n. 4, 96.

133 E.A. Posner, above n. 4, 547–548 and 570–571.

134 G.M. Cohen, above n. 4, 96.

4. CONCLUSION

Economic agents enter contracts with a view to maximising the joint surplus. A key purpose of every contract is to describe the rights and obligations that each party undertakes in the pursuit of the joint welfare maximisation aim. Contracts typically do not provide for all variables and contingencies that are of potential relevance to performance. Incompleteness is a central, rather than tangential, feature of commercial contracts and a key theme in the economic literature on contract interpretation. When performance unfolds over time, parties cannot foresee and bargain ex ante over every relevant contingency, due to high transaction costs or bounded rationality. Even under low transaction costs and perfect rationality, parties may choose to leave potentially contentious points for future negotiations, to withhold information for strategic purposes, or to delegate contractual completion to courts, should a particular contingency arise.

When contracts are incomplete and their terms are ambiguous or contradictory, interpretation is necessary to ascertain the parties' intentions at the time of contract formation. Disputes about the existence or meaning of terms are bound to arise even in the most carefully drafted contracts, especially when a party's liability is at stake. The interpretive process is expected to be goal neutral, in the sense of facilitating the achievement of parties' goals. The principle of court neutrality in determining the parties' intentions implies that a high degree of accuracy in interpretation is desirable. Contract writing and litigation are costly, however, and an optimal interpretive method must discount the benefit of accuracy with contract-writing and adjudication costs. A long-standing controversy exists over which interpretive strategy is more effective in approximating the parties' intentions.

Textualism has the advantage of predictability, celerity and low litigation costs, at the expense of interpretive accuracy and ex ante transaction costs. Contextualism saves bargaining and drafting costs and maximises accuracy but comes with uncertainty and high litigation costs. An emerging approach to the problem of identifying the optimal interpretive regime places the choice of interpretive method with contractual parties rather than courts or legislators. In this view, textualism is not opposed to contextualism. The question is not one of relative superiority, but one of efficient choice. Contracting parties are in a better position to make an efficient trade-off between their costs and the benefits of increased accuracy in interpretation. The efficient choice between formal and substantive interpretive regimes depends on multiple variables, including the parties' degree of sophistication, the length and complexity of their relation, and the need to prevent opportunism or judicial error.

INTERPRETATION IN THE PRINCIPLES OF EUROPEAN CONTRACT LAW, THE DRAFT COMMON FRAME OF REFERENCE AND THE COMMON EUROPEAN SALES LAW

Lorna RICHARDSON

1. INTRODUCTION

No law or other normative ordering at the European level exists for the interpretation of contracts. The closest the European Union (EU) Institutions came to producing a legal instrument containing rules on contract interpretation, was the Proposal for a Common European Sales Law (CESL).[1] The CESL was not adopted.[2] The two succeeding legislative proposals[3] do not deal with interpretation of contracts. Nonetheless, it seems likely that any future European instrument would not stray too far from the interpretation principles and rules set out in the CESL, given that the provisions of the CESL build upon the work carried out in creating the Principles of European Contract Law[4] (PECL) and the

1 The Proposal for a Regulation of the European Parliament and of the Council on a Common European Sales Law, COM/2011/0635. The consolidated text of the CESL is available at http://www.europarl.europa.eu/sides/getDoc.do?pubRef=-//EP//TEXT+TA+P7-TA-2014-0159+0+DOC+XML+V0//EN#BKMD-41. This version of the CESL is the position of the European Parliament adopted on 26 February 2014. Shortly thereafter the CESL was withdrawn, see footnote 2 below.

2 It was withdrawn by the EU Commission in December 2014 with a decision to focus on e-commerce: see Directive (EU) 2019/770 of the European Parliament and of the Council of 20 May 2019 on certain aspects concerning contracts for the supply of digital content; and Directive (EU) 2019/771 of the European Parliament and of the Council of 20 May 2019 on certain aspects concerning contracts for the sale of goods, amending Regulation (EU) 2017/2394 and Directive 2009/22/EC and repealing Directive 1999/44/EC. It may be noted that the sale of goods Directive applies to all sales, whether in person or distance sales.

3 Directive on sale of goods, *ibid*; and Directive on supply of digital content, *ibid*.

4 For the text, including comments and comparative notes see O. Lando and H. Beale (eds.), *Principles of European Contract Law Part I and II* (The Hague/London/Boston: Kluwer Law International, 2000) and O. Lando, E. Clive, A. Prüm and R. Zimmermann (eds.), *Principles of European Contract Law Part III* (The Hague/London/Boston: Kluwer Law International, 2003). The text of the PECL is available at https://www.trans-lex.org/400200/_/pecl/.

Draft Common Frame of Reference[5] (DCFR). To obtain a deeper appreciation of what a pan-European regime for contract interpretation might look like, this chapter considers the rules and principles of interpretation found in the PECL, the DCFR and the CESL.

The aim of the PECL and the DCFR was to create a set of non-binding model rules, following a significant comparative survey of the legal rules of each Member State.[6] The rules of both instruments aim to set out optimum rules on the law of contract,[7] including rules on interpretation, and not simply a compromise among the national rules. That said, many of the rules of the PECL and DCFR and thus the CESL are a compromise or a combination of the rules found in the laws of the Member States.[8] The aim of the CESL was to provide an optional instrument that parties could use to govern their cross-border distance contracts for the sale of goods or supply of digital content. The CESL was not to be a twenty-ninth legal regime within the EU, but rather to provide a second contract law regime within each Member State, that could be utilised by contracting parties to govern their contract.[9]

The rules on interpretation in all three instruments are similar. This is not surprising, given the DCFR progressed and further developed the work that was carried out to produce the PECL. In turn, the work that was carried out in producing the DCFR was used in formulating the CESL. However, the rules are not identical. In two important respects the rules differ. These differences are discussed in detail in sections 2.3 and 5. It is worth pointing out that the PECL refers to its provisions as 'principles', the DCFR refers to its provisions as 'model rules', and the CESL uses 'rules'. The term 'rules' will be used in this chapter to refer to the provisions of all three instruments.[10]

---

5 For the text, including comments and comparative notes see C. von Bar, E. Clive and H. Schulte-Nölke, *Principles, Definitions and Model Rules of European Private Law, Draft Common Frame of Reference (DCFR)*, Full Edition (Munich: Sellier, 2009).

6 It seems that the purpose of the instruments was different, with the PECL being intended for use by parties who wished to use the PECL as part of or to govern their contract (see Art. 1:101 PECL), whereas the DCFR was intended as a stepping-stone to a political Common Frame of Reference and as a reference and source of inspiration for the development of European and national private law: see Intr. 4, 6 and 7 of the DCFR (Outline Edition).

7 The DCFR goes beyond the law of contract, producing rules in relation to other areas of law, including non-contractual liability and unjustified enrichment: see Books V–X of the DCFR.

8 The Introduction to the DCFR notes that the DCFR will help to show how much the national rules resemble one another and have provided mutual stimulus for development, as well as to what extent the laws may be regarded as regional manifestations of an overall common European legacy – see Intr. 7 (Outline Edition).

9 See the explanatory memorandum to the Proposal for a Regulation of the European Parliament and of the Council on a Common European Sales Law, COM/2011/0635. See: https://eur-lex.europa.eu/LexUriServ/LexUriServ.do?uri=COM:2011:0635:FIN:en:PDF.

10 The DCFR discusses principles underlying and inspiring the model rules in Princ 1–62 (Outline Edition) found at the beginning of the text.

Section 2 of this chapter considers the rules on the approach to contractual interpretation. In this part the protection afforded to third-party reliance on the apparent meaning of the contract, found in the DCFR, but not the PECL or CESL, will be discussed. Section 3 considers the factors which the person tasked with interpreting the contract (the interpreter) can take into account in interpreting a contract. In section 4 specific interpretive rules are discussed. Section 5 considers the rules on interpreting unilateral statements or conduct, which are significantly more developed in the DCFR and CESL than they are in the PECL. Concluding comments are set out in section 6.

2. THE APPROACH TO CONTRACTUAL INTERPRETATION

The rules of interpretation are found in chapter 5 of the PECL, chapter 8 of Book II of the DCFR and chapter 6 of Part III of the CESL. The commentaries to the PECL and DCFR note that the rules apply to all types of contract, including oral contracts and contracts concluded on standard terms.[11] However, the scope of application of these instruments must be taken into account. The DCFR specifically provides that its rules, including those on interpretation, are not intended to be used, or used without modification or supplementation, in relation to certain areas of law, including wills and succession, employment relationships, negotiable instruments or the ownership or security over immoveable property.[12] There is no provision in the PECL seeking to limit or exclude its rules from certain areas of law. In contrast, the scope of the CESL is much more limited. The CESL only applies to cross-border contracts for the distance sale of goods, digital content or related services.[13] The CESL does not require contracts to be in any particular form[14] and makes provision for contracts concluded on standard terms,[15] thus the rules of interpretation discussed below would apply to contracts concluded on standard terms.

---

11 See PECL, *supra* n. 4, p. 287; Full Edition of the DCFR, *supra* n. 5, p. 554.

12 Art. I-1:101(2) DCFR. This is important when considering the approach to interpreting contracts that are routinely relied on by third parties. This issue is discussed further in section 2.3 below. Within the DCFR there are special rules of interpretation set out in relation to trusts only – see Arts. X-2:203 and X-4:101 DCFR.

13 Arts. 4 and 5 of the Proposal for a Regulation of the European Parliament and of the Council on a Common European Sales Law, COM/2011/0635.

14 Art. 6 CESL.

15 See for instance Arts. 7 and 62 CESL.

2.1. THE SEARCH FOR COMMON INTENTION

In all three instruments, the first rule is that the interpreter must interpret the contract according to the common intention of the parties, even if that differs from the literal meaning of the words.[16] The commentaries to the PECL and the DCFR state that this rule seeks to combine the subjective and objective approach to interpretation.[17] However, seeking the common intention of the parties makes no reference to external factors or actors,[18] such as how the words would reasonably be understood or what they would mean to the reasonable man.[19]

It may perhaps be said that there is a spectrum of interpretation, beginning at (i) a subjective approach to interpretation in terms of which each party's understanding is sought, moving to (ii) a less subjective approach, where the parties' common intention is the focus,[20] to (iii) a more objective interpretation but which nonetheless contains a subjective element: where the reasonable person knows what the actual parties knew at the time of contract formation, to finally (iv) an objective approach to interpretation where the interpreter simply asks what the reasonable person would understand the words to mean without any reference to the position or knowledge of the actual parties. The rules set out in Art. 5:101(1) PECL, Art. II-8:101(1) DCFR and Art. 58(1) CESL require the interpreter to seek the parties' common intention, and not either party's subjective intention. As such, the primary rule of interpretation under the instruments could be said to be at point (ii) of this continuum, closer to the subjective end of the interpretation spectrum.

The interpreter must seek to discover the parties' common intention at the time of contract formation, not at a later time.[21] It is therefore important that the interpreter does not look back to the time of formation with the benefit of hindsight and use what is known at that later stage, for instance changes to the law or scientific developments, in interpreting the contract. However, as discussed in section 3.2 below, the interpreter can take account of the conduct of the parties subsequent to contract formation to interpret the contract.

---

16 Art. 5:101(1) PECL; Art. II-8:101(1) DCFR; Art 58(1) CESL.

17 PECL, *supra* n. 4, p. 288; Full Edition of the DCFR, *supra* n. 5, p. 554.

18 However the interpreter may take certain factors into account in interpreting the contract (discussed in section 3), some of which may be said to be objective.

19 The commentaries to both instruments note that the subjective method gives pre-eminence to the parties' common intention, whereas an objective method takes an external view by reference to objective criteria such as reasonableness and good faith – see PECL, *supra* n. 4, p. 288; Full Edition of the DCFR, *supra* n. 5, p. 554.

20 Indeed the commentary to Art. II-8:201 DCFR (discussed in detail in section 5 below) states that the primary rule in the interpretation of contracts, in referring to the common intention of the parties, introduces an element of objectivity, different from the secret uncommunicated individual intention – see Full Edition of the DCFR, *supra* n. 5, p. 572.

21 PECL, *supra* n. 4, p. 288; Full Edition of the DCFR, *supra* n. 5, p. 554.

The desire to give effect to the will of the parties, as demonstrated by their common intention, is evident when the use of 'code words' is considered. Code words exist when parties use certain words in their contract that have a hidden or private meaning. This special meaning will not be apparent to anyone else reading the contract. The commentary to the DCFR provides that where the parties have used code words in the contract, effect will be given to those code words, and what they mean to the parties, rather than to the apparent meaning of the words that have been used in the contract.[22] Such a situation raises parallels with the doctrine of simulation.[23] Simulation has a wide scope. It includes cases where parties seemingly enter into an agreement which they have no intention of actually concluding, for example, where A's creditor threatens action in relation to goods A owns, to recover payment of debts due to the creditor and A enters into a fictitious sale of the goods to B to defeat his creditor's action. Simulation also includes situations where the nature of the transaction appears differently in the contract from the reality, for example, an apparent sale of goods, but with a secret agreement that the goods are not paid for, such that the transaction is, in fact, a gift. In addition, simulation can relate to the contents of an agreement; for instance, the price set out in the contract may not be what the parties have actually agreed will be paid. It is in this final respect that simulation overlaps with interpretation.

The commentary to the PECL states that simulation and interpreting a contract by seeking the parties' common intention are different. According to the commentary, with simulation there are, in effect, two contracts: (i) the sham contract and (ii) the overt contract. Where the issue is one of interpretation, there is only one agreement, the meaning of which is ambiguous or vague.[24] This position does not seem tenable. A contractual provision may, on its face, be perfectly clear and in no way vague, yet in looking at the parties' common intention it is clear that what has been set out in the contract is not what the parties actually meant. This can be seen in the example above of the price being noted incorrectly in the parties' contract. The classic example is the German case of the parties who contracted intending the subject matter of the contract to be whale meat, but used the Norwegian word *haakjöringskod*, which in fact

22 Full Edition of the DCFR, *supra* n. 5, p. 554. A similar comment is not made in the commentary to the PECL. Commentary on the CESL gives the famous example of the parties using the term 'shark meat' when they meant 'whale meat', discussed below, noting that the contract would be held to be about whale meat regardless of the language used in the contract: see C. Wendehorst, 'Interpretation' in R. Schulze (ed.), *Common European Sales Law (CESL) Commentary*, (Baden-Baden: Nomos, 2012), p. 305.

23 This is a doctrine which is not known to Scots or English law, and is dealt with by other legal rules, for instance rules on identifying the true content of contracts, illegality and estoppel (England) and personal bar (Scotland). The rules on simulation can be found in Art. 6:103 PECL and Art. II-9:201 DCFR. Simulation is not dealt with in the CESL.

24 PECL, *supra* n. 4, p. 386.

means shark meat, in their contract.[25] The court upheld the parties' intention that the contract was for whale meat. Even in legal systems such as Scotland and England where a more objective approach to interpretation has generally been taken to that in continental legal systems, the courts will not hold the parties to a contractual provision if that is clearly not what they intended.[26] The court will give effect to their common intended meaning of the term in question. This is sometimes referred to as the 'private dictionary' rule or principle.[27]

The position adopted in the DCFR, in recognising the overlap between interpretation and simulation, is therefore to be preferred. The commentary to the DCFR gives the example of parties deciding to use the word 'refrigerators' in their contract when they really mean some commercially sensitive new equipment, so that anyone reading the contract will not know the true subject matter of the contract.[28] In such a situation, there would be a choice on whether the rules of interpretation or simulation would apply.[29]

2.2. RELEVANCE OF KNOWLEDGE OF INTENDED MEANING

Art. 5:101(2) PECL provides that where it is established that A intended the contract to have a particular meaning, and at the time of conclusion of the contract B could not have been unaware of A's intention, the contract is to be interpreted in the way A intended. The DCFR is to similar effect stating that if A intended the contract, or a term or expression used in it, to have a particular meaning, and at the time of concluding the contract B was aware or could reasonably be expected to have been aware of A's intention, the contract is to be interpreted in the way A intended.[30] The CESL follows the DCFR in providing that 'where one party intended an expression used in the contract or equivalent conduct to have a particular meaning, and at the time of conclusion of the contract the other party was aware, or could be expected to have been aware, of that intention, the expression or equivalent conduct is to be interpreted

25 RG, 8 June 1920 (II) Ziv RGZ 99, 147.

26 *Investors Compensation Scheme Ltd v West Bromwich Building Society Ltd (No. 1)* [1998] 1 WLR 896 per Lord Hoffmann at 913. While both Scots and English law allow rectification of documents which do not set out the parties' true agreement, the issue may also be determined by interpretation.

27 See the discussion of the limits of this principle in English law in *Chartbrook Ltd v Persimmon Homes Ltd* [2009] 1 AC 1101; for the position in Scots law, see *Hunter v Baron's Trs* (1886) 13R 883.

28 Full Edition of the DCFR, *supra* n. 5, p. 612.

29 The rules on interpretation and simulation are similar: both give effect to the parties' true intention except where this would adversely impact on a third party's good faith reliance on the contract (as to which see section 2.3 below).

30 Art. II-8:101(2) DCFR.

in the way intended by the first party'.[31] There is a requirement of reasonableness as to what is expected of the second party.[32]

It appears that this approach to interpretation is closer to the subjective end of the continuum, discussed in section 2.1 above, close to point (i). The interpretation to be preferred is that which *one* of the parties intended, provided the other party knew or should have known of it. In this way it is not entirely subjective, but it is close to it.

Such an approach may result in party B having to rebuff interpretations of the contract or its terms put forward by A that B does not agree with and vice versa. In complex and protracted contractual negotiations, with lots of discussion and communication between the parties, and indeed perhaps a number of people conducting the negotiations for each party, this may be an onerous task. Each party would have to be alert to interpretations put forward by the other during the negotiation process and to correct those where they did not accord with their own view as to the meaning of a word or phrase. Yet the rule goes further than that: it applies not only where B knew of A's interpretation but also where he could not have been unaware of it (in terms of the PECL) or could reasonably be expected to have known it (under the DCFR and CESL). It is unclear from the rules when this will be the case and as such there is uncertainty about when, in any given case, it may be said that B should have been aware of A's interpretation.

However, some assistance may be gleaned from the illustration provided regarding the operation of this rule in the commentaries to the PECL and DCFR. The same illustration is used in both: A, a fur trader, offers to sell B, also a fur trader, hare skins at £1 per kilo. This is a typing error: A meant to stipulate £1 per piece. In the fur trade, skins are usually sold per piece. As there are about six skins to the kilo, the price proposed by A is absurdly low. B accepts A's offer. There is a contract at £1 per piece as A intended.[33] The illustration suggests that A will have to reach a fairly high threshold to show that B knew or could not have been unaware (or should reasonably have known) of A's meaning of the

31 Art 58(2) CESL.

32 Art 5(2) CESL.

33 PECL, *supra* n. 4, p. 289; Full Edition of the DCFR, *supra* n. 5, p. 555. The illustration is based on the English case of *Hartog v Colin & Shields* [1939] 3 All ER 566. However, the case was dealt with as one of error, not interpretation. The court held that there was no contract between the parties as a result of A's mistake, due to the fact that B must have known of A's error. It has however been suggested that under English law A would be able to enforce the contract, according to his intended meaning because not only did B know that a mistake had been made, he knew what A had intended to offer: H. Beale (ed.), *Chitty on Contracts* (33rd edn, London: Thomson Reuters, 2018), vol. I, para. 3.029. Scots law would also tend to look to the law of error in such a situation: in *Phil Wills v Strategic Procurement (UK) Ltd* [2013] CSOH 26 a contract was held to be voidable where A made a mistake in an essential matter in the offer, which mistake was known to the other party – although an interpretation based on A's intended meaning would also be possible.

contract or term, given the term related to a practice established in the relevant trade. A high standard has also been suggested as applying to Art. 58(2) of the CESL.[34] However, the position is not free from doubt.

It is suggested that the PECL's formulation, using 'could not have been unaware', is to be preferred. It is likely to create less uncertainty in relation to what B is deemed to know. The formulation in the PECL does not suggest any positive action on B's part to become aware of A's intended meaning. The form of words used in the DCFR and CESL suggests that B may be required to take some action to become aware of A's intended meaning, which seems unduly onerous. It should be noted that where B did not know of A's intended meaning, the effect of the rule in Art. 5:102 PECL, Art. II-8:101(2) DCFR and Art. 58(2) CESL is that B is bound to a contract that he may never have agreed to enter into. It is therefore suggested that only where B knew or could not have been unaware of A's intended meaning should he be held to the contract with A's intended meaning. That is not to say that where B should reasonably have been aware of A's intended meaning, perhaps by making some enquiries, there is no effect on the contract. It is suggested that in such a situation the contract may be void or voidable.[35]

The rule of interpretation in these articles may be considered an expression of the principle of good faith and fair dealing between the parties,[36] with B having to correct A when A proposes an interpretation of the contract or a term that B does not agree with, and failing which B will be bound to a contract having the meaning intended by A. Unlike continental legal systems, there is no overriding principle of good faith in Scots or English contract law.[37] That does not however mean that where A's intended meaning of a term is different from its apparent meaning, and B is aware of A's intended meaning, that B can rely on the term's apparent meaning. In some situations, it may be that B will be held to the contract on the basis of A's intended meaning[38] or the law of error may be used. The situation referred to in the illustration above, where B attempts to snatch at a bargain, would be dealt with by the law of error, rather than interpretation,

34 Wendehorst, *supra* n. 22, p. 305.

35 This is a suggested approach when considering the effect of unilateral error on a contract in English law: see *Chitty*, *supra* n. 33, vol. I, para. 3.034.

36 Wendehorst, *supra* n. 22, p. 305. This can also be seen from the commentary to the equivalent rule of interpretation in relation to statements or conduct other than contracts, discussed in section 5.2 below; see Full Edition of the DCFR, *supra* n. 5, p. 572.

37 This issue is discussed more fully in section 3.7 below.

38 For Scots law see *Sutton & Co v Ciceri & Co* (1890) 17 R (HL) 40; *Houldsworth v Gordon Cumming* 1910 SC (HL) 49. The position in English law is less clear, with the Court of Appeal in *Winwood v Biffa Waste Services Ltd* [2011] EWCA Civ 108 noting that it was not legitimate to invoke in aid of interpretation what Biffa had told Winwood its intentions were regarding the clause in dispute.

in Scots and English law.[39] The outcome of such an approach is that the parties are not held to the contract based on its apparent meaning or the meaning intended by A.

2.3. A MOVE TO A MORE OBJECTIVE APPROACH TO INTERPRETATION

Art. 5:101(3) PECL provides that if an interpretation cannot be established according to paragraphs (1) and (2), discussed in section 2.1 and 2.2 above, the contract is to be interpreted according to the meaning that reasonable persons of the same kind as the parties would give to it in the same circumstances. Art. II-8:101(3)(a) DCFR provides that if an intention cannot be established according to paragraphs (1) or (2), the contract is to be interpreted according to the meaning a reasonable person would give to it. Art. 58(3) CESL is in the same terms. The rules suggest a divergent treatment, with the PECL taking an objective approach with some subjectivity, given that the reasonable person is of the same kind and in the same circumstances as the parties. This would appear at point (iii) of the continuum discussed in section 2.1 above. The DCFR and CESL, on the other hand, appear to adopt a wholly objective approach, with no reference to the position of the parties (at point (iv) of the continuum).

However, further investigations show this is not the case. The commentary to the DCFR notes that a reasonable person would take into account the objective circumstances in which the contract was concluded and the nature of the parties.[40] This therefore suggests an approach that is not completely objective, but which takes into account who the parties are and the factual background at the time of contract formation. It is therefore similar to the test in the PECL, albeit that the reference to the reasonable person being of the same kind as the parties in the PECL suggests a slightly more subjective approach to that in the DCFR. It has been suggested that the difference in formulation of the rules in the PECL and the CESL is not meant to denote a difference in meaning.[41] It should also be noted that in terms of all three instruments various factors can be taken into account as part of the process of interpretation, including the circumstances in which the contract was concluded and the conduct of the parties. This is discussed further in section 3 below.

Both the PECL and the DCFR are clear that the use of an objective approach to interpretation does not empower the interpreter to overturn the effect of a contract under the guise of interpretation, or to go against the unequivocal

[39] See *supra* n. 33 for more detail.
[40] Full Edition of the DCFR, *supra* n. 5, p. 556.
[41] Wendehorst, *supra* n. 22, p. 306.

will of the contracting parties.[42] This warning is important. While an objective approach is not the primary route to interpretation (that being the parties' common intention, followed by awareness of the other party's real intentions, discussed in sections 2.1 and 2.2), it is likely to be a common method of interpretation applied by the courts. This is because parties will frequently not have any special intention as to the meaning of the contract or its terms,[43] thus an objective approach will have to be taken to determine what the term in dispute means.

An objective approach to interpretation is required in terms of Art. II-8:101(3)(b) DCFR where a third party has reasonably and in good faith relied on the contract's apparent meaning.[44] There is no equivalent provision in either the PECL or the CESL. As such, third-party reliance is given greater emphasis in the DCFR. The importance of third-party reliance is clear from the principles underpinning the DCFR, with Principle 17 noting that an ingredient of contractual security[45] is the protection of reasonable reliance and expectations in situations not covered by the doctrine of contractual loyalty.[46]

Art. II-8:101(3)(b) DCFR protects third parties who are completely external to the contract. It does not protect third parties in the sense of parties who were not initially parties but have become parties to the contract after formation, for instance by way of assignation. This is not particularly clear from the terms of the article, which stipulate that an objective approach to interpretation is to be taken where 'a person, not being a party to the contract or a person who by law has no better rights than such a party, who has reasonably and in good faith relied on

---

42 PECL, *supra* n. 4, p. 289; Full Edition of the DCFR, *supra* n. 5, p. 556. It has been suggested that the Scottish courts have done so in a controversial case: *Grove Investments Ltd v Cape Building Products Ltd* 2014 Hous LR 35. For discussion of the case see L. Macgregor, 'Crossing the Line between Business Common Sense and Perceived Fairness in Contractual Interpretation' (2015) 19(3) *Edinburgh Law Review* 378.

43 Full Edition of the DCFR, *supra* n. 5, p. 556.

44 See also the discussion of Art. II-8:102(2) DCFR in section 3.8 below.

45 Which is not set out explicitly in B. Fauvarque-Cosson and D. Mazeaud, *Principes Directeurs du Droit Européen du Contrat* (Paris: Association Henri Capitant, 2008) and G. Wicker, J.B. Racine, L. Sautonie-Laguionie and F. Bujoli (eds.), *Principes Contractuels Commun. Projet de Cadre Commun de Référence* (Paris: Association Henri Capitant, 2008); B. Fauvarque-Cosson, D. Mazeaud and A. Tenenbaum, *Terminologie Contractuelle Commune. Projet de Cadre Commun de Référence* (Paris: Association Henri Capitant, 2008). These studies have been published in English as B. Fauvarque-Cosson and D. Mazeaud (eds.), *European Contract Law. Materials for a Common Frame of Reference: Terminology, Guiding Principles, Model Rules* (Munich: Sellier, 2008), from which the DCFR draws significantly in setting out its four underlying principles – see the discussion in Intr. 3 and 11–14 of the DCFR (Outline Edition).

46 Contractual loyalty includes duties to behave in accordance with the requirements of good faith, to cooperate when necessary for the performance of contractual obligations and not to act inconsistently with prior declarations or conduct on which the other party has relied – see Princ. 17 DCFR (Outline Edition). Given third parties are, by definition, not parties to the contract, their reliance on the contract is a separate principle, protected under the DCFR.

the contract's apparent meaning.' Some clarity is provided by the commentary, which provides that Art. II-8:101(3)(b) preserves the rule that an assignee takes no better rights against the other contracting party than the assignor. To allow an assignee to take advantage of an apparent meaning of a term, when its real meaning as between the original contracting parties is something else, would allow one party to the contract to take advantage of the other party simply by assigning the contract to a third party. This would be contrary to good faith and fair dealing.[47] So the DCFR seeks to keep the status quo as between the contracting parties and any assignee, but to protect those external to the contract who may nonetheless have relied upon it. An assignee is therefore in a vulnerable position. He does not benefit from the use of an objective approach to interpretation, unless common intention or knowledge of intended meaning (discussed in sections 2.1 and 2.2 above) do not determine the meaning of the contract. An assignee must therefore take steps to protect himself by making inquiries of the assignor to ensure that he understands anything that passed between the parties that may affect the meaning of the contract,[48] and ensure he has appropriate rights against the assignor in the event that the assignor conceals something from him that affects the operation of the contract.[49] Ultimately it may be that this problem is more theoretical than real, given the majority of contracts are likely to be interpreted using the objective approach, since parties are unlikely to have a special intention as to the meaning of the contract or its terms, as noted above.

It seems more likely that third parties will rely on contracts that are designed to be provided to or be available to third parties, such as negotiable instruments, or contracts that are or have to be published in a public register, such as documents relating to immoveable property. It will be remembered that the rules of the DCFR do not apply to certain areas of law, including negotiable instruments and immoveable property.[50] In areas of law where the rules do apply, for instance in relation to ownership of goods, and where registration is required,[51] a third party would be protected from a 'private' understanding of the contract by virtue of the objective approach to interpretation, provided his reliance was reasonable and in good faith.[52]

---

47 Full Edition of the DCFR, *supra* n. 5, p. 556.

48 This point was made in the English House of Lords case *Chartbrook Ltd v Persimmon Homes Ltd* [2009] 1 AC 1101.

49 Full Edition of the DCFR, *supra* n. 5, p. 556.

50 Art. I-1:101(2) DCFR.

51 Art. VIII-1:102 DCFR notes that whether ownership and the transfer of ownership of certain categories of goods may be or have to be registered in a pubic register is to be determined by national law.

52 Art. VIII-1:104 DCFR provides that where proprietary effects are determined by an agreement Books I–III apply where appropriate.

Thus, the contract can be interpreted in different ways depending on whether or not a third party, reasonably and in good faith, has relied on the contract's apparent meaning. It seems a little strange that the interests of the contracting parties, and the meaning which they ascribe to their contract, are subordinated to the interests of a third party.[53] While there is undoubtedly a need to protect certain third-party reliance, Art. II-8:101(3)(b) DCFR affords wide protection to third parties to the potential detriment of the contracting parties. Art. II-8:101(3)(b) comes into play even where the contract is not intended to be relied on by a third party[54] (although this may raise the question of whether such reliance was reasonable); or where the third party's reliance is not to his detriment, there being no requirement for detriment or prejudice to the third party before the objective approach to interpretation must be taken.[55] It is suggested that the desire to protect third-party reliance has gone too far and some further qualification on third-party reliance, beyond it being reasonable and in good faith, should be required before the understanding of the contract held by the parties to it is subordinated. This would give effect to the will of the contracting parties while continuing to provide protection to third-party reliance.

3. FACTORS TO BE CONSIDERED WHEN INTERPRETING A CONTRACT

All three instruments set out factors to be taken into account when interpreting a contract. Having considered the general approach to interpretation in section 2, these factors will now be explored. The instruments set out a near-identical list of factors to be considered when seeking to interpret a contract. These factors apply when the contract is being interpreted either by reference to the parties' common intention or when the more objective approach to interpretation

---

53 See the criticism of third-party protection in the DCFR in G. McMeel and H.C. Grigoleit, 'Interpretation of Contracts' in G. Dannemann and S. Vogenauer (eds.), *The Common European Sales Law in Context: Interactions with English and German Law* (Oxford: Oxford University Press, 2013), p. 354.

54 The comparative notes to Art. II-8:101(3) DCFR note that in Dutch law objective interpretation is the overriding approach where the contract is intended to affect the position of (a potentially large number of) third parties, not involved in the conclusion of the contract who could not be aware of the intentions of the parties: Full Edition of the DCFR, *supra* n. 5, p. 560.

55 In Scots law a contract that does not set out the common intention of the parties can be rectified. The court will rectify the contract, provided a person who has acted or refrained from acting in reliance on the contract would not be adversely affected to a material extent – see s. 9 of the Law Reform (Miscellaneous Provisions) (Scotland) Act 1985.

is taken.[56] The list is not exhaustive and so factors beyond those set out can also be considered.[57] The approach of the instruments to the list of factors is however different, with the PECL directing the interpreter to take account of these factors, using the mandatory term 'shall', whereas the DCFR and the CESL are permissive, noting that the interpreter 'may' take the factors into account. Each of the factors will be considered in turn.

3.1. THE CIRCUMSTANCES IN WHICH THE CONTRACT WAS CONCLUDED[58]

It is in relation to this factor that there is a difference between the instruments. Both the PECL and the DCFR provide that the circumstances in which the contract was concluded, including the preliminary negotiations, be taken into account. The commentaries to both instruments note that the rule[59] is consistent with any rule of law that forbids proof of matters in addition to or contrary to a written contract. The interpreter is able to take account of the circumstances at contract formation, not to seek further terms of the contract or to seek evidence that other terms contradict the contractual provisions, but to help him understand the terms of the contract.[60] Thus the surrounding circumstances can only be used to assist in understanding what the parties meant by the words used in their contract, on the basis that words do not exist in a vacuum and are used against a particular factual backdrop.

In the CESL account may be taken of the circumstances in which the contract was concluded but there is no reference to the preliminary negotiations. The text of the CESL originally contained reference to preliminary negotiations but that was deleted when the European Parliament voted on the CESL in February 2014. No justification for the deletion is given in the Report of the Committee on Legal Affairs which preceded the debate in Parliament.[61]

---

56 That the list applies to both methods of interpretation is clear from the commentary – see PECL, *supra* n. 4, p. 291; Full Edition of the DCFR, *supra* n. 5, p. 561.

57 See the use of 'in particular' in Art. 5:102 PECL, Art. II-8:102 DCFR and Art. 59 CESL. See also the commentary to the articles: PECL, *supra* n. 4, p. 291; Full Edition of the DCFR, *supra* n. 5, p. 561; Wendehorst, *supra* n. 22, p. 307.

58 Art. 5:102(a) PECL; Art. II-8:102(a) DCFR; Art. 59(a) CESL.

59 And, indeed, any of the factors set out under Art. 5:102 PECL and Art. II-8:102 DCFR.

60 PECL, *supra* n. 4, p. 288; Full Edition of the DCFR, *supra* n. 5, p. 554.

61 Report of 25 September 2013, http://www.europarl.europa.eu/sides/getDoc.do?type=REPORT&reference=A7-2013-0301&language=EN. In the same report Art. 59(b) is amended to refer to the conduct of the parties *prior, during and* subsequent to the conclusion of the contract (amendments in italics). The justification given for the amendment is clarity of wording. As such it does not appear that a substantive change was intended that would permit preliminary negotiations to be considered in terms of Art. 59(b).

While it is not clear, it appears that the CESL does not permit reference to the parties' preliminary negotiations for the purpose of interpreting a contract. This is in contrast to the position in most civilian legal systems in Europe and perhaps indicates an influence of common law jurisdictions on the process of interpretation as the CESL passed through the legislative process.

The laws of Scotland and England stand apart from most Members States on this matter. The comparative notes in the PECL and DCFR state that English law is different to other Member States in not permitting pre-contractual negotiations to be taken into account in the interpretive exercise.[62] The commentaries differ on the position in Scots law, with the PECL noting that Scots law does permit pre-contractual negotiations to be taken into account[63] and the DCFR noting that Scots law was reluctant to allow reference to pre-contractual negotiations but that there are now exceptions.[64]

It is suggested that the commentaries are somewhat misleading on this matter. On this issue Scots and English law are the same and, more importantly, the systems are not as different to other jurisdictions as the comparative notes to the PECL and DCFR suggest. In both Scots and English law, reference can be made to the parties' pre-contractual negotiations to show that a matter was known to both of the parties, such as a fact or the state of the law or regulation in an area of activity. In neither Scots nor English law can reference be made to pre-contractual negotiations to show what one of the parties thought the contract or a term of it meant.[65] Scots and English law therefore differentiate between references to the parties' negotiations for objective reasons, which is permitted, and for subjective reasons, which is not permitted. As such, the position in Scots and English law on pre-contractual negotiations is not so different from the law of other systems in permitting reference to the parties' pre-contractual negotiations, albeit for a limited purpose.

The commentary to the DCFR notes that not all Member States allow evidence of pre-contractual negotiations to be taken into account in interpreting the contract, on the grounds that what one party said was meant is not useful evidence, as the other contracting party might not agree with that interpretation. However, the better approach, according to the commentary, is not to exclude this from the evidence but to allow the court to assess it for what it is worth.[66]

---

62 PECL, *supra* n. 4, p. 293; Full Edition of the DCFR, *supra* n. 5, p. 563.

63 Ibid.

64 Full Edition of the DCFR, *supra* n. 5, p. 564.

65 *The Centre for Maritime and Industrial Safety Technology Ltd v Ineos Manufacturing Scotland Ltd* [2014] CSOH 5 (Scotland); *Chartbrook Ltd v Persimmon Homes Ltd* [2009] 1 AC 1101 (England).

66 Full Edition of the DCFR, *supra* n. 5, p. 561.

One doubts whether that is really the best approach. Taking into account one party's subjective understanding of the contract is contrary to the approach to interpretation set out in all three instruments, where the interpreter is directed to the parties' common intention (point (ii) on the continuum discussed in section 2.1 above), not the subjective intention of one of the parties (point (i) of the continuum). The subjective understanding of one of the parties is also not, without more, useful in interpreting the contract on the basis that one party's intended meaning should not prevail (discussed in section 2.2 above). Evidence would also have to be led that the other party knew or should have known of his contracting partner's intended meaning.

Furthermore, the parties' pre-contractual negotiations include all of the parties' discussions to get to the point where they reach *consensus in idem* and form their contract. In allowing pre-contractual negotiations to be taken into account, the interpreter may have to consider evidence which is irrelevant to the actual contract the parties entered into. It is the essence of negotiations that things will change and evolve until the parties reach agreement. Analysing evidence prior to contract formation, other than to show objective factors, such as that a certain fact was known to both parties, is to analyse something other than the actual contract the parties entered into.[67]

While both the PECL and the DCFR allow pre-contractual negotiations to be considered, both instruments also allow the parties to agree to exclude reference to these discussions in interpreting the contract. The parties can specify in an individually negotiated[68] merger clause[69] that their pre-contractual negotiations may not be used for the purpose of interpreting their contract.[70] In this way, the parties can agree how the contract is to be interpreted. This will be surprising to those from jurisdictions where interpretation is a matter of law, not fact.[71] While it is common for parties to agree, by the terms of their contract, that certain default rules will not apply, for example by making provision as to their contractual relationship which differs from the default rules, it is a different matter to permit parties to be able to dictate to the interpreter how to go about interpreting the contract, where that is a question of law.

---

67 This point was made by Lord Wilberforce in the English House of Lords case *Prenn v Simmonds* [1971] 1 WLR 1381 at 1384.

68 A non-individually negotiated merger clause will not have this effect – see Art. 2:105(3) PECL and Art. II-4:104(3) DCFR.

69 A merger clause states that the document embodies all of the terms of the contract: Art. 2:105 PECL and Art. II-4:104 DCFR. Such a clause may be known as an entire agreement clause in some jurisdictions.

70 Art. 2:105(3) PECL and Art. II-4:104(3) DCFR.

71 See the discussion of this issue in PECL, *supra* n. 4, p. 290; Full Edition of the DCFR, *supra* n. 5, pp. 556–557.

3.2. THE PARTIES' CONDUCT, EVEN SUBSEQUENT TO CONTRACT CONCLUSION[72]

It is suggested that the parties' conduct prior to the conclusion of the contract would form part of the circumstances existing at contract formation (discussed in section 3.1 above).[73] However, what makes this factor different is the reference to parties' post-formation conduct as a factor relevant to interpreting a contract.

As with pre-contractual negotiations, Scots and English law differ from most Member States in not taking post-contractual conduct into account in interpretation.[74] Such conduct is relevant to the question of whether a contract has been formed[75] but not to its interpretation. However, in a number of Scottish cases, post-contractual conduct has been taken into account insofar as it shows what was known to the parties at contract formation.[76]

The exclusion of post-contractual conduct from the process of interpreting a contract does not mean that such conduct is irrelevant to the operation of the contract between the parties in Scots and English law. It may be that the parties' actings following the conclusion of the contract result in a variation of the contract by conduct[77] or allows personal bar or estoppel to be pled.[78]

Taking into account the post-formation conduct of the parties is contrary to the principle that interpretation seeks to discover the meaning of the contract, at the time of formation of the contract, which is what the interpreter is required to do.[79] That is not to suggest that post-formation conduct is irrelevant – indeed it may show that the parties have varied or novated the contract – but, unless post-contractual conduct is limited to deducing from it what parties knew at the

---

72 Art. 5:102(b) PECL; Art. II-8:102(b) DCFR; Art. 59(b) CESL.

73 Art. 59(b) CESL provides that the parties' conduct prior, during and subsequent to the conclusion of the contract can be taken into account.

74 PECL, *supra* n. 4, p. 293; Full Edition of the DCFR, *supra* n. 5, pp. 563–564.

75 *Morgan Utilities Ltd v Scottish Water Solutions Ltd* [2011] CSOH 112 at para. 52 (Scotland); *ED&F Man Commodity Advisors Ltd v Fluxo-Cane Overseas Ltd* [2009] EWCA Civ 406 at paras. 20–21 (England).

76 *Cameron (Scotland) Ltd v Melville Dundas Ltd* 2001 SCLR 691 at paras. 30–31; *Wincanton Group Ltd v Reid Furniture plc* [2008] CSOH 109 at para. 16.

77 This may be more difficult where there is a term of the contract which requires variations to be dealt with in a certain way, e.g. to be in writing and signed by the parties; for interesting recent developments on this issue in English law see the Supreme Court's decision in *MWB Business Exchange Centres Ltd v Rock Advertising Ltd* [2018] 2 WLR 1603.

78 Personal bar applies in Scotland, estoppel in England. Estoppel by representation applies only as a defence, not as a cause of action. Personal bar generally operates defensively in Scots law; for more details see E. Reid and J Blackie, *Personal Bar* (Edinburgh: W. Green, 2006) paras. 5.21–5.25. The illustration of this rule provided in the commentaries (PECL, *supra* n. 4, p. 292; Full Edition of the DCFR, *supra* n. 5, p. 561) would likely raise personal bar or estoppel.

79 As noted in section 2.1 above.

time of contract formation, it considers matters after contract formation, which is not the critical point in time so far as interpretation is concerned.

3.3. THE INTERPRETATION ALREADY GIVEN TO THE SAME/SIMILAR TERMS BY THE PARTIES AND THE PARTIES' PRACTICES[80]

In relation to this factor, the text of the instruments differ slightly. The PECL refers to the interpretation given to similar clauses by the parties as a factor to consider. The DCFR and CESL provide that if *the same term/expression* or a similar term/expression has been interpreted by the parties to have a particular meaning, this may be taken into account. This, of course, makes sense. When parties are dealing with each other, it is likely that terms used will be given the same meaning across their contracts, unless the circumstances of the contract or its terms suggest otherwise. This factor may be of particular importance when the parties deal on standard terms and conditions.

All three instruments also mention the practices the parties have established between themselves as a factor to be taken into account. Further information on what is meant by a practice can be found in the commentaries to Art. 1:105 PECL and Art. II-1:104 DCFR, which provide that such practices may arise as a result of a sequence of previous conduct in relation to a particular transaction or a particular kind of transaction between the parties.[81] Commentary to the CESL notes that practices are likely to be factual habits the parties have established.[82] It is therefore clear that a practice is not limited to a particular contract but may operate in relation to particular types of contract.[83] The practice is established when the parties' conduct may fairly be regarded as a common understanding between them. While no period is mentioned, it appears that there would need to be conduct over a reasonable period of time or in relation to a reasonable number of contracts before a common understanding could be said to be established. The number of contracts between the parties in any period would, of course, depend on the parties and their relationship. It seems that parties' conduct must be consistent for a practice to be established.[84] The commentaries

80 Art. 5:102(d) PECL; Art. II-8:102(c) DCFR; Art. 59(c) CSEL (interpretation already given); and Art. 59(e) CESL (practices).

81 PECL, *supra* n. 4, p. 104; Full Edition of the DCFR, *supra* n. 5, p. 138.

82 Wendehorst, *supra* n. 22, p. 311.

83 PECL, *supra* n. 4, p. 104; Full Edition of the DCFR, *supra* n. 5, p. 138.

84 Practices established between the parties are also a basis on which a term may be included in the parties' contract, as a tacitly agreed term, under the DCFR (Art. II-9:101(1)). Likewise a practice established between traders in a B2B contract would be a term of the contract under the CESL: see Arts. 66(b) and 67(1) CESL. There is no equivalent provision in the PECL.

to the PECL and DCFR note that the practices established between the parties are often decisive.[85]

3.4. THE MEANING COMMONLY GIVEN TO TERMS IN THE BRANCH OF ACTIVITY[86]

There is a slight difference in the wording of this factor between the PECL and DCFR, on the one hand, and the CESL on the other. The relevant Articles in the PECL and DCFR go on to provide 'and the interpretation such terms may have already received' will be taken into account. It is thought that the difference in wording does not denote a substantive difference between the instruments, given that an interpretation given to a term will affect the meaning given to it in the branch of activity concerned.

This factor allows reference to be made to meanings, not as established between the parties, but interpretations that have been given to terms or expressions in the branch of activity in which the contract is to be performed. It is suggested that this factor is essentially a facet of the circumstances in which the contract is concluded (discussed in section 3.1 above). It of course makes sense to take account of a meaning established within the environment or market in which a contract is to operate in order to determine what the words used in the contract mean. In many sectors particular words will not have the meaning that would be given to them by laymen, but have a specialised meaning which anyone operating in that field of activity would understand the term to mean.

Taking account of this factor accords with the fact that in interpreting a contract the interpreter is seeking to determine the parties' common intention or to interpret the contract in a way that is not entirely objective, but that takes account of the parties and the position they were in at contract formation.

3.5. THE NATURE AND PURPOSE OF THE CONTRACT[87]

This is an uncontroversial factor to be considered in interpreting a contract. All three instruments provide that terms are to be interpreted in light of the contract as

This may be likened to implied terms in fact in Scots and English law on the basis that the term is so obvious that it goes without saying: see *Shirlaw v Southern Foundries (1926) Ltd* [1939] 2 KB 206; or that the practice is a term of the contract based on a course of dealing between the parties.

85 PECL, *supra* n. 4, p. 292; Full Edition of the DCFR, *supra* n. 5, p. 562.

86 Art. 5:102(e) PECL; Art. II-8:102(d) DCFR; Art. 59(f) CESL.

87 Art. 5:102(c) PECL and Art. II-8:102(e) DCFR; Art. 59(g) CESL.

a whole[88] and that contractual provisions should be interpreted in such a way that the terms of the contract are lawful and effectual.[89] This factor complements those rules by considering why the parties entered into the contract and what the contract seeks to achieve.

3.6. USAGES[90]

Usages are also a factor to be taken into account in interpreting the parties' contract.[91] A usage may be agreed between the parties, but may also be imposed upon the parties. The latter occurs where there is a usage which would generally be considered applicable to persons in the same position as the parties, except where application of the usage would be unreasonable.[92] To be relevant the usage must not conflict with the express or implied terms of the parties' contract.[93]

The commentaries to both the PECL and the DCFR further explain that usages may be understood as a course of dealing or a line of conduct which is, and has for a certain period of time been, generally adopted by those engaged in a trade or other activity.[94] The usage must be so well established and have such

88 See the discussion of Art. 5:105 PECL; Art. II-8:105 DCFR; Art. 58(3)(a) CESL in section 4 below.

89 See the discussion of Art. 5:106 PECL; Art. II-8:106 DCFR; Art. 61(a) CESL in section 4 below.

90 Art. 5:102(f) PECL; Art. II-8:102(f) DCFR; Art. 59(d) CESL.

91 As with practices established between the parties (discussed at section 3.3 above), usages can be a basis on which a term may be included in the parties' contract, as a tacitly agreed term, under the DCFR (Art. II-9:101(1)) and in B2B contracts in terms of Arts. 66(b) and 67 CESL. There is no equivalent provision in the PECL.

92 Considering the general rule on usages found in Art. 1:105 PECL and Art. II-1:104 DCFR. In the general provisions part of the instruments, where these articles are to be found, usages and practices established between the parties are considered together, yet in the factors to be taken into account in interpreting the contract they are dealt with separately. This perhaps signifies that practices are those personal to the parties, whereas usages can be personal to the parties but may also be external, in that the parties may be bound by a usage generally applicable to persons in the same position as the parties. There is no reference to the usage having to be reasonable in the CESL, however, it seems difficult to envisage a situation in which the usage would be applicable to persons in the same position as the parties yet would be unreasonable to apply to the parties.

93 The discussion at p. 104 of the PECL (*supra* n. 4) suggests that the usage need only be consistent with the express terms of the parties' contract, as does the discussion at p. 138 of the Full Edition of the DCFR (*supra* n. 5). However, p. 140 of the Full Edition of the DCFR makes clear that the implied terms should also be considered. It is suggested that clearly extending consideration to implied terms is the correct approach, given it seems likely that a usage that conflicts with the implied terms of the contract would be unreasonable and therefore inapplicable to the parties' contract. The usage must be consistent with the agreement of the parties in terms of Art. 67(3) CESL. A term will not be implied into a contract where there is a usage or practice which applies: Art. 68 CESL. As such a usage will take precedence over implied terms under the CESL.

94 PECL, *supra* n. 4, p. 104; Full Edition of the DCFR, *supra* n. 5, p. 138.

general application among those engaged in the trade or activity that persons in the same situation as the parties would consider it applicable to them.[95] In this way the contract may be affected by usages applicable to all trades and/or those that apply to certain trades, where the contract is to operate in that trade.[96] Usages encompasses local, national and international usages.[97] The usages that apply are those current at the place where the contract is made.[98]

It is unsurprising that usages agreed between the parties are considered in interpreting the parties' contract. What is more surprising is that usages applicable to other parties in the same position as the contracting parties are taken into account where the interpreter is seeking the parties' common intention (as discussed in section 2.1 above). Considering the position of third parties in the same position as the contracting parties includes an objective element, which may not accord with the parties' understanding of the contract.[99] This is emphasised in the commentaries to the PECL and DCFR, which provide that usages may be referred to whether the parties may be considered to have contracted by reference to the usage *or* when the usage forms the basis of a reasonable interpretation that can be used to resolve an uncertainty about the meaning of a contract.[100] This is, of course, less of an issue where an objective approach is taken to the interpretive exercise (as discussed in section 2.3 above).

3.7. GOOD FAITH AND FAIR DEALING[101]

The final factor listed in all three instruments is good faith and fair dealing. The term 'good faith and fair dealing' is defined in the DCFR as referring to a standard of conduct characterised by honesty, openness and consideration for the interests of the other party to the transaction or relationship.[102] A similar definition is found in the CESL: a standard of conduct characterised by honesty, openness and, in so far as may be appropriate, reasonable consideration for the interests of the other party to the transaction or relationship in question.[103]

---

95 PECL, *supra* n. 4, p. 105; Full Edition of the DCFR, *supra* n. 5, p. 140.
96 Ibid.
97 Ibid.
98 PECL, *supra* n. 4, p. 293; Full Edition of the DCFR, *supra* n. 5, p. 562.
99 Although if the parties consider the usage applies to them, then this is not an objective factor.
100 PECL, *supra* n. 4, p. 292–293; Full Edition of the DCFR, *supra* n. 5, p. 562.
101 Art. 5:102(g) PECL; Art. II-8:102(g) DCFR; Art. 59(h) CESL.
102 Art. I-1:103 DCFR.
103 Art. 2(fe) of the Proposal for a Regulation of the European Parliament and of the Council on a Common European Sales Law. The definition is not found in the text of the CESL itself. Prior to the changes made to the Proposed Regulation by the European Parliament in February 2014, the definition was the same as that in the DCFR. No justification is provided in the Report of the Committee on Legal Affairs which preceded the Parliament's amendments: Report of 25 September 2013, *supra* n. 61.

No definition is provided within the rules of the PECL; however, the meanings of 'good faith' and, separately, 'fair dealing' are discussed in the commentary to Art. 1:201 PECL. This provides that 'good faith' means honesty and fairness in mind, which are subjective concepts. 'Fair dealing' means observance of fairness in fact, which is an objective standard.[104] The commentary to the DCFR notes that the composite term 'good faith and fair dealing' has a different meaning to 'good faith' alone.[105] 'Good faith' in the DCFR refers to a subjective state of mind generally characterised by honesty and a lack of knowledge that an apparent situation is not the true situation.[106] It is therefore clear that by using 'good faith and fair dealing' the interpreter is directed to an objective, rather than subjective standard.

Interpretation is, of course, not the only place within the instruments where the concept of good faith and fair dealing arises. Good faith and fair dealing is a fundamental general concept in all of the instruments.[107] This is clearly demonstrated by the number of references to good faith and fair dealing within the rules in all three instruments, together with the central importance given to good faith and fair dealing in rules of general application. For instance, Art. 1:201 PECL and Art. 2(1) CESL stipulate that each party must act in accordance with good faith and fair dealing, which rule cannot be excluded or limited. Art. III-1:103 DCFR provides that parties must act in accordance with good faith and fair dealing in performing an obligation, exercising a right to performance, pursuing or defending a remedy for non-performance, or exercising a right to terminate an obligation or contractual relationship.[108]

---

104 PECL, *supra* n. 4, pp. 115–116.

105 The same point is made in a commentary to the CESL: see Wendehorst, *supra* n. 22, p. 90.

106 It is noteworthy that the examples of good faith provided in the commentary to the DCFR are examples provided in the commentary to the PECL as *not* exemplifying what is meant by good faith in the latter instrument: PECL, *supra* n. 4, p. 116; Full Edition of the DCFR, *supra* n. 5, p. 89.

107 However, it appears that good faith plays a less fundamental and pervasive role in the DCFR and CESL to that envisaged by the PECL. This can be seen in the difference between Art. 1:102 PECL and Art. II-1:102 DCFR. The former provides that parties are free to enter into a contract and determine its contents, subject to *the requirements of good faith and fair dealing, and* the mandatory rules set out in the PECL. In Art. 1:102 DCFR the words in italics in the previous sentence are omitted (and the reference to mandatory rules are to those under the DCFR). This change appears to have occurred fairly late in the development of the DCFR, as the Interim Outline Edition (C. von Bar, E. Clive and H. Schulte-Nölke (eds.), *Principles, Definitions and Model Rules of European Private Law: Draft Common Frame of Reference (DCFR)*, Interim Outline Edition (Munich: Sellier, 2008), published a year before the Full Edition, qualifies the parties' freedom to enter contracts by reference to good faith and fair dealing, as well as the mandatory rules of the DCFR. There is also a marked difference in the discussion of good faith and fair dealing in the commentary to Art. 1:201 PECL (*supra* n. 4, pp. 113–116) and the discussion in the commentary to Art. III-1:103 DCFR (Full Edition, *supra* n. 5, pp. 676–679). Art. 1(1) CESL is in the same terms as Art. II-1:102 Outline Edition DCFR.

108 Art. II-3:301 DCFR requires parties to negotiate in accordance with good faith and fair dealing.

As with the other instruments, this rule cannot be excluded or limited by the parties. The commentaries to the instruments make clear that these articles set out a basic principle.[109]

The commentaries to both the PECL and the DCFR note that good faith and fair dealing will often determine the interpretation of a contract.[110] Yet no reason is given as to why this is the case. It may be obvious that good faith and fair dealing will often be the determining factor to those from a legal system with a general doctrine of good faith, but it is far from clear why this should be the case under the PECL or DCFR without further explanation. To those from a legal system without a general doctrine of good faith, such as England and Scotland,[111] the priority given to this factor in the interpretive exercise is far from clear. Those unfamiliar with a general duty of good faith will not be reassured to find that the term 'duty' is used, rather than 'obligation', because 'of the rather vague, supplementary and all-pervasive nature of what is expected from the parties'.[112] How can such a duty frequently be the decisive factor in contractual interpretation? Conversely, commentary on the CESL suggests a much more limited role for good faith and fair dealing in the interpretive exercise: as simply one of the factors to be considered, and one that may be superfluous.[113]

There have been attempts to bring good faith into contract law in Scots and English law in recent years. In 2014 the Inner House of the Court of Session[114] held that contracts should be interpreted on the basis that contracts are cooperative enterprises for parties' mutual benefit, such that it would be difficult to persuade the court that an interpretation which provided a windfall burden or benefit for either of the parties was correct.[115] The case has been criticised[116] and subsequent cases have noted, in strong terms, that this is not

109 PECL, *supra* n. 4, p. 113; Full Edition of the DCFR, *supra* n. 5, p. 676; Wendehorst, *supra* n. 22, p. 90.

110 PECL, *supra* n. 4, p. 293; Full Edition of the DCFR, *supra* n. 5, p. 563.

111 It might be said that Scots law has an underlying doctrine of good faith, upon which many specific contractual (and other rules) are based; for further discussion see H. MacQueen, 'Good Faith in the Scots Law of Contract: An Undisclosed Principle?' in A.D.M. Forte, *Good Faith in Contract and Property Law* (Oxford: Hart Publishing, 1999).

112 Full Edition of the DCFR, *supra* n. 5, p. 676.

113 Wendehorst, *supra* n 22, p. 311.

114 This is an appellate court and the highest civil court in Scotland, although Scottish civil cases can be further appealed to the Supreme Court of the UK.

115 *Grove Investments Ltd v Cape Building Products Ltd* 2014 Hous LR 35. The Inner House restricted its comments on interpretation to the ancillary, rather than the main, terms of the contract; however, later cases went further and appeared to use this approach to deal with all terms of a contract: see *Mapeley Acquisitions Co (3) Ltd v City of Edinburgh Council* [2015] CSOH 29.

116 See for instance L. Macgregor, *supra* n. 42.

the correct approach to interpretation.[117] It seems unlikely that this approach to interpretation will progress.[118]

In England there have been a number of cases where a party to a contract has sought to persuade the court that their contractual partner owes them obligations based on a duty of good faith. This has been attempted by seeking to imply a duty of good faith into the contract.[119] To date, the term has been implied into only certain 'relational contracts', that is contracts where the parties require a high degree of communication, cooperation and loyalty from each other and where contractual performance is based on mutual trust and confidence.[120] The case law shows no signs of a duty of good faith being implied into other types of contract, or that the court will permit implication of such a term other than exceptionally.[121]

3.8. PROTECTION OF THIRD-PARTY RELIANCE

Following the list of factors that the interpreter may take into account, the DCFR provides:

> in a question with a person, not being a party to the contract or a person such as an assignee who by law has no better rights than such a party, who has reasonably and in good faith relied on the contract's apparent meaning, regard may be had to the circumstances discussed in [sections 3.1 to 3.3 above] only to the extent that those circumstances were known to, or could reasonably be expected to have been known to, that person.[122]

---

117 *@Sipp (Pension Trustees) Ltd v Insight Travel Services Ltd* 2016 SC 243.

118 Particularly in light of recent UK Supreme Court cases such as *Arnold v Britton* [2015] AC 1619 and *Wood v Capita Insurance Services Ltd* [2017] 2 WLR 1095, which have been followed in Scotland.

119 The spate of cases on this topic follow on from the decision in *Yam Seng Pte Ltd v International Trade Corp Ltd* [2013] EWHC 111 (QB). Cases include *National Private Air Transport Services Co. (National Air Services) Ltd v Creditrade LLP* [2016] EWHC 2144 (Comm); *Hamsard 3147 Ltd (t/a Mini Mode Childrenswear) v Boots UK Ltd* [2013] EWHC 3251 (Pat); *Emirates Trading Agency LLC v Prime Mineral Exports Private Ltd* [2014] EWHC 2104 (Comm); *British Groundschool Ltd v Intelligent Data Capture Ltd* [2014] EWHC 2145 (Ch); *Monde Petroleum SA v Westernzagros Ltd* [2016] EWHC 1472 (Comm); and *Al Nehayan v Kent* [2018] EWHC 333 (Comm).

120 This is how relational contracts were described in *Yam Seng Pte Ltd v International Trade Corp Ltd* [2013] EWHC 111 (QB) at para. 142. Examples might include joint venture agreements, franchise agreements and long-term distributorship contracts.

121 Usually where the term is necessary for the contract to work, the so-called business efficacy test: see *Marks and Spencer plc v BNP Paribas Securities Services Trust Co (Jersey) Ltd* [2015] 3 WLR 1843 and *Monde Petroleum SA v Westernzagros Ltd* [2016] EWHC 1472 (Comm).

122 Art. II-8:102(2) DCFR.

No such provision is made in either the PECL or the CESL. As noted in section 2 above, Art. II-8:101(3)(b) DCFR stipulates that an objective approach to interpretation should be taken when a third party has, reasonably and in good faith, relied on a contract's apparent meaning. The approach to the factors to be taken into account in Art. II-8:102(2) corresponds to that rule and seeks to protect third parties who did not know what the parties knew at or before contract formation, and afterwards, insofar as post-contractual conduct is concerned. It is suggested that the wording of Art. II-8:102(2)[123] is not especially clear. In particular, from its formulation it is not immediately clear whether the third-party protection extends to assignees or not. Greater clarity on this point in the rules would be beneficial.

4. SPECIFIC RULES OF INTERPRETATION

As well as setting out the general approach to interpreting contracts and the factors to be taken into account in doing so, the instruments contain a number of specific rules of interpretation, which are discussed in this section. Given that the rules are fairly uncontroversial, they can be dealt with fairly briefly.

4.1. INTERPRETATION AGAINST THE SUPPLIER OF A TERM

All three instruments provide that where there is doubt about the meaning of a contract term which has not been individually negotiated, an interpretation against the party who supplied the term is to be preferred.[124] This is, of course, the *contra proferentem* rule of interpretation.[125] The DCFR specifies that a term supplied by one party is not individually negotiated if the other party has not been able to influence its content, in particular because it has been drafted in advance, whether or not as part of standard terms.[126] Similarly, the CESL states that a contract term is not individually negotiated if it has been supplied by one party and the other party has not been able to influence its content.[127] While this rule may often be used where the parties have contracted on standard terms, its remit is wider than that.

123 As with Art. II-8:101(3)(b), discussed in section 2.3 above.

124 Art. 5:103 PECL; Art. II-8:103(1) DCFR; Art. 62(1a) CESL. Art. 62(1a) CESL is subordinate to Art. 61b, discussed below.

125 Indeed, the article in the PECL is headed: '*Contra Proferentem* Rule'.

126 Art. II-1:110(1) DCFR. No detail is given as to the meaning of 'terms not individually negotiated' in the PECL.

127 Art. 7(1) CESL.

The commentaries to the PECL and DCFR note that the rule applies not only where one of the parties has drafted the disputed term, but also where a party uses pre-drafted clauses which have been drafted by a third party. As such, where a contracting party seeks to use the standard clauses prepared by a professional or trade association to which he belongs, any ambiguity in the meaning of those terms may mean that the term is interpreted against him.[128] It is to be noted that an interpretation against the party who provided the non-negotiated contract term is to be preferred, thus it is not inevitable that the contract will be interpreted against him.[129]

Art. II-8:103(2) DCFR provides a further interpretive rule.[130] It stipulates that where there is doubt about the meaning of any other term, and that term has been established under the dominant influence of one party, an interpretation of the term against that party is to be preferred. This rule is said to be an extension of the *contra proferentem* rule, but will apply to terms of the contract that have been individually negotiated. It is not clear how dominant the contracting party's influence needs to be to engage the rule, other than the commentary providing that the rule is not restricted to business-to-consumer contracts. No such rule appears in the PECL or CESL.

The CESL provides a further rule for the protection of consumers. Art. 61b states that where there is any doubt about the meaning of a contract term in a B2C contract, the interpretation most favourable to the consumer shall prevail unless the term was supplied by the consumer.[131] This rule cannot be excluded, derogated from or its effect varied to the detriment of the consumer. Neither the PECL nor the DCFR contains such a rule.

It must be noted that the rules discussed in this section only apply where there is doubt as to the meaning of a contractual term. In many cases, by utilising the general approach to contractual interpretation (discussed in sections 2 and 3) the meaning of a disputed provision will be clear to the interpreter, such that the use of the specific rules in this section will be limited.[132]

---

128 PECL, *supra* n. 4, p. 294; Full Edition of the DCFR, *supra* n. 5, p. 564. The same can be said about the CESL given the use of 'supplied' rather than 'drafted' in the rule. Both the DCFR and the CESL expressly provide that in a contract between a business and a consumer, terms drafted by a third person are considered to have been supplied by the business, unless the consumer introduced them to the contract: Art. II-1:110(5) DCFR and Art. 7(5) CESL.

129 PECL, *supra* n. 4, p. 294; Full Edition of the DCFR, *supra* n. 5, p. 565.

130 This rule did not appear in the Interim Outline Edition of the DCFR published in 2008 (*supra* n. 107).

131 In the UK a similar rule applies: s 69, Consumer Rights Act 2015.

132 Full Edition of the DCFR, *supra* n. 5, p. 565. Similar comments have been made in relation to the *contra proferentem* rule in Scots and English law. For a recent example see *Transocean Drilling UK Ltd v Providence Resources plc* [2016] EWCA Civ 372.

4.2. PREFERENCE FOR NEGOTIATED TERMS

Art. 5:104 PECL and Art. II-8:104 DCFR provide that terms which have been individually negotiated take precedence over terms that have not.[133] The wording of the rule in the CESL is slightly different, providing that to the extent there is an inconsistency, negotiated terms prevail over those that have not been individually negotiated.[134] It is suggested that the difference in wording does not affect the substance of the rule. It is an uncontroversial rule, based on the assumption that where parties have negotiated a term it is more likely to represent their common intention than terms that have not been negotiated. However, it is suggested that the rule should include provision that the parties can prove the contrary.[135] None of the instruments provide that this rule cannot be excluded or modified, and as such it is likely that parties with strong negotiating positions may seek to exclude the application of the rule when dealing on their standard terms.

The preference for negotiated terms applies to printed terms which are modified, either by hand or in some other way, including oral modifications.[136] The commentaries to the PECL and DCFR provide that the rule operates as a rebuttable presumption that such modifications were negotiated.[137]

4.3. CONTRACT TO BE INTERPRETED AS A WHOLE[138]

All of the instruments provide that terms are to be interpreted in light of the contract as a whole.[139] This is also an uncontroversial rule, requiring the disputed term to be read in the context of the entire contract in which it appears, rather than homing in on the disputed term or passage and interpreting the term in isolation. This rule assumes that the terms of the contract will be coherent and

---

133 The rule will not assist where there is doubt as to which set of terms the parties intend to contract on, where both parties seek to use their own standard terms – the so-called battle of the forms.

134 Art. 62(1) CESL.

135 It is not inconceivable in a contract in relation to which some of the terms have been negotiated and some are standard that the parties wish the contract to be governed by the standard terms, as opposed to the negotiated terms.

136 PECL, *supra* n. 4, p. 295; Full Edition of the DCFR, *supra* n. 5, p. 567; Wendehorst, *supra* n. 22, p. 316.

137 PECL, *supra* n. 4, p. 295; Full Edition of the DCFR, *supra* n. 5, p. 567.

138 In the CESL this rule does not appear as a specific rule of interpretation but appears in the general rules of contract interpretation, discussed in section 2 above.

139 Art. 5:105 PECL; Art. II-8:105 DCFR; Art. 58(3a) CESL.

should not contradict each other, and that the same word or expression will not have different meanings in different parts of the contract.[140]

The commentaries further provide that the rule can be applied to certain groups of contracts, such as a framework agreement and the various contracts made under it.[141] The commentaries do not specify that the rule would apply in such situations unless the terms of the contracts or circumstances of the case suggests otherwise. Presumably, however, the rule would not apply in those situations, particularly where the terms of the contract state otherwise.

4.4. TERMS TO BE GIVEN EFFECT

The final specific rule of contractual interpretation found in all three instruments is that there is a preference for an interpretation which renders the terms of the contract lawful or effectual, as opposed to an interpretation which does not.[142] Again, this is an uncontroversial rule which assumes that the contracting parties wish their contract to be fully effective.[143]

The commentaries to the rule suggest that this rule only becomes effective where there is doubt as to the meaning of the term, such that there is more than one possible interpretation.[144] That this is so might have been usefully set out in the rules themselves, rather than left to the commentaries.[145]

Insofar as the PECL is concerned, there are no further provisions in relation to interpretation.[146] That is not the position under the DCFR or CESL, where Arts. II-8:201 and II-8:202 DCFR and Art. 12 CESL set out the rules of interpretation applicable to legal acts or statements other than contracts. These are discussed in the next section.

---

140 PECL, *supra* n. 4, p. 296; Full Edition of the DCFR, *supra* n. 5, p. 568; Wendehorst, *supra* n. 22, pp. 312–313.

141 Ibid.

142 Art. 5:106 PECL; Art. II-8:106 DCFR; Art. 61a CESL.

143 Although it should be noted that in relation to Art. 7(2) of the European Directive on Unfair Terms in Consumer Contracts (93/13/EEC) the rule does not apply: that article allows enforcement bodies to seek decisions on whether terms put to general use by suppliers are unfair.

144 PECL, *supra* n. 4, p. 297; Full Edition of the DCFR, *supra* n. 5, p. 566; Wendehorst, *supra* n. 22, p. 318.

145 In the UK, this rule is referred to as the business common sense approach to interpretation. The importance of this approach has recently been affirmed by the UK Supreme Court: see *Wood v Capita Insurance Services Ltd* [2017] 2 WLR 1095; however, it is clear that there must be a true ambiguity before the court can seek to utilise business common sense: see *Arnold v Britton* [2015] AC 1619.

146 Other than provisions where contract documents appear in more than one language in Art. 5:107 PECL.

5. INTERPRETING ACTS OR STATEMENTS OTHER THAN CONTRACTS[147]

5.1. THE PECL

No specific provision is made on the approach to interpretation other than in respect of contracts. However, that is not to say that no provision is made on the approach to interpreting other actions or statements indicating intention. Art. 1:107 PECL provides that the rules found in the PECL apply with appropriate modifications to agreements to modify or end a contract, to unilateral promises and to other statements and conduct indicating intention. The commentary to this article states that adaptions will have to be made to the rules of interpretation. But just what those adaptations will be are not specified. The commentary notes that it may be necessary to consider simply the intention of the party making the declaration, although, on the other hand, it will be necessary to consider how the recipient of the declaration understood or should have understood it.[148] The commentary to Art. 2:107 PECL provides that promises binding without acceptance are to be treated as contracts, albeit with some modifications.[149] Again, no detail is given as to what those modifications may be or how they are to operate.

5.2. THE DCFR AND THE CESL

The position is different in the DCFR and the CESL. The DCFR uses the term 'juridical act' to refer to statements or conduct indicating intention. Art. II-1:101 defines a juridical act as any statement or agreement, express or implied from conduct, which is intended to have legal effect as such. It may be unilateral, bilateral or multilateral. The DCFR makes provision for interpreting juridical acts other than contracts, whereas the CESL makes provision for interpreting unilateral statements or conduct indicating intention. As such the scope of the rules is, at least theoretically,[150] narrower in the CESL.

---

[147] The DCFR uses the term, 'juridical acts' for such actions or statements.

[148] PECL, *supra* n. 4, p. 110. The commentary goes on to note that the guidance on interpretation given by Art. 5:103(d), (e) and (f) will be very useful here. This seems to be a typographic error, intending to refer to Art. 5:102. It is not clear why the guidance on the factors to be taken into account in interpretation set out in paras. (d), (e) and (f) (discussed in sections 3.3, 3.4 and 3.6 above, respectively) are more helpful than the other factors.

[149] PECL, *supra* n. 4, p. 157.

[150] There is unlikely to be any practical difference given acts or statements indicating intention are likely to be either contracts; unilateral statements or conduct; or variations to contracts (to which the rules on interpretation of contracts would apply).

Both the DCFR and the CESL set out the general approach to interpreting a unilateral juridical act; then the approach to be taken where the addressor's intended meaning was known, or should have been known, to the addressee. The DCFR goes on to set out the approach to be taken to interpretation where the rules just mentioned do not apply; and finally how a juridical act should be interpreted where there has been reliance upon it by a third party. The rules will be considered in turn.

Art. II-8:201(1) DCFR provides that a unilateral juridical act is to be interpreted in the way in which it could reasonably be expected to be understood by the person to whom it is addressed. Art. 12(1) CESL provides that a unilateral statement indicating intention is to be interpreted in the way in which the person to whom it is addressed could be expected to understand it. At first sight the CESL appears to take a more subjective approach than the DCFR. However, this is not the case given Art. 5(2) CESL provides that any reference to what can be expected of or by a person, or in a particular situation, is a reference to what can reasonably be expected. As such in both instruments an element of objectivity is included given the requirement of reasonableness on the part of the addressee. It is suggested that this approach to interpretation sits close to point (iii) of the continuum, discussed in section 2.1 above. As such, the primary approach to interpreting unilateral juridical acts is more objective than the primary approach to interpreting contracts, where the parties' common intention is initially sought.

The commentaries to the rules suggest that, in fact, the rule is even more objective than it first appears. The commentaries note that account can be taken of the characteristics of the addressee. However they go on to note that this reflects the policy that the addressee of a communication intended to have legal effect is entitled to rely on it having the meaning which *any recipient of the same type* could reasonably be expected to place on it.[151] It thus appears that there is not much difference between the primary approach to interpreting unilateral juridical acts and the objective approach to interpreting such acts, discussed below.

Art. II-8:201(2) DCFR provides that if the person making the juridical act (the addressor) intended the act, or a term or expression used in it, to have a particular meaning, and at the time of the act the addressee was aware, or could reasonably be expected to be aware, of the addressor's intention, the act

[151] Full Edition of the DCFR, *supra* n. 5, p. 572. Emphasis added. The commentary to the CESL is in similar terms: the interpretation a reasonable recipient of the same type as the actual recipient would give to it in the same circumstances, Wendehorst, 'Interpretation', *supra* n. 22, p. 122.

is to be interpreted in the way intended by the addressor. Art. 12(2) CESL is in similar terms.[152] The provisions mirror the equivalent provision on interpreting contracts, discussed in section 2.2 above. As such, the comments made in that section apply equally here, with one exception. It is suggested that in the case of a unilateral juridical act, where the addressee receives a benefit from the addressor, with no corresponding obligation on the part of the addressee for this benefit, there may be stronger grounds for allowing the unilateral juridical act to be interpreted in the way the addressor intended where the addressee was aware or could reasonably be expected to have been aware[153] of the addressor's intended meaning. There may, of course be situations where the unilateral juridical act is part of a transaction involving other contracts and commitments, for example where a personal guarantee is provided by a company director for the company's debts, such that there are corresponding obligations on the addressee, which are found in those other contracts. In that situation, however, this background and the other contracts making up the whole transaction would be part of the circumstances to be considered in interpreting the guarantee and could therefore be taken into account.[154]

Art. II-8:201(3)(a) DCFR provides that a juridical act is to be interpreted according to the meaning which a reasonable person would give to it if neither of the rules discussed above apply. There is no equivalent provision in the CESL.[155] At first sight, this appears to be a completely objective approach to interpreting the act.[156] However Art. II-8:202 provides that the rules in section 1, apart from the first article (i.e. Art. II-8:101), apply with appropriate modifications to interpreting juridical acts. As such, the factors set out in Art. II-8:102, discussed in section 3 above, would apply, including the circumstances in which the juridical act is made and the conduct of the parties. This is therefore not a wholly objective approach, as the reasonable person can take account of the parties' positions and knowledge available to them when the juridical act was made. This therefore sits at point (iii) of the continuum discussed in section 2.1. As noted above, there does not seem to be much difference in the approach to

---

152 Although Art. II-8:201(2) DCFR benefits from specifying that the relevant point in time at which the addressee is or should have been aware is at the time of the juridical act.

153 This is contrary to the position advocated in section 2.3 for the approach to the equivalent rule of contractual interpretation, where it was argued that the test specified in Art. 5:101(2) PECL – 'could not have been unaware' – is preferable to the test in the DCFR and the CESL.

154 Art. II-8:202 DCFR applies the rules of section 1 of the article to interpreting juridical acts.

155 Although Art. 58(3b) CESL provides that the rules in chapter 6 (on the interpretation of contracts) is to apply to the interpretation of an offer, acceptance or other unilateral statement indicating intention, or equivalent conduct, with appropriate adaptations. As noted in Part section 2.3, Art. 58(3) provides that a contract is to be interpreted according to the meaning a reasonable person would give to it.

156 As is the equivalent provision in relation to contracts, Art. II-8:101(3)(a) DCFR, discussed in section 2.3 above.

interpretation required by this article and Art. II-8:201(1). This is reflected in the commentary, which states that in most cases Art. II-8:201(3)(a) will produce the same result as the rule in Art. II-8:201(1). However, Art. II-8:201(3)(a) was thought necessary to deal with cases where there was no identifiable addressee.[157]

Finally, Art. II-8:201(3)(b) DCFR provides that an objective approach to interpretation be adopted if a question arises with a third party who has reasonably and in good faith relied upon the contract's apparent meaning. This appears to be a typographic error and should instead refer to the third party having relied on the juridical act's apparent meaning. This provision mirrors Art. II-8:101(3)(b) and as such the comments made in section 2.3 are relevant to this article also. However, given the more objective approach taken to the interpretation of unilateral juridical acts, as discussed above, taking an objective approach due to third-party reliance is likely to be less of an issue. As pointed out previously, neither the PECL nor the CESL contain specific provisions covering third-party reliance.

6. CONCLUDING REMARKS

The discussion above of the rules of interpretation found in the PECL, the DCFR and the CESL shows that while there are many similarities between the instruments, there are some important differences. Many of the developments found in the DCFR and the CESL are welcome, in that they deal with matters that had been raised by the PECL, but which had not been fully determined by the rules or commentary to that instrument. This is particularly the case in relation to the approach to interpreting statements or conduct other than contracts, where more detailed rules are to be found in the DCFR and the CESL. The analysis of the rules in these instruments shows a more objective approach to the interpretation of juridical acts than to contracts, where the interpreter is tasked with first seeking to find the parties' common intention.

Another marked difference between the instruments is the inclusion of rules of interpretation to protect third-party reliance in the DCFR. While there is no doubt that third-party reliance is an important consideration, a balance must be struck between the interests of the parties to the contract or juridical act and third parties. In this chapter, it has been argued that the rules seeking to protect such reliance, especially the rule in relation to the interpretation of contracts, goes too far. It has been suggested that to engage the protection of an objective interpretation, the third party should have to have suffered some prejudice or detriment, as well as being able to show that such reliance was reasonable and in good faith.

---

157 Full Edition of the DCFR, *supra* n. 5, p. 572.

OPENING REMARKS ON THE NATIONAL REPORTS

1. INTRODUCTION

This chapter contains Opening Remarks written by each national reporter describing the interpretative process in their legal system. The editors asked these to be prepared with specific aims in mind.

First, the Opening Remarks perform the function of 'setting the scene' for the more detailed answering of questions which is to follow. To this end, reporters were asked to discuss more general matters relating to contract interpretation that they believed the reader should know about their legal system in advance. Starting with a country-specific introduction helps the reader to understand the answers to the questions better.

Second, they provide reporters with an opportunity to inform the reader of the cultural particularities of their respective legal systems without being confined by the parameters of questions and cases. It compensates for the reporter's experience that the inescapable presumptions of the questionnaire have a restrictive effect on her or his answers.

Third, allowing the reporters to clarify matters that the questionnaire would otherwise prevent them from doing advances the reliability of the output of the comparative analysis. Again, one of the comparatist's most likely pitfalls is the need for comparability and comprehensibility accidentally covering up the subtler differences and peculiarities. After all, if different reporters add different details that are not directly relevant to the question at hand, their reports would contain incomparable data. Nevertheless, the fact that comparability is not the objective of this chapter does not prevent consideration of the differences and similarities between the key characteristics of contract interpretation that the various opening remarks address. Therefore, the editors conclude this chapter with several comparative observations in which they focus specifically on the nature, aims, and means of contract interpretation.

2. CROATIA

In the Croatian legal system, the general provisions of contract law on interpretation of contracts are laid down in Arts. 319–321 of the Civil Obligations

Act (COA).[1] Because the COA is based on a monistic system, it sets the rules on interpretation for all types of contracts, both contracts characterised as civil law ones and those characterised as belonging to commercial law.[2] Moreover, the rules on interpretation are also applicable *mutatis mutandis* to other legal transactions (Art. 14(3) of the COA). While Art. 319 prescribes the general rule on interpretation, Art. 320(1) of the COA contains the special rule on interpretation of pre-formulated standard contracts (the *contra proferentem* principle or the principle known as *in dubio contra stipulatorem*).[3] The judicial control over the latter is regulated by Arts. 295–96 of the COA.[4] Art. 320(2) of the COA contains provisions on interpretation of unclear clauses in lucrative and onerous contracts[5] and Art. 321 of the COA concerns the out-of-court interpretation of contracts.[6]

---

1 Civil Obligation Act, OG Nos. 35/05, 41/08, 125/11, 78/15 and 29/18. See Part Two, Title VIII on Contractual Obligations, Chapter 1 General Provisions. These provisions correspond to Arts. 99–102 of the former COA, OG Nos. 53/91, 73/91, 111/93, 3/94, 107/95, 7/96, 91/96, 112/99 and 88/01. This Act was essentially the former Yugoslav Civil Obligations Act (OJ SFRJ 29/78, 39/85, 46/85, 45/89 and 57/89), transposed into the Croatian legal system by means of the Transposition of Civil Obligation Act, OG No. 53/91. The COA of 1978 was repealed by the new COA enacted in 2005, OG Nos. 35/05, 41/08, 125/11, 78/15 and 29/18.

2 In the Croatian legal system, there is no dualism in legal regulation of these types of contracts. According to the monistic theory, commercial legal transactions are regulated by the COA as a single and general act on obligations. The same provisions on obligations apply irrespective of whether the contract parties are subject to commercial law or civil law, except when the special characteristics of commercial contracts require different regulation. According to Art. 14(1), the COA provisions on contracts apply to all types of contracts, unless explicitly provided otherwise for commercial contracts. Art. 14(2) of the COA lays down that, within the meaning of the COA, commercial contracts are contracts entered into by traders between themselves in pursuing activities which fall under the scope of activities of at least one of them or which are related to the pursuit of such activities.

3 Pursuant to this principle, where a contract is concluded based on previously printed content or was prepared and proposed by one contracting party, the court has to interpret any unclear clause in favour of the other contracting party. See County Court in Varaždin, Gž. 1359/08-2 of 8 December 2008.

4 The provisions of Arts. 295–296 concern the control of general contract conditions in standard pre-formulated contracts and are regulated under Title VII General Contract Conditions in Part Two, Title VIII on Contractual Obligations, Chapter 1 General Provisions. See Petrić, 'Koncept nepoštenih ugovornih odredbi s posebnim osvrtom na potrošačke ugovore', p. 15.

5 According to Art. 320(2) of the COA, any unclear clauses in a lucrative contract are to be interpreted in a manner which is less onerous for the debtor, whereas any unclear clauses in a contract with consideration must be interpreted in order to establish an equitable exchange of mutual performances.

6 According to Art. 321 of the COA, contracting parties may agree that, in the event of disagreement with regard to the meaning and scope of any contract clauses, a third person must interpret their contract, in which case the contracting parties may not start the proceedings before a court or other competent authority prior to obtaining such interpretation, except where the third party refuses to provide the requested interpretation of the contract.

Under the title 'Application of Provisions and Interpretation of Controversial Clauses', the general rule on interpretation combines elements of both objective and subjective methods of interpretation. According to Art. 319(1) of the COA, contract clauses apply as they read, meaning that there is no room for contract interpretation, when the contract clearly and undoubtedly expresses the intention of the contracting parties (*in claris non fit interpretatio*).[7] However, in interpreting disputed clauses, it is the mutually agreed intention of the parties that should be explored and considered rather than the literal meaning of the particular expressions used (subjective criterion), and the disputed clause must be construed in accordance with the principles of the law on obligations established by the COA (objective criterion)[8] (Art. 319(2) of the COA).[9] These basic principles include, inter alia, 'sloboda uređivanja obveznih odnosa' [freedom to regulate obligations relationships], which is the Croatian equivalent of freedom of contract,[10] 'ravnopravnost sudionika u obveznom odnosu' [equality of the parties to the obligations relationship],[11] 'načelo savjesnosti i poštenja' [principle of conscientiousness and honesty], which is the Croatian equivalent to good faith and fair dealing, etc.[12] When it comes to obligations between traders, the principles of the law on obligations also include provisions

7 See VTSRH, Pž-2531/05 of 9 May 2007, where the court established that in circumstances when the will of the other contracting party is clearly and undoubtedly expressed in the contract, there is no need for contract interpretation and its provisions are to be interpreted as they read. The court stated that when the words of a written document are clear, one cannot prove that the will of the drafter was different, since interpretation of clear contractual terms is against the concept and sense of interpretation and would violate the basic principle of freedom to regulate contractual relationships. See also County Court in Dubrovnik, Gž-2316/07 of 24 March 2010; VSRH, Rev 1369/07-2 of 1 April 2009; VTSRH, Pž-2531/05, of 9 May 2007; VSRH, Rev 698/06-2 of 26 July 2006.

8 It must be emphasised that Croatian legal scholars and the judiciary speak about the above-mentioned 'objective criterion', which differs from and does not correspond to so-called 'objective interpretation' (textualism) according to which the words of the contract govern its interpretation. See Mišćenić, 'Uniform Interpretation of Article 4(2) of UCT Directive in the Context of Consumer Credit Agreements: Is it possible?', p. 150.

9 See the rulings of the Constitutional Court in cases USRH, U-III-2027/2018 of 4 July 2018 and USRH, U-III-4697/2005 of 21 November 2007. See also PS, Pž-2417/89 of 14 November 1989, PSP-44/188, where the court established that clear contract provisions are to be applied and enforced as they read (the theory of declaration), and only ambiguous provisions must be interpreted and enforced in accordance with the true will of the contracting parties (the will theory), in accordance with the principles of the law on obligations.

10 Art. 2 of the COA. The principle of private autonomy in the law on obligations is termed 'freedom of contract' and includes the freedom to regulate obligations relationships according to which the parties are free to regulate their obligations, and these obligations cannot be regulated contrary to the Constitution of the Republic of Croatia, mandatory laws and the morals of society (Art. 2 of the COA).

11 Under Art. 3 COA, parties to obligations are equal.

12 Basic principles are regulated in Part I, General Part, Title I (Arts. 1–15). There is an objective criterion prescribed more narrowly than in other legal systems, which usually refer to 'general legal principles'.

on the application of trade usages and mutually developed practices pursuant to Art. 12 of the COA.

With regard to interpretation of contracts, the established court practice and legal theory have given the utmost importance to the principle of conscientiousness and honesty. In contracts, as the embodiments of the contracting parties' intentions, this principle determines the considerations that both parties should have towards each other, by integrating the principle of confidence into their contractual relationship. The latter principle is based on the idea of responsibility, according to which each contracting party is responsible for its own words and the other party should have confidence in the statement. The idea of protection of confidence derives from the general and most important principle of conscientiousness and honesty and represents its fundamental content.[13] The principle of conscientiousness and honesty plays an important role in the determination of the actual and true intention of contracting parties as the main goal of contract interpretation.[14]

Settled Croatian case law corresponds to interpretation of the above-mentioned statutory provisions as developed in legal theory. Both case law and legal theory have developed additional special principles and criteria for contract interpretation building on the general statutory principles, which enable the individualisation of the contract to be interpreted.[15]

3. ENGLAND AND WALES

For the modern approach to interpretation, which is contextual and purposive rather than solely textual and literalist, English courts turn to the authoritative

---

13 See Baretić, 'Načelo savjesnosti i poštenja u obveznom pravu', p. 571; Perović and Stojanović, *Komentar zakona o obligacionim odnosima*, p. 346; Blagojević and Krulj, *Komentar zakona o obligacionim odnosima*, p. 274. This principle is the fundamental principle of Croatian contract law and is regarded as an equivalent of 'good faith' or for 'good faith and fair dealing', although these are not identical concepts. Art. 4 of the COA requires parties to observe this principle when creating obligations and exercising the rights and obligations resulting from such obligations. See Mišćenić, 'Legal Translation vs. Legal Certainty in EU Law', p. 87.

14 This principle played an important role in the first Croatian collective redress proceedings in the case 'Franak' dealing with unfair contract terms in credit agreements. See the following rulings: Commercial Court in Zagreb, P-1401/12 of 4 July 2013; VTSRH, Pž-7129/13-4 of 13 June 2014; VSRH, Revt 249/14-2 of 9 April 2015; USRH, U-III – 2521/2015 et al. of 13 December 2016; VSRH, Revt 575/16-5 of 3 October 2017; VTSRH, 43 Pž-6632/2017-10 of 14 June 2018. See Mišćenić, 'Croatian Case "Franak:" Effective or "Defective" Protection of Consumer Rights?', p. 184.

15 Both legal theory and court practice developed certain rules and methods: no necessity of interpretation of clear provisions, necessity of taking into account circumstances under which the contract was concluded, or of intent of the contract parties, taking into account the purpose(s) of the contract (teleological method), extensive or restrictive interpretation, *argumentum a contrario*, etc. See Gorenc et al., *Komentar Zakona o obveznim odnosima*, p. 467.

summary by Lord Hoffmann in the 1997 House of Lords' decision in *Investors Compensation Scheme v West Bromwich Buildings Society.*[16] Although judicial explanation and not legislation, it has been universally adopted and applied and would form the starting point for an English court for all the cases in this volume.

The main points of the English law of interpretation, many of which were summarised in the *Investors Compensation Scheme* decision, are as follows:

(1) The correct test of interpretation is an objective one, as to what a reasonable person in the position of the parties and knowing what they both know (but not what only one of them knows) would have understood the contract to mean. The subjective understanding of the parties is in general terms irrelevant and inadmissible.
(2) The background or 'matrix of fact' that is ascribed to the reasonable person includes everything that both of the parties knew and that affects the way a reasonable person would understand the contract.
(3) The main exception to point (2) is that, for policy reasons, evidence of pre-contractual negotiations between the parties is inadmissible, even if such negotiations would have had a bearing on the way a reasonable person would understand the contract.[17] The distinction between admissible matrix of fact, including evidence relating to the nature and object of the contractual venture, and inadmissible pre-contractual negotiations, comprising evidence of the terms for which each party was contending in the course of negotiations,[18] is not always an easy one.
(4) Despite the previous point, there are two doctrines which form part of the substantive English law of interpretation, although they are formally or taxonomically considered to be separate to the rules of interpretation. The doctrines are those of estoppel by convention and rectification. The main effect of the doctrines is to abrogate the rule against admission of pre-contractual negotiations. The minute detail of the doctrines is unimportant, but both doctrines operate to give effect to a pre-contractual outward expression of consensus as to the meaning of a term in the contract,[19] although in the case of rectification the consensus must be subjectively held by the parties and not merely apparent on an objective analysis (unless there was a binding pre-contractual agreement as to the terms that would

[16] [1998] 1 WLR 896 (HL) at 912–913.
[17] See especially *Chartbrook v Persimmon Homes Ltd* [2009] 1 AC 1101 (HL).
[18] *The 'Tychy' No. 2* [2001] 2 Lloyd's Rep 403 (CA), per Lord Phillips MR at 409.
[19] See in particular *Amalgamated Investment & Property Co Ltd (In Liquidation) v Texas Commerce International Bank Ltd* [1982] QB 84 (CA) on estoppel. Estoppel can also arise out of post-contractual conduct.

be entered into).[20] By these doctrines, subject to some discretion of the court, the parties are bound to treat the relevant term as meaning what the pre-contractual consensus was that it would mean. Estoppel operates as a rule of evidence, preventing ('estopping') the parties from maintaining a rival construction; rectification operates to allow the court to actually rewrite ('rectify') the written agreement to reflect the agreed meaning the parties had for whatever reason failed properly to record.[21]

(5) Sometimes the reasonable person would conclude that the words or syntax used are mistaken and do not reflect what the drafters intended. In those circumstances, the meaning of the contract is what the reasonable person would think *was* intended despite the words used, where the intended meaning can be identified. The reasonable person would not lightly reach the conclusion that a mistake has been made, particularly in formal documents, but sometimes (including because of the absurdity of the effect of the words that were used) this is the most reasonable conclusion.

(6) The main tension in construing contracts is usually between the interpretation that is most faithful to the words actually used (e.g. the interpretation that selects the more obvious of the two meanings of an ambiguous term, and/or does not require words to be ignored as mistaken), and the interpretation that gives a result that makes the most commercial sense (although perhaps at the cost of a slightly more strained construction, when only the words themselves are considered).[22]

(7) There is no general principle of good faith in the interpretation of commercial contracts in English law, although where circumstances support an expectation of honesty or cooperation or reasonableness or not derogating from the grant in the contract, the courts will imply such an obligation or construe clauses in the light of such a norm.[23]

---

20 *FSHC Group Holdings Ltd v GLAS Trust Corp Ltd* [2019] EWCA Civ 1361, [2020] 1 All ER 505 (CA), disapproving obiter comments in *Chartbrook v Persimmon Homes Ltd* [2009] 1 AC 1101 (HL).

21 These are equitable doctrines, meaning they originated in the separate courts of Equity and not of Law, back before the two were fused in the late 19th century. The laws of Equity were typically (as with these doctrines) rules that allow a court, within a discretion, to ameliorate the strict effect of the rules of Law. These doctrines still reflect that historical origin, in that they are discretionary doctrines treated as operating outside the legal rules of interpretation, and after the interpretation of the contract has been identified (which itself is a non-discretionary process of legal principle).

22 See further the discussion in the Supreme Court of this tension or balance in *Wood v Capita Insurance Services Ltd* [2017] UKSC 24; [2017] AC 1173 (SC).

23 The point was reviewed in some detail in the case of *Yam Seng Pte Ltd v International Trade Corporation Ltd* [2013] EWHC 111 (QB) (Leggatt J). See also *Bates v Post Office Ltd* [2019] EWHC 606 (QB) (Fraser J).

4. FINLAND

In Finland, there are no written rules on 'Fi. sopimuksen tulkinta', the interpretation of contracts. In fact, like Sweden, the Contracts Act [228/1929, Fi. laki varallisuusoikeudellisista oikeustoimista] is categorically silent on the matter. However, its preparatory works – and particularly the Commission's Report of 1990[24] – contain important information on how contracts should be interpreted.[25] Furthermore, there are certain rules governing certain contract types, but as mentioned, no general rules exist.[26]

In practice, case law is the primary source of law as far as interpretation of contracts is concerned. However, the Finnish courts, including the Supreme Court, have been rather reluctant to provide precise instructions on how contracts should be interpreted. In other words, the factual circumstances of the individual case have typically lain at the centre of the court's attention. That said, the main interpretation rules have been explained in several Supreme Court decisions.[27] In particular, when it comes to commercial (i.e. B2B) contracts, the main rule is that a contract should be interpreted by paying close attention to its wording, unless it is evident that the parties have intended something else. This intention is typically ascertained from materials, such as emails, recordings and contract drafts and, of course, by hearing witnesses. Furthermore, as shown by Supreme Court decision 2003:26, any commonly applied practices in the concerned field of business may have an impact on how unclear contracts are interpreted.[28] All in all, the main objective of contract interpretation is to search for the mutual intention of the parties at the time the contract was made.

The primary method of contract interpretation, as described briefly above, is called 'Fi. osapuolisuuntautunut tulkinta' [part-oriented interpretation]. There are, however, situations, where supplementary interpretation rules are needed. These rules, including the rule of ambiguity, 'Fi. minimisääntö' [the minimum rule], 'Fi. tavallisuussääntö' [the rule of normality] and

24 Oikeustoimilakitoimikunnan mietintö 1990:20.

25 It is, however, important to note that the Commission's Report did not lead to any legislative amendments, although it was proposed that rules on the interpretation of contracts should be included in the Contracts Act.

26 For example, the Finnish Consumer Protection Act (38/1978, Fi. kuluttajansuojalaki) contains the so-called rule of ambiguity, which reads as follows: 'If a term in a contract referred to in this Act has been drafted in advance without the consumer having been able to influence its contents and if uncertainty arises as to the significance of the term, the term shall be interpreted in favour of the consumer.'

27 See e.g. Supreme Court decisions KKO 2010:69, KKO 2011:13, KKO 2015:26 and KKO 2016:10.

28 Moreover, the behaviour of the parties after the contract was made may indicate how they have understood their contractual obligations.

'Fi. pätevyyssääntö' [the rule of validity], are called 'Fi. tavoitteelliset tulkintasäännöt' [objective-oriented interpretation rules].[29] These rules, and especially the rule of ambiguity,[30] are quite often used by Finnish courts, as it may be difficult – or even impossible – to determine the mutual intention of the parties if the wording of their contract is unclear or incomplete.

Finally, it should be stressed that since there are no strict rules on how contracts should be interpreted, Finnish courts have a relatively wide discretion in the matter. Then again, the main guidelines, elaborated by the Supreme Court, are followed rather precisely by the lower courts and by arbitral tribunals. This means that legal certainty regarding interpretation disputes is quite high in Finland. Besides case law, Finnish judges and arbitrators often utilise legal literature and expert opinions to determine what factors should be taken into account when interpreting a contract. As in Sweden, in Finland there is nowadays much published literature on the topic.[31]

5. FRANCE

5.1. THE 2016 REFORM

The provisions of the French Civil Code (Cciv) on the law of contract have recently been reformed by the government in the Ordonnance no. 2016-131,[32] which was then ratified by Parliament in the Loi no. 2018-287.[33] As a consequence of the reform, the interpretation of contracts concluded before 1 October 2016 is still governed by the old provisions of the Code, whereas the interpretation of contracts and contractual amendments concluded from 1 October 2016 is governed by the new provisions.[34] The content of the rules has not substantially changed, even though some of the provisions of the Code have been partially rephrased, rearranged and shortened.

---

29 Hemmo, *Sopimusoikeus I*, pp. 602–656.

30 See e.g. Supreme Court decision KKO 2010:69, where the court applied the rule of ambiguity in a dispute concerning two entrepreneurs.

31 See e.g. Aho, *Varallisuusoikeudellisen oikeustoimen tulkinnasta*; Annola, *Sopimustulkinta*; and Hemmo, *Sopimusoikeus I*, pp. 602–656.

32 Ordonnance no. 2016-131 de 10 février 2016 portant réforme du droit des contrats, du régime général et de la preuve des obligations.

33 Loi no. 2018-287 de 20 avril 2018 ratifiant l'ordonnance n° 2016-131 du 10 février 2016. Although the Loi no. 2018-287 introduced some amendments to the 2016 reform, none of them affect the rules on contractual interpretation.

34 See Art. 9, Ordonnance no. 2016-131 de 10 février 2016 portant réforme du droit des contrats, du régime général et de la preuve des obligations.

5.2. DOMESTIC CONTRACTS

Interpretation of domestic contracts relies essentially on Arts. 1188–1191 (formerly Arts. 1156–1164) Cciv. However, these articles are mere recommendations rather than real legal rules. They were drafted with the view to guiding judges rather than constraining them. Therefore, an alleged violation of them may not serve as a legal basis for an action in cassation.[35]

Like former Art. 1156, new Art. 1188 (1) Cciv exhorts judges to interpret contracts in compliance with the common intention of the parties,[36] which implies that the latter have actually expressed their intention.[37] In the case of uncertainty as to the common intention of the parties, new Art. 1188 (2) urges judges to determine how a 'reasonable person in the same situation' would objectively interpret the contract. This reference to a general reasonableness test is new and opportunely introduces the series of objective rules of interpretation provided by the Civil Code as guidelines. According to these rules, the interpretation of equivocal terms should follow either (1) the meaning that ensures consistency between the terms of the contract or group of contracts (Art. 1189, formerly Art. 1161), or (2) the meaning that preserves the validity and effectiveness of the contract (Art. 1191, formerly Art. 1157),[38] or (3) an extended version of the *contra proferentem* rule under which negotiable contracts should be interpreted against the creditor, whereas contracts containing a set of non-negotiable terms imposed by one party should be interpreted against that party (Art. 1190, formerly Art. 1162). Before the reform, the Code provided five other rules that have been removed, although they are still applicable to contracts concluded before 1 October 2016 and potentially also to contracts concluded after that date, as long as a reasonable person would consider them. These rules refer to (1) the most appropriate meaning considering the subject matter of the contract (former Art. 1158), (2) the meaning that is consistent with the usages governing the contract (former Arts. 1159–1160), and (3) the advice to restrict the meaning of broad terms or extend the meaning of narrow terms wherever needed in view of the subject matter of the contract (former Arts. 1163–1164).

In situations where the judge is not asked to interpret existing terms but to fill gaps in the contract, new Art. 1194 Cciv carries on the rule previously expressed in Art. 1135 Cciv, according to which the contracting parties are bound not

35 Req., 18 March 1807, *S.* (1807) 361; Civ. 1, 6 March 1979, *Bull. civ.* (1979) no. 81.

36 Subject to contractual terms that would be imposed by the law.

37 See e.g. Ph. Simler in *JCl. Civil Code*, Art. 1188 à 1192, Fasc. 10, no. 10.

38 Illustrations of the implementation of this interpretation rule in particular situations can be found in other provisions of the Code, such as the new Arts. 1119 (conflict between general clauses or between general clauses and particular terms) and 1167 (substitution of a non-existent price index stipulated in the contract).

only by the obligations expressed in their contract but also by those deriving from the contract on the basis of equity (reasonableness, fairness), usages or law. This rule can be used in combination with the rule expressed in Art. 1104 Cciv (formerly Art. 1134 (3)), according to which contracts must be performed in good faith. Interestingly, under French law, although these two rules have long been considered as rules of interpretation, they have now gained autonomy and are considered as rules on performance. As such, they would help determine how to perform the contract rather than what is in the contract.[39]

5.3. INTERNATIONAL SALE CONTRACTS

In 1982, France approved the CISG, which then came into force in 1988. The CISG is now the French legal regime for contracts of international sale of goods and will be considered briefly whenever appropriate. In a nutshell, one may consider that the main difference in the approach to contractual interpretation between the CISG and the French Civil Code comes from the fact that, in the CISG, the focus is not on the common intention of the parties but on the intent of each party as far as the other party knew or could not have been unaware of it (Art. 8(1)). This subjective test may, however, be completed by objective tests that are less detailed but equivalent to the domestic ones (Arts. 8(2), (3) and 9).[40]

5.4. ROLE OF THE COUR DE CASSATION

The interpretation of contracts raises questions of fact. As the 'Cour de cassation' [French Supreme Court for civil and commercial matters] rules only on law and not on facts,[41] the interpretation of contracts is reserved to judges of first instance and of appeal.[42]

There are, however, three limitations to this principle. First, the Cour de cassation has jurisdiction over cases of 'dénaturation' [distortion] of contractual terms. *Dénaturation* typically results from decisions of lower courts who erred

---

[39] See e.g. Y. Picod in *JCl. Civil Code*, Art. 1134 et 1135, Fasc. unique (unrevised), no. 7.

[40] See e.g. P. Schlechtriem and C. Witz, Convention de Vienne sur les contrats de vente internationale de marchandises, nos. 92–98.

[41] Art. L 111411-2 COJ, which incorporates into the Code of Judicial Organisation a rule initially expressed in a statute of 1790. In the same way, judges hearing applications for interim measures cannot rule on the interpretation of contracts since they are only entitled to rule on what is obvious and unambiguous: CA Aix-en-Provence, 6 April 2004, *JurisData* no. 2004-251458 – for further references, Ph. Simler in *JCl. Civil Code*, Art. 1188 à 1192, Fasc. 20.

[42] Ch. réun., 2 February 1808, *GAJC* no. 160.

in their interpretation of clear, precise and unambiguous terms.[43] According to Art. 1103 Cciv (former Art. 1134 (1)), agreements lawfully entered into have the same binding force as law between the parties. Distorted misinterpretation violates Art. 1103 Cciv, which provides a valid legal ground for the parties to bring an action in cassation.[44] The Cour de cassation has jurisdiction over distorted interpretation not only of written contracts but also of any written documents – correspondence, invoices, expert reports, testimonies,[45] etc. Conversely, as oral contracts are considered to be ambiguous by nature,[46] they will generally give rise to judicial interpretation rather than to an action for distortion.

Second, the Cour de cassation also has jurisdiction over cases of 'objective gap-filling interpretation'. Indeed, in cases requiring the court to fill gaps in a contract, contractual construction relies on objective rules of construction[47] and default rules of contract law. In such cases, interpretation does not derive from the common intention of the parties but rather from the law itself, which explains why the Cour de cassation may exercise control.[48]

Third, in the past the Cour de cassation has occasionally agreed to control the interpretation of standard contracts.[49] Building on this experience, Art. L. 441-4 Code of the Judicial Organisation (COJ) has since 2016[50] offered the possibility for courts to request from the Cour de cassation an opinion on the interpretation of a convention or a collective agreement when the issue to be decided is serious and likely to affect a large number of cases in the future. The rationale behind this provision is thus to prevent judicial divergences of interpretation in recurring types of contractual disputes.

---

43 This definition is now codified in the new Art. 1192 Cciv.

44 Civ., 15 April 1872, *GAJC* no. 161. This enables the Cour de cassation to control whether a lower court has rewritten a clear and unambiguous contract, which some judges might be tempted to do when a contract is manifestly unbalanced, and the disadvantaged party has no legal remedy. In practice, this type of appeal is quite common but less frequently successful.

45 Respectively Civ. 1, 4 November 1968, *Bull. civ.* (1968) no. 262; Com., 31 January 1995, *JCP G* (1995) no. 22385; Civ. 1, 3 June 1958, *Bull. civ.* (1958) no. 282; Civ. 2, 8 October 1975, *Bull. civ.* (1975) no. 243.

46 See in this respect the statement of the Cour de cassation in Com., 5 December 1984, *Bull. civ.* (1984) no. 332.

47 Namely, new Arts. 1104 and 1194, formerly Arts. 1134 (3) and 1135 Cciv.

48 For further insights, see F. Terré, Ph. Simler, Y. Lequette, F. Chénedé, *Droit civil: les obligations*, no. 620; Ph. Simler in *JCl. Civil Code*, Art. 1188 à 1192, Fasc. 10, no. 55.

49 See e.g. Civ., 18 March 1942, *S.* (1943) 13 (insurance contract); Civ., 20 June 1950, *Bull. civ.* (1950) no. 221 (patents); Civ. 1, 24 January 1984, *Bull. civ.* (1984) no. 28 (insurance contract); Civ. 1, 2 May 1990, *Bull. civ.* (1990) no. 89 (insurance contract); Civ. 1, 16 May 1995, *D.* (1995) 349 (insurance contract); Soc., 6 November 1942, *JCP G* (1943) 6220 (collective labour agreement); contrast Com., 7 July 1981, *Bull. civ.* (1981) no. 310 (patents); Com., 17 December 1991, *Bull. civ.* (1981) no. 396 (gas station leasing contract).

50 This provision was introduced by the Loi no. 2016-1088 of 8 August 2016.

6. GERMANY

As a starting point, it is the task of legal interpretation to identify the meaning of a legal rule.[51] However, the function of interpretation depends on how comprehensive the legal order is.[52] Codified German law is characterised by a comprehensive body of legislation. Therefore, the usual function of a contract clause is to deviate from non-mandatory law.[53]

6.1. MATTER OF FACT NOT OF LAW

The interpretation of contracts is not a part of the application of the law,[54] but a matter of the finding of facts.[55] In detail, the finding of the relevant facts[56] as a necessary first requirement consists of establishing a declaration of intent, the clarification of its wording and the surrounding circumstances.[57] The investigation of the common intention is affected by the possible legal consequences, for example if the established facts do not unambiguously confirm a common intention of the parties.[58]

6.2. FREE CONSIDERATION OF EVIDENCE

The 'Freie Beweiswürdigung' [free consideration of evidence] under §286 Zivilprozessordnung (ZPO) is highly relevant for contract interpretation by the judge. The judge may estimate the concrete value of evidence under free consideration,[59] such as all relevant facts, as well as the will, deliberate intention

---

51 F.J. Säcker, 'Einleitung' in K. Rebmann and F.J. Säcker (eds.), *Münchener Kommentar zum Bürgerlichen Gesetzbuch*, m.n. 153.

52 A. Lüderitz, *Auslegung von Rechtsgeschäften*, p. 10.

53 E. Rehbinder, *Vertragsgestaltung*, p. 9; in fact, the interpretation has to show how far the parties effectually deviated from the law: A. Lüderitz, *Auslegung von Rechtsgeschäften*, p. 24. In relation to non-mandatory law, German courts prefer to use non-mandatory law to solve a case rather than use interpretation, because in interpretation evidence is rather hard to store and check (cf. Case 10).

54 A. Lüderitz, *Auslegung von Rechtsgeschäften*, p. 20.

55 J. Busche, '§133 BGB' in K. Rebmann and F.J. Säcker (eds.), *Münchener Kommentar zum Bürgerlichen Gesetzbuch*, m.n. 55; the finding of facts is supplemented by legal considerations only to a very limited extent: BGH, 07.14.2004, *NJW* 2004, 2751.

56 For the relation between declaration of intent, clarification of wording and surrounding circumstances, see sections 5.3 and 5.4 below.

57 J. Ellenberger, '§133' in O. Palandt (ed.), *Palandt Bürgerliches Gesetzbuch mit Nebengesetzen – Kommentar*, m.n. 5.

58 BGH, 14.07.2004, *NJW* 2004, 2751 m.n. 17.

59 H.-W. Laumen, '§286 ZPO' in H. Prütting and M. Gehrlein (eds.), *ZPO Kommentar*, m.n. 2.

or knowledge of the parties.[60] There is no rule which sets a specific evidential value on pieces of evidence.[61]

6.3. NO STRONG RULE IN FAVOUR OF LITERAL INTERPRETATION

Though the wording of a declaration is the practical starting point of interpretation,[62] it limits neither the 'erläuternden' [explanatory] interpretation nor the 'ergänzenden' [supplementary] interpretation.[63] As the parties' common intention prevails anyway,[64] the wording of the contract sets no absolute limit on contract interpretation, as long as some minimal basis of a certain interpretation may be found in the text – 'Trittstufentheorie'[65] [footstep theory]. The ambiguity of a term or clause is, therefore, usually irrelevant to the process of interpretation under German law.[66]

German law recognises the *contra proferentem* rule,[67] which states that an ambiguous contract term shall be interpreted to the detriment of the contracting party who proposed it.[68]

Furthermore, German law does not exclude material that is not found in the four corners of the contractual deed from being relevant. There is a rebuttable presumption that the deed containing the contract mirrors the contract

60 BGH, 08.12.1982, *NJW* 1983, 672.

61 The judge rules freely and decides him/herself if there is a different weight to be given to pieces of evidence: U. Foerste, '§286 ZPO' in H.-J. Musielak (ed.), *Zivilprozessordnung mit Gerichtsverfassungsgesetz – Kommentar*, m.n. 9.

62 BGH, 03.04.2000, *NJW* 2000, 2099.

63 W. Hefermehl, '§133 BGB' in H.-T. Soergel, *Bürgerliches Gesetzbuch mit Einführungsgesetz und Nebengesetzen*, vol. II, m.n. 27; however, under German law, supplementary interpretation requires (following case law and the majority of academic writing) a 'Planwidrige Regelungslücke' [unintended gap]: see BGH, 20.04.2017, BGHZ 214, 340.

64 The wording also may be overcome by the content of the whole contract and the behaviour of the parties making the declarations: J. Busche, '§133 BGB' in K. Rebmann and F.J. Säcker (eds.), *Münchener Kommentar zum Bürgerlichen Gesetzbuch*, m.n. 54.

65 BGH, 04.09.1981, *NJW* 1981, 1736. This limitation of the literal interpretation is supported by legal scholars who stress what is systematically self-evident, namely that terms must not be interpreted by words only (Verbot der Buchstabendeutung): J. Busche, '§133 BGB' in K. Rebmann and F. J. Säcker (eds.), *Münchener Kommentar zum Bürgerlichen Gesetzbuch*, m.n. 54, 59.

66 The only exception to this irrelevance of ambiguity is the famous *contra proferentem* rule: cf. Case 1.

67 J. Busche, '§157 BGB' in K. Rebmann and F. J. Säcker (eds.), *Münchener Kommentar zum Bürgerlichen Gesetzbuch*, m.n. 8.

68 However, from the wording of the Civil Code this rule applies only to previously formulated standard terms of that contract, in which case the rule is laid down especially in §305c (2) BGB, and not also to cases of individually negotiated contract terms. This rule was developed by the former German Supreme Court even before codification: Reichsgericht, RGZ 145, 21; Reichsgericht, 10.01.1928, RGZ 120, 18; BGH, 02.12.1952, BGHZ 5, 111.

completely and correctly,[69] which may be overcome by reference to proven circumstances at the time of the conclusion of the contract.[70]

6.4. SUBJECTIVE APPROACH

German law adopts the subjective approach to the process of interpretation. As a starting point of interpretation, one has to establish the real and common[71] intentions of the parties.[72]

The subjective approach is considered to be so important that there is a rule of *falsa demonstratio non nocet*, which says that if both parties agree on one meaning of the declaration, there is no reason to overrule this by the objective meaning of the declaration.[73]

6.5. METHODS OF OBJECTIVE INTERPRETATION

If the subjective interpretation fails to identify a common intention of the parties, one has to discover the objective meaning of the contract clause from the perspective of a reasonable recipient. In the style of interpretation of law,[74] there are also four methods[75] which apply in the case of contract interpretation.[76] Those methods[77] suggest that a term may be interpreted: (1) literally; (2) historically; (3) systematically; and in accordance with (4) the purpose of the contract.[78]

---

69 BGH, 07.05.2002, *NJW* 2002, 3164 (acquisition of property).

70 Cf. Case 3.

71 M. Wolf, '§157 BGB' in H.-T. Soergel, *Bürgerliches Gesetzbuch mit Einführungsgesetz und Nebengesetzen*, vol. II, m.n. 29; furthermore, the motive, purpose and interest of the parties have to be identified (A. Lüderitz, *Auslegung von Rechtsgeschäften*, p. 316).

72 A. Lüderitz, *Auslegung von Rechtsgeschäften*, p. 309.

73 R. Singer '§133 BGB' in N. Habermann (ed.), *J. von Staudingers Kommentar zum Bürgerlichen Gesetzbuch*, vol. III, m.n. 13; cf. Case 6.

74 A. Lüderitz, *Auslegung von Rechtsgeschäften*, p. 10.

75 Ibid., p. 64: it is worth mentioning that this objective approach is an antagonism to the basic subjective approach and does not exclude facts pointing to the real intention of the parties from being relevant.

76 J. Busche, '§133 BGB' in K. Rebmann and F.J. Säcker (eds.), *Münchener Kommentar zum Bürgerlichen Gesetzbuch*, m.n. 6, 7: this variety of factors shows very clearly that even where an objective interpretation applies, German legal rules on interpretation are far removed from a system that affords formal prevalence to a literal interpretation.

77 However, if there are several interpretation options, the economic purpose of the contract prevails and the interpretation which renders the clause legally relevant is applicable: H. Reichhold, '§133 BGB' in M. Herberger, M. Martinek and H. Rüßmann, *jurisPraxisKommentar-BGB*, vol. II, m.n. 21.

78 J. Busche, '§133 BGB' in K. Rebmann and F.J. Säcker (eds.), *Münchener Kommentar zum Bürgerlichen Gesetzbuch*, m.n. 7.

6.6. VARIETY OF FACTORS

There is a broad variety of factors to be taken into account by the judge that assist in identifying the objective content of the contract as well as the common intention of the parties. The good faith principle under §242 Bürgerliches Gesetzbuch (BGB) serves as a general guideline for interpretation, see §157 BGB. However, the sense of the behaviour of the parties may not be overruled by the good faith principle.[79] These factors are:

(i) alignment with the subject of the contract;[80]
(ii) interpretation of the contract as a whole;[81]
(iii) negotiations and circumstances of contract formation;[82]
(iv) foreseeability and recognition as circumstances;[83]
(v) usual meaning;[84]

---

79 Therefore, the reasonable and skilful understanding of the recipient is a decisive factor in interpreting the contract: M. Wolf, '§157 BGB' in H.-T. Soergel, *Bürgerliches Gesetzbuch mit Einführungsgesetz und Nebengesetzen*, vol. II, m.n. 55.

80 A. Lüderitz, *Auslegung von Rechtsgeschäften*, p. 48: the function of the interpretation depends on the function of the contract to be interpreted; the function of contract law is it to determine the extent of the 'Privatautonomie', to limit the domain of decisions of the parties. A. Lüderitz, *Auslegung von Rechtsgeschäften*, p. 90. Furthermore, it is the function of contract law to define the intention of the parties and to rule if the intention is binding.

81 M. Wolf, '§157 BGB' in H.-T. Soergel, *Bürgerliches Gesetzbuch mit Einführungsgesetz und Nebengesetzen*, vol. II, m.n. 29; M. Schmidt-Kessel, 'Art. 8 CISG' in P. Schlechtriem and I. Schwenzer (eds.), *Kommentar zum Einheitlichen UN-Kaufrecht – Das Übereinkommen der Vereinten Nationen über Verträge über den internationalen Warenkauf (CISG)*, m.n. 29: there is no interpretation of isolated terms but rather within the whole context of the contract, cf. Case 1; BGH, 22.10.1990, *NJW-RR* 1990, 613: in principle there is no hierarchy among contract terms. There are however some exceptions to this principle, in particular the freedom of the parties to establish a hierarchy, the precedence of individual agreed-upon terms (cf. Case 5), restrictive interpretation of exceptions and precedence of a more specific provision (M. Schmidt-Kessel, 'Art. 8 CISG' in P. Schlechtriem and I. Schwenzer (eds.), *Kommentar zum Einheitlichen UN-Kaufrecht – Das Übereinkommen der Vereinten Nationen über Verträge über den internationalen Warenkauf (CISG)*, m.n. 30).

82 M. Wolf, '§157 BGB' in H.-T. Soergel, *Bürgerliches Gesetzbuch mit Einführungsgesetz und Nebengesetzen*, vol. II, m.n. 36: the positions of the parties are influenced by the previous negotiations and the circumstances of contract formations; BGH, 23.02.1987, *NJW* 1987, 2437: in regard to this, formless agreements have to be considered as well.

83 M. Schmidt-Kessel, 'Art. 8 CISG' in P. Schlechtriem and I. Schwenzer (eds.), *Kommentar zum Einheitlichen UN-Kaufrecht – Das Übereinkommen der Vereinten Nationen über Verträge über den internationalen Warenkauf (CISG)*, m.n. 40: a party that has foreseen certain circumstances in concluding a contract has also considered them. Furthermore, a party that foresees a circumstance and fails to protect itself through agreement bears the risk of this circumstance occurring.

84 M. Schmidt-Kessel, 'Art. 8 CISG' in P. Schlechtriem and I. Schwenzer (eds.), *Kommentar zum Einheitlichen UN-Kaufrecht – Das Übereinkommen der Vereinten Nationen über*

(vi) practices between the parties;[85]
(vii) usages;[86] and
(viii) subsequent conduct of the parties.[87]

6.7. MECHANISMS TO CORRECT THE RESULTS OF INTERPRETATION

The rules on vitiated consent or intention serve as a means of correcting the results of interpretation by protecting both the party in error and the reliance of the other party. The party in error may avoid the contract under §119 (1) 1. Var. BGB.[88] The other party, who relied on the existence of the contract, may claim damages from the party in error.

6.8. RELATIONSHIP TO IMPLICATION OF TERMS

The relationship between the implications of terms on the basis of 'Guter Glaube' [good faith] to supplementary interpretation is much disputed.[89] As a result of comparison of law, there is no such broad instrument of supplementary interpretation of contracts like implication of terms under German law.

Verträge über den internationalen Warenkauf (CISG), m.n. 40: reference to standard terms or conditions indicates that the parties intended the usual interpretation of these terms to apply; BGH, 23.11.1994, *NJW-RR* 1995, 364: as a second step, the language use of the specific communication sphere in which the contract was concluded (e.g. a certain branch or market) that deviates from the usual meaning is taken into account; J. Ellenberger, '§133' in O. Palandt (ed.), *Palandt Bürgerliches Gesetzbuch mit Nebengesetzen – Kommentar*, m.n. 14: furthermore individual characteristics in the language use may affect the interpretation, if the addressee is aware of these individual characteristics.

85 Practices established between the parties are usually not in themselves binding on the parties but serve as a key element of the interpretation of contracts concluded between them, cf. Case 8. BGH, 01.29.2003, *NJW-RR* 2003, 926: the development of the ongoing business relationship is a key element of the interpretation. In contrast to that, a custom between the parties in an employment contract may become binding on the parties, see C. Picker, *Die betriebliche Übung*.

86 Local usage under German law may both, first, serve as an argument for interpretation of contracts and, second, complement the contract by implying terms under §346 HGB, cf. Case 9. BGH, 30.03.1990, *NJW* 1990, 1724: a local usage or custom which is followed for some period of time may serve as an argument in the process of interpretation, if the local usage concerns the branch or activity of the parties (BGH, 30.09.2009, *NJW* 2010, 1136).

87 BGH, 16.10.1997, BGH IX ZR 164/96, *NJW-RR* 1998, 259: if there is subsequent conduct of the parties after concluding the contract, it may not change the expressed intention of the parties at the time of the conclusion, but it may show the real intention of the parties.

88 Cf. Case 1.

89 M. Schmidt-Kessel, 'Implied Terms – auf der Suche nach dem Funktionsäquivalent', p. 141.

6.9. INTERPRETATION OF STANDARD TERMS

The general approach of subjective interpretation which may come back to objective interpretation (see above) does not apply without restrictions in the case of the interpretation of standard terms or general contract conditions.[90]

However, even in the interpretation of general contract terms, subjective elements retain their importance.[91]

7. GREECE

7.1. LEGAL FRAMEWORK OF INTERPRETATION OF 'ΔΗΛΏΣΕΙΣ ΒΟΎΛΗΣΗΣ' [DECLARATIONS OF WILL] UNDER GREEK LAW

The interpretation of contracts in Greek law relies upon two core provisions codified in the Greek Civil Code (CC): Arts. 173 and 200 CC, which regulate the interpretation of 'δηλώσεις βούλησης' [declarations of will] and 'συμβάσεις' [contracts] respectively. The first provision prescribes that, when interpreting a legally relevant declaration of intent, the interpreter seeks to determine the true intention of the person, as contained in their externalised declaration, without holding fast to the wording used and that alone. Pursuant to the second provision, contracts are to be interpreted according to the principle of 'καλή πίστη' [good faith], whereby the 'συναλλακτικά ήθη' [transactions usages or trade customs] are also to be taken into account. The concept of 'καλή πίστη' constitutes a prime example of the so-called 'γενικές ρήτρες' [general clauses], cornerstone legal principles which apply throughout Greek civil law and the precise normative

90 This becomes clear in the case of an injunction applied for by a consumer organisation and comparative cases of collective redress: when the court has to decide on the prohibition of a clause alleged to be unfair by the consumer organisation, an objective approach to interpretation applies. The guideline of this interpretation is to interpret the clause to the disadvantage of the consumer for the purpose of the unfairness test. In this case the *contra proferentem* rule is not to be applied. The interpretation has to be driven in the opposite direction. If in an individual case between a consumer and a business the interpretation of general standard terms becomes relevant, the rules on interpretation differ from the general rules under §§133, 157 BGB. First, the aforementioned *contra proferentem* rule under §305c (2) BGB applies. Second, where the validity of the clause under the rules on unfair contract terms is at stake, the aforementioned rule of interpreting the clause to the detriment of the consumer applies.

91 The first element of subjective interpretation is the relevance of the circumstances of the conclusion of the contract for the judgment on the fairness or unfairness of the clause under §310 (3) No. 3 BGB. In addition to that, individually agreed clauses prevail over general conditions, see §305b BGB.

content of which is defined by reference to the statutory rule that cites them and the particular sets of circumstances in which they are applicable.[92]

According to case law, the concept of 'καλή πίστη' refers to an honest and reasonable person's behaviour that is objectively expected when participating in legal transactions, while the 'συναλλακτικά ήθη' are the courses of action usual in commercial practice, either in specific categories of transactions or a specific circle of professionals or in a specific area.[93] The 'συναλλακτικά ήθη' are treated as a means to concretise the 'καλή πίστη', not as an independent element of interpretation operating in parallel to the latter.[94]

Apart from those general provisions, the Greek CC also contains a number of particular rules of interpretation that apply to specific contracts only (e.g. Art. 370 CC provides that, 'in case of doubt', an agreement for the sale or pledging of a thing includes its fixtures).[95] Those rules apply either when the declaration of the parties is unclear as to its meaning or extent (e.g. Art. 480 CC specifying that an obligation owed by many parties is not joint and several) or when the parties did not make any provision for the point in question (e.g. the aforementioned Art. 370 CC or Art. 295 CC, according to which, if the parties simply provided that a monetary claim shall be subject to interest, such interest will be that defined by law and due on an annualised basis). Their relation to the general rules of Arts. 173 and 200 CC is disputed: according to one view, the specific rules of interpretation become applicable only if the will of the parties cannot be determined on the basis of Arts. 173 and 200 CC;[96] another view suggests that the specific rules always prevail over Arts. 173 and 200 CC (*lex specialis derogat lege generali*), unless the agreement in question substantially deviates from the contractual type which the specific rules regulate.[97]

---

92 For the concept of good faith, see, among others, Papantoniou, *Η καλή πίστις εις το αστικόν δίκαιον [Good faith in civil law]*, *passim*; see also Georgiades, *Γενικές Αρχές Αστικού Δικαίου [General Principles of Civil Law]*, §5 no. 10, §2 nos. 10–12.

93 See e.g. AP 1345/2012, EEmpD 64 (2013), 109; AP 819/2012, first published in NOMOS; for the 'συναλλακτικά ήθη', see e.g. AP 678/1996, EEN 65 (1998), 38; Stathopoulos, 'Arts. 173 and 200' in Georgiades and Stathopoulos (eds.), *Αστικός Κώδιξ: ερμηνεία κατ' άρθρο – νομολογία – βιβλιογραφία, Τόμος 1^B: Γενικές Αρχές [Astikos Kodex: Commentary by Article – Case Law – Bibliography, Volume 1^B: General Principles]*, nos. 107–112.

94 AP 1199/1986, NoV 35 (1987), 903; Balis, *Γενικαί Αρχαί του Αστικού Δικαίου [General Principles of Civil Law]*, §88; Stathopoulos, *Civil Code*, vol. 1^B, Arts. 173 and 200 nos. 113–117; Karakostas, *Αστικός Κώδικας: Ερμηνεία – Σχόλια – Νομολογία, Τόμος Δεύτερος: Γενικές Αρχές (άρθρα 127/286) [Astikos Kodikas: Commentary – Gloss – Case law, Volume II: General Principles (Articles 127-286)]*, Arts. 173, 200 no. 879.

95 Georgiades, *General Principles*, §41 no. 20; Karakostas, *Civil Code*, vol. II, Arts. 173, 200 no. 887.

96 Georgiades, *General Principles*, §41 no. 20.

97 AP 2106/1990, NoV 39 (1991), 743; Karakostas, *Civil Code*, vol. II, Arts. 173, 200 no. 887; cf. Balis, *General Principles*, §91, who affirms the prevalence of the specific rules of interpretation, but stresses that the parties may prove that they actually had a different result in mind.

7.2. BRIEF OUTLINE OF THE INTERPRETATION PROCESS

When examining an agreement, a judge will begin with its letter, namely apply in the first place a strict grammatical interpretation.[98] This approach relies upon the applicability of the general principles of interpretation of the law also to declarations of intent and the underlying thought that, in spite of (or in parallel to) the wording of Art. 173 CC, the letter of the agreement offers, at least at the outset, a solid basis and the necessary starting point for discerning the true intent of the parties.[99]

If the grammatical interpretation does not allow the will of the parties to readily be assessed,[100] the judge will proceed to interpretation per se, which is articulated in two steps, namely the subjective and the objective criterion. In the first step, the judge tries to discover the true intent of the parties, namely their subjective understanding of a controversial clause or the contract as a whole. If both parties shared a common understanding of the agreement, this common understanding will prevail, even if it is contrary to the understanding of an average reasonable observer or if both parties were under a common misunderstanding as to the meaning of the wording used, but they aimed at the same result (*falsa demonstratio non nocet*). In practice, the judge will examine the allegations of each party without having to resort yet to evidence. If those allegations essentially coincide, his interpretative task comes to an end; if, on the other hand, those diverge, the judge will order the parties to present evidence with regard to their respective subjective understanding of the agreement. If each party's understanding thus established differs from that of the other, or when the evidence cannot offer conclusive results, the judge proceeds to the objective criterion, namely he/she discerns the normative meaning of the agreement before him and examines two parallel questions: what the person making a declaration of intent ought to have understood his declaration to mean and what the addressee of that declaration ought to have understood, taking due account of the specific circumstances of the parties.[101]

---

98 Balis, *General Principles*, §88.

99 Georgiades, *General Principles*, §41 no. 4, §6 nos. 3 et seq.; Stathopoulos, *Civil Code*, vol. 1^{B}, Arts. 173 and 200 nos. 100–102; cf. Karassis, *Γενικές Αρχές του Αστικού Δικαίου – Δικαιοπραξία [General Principles of Civil Law – Juridical Act]*, vol. I, § Γ 263.

100 Although it is sometimes suggested, especially in case law (see e.g. AP 521/1999, ArchNom 51 (2000), 92), that a clear declaration of intent is not apt to be interpreted, this is not entirely true; even a clear and unambiguous declaration of intent is susceptible to that minimum of interpretation that allows it to elicit its normative content. The hermeneutic work becomes more challenging the greater the ambiguity; in other words, it is a question of grade. See Stathopoulos, 'Περί της μεθόδου ερμηνείας της δηλώσεως βουλήσεως' [On the method of interpretation of the declaration of intent], p. 30; Ladas, *General Principles of Civil Law [Γενικές Αρχές Αστικού Δκαίου]*, vol. II, §34 nos. 12–13.

101 See Karassis, *General Principles*, § Γ 291, 295–296; Georgiades, *General Principles*, §41 nos. 16–19; Balis, *General Principles*, §88; Ladas, *General Principles*, §34 nos. 4, 6–7, 22, 26–32;

Although the two criteria seem incompatible at first sight, they actually operate in a complementary manner and form an integral, gradual scheme for the interpretation of juridical acts.[102] As stated above, the objective criterion steps in and becomes applicable once the subjective criterion has failed to deliver results because the parties have understood a disputed contractual term in a different manner.[103] The cornerstones of the objective criterion are the 'καλή πίστη' and the applicable 'συναλλακτικά ήθη'.[104] When implementing this criterion, the judge turns to the so-called normative meaning of the agreement, namely the meaning that each party could and ought to have attributed to the disputed term in accordance with the perceptive capacity of each party and their respective responsibility towards each other for proper language usage and understanding. As was the case with the first step, the judge will take for granted what both parties commonly accepted, and he will have to order evidence with regard to the disputed aspects of the case. This normative meaning of the agreement actually has a dual scope: each party is not only under a duty to make best efforts to understand what they could and ought to have understood, but they must also ensure that they formulate their own declaration of intent in a manner understandable for the other, always in the context of the particular circumstances surrounding the specific transaction.[105]

In the event that it is impossible to reach a definitive interpretation of the disputed term that is at least in part in conformance with the understanding of each party, and if both parties were justified in understanding a term or a clause in different ways, there is no valid declaration of intent or, respectively, contract due to dissent (Art. 195 CC); the relevant declaration of intent or contractual

---

Stathopoulos, *Civil Code*, vol. 1^B, Arts. 173 and 200 nos. 81–84; Stathopoulos, 'On the method of interpretation', pp. 40–43, 55. In certain cases, only the subjective criterion applies, such as the interpretation of testaments or occupation of land or goods with no owner; Georgiades, *General Principles*, §41 nos. 22–24; Karakostas, *Civil Code*, vol. II, Arts. 173, 200 nos. 872–874; cf. Ladas, *General Principles*, §34 nos. 8, 9–11 (distinguishing various cases); also cf. Stathopoulos, *Civil Code*, vol. 1^B, Arts. 173 and 200 no. 58, observing that 'πράξεις βουλήσεως' [acts of intent], i.e. cases where a declaration of intent is expressed through external acts (e.g. occupation of land or goods), are subject to proof rather than interpretation.

102 Papanikolaou, *Μεθοδολογία του Ιδιωτικού Δικαίου και Ερμηνεία των Δικαιοπραξιών [Private Law Methodology and Interpretation of Juridical Acts]*, §§504–509; Karassis, *General Principles*, §§ Γ 289–299; Georgiades, *General Principles*, §41 no. 13.

103 Papanikolaou, *Methodology*, §§505–509; Karassis, *General Principles*, §§ Γ 283–299; Stathopoulos, 'On the method of interpretation', pp. 43–52.

104 For the relation of trade customs to the general standard of good faith under Art. 200 CC and the role the former play in the concretisation of the standard of good faith in each particular case, see Case 9.

105 Papanikolaou, *Methodology*, §§460–461; Georgiades, *General Principles*, §41 nos. 11, 15, 18; Stathopoulos, 'On the method of interpretation', p. 35; Karassis, *General Principles*, § Γ 292, with further references.

provision is deemed to be null and void.[106] In practice, such cases are rare by virtue of the principle of *favor contractus*, which aims at safeguarding the validity of the contract; in such cases, the party feeling disadvantaged may still try to avoid the contract on grounds of error.[107]

7.3. UNDERLYING PRINCIPLES

On the one hand, Art. 173 CC gives full precedence to the 'αρχή της ιδιωτικής αυτονομίας' [principle of private autonomy], namely the freedom of the persons to shape their private-law relations as they wish, which is a central axiom of the Greek legal system. Art. 200 CC, on the other hand, takes a step further and also considers the 'αρχή της εμπιστοσύνης' [principle of trust] and the 'αρχή της ασφάλειας των συναλλαγών' [principle of certainty in transactions], namely principles aiming at the frictionless function of the market and the smooth implementation of legal transactions. The very nature of contracts requires that the interests and expectations of both parties must be taken into account and both parties are accountable for their legally meaningful acts in law and their conduct altogether ('αρχή της αυτοευθύνης' [principle of self-responsibility]), in the sense that they must show due diligence both in making their declarations clear and understandable for their counterparty and in interpreting the declarations addressed to them.[108] The criterion of Art. 173 CC is obviously subjective in nature, whereby Art. 200 CC adopts a more objective perspective (albeit still strongly attached to the specific contracting parties).[109]

Consequently, the judge always undertakes a logical evaluation of the case before him, but the nature of such evaluation differs in each step of the interpretation process: under Art. 173 CC, the judge performs an ontological evaluation: he reaches a conclusion as to what the situation really is on the basis of the private autonomy of the parties; whereas the objective interpretation of Art. 200 CC is deontological in nature and relies upon a logical compromise

---

106 See AP 33/1962, NoV 10 (1962), 562; Georgiades, *General Principles*, §41 nos. 18–19; Karakostas, *Civil Code*, vol. II, Arts. 173, 200 no. 871; Filios, *Γενικές Αρχές Αστικού Δικαίου [General Principles of Civil Law]*, §241 Δ. α).

107 Stathopoulos, *Civil Code*, vol. 1^B, Arts. 173 and 200 no. 93–94; Georgiades, *General Principles*, §41 no. 18; Balis, *General Principles*, §89. The present report focuses on contractual interpretation that seeks to safeguard the validity of a contract; cases of invalidity due to dissent, voidable contracts, etc. are beyond its scope.

108 Papanikolaou, *Methodology*, §461; Karassis, *General Principles*, §§ Γ 286, 292; Ladas, *General Principles*, §34 nos. 19, 22; Filios, *General Principles*, §243; Stathopoulos, 'On the method of interpretation', 5–6.

109 AP 490/1994, NoV 43 (1995), 546 (on Art. 173 CC), stressing that the perception of third parties on the declaration of intent in question is irrelevant; AP 844/1998, EllDni 40 (1999), 145; Papanikolaou, *Methodology*, §465, §§472 et seq., 492 et seq.; Karassis, *General Principles*, §§ Γ 283–288.

between the rule of private autonomy, on the one hand, and the principles of trust, certainty of transactions and self-responsibility of the parties, on the other hand.[110]

In the same sense, the old controversy between the so-called subjective and objective theories of interpretation, relying respectively only upon the will of the person expressing a declaration of intent or only upon how this would be understood by an objective observer or circle of observers, cannot be decided solely in favour of one or the other school. The correct approach lies somewhere in the middle: the subjective criterion may not be decisive on its own, because declarations of intent are in the majority of cases[111] addressed to another person, but this 'objectivisation' of the declaration of intent may not go beyond the sense attributed to it when taking due account of the specific parties and set of circumstances.[112]

7.4. TERMINOLOGICAL AND CONCEPTUAL CLARIFICATIONS

A few more points should be stressed. It was noted above that Art. 173 CC refers to declarations of intent, and Art. 200 CC to contracts; however, the letter of the law is misleading, since it is commonly accepted that both provisions apply to all kinds of juridical acts, regardless of whether they are unilateral or contractual, and Greek courts generally tend to cite and apply them together in their rulings.[113]

It was also mentioned at the outset that Art. 173 CC seeks to elicit the true meaning of a declaration of intent without holding fast to the wording used. The reference to the wording in this provision already indicates that the critical content of a declaration of intent must have somehow been externalised, expressed in a manner perceptible for third parties. The principle of private autonomy does not reach as far as imposing that what the person intended, but did not explicitly express and sufficiently externalise, can prevail.[114]

---

110 Karassis, *General Principles*, §§ Γ 292, 298–299.

111 See n. 101 above for exceptions.

112 Stathopoulos, 'On the method of interpretation', 39; see, for a brief account of the relevant theories and the prevailing doctrinal view, Stathopoulos, *Civil Code*, vol. 1^{B}, Arts. 173 and 200 nos. 15–27.

113 AP 27/1997, NoV 46 (1998), 763; Karassis, *General Principles*, § Γ 279; Balis, *General Principles*, §88; Stathopoulos, *Civil Code*, vol. 1^{B}, Arts. 173 and 200 no. 6; Georgiades, *General Principles*, §41 no. 12; Karakostas, *Civil Code*, vol. II, Arts. 173, 200 nos. 865, 876; Ladas, *General Principles*, §34 nos. 19, 25; see also Papanikolaou, *Methodology*, §§475–477, 492. Greek legal doctrine tends to be critical of the split between the two provisions, which relies upon the similar construction of the German BGB and is generally regarded as somewhat impractical and anachronistic.

114 Georgiades, *General Principles*, §41 no. 5; Stathopoulos, *Civil Code*, vol. 1^{B}, Arts. 173 and 200 nos. 18–19, 24; Ladas, *General Principles*, §34 nos. 17–18.

Regarding the principle of 'καλή πίστη', case law treats it as referring to the behaviour of an honest and reasonable person participating in the pertinent transaction setting.[115] Legal doctrine generally affirms this view, but stresses that a contract must be interpreted in the light of the circumstances and purpose of the specific contracting parties in question, not solely of some abstract concept of an honest and reasonable transactor.[116]

On a final note, the importance of the specific transactional setting highlights how the principle of private autonomy is of paramount importance for both interpretative criteria. Even when resorting to Art. 200 CC, the applicable interpretation benchmark, i.e. what should be objectively expected from a reasonable, average person, may not lead to conclusions that deviate to an excessive extent from the expressed will of the parties and how the parties commonly understood or should have understood such an expression of intent, taking due account of their circumstances. The reasonable compromise between the principle of private autonomy and the principles of trust and certainty of transactions is achieved by reference to the specific transacting parties.[117]

8. ITALY

The Italian Codice civile (c.c.) [Civil Code] contains a set of specific rules on the interpretation of contracts. An ancient scholarly position used to regard those rules not as real legal rules but as mere recommendations to the judge. As the interpretation of contract should be essentially aimed at unfolding the intention of the parties, it was argued, it is this sole purpose that should lead the judge, and once the judge realises that the 'rules' provided for by the Civil Code do not help in finding the parties' will, she would be allowed to disregard them.[118] This opinion did not gain widespread acceptance and the rules on the interpretation of contracts are now unanimously regarded as actual legal rules.

---

115 See n. 93 above.

116 See e.g. Stathopoulos, *Civil Code*, vol. 1^B, Arts. 173 and 200 nos. 107, 110; Karakostas, *Civil Code*, vol. II, Arts. 173, 200 nos. 865, 877; Balis, *General Principles*, §88 *in fine*; Papanikolaou, *Methodology*, §494; Georgiades, *General Principles*, §41 nos. 9, 14.

117 Stathopoulos, *Civil Code*, vol. 1^B, Arts. 173 and 200 no. 31; Papanikolaou, *Methodology*, §§493–495.

118 Giorgi, *Teoria delle obbligazioni*, IV, p. 181; Pacifici Mazzoni, *Istituzioni di diritto civile italiano*, p. 189; Pacchioni, *Dei contratti in generale*, p. 156 (those authors referred to the previous Civil Code, enacted in 1865 and in force until 1942). Under the 1942 Civil Code: Carresi, *Il contratto*, p. 500; Carresi, *L'interpretazione del contratto*, p. 552. For comments, see Sacco, *Contratto*, p. 1329 ff.; for a recent comprehensive account of the history and theories of interpretation of contracts see Gentili, *Senso e consenso*, *passim* (esp. for the debate on the 'nature' of the rules on interpretation of contract at p. 444 ff.).

Arts. 1362–1371 c.c. indicate several factors that one must take into account in order to determine the legally relevant meaning of contractual terms.[119] Those articles are usually classified in two different groups, each purportedly giving rise to a different interpretation process, namely subjective interpretation and objective interpretation. The former purports to construe the legal meaning of the contract according to the actual intention of the parties. The latter is aimed at assigning to the contract an 'objective' meaning, according to legal rules whose function is to provide the contract with a workable and reasonable meaning.

Both scholars and courts generally share the opinion that those rules must be applied according to a certain hierarchical order that is commonly referred to as 'gradualismo' or 'gerarchia' [graduation or hierarchy] of the interpretation criteria.[120] As the will of the parties is the basic source of contractual obligations, the legal meaning of the contract should be ascertained, in the first instance, through the application of rules of 'subjective' interpretation. Those rules, according to a widely shared opinion, address some factors that the law considers relevant in order to provide the contract with content as close as possible to the parties' actual intentions. If the 'subjective' interpretation rules do not suffice to uncover unambiguous contractual content, then it would be possible to look at the 'objective' interpretation rules. Those rules provide further criteria for the definition of a legal meaning of the contract, which are tailored to general considerations of reasonableness and business efficacy.

The distinction between rules of subjective interpretation and rules of objective interpretation, the idea of the priority of some interpretive factors and the consequent hierarchy of the respective rules have a scholarly origin and they were conceived when the previous Codice civile was in force.[121] Those ideas, now accepted by the majority of scholars, have been followed by the drafters of the new Codice civile (enacted in 1942)[122] and are consistently applied by

[119] Interpretation of contracts was defined as the search for the legally relevant meaning of the contract initially by Grassetti, *L'interpretazione del negozio giuridico*, pp. 17, 59, 99; this definition has displaced more traditional positions which had defined the interpretation of contract as the ascertainment of the will of the parties: see Sacco, *Contratto*, p. 1329 ff.; Bianca, *Contratto*, pp. 407–9.

[120] For critical remarks on the distinction between subjective and objective rules and on a strict application of the hierarchy principle see e.g. Rizzo, *Interpretazione del contratto*, p. 498; Bigliazzi Geri, *L'interpretazione*, p. 39 ff.; Costanza, *Profili dell'interpretazione del contratto*, p. 11; Alpa, *Unità del negozio e principi di ermeneutica contrattuale*, p. 1508; Scognamiglio, *Interpretazione del contratto*, *passim*; for a comprehensive account of doctrinal opinions see Gentili, *Senso e consenso*, p. 425 ff.

[121] Grassetti, *L'interpretazione del negozio giuridico*; Grassetti, *Interpretazione dei negozi giuridici 'inter vivos'*, pp. 905–906; Oppo, *Profili dell'interpretazione oggettiva del negozio giuridico*; the first reported decision adopting the hierarchy principle appears to be Cass. 24 June 1940 no. 2079, in Foro it. 1941, I, 512.

[122] *Relazione al Codice Civile* no. 622; see Gentili, *Senso e consenso*, pp. 377 ff., 409 ff.

courts, even though scholars do not always agree as to the proper classification of each rule.

The hierarchy principle also receives some textual support from the wording of the relevant articles of the Codice civile. While the first article of the chapter on the interpretation of contracts (Art. 1362) points to the search for the intention of the parties as the primary aim of the interpretation process, other rules, usually regarded as rules of objective interpretation, expressly make their application conditional upon the existence of some 'doubt' or 'ambiguity' as to the meaning of the contract. It thus follows that the rules on objective interpretation should be applied only if the application of rules aimed at understanding the parties' actual will have not succeeded to uncover a clear and unambiguous contractual meaning. In any event, regardless of the reliability of this textual basis, this distinction, as well as the hierarchy principle, are accepted and routinely applied by courts.[123]

It is a firm judicial position that the outcome of the interpretation process raises a question of fact, whose solution is reserved to trial judges (tribunals and courts of appeal), while the way the judge interprets and applies the rules regulating the interpretation process is a question of law.

As the rules regarding interpretation of contracts are actual legal rules, the way they are interpreted and applied is a question of law subject to review by the 'Corte di Cassazione' [the court of last instance]. The Corte di Cassazione cannot assess facts but only the proper interpretation and application of the law by lower judges. Therefore, the Corte di Cassazione cannot question or supersede the way in which the trial judges interpreted a contract as long as the trial judges have correctly interpreted and applied legal rules on the interpretation of contracts, including the hierarchy principle. If a lower court has violated or misunderstood the legal rules on interpretation, then the Corte di Cassazione has the power to annul the judgment from the lower court and remand the matter to a different lower court.

Therefore, a party who wants the decision of a lower judge to be annulled by the Corte di Cassazione cannot simply plead a wrong interpretation of the contract and rely on the Corte di Cassazione for an alternative interpretation. The complaining party must indicate the specific rules that the lower judge has infringed and, if the Corte di Cassazione is persuaded that the decision is wrong as a matter of law, the case will be remanded to a different lower court, which will interpret the contract according to the instructions of the Corte di Cassazione.[124]

---

123 See e.g. Cass. 11 March 2014 no. 5595; Cass. 8 November 2013 no. 25243; Cass. 24 January 2012 no. 925; Cass. 12 June 2007 no. 13777.

124 See recently Cass. 14 March 2018 no. 6311; Cass. 20 January 2017 no. 1587; Cass. 22 July 2016 no. 15253; Cass. 26 May 2016 no. 10896.

9. NETHERLANDS

The Burgerlijk Wetboek [Civil Code] of the Netherlands of 1992 contains no general provisions on contract interpretation. In contrast to the codification of 1838, such provisions were considered by the drafters of the new code to be superfluous and too general and therefore of little use in an interpretation dispute.[125] Instead, the development of interpretation norms was left to the courts and doctrine.[126]

The Supreme Court's judgment in the *Haviltex* case has dominated the legal landscape with respect to contract interpretation since 1981.[127] In that case, the Court rejected a purely linguistic approach to interpretation, as well as an interpretation of the contract exclusively based on the subjective intentions of the parties.[128] Instead, it laid down a norm for the interpretation of contracts that requires courts to have regard to the meaning that the respective parties, in the given circumstances, could reasonably have attributed to the provisions of the contract and to that which in that respect they could reasonably have expected from each other.[129] With this norm, the Court essentially subjects contract interpretation to the 'wilsvertrouwensleer' [will-reliance theory] encapsulated in Arts. 3:33 and 3:35 BW and the principle of 'redelijkheid en billijkheid' [reasonableness and fairness].[130] In doing so, it reveals the close relationship between the requirements for contract formation and the approach to contract interpretation.[131]

During the interpretation process, a court should not only consider what meaning each party attributes to the contractual terms, but also whether that meaning is reasonable in the given circumstances also taking into account what meaning each party could reasonably believe the other party attributes to the wording.[132] Consequently, each party is protected in its justified reliance on

125 Parlementaire Geschiedenis Boek 6, 916; see Asser/Sieburgh, *Algemene leer der overeenkomsten*, 6-III, no. 354. It should be noted that there are still statutory interpretation rules for wills and testaments, see Art. 4:46 BW, and the *contra proferentem* rule has been incorporated into Art. 6:238 (2) BW as a result of Council Directive 93/13 of 5 April 1993 on unfair terms in consumer contracts, *OJ* L 95/93.

126 Asser/Sieburgh, *Algemene leer der overeenkomsten*, 6-III, no. 354.

127 Hoge Raad 13 March 1981, *NJ* 1981, 635 (Ermes/Haviltex).

128 See Wissink, 'Uitleg volgens Haviltex of de cao-norm? Over een vloeiende overgang en de noodzaak om toch te kiezen'.

129 The Dutch wording from the Supreme Court in the *Haviltex* case is as follows: '[D]e zin die partijen in de gegeven omstandigheden over en weer redelijkerwijs aan deze bepalingen mochten toekennen en op hetgeen zij te dien aanzien redelijkerwijs van elkaar mochten verwachten'.

130 See Valk in Schelhaas/Valk, *Uitleg van rechtshandelingen*, p. 16.

131 Tjittes, 'Uitleg van schriftelijke contracten', p. 3; Wissink, 'Uitleg volgens Haviltex of de CAO-norm? Over een vloeiende overgang en de noodzaak om toch te kiezen', p. 407.

132 Wissink, 'Chapter 5: Interpretation. Art. 5:101-5:107', p. 245.

the meaning it gave to the words, provided its expectation that the other party shared that meaning is also justified. To this end, the court may have regard to a wide range of relevant circumstances, including the nature and purpose of the contract, the negotiation and drafting history, the parties' statements and conduct, the parties' subsequent conduct after the conclusion of the contract, the nature of the contracting parties and trade usages.[133]

In the 1990s, the Supreme Court developed a more textual interpretation norm for collective employment agreements and similar types of contracts, the so-called CAO norm.[134] The aim of these types of contract is to regulate uniformly the rights and obligations of a large number of parties who were not present during the negotiations. These parties generally lack the background information that could shed light on the nature of the rights and duties contained in the contract, for which reason contract interpretation is to be based on more objective factors, in particular the wording of the provisions and the overall text of the contract. The intentions of the contracting parties are only relevant to the extent that they stem from the text of the contract and the explanatory text available to third parties and other relevant information that is publicly available.[135]

Although the Supreme Court appears to have developed two seemingly contradictory interpretative norms, in its 2004 *DSM-Chemie/Fox* decision[136] the Court clarified the relationship between the *Haviltex* and CAO norms by positioning them on a sliding scale on which they transition smoothly into each other. The Court explained that these norms share a common foundation, namely that all the circumstances of the individual case, assessed in light of the standards of 'redelijkheid en billijkheid' [reasonableness and fairness], are decisive for the interpretation of contracts.[137] In its *DSM-Chemie/Fox* decision, the Supreme Court explained that on this sliding scale, depending on the circumstances, the *Haviltex* norm can be applied in a more objective manner, meaning that objective circumstances, such as the text, structure and public

---

133 Tjittes, *Uitleg van schriftelijke contracten*, p. 32 ff.

134 Hoge Raad 17 September 1993, *NJ* 1994, 173 (Gerritse/HAS) and Hoge Raad 24 September 1993, *NJ* 1994, 174 (Hol/EIM). See also Hoge Raad 31 May 2002, *NJ* 2003, 110 and Hoge Raad 28 June 2002, *NJ* 2003, 111. CAO is the abbreviation for 'collectieve arbeidsovereenkomst', which means collective employment contract.

135 Asser, Hartkamp and Sieburgh, *Algemene leer der overeenkomsten*, 6-III, no. 374; Wissink, 'Uitleg volgens *Haviltex* of de CAO-norm? Over een vloeiende overgang en de noodzaak om toch te kiezen', p. 407.

136 Hoge Raad 20 February 2004, NJ 2005, 493 (DSM-Chemie/Fox).

137 The Dutch wording from the Supreme Court in the *DSM-Chemie/Fox* case is as follows: '4.5 De hiervoor in 4.2–4.4 weergegeven rechtspraak heeft als gemeenschappelijke grondslag dat bij de uitleg van een schriftelijk contract telkens van beslissende betekenis zijn alle omstandigheden van het concrete geval, gewaardeerd naar hetgeen de maatstaven van redelijkheid en billijkheid meebrengen.'

explanatory texts, as well as the probability of the legal consequences of one of the interpretations of the wording, may be given greater weight. The formulation of this common foundation has been criticised, in particular in the context of commercial contracts, for being uninformative and lacking any differentiating ability, for being too vague, artificial and unnecessary and consequently for jeopardising the certainty and predictability of contract interpretation often sought in commercial contracts.[138]

In subsequent decisions,[139] the Supreme Court has clarified the approach for commercial contracts. The *Haviltex* norm is leading and applies to the interpretation of all commercial contracts. However, in accordance with the *Pont Meyer* and *Lundiform/Mexx* decisions, when applying that norm in the case of a carefully drafted, comprehensive and detailed commercial contract between professional parties that has been the subject of extensive negotiations and which was concluded with legal advice, and in particular where it contains an entire agreement clause, courts may attach great weight to the 'taalkundige betekenis' [linguistic meaning] of the wording. It remains open for the party relying on an alternative meaning to provide evidence of relevant facts and circumstances that reveal that it was reasonable for it to attribute a different meaning to the contractual expression and that it was reasonable to expect the other party to share this meaning. It should be noted that for contracts that fall within this category there is a freedom for the court to attach great weight to the linguistic meaning of the wording, subject to evidence to the contrary, but the court is not under a duty to so. Where the commercial contract does not fall within this category, for instance the parties did not take great care when formulating the contract with a view to having the contract reflect precisely their intentions, or where they were not supported by legal advisors, the 'ordinary' *Haviltex* norm will apply, whereby courts will weigh all the relevant facts and circumstances in accordance with the standards of reasonableness and fairness to establish what meaning each party could reasonably have attached to the wording and reasonably have expected the other party to have attributed to the wording.

The interpretation of a contract is to a large extent a question of fact. The control by the Supreme Court is limited to determining whether the correct interpretation norm has been used, whether all the relevant circumstances were taken into account, whether the procedural rules have been followed and

---

138 Hartlief, 'De uitleg van contracten. Haviltex revisited'; Wissink, 'Uitleg volgens Haviltex of de cao-norm? Over een vloeiende overgang en de noodzaak om toch te kiezen', p. 407; also see Tjittes, 'Uitleg van schriftelijke contracten'; Grosheide, 'Lees maar, er staat wat er staat', pp. 5–13.

139 Hoge Raad 19 January 2007, *NJ* 2007, 575 (Pont Meyer); Hoge Raad 29 June 2007, *NJ* 2007, 576 (Derksen/Homberg); Hoge Raad 9 April 2010, *JOR* 2010, 179 (UPC/Land); Hoge Raad 5 April 2013, *NJ* 2013, 214 (Lundiform/Mexx).

whether the lower court's judgment is grounded on sufficient reasoning.[140] Where the parties do not agree on the meaning to be given to a term in the contract, courts may interpret the term itself. In doing so, it is not restricted to the interpretations defended by the parties,[141] unless the parties have requested the court to choose between certain potential interpretations.[142] Within the framework of the applicable norm, the court is free in the choice of factors it takes into account in order to establish the meaning to be attributed to the terms of the contract as well as the weight to attribute to them.[143] The court may take an array of surrounding circumstances into account. It may call for witness evidence to prove certain facts and circumstances, if necessary.[144] Where such information is not available, the court will have to rely on more objective sources of information to inform its interpretation. In that case, interpretation will be relatively textual, in the sense that the court may rely on ordinary linguistic usage, the contractual documentation, the nature and purpose of the contract, the nature of the contracting parties and generally known facts and circumstances. In the end, the foundation for the court's interpretation will lie in its weighing of 'all the relevant circumstances' in light of the standards of 'redelijkheid en billijkheid' [reasonableness and fairness].

10. POLAND

The current standard of interpreting contracts is explained as the 'metoda kombinowana' [mixed method].[145] Its theoretical foundations can be found in legal writing (Longchamps de Berier,[146] Wolter[147] and Radwański[148]) and

140 Hoge Raad 17 February 2006, NJ 2006, 378 (Royal & Sun Alliance/Universal Pictures); Tjittes, *Uitleg van schriftelijke contracten*, p. 50; also see e.g. Hoge Raad 5 April 2013, *NJ* 2013, 214, A-G Timmerman (no. 3.2).

141 Hoge Raad 16 February 1996, *NJ* 1997, 327 (Van Genk/De Wild); Asser/Sieburgh, *Algemene leer der overeenkomsten*, 6-III, no. 377; Tjittes, *Uitleg van schriftelijke contracten*, p. 55.

142 Hoge Raad 20 January 1984, *NJ* 1987, 295; Asser/Sieburgh, *Algemene leer der overeenkomsten*, 6-III, no. 377; Tjittes, *Uitleg van schriftelijke contracten*, p. 55.

143 Asser/Sieburgh, *Algemene leer der overeenkomsten*, 6-III, no. 377.

144 Ibid., no. 377.

145 Judgment of SN of 20.05.2004, II CK 354/03; Judgment of SN of 02.07.2004, II CK 271/04; Judgment of SN of 05.10.2005, II CK 122/05; Judgment of SN of 17.12.2008, I CSK 250/08; Judgment of SN of 17.06.2009, IV CSK 90/09; Judgment of SN of 09.02.2012, III CSK 179/11; Judgment of SN of 06.02.2013, V CSK 162/12; Judgment of SN of 10.05.2013, I CSK 74/13; Judgment of SN of 23.05.2013, I CSK 569/12; Judgment of SN of 18.11.2016, I CSK 802/15; E. Rott-Pietrzyk, 'Interpretacja oświadczenia woli (uwagi na tle rozwiązań projektu księgi I kodeksu cywilnego)', TPP 4/2010, p. 45.

146 R. Longchamps de Berier, *Zobowiązania*, pp. 146–147.

147 A. Wolter, *Prawo cywilne, Zarys części ogólnej*, p. 299.

148 Z. Radwański, *Wykładnia oświadczeń woli składanych indywidualnym adresatom.*

over time it has been adopted by case law.[149] This interpretation method acknowledges both the (free) will of the person declaring his intentions, and the trust (reliance) that the declaration awakens in other parties. This approach reflects the importance of the principle of the parties' autonomy in forming their contractual relationship, and recognises that the parties to the contract have the best knowledge about the desired and most appropriate content of their contractual relationship, from the point of view of fulfilling their individual interests.[150]

The interpretation process has two stages: subjective and objective. In the subjective stage, the common intention of the parties has priority and prevails over the literal wording of the contract (Art. 65 para. 2 of the 'Kodeks Cywilny' (KC) [Civil Code]).[151] Polish courts recognise that in order to 'odtworzyć' [re-create] the common intention of parties at the moment of concluding the contract, pursuant to which the contractual relationship should be regulated and contractual terms should be interpreted, any evidence may be presented in court.[152] In a recent judgment, the 'Sąd Najwyższy' (SN) [Supreme Court] stated, however, that recreating the intention of parties at the moment of concluding the contract should not have an absolute character.[153] Pursuant to this judgment, Polish courts need to account for the fact that, with the lapse of time from the conclusion of the contract, the relationship between the parties and their economic interests might have evolved in a way that could not have been anticipated at that time. In order to provide the parties with just and effective dispute resolution, which would preserve their interests, the directive to base the interpretation process on the reconstruction of the original intention of parties should not be too strictly observed. While the interpretive

---

149 Judgment of SN of 20.05.2004, II CK 354/03; Judgment of SN of 02.07.2004, II CK 271/04; Judgment of SN of 05.10.2005, II CK 122/05; Judgment of SN of 17.12.2008, I CSK 250/08; Judgment of SN of 17.06.2009, IV CSK 90/09.

150 B. Kaczorowska, 'Wizja wykładni umów w projekcie księgi pierwszej kodeksu cywilnego', TPP 2/2011, p. 15.

151 E.g. Judgment of SN of 23.05.2013, I CSK 569/12.

152 Judgment of SN of 04.07.1975, III CRN 160/75; Decree of SN of 29.06.1995, III CZP 66/95; Judgment of SN of 21.11.1997, I CKN 825/97; Judgment of SN of 03.09.1998, I CKN 815/97; Judgment of SN of 08.10.2004, V CK 670/03; Judgment of SN of 05.10.2005, II CK 122/05; Judgment of SN of 15.06.2007, V CSK 63/07; Judgment of SN of 17.12.2008, I CSK 250/08; Judgment of SN of 17.06.2009, IV CSK 90/09; Judgment of SN of 13.06.2012, II CSK 608/11; Judgment of SN of 14.06.2012, I CSK 485/11; Judgment of SN of 06.02.2013, V CSK 162/12; Judgment of SN of 27.03.2013, I CSK 403/12; Judgment of SN of 10.05.2013, I CSK 74/13; Ł. Węgrzynowski, 'Sądowe ustalanie treści stosunku umownego', PPH 2007/5/44–49; B. Kaczorowska, 'Wizja wykładni umów w projekcie księgi pierwszej kodeksu cywilnego', TPP 2/2011, pp. 14–15; M. Romanowski, 'Ogólne reguły wykładni kontraktów w świetle zasad europejskiego prawa kontraktów a reguły wykładni umów w prawie polskim', PPH 2004/8; M. Romanowski, 'Szczegółowe reguły wykładni kontraktów w świetle zasad europejskiego prawa kontraktów a reguły wykładni umów w prawie polskim', PPH 2004/9/12–18.

153 Judgment of SN of 05.02.2014, V CSK 125/13.

directive of reconstructing the intention of parties at the moment of concluding the contract should not be perceived as absolute, it is, however, perceived as controversial that the SN encourages courts to interpret a contract in a way that most effectively reconciles the parties' economic interests.[154] In practice, this gives courts the authority to determine the scope and content of the contract, whereas the parties' intention and will should prevail.

Only when the parties' common intention cannot be established are objective interpretation criteria introduced, in Art. 65 para. 1 KC.[155] A contract is then interpreted in accordance with (1) the circumstances in which it was made, (2) the 'zasady współżycia społecznego' [the principles of community life] and (3) the established customs. The court determines what the recipient of the declaration would and should have understood under it, if interpreting the contract with due diligence.[156] Protecting the recipient's trust prevails over the intentions of the party making the declaration. Since the maker of the declaration formulates or drafts it, he should do it in a way that allows the declaration to be understood by its recipient according to the drafter's intention.[157] The 'zasada dobrej wiary' [principle of good faith] is a general paradigm for all interpretation criteria in Polish law, and as such is not separately considered by judges or in academic literature as an interpretation criterion.

The KC does not use the terms 'intepretacja' [interpretation] or 'wykładnia' [explanation], but rather 'tłumaczenie' [translation] in relation to establishing the content of the declaration of the parties' intentions. The academic literature and case law use these terms interchangeably.[158]

The first draft of the new Book I of the KC,[159] published in 2008, proposed substantial changes to the interpretation rules. The drafters of the new KC

154 P. Sobolewski, 'Komentarz do art. 65 KC' in K. Osajda (ed.), *Kodeks cywilny. Komentarz*, point 43.

155 Decree of SN of 29.06.1995, III CZP 66/95; Judgment of SN of 08.10.2004, V CK 670/03; Judgment of SN of 17.12.2008, I CSK 250/08; Judgment of SN of 17.06.2009, IV CSK 90/09; Judgment of SN of 14.06.2012, I CSK 485/11; Judgment of SN of 18.11.2016, I CSK 802/15; Ł. Węgrzynowski, 'Sądowe ustalanie treści stosunku umownego', PPH 2007/5/44–49; M. Romanowski, 'Ogólne reguły wykładni kontraktów w świetle zasad europejskiego prawa kontraktów a reguły wykładni umów w prawie polskim', PPH 2004/8.

156 Decree of SN (7) of 29.06.1995, III CZP 66/95; Judgment of SN of 05.10.2005, II CK 122/05; Judgment of SN of 17.06.2009, IV CSK 90/09; Judgment of SN of 09.02.2012, III CSK 179/11; Judgment of SN of 14.06.2012, I CSK 485/11; Judgment of SN of 06.02.2013, V CSK 162/12; Judgment of SN of 27.03.2013, I CSK 403/12; Judgment of SN of 23.05.2013, I CSK 569/12; Judgment of SN of 18.11.2016, I CSK 802/15.

157 Decree of SN (7) of 29.06.1995, III CZP 66/95.

158 B. Kaczorowska, 'Wizja wykładni umów w projekcie księgi pierwszej kodeksu cywilnego', TPP 2/2011, p. 12.

159 The Civil Law Codification Commission, consisting of academics and judges of higher courts, has been drafting the new KC for several years now. The draft Book I was published back in 2009 (see Komisja Kodyfikacyjna Prawa Cywilnego działająca przy Ministrze Sprawiedliwości, Księga pierwsza Kodeksu cywilnego).

criticised the current interpretation rules as being eclectic, disorganised and not transparent. They claim that there is no clear hierarchy or preference given to any specific interpretation rule or form of evidence on the basis of which the parties' common intentions can be established.[160] The proposed changes were further reformulated in the second draft of Book I.[161]

11. PORTUGAL

The Portuguese Código Civil (CC) [Civil Code] has four articles devoted to the interpretation of contracts (236.°, 237.°, 238.° and 239.°). Art. 236.°/1 determines that the declaration must be interpreted in the manner a 'declaratário normal' [reasonable person] in the position of the 'real declaratário' [real addressee] would interpret it based on the behaviour of the author of the declaration, unless the former could not rely on it. Art. 236.°/2 states that if the addressee knows the real intention of the author of the declaration, then it is according to that intention that the declaration must be interpreted.

Art. 237.° stipulates that in the context of gifts or donations, the meaning that is the least onerous to the donor prevails. In onerous contracts, the meaning that leads to a more balanced contract prevails. Art. 238.°/1, which applies to written contracts, states that the declaration must be interpreted in a way that has a minimum degree of correspondence with the text of the document, even if the document does not express the declaration clearly. Art. 238.°/2 acknowledges that in the case of written contracts, the parties' real intention can also be relevant, unless it is contrary to formal legal reasons. Art. 239.°, with regard to the integration of contracts, states that omissions in contracts must be integrated according to the intention that the parties should have had and according to 'boa fé' [good faith].

Portuguese law relies on a method of interpretation which combines elements of both objective and subjective theories. In fact, the Portuguese system also stresses the importance of the subjective intention of the parties.[162] That results clearly from Arts. 236.°/2, 238.°/2 and 239.° CC.

According to Art. 236.°/1, the standard for assessing the conduct of the parties is not internal but external. In other words, the court will look at the

160 B. Kaczorowska, 'Wizja wykładni umów w projekcie księgi pierwszej kodeksu cywilnego', TPP 2/2011, p. 13; E. Rott-Pietrzyk, 'Interpretacja owiadczenia woli (uwagi na tle rozwiza projektu księgi I kodeksu cywilnego)', TPP 4/2010, p. 46.

161 http://www.projektkc.uj.edu.pl/dokumenty/Projekt_Komisji_Kodyfikacyjnej_Ksiega_I_z_uzasadnieniem.pdf.

162 See Pais de Vasconcelos, *Teoria Geral do Direito Civil*, pp. 246–247; Rei, *Da interpretação da declaração negocial no Direito Civil Português*, p. 476; Santos Junior, *Sobre a Teoria da Interpretação dos negócios jurídicos*, p. 226.

outward appearance of the agreement and will endorse what the parties objectively appear to have intended. After all, the meaning of the terms of a contract do not depend upon the state of the parties' minds. Portuguese case law on Art. 236.°/1 CC has affirmed the relevance of objective elements in the interpretation of contract. There are several decisions that underline this interpretation of Art. 236.°/1 CC.[163]

However, under Art. 236.°/2, Portuguese courts also take into account subjective elements of the parties' intention. Portuguese scholarship on the four articles referred to above observes a mixed model of contract interpretation, which combines objective and subjective elements concerning the interpretation of contract. For example, Castro Mendes considers that the Art. 236.°/1 CC must be interpreted by giving weight to what the author of the declaration wanted and expressed.[164] This position is much more subjective than the one that is suggested by Pires de Lima, Antunes Varela[165] and Mota Pinto,[166] for whom the Portuguese Civil Code has adopted an objective method of interpretation. Ferreira de Almeida also supports the objective model.[167]

Heinrich Ewald Hörster[168] suggests that Art. 236.°/1 CC seeks to conciliate the interests of the parties. The scope of interpretation is the meaning of the declaration as an expression of the will in the same direction of the position defended by Castro Mendes, giving relevance to the intention from the author of the declaration. The standard of the 'declaratário normal' [reasonable person] is also relevant to evaluate how the recipient could have understood the declaration. Here, the text and its content are important factors, as well as the diligence required to obtain all the elements that can help to discover the real intention of the author of the declaration.[169] In the Portuguese system, courts tend to only give special weight to the subjective (internal) intent if this intent is communicated to the other party or if the other party (acting in a reasonable way) can deduce from that intent.

When interpreting commercial contracts in Portugal, the court will focus on both the subjective intent and objective factors. But there is not just one formula

---

163 Such as RCb 20 December 1990 (Dias Simão), CJ XV (1990) 5, 100–102; STJ 13 April 1994 (Martins Valada) CJ/Supremo II (1994) 2, 32–37; RLx 15 February 1996 (Almeida Valadas), CJ XXI (1996) 1, 121–124; STJ 11 March 1999 (Pinto Monteiro), CJ/Supremo VII (1999), 156–158; STJ 13 March 2001 (Silva Paixão), CJ/Supremo IX (2001) 1, 163–168; STJ 11 February 2003 (Afonso Correia), CJ/Supremo XI (2003) 1, 88–93; STJ 19 January 2017 (António Joaquim Pirraça). See Menezes Cordeiro, *Tratado de Direito Civil Português*, I, Parte Geral, II, p. 617.

164 Castro Mendes, *Teoria Geral do Direito Civil*, pp. 366–367.

165 Pires de Lima/Antunes Varela, Código Civil Anotado, I, 4.ª ed, 1997, p. 233.

166 Carlos Mota Pinto, Teoria Geral do Direito Civil, (António Pinto Monteiro e Paulo Mota Pinto), 4.ª ed, 2005, pp. 441–454.

167 Ferreira de Almeida, *Texto e Enunciado na Teoria do Negócio Jurídico*, p. 189.

168 Hörster, *A Parte Geral do Código Civil Português*, pp. 509–510.

169 Ibid., pp. 509–510.

to interpret contracts. Interpretation is a complex operation with different important factors, such as concrete declarations, the whole of the contract, the context of its formation, the self-executing rules that the contract prescribes, contractual practice, preliminary negotiations, the text of the declarations, the way the contract is executed and the subsequent acts of the execution, the type of contract, and how the contact fits in with similar contracts concluded between the parties.[170]

The formula of Art. 236.°/1 *in fine* introduces and underlines the importance of good faith (the declaration of one party is understood in the sense that the other party, acting in a reasonable way, could attribute to it). Good faith can be also inferred from Art. 236.°/1 CC in conformity with the sense which he could reasonably attribute to it in the circumstances, as a declaration of a particular tenor made to him by that other person. To determine what one party could reasonably expect from the other, all types of proof can be used. In two important decisions, Portuguese courts have determined that contractual interpretation must comply with good faith.[171] Because the four articles concerning the interpretation of contract might not be enough to arrive at an interpretation of a contract, good faith has an enormous role in helping to solve cases that are not directly solved by the rules concerning interpretation of contract.[172]

The Portuguese Civil Code does not specifically address the issue of extrinsic evidence. However, Art. 236.°/1 CC states that all relevant circumstances of the case, including the negotiations, any practices the parties have established between themselves, usages and the subsequent conduct of the parties can be taken into consideration when assessing the intention of the parties. Portuguese courts appeal to a contractual interpretation that not only gives importance to literal aspects but is also capable of giving relevance to concrete circumstances.[173] The meaning and the effect of the written agreement will also be determined by the literal interpretation of the words. If the contract is unambiguous, the court will not even admit evidence of what the parties may have thought the meaning to be.

12. SCOTLAND

The law of interpretation of contract in Scotland is part of the common law, i.e. the rules have been developed incrementally over time in a multitude of cases.

---

170 Menezes Cordeiro, *Tratado de Direito Civil Português*, p. 717.

171 RLx 2 October 1997 (Eduardo Baptista), CJ XXII and RLx 22 January 1998 (Soares Curado).

172 RLx 22 January 1998 (Soares Curado), CJ XXIII (1998), 1, 89–93; STJ 27 January 2015 (Maria Clara Sottomayor); STJ 7 December 2016 (Olindo Geraldes). See Menezes Cordeiro, *Tratado de Direito Civil Português*, p. 717.

173 Menezes Cordeiro, *Tratado de Direito Civil Português*, p. 717.

The authoritative cases are principally those decided by the higher levels of the Scottish courts, namely the Inner House of the Court of Session and the House of Lords/UK Supreme Court. In an area such as this where there are few (if any) structural differences between Scots and English law, English cases are highly persuasive, and are treated as leading authorities in Scots law. Legislation has a marginal role to play.[174]

Interpretation in the Scottish courts is a unitary exercise,[175] in which the court seeks to give to contract terms their natural and ordinary meaning,[176] in light of the terms of the contract as a whole.[177] The court will take into account the way in which the disputed clause inter-relates with the other clauses of the contract.

The court will also take into account the context, sometimes described as the factual matrix, including the circumstances surrounding the formation of the contract: 'what the parties said or did at the time, and all relevant contemporary circumstances'.[178] The court considers the background knowledge of the parties or the background knowledge which ought reasonably to have been available to them at the time they entered into the contract. That background material is interpreted objectively, i.e. in light of what reasonable contracting parties in the position of the contracting parties would have understood the material to mean. The courts do not seek to apply what the parties themselves subjectively understood it to mean.

Arguably, the contextual approach to interpretation reached its high-water mark in the UK in 1998 in *Investors Compensation Scheme Ltd v West Bromwich Building Society*.[179] Context continues to be important: Lord Hodge stated in the Supreme Court case *Wood v Capita Insurance Services Ltd* in 2017:

> it is necessary to place the clause in the context of the contract as a whole, to examine the clause in more detail and to consider whether the wider relevant factual matrix gives guidance as to its meaning in order to consider the implications of the rival interpretations.[180]

---

174 Contract (Scotland) Act 1997. The main relevance of this Act to interpretation lies in its regulation of entire agreement clauses, see s. 1.

175 *Rainy Sky SA v Kookmin Bank* [2011] UKSC 50; [2011] 1 WLR 2900, paras. 20–21 per Lord Clarke.

176 *Charter Reinsurance v Fagan* [1997] AC 313 at 384 per Lord Clyde; McBryde, *The Law of Contract in Scotland*, para. 8-25.

177 *Taylor v Secretary of State for Scotland* 2000 SC (HL) 139; *Modern Engineering v Gilbert-Ash* [1974] AC 689, 703 per Lord Morris; McBryde, *Contract*, para. 8-18.

178 McBryde, *Contract*, para. 8-23.

179 [1998] 1 WLR 896.

180 *Wood v Capita Insurance Services Ltd* [2017] UKSC 24; [2017] 2 WLR 1095 at para. 26.

Since the *ICS* decision, however, there has been a perceptible decrease in the emphasis of the context and concomitant reassertion of the importance of the actual wording of the contract.[181]

A particularly controversial issue has been the use by the courts of a 'commercially sensible construction'. Historically, such an approach has involved ascertaining the meaning which the terms of that contract would convey to a reasonable and objective businessperson standing in the shoes of the contracting parties.[182] The role of business common sense has fluctuated in several UK Supreme Court appeals. In *Rainy Sky SA v Kookmin Bank*, Lord Clarke suggested that, where there are two competing possible constructions, the court is entitled to select the one which accords with commercial common sense.[183] While *Rainy Sky* remains authoritative, in later cases the Supreme Court has qualified it in certain respects. In *Arnold v Britton*, the Court emphasised the importance of language and warned against the parties and the courts inventing drafting infelicities in order to be able to have recourse to commercial common sense.[184] Following this case, it seemed to be more difficult to persuade the court that there were, in fact, two competing interpretations. In *Wood v Capita Insurance Services Ltd*, while suggesting that commercial common sense could help to identify the purpose of a provision and how it would operate in practice, Lord Hodge stated: '[b]ut in the tug o' war of commercial negotiation, business common sense can rarely assist the court in ascertaining on which side of the line the centre line marking on the tug o' war rope lay, when the negotiations ended'.[185]

The rise and fall of commercial common sense in the UK Supreme Court has been mirrored in the Scottish courts. In *Grove Investments Ltd v Cape Building Products Ltd* the Inner House, using the commercially sensible construction, came close to substituting for the disputed clause the court's conception of what would be reasonable in the circumstances.[186] Influenced by the Supreme Court's narrower approach in *Arnold v Britton*, a differently constituted bench of the same court later appeared to deliver a rebuke: '[c]are must be taken to avoid

---

181 For example, in *Arnold v Britton* [2015] UKSC 36; [2015] AC 1619.

182 *Investors Compensation Scheme Ltd v West Bromwich Building Society* [1998] 1 WLR 896, 912–913; *Rainy Sky SA v Kookmin Bank* [2011] UKSC 50; [2011] 1 WLR 2900, 2908E–G per Lord Clarke; *Melville Dundas Ltd v Hotel Corporation of Edinburgh Ltd* 2007 SC 12, 23 at para. 17 per Lord Drummond Young.

183 [2011] UKSC 50; [2011] 1 WLR 2900, 2908E–G.

184 [2015] UKSC 36; [2015] AC 1619; Connal, 'Has the Rainy Sky Dried up? Arnold v Britton and commercial interpretation'.

185 [2017] UKSC 24; [2017] 2 WLR 1095 at para. 28.

186 *Grove Investments Ltd v Cape Building Products Ltd* [2014] CSIH 43; 2014 Hous LR 35, and see Macgregor, 'Crossing the line between business common sense and perceived fairness in contractual interpretation'.

reading anything said in *Grove Investments* as being to the effect that the court can correct a bad bargain or even an unfair one; there is no general rule that a commercial contract requires to be fair'.[187] Although most recent Scottish Inner House cases have followed *Arnold v Britton*, giving to commercial common sense a relatively narrow role,[188] there are examples of cases in which Scottish judges have failed to follow the Supreme Court.[189] It appears that the role of commercial common sense in Scotland is not yet settled.

Certain types of evidence are not admissible in the interpretative exercise, namely evidence of subjective intentions of the parties,[190] pre-contractual negotiations (what are generally known as 'prior communings'),[191] and the conduct of the parties post-dating formation.[192] The attitude of the courts to this final type of evidence has not always been consistent. Despite a number of judicial statements confirming its exclusion,[193] it has in several cases been admitted.[194] Confirmation that it is excluded was given in a Scottish appeal to the Supreme Court.[195]

---

187 *@SIPP Pension Trustees Ltd v Insight Travel Services Ltd* [2015] CSIH 91; 2016 SC 243 per Lady Smith, delivering the opinion of the Court, para. 44; Richardson, 'Commercial common sense revisited: further developments in contract interpretation and commercial leasing'.

188 *@SIPP Pension Trustees Ltd v Insight Travel Services Ltd* [2015] CSIH 91; 2016 SC 243; *Gyle Shopping Centre General Partners Ltd v Marks & Spencer plc* [2016] CSIH 19; *AWG Business Centres Ltd v Regus Caledonia Ltd and Cheshire West and Cheshire Council* [2017] CSIH 22; *Hill v Stewart Milne Group Ltd and Anor* [2016] CSIH 35; 2017 SCLR 92;

189 See, for example, Lord Drummond Young in *Grant v International Insurance Company of Hanover* [2019] CSIH 9; and Lord President Carloway in *Scanmudring AS v James Fisher MFE Ltd* [2019] CSIH 10. See also *HOE International Ltd v Andersen* [2017] CSIH 9; 2017 SC 313, criticised in this respect by Richardson, 'Commercial common sense in contractual interpretation: further views from the Inner House'.

190 Gloag, *The Law of Contract*, p. 398.

191 *Inglis v Buttery* (1877) 5 R 58 per Lord Gifford at 59–60, approved by Lord Blackburn 5 R HL 87 at 102; *Prenn v Simmonds* [1971] 1 WLR 1381, 1384 per Lord Wilberforce.

192 McBryde, *Contract*, paras. 8-30–8-33.

193 *Eurocopy Rentals v Streamline Shipping Agencies Ltd* (2001) GWD 28-1121; *Quantum Claims Compensation Specialists Ltd v Wren Insurance Services* (2011) CSOH 61 per Lord Hodge at para. 26, and see Gloag, *Contract*, p. 375.

194 The Scottish Law Commission Report, *Interpretation in Private Law* (Scot Law Com No. 160, 1997), lists (at para. 2.27, n. 55) the following cases in which such evidence was admitted: *Heriot's Hospital v McDonald* (1830) 4 W & S 98; *Scott v Howard* (1881) 8 R (HL) 59 at 67; *Clyde Navigation Trs v Laird & Son* (1883) 10 R (HL) 77; *Hunter v Barron's Trs* (1886) 13 R 883 at 892; *Jopp's Trs v Edmond* (1888) 15 R 271 at 282; *Dowling v Henderson* (1890) 17 R 921; *Mackenzie v Lidell* (1893) 10 R 705 at 714; *Macgill v Park* (1899) 2 F 272 at 275; *North British Railway Co v Magistrates of Edinburgh* 1920 SC 409 at 425; *Welwood's Trs v Mungall* 1921 SC 911 at 929; *Watters v Watters* 1927 SC 310; *A M Carmichael Ltd v Lord Advocate* 1948 SLT (Notes) 88; and *Smith v Johnstone* 1949 SLT (Notes) 11.

195 *Lloyds TSB Foundation for Scotland v Lloyds Banking Group plc* [2013] UKSC 3; [2013] 1 WLR 366 at para. 17 per Lord Mance.

13. SOUTH AFRICA

The South African Supreme Court of Appeal has recently pronounced on the correct approach to interpretation.[196] The purpose of the process is to ascertain the meaning which a provision would convey to a reasonable person in the position of the contracting parties.[197] The point of departure is to consider the language of the provision itself, read in context and taking into account its apparent purpose and the 'background to the preparation and production of the document'[198] (evidence relating to the last factor has also been described as evidence of the circumstances surrounding the conclusion of the contract[199] or, more concisely, the 'factual matrix' or 'context'[200]). If a provision has more than one possible meaning, each possibility should be considered in light of all these factors.[201]

This description merits some explanatory comment. First, interpretation is regarded as a matter of law.[202] Secondly, the process is objective.[203] Thirdly, no reference is made to the purpose of interpretation as involving the search for the parties' common intention, because such a search is thought to be counter-productive.[204] Finally, ambiguity or uncertainty of meaning is no

196 In judgments delivered by Wallis JA in *Natal Joint Municipal Pension Fund v Endumeni Municipality* 2012 4 SA 593 (SCA) and *Bothma-Batho Transport (Edms) Bpk v S Bothma & Seun Transport (Edms) Bpk* 2014 2 SA 494 (SCA). The correctness of the approach adopted in these judgments has also been confirmed by the Constitutional Court, most recently in *Airports Company South Africa v Big Five Duty Free (Pty) Ltd* [2018] ZACC 33 para. 29. In Wallis, 'What's in a word?', pp. 683–685, it is clear that the author's views are closely aligned with those of Lord Hoffmann, either writing extra-judicially (Hoffmann, 'The intolerable wrestle with words and meanings', p. 656) or in judgment (*Investors Compensation Scheme v West Bromwich Building Society* [1998] 1 WLR 896 (HL)).

197 *Comwezi Security Services (Pty) Ltd v Cape Empowerment Trust Ltd* (759/11) [2012] ZASCA 126 (21-09-2012) para. 15; Wallis 'What's in a word?', pp. 682, 686.

198 *Natal Joint Municipal Pension Fund v Endumeni Municipality* 2012 4 SA 593 (SCA) para. 18.

199 Ibid.

200 *KPMG Chartered Accountants (SA) v Securefin Ltd* 2009 4 SA 399 (SCA) para. 39.

201 *Natal Joint Municipal Pension Fund v Endumeni Municipality* 2012 4 SA 593 (SCA) para. 18. These are the primary interpretative factors; secondary factors are discussed in Case 2, Question 1 and tertiary factors in Case 5, Question 2.

202 *KPMG Chartered Accountants (SA) v Securefin Ltd* 2009 4 SA 399 (SCA) para. 39.

203 Apparently, this accords with the objective approach adopted to contract formation as well as the objective determination of the content of a contract (e.g. whether it contains a 'tacit' term, that is, a term which is based on the presumed intention of the parties) – see Wallis, 'What's in a word?', p. 676. The correctness of these assumptions is debatable (for tacit terms, see Case 10; for the view that the point of departure to contract formation in South African law is subjective, see Van Huyssteen et al., *Contract*, p. 21; Hutchison, 'Nature and basis of Contract', p. 20).

204 The traditional approach to contractual interpretation in South African law emphasised that the goal of interpretation was to ascertain the common intention of the parties, albeit from the language used in the contract (*Coopers & Lybrand v Bryant* 1995 3 SA 761 (A) 767D). Such a statement is now thought to be misleading because, amongst other things, the parties often have not thought about the possibility of a dispute as to the meaning of a provision

longer a prerequisite for the consideration of extrinsic evidence. Traditionally,[205] evidence explaining the origin and purpose of a provision could only be considered if an examination of the literal meaning and the intra-contractual context did not yield a definitive result. This was regarded as evidence of 'background circumstances'. Only if the contractual provision remained ambiguous after a consideration of this evidence could a court consider evidence of 'surrounding circumstances', including evidence of the parties' prior negotiations and their conduct subsequent to contract conclusion.[206] This distinction between 'background' and 'surrounding' circumstances was abolished in *KPMG Chartered Accountants (SA) v Securefin Ltd*,[207] for an approach which allows evidence of 'context' or the 'factual matrix' as a matter of course. Although the exact scope of the evidence which may be considered as part of the context remains unclear,[208] the abolition of the distinction between different kinds of extrinsic evidence means that the language of the provision and the context are considered from the outset, with neither predominating over the other.[209]

While it is generally agreed that the revised approach to interpretation is 'a unitary endeavour requiring the consideration of text, context and purpose',[210] some judgments nevertheless continue to refer to the search for the parties' common intention as the primary aim of the interpretative exercise.[211] To what extent this preference for a subjective approach to contractual interpretation serves as implicit criticism of the current objective approach is uncertain; whether the former approach would result in a more liberal attitude towards the admissibility of extrinsic evidence now that ambiguity is no longer a requirement is equally uncertain.

One final comment should be made. The South African common law is the primary source of the rules regarding interpretation. This bears emphasising,

---

and therefore a search for a 'common intention' is rendered nugatory. Further reasons for the statement in the main text are provided in Wallis, 'What's in a word?', p. 675; *Natal Joint Municipal Pension Fund v Endumeni Municipality* 2012 4 SA 593 (SCA) paras. 20–24.

205 The rules relating to the admission of extrinsic evidence to aid interpretation are summarised in *Coopers & Lybrand v Bryant* 1995 3 SA 761 (A) 768B–E.

206 These rules were not applied consistently – cf. the judgments of Heher AJA and Lewis AJA in *Van der Westhuizen v Arnold* 2002 6 SA 453 (SCA), in which both judges, using the same rules relating to extrinsic evidence, came to different conclusions regarding the meaning of a clause.

207 2009 4 SA 399 (SCA) para. 39. According to Harms DP, the distinction was artificial and the terms vague and confusing.

208 See Case 3, Question 1.

209 *Natal Joint Municipal Pension Fund v Endumeni Municipality* 2012 4 SA 593 (SCA) para. 19.

210 *Butterbridge (Pty) Ltd v Masilo and Others NNO* 2015 2 SA 396 (GNP) para. 8.

211 *North East Finance (Pty) Ltd v Standard Bank of South Africa Ltd* 2013 5 SA 1 (SCA) paras. 24–25; *Novartis SA (Pty) Ltd v Maphil Trading (Pty) Ltd* 2016 1 SA 518 (SCA) para. 27; *Unica Iron and Steel (Pty) Ltd v Mirchandani* 2016 2 SA 307 (SCA) para 21. An attempt to explain this lack of unanimity is provided by Myburgh, 'Contractual interpretation', p. 514.

because it is not clear how the revised approach to contractual interpretation will affect accepted conclusions relating to certain interpretation problems. As a result, some of the answers to the questions posed are necessarily speculative.

14. SPAIN

14.1. LEGAL FORMANTS

14.1.1. Rules on Interpretation of Contracts in Spanish Law

The legal rules on interpretation of contracts in Spanish law are contained in Arts. 1.281–1.289 of the Código Civil (CC) [Civil Code] (in Book IV: Obligations and contracts), which are applicable to civil contracts and business contracts. The Código de Comercio (CCom) [Code of Commerce] does not contain a specific set of rules on interpretation for business contracts. However, there are two specific rules on interpretation for business contracts: Arts. 57 and 59. For the rest of the questions, the interpretation formants for business contracts are ruled by the CC. Art. 50 CCom claims that 'business contracts, in all matters related to … interpretation, shall be governed in all matters not specifically set forth in this Code or in the special laws, by the general rules of ordinary Civil Law'. Therefore, the CC is of subsidiary application. Finally, Art. 6 of the Ley General de Condiciones, Generales de la Contratación (LGCGC) [Standard Contracts Act] is applicable to both business contracts and civil contracts.

14.1.2. Subjective Method of Interpretation versus Objective Method

The rules of interpretation included in the CC combine the subjective method, according to which pre-eminence is given to the common and real intention of the parties, and the objective method, which uses different references to objective *criteria* to attribute a certain meaning in order to overcome any ambiguity or obscurity.[212]

14.1.3. Specific Rules on Interpretation of Business Contracts in the CCom

Art. 57 CCom contains the principle of 'buena fe' [good faith]:

(1) Business contracts must be performed and fulfilled in good faith, pursuant to the terms under which they were made and drafted, with mutual confidence. This rule implies good faith in objective terms.

---

212 Díez-Picazo, *Fundamentos*, p. 497.

(2) The interpreter must pay attention mainly to the terms under which they were made and drafted, without misinterpreting them through arbitrary constructions of the correct, proper and usual sense of the words said or written. Additionally, attention must be paid to the economic function of the contract that both parties pursued.[213]
(3) The interpretation should not restrict the effects naturally arising from the way in which the parties would have explained their will and contracted their obligations.

Art. 59 CCom is a closing rule for business contracts insofar as where any doubts arise that cannot be resolved according to the terms established in Art. 2 CCom, the matter shall be decided in favour of the debtor (*favor debitoris* principle).

14.1.4. Most Important and General Principles on Interpretation of Contracts

These are as follows:

(1) the search for the real and common intention of the parties at the time of the conclusion of the contract, according to Arts. 1.281 and 1.282 CC;[214]
(2) the principle of maintenance of the contract (Art. 1.284 CC), in consequence of which all useless interpretations shall be rejected;[215]
(3) the principle of 'buena fe' [good faith].

The CC does not contain the good faith principle among the rules on interpretation of contracts, but no doubt exists as to the relevance of that principle for the interpretation of any contract.[216] Scholars and case law consider that Art. 1.258 CC provides the general legal reference to 'buena fe'. According to this article, contracts bind the parties, not just to the performance of the matters expressly agreed therein, but also to all consequences which, by their nature, are in accordance with good faith, custom and the law.[217]

Another provision, Art. 1.288 CC, is an application of this principle because it includes the classical rule of *interpretatio contra proferentem* or

213 Uría et al., *Curso*, p. 44; Sánchez Calero, *Instituciones*, p. 135.
214 López y López, *Comentarios*, pp. 24–28.
215 The maintenance of contract principle may be found explicitly here: STS 22.04.2013, ECLI:ES:TS:2014:2246; STS (Plenary Session), 15.01.2013, ECLI: ES:TS:2013:1153; STS 29.01.2015, ECLI:ES:TS:2015:835 – this decision quotes the PECL and Vienna Convention.
216 Díez-Picazo, *Fundamentos*, pp. 499–500.
217 On good faith in contractual interpretation: STS 30.01.2003 (RJ 2003\2024); STS 30.01.2017 (RJ 2017\371).

contra stipulatorem.[218] Therefore, the 'buena fe' principle may determine the interpretation of a contract, especially regarding obscure clauses or ambiguous clauses, terms or expressions.[219] It makes one party responsible for her or his declaration because it creates confidence in the other party, who trusts in what is said and done by the former (confidence principle).[220]

14.2. SIGNIFICANT RECENT DEVELOPMENTS IN THE INTERPRETATION OF CONTRACTS

In January 2009, the Minister of Justice published a Proposal for the Modernisation of the Spanish Civil Code on Obligations and Contracts, containing a set of rules on interpretation of contracts (Arts. 1.278–1.281). This reform was never enacted. As its Preamble said, it was inspired by the CSIG and PECL (i.e. Art. 1.279 is practically identical to Art. 5:102 PECL, and Art. 1281 is identical to Art. 5:107 PECL on linguistic discrepancies).

14.3. DOCTRINAL CONSIDERATIONS

14.3.1. Nature of Interpretation Rules

At the beginning of the 20th century, the interpretation rules were considered mere pieces of advice based on common sense addressed to the judges as an orientation guide to help them in their daily task of interpretation. Since the 1960s, interpretation rules have been considered truly legal rules and binding.[221]

14.3.2. Types of Interpretation

Parties may carry out an interpretation of their own contract after its conclusion. This is called 'interpretación auténtica' [authentic interpretation]. The interpretation carried out by the judge is binding, but one by scholars is not binding ('auténtica').

218 On this rule, see: STS 15.01.2013, ECLI:ES:TS:2013:1153; STS 12.04.2013, ECLI:ES:TS:2013:1899; STS 01.07.2015, ECLI:ES:TS:2015:3152; STS 09.09.2015, ECLI:ES:TS:2015:3711; Auto 30.03.2016, ECLI:ES:TS:2016:2340A; STS 04.05.2017, ECLI:ES:TS:2017:1858.

219 López y López, 'De la interpretación', p. 609.

220 On the good faith principle as a decisive criterion on interpretation and execution of a contract: STS 14.01.2014.

221 De Castro y Bravo, *El negocio jurídico*, p. 80.

14.3.3. *Rationale and Historical Origin*

The legal rules on interpretation of contracts contained in the CC have their remote origin in Roman law, but it was the ideas of the French jurist, Pothier, which influenced the Spanish rules on interpretation.[222] He summarised Domat's thinking in 15 rules based on the *Corpus Iuris Civilis* (Emperor Justinian, ca. 533 AD).[223]

Federico de Castro y Bravo,[224] one of the leading scholars of the 20th century, was greatly influential on the issue of interpretation, and the Italian scholar Emilio Betti was very influential in legal scholarship in Spain as well.

14.3.4. *Question of Law or Question of Fact*

Interpretation of contracts is considered a question of fact. As a consequence, it is a function attached to 'tribunales de instancia' [instance courts] and cannot be revised by the Tribunal Supremo (TS) [Supreme Court], which can only resolve questions related to interpretation whenever one party to the contract can demonstrate that the meaning given to it by an instance court is illogical, irrational, arbitrary or absolutely against the legal rules on interpretation of contracts. Thus, the TS only considers legal issues related to interpretation, because the interpretation itself is carried out by the instance courts. This is repeated constantly in Supreme Court resolutions.[225]

An interesting nuance is that the interpretation given by the judge at first or second instance prevails even if there are reasonable doubts about its accuracy, unless, as noted above, it is absurd, arbitrary, illogical or infringes legal precepts. Therefore, the interpretation of the trial judge prevails even if the interpretation accepted in the judgment is not the only one possible, or if there could be

---

[222] *Traité des obligations*, in Oeuvres de Pothier II 8 (1883) 48 et seq.

[223] J. Miquel, 'La interpretación de los contratos. Vinculación entre teoría y práctica', p. 799.

[224] *El negocio jurídico* and *El Derecho civil de España* (2 vols.).

[225] The most recent Supreme Court cases are: STS 12.02.2013, ECLI:ES:TS:2013:594; STS 25.02.2013, ECLI:ES:TS:2013:672; STS 20.05.2013, ECLI:ES:TS:2013:2261; STS 26.11.2013, ECLI:ES:TS:2013:5647; STS 17.01.2014, ECLI:ES:TS:2014:192; STS 23.01.2014, ECLI:ES:TS:2014:227; STS 23.05.2014, ECLI:ES:TS:2014:2134; STS 05.11.2014, ECLI:ES:TS:2014:5491; STS 04.11.2014, ECLI:ES:TS:2014:4255; STS 19.11.2014, ECLI:ES:TS:2014:4846; STS 06.02.2015, ECLI:ES:TS:2015:264; STS 04.02.2015, ECLI:ES:TS:2015:204; STS 17.03.2015, ECLI:ES:TS:2015:1706; STS 18.03.2015, ECLI:ES:TS:2015:1081; STS 25.03.2015, ECLI:ES:TS:2015:1088; STS 01.04.2015, ECLI:ES:TS:2015:1236; STS 15.06.2015, ECLI:ES:TS:2015:2575; STS 29.06.2015, ECLI:ES:TS:2015:3150; STS 30.12.2015, ECLI:ES:TS:2015:5803; STS 16.12.2015, ECLI:ES:TS:2015:5686; STS 28.01.2016, ECLI:ES:TS:2016:333; STS 07.04.2016, ECLI:ES:TS:2016:1501; STS 05.05.2016, ECLI:ES:TS:2016:1904; STS 27.06.2016, ECLI:ES:TS:2016:3137; STS 20.07.2017, ECLI:ES:TS:2017:3023.

reasonable doubt about its accuracy. It is not about whether there is a better interpretation, but that the first or second instance interpretation is accepted.[226]

Consequently, it is only exceptionally that the Supreme Court will agree to revise the interpretation of the contract, and rarely will it correct the interpretation given by the trial judge. In fact, it only does so when there is an error of legal evaluation in the interpretation of the contract.[227]

14.3.5. *Hierarchy of the Interpretative Formants*

It is generally understood that there is no hierarchy between the different interpretation rules. All the interpretation rules are concurrent and there is no preference for one or another in the sense that subjective interpretation factors have no preference to objective ones. Any rule can play a role in a combined way in discovering the common intention of the parties. This is commonly accepted by doctrine,[228] with some exceptions, including those who think that the subjective method must prevail and the interpreter can only turn to objective rules in a subsidiary way.[229]

In interpreting the contract, the real common intention of the parties must be found projected through the whole of the contract, which is considered as a logical unit and not as a mere collection of clauses.

The general rules for interpretation are that there should first be a literal interpretation of the contract carried out using the grammatical meaning of the terms.[230] This 'grammatical' interpretation is based on the literal.[231] The literal interpretation prevails if the terms are clear and do not leave any doubt about what the intention of the contracting parties is.[232] In these cases, the

---

226 This affirmation may be found in these judgments: STS 12.04.2013, ECLI:ES:TS:2013:207; STS 06.05.2013, ECLI:ES:TS:2013:2491; STS 16.10.2013, ECLI:ES:TS:2013:5472; STS 08.04.2015, ECLI:ES:TS:2015:1410; STS 10.03.2016, ECLI:ES:TS:2016:970.

227 For example in these cases: STS 08.04.2013, ECLI:ES:TS:2013:3513 (in this case the interpretation was corrected in cassation because the interpretation of the contractual clause contradicted the literal wording that clearly reflected the will of the contracting parties); STS 16.04.2015, ECLI:ES:TS:2015:2213 (this is an important sentence because it stablishes the 'doctrina jurisprudencial sobre interpretación'); STS 02.07.2015, ECLI:ES:TS:2015:3203; STS 02.12.2015, ECLI:ES:TS:2015:5149; STS 09.05.2016, ECLI:ES:TS:2016:2063; STS 14.03.2017, ECLI:ES:TS:2017:978.

228 De Castro y Bravo, *El negocio*, pp. 62–65; Díez-Picazo, *Fundamentos*, p. 497; Jordano Barea, *Comentario*, p. 15.

229 López y López, 'De la interpretación', p. 697. A summary of Spanish doctrine on contractual interpretation can be found in: STS 16.04.2015, ECLI:ES:TS:2015:2213. It is one of the most important judgments given in recent years and establishes the governing jurisprudence on contractual interpretation.

230 STS 01.03.2018, ECLI:ES:TS:2018:647.

231 STS 12.11.2014, ECLI:ES:TS:2014:4892.

232 STS 19.04.2013, ECLI:ES:TS:2013:2158; STS 22.04.2013, ECLI:ES:TS:2013:2411; STS 14.05.2014, ECLI:ES:TS:2014:1914; STS 06.02.2013, ECLI:ES:TS:2013:428; STS

Supreme Court states that 'the literal interpretation is the starting point and also the point of arrival'.[233] However, when interpreting the contract, the grammatical interpretation is not sufficient: the real common intention of the parties must be found using the other legal rules,[234] such as considering the contract as a whole and the rest of the objective criteria.[235]

15. SWEDEN

The question of 'avtalstolkning' [contract interpretation] is left unaddressed by the Swedish legislator.[236] The Contracts Act (1915:218) – the principal piece of legislation in the field of 'avtalsrätt' [contract law] – is silent on the matter, and the preparatory works, normally a source of law of great importance to Swedish lawyers, simply state that, when interpretation is due, all relevant circumstances should be considered.[237]

Given this state of affairs, *case law* is, in effect, the primary source of law as far as 'avtalstolkning' is concerned. Traditionally, however, the courts have been reluctant to address these issues at the abstract level. As a result, there really is no system of explicit norms in the field. The factual circumstances of the individual case – the text and context – are typically at the centre of the courts' attention and, by extension, interpretation becomes a matter of *letting* these circumstances speak. As the Supreme Court stated in NJA 2018 p. 834, several diverse factors are to be considered when interpreting a contract, and which factor is to be accorded decisive weight cannot be stated in general terms – the decision must be made on the basis of an overall assessment in the individual case.

20.02.2014, ECLI:ES:TS:2014:631; STS 24.11.2014, ECLI:ES:TS:2014:5756; STS 23.02.2015, ECLI:ES:TS:2015:1079; STS 14.12.2015, ECLI:ES:TS:2015:5440; STS 21.03.2018, ECLI:ES:TS:2018:1046.

233 STS 22.02.2013, ECLI:ES:TS:2013:423; STS 16.04.2015, ECLI:ES:TS:2015:2213 (important sentence); STS 28.03.2016, ECLI:ES:TS:2016:1320.

234 STS 05.06.2013, ECLI:ES:TS:2013:3126; STS 13.10.2014, ECLI:ES:TS:2014:3909; STS 09.03.2015, ECLI:ES:TS:2015:1403; STS 08.06.2016, ECLI:ES:TS:2016:2624; STS 04.02.2016, ECLI:ES:TS:2016:332; STS 03.03.2016, ECLI:ES:TS:2016:978.

235 STS 19.05.2015, ECLI:ES:TS:2015:2055; STS 11.06.2015, ECLI:ES:TS:2015:2453; STS 09.12.2014, ECLI:ES:TS:2014:5419; STS 18.07.2013, ECLI:ES:TS:2013:4245; STS 29.01.2015, ECLI:ES:TS:2015:835; STS 20.05.2015, ECLI:ES:TS:2015:3159; STS 03.06.2016, ECLI:ES:TS:2016:256; STS 13.04.2016, ECLI:ES:TS:2016:1648; STS 30.03.2016, ECLI:ES:TS:2016:1323.

236 Outside of the commercial sphere, there is one exception (found in Section 10 of the Contract Terms in Consumer Relations Act (1994:1512) which contains a variation of the 'oklarhetsregel' [unclarity rule]).

237 Förslag till lag om avtal (1914) p. 140.

Granted, in the pioneering case NJA 1999 p. 35, the Supreme Court asserted a hierarchy of sorts, a hierarchy of norms, or a list of considerations to be made,[238] and this decision has been followed by a string of cases reinforcing the pattern.[239] Generally, this development echoes the manner in which the subject of contract interpretation is typically treated in legal doctrine.[240] Prevalence, the textbooks inform us, shall be given to the common intention of the parties, where it is possible to establish such an intention.[241] This is the principle of 'den gemensamma partsviljans företräde' [prevalence of the common intention of the parties]. An accessory to this principle is the 'dolusregeln' [dolus rule][242] – a rule of qualified bad faith: the concept of dolus entails insight into, i.e. factual knowledge of, some state of affairs, in the current context the understanding that the other party had of the agreement at the time of conclusion. The 'dolusregeln' holds the knowing party to the understanding of his counterpart. As can be gained from this, Swedish jurisprudence accords subjective elements priority, where possible to ascertain. If the materials available do not allow any conclusion as to the subjective content of the contract, recourse must be had to objective methods – a close reading of the contract with due reference to the relevant context, making use of the economic rationale of the contract, its purpose, the nature of things and other such objective standards. Up to this point, the methodological declarations offered by the Supreme Court in recent years conforms, roughly, with received academic opinion.

In addition, legal doctrine provide a few maxims of interpretation – rules of thumb to be used as a last resort. The most well-known are the 'oklarhetsregeln' [unclarity rule] and 'minimumregeln' [minimum rule]. They suggest, respectively, that the contract, when unclear, should be read against the party responsible for the lack of clarity and that, when determining the scope of a contractual obligation, the interpretation least burdensome for the party

---

238 The decisions in NJA 1991 p. 319 and NJA 1997 p. 382 can be regarded as precursors.

239 See e.g. NJA 2007 p. 35; NJA 2012 p. 3; NJA 2012 p. 597; NJA 2013 p. 271; NJA 2014 p. 960; NJA 2015 p. 741; NJA 2015 p. 862.

240 This is, perhaps, no coincidence. The 'referent' in NJA 1999 p. 35, i.e. the judge responsible for preparing the case, was Justice Håstad – a former professor of private law.

241 Adlercreutz and Gorton, *Avtalsrätt II*, p. 57 ff., Bernitz, *Standardavtalsrätt*, p. 78; Fohlin, *Avtalstolkning*, p. 36 ff.; Lehrberg, *Avtalstolkning*, p. 39 ff.; Samuelsson, *Tolkningslärans gåta*, p. 190. The importance and relevance of the common intention has been contested; see e.g. Grönfors, *Tolkning av fraktavtal*, p. 36 ff.; J. Ramberg and C. Ramberg, *Allmän avtalsrätt*, p. 147 ff.; J. Ramberg, *Avtalsautonomi och den dispositiva rätten*; J. Ramberg, *Avtalstolkningsmetoder*, p. 499 ff.

242 See Adlercreutz and Gorton, *Avtalsrätt II*, p. 132 ff.; Fohlin, *Avtalstolkning*, p. 52 ff.; Lehrberg, *Avtalstolkning*, p. 49 ff.; Vahlén, *Avtal och tolkning*, p. 292 ff. The leading case is NJA 1951 p. 282. The rule is confirmed by the Supreme Court in NJA 1999 p. 35; see also the special opinion of Justice Håstad in NJA 2006 p. 638. Cf. Section 6(2) of the Contracts Act.

subject to the obligation in question should be preferred.[243] Of these two, the courts only recognise the 'oklarhetsregeln' explicitly,[244] but it is seldom treated as a rule in any stricter sense; rather it figures as a recurring, to some extent formalised, argument, that factors in when the final judgment is made.[245]

In all, methodological declarations aside, the interpretation of contracts as it is actually performed by Swedish courts is very much a free-form exercise. Jan Hellner, arguably the leading authority on Swedish private law in the last hundred years, sums it up nicely when he concludes that 'the interpretation of contracts cannot be captured, not even in some general remarks'.[246]

16. EDITORIAL COMPARATIVE OBSERVATIONS

A comparison of the opening remarks of the various national reports brings to the fore several differences and similarities concerning some of the basic tenets of contract interpretation. These involve at least three aspects: the nature of the interpretation question, and the aims and the modalities of the methods of contract interpretation, or: the *what*, *why*, and *how*.

16.1. THE NATURE OF THE INTERPRETATION QUESTION

As to the nature of contract interpretation, the national reports indicate that it is a matter of fact, of law, or a combination of both. In France, Germany and Sweden, contract interpretation is primarily a factual matter. Consequently, notwithstanding certain judicial practices and scholarly reflections, no legally prescribed strategy for interpreting contracts exists. The Swedish and Netherlands reports indicate that, *ultimately, a court is free to weigh evidence.*

Most of the other reports, however, demonstrate a hybrid notion of contract interpretation. The Netherlands report observes that in the Dutch jurisdiction, interpretation is a matter of fact, in the sense that the Supreme Court will not review the lower court's interpretation. However, that report does point out that the Supreme Court can indeed review the procedural rules and legal reasoning the lower court employed. In that respect, the methods of contract interpretation have a legal dimension in the Netherlands. Likewise, the Italian reporter points

243 See Adlercreutz and Gorton, *Avtalsrätt II*, p. 110 ff.; Bernitz, *Standardavtalsrätt*, p. 88 ff.; Lehrberg, *Avtalstolkning*, p. 169 ff.; Vahlén, *Avtal och tolkning*, p. 271 ff. Cf. J. Ramberg and C. Ramberg, *Allmän avtalsrätt*, p. 170 f.

244 See e.g. NJA 1950 p. 86, NJA 1979 p. 483, NJA 1981 p. 323. Cf. NJA 2006 p. 53, NJA 2010 p. 416, where the Supreme Court emphasises that the 'oklarhetsregel' is to be used with caution.

245 NJA 2012 p. 3 offers a conspicuous example of this technique; see also NJA 2018 p. 834.

246 Hellner, 'The parol evidence rule och tolkning av skriftliga avtal i svensk rätt', p. 205.

out that even though any interpretation of a contract is answering a factual question, a higher court may review a lower court's interpretation methods by the applicable principles and rules of contract interpretation. The Spanish and South African reports seem to allude to a similar view. So does the Spanish report, with the qualification that a higher court may step in if the lower court's interpretation is absurd, arbitrary or illogical. In contrast, the French Supreme Court may only review a lower court's interpretation of unambiguous terms in a claim that this interpretation was made in error.

The reports additionally explicate the formal sources of the legal rules that apply to contract interpretation. They entail either case law alone, or a combination of case law and private law legislation. The civil code of several jurisdictions contains several rules for the interpretation of contracts, including in Croatia, France, Germany, Greece, Italy and Spain. If the Civil Code offers only general rules, these might further be supplemented with underlying principles and specific rules in case law, for example, in Spain. The fact that the Civil Code contains rules of interpretation does not necessarily make contract interpretation a matter of fact. In France, for example, the rules are guidelines rather than stipulations. Furthermore, the rules of the Civil Code might also have originated and thus been developed in case law preceding codification, such as in Poland. In contrast, in England and Wales, the Netherlands, Scotland and South Africa, the doctrines of contract interpretation have been developed solely through case law.

16.2. THE AIMS OF CONTRACT INTERPRETATION

As to the second aspect the opening remarks touch upon, the national reports suggest roughly three different aims of interpreting contracts. First, in most jurisdictions, the interpretation of a contract entails retrieving what the specific contracting parties actually intended the provisions of their contract to mean. The aim here is the common intention of the parties. The reports from Croatia, Finland, France, Germany, Greece, Italy, Poland, Spain and Sweden indicate as much.

Second, contract interpretation in other jurisdictions aims to establish instead what a reasonable person in the position of the actual parties would likely have understood the contractual provisions to mean. Courts take this approach in the common law jurisdiction of England and Wales and the mixed legal system of Scotland. The situation in South Africa is less clear, as some courts have referenced the actual intentions of the parties as the aim of contract interpretation. In any event, the difference between looking for the meaning the parties in fact attributed to the contractual language and how a reasonable person in their position would have intended the contract to mean is subtle. The Scottish respondents emphasise that the second aim, too, involves ascertaining the mutual intentions of the parties. Nonetheless, the criterion is not the meaning that the parties as a matter of fact attributed to the contract, but the meaning that they would have reasonably ascribed to the contract. In jurisdictions such as France, courts would only turn to seeking the meaning a reasonable person would attribute to the contract *after* the factual intentions of the parties could not be established.

The third type of aim is found in the Netherlands and Portuguese reports. In the Netherlands, the goal of contract interpretation is neither to retrieve the parties' actual intentions nor to establish their reasonable intentions, but rather to establish which meaning is reasonable for the parties to attribute to the contract. The difference between the second and third kind of interpretation aims might be obscured by the word 'reasonable', which appears in both descriptions. To clarify, the 'reasonable' intentions in the common law jurisdictions must be understood as sensible or rational intentions, while in the Netherlands jurisdiction 'reasonable' connotes fair or just expectations of the other parties' intentions. That is to say, in the Netherlands the question is upon which intentions the other parties could justifiably rely. The Greek report, which refers to standards of good faith as a secondary aim, refers to this approach as seeking 'normative meaning'. The Portuguese courts combine both forms of reasonableness: here the interpreter looks for the meaning that a reasonable as in sensible or rational person would attach to the contractual language, yet only if that reading is reasonable in terms of fair or just.

16.3. THE MODALITIES OF CONTRACT INTERPRETATION

When we turn to the modalities of contract interpretation, i.e. how the respective aims are to be achieved, we distinguish subjective interpretation factors, i.e. those that involve the intentions or expectations of the contracting parties, and objective factors, which are indicators of meaning beyond the parties' subjective experience.

As expected, among the national reports that have indicated that contract interpretation is aimed at uncovering the actual intentions of the specific contracting parties, most mention the significance of subjective elements. For example, in Croatia, Germany and Poland alike, the focus of contract interpretation is on uncovering the meaning that the contracting parties in reality agreed upon, rather than the semantic meaning of the contractual language. It is also no surprise that in the jurisdictions in which contract interpretation aims are to establish what a reasonable person would take the contract to mean, interpretation leans on objective rather than subjective elements.

However, the differences between the various jurisdictions are more nuanced than it appears on face value. First, looking to the parties' actual intentions does not exclude consideration of objective elements. For example, the Italian, Croatian, German, Greek, French and Polish reporters observe alike that when courts fail to establish the actual intentions of the contracting parties with sufficient certainty, the interpretation of contracts may take on a more objective character. Still, these reports point to different objective factors, ranging from considerations of reasonableness and business efficacy to legal principles of private law and established customs.

Second, in jurisdictions where courts will look to objective elements, the primary focus is not necessarily on the semantic meaning of the contractual language. The English and Scottish reporters all observe that the context and circumstances surrounding the closing or formation of a contract – the factual matrix – as well as the purpose of the contract play a more significant role than the textual or literal meaning of the contractual words. Likewise, although the South African reporter does point out that in this jurisdiction the language of the provision is the starting point of contract interpretation, this approach does not preclude taking account of extrinsic evidence of the purpose and context of the contract if the text turns out to be ambiguous. The Spanish report indicates a similar approach, observing that courts will hold the textual analysis to prevail over contrary extrinsic evidence if the contractual language is unambiguous.

Third, the aim of uncovering the actual intentions of the contracting parties does not prove inconsistent with methods that focus on the textual meaning of the contractual language. The Finnish report, for example, indicates that, even though the aim is retrieving the parties' common intention, the starting point of interpretation is an objective one: the words of the contract. Moreover, the Finnish and Spanish reports note that a court would not take into consideration extraneous evidence if the contractual language itself is unambiguous. Still, in Finland, the textual meaning is trumped by any diverging subjective meaning: the meaning that the parties actually intended to attribute to the contract. If a court fails to establish this subjective meaning, it will turn toward a more objective interpretation method, emphasising the meaning a reasonable person in the same circumstances as the parties would ascribe to the contract, similar to the primary aim of contract interpretation in the common law jurisdictions.

Similarly, the German, Greek and Swedish reports observe that uncovering the true intentions of the actual contracting parties begins with interpreting the textual meaning of the contract language. For instance, the German national reporters emphasise that contract interpretation is based on a rebuttable presumption that the contract reflects the will of the parties correctly and completely. Similarly, the Croatian report highlights that usually a court would first consider the will of the parties as expressed in the contract itself, and only then contextual circumstances. Additionally, the Netherlands respondent explains that under certain circumstances a Dutch judge might prioritise the meaning of the contractual language as well, namely when professional parties have negotiated extensively and have drafted a comprehensive contract or when the contract has legal consequences for parties who were not part of the negotiations. In Greece, Germany and Sweden, other factors will play a role only when the text supports multiple contrary interpretations. Here the various jurisdictions diverge, however. In Greece, the interpreter then turns to subjective factors, i.e. the actual intentions of the contracting parties in question. Still, a German and Swedish court would focus on objective elements instead, such as how the contract came to pass, and what the agreement purports to achieve. Likewise, in France, interpretation factors include, for example, consistency of the interpreted terms with other terms of the contract and with relevant usages.

In conclusion, it is worth pointing out that standards of good faith not only play a notable role in the Dutch and the Portuguese jurisdictions, i.e. the two jurisdictions where the aim of contract interpretation is establishing the intentions or expectations on which the contracting parties could justifiably rely. Good faith may also be a factor in jurisdictions where the interpretation of contracts serves other aims. In Greece, when the textual meaning of the contract and evidence of the actual intentions do not suffice to solve the interpretation question, the central objective factor will be the principle of good faith ('καλή πίστη'). Furthermore, the Polish and Spanish reporters point out that a principle of good faith plays into the principle of party autonomy, resulting in the standard that one party is bound by the trust or reliance that she or he freely decides to invoke in her/his contracting partner.

PART II

CASE STUDIES

CASE 1: JEWELLERS KING

'Premier' is the owner of numerous retail units in a local shopping centre. At present, it leases two units to two jewellers. It decides to lease a third unit for 15 years to 'Jewellers King', a company also operating a retail jewellery sales business. Clause 12(d) of the lease contract with Jewellers King provides: 'With regard to any of its retail units, Premier shall not lease any such unit – other than Jewellers King's unit and two other units only – for a use entailing the retail sale of jewellery.' Within 19 months of entering into the lease contract, Premier grants a lease of one of its other retail units to a fourth jeweller. Jewellers King is infuriated. It argues that Clause 12(d) prohibits Premier from granting another lease at the shopping centre to a jeweller. Premier is surprised. It argues that the phrase 'two other units only' refers to two units in addition to the three units that it is already leasing to Jewellers King and the two other jewellers. In effect, it concludes, under Clause 12(d) it is therefore permitted to let up to a total of five jewellery retail units. Jewellers King disagrees. It argues that the phrase 'two other units only' is a reference to the two units that were already *let to jewellers. Hence, since Jewellers King was the third jeweller to lease one of Premier's retail units, the total number of three jewellery retail units had been reached. Premier was thus prohibited from leasing any more retail units to other jewellers. Premier stands firm. In order to support its reading of Clause 12(d), it refers to the fifth recital of the preamble of the lease contract, which reads: 'Whereas Premier intends to let no more than a total of five units at the shopping centre for the purposes of the retail sale of jewellery'. Therefore, Premier argues, Clause 12(d) cannot be interpreted as having the effect that it is in breach of the lease contract by letting a fourth retail unit to a jeweller.*

1. *[Preamble] Assume that the language of Clause 12(d) is ambiguous. What role, if any, may the preamble play in corroborating Premier's interpretation of Clause 12(d)? Would it make a difference if it involved not a preamble but another Clause in the contract?*
2. *[Information Brochure] Would your answer be different if Premier had not referred to the preamble but rather to Premier's information brochure with similar text?*
3. *[The Contract's Purpose] Assume that neither the preamble nor an information brochure had mentioned anything relating to the purpose of Clause 12(d) of the lease contract. What role, if any, may Premier's reliance on the purpose or*

objective of Clause 12(d) of the lease contract, being that it was restricted to letting five units at the shopping centre, still have played in the interpretation of Clause 12(d)?

1. KEY ISSUES

The case concerns a dispute between a landlord and a tenant which takes place in the context of a retail park.[1] It is designed to provoke analysis of how a contractual purpose or objective can be relevant to the exercise of interpretation. In the first of the two questions asked, reporters were directed to consider the impact of information contained in (a) a preamble; and (b) another clause of the contract. A preamble might be useful not just because it 'sets the scene', but because it potentially reflects shared assumptions held by the contracting parties on the meaning and purpose of the contract. Of course, preambles may not be used in certain legal systems or, if they are, they may not be treated as legally relevant. By including alternatives (a) and (b), the case allows reporters to compare and contrast the effect of a preamble, on the one hand, and an ordinary clause of the contract on the other. This should highlight whether preambles, in the legal system in question, have a status which differs from ordinary clauses of the contract. In the second question, the focus moves beyond the four walls of the contract itself, directing reporters to consider the effect of an information brochure provided by the landlord to the tenant. This should highlight whether, in the legal system concerned, information drawn from the contract itself relating to purpose is treated differently from information outside the contract. Finally, in this case, reporters were asked to consider the relevance of the contractual purpose in the abstract, assuming instead that there is no evidence to support the existence or the import of that purpose.

2. CROATIA

Question 1: Preamble

Although the content of a contract is determined by the contracting parties themselves (within the limits set by the law), it is possible, as in the case at hand, that a dispute arises between them about the exact content of the contract, because they understand certain contractual clauses or the whole contract differently. In this case where the language of Clause 12(d) is disputed, the Croatian courts would apply the interpretation method envisaged under

---

1 The facts of Case 1 are loosely based on the case of *Warren James (Jewellers) Ltd v Overgate GP Ltd* [2010] CSOH 57, 2010 GWD 17–348 decided by the Scottish courts.

Art. 319(2) of the COA.[2] According to the prevailing opinion in legal scholarship, this statutory provision instructs the courts to look for the true common will of the contracting parties as the primary criterion (subjective criterion).[3] If this subjective criterion would result in two or more conflicting interpretations of the disputed contractual clause, the objective criterion should step in and point to the interpretation which is more in accordance with principles of the law on obligations (this combination of subjective and objective criteria is often referred to as mixed interpretation). The reason for this approach is the search for the true meaning and scope of a certain contractual clause, mentioned in the Opening Remarks, by considering, inter alia, the objective of the clause and the purpose the parties intended to achieve with it. According to legal scholarship and settled case law, in order to establish the common and true will of the parties, all contractual clauses need to be taken into account and considered together, irrespective of whether they form part of the contract or preamble.[4] This leads to the conclusion that Croatian judges would certainly take other clauses in the contract or preamble into account in interpreting Clause 12(d).

Question 2: Information Brochure

The answer would be the same if Premier had referred to Premier's information brochure with similar text. The *ratio* and the scope of a certain contractual clause are determined depending on the content of other contractual clauses or even clauses additional to the contract.[5] Since the parties can demonstrate

2 Although not relevant for this study on contract interpretation, it should be emphasised that prior to determining the common will of the parties, the courts will observe *ex officio* whether a contractual clause containing restrictions on leasing to other jewellers other than Jewellers King is valid in the context of competition law. Of relevance here are limits on the freedom to regulate obligations relationships and limits set by Art. 322(1) of the COA, according to which a contract that is contrary to the Constitution of the Republic of Croatia, to mandatory laws or to the morals of society is null and void unless the objective of the infringed rule refers to some other legal consequence or the law provides otherwise in such a case. Although there is no relevant provision within the *lex specialis*, namely the Lease and Sale of Business Premises Act (OG 125/11 and 64/15), such contractual clauses could be characterised as agreements distorting free market competition and thus contrary to the mandatory provisions of the Protection of Market Competition Act (OG Nos. 79/09 and 80/13), rendering such contracts null and void.

3 See County Court in Varaždin, Gž. 1212/08-2 of 10 February 2009; VSRH, Revr 434/08-2 of 24 September 2008; VSRH, Rev 946/05-2 of 4 July 2007; County Court in Varaždin, Gž. 1440/05-2 of 5 September 2005; VSRH, II Rev-17/01-2 of 11 December 2002; VSRH, Rev 2285/1995-2 of 21 September 1995; VTSRH, Pž-1370/93 of 15 June 1993. See also VSRH, Revt-95/2006-2 of 6 September 2007, where the court established that the contractual clause cannot be interpreted against the rules of logical thinking and against expected behaviour of persons who professionally pursue economic activity.

4 See VSRH, Rev 1422/2009-2 of 18 May 2011.

5 Perović, *Obligaciono pravo*, p. 372. See VSRH, Revr-291/03-2 of 26 November 2003. See also VSRH, Rev 1109/1994-2 of 7 September 1995, where the court established that the common

their will in various ways (Art. 249 of the COA), their motives, intent and goals can be determined from the words they used in the contract, but also from other forms in which they express their will,[6] such as the circumstances before or at the time the contract was concluded. According to Art. 256 of the COA,[7] Premier's information brochure would be qualified as an invitation to make an offer, which is relevant for the contract conclusion and consequently its interpretation. Ambiguous clauses must be interpreted in a way which corresponds to the content of the contract in general, its nature and subject matter and in the manner which would enable the contract to remain in force (*pacta sunt servanda*). Thus, in interpreting the contract or its clauses, the courts have a duty to aim at preserving the contract and its clauses rather than deprive them of their legal effects.

Question 3: The Contract's Purpose

Under the assumption that neither the preamble nor an information brochure had mentioned anything relating to the purpose of Clause 12(d) of the lease contract, Premier's reliance on the *purpose* or *objective* of Clause 12(d) of the lease contract, namely to allow for only five units at the shopping centre, would still have played an important role in the interpretation of Clause 12(d) and in the determination of the true common will of the parties. As already mentioned, in interpreting ambiguous contract terms, the Croatian courts apply additional special principles and criteria for contract interpretation developed by the case law and legal theory.[8] These criteria, which build on the general statutory principles, include inter alia reliance on the teleological method of interpretation in order to determine the purpose of the contract. Although the object of the interpretation is normally the parties' intent expressed and determined in the contract, the circumstances under which the contract was concluded, motives,

---

intention of the contracting parties has to be examined for the purpose of determining the true nature of the concluded contract and to eliminate conflicts between certain contracting provisions and to determine obligations deriving from these provisions for both parties. See also VSRH, Revr 187/03-2 of 3 December 2003, where the court established that an unclear contractual provision has to be interpreted in the context of the contract as a whole, especially its introductory part.

6 See VTSRH, Pž-2531/05 of 9 May 2007, where the court established that the parties' will can be expressed in different ways and consequently every form in which the will is manifested should be taken into account in interpreting the contract.

7 According to Art. 256(1) of the COA, any dispatch of catalogues, price lists, tariffs and other publications as well as advertisements in the press, leaflets, on the radio, television, by means of electronic media or any other means shall not be deemed to constitute an offer to enter into a contract, but only an invitation to make an offer under the conditions made public, unless such statements of intent indicate otherwise.

8 See Opening Remarks, n. 15.

aims, goals, etc. will also be taken into account in the course of interpreting the contract. This is because these elements make it easier to observe and appreciate what was expressed in the contract.[9] The courts would also apply the additional rules and methods of contract interpretation within the limits of *bona fides* and combine them in order to establish the true intention of the contracting parties, at the same time attempting to preserve the contract.

3. ENGLAND AND WALES

Question 1: Preamble

The preamble of a contract, containing recitals of agreed facts, understandings or intentions, is admissible in construing the obligation-creating provisions of a contract. The case law provides that clear recitals can assist in resolving ambiguities in the main part of the contract, but that if the recitals and operative part of the contract are both clear but inconsistent with each other the latter prevails.[10] Given that Clause 12(d) is ambiguous (probably stemming from the ambiguity in the objects to which the word 'other' refers), the recital, if unambiguous, would be of significant weight in determining the interpretation to be applied (i.e. the interpretation that a reasonable person would put on Clause 12(d), as discussed in the Opening Remarks).

If the preamble text were contained in another clause in the contract, then the court would give even more weight to it: other clauses are more powerful factors in interpreting a clause than a preamble is, and the court would attempt to construe Clause 12(d) so that it is consistent with the other clause (and vice versa).

Question 2: Information Brochure

If the text was in Premier's information brochure, then things are very different. The importance of a preamble stems from its forming part of the final written contract of the parties. This is the document signalling to the court the parties' intended agreement, and the court will not lightly conclude that any of the document, including the preamble, is inconsistent with any other part, and therefore will construe the document (including the operative clauses such as Clause 12(d)) to avoid such inconsistency.

---

9 Gorenc et al., *Komentar Zakona o obveznim odnosima*, p. 468; Perović, *Stojanović, Komentar zakona o obligacionim odnosima*, p. 349.

10 *Re Moon, ex p Dawes* (1886) 17 QBD 275 (CA), 286 per Lord Esher MR.

A brochure, however, being a document that passed between the parties prior to their entering into the contract, would probably amount to part of the pre-contractual negotiations and so be inadmissible when construing the contract (see point (3) in the Opening Remarks), unless it were referred to in the contract itself.

The first possible way around this result for Premier would be if it is able to rely on the brochure as identifying the 'general objective' of Clause 12(d), which objective can then be taken into account when construing the clause,[11] although there is some doubt as to whether this principle survived the comments of the House of Lords in *Chartbrook v Persimmon Homes Ltd.*[12]

The second way around this result for Premier would be for it to argue that the brochure demonstrates a common consensus as to what was to be agreed in the contract, and therefore that Jewellers King is estopped from relying on its interpretation of Clause 12(d) or that clause should be rectified (rewritten) to make Premier's interpretation clear (see point (4) in the Opening Remarks). The latter route (rectification) would only be available if the court found that Jewellers King (as well as Premier) actually understood the parties as intending to allow for five and not three jewellers.[13]

Question 3: The Contract's Purpose

The *apparent* purpose or objective or commercial sense of Clause 12(d) are important factors in any interpretation dispute. It is only the objectively apparent purpose – apparent from all the shared circumstances, admissible documents or outward statements, and general commercial sense – that is admissible and so important. Any purpose that Premier actually had in drafting the clause (if it drafted it) or agreeing it is, if unexpressed or not the purpose that the reasonable person would discern from the clause and the circumstances, irrelevant.

It would be open to the court to find that the apparent purpose in this case does not point in either direction, for example because the apparent purpose of the clause is to protect Jewellers King against too much competition from jewellers pre-dating or post-dating its taking up the lease, but that this does not allow the court to decide between the two competing interpretations as to how much competition is permitted. If, however, the reasonably apparent purpose is to restrict Premier to letting five units at the shopping centre for the sale of

---

11 *Investec Bank (Channel Islands) Ltd. v The Retail Group plc* [2009] EWHC 476 (Ch) (Sales J) at paras. 75–76.

12 See the comments in *Excelsior Group Productions Ltd v Yorkshire Television Ltd* [2009] EWHC 1751 (Comm) (Flaux J) at para. 25.

13 *FSHC Group Holdings Ltd v GLAS Trust Corp Ltd* [2019] EWCA Civ 1361, [2020] 1 All ER 505 (CA).

jewellery, then this would have significant (and possibly, in this case, conclusive) weight in the court's interpretation of the clause.

4. FINLAND

Question 1: Preamble

In this case, the intention of Premier is indicated in the preamble of the contract. The preamble is a part of the contractual documents and it indicates the nature and purpose of the contract. Therefore, the ambiguous wording of the Clause 12(d) is to be interpreted together with the preamble in order to find out the contents of the contract. As the preamble indicates that Premier intended to let up to five units for the purposes of the retail sale of jewellery, the wording of Clause 12(d) stating 'two other units only' is reasonably interpreted to allow Premier to let up to a total five jewellery retail units. The preamble can hence be seen to support Premier's interpretation.

Question 2: Information Brochure

The basic rule is that all communications between the parties are to be taken into account in interpreting the contract.[14] It is therefore irrelevant whether Premier's intention was declared in the contractual documents or in the information brochure. In this case it is relevant whether Jewellers King knew or could not have been unaware of Premier's intentions. If Jewellers King learnt of the information brochure before the conclusion of the contract, they could not have been unaware of Premier's intentions. However, as the primary source for the interpretation is the contractual document, Premier's standpoint would be more difficult to prove as the information brochure is not a term of the contract as such.

Question 3: The Contract's Purpose

As mentioned above, all the communications between the parties, unless otherwise agreed, are to be taken into account in interpreting a contract. Therefore, the purpose or objective of the lease contract can be considered if this objective or purpose was communicated to the other party. The objective or purpose of the contract is also to be taken into account if the other party would not have been unaware of that objective or purpose. If the purpose or objective was not made clear for Jewellers King or it was not otherwise evident, the objective or purpose has no role to play in the interpretation of Clause 12(d) and the literal interpretation prevails.

---

14 See e.g. Pönkä, 'Tavoitteellisten tulkintasääntöjen merkityksestä liikesopimusten tulkinnassa', pp. 921–922. See also the Finnish Supreme Court's decision KKO 2001:34.

5. FRANCE

Question 1: Preamble

The principle is that the meaning of Clause 12(d) will be assessed against the common intention of the parties according to the terms of Art. 1188 Cciv (formerly Art. 1156). In this particular case, however, a reference to Art. 1189 Cciv (formerly Art. 1161) would give more insights into what should concretely be done. Indeed, this provision addresses scenarios where the meaning of a clause is either clear in itself but ambiguous when combined with other clauses or – as is the case here – where the meaning of a clause is ambiguous except when interpreted in the light of the other provisions of the contract.[15]

Art. 1189 indeed requires that all clauses be interpreted in the light of each other, in a systematic manner. Clause 12(d) should thus be considered by taking account of the whole contract, and even of the whole transaction. This is understood quite broadly by the courts[16] as covering not only the contractual terms *stricto sensu* but also the preamble of the agreement, pre-contractual negotiations and related documents, and more generally any relevant expression of will. The assumption here is that the formal contract constitutes the final expression of the agreement but may or may not accurately reflect the common intention of the parties.

In our case it would thus make perfect sense to interpret Clause 12(d) by reference to the preamble of the lease contract, all the more so since preambles are often used by the parties to provide a framework for the interpretation of the contract by clarifying their intentions and the circumstances surrounding the conclusion of their agreement, as well as by identifying the key factors to be taken into account for the construction of the contractual terms.[17] Of course, this does not mean that the preamble itself is exhaustive or that the judge should not contemplate other sources in order to assess the common intention of the parties. As a consequence, the preamble will be taken into account as one element among others – most likely a significant one given its wording.

The reasoning and the result would be similar if the statement was incorporated not in the preamble but in another clause of the contract.

---

15 Interestingly, the courts traditionally tended to see Art. 1161 Cciv as a mere development of Art. 1156 Cciv and therefore to simply refer to the interpretation of the intention of the parties in decisions where a reference to Art. 1161 Cciv would have appeared appropriate and more explanatory. Civ. 1, 13 October 1965, *Bull. civ.* (1965) no. 541; Com., 29 November 1965, *Bull. civ.* (1965) no. 612; Com., 26 January 1970, *Bull. civ.* (1970) no. 29.

16 In line with ideas developed by Domat and Pothier, who both inspired the French Civil Code.

17 G. Chantepie, 'L'exigence de clarté dans la rédaction du contrat', *RDC* (2012) 1010.

Question 2: Information Brochure

The reasoning would be partly similar if the statement was incorporated in Premier's information brochure instead of the preamble or the core of the contract. However, an information brochure typically contains statements made by one party before negotiations are entered into. It does not, as such, reflect any common intention of the parties and its significance would thus have to be all the more carefully assessed against subsequent expressions of intention made by one or both parties, as well as against the contract itself. In other words, Premier's information brochure may be taken into account by the court for the interpretation of the contract, but only to the extent that its content is found to represent the common intention of the parties. At the very least, there must be evidence that Premier's intention as expressed in the information brochure has been understood and has not been contested by Jewellers King.[18]

Question 3: The Contract's Purpose

As Clause 12(d) shall be interpreted by reference to the common intention of the parties, the reliance by Premier on the *purpose* or *objective* of the clause will essentially be effective if such a purpose or objective appears to be common to both parties, which would have to be corroborated by contractual and/or pre-contractual documents or other declarations of intent made by either one or both parties. As previously mentioned, the Civil Code provides other rules of interpretation, but they do not seem to be of any assistance in this last scenario since there is no 'effective' meaning in the sense of Art. 1191 Cciv (formerly Art. 1157), nor any reason to think that the *contra proferentem* rule of Art. 1190 Cciv (formerly Art. 1162) would be applicable.

6. GERMANY

Question 1: Preamble

Under German law, the preamble may play a role in the 'erläuternde Auslegung' [explanatory interpretation] of the contract under §§157, 133 BGB. In particular, the purpose and objective may be drawn from the preamble and these can serve as arguments in the interpretation process. Arguments based on the preamble may also help to fill gaps in the contract by complementary interpretation or implication of terms.

From the German perspective, Premier and Jewellers King most likely would have concluded a lease contract under §581 BGB. Assuming Clause 12(d)

[18] See e.g. Ph. Simler in *JCl. Civil Code*, Art. 1188 à 1192, Fasc. 10, no. 43.

formulates a non-competition clause, under German law, protection against competition in the case of lease contracts is guaranteed by the principle of good faith, according to §242 BGB.[19] Therefore, under German law, parties to a lease contract would not need to agree on a non-competition clause.[20] Case law does not specify, however, the threshold as to the number of competitors as tenants that is contrary to good faith.[21]

The case assumes that Clause 12(d) is an ambiguous clause and evokes different interpretations for Jewellers King and Premier. German law contains an 'Unklarheitenregel' or '*contra proferentem* Regel' [ambiguity rule], which states that ambiguous contract terms that are proposed by one of the contract parties shall be interpreted to the detriment of that party.[22] Independently from the exact scope of application of the 'Unklarheitenregel' [ambiguity rule] under German law, the rule presupposes ambiguity. Therefore, the rules on 'erläuternde Auslegung' [explanatory interpretation] have priority over the 'Unklarheitenregel' [ambiguity rule] if they lead to a non-ambiguous result.[23]

The preamble could play an important role in the 'erläuternde Auslegung' [explanatory interpretation] because the contract has to be interpreted as a whole, including the preamble[24] The impact of a preamble in the interpretative exercise is an issue which remains unexplored in German academic literature. However, one can find information about the significance of a preamble of a contract in literature for legal practitioners.[25] A preamble most commonly forms part of a contract with a rather complicated structure. It is assumed that it both explains and documents the motives of the parties.[26] It usually shows the intention of the parties and lays down the interests, purposes and objectives of the parties in written form.[27] In case of doubt about the meaning of a clause of the contract, the clause must be interpreted in light of

19 OLG Karlsruhe, 07.04.1989, *NJW-RR* 1990, 1234, 1235 (lease of a pub).

20 M.G. Häublein, '§535 BGB' in K. Rebmann and F.J. Säcker (eds.), *Münchener Kommentar zum Bürgerlichen Gesetzbuch*, m.n. 180.

21 Without a non-competition clause, how this case would be decided under German law is not predictable.

22 BGH, 25.10.2016, BGHZ 212, 329, BGH, 24.10.2017, *NJW* 2018, 455, BGH, 23.08.2018, *BB* 2018, 2317, see also J. Busche, '§157 BGB' in K. Rebmann and F.J. Säcker (eds.), *Münchener Kommentar zum Bürgerlichen Gesetzbuch*, m.n. 8.

23 R. Singer '§133 BGB' in N. Habermann (ed.), *J. von Staudingers Kommentar zum Bürgerlichen Gesetzbuch*, vol. I, m.n. 63.

24 M. Wolf, '§157 BGB' in H.-T. Soergel, *Bürgerliches Gesetzbuch mit Einführungsgesetz und Nebengesetzen*, vol. II, m.n. 29; M. Schmidt-Kessel, 'Art. 8 CISG', in P. Schlechtriem and I. Schwenzer (eds.), *Kommentar zum Einheitlichen UN-Kaufrecht – Das Übereinkommen der Vereinten Nationen über Verträge über den internationalen Warenkauf (CISG)*, m.n. 29.

25 T. Beck, *Anwaltsstrategien bei der Vertragsgestaltung*, p. 123; K.-O. Schmittat, *Einführung in die Vertragsgestaltung*, vol. 2, m.n. 163.

26 T. Beck, *Anwaltsstrategien bei der Vertragsgestaltung*, p. 123.

27 Ibid.

these interests, purposes and objectives of the parties,[28] because the preamble shows that they share aspects of the common intentions of the parties.

This means, therefore, that Clause 12(d) in this case has to be interpreted in the light of the preamble. As a result, the preamble supports the interpretation of Premier, which argues that the phrase 'two other units only' refers to two units in addition to the three existing ones. In consequence, the preamble plays a decisive role in the 'erläuternde Auslegung' [explanatory interpretation] under §133, 157 BGB and supports the interpretation of Premier.

If, however, the rules on the 'erläuternde Auslegung' [explanatory interpretation] would lead to an ambiguous result, the 'Unklarheitenregel' [ambiguity rule] could be applied. Still, it is debated whether this ambiguity rule also applies to cases of individually negotiated contract terms or only to previously formulated general conditions of that contract, in which case the rule is laid down especially in §305c (2) BGB. Whereas for some specific cases ambiguity of contractual terms may even lead to a lack of consensus and because of that to 'Nichtigkeit' [inoperativeness] of the contract,[29] different points of view may be found on a general *contra proferentem* rule which would go beyond 305c (2) BGB. Some authors advocate a general *contra proferentem* rule,[30] while others emphasise that there is no such thing as a general principle of ambiguity in German law.[31] As the scope of application of the rule is in any event limited by the restriction of the unilateral origin of the clause, this debate is of restricted practical effect bearing in mind that court decisions have broadened the notion of general conditions in the sense of §§305, 305c BGB considerably. However, there is a line of older case law on which an analogy perhaps could be based, if there are comparable conditions of structural superiority.[32] Therefore, a general *contra proferentem* rule may not be accepted under German law, because it would be incoherent with the subjective approach and with the free consideration of evidence under §286 ZPO.

In the event that one party (Premier) has formulated the text of a contract unilaterally and the other party (Jewellers King) had no other choice than to sign it, this could possibly lead to an application of the '*contra proferentem*

28 M. Wolf, '§157 BGB' in H.-T. Soergel, *Bürgerliches Gesetzbuch mit Einführungsgesetz und Nebengesetzen*, vol. II, m.n. 57.

29 R. Singer '§133 BGB' in N. Habermann (ed.), *J. von Staudingers Kommentar zum Bürgerlichen Gesetzbuch*, vol. I, m.n. 63. Just to give an example: to say, 'I would like to book two rooms with three beds' is ambiguous. For it could mean 'two rooms with three beds altogether' or 'two rooms with three beds each'.

30 K. Larenz and M. Wolf, 'Allgemeiner Teil des Bürgerlichen Rechts: Ein Lehrbuch', §28 m.n. 56.

31 J. Busche, '§157 BGB' in K. Rebmann and F. J. Säcker (eds.), *Münchener Kommentar zum Bürgerlichen Gesetzbuch*, m.n. 8.

32 BGH, 12.02.1952, *NJW* 1952, 657; BGH, 19.11.1970, VII ZR 238/68, *VersR* 1971, 172.

Regel' [ambiguity rule].[33] This assumption would qualify the non-competition clause as forming part of Premier's general conditions; §305c (2) BGB should apply directly, therefore. Even if a court would hold otherwise, the ambiguity rule should probably be applied by analogy because of the predominant position of Premier as a landlord. At this stage, the above-mentioned discussions on the scope of the ambiguity rule are, therefore, of no relevance.

It is worth mentioning that Jewellers King may have a right to avoid the contract for 'Inhaltsirrtum' [mistake about the content of the contract] according to §119 (1) first alternative BGB. Despite the fact that it is not protected by the ambiguity rule, it would however be a question if the preamble shifts the risk of error to Jewellers King, and thereby excludes the right to avoid the contract. Nevertheless, 'Anfechtung' [avoidance] would not leave Premier without any protection because it would be protected by a claim for damages for the reliance loss suffered by Premier under §122 BGB. Additionally, 'Anfechtung' [avoidance] would not operate retrospectively in case of the lease contract but only bring the contract to an end at the time of the 'Anfechtung' [avoidance].

If Clause 12(d) was to be considered a non-competition clause, it deviates from the aforementioned general rule derived from the 'Grundsatz von Treu und Glauben' [good faith principle], which most probably would not apply at least to five competitors. If the clause is treated as forming part of Premier's general conditions, it may be void as an unfair contract term under §307 BGB.[34] Before the application of this unfairness test, the clause controlled has to be interpreted in the sense most detrimental to the other party. Here again the preamble would have a decisive effect by allowing leases to five competitors. Whereas some case law basically supports the view that clauses like Clause 12(d) may be upheld under §307,[35] courts may find the clause void as unfair because of its lack of transparency in the sense of §307 (1) second sentence BGB. Here the ambiguity of the clause may 'step through the back door' of invalidity and ultimately lead to the preamble having no effect. As a result, the non-competition rule derived from the principle of good faith may even lead to a complete prohibition of any lease competitors. Premier should be advised, therefore, not to insist on its interpretation based on the preamble.

---

33 In the case at hand, Premier is the owner of numerous retail units in the shopping centre. Before concluding the contract with Jewellers King, it let two units to other jewellers. Under these conditions a unilaterally formulated contract may be assumed; OLG Frankfurt a. M., 06.12.1972, *OLGZ* 1973, 229.

34 C. Grüneberg, '§307' in O. Palandt (ed.), *Palandt Bürgerliches Gesetzbuch mit Nebengesetzen – Kommentar*, m.n. 10.

35 OLG Hamm, 02.13.1997, *NJWE-MietR* 1997, 180; BGH, 13.03.1979, *NJW* 1979, 1605; P. Ulmer, E. Brandner and H.-D. Hensen, *AGB-Recht*, m.n. 608.

A more typical role of a preamble, the use of which is quite self-evident as far as interpretation is concerned, would be the implication of terms or so-called supplementary interpretation to the contract.[36] This would presuppose that the content of the contract is otherwise incomplete.[37] In the case at hand, Clause 12(d) is ambiguous but leaves no gap to be closed by supplementary interpretation. Therefore, this second interpretative function of a preamble does not apply here.

Question 2: Information Brochure

Referring to Premier's information brochure could lead to slightly different results: it has to be said that German law does not exclude the possibility that extra-contractual material can be used in the interpretative process. Indeed, there is a rebuttable presumption that the deed, which contains the contract, mirrors the contract completely and correctly ('Vermutung der Vollständigkeit und Richtigkeit der Urkunde' [presumption of completeness and correctness of the deed]).[38] However, assuming Clause 12(d) is ambiguous, this presumption could be rebutted by an information brochure, which may be useful for the interpretation process.

Under German law an information brochure does not legally bind the parties, since it is only an '*invitato ad offerendum*' [invitation to submit an offer].[39] However, there could be a legal effect anyway, if the information brochure shows the intention of the parties and therefore turns out to be a relevant circumstance of contract formation itself.[40] In fact, the information brochure may affect the interpretation, if the addressee is aware of the information it provides.[41]

When both parties know or are capable of knowing this information, it also needs to influence the declarations of intent.[42] Given Jewellers King was aware of the information the brochure provides and this information influenced its declaration of intent by forming the contract, the result of interpretation would, therefore, be no different from Question 1.

---

36 See e.g. BGH, 15.10.2014, in *NZM* 2015, 211, in which the German Federal Court uses the preamble for interpretation without discussing the theoretical background of taking the preamble into account, K.-O. Schmittat, *Einführung in die Vertragsgestaltung*, vol. 2, m.n. 163.

37 D. Medicus, *Allgemeiner Teil des BGB*, §9 m.n. 19; BGH, 17.04.2002, *NJW* 2002, 2310.

38 BGH, 11.05.2017, *BeckRS* 2017, 126042, BGH, 05.07.2002, *NJW* 2002, 3164.

39 H. Köhler, *BGB Allgemeiner Teil*, §8, m.n. 9.

40 K.-H. Below, *Bürgerliches Recht Allgemeiner Teil*, p. 108, 109; K. Riesenhuber, *Europäisches Vertragsrecht*, §17, m.n. 469; BGH, 25.10.2007, *NJW-R* 2008, 258.

41 J. Ellenberger, '§133' in O. Palandt (ed.), *Palandt Bürgerliches Gesetzbuch mit Nebengesetzen – Kommentar*, m.n. 15.

42 Ibid., m.n. 18.

Question 3: The Contract's Purpose

The purpose or objective of the contract is a factor which can be taken into account in the interpretative process.[43] These factors do not need to be mentioned somewhere in the written text of the contract. In practical terms, however, it would be much more difficult to prove the objective or purpose of the contract if they are not specifically mentioned.

7. GREECE

Question 1: Preamble

When evaluating an ambiguous contractual clause like Clause 12(d), the deciding judge will resort to the interpretation scheme explained in the Opening Remarks. In this case, the parties apparently have a different understanding of the clause in question. Therefore, the subjective criterion is not helpful, and the objective criterion of Art. 200 CC becomes decisive.

An issue preceding the determination of the normative meaning of the clause in question is whether the preamble can be of use to the court in detecting that meaning. More specifically, when trying to determine the importance of the preamble for the lease agreement between Premier and Jewellers King, the court would begin by examining whether the preamble forms an integral part of the lease agreement between them, namely whether the content of the preamble is covered by the consent of the parties. For the deciding judge it makes no difference whether the clause in question allowing Premier to lease five units altogether for the purposes of the retail sale of jewellery was included in the preamble or in the main text of the agreement. What interests the court is whether both parties acknowledged and affirmed the terms included in their agreement before concluding it, regardless of whether the terms in question were included in the preamble or the main text, because contracts are concluded by consensus of the parties (Arts. 192–193 CC).

Therefore, it is possible to use the preamble in order to interpret Clause 12(d), and this 'systematic' interpretation remains unaffected by the position of the interpreted components in the agreement, since under Greek law there seems to be no hierarchical graduation of clauses in terms of their relative strength depending on where they are placed. The only issue that matters is whether all terms are covered by the consensus of the parties. This is what the court would examine, especially regarding a written agreement and its parts, introductory or otherwise. Since the text of Clause 12(d) is understood differently by the parties, its interpretation in the light of the fifth recital of the preamble should

---

[43] M. Wolf, '§157 BGB' in H.-T. Soergel, *Bürgerliches Gesetzbuch mit Einführungsgesetz und Nebengesetzen*, vol. II, m.n. 57.

allow for a more specific and comprehensive understanding of the clause and this is the most likely route for the judge to take when evaluating the case.[44] Consequently, the court will have to weigh eventual claims by Jewellers King against the normative value of its consent.[45] The court would, for example, have to determine whether Jewellers King can plausibly claim that it never became aware of the content of the fifth recital of the preamble or that it considered Clause 12(d) to be superior to the preamble.[46] For any allegation brought forward, Jewellers King will have to discharge the relevant burden of proof (see Arts. 216, 237 Code of Civil Procedure (CPC)).[47]

Question 2: Information Brochure

The answer with regard to information included in Premier's information brochure is essentially the same as for Question 1. As mentioned in the Opening Remarks, when interpreting a contract, especially one not subject to a specific form,[48] the first issue to be identified is whether the term in question indeed became part of the agreement of the parties, and the answer to this depends on the proof that the parties can present. If this is the case, it makes no difference how exactly the term in question was incorporated into the agreement of the parties, provided that the true intent of the parties did find some form of external expression, even during for example pre-contractual negotiations – as is the case here with an information brochure shared and discussed between the parties – and did not remain a purely internal

---

44 For the applicability of the classical methods of interpretation of the law also to contracts and other juridical acts (namely the grammatical, historical, systematical and teleological method of interpretation), see Papanikolaou, *Methodology*, §465.

45 Papanikolaou, *Methodology*, §§460–461.

46 An additional question that arises is whether the importance attributed to the recital in question by Jewellers King is enough to suggest that it would not have concluded the contract had it been aware of the term in question; cf. Art. 141 CC.

47 Jewellers King could eventually also resort to the avoidance of the agreement on the grounds of error (Arts. 140 et seq. CC). The issue of avoidance for error raises in its turn a series of further questions, such as whether the error was substantial enough to lead to the avoidance of the whole lease agreement, and in any case falls out of the scope of the present case study, since determining the existence and extent of a possible error forms a logical step that follows the interpretation of the agreement; see Karassis, *General Principles*, § Γ 292 fn. 166 *in fine*.

48 If a contract is subject *ex lege* to written or notarial form, elements outside the written agreement or the notarial deed may not, as a rule of thumb, be taken into account in order to supplement the will of the parties, but only in order to clarify it (in practice the distinction may become difficult); AP 154/2002, EllDni 43 (2002), 1638; CA Athens 3933/2002, EDPol 19 (2003), 36; Balis, *General Principles*, §91; see Georgiades, *General Principles*, §41 no. 25, Ladas, *General Principles*, §34 no. 42–43 and Filios, *General Principles*, §245, who concur but also note certain exceptions. In Greek law, the default rule is that no form is required for juridical acts, unless otherwise provided in the law; see Art. 158 CC ('αρχή του ατύπου της δικαιοπραξίας' [principle of the formlessness of juridical acts]); cf. also e.g. PD 34/1995 on professional leases *e contrario*, which does not require any form for a professional lease.

predisposition.[49] However, it must be noted that the connection of an information brochure not attached to or mentioned in the pertinent agreement may be somewhat more tenuous than that of its preamble. This is a factor that would most probably be weighed when the judge evaluates whether Clause 12(d) can be construed in the sense of a text that is not integrated into the lease agreement itself.[50]

Question 3: The Contract's Purpose

Assuming that neither a preamble nor an information brochure contains anything relating to Clause 12(d), the court will have to objectively evaluate the intent of the parties on the basis of the purported purpose of the contract, according to the rules described in the Opening Remarks. More specifically, the deciding judge will probably turn to the normative meaning of the clause in question, and he will have to do that not by reference to any abstract notion of the 'average' contracting parties, but according to what the specific parties in question could and ought to have understood with regard to their stipulations.[51] For the purpose of interpreting Clause 12(d), the court would possibly address the question whether that purpose covered, apart from the main objective of letting business premises, the protection of the lessee's business interests and, if so, to what extent. The two parties have concluded a lease agreement. The content of the agreement is primarily the letting of business premises, whereby the protection of the business interests of the lessee seems to be taken into account in view of Clause 12(d) in the form of a passive obligation on behalf of Premier. Such considerations could be examined by the court in an effort to determine the scope and purpose of the contract in general and the specific clause in particular, especially since the other standards of evaluation under Art. 200 CC – namely the 'καλή πίστη' [good faith] and the 'συναλλακτικά ήθη' [transactions usages or trade customs] – do not seem to prescribe something else in the case at hand. Most importantly, Premier's internal intent may not be decisive, if it had not somehow been externalised towards Jewellers King at some stage of their negotiations regarding the conclusion of the lease agreement.[52]

---

49 Georgiades, *General Principles*, §41 nos. 5–6; Balis, *General Principles*, §88; Karakostas, *Civil Code*, vol. II, Arts. 173, 200 nos. 867, 870; cf. Stathopoulos, *Civil Code*, vol. 1^B, Arts. 173 and 200 nos. 120, 124–125.

50 Cf. AP 413/2008, NoV 56 (2008), 1889: an advertising brochure was evaluated among other documents by the court in order to determine the precise extent of an employee's workdays and working hours.

51 Karassis, *General Principles*, § Γ 292, with further references; Stathopoulos, *Civil Code*, vol. 1^B, Arts. 173 and 200 nos. 107, 110; Georgiades, *General Principles*, §41 nos. 9, 14.

52 Stathopoulos, *Civil Code*, vol. 1^B, Arts. 173 and 200 no. 24; Ladas, *General Principles*, §34 nos. 17–18.

8. ITALY

Question 1: Preamble

Art. 1362 c.c. provides the fundamental rule for the interpretation of contracts.[53] This article provides the general aim of the interpretation process (ascertaining the common intention of the parties) and points at two factors that must be considered first, in order to pursue an interpretation aimed at the discovery of the common will of the parties. The first relevant factor is the literal meaning of the words used by the parties. The contractual wording must be considered as the first clue for a proper understanding of the legal meaning of the contract. However, the court will not necessarily limit itself to the examination of the literal contractual wording because the search for the parties' intention might also require the court to consider the parties' conduct, both preceding and subsequent to the making of the contract.

Art. 1363 provides the second rule on contract interpretation, usually referred to as the principle of 'systematic' interpretation because it requires that each contractual clause be interpreted in light of other clauses and of the contract as a whole.[54] This rule is regarded as a 'subjective' and literal interpretation rule, because reference to the contract as a whole is regarded as a means to provide each contractual clause with a meaning consistent with the actual intention of the parties as expressed by the overall textual provisions of the contract.

Based on Art. 1363 c.c., the preamble of the lease contract would certainly play a role in the interpretation of Clause 12(d). In order to apply the systematic interpretation rule (Art. 1363), it would not be necessary to assume that the clause be ambiguous. Systematic interpretation is indeed regarded as a form of literal interpretation and for this reason it must be plainly applied by the judge and does not need any particular justification such as the ambiguity of the text. This means that a judge should look at the contract as a whole even to interpret specific clauses that are not particularly obscure at first sight and, relying on such systematic interpretation, the judge has the power to assign to such clauses a meaning which may differ from their seemingly clear literal meaning.[55]

---

53 Art. 1362 c.c.: '(1) In the interpretation of the contract one must look for the parties' common intention and must not restrain the analysis to the literal meaning of the words. (2) In order to ascertain the common intention of the parties, one must consider their overall conduct, also subsequent to the conclusion of contract.'

54 Art. 1363 c.c.: 'Each clause of the contract must be interpreted by means of other clauses, and each clause must be given the meaning which results from the contract as a whole'; see Astone, 'Dell'interpretazione del contratto (sub art. 1363)', p. 444 ff.

55 See Cass. 30 January 2018 no. 2267; Cass. 10 May 2016 no. 9380; Cass. 14 November 2014 no. 24333; Cass. 30 June 2011 no. 14460; Cass. 28 August 2007 no. 18180; Cass. 25 October 2006 no. 22899; Cass. 24 April 1990 no. 3439; Bianca, *Contratto*, p. 432; Sacco, *Contratto*, p. 1353. In contrast, the majority of judicial decisions require some ambiguity of the contractual text in order to apply further criteria, other than the literal meaning of the words,

Judges and scholars[56] usually regard the preamble, as well as documents possibly attached to the contract, as parts of the contract and therefore consider them as relevant interpretation factors pursuant to Art. 1363 c.c.

Question 2: Information Brochure

The conclusion could be different if Premier had referred to its information brochure rather than to the preamble, because the brochure should probably not be regarded as part of the contract, but only as a pre-contractual representation.

Nevertheless, the brochure could be deemed relevant under Art. 1362 c.c., as a representation or a 'behaviour' evidencing the common intention of the parties, if it can be proved that Jewellers King did know about the brochure and had in some way accepted its content while making the contract. In such a case, Art. 1366 c.c., which provides for the principle of interpretation 'secondo buona fede' [according to good faith],[57] could also help support Premier's interpretation.

Scholars disagree as to the proper classification of Art. 1366 c.c. within either one or the other of the two patterns of subjective or objective interpretation. The 'Relazione al codice civile' [report accompanying the civil code when it was enacted] depicts 'buona fede' as a synthesis of subjective and objective aspects of the interpretation process, and it defines Art. 1366 as the 'suture stitch' between subjective and objective interpretation.[58]

Scholars and courts usually explain the concept of contractual good faith in general as a rule of fair dealing which calls for a reasonable and equitable consideration of the interests of both parties.[59] Basically, this implies that in the interpretation of contracts the good faith standard prevents each party

---

such as the reference to the parties' overall conduct. According to this judicial position, when the literal wording of the contract looks clear and unambiguous, the judge should not resort to any other criteria and should give the contract the legal meaning which results from such clear text (this principle is sometimes expressed with the trite Latin maxim *in claris non fit interpretatio*), see e.g. Cass. 11 March 2016 no. 4832; Cass. 25 March 2013 no. 7472; Cass. 11 March 2014 no. 5595; Cass. 19 October 2009 no. 22124; Cass. 12 June 2007 no. 13777. Scholars usually disagree with this position and deny the possibility that any given contractual text can be ever so 'clear' as to exclude the need for extra-literal interpretation; see Roppo, *Il contratto*, p. 444 ff.; Bianca, *Contratto*, p. 420–422; Sacco, *Contratto*, p. 1354 ff.; Bigliazzi Geri, *L'interpretazione del contratto*, p. 93 ff.; Gentili, *Senso e consenso*, p. 410 ff., 511 ff.; another stream of judicial precedents, whose influence seems to be increasing, more consistently with the wording of Art. 1362, adopt this latter perspective: see e.g. Cass. 6 July 2018 no. 17718; Cass. 15 July 2016 no. 14432; Cass. 23 May 2014 no. 11533; Cass. 10 December 2008 no. 29029.

56 Roppo, *Contratto*, p. 449; Cass. 14 June 2011 no. 12950.

57 Art. 1366 c.c.: 'The contract must be interpreted according to good faith'.

58 Relazione al codice civile no. 622; Betti, *Teoria generale*, p. 349.

59 See Bianca, *La nozione di buona fede*; Roppo, *Contratto*, p. 450; for a deeper account of contractual good faith, see M. Barcellona, *Clausole generali e giustizia contrattuale*.

from denying the contractual meaning the other party has reasonably relied on. Some scholars argue that this rule leads to a 'subjective' interpretation.[60] Other scholars, though, tend to stress the 'objective' character of such a 'good faith interpretation', in that it gives priority to the most reasonable and fair contractual meaning in light of all the relevant circumstances.[61]

If Premier can show that its reliance on a certain meaning of Clause 12(d) is reasonable because Jewellers King did in fact know about the brochure, then the good faith standard of Art. 1366 may prevent Jewellers King from asserting a different meaning.

Question 3: The Contract's Purpose

The purpose or objective of the contract may be relevant under Art. 1369,[62] which refers to the 'nature' and 'object' of the contract (but not of the specific controversial clause) as a means for its interpretation 'in case of doubt'.

The reference to the 'natura del contratto' [nature or purpose of the contract] is usually understood as indicating the need to consider the 'causa' [cause] of the contract.[63] This basically means that the contractual meaning must be construed consistently with the structure and the economic purpose of the intended specific transaction.

According to another scholarly position, the 'nature' of the contract should be understood as the 'tipo contrattuale' [contractual type] and it would therefore refer to the statutory regulation of those model transactions ('contractual types' or 'nominated contracts') specifically regulated by the Civil Code.[64] The 'object' is the entirety of the legal effects that the contract is intended to produce.

The rule of Art. 1369 is usually considered, by courts and the majority of scholars, as a rule of 'objective' interpretation, because reference to the objective structure and purpose of the contract would not be intended as a means of investigating the actual will of the parties but as a means of providing the contract with a reasonable and workable meaning, according to its basic economic purpose, when the parties' actual intention cannot be ascertained.

Scholars, though, warn that this article shows the inevitable 'circularity' of the interpretation process, because, in order to ascertain the purpose or subject matter of the contract, one must first investigate the parties' will, then

---

60 Bianca, *Contratto*, p. 422.

61 Roppo, *Contratto*, p. 450; for deeper accounts see: Bessone, *Adempimento e rischio contrattuale*; Bigliazzi Geri, *Note in tema di interpretazione*; Costanza, *Profili*; Turco, *Note in tema di ermeneutica*; Scognamiglio, *Interpretazione*.

62 Art. 1369 c.c.: 'Expressions which may have different meanings, in case of doubt, must be understood in accordance with the nature and the object of the contract'

63 Roppo, *Contratto*, p. 451; Bianca, *Contratto*, p. 433; Alpa, *Unità*, 1509.

64 Ziccardi, *Interpretazione*, 8.

such a purpose or subject matter will help enlighten those aspects that a bare examination of the parties' expressed will has left unclear.[65] This idea leads some scholars to argue that Art. 1369 in fact provides a rule of subjective interpretation.[66]

The application of this rule is expressly made conditional upon the existence of some 'doubt' or ambiguity as to the proper meaning of the contractual term.

It is not clear whether the application of Art. 1369 turns in favour of the lessor or of the lessee. What has to be considered is the 'nature' of the contract, because this is the legal concept that can give relevance to the purpose of the transaction. If the 'nature' of the contract is intended as its 'cause', the judge should examine all the relevant terms of the specific agreement in order to determine whether the fulfilment of the economic purpose of the contract requires the acknowledgement of a sort of relatively 'exclusive' right to the lessee so that such purpose would be substantially frustrated if the owner of the units maintains the right to lease further units to jewellers. If, according to the other scholarly position, the nature of the contract should be intended as a reference to the contractual type, then the judge should look to the statutory regulation of the lease contract in order to ascertain whether existing legal rules support one or the other interpretation.

In addition, reliance on a particular purpose of a specific contractual clause may be a relevant interpretation factor under the standard of 'buona fede' [good faith] of Art. 1366 c.c.

If Premier manages to convince the court that Premier has relied on the purpose of Clause 12(d) being that five units could be let to jewellers, and if there is some element that treats such reliance as reasonable and worthy of protection, then the standard of 'buona fede' could help support Premier's contentions.

9. NETHERLANDS

Question 1: Preamble

To establish the meaning to be given to Clause 12(d), it is necessary to apply the interpretation norm laid down in the *Haviltex* judgment.[67] The court will look to ascertain the meaning each party could reasonably attach to Clause 12(d) and the meaning they each could reasonably expect the other party to have given to the clause having regard to all the relevant facts and circumstances

65 Bianca, *Contratto*, p. 434; Bigliazzi Geri, *L'interpretazione del contratto*, p. 346;

66 Oppo, *Profili*, p. 42; Bianca, *Contratto*, p. 433; but see Bigliazzi Geri, *L'interpretazione*, p. 351; for a critical review of scholarly opinions, see Gentili, *Senso e consenso*, p. 597 ff.

67 Hoge Raad 13 March 1981, *NJ* 1981, 635 (Ermes/Haviltex) read in light of Hoge Raad 20 February 2004, *NJ* 2005, 493 (DSM-Chemie/Fox).

assessed in light of the standards of 'redelijkheid en billijkheid' [reasonableness and fairness].

The preamble of the contract constitutes an important and relevant factor for interpretation. After all, a clause in a contract does not exist in a vacuum; it forms part of the contract and must therefore be interpreted in light of the contract as a whole.[68] The preamble also constitutes part of the contract and is therefore relevant to the interpretation of clauses within it.[69] This is of particular importance if the parties have laid down the particular commercial purpose of the contract in the preamble, since it can be expected that such statements influence the expectations the parties will have with respect to the meaning to be attributed to the individual term in the contract.[70] If the preamble is clear and the body of the contract is unclear, the preamble will provide direction for the interpretation; if the preamble is unclear and the body of the contract is sufficiently clear, the clause will prevail; if the preamble and the body of the contract are contradictory, the body of the contract will prevail.[71] In addition, where a more objective application of the *Haviltex* norm is adopted, in the context of a carefully drafted, detailed contract concluded between professional parties following extensive negotiations and with the assistance of legal advisors, the preamble will still provide relevant information for establishing the meaning of Clause 12(d). The same would be true if the interpretation were corroborated by another clause in the contract because the contract should be read as a whole and words used elsewhere in the contract are relevant to interpretation since a contract is not considered to be internally contradictory.[72]

Question 2: Information Brochure

Under the *Haviltex* norm, all relevant circumstances will be taken into consideration in order to establish the meaning the parties could reasonably attach to the provision of the contract and could reasonably have expected the other party to have attributed to it. Such relevant circumstances will include an information brochure that was provided by Premier. Where that information brochure outlines the purpose of the contract and provides additional explanations and background to the parties' rights and obligations, it will constitute relevant information for the court to consider when establishing what meaning Premier and Jewellers King each could reasonably attribute to Clause 12(d) and whether they could reasonably expect the other to share that meaning.

---

68 Hoge Raad 8 November 1983, *NJ* 1984, 272 (Kluft/B en W Supermarkten); Tjittes, 'Uitleg van schriftelijke contracten', p. 16.

69 Hoge Raad 30 November 1951, *NJ* 1953, 75 (Van Stijverden/Olst); Tjittes, *Uitleg van schriftelijke contracten*, p. 36; Valk, 'Kijk naar jezelf', p. 57; Tjittes, *Commercieel Contractenrecht*, p. 308.

70 Tjittes, *Uitleg van schriftelijke contracten*, p. 36.

71 Tjittes, *Commercieel Contractenrecht*, p. 308.

72 Ibid., p. 306.

Assuming Premier provided Jewellers King with the information brochure during the contract negotiations, it is reasonable for the court to take it into account as a relevant circumstance and as evidence of the purpose and objective of the contract.

Question 3: The Contract's Purpose

Even in the absence of written evidence of the purpose of the contract, for example in the preamble or an information brochure, the courts would look to the nature and purpose of the contract in order to establish the meaning the parties could reasonably have attributed to and expected the other party to attribute to a particular provision in the contract.[73] After all, the contract is concluded with a particular purpose which shapes the parties' understanding and expectations. An interpretation that is more in line with the commercial purpose of the contract would likely prevail.[74] This is also relevant in the context of the particular purpose or objective of a clause in the contract. The court would consider as a relevant factor the purpose and objective of a particular clause in a contract to the extent that it would shape the respective parties' understandings of the contractual provision. It would be necessary for the court to consider whether it was reasonable in the given circumstances for Premier to rely on the purpose of Clause 12(d) to restrict it to letting five units at the shopping centre and whether it could reasonably expect Jewellers King to understand that to be the purpose or objective of the provision. If we assume that there is no further evidence suggesting that Jewellers King was aware of this purpose or objective, then it is likely that the court would not regard it as reasonable for Premier to expect Jewellers King to share this understanding of Clause 12(d).

10. POLAND

Question 1: Preamble

The Opening Remarks explain that Polish courts may consider any evidence presented by the parties in order to establish the parties' common intentions. The preamble to a contract constitutes a part of the contract and should be seen as a part of the same act in law conducted by the parties. The document's text is the main evidence as to the parties' intentions, as declared therein.[75] Applying the interpretation rules, the court examines the ambiguous term,

---

73 Ibid., pp. 36–37; see e.g. Hoge Raad 17 September 2004, *NJ* 2005, 169 (Wessanen/Nutricia).

74 Ibid., p. 37; Tjittes, *Commercieel Contractenrecht*, p. 312.

75 Decree of SN of 29.06.1995, III CZP 66/95; Judgment of SN of 09.02.2012, III CSK 179/11; Judgment of SN of 16.01.2013, II CSK 302/12; Judgment of SN of 06.02.2013, V CSK 162/12; Judgment of SN of 23.05.2013, I CSK 569/12.

Clause 12(d), and tries to determine its meaning not only based on the understanding of the term by the parties, but also taking into account the context in which it was used, and the connections to other provisions in the contract.[76] A specific contractual term, together with other terms of the contract, creates a specific functional unit, with the general rule that all contractual provisions are equally important, regardless of where they are located in the contract.[77] However, it is possible that parties to a contract would decide on the hierarchy of contractual provisions by making a distinction between general and specific terms or, for example, distinguishing the basic objectives of the contract in its preamble. Then the interpretation process should take into account the contract's specific structure that the parties have adopted, which reflects their expectations and assumptions as to the results of the concluded contract.[78]

The wording of the preamble, or of any other clause in the contract, should be treated by the Polish courts as corroborating Premier's interpretation of Clause 12(d). For example, the SN criticised the lower courts for interpreting a contractual term in isolation from other terms of the contract that were related to it and put it in another context.[79] Therefore, it is unlikely that an interpretation of Clause 12(d) that goes against other contractual provisions would be adopted, since that would undermine the logical assumption that the parties to the contract acted rationally while drafting it. The assumption of the contractual partners' rationality is what the subjective interpretation of a contract is based upon.[80] Premier would therefore be likely to rely on its interpretation of Clause 12(d).

Question 2: Information Brochure

As mentioned in the Opening Remarks, in order to establish the common intention of the parties, any evidence may be presented in a Polish court.

---

76 Decree of SN of 29.06.1995, III CZP 66/95; Judgment of SN of 21.11.1997, I CKN 825/97; Judgment of SN of 08.07.2004, IV CK 582/03; Judgment of SN of 05.10.2005, II CK 122/05; Judgment of SN of 17.06.2009, IV CSK 90/09; Judgment of SN of 09.02.2012, III CSK 179/11; Judgment of SN of 16.01.2013, II CSK 302/12; Judgment of SN of 06.02.2013, V CSK 162/12; Judgment of SN of 23.05.2013, I CSK 569/12; Judgment of SN of 18.11.2016, I CSK 802/15; Ł. Węgrzynowski, 'Sądowe ustalanie treści stosunku umownego', PPH 2007/5/44–49; B. Kaczorowska, 'Wizja wykładni umów w projekcie księgi pierwszej kodeksu cywilnego', TPP 2/2011, p. 23; E. Rott-Pietrzyk, 'Interpretacja owiadczenia woli (uwagi na tle rozwiza projektu księgi I kodeksu cywilnego)', TPP 4/2010, pp. 54–55.

77 Ł. Węgrzynowski, 'Sądowe ustalanie treści stosunku umownego', PPH 2007/5/44–49; B. Kaczorowska, 'Wizja wykładni umów w projekcie księgi pierwszej kodeksu cywilnego', TPP 2/2011, pp. 23–24.

78 B. Kaczorowska, 'Wizja wykładni umów w projekcie księgi pierwszej kodeksu cywilnego', TPP 2/2011, p. 23.

79 Judgment of SN of 03.09.1998, I CKN 815/97.

80 Decree of SN of 11.09.1997, III CZP 39/97; Judgment of SN of 19.11.2002, IV CKN 1474/00; Judgment of SN of 08.10.2004, V CK 670/03; Judgment of SN of 05.10.2005, II CK 122/05; Judgment of SN of 17.06.2009, IV CSK 90/09.

Even if Premier's information brochure would not be seen as a part of the contract and would not have a binding character, it would still be admitted as evidence of the parties' common intentions, if it were proven that neither party objected to its content. In the same way, Polish courts will admit evidence from the minutes of pre-contractual negotiations, which are also not binding in character.[81] Moreover, for interpretation purposes, the courts may use circumstances existing at the time when the declaration of intentions expressed in a contract was made. Such circumstances may be established based on evidence other than the text of the contract itself, for example as stated in the information brochure. Therefore, Premier may corroborate its claim with the wording of the information brochure. However, contrary to the answer given in the first question, since the wording of the information brochure is not binding, it could have been replaced by newer contractual provisions, which would be for Jewellers King to prove.

Question 3: The Contract's Purpose

Determining the purpose or objective of the contract through indicating the parties' common intention, upon which the contractual relationship was formed, is done on the basis of applying Art. 65 para. 2 of the 'Kodeks Cywilny' [Civil Code]. When interpreting the contractual terms, it requires the court to consider the common intention of the contractual parties and the purpose of the contract, rather than the literal meaning of the terms used.[82] Theoretically speaking, the evaluation of the contract's purpose and objective should be conducted according to the principles of reasonableness[83] and fairness;[84] in practice, however, the courts are rather hesitant to use this kind of general clause. Moreover, the Polish courts would not only take into account the purpose or objective of the declaration of intentions explicitly expressed in the contract but would also try to establish it based on the content of the contract, and on such things as pre-contractual negotiations.[85]

---

81 Judgment of SN of 04.07.1975, III CRN 160/75; Judgment of SN of 02.07.2004, II CK 271/04; Judgment of SN of 05.10.2005, II CK 122/05; Judgment of SN of 17.12.2008, I CSK 250/08; Judgment of SN of 17.06.2009, IV CSK 90/09; Judgment of SN of 14.06.2012, I CSK 485/11; Judgment of SN of 10.05.2013, I CSK 74/13.

82 E.g. Judgment of SN of 16.01.2013, II CSK 302/12; Judgment of SN of 10.05.2013, I CSK 74/13; Judgment of SN of 23.05.2013, I CSK 569/12; Judgment of SN of 13.01.2016, V CSK 277/15; Judgment of SN of 18.11.2016, I CSK 802/15.

83 Z. Radwański, *System prawa cywilnego*, vol. 2, p. 74.

84 B. Kaczorowska, 'Wizja wykładni umów w projekcie księgi pierwszej kodeksu cywilnego', TPP 2/2011, pp. 19–20; M. Romanowski, 'Szczegółowe reguły wykładni kontraktów w świetle zasad europejskiego prawa kontraktów a reguły wykładni umów w prawie polskim', PPH 2004/9/12–18.

85 Judgment of SN of 21.11.1997, I CKN 825/97; Judgment of SN of 03.09.1998, I CKN 815/97; Judgment of SN of 08.07.2004, IV CK 582/03; Judgment of SN of 05.10.2005, II CK 122/05; Judgment of SN of 17.12.2008, I CSK 250/08; Judgment of SN of 17.06.2009, IV CSK 90/09;

For example, in the judgment of the SN of 7 December 2000,[86] the parties argued as to whether and when a contract binding them could be terminated. The contract did not contain a clear provision on this subject. The SN decided that, in the interpretation process, the purpose of the contract, namely the fact that the services were to be delivered only seasonally, should also be considered.

Pursuant to the above, the purpose or objective of a contract can definitely play a role in the corroboration of Premier's interpretation of Clause 12(d) in Polish law (see further our comments to Case 10).[87] Premier would have to prove, however, that Jewellers King was aware of that purpose of Clause 12(d) and did not oppose it.

11. PORTUGAL

Question 1: Preamble

The preamble, as an interpretation factor, is less relevant for the interpretation of the contract than a clause inserted in the contract, but it is an element among others that can be relevant to discovering the meaning of Clause 12(d). The reason is that, following the 'Código Civil' (CC) [Civil Code] (Art. 236.°/1), Clause 12(d) should be interpreted according to the meaning given to it by a 'declaratário normal' [reasonable person] who receives the declaration in the context of the relevant factual situation.

The Portuguese system of interpretation of contract contained in Arts. 236.°, 237.°, 238.° and 239.° CC does not expressly mention the preamble as a relevant element for the interpretation of the contract. This approach would apply in this case, for the interpretation of Clause 12(d). Nevertheless, all formal elements can be used to support a particular interpretation from the text of the clause. One must ask what this person could understand from the behaviour of the other party to the contract, unless it was not reasonable for her to rely on it. Still, if Jewellers King knew Premier's real intention based on other elements,

---

Judgment of SN of 14.06.2012, I CSK 485/11; Judgment of SN of 06.02.2013, V CSK 162/12; Judgment of SN of 10.05.2013, I CSK 74/13; Ł. Węgrzynowski, 'Sądowe ustalanie treści stosunku umownego', PPH 2007/5/44–49; B. Kaczorowska, 'Wizja wykładni umów w projekcie księgi pierwszej kodeksu cywilnego', TPP 2/2011, pp. 19–20.

86 Judgment of SN of 07.12.2000, II CKN 351/00.

87 Decree of SN of 29.06.1995, III CZP 66/95; Decree of SN of 11.09.1997, III CZP 39/97; Judgment of SN of 03.09.1998, I CKN 815/97; Judgment of SN of 25.03.2004, II CK 116/03; Judgment of SN of 08.07.2004, IV CK 582/03; Judgment of SN of 05.10.2005, II CK 122/05; Judgment of SN of 17.06.2009, IV CSK 90/09; Z. Radwanski, *System prawa cywilnego*, vol. 2, p. 54; B. Kaczorowska, 'Wizja wykładni umów w projekcie księgi pierwszej kodeksu cywilnego', TPP 2/2011, pp. 19–20; M. Romanowski, 'Szczegółowe reguły wykładni kontraktów w świetle zasad europejskiego prawa kontraktów a reguły wykładni umów w prawie polskim', PPH 2004/9/12–18.

or even if that intention was revealed in the formation of the contract, then it is according to that intention, revealed in the preamble, that the declaration must be interpreted (Art. 236.°/2). In fact, written contracts must be interpreted in accordance with the sense that has a minimum correspondence with the text even if it is imperfectly expressed. This is the relevant factor of interpretation according to Art. 238.°/1 CC.

In this case, the preamble refers to the real intention of Premier. Therefore, it is possible to argue that, despite the ambiguous words used in Clause 12(d), the preamble reveals that Jewellers King knew of Premier's intention to lease five retails units in the shopping centre to jewellery businesses. Therefore, the preamble can be used to prove that knowledge according to Arts. 236.°/1 and 236.°/2 CC.

Question 2: Information Brochure

If Premier had referred only to an information brochure with the same text, the answer would be the same in the Portuguese system of contract interpretation. For the same reasons as discussed above, an information brochure can be used as evidence to show that Jewellers King knew of Premier's intention according Art. 236.°/2 CC.

Question 3: The Contract's Purpose

If neither the preamble nor an information brochure had mentioned anything relating to the purpose of the contract, the purpose could still be relevant as an interpretation factor if it is referred to in the text of the contract (Art. 238.°/1 CC) or if Jewellers knew of Premier's real aim at the formation of the contract (Arts. 236.°/2 and 238.°/2 CC). This holds even if there is no written document. In this case, the court will need to appeal to other kinds of proof such as witness testimony (Art. 393.° CC). Art. 393.° expressly admits witness testimony concerning contracts, which do not need to be written, and moreover, even if there is a written contract, the witness testimony can be used to interpret the context of the contract.

12. SCOTLAND

Question 1: Preamble

Clause 12(d) protects Jewellers King from future competition at the shopping centre owned by Premier. The question concerns the precise point in time at which that protection from competition commences, i.e. whether it is operative as soon as the lease contract has been concluded or only after Premier has let out a fifth jewellery store.

Since it is a central interpretative criterion that the contract must be construed as a whole, as Lord Reed noted in the case of *Macdonald Estates plc v Regenesis (2005) Dunfermline Ltd*,[88] the preamble and recitals of a contract form part of the contract itself and have a role to play here. Therefore, the Scottish courts may derive assistance from the terms of the preamble in order to resolve any ambiguity in the operative provisions of a contract. However, they are unable to override the operative terms of a contract where the latter are clear.[89] On the assumption that Clause 12(d) is ambiguously drafted, the terms of the preamble could be used to sustain Premier's reading of the position. However, if it had been the case that Clause 12(d) was unambiguous, then the courts would not have permitted the preamble to supersede the ordinary and natural meaning of the words in the clause.[90]

Question 2: Information Brochure

If Premier had not referred to the preamble but rather to an information brochure to the lease contract with similar text, matters would be different. Since an information brochure does not form part of the contract itself, it would be treated as extrinsic evidence and merely a single isolated part of the overall factual context. Irrespective of whether they find Clause 12(d) to be ambiguous or not as the case may be, the Scottish courts are prepared to adopt an objective and contextual approach by taking into account the surrounding circumstances when the contract was entered into, including the background knowledge which was, or ought reasonably to have been, available to the contracting parties and the overall factual matrix/context. Since the agreement is a commercial lease, the Scottish courts could have recourse to the commercially sensible construction. Applying that interpretative tool to this case would result in a finding in favour of Jewellers King since a tenant who is successful in securing an anti-competition clause would hardly be likely to agree to an additional two units beyond their let.[91] However, that commercially sensible construction would clash with the provisions of the information brochure and the question is how the Scottish courts would resolve that inconsistency. Recently, the Supreme Court has re-emphasised

---

88 2007 SLT 791, 818.

89 *Young v Smith* (1865) LR 1 Eq 180, 183 per Sir J Romilly MR; *Re Moon, ex p Dawes* (1886) 17 QBD 275; *Commissioners of Inland Revenue v Raphael, re Sassoon* [1933] 1 Ch 858, 879 per Lord Hanworth MR; *Rutter (Inspector of Taxes) v Charles Sharpe & Co Ltd* [1979] 1 WLR 1429; *T&N Ltd (in administration) v Royal & Sun Alliance plc* [2003] EWHC 1016 (Ch); [2003] 2 All ER (Comm) 939; *Gallaher International Ltd v Tlais Enterprises Ltd* [2008] EWHC 804 (Comm); and *Brookfield Construction Ltd v Foster & Partners Ltd* [2009] EWHC 307 (TCC); [2009] BLR 246.

90 *Macdonald Estates plc v Regenesis (2005) Dunfermline Ltd* 2007 SLT 791, 818 per Lord Reed.

91 *Warren James (Jewellers) Ltd v Overgate Group Ltd* [2007] CSIH 14.

the importance of the actual wording of the contract and placed important qualifications on the use of the commercially sensible construction.[92] They warned that the parties must not invent drafting infelicities in order to be able to have recourse to the commercially sensible construction.[93] It is only one of the tools available to the Scottish court and is not given a pre-eminent role in any hierarchy of interpretative norms. The commercially sensible construction could be used by the court, but it is unlikely to be given any greater weight in the interpretative process than the information brochure (which would be considered part of the factual matrix).

Question 3: The Contract's Purpose

In the situation where neither the preamble nor an information brochure had mentioned anything relating to the purpose of the lease contract, the *purpose* or *objective* of the lease contract would be taken into account in the interpretation of Clause 12(d). This would be done through a commercially sensible construction of the lease which, as the Supreme Court recently recognised, can assist in the identification of the purpose or objective.[94]

13. SOUTH AFRICA

Question 1: Preamble

In terms of the traditional approach to contractual interpretation, a South African court could consider the preamble in order to assist in the interpretation of a contractual provision provided the meaning of the latter was ambiguous.[95]

In the absence of ambiguity, the preamble was not taken into account (even if the recital displayed a contrary intention to that contained in the operative part[96]) because it was regarded as subordinate to the operative part.[97] This rule was criticised on the basis that the better view is to consider the preamble as an integral part of the contract and therefore always to be considered, even in the absence of ambiguity.[98] In view of the current approach to interpretation, with

---

92 *Arnold v Britton* [2015] UKSC 36; [2015] AC 1619.

93 Ibid.; C. Connal, 'Has the Rainy Sky Dried up? *Arnold v Britton* and commercial interpretation'.

94 *Wood v Capita Insurance Services Ltd* [2017] UKSC 24; [2017] 2 WLR 1095, per Lord Hodge at para. 28.

95 *Agricultural Supply Association v Olivier* 1952 2 SA 661 (T) 664B-E; *Logista Inc. v Van der Merwe* 2010 3 SA 105 (WCC) para. 7.

96 The operative part of the contract is regarded as that part which creates rights and duties – *Consol Ltd t/a Consol Glass v Twee Jonge Gezellen (Pty) Ltd* 2005 6 SA 1 (SCA) para. 13.

97 *Agricultural Supply Association v Olivier* 1952 2 SA 661 (T) 664B-E; *Logista Inc. v Van der Merwe* 2010 3 SA 105 (WCC) para. 7; Bradfield, *Christie's Law of Contract*, p. 251.

98 Lubbe and Murray, *Farlam & Hathaway*, p. 454 n. 5; Cornelius, *Interpretation*, p. 176; *Wijtenburg Holdings t/a Flamingo Dry Cleaners v Bobroff* 1970 4 SA 197 (T) 207D-E.

its emphasis on context, this criticism probably indicates the correct point of departure and the preamble will be considered as a matter of course (although a court will presumably continue to give greater weight to the operative part of the contract).

Whether the answer would be different if a court were not dealing with the preamble, but rather with another clause in the contract, would depend on the formulation of that clause. If the wording of the clause has remained the same as that of the fifth recital in the preamble, then it is likely that a court will still treat the clause as merely introductory and of less weight than Clause 12(d) and the rest of the operative part of the contract.[99] However, if it were formulated in a manner that it creates a right for Premier to let five units in total, then it will constitute an operative part of the contract and be read together with Clause 12(d).[100]

Question 2: Information Brochure

Premier's information brochure would be taken into account in interpreting the clause,[101] provided Jewellers King was aware of its contents. If so, the information brochure would be regarded as part of the broader context or factual matrix because it establishes a fact known to both parties[102] and therefore indicates how a reasonable person, in the position of the contracting parties, would interpret the clause.

Question 3: The Contract's Purpose

The commercial purpose of a contract or a clause therein may be taken into account during the process of interpretation.[103] Furthermore, where a contract or clause is reasonably capable of being interpreted in a manner that does not lead to absurd practical or commercial consequences, a court will favour a commercially sensible meaning above a meaning which is not.[104] A court may not, however, impose its own view of what it considers to be a commercially sensible meaning on the words actually used by the parties. To do so would

---

99 *Consol Ltd t/a Consol Glass v Twee Jonge Gezellen (Pty) Ltd* 2005 6 SA 1 (SCA) para. 13.

100 *Logista Inc. v Van der Merwe* 2010 3 SA 105 (WCC) para. 11.

101 See e.g. *Seven Eleven Corporation of SA (Pty) Ltd v Cancun Trading No 150 CC* 2005 5 SA 186 (SCA) para. 22, where the court held that information contained in a disclosure document issued to a prospective franchisee formed part of the background to the conclusion of the contract and could be considered in interpreting the latter.

102 A prerequisite for evidence to be regarded as part of the factual matrix – see *Seven Eleven Corporation of SA (Pty) Ltd v Cancun Trading No 150 CC* 2005 5 SA 186 (SCA) para. 22; *Natal Joint Municipal Pension Fund v Endumeni Municipality* 2012 4 SA 593 (SCA) para. 18.

103 *Natal Joint Municipal Pension Fund v Endumeni Municipality* 2012 4 SA 593 (SCA) para. 18; *Novartis SA (Pty) Ltd v Maphil Trading (Pty) Ltd* 2016 1 SA 518 (SCA) paras. 27–31.

104 *Natal Joint Municipal Pension Fund v Endumeni Municipality* 2012 4 SA 593 (SCA) paras. 18, 26.

amount to the creation of a contract for the parties, rather than the enforcement of the contract that the parties had, in fact, concluded.[105]

The purpose of the lease contract may be discerned from the contract as a whole, as explained by evidence of the factual matrix. The fact that Premier intended to conclude lease contracts with five retail jewellers would be irrelevant to establishing the purpose of the contract, unless Jewellers King knew of this.[106] However, the fact that Premier had already leased two units to retail jewellers (of which Jewellers King is aware) may be relevant to explaining the purpose of the lease and the meaning of the clause.

14. SPAIN

Question 1: Preamble

The preamble is usually taken into account by Spanish courts because of the systematic interpretation factor set out in Art. 1.285 CC, which says clauses must be interpreted in connection with each other, attributing to any doubtful clauses the meaning resulting from the whole. This rule is widely known as 'canon de la totalidad' [systematic and contextual interpretation rule].[107] Therefore, this legal rule requires the court to pay attention to the whole contract, which must be read as a whole. From the preamble to the additional and final clauses, every single part of the contract plays an important role in interpretation.

This article belongs to the so-called 'subjective interpretation', which permits considering the common intention of the parties. This intention, this common contractual consent, is found not only in every single clause, but also in the all organic text.

Art. 1.285 is applicable even though the preamble is not a clause itself. This is because the term 'cláusula" [clause] used by Art. 1.285 is read in a very broad sense as part of the contract. Thus, if the preamble of a contract is part of a contract, then it can be used as an interpretative element which can shed light on and give sense to doubtful clauses. Furthermore, some scholars, such as Díez-Picazo,[108] state that Art. 1.285 could also enter into play provided that different contracts are connected by the same economic function or persons, as happened in STS 20.05.1986 (RJ 1986\2735).

Systematic interpretation is a consequence of the logical unit of the contract, the spirit of which is always indivisible. In conclusion, the whole

105 Ibid., para. 18.

106 See Question 2.

107 Spanish doctrine uses this expression coined by the Italian jurist E. Betti. See Spanish scholars like: Díez-Picazo, *Fundamentos*, p. 503; Jordano Barea, *Comentario*, p. 515; Rodríguez Marín, 'De la interpretación de los contratos', p. 2284.

108 Díez-Picazo, p. 502.

contract serves to identify the common intention of the parties (Art. 1.281 CC), which is the basic aim of contractual interpretation, and facilitates overcoming and avoiding contradictions and antinomies.

Jurisprudence confirms these considerations. Spanish courts confirm this view of the contract as an organic whole and not as a mere collection of clauses. As a result, they require a connection between the different parts of the contract and its systematic analysis. Some judicial decisions use the systematic interpretative element and prohibit a contractual interpretation based on an isolated clause.[109] Jurisprudence states that when interpreting the contract, grammatical interpretation is not sufficient, and the real common intention of the parties must be found with the other legal rules.[110]

Question 2: Information Brochure

Regarding whether the answer would be the same were the text not in the preamble but in an information brochure, the answer might be more controversial before a Spanish court. A brochure is outside the contract itself. It has contractual value but it is not in the contract itself and therefore it becomes difficult for Art. 1.285 to be applied.

Nevertheless, we can evoke another important factor in interpretation: the way in which the contract was drawn up and the parties' behaviour. Art. 1.282 CC states that in order to judge the intention of the contracting parties, their behaviour at the time of and subsequent to the contract shall be mainly taken into account. This is usually called historical interpretation.[111] Spanish courts can search for the common intention of the parties 'outside' the contract. 'Acts' are meant in a broad sense, and documents, notes or preliminary drafts are included in this kind of historical interpretation. In this sense, an information brochure is a document that can be analysed as one of the external elements in order to discover the intention of the parties. It can be a relevant sign to identify the real meaning for both parties of Clause 12(d).

However, the brochure is a unilateral draft and can only be the expression of a common intention in the event that it was known to and accepted by the other.[112]

---

109 See STS 28.11.2013, ECLI:ES:TS:2013:5821.

110 STS 05.06.2013, ECLI:ES:TS:2013:3126; STS 13.10.2014, ECLI:ES:TS:2014:3909; STS 09.03.2015, ECLI:ES:TS:2015:1403; STS 03.03.2016, ECLI:ES:TS:2016:978.

111 STS 04.03.2014, ECLI:ES:TS:2014:849; STS 17.02.2015, ECLI:ES:TS:2015:1402; STS 16.04.2015, ECLI:ES:TS:2015:2213; STS 30.03.2016, ECLI:ES:TS:2016:1297; STS 07.06.1989; STS 07.07.1994.

112 Díez-Picazo, *Fundamentos*, p. 504; Jordano Barea, *Comentario*, p. 512.

Question 3: The Contract's Purpose

Regarding the role, if any, that the purpose or objective of the lease contract in the interpretation of Clause 12(d) may play, assuming that neither the preamble nor a brochure had mentioned anything, two articles of the Spanish CC can be taken into account, but none of them in this case may offer an easy solution to the question.

First, Art. 1.286 CC, as a legal rule, contains an objective interpretation element. This provision says that words that may have different meanings shall be understood as having the meaning which is most in accordance with the nature and subject matter of the agreement. Therefore, attention must be focused on the nature and subject matter of the agreement. 'Nature' here is understood as the type of contract and 'subject' must be read as the purpose or concrete economic function of the contract – its practical aim. Thus, this rule consists of a finalist or teleological interpretative factor.[113] Although the article uses the term 'palabras' [words], this is meant in a broad sense in terms of legal doctrine and judicial decision.

Second, Art. 1.289 CC, which is a closing clause, may also enter into play because it says that in the event that it is absolutely impossible to resolve any doubts, if such doubts are about accidental circumstances of the contract, and the contract is gratuitous in the sense of a commodatum whereby a party conveys moveable or immoveable property to another without charge, they shall be resolved in favour of the least transfer of rights and interests. If the contract is onerous, as in this case, the doubt shall be resolved in favour of the greatest reciprocity of interests or the least relinquishment of rights. This is an obscure provision not often applied by courts.[114]

15. SWEDEN

Question 1: Preamble

Swedish courts will consider the preamble relevant. It can hardly be overlooked in the textual analysis – and, in this case, textual analysis will be the natural starting point when interpreting the contract.[115] However, it is not possible to specify beforehand exactly *what* role the preamble will play – simply because, even though it might seem to corroborate Premier's interpretation of Clause 12(d), it does not do so conclusively.

---

113 López y López, 'De la interpretación', p. 702; Díez-Picazo, *Fundamentos*, p. 507; Jordano Barea, *Comentario*, p. 515. See STS 17.04.2015, ECLI:ES:TS:2015:1705; STS 25.03.2013, ECLI:TS:2013:4910.

114 See STS 28.05.2001 (RJ 2001\3435).

115 See the Opening Remarks and, especially, the Supreme Court cases referred to in n. 238.

It is certainly possible for the courts to construe the relation between clause and preamble in other ways. For instance, the language of the fifth recital of the preamble is rather vague, at least assessed from the viewpoint of the doctrine of formation of contracts: there is talk of the *intentions* of *one* of the contracting parties. According this recital decisive weight when attributing sense to the *mutual agreement* seems questionable. And considering the nature of preambles (they tend to be composed of fairly lofty statements) it could well be argued that the fifth recital is no more than an 'avsiktsförklaring' [declaration of intent]. On this reading, Premier has *declared its intent* to lease to no more than five jewellers, but has *promised* Jewellers King not to lease to more than three.[116] Proponents of this interpretation will, of course, have to produce an alternative explanation of the occurrence of this 'declaration of intent' in the preamble – seeing as the result is a somewhat less coherent text. Whether or not this can be accomplished will depend on the circumstances. The dictum that the text is to be regarded as a coherent whole provides, as is generally acknowledged, but a presupposition,[117] and carries no real normative force. After all, in practice contracts might be quite incoherent.

In addition, there is a normative trait in the general doctrine of interpretation of contracts and other juridical acts – a most indeterminate body of principles on occasion referred to by the Swedish Supreme Court as 'vanliga principer för avtalstolkning' [the usual principles of contract interpretation] (or some variation of that expression)[118] – working against Premier here. Even though we are dealing with the preamble to a bilateral 'rättshandling' [juridical act],[119] the declaration under consideration, in the fifth recital, has a unilateral flavour to it, and in as far as the wording is considered inaccurate, the courts will tend to read it against the stipulating party, especially when the stipulation in question can be understood as a would-be attempt to delimit an obligation

116 On the distinction between non-binding declarations of intent and legally binding promises, see the Supreme Court cases NJA 1992 p. 375; NJA 1994 p. 204; NJA 1995 p. 586. The line is, according to the Supreme Court, to be drawn using the usual principles of contract interpretation, which is to say that the line has to be drawn ad hoc, the decisive question being whether the declaring party did intend to issue a binding promise or not, and that is not a question of (legal) principle.

117 This principle has been referred to by the Supreme Court in a series of cases – see NJA 1990 p. 24, NJA 1992 p. 403 and NJA 2007 p. 35; cf. NJA 2017 p. 237.

118 See e.g. NJA 1995 p. 586; NJA 1997 p. 382; NJA 2004 p. 363; NJA 2018 p. 805; NJA 2019 p. 195. Though on occasion referred to, and sometimes described, these principles have never been exhaustively enumerated, let alone defined, by the Supreme Court; cf. NJA 1999 p. 35; NJA 2018 p. 834; NJA 2019 p. 638.

119 'Rättshandling' is a basic concept of Swedish contract law. It is defined as any 'viljeförklaring' [will declaration] aimed at achieving a legal effect. The concepts of 'rättshandling' and 'viljeförklaring' are nowadays typically seen as dogmatic remnants of an age gone by; see e.g. Adlercreutz and Gorton, *Avtalsrätt I*, p. 24.

of that party defined elsewhere.[120] Whether or not it can be so understood is an open question. The fifth recital of the preamble will have to be read against Clause 12(d) and vice versa. All will depend on *how* clear, or unclear, Clause 12(d) is deemed to be, and this can be decided only with reference to the context. Basically, if Jewellers King is, all relevant matters (such as the economic stakes) considered, justified in concluding from Clause 12(d) that Premier is prohibited from leasing to more than three jewellers, then the declaration of Premier's intent, in the preamble, to lease to no more than five, is of no consequence. Should, however, Clause 12(d), in the final analysis, be deemed to be radically ambiguous, or if the reading preferred by Premier is, to any degree, considered to be more sound, then, most likely, the fifth recital will form an integral part of the interpretation that the court will forge in order to decide the case.

Swedish law, as such, sides with neither party. All it decrees is that there are no formal constraints on interpretive data.[121] Everything relevant should be considered. Preambles are typically relevant.[122] *What* role they will play is a matter of the interpreters' discretion. And – this is an important point – it is not possible to decide on the role of the preamble in this case – or of the role of *any* matter relevant to *any* interpretive question arising under Swedish law – without actually engaging in interpretation.

And what if the information that Premier intends to let to no more than five jewellers in total was included in the contract as such, in a separate clause? That would change things. It is acknowledged by the Supreme Court that the location of a provision within the contract text matters when assessing its import.[123] In this case, including the text in the contract makes its unilateral character somewhat less tangible, and the courts will, accordingly, be more inclined to hold both parties responsible, jointly, for the wording – for instance, vagueness will be less important, as a factor, in deciding in whose favour the contract should be read. Still, this does not entail that the information in question will be decisive when the courts interpret the contract.[124] There are – as is well known in the theory of interpretation of contracts – limits to what can be achieved by including, in the contract itself, explanations, definitions and other attempts at controlling the interpretation of the contract.[125] Context is everything, and the decision is always, in the end, in the hands of the court.

---

120 Cf. for instance NJA 1951 p. 282; on this case see Vahlén, *Avtal och tolkning*, p. 294 ff. See also the recent case NJA 2012 p. 3. The argument is clearly related to the 'oklarhetsregel' mentioned in the Opening Remarks.

121 See the Opening Remarks, n. 237.

122 In NJA 1993 p. 436 the Supreme Court held that an enunciation – a statement of fact – found in a preamble to a sales contract was not to be treated as a contract term. Cf. NJA 1990 p. 24.

123 See NJA 1964 p. 152 and NJA 1985 p. 397.

124 Cf. NJA 2007 p. 35, where an explanatory note was accorded some weight by the Supreme Court.

125 See e.g. Samuelsson, *Tolkningslärans gåta*, p. 163.

Question 2: Information Brochure

Suppose Premier had referred not to the preamble but rather to an information brochure with similar text? That would pose an additional problem. Before engaging in any interpretative activity, the courts would now have to decide whether the information brochure ought to be included at all in the relevant context when interpreting Clause 12(d) of the contract. If not, the information in question should be ignored.[126]

The question is not, from the point of view of Swedish law, about the formal nature of the data considered, i.e. whether we are dealing with a 'preamble' or a 'brochure', or with something else. The question is whether, under the circumstances, the parties have 'fog' [reason] to include the matter in the context when attributing sense to their agreement. Their 'befogade tolkning' [reasonable interpretation] is protected by the courts.[127] And the frame is intersubjective. The parties – both parties, jointly – must have had reason to consider the matter in question as relevant.[128] It is, for example, one thing if the information brochure was presented to Jewellers King during negotiations, quite another if the brochure was merely available, for instance online or at Premier's offices.[129]

If the brochure is considered relevant, the situation will be somewhat similar to the one detailed in the original case description. However, the text will now most likely be regarded by the courts as unilateral and non-binding. If deemed to have an impact on the understanding of Clause 12(d) this will probably be in the form of *evidence* – of the eventual fact that Premier, at the time of formation of the contract, did read Clause 12(d) the way Premier now claims it is to be read, and, possibly, of the additional, eventual fact that Jewellers King was in 'ond tro' [bad faith] with regard to Premier's reading. 'Ond tro' is, in effect, a standard of conduct.[130] If these facts can be established, especially if Jewellers King is held to be 'dolösa' [in qualified bad faith], i.e. if Jewellers King knew, or must have known, of Premier's understanding of Clause 12(d)), the courts have the option to apply 'dolusregeln', holding Jewellers King to the interpretation made by Premier at the time of the formation of the contract.

126 Cf. e.g. NJA 1941 p. 563; NJA 1964 p. 239; NJA 1984 p. 280.

127 This is in line with the rule on mistake found in Section 32(1) of the Contracts Act. Cf. Lehrberg, *Avtalstolkning*, p. 22 ff. See, for a classic statement to this effect in the preparatory works, SOU 1929:22 p. 204 f.

128 See e.g. Adlercreutz andGorton, *Avtalrätt II*, p. 54 ff.

129 Cf. NJA 1978 p. 432, where the Supreme Court considered standard terms, found in a travel brochure available to customers at the travel agency, part of the contract between traveller and travel agency, in spite of the fact that the traveller had not read the brochure. However, the decision was based, inter alia, on the fact that travellers – consumers – generally are aware of the existence of standardised travelling terms. See Bernitz, *Standardavtalsrätt*, p. 58 ff.

130 The concept is frequently used in statutory provisions. An authoritative explanation is offered by Adlercreutz, *Avtalsrätt I*, p. 43 ff.

Question 3: The Contract's Purpose

Had neither the preamble nor an information brochure mentioned anything relating to the purpose of Clause 12(d) of the lease contract, the 'avtalets syfte' [contract's purpose] might still, if possible to establish, have a role to play. Indeed, Swedish courts are quite fond of construing contracts teleologically, where the approach is appropriate[131] – especially in circumstances like these, i.e. in a commercial context, where there are no direct indications of what content the parties envisioned, where the wording is ambiguous and where there is little hope of doing away with the ambiguity by means of textual analysis in any stricter sense.[132]

However, it should be borne in mind that the 'purpose' of the contract is a construction, arrived at by means of interpretation, and not in itself a fact, somehow objectively given. Where the notion of 'purpose' is employed by the courts, it is typically in order to affirm a reading aligned with the particular purpose thus ascribed to the contract.[133] Moreover, the purpose of the contract will typically reflect the reciprocity of the contract instrument. The fact that a specific clause is ascribed a specific purpose by *one* of the parties is in itself of no consequence, even if the clause in question was stipulated by, or provided by, that party. 'Avtalets syfte' is to be constructed objectively – with reference to circumstances visible to both parties at the time of conclusion of the contract and, where appropriate, to objective standards such as functionality and economic rationality.[134]

Premier's reliance on the purpose that *Premier* has ascribed to Clause 12(d) is of no consequence when interpreting the contract – unless, again, it can be shown that Jewellers King was aware, at the time of conclusion of the contract, that Premier did ascribe this purpose to the clause.[135]

16. EDITORIAL COMPARATIVE OBSERVATIONS

Reporters for most of the jurisdictions have reached the same conclusion in this case as to the role of the preamble, the information brochure or the purpose of Clause 12(d): the court is likely to have regard to each of these items/factors in order to interpret Clause 12(d). However, in each jurisdiction,

---

131 See e.g. NJA 1974 p. 526; NJA 1991 p. 319; NJA 1992 p. 439; NJA 1997 p. 382; NJA 2015 p. 991; NJA 2017 p. 237; cf. NJA 2011 p. 316 (non-commercial context).

132 See generally Adlercreutz and Gorton, *Avtalrätt II*, p. 66; Lehrberg, *Avtalstolkning*, p. 112 ff.; J. Ramberg and C. Ramberg, *Allmän avtalsrätt*, p. 156 ff.

133 See e.g. NJA 2015 p. 991.

134 See e.g. NJA 1997 p. 382.

135 See Lehrberg, *Avtalstolkning*, p. 117.

the route adopted to reach that result will vary. Irrespective of whether a jurisdiction begins the interpretative enquiry by having regard to the subjective or objective contextual meaning of an expression in the contract, in the lion's share of the jurisdictions reviewed, recourse to the terms of the preamble, information brochure (with the exception of England and Wales, Scotland and Sweden) and the contractual purpose or objective will be adopted as a matter of course by virtue of particular interpretative rules in play in those jurisdictions.

Some jurisdictions reach this solution by the application of civil code provisions. This would include Croatia, France, Germany, Greece, Italy, Poland, Portugal and Spain. In other jurisdictions, there is no specific legislative provision which governs the solution. There, courts may make reference to precedents or legal cases which would guide the court towards the correct result. This would include England, the Netherlands, Poland, Scotland, South Africa and Sweden. In these cases, precedents are used perhaps because interpretation falls outside the civil code (the Netherlands) or because the jurisdiction is not codified (England, Scotland and South Africa). Poland makes use of both codal provisions and precedents.

In France, Germany, Portugal, Finland, Sweden and Spain, academic writings and legal practice would exert an influence on the outcome of the case. Meanwhile, in Germany, Greece and Italy, various principles would be relevant criteria in interpreting the provisions of a contract. For example, principles of good faith, trust, and certainty in transactions would have an impact on the case, as would the 'causa' of the contract.

As to the reason for giving weight to the preamble, information brochure or purpose of a clause, it is possible to see a split between the legal systems in which the aim of the interpretative exercise is to reach the true, subjective common intention of the parties, and those in which a more objective aim is pursued. The majority of the legal systems fall into the former category, whereas in England, Scotland and South Africa, the aim is to adopt an objective construction in order to discover what the contract would mean to a reasonable person in the position of the contracting parties. The Netherlands would appear to adopt a midway position, where the correct technique is not to adopt a subjective or literal approach, but to take into account the meaning that the respective parties, in the particular circumstances, could reasonably have attributed to the provisions of the contract and to that which in that respect they could reasonably have expected from each other. As for the status of the preamble, most jurisdictions would treat it as admissible material. The principal ground for doing so is that the preamble would be considered an integral part of the contract. Therefore, in accordance with the notion of 'systematic interpretation', particular terms of a contract would be interpreted in accordance with the terms of the contract as a whole, i.e. other parts of the contract. For example, this is an approach that is quite clearly adopted in France,

Spain and Italy. Other jurisdictions, however, would account for the preamble on different grounds. For example, in Poland, it would be treated as part of the surrounding context of the contract. As such, the admissibility of the preamble is a finding that is common to both civilian and common law countries alike in this study. The only outlier jurisdiction is Sweden, where the contents of the preamble may occasionally be ruled as non-conclusive on the basis that its terms would be treated as a unilateral declaration by one of the parties only and non-binding.

The treatment of the preamble can be contrasted with that of the information brochure. For example, some of the jurisdictions would not take into account the content of the information brochure on the basis that it is inadmissible material, for example England. In English law, it would not be considered part of the contract and instead would constitute a component of the inadmissible pre-contractual negotiations between the contracting parties. Of course, English law is the embodiment of the common law system, which can be contrasted with South Africa – another jurisdiction influenced by the common law – where the information brochure would be admitted as evidence without demur. In fact, generally speaking, the majority of the jurisdictions in the study would take into account the content of the information brochure as a matter of course, for example Croatia, Finland, Germany, the Netherlands, Poland, Portugal, South Africa and Spain, although in some jurisdictions, such as Greece, the status of an information brochure may be somewhat more tenuous than that of a preamble if it is not appended to or mentioned in the agreement. However, the grounds for admitting the information brochure in each of the aforementioned countries would vary. In certain cases, the juridical grounds for doing so – beyond a simple statement that certain provisions of the Civil Code or a case authority would apply – are not altogether clear, for example in Croatia, Finland, Germany, the Netherlands, Poland and Portugal. Meanwhile, in Italy, the principle of good faith would be applied to prevent Jewellers King from relying on an interpretation that is inconsistent with the terms of Premier's information brochure. This doctrine may well be operating as a functional equivalent of 'estoppel' or 'personal bar' in English or Scots law in this particular context. As for Greece, the justification for the admissibility of the information brochure would be based on the fact that it amounted to an external expression of the true common intent of the parties.

Finally, in all the jurisdictions, the purpose or objective of Clause 12(d) would indeed be relevant as an interpretative criterion. In some jurisdictions, this 'purpose or objective' would be identified by adopting an objective evaluation, for example in England and Scotland. In Sweden, however, it would have to amount to a mutually understood or accepted objective.

Interestingly, in Scotland, the information brochure which is indicative of the purpose or objective of Clause 12(d) would be treated as background material that would only be considered as part of the interpretative exercise if it did not form part of the pre-contractual negotiations between the parties. The same point applies in England. This can be contrasted with the civilian jurisdictions, where there is no embargo on consideration of the information brochure, since it would not be categorised as inadmissible background material, but as providing evidence of the parties' understanding of the purpose of objective of the contract.

As for the corresponding weight to be attached to the preamble, the information brochure and the purpose or objective of the Clause 12(d), it is the former that is undoubtedly the most influential as an interpretative factor. Meanwhile, the information brochure is the least weighty in terms of importance, partly because it is treated as peripheral to the contract in many jurisdictions.

CASE 2: BOTANICAL FRUITS

'Imperial Real Estate' owns a small food court and lets spaces to various vendors. It enters into a lease agreement with 'Botanical Fruits', a store which sells fruits and fruit juices. The mall already includes a vegetable vendor. Because Imperial strives for the biggest possible variety of products sold in its small shopping mall, the director of Imperial requires that Clause 8 of the lease contract reads: 'Botanical Fruits will abstain from selling: ... (g) any vegetables or vegetable products.' Botanical Fruits accepts. Soon after Botanical Fruits opens business, Imperial discovers that Botanical Fruits is selling aubergines, tomatoes and cucumbers, as well as juices containing these products, in large quantities. After warning Botanical Fruits numerous times that, under Clause 8(g) of the lease contract, the latter is to cease selling aubergines, tomatoes and cucumbers immediately, Imperial holds Botanical Fruits in breach of its obligations and terminates the lease contract. Botanical Fruits disagrees that it breached its contractual obligations and contests the termination of the contract. As Botanical Fruits tried to tell Imperial recently, botanically speaking, cucumbers are ripened ovaries of a flowering plant, and botanical experts therefore classify aubergines, tomatoes and cucumbers as fruits. Imperial had heard Botanical Fruits' arguments before but found them simply preposterous. In ordinary, common language for everyday purposes, Imperial contends, aubergines, tomatoes and cucumbers are considered vegetables.

1 *[Technical and Ordinary Meaning] Assume that both Imperial and Botanical Fruits are correct; the technical, botanical meaning of 'vegetables' excludes aubergines, tomatoes and cucumbers, and the common or ordinary meaning of 'vegetables' includes these items. What relative weight will be attached to both the technical or ordinary meaning play in the interpretation of Clause 8(g)?*
2 *[Expertise] Would your answer to Question 1 be different if Imperial had many decades of experience in the food retail industry, and its director had an academic background in botanical studies?*

1. KEY ISSUES

The case concerns a dispute between a landlord and tenant in the context of a lease within a small food court. The case is designed to provoke discussion of whether a literal, technical meaning of a term is or is not to be preferred to an ordinary, common sense meaning. The tenant in the case seeks to rely on an interpretation which some might consider overly scientific, namely that, botanically speaking, aubergines, tomatoes and cucumbers are fruits. If this is the case, they will fall within the definition of the goods the tenant is entitled to sell in terms of the lease. This botanical meaning is very different from the common or ordinary meaning. The first question asks reporters to outline the relative weight which will be attached to both meanings in the interpretative process. The second question adds a further dimension, asking whether the answer would be different if the landlord had many decades of experience in the food retail industry, and its director had an academic background in botanical studies. It is the tenant who seeks to rely on the botanical meaning. This question allows reporters to examine whether specialist knowledge on the part of the other party, the landlord, might be relevant to the interpretative process. If the landlord is aware of the botanical meaning, this factor might weigh in favour of the tenant's interpretation.

2. CROATIA

Question 1: Technical and Ordinary Meaning

Under the assumption that both Imperial and Botanical Fruits are correct and the technical, botanical meaning of 'vegetables' excludes aubergines, tomatoes and cucumbers, and the common or ordinary meaning of 'vegetables' includes these items, the Croatian judge would have to interpret the contractual Clause 8(g) and establish what meaning – the technical or ordinary – corresponds to the actual and common intent of the contract parties. If the actual intent of the contracting parties cannot be determined, the judge would most likely resort to the so-called 'reasonable intent'. Applying the criterion of reasonableness,[1] courts regularly interpret statements and the conduct of a party by taking into account all relevant circumstances of the case, in accordance with the understanding that a reasonable person in the same position and acting in good faith would have

1 See more about the criterion of 'reasonableness' in Art. 8(2) of the CISG and Art. 1:302 of the PECL on www.cisg.law.pace.edu/cisg/text/reason.html#view, where it is stated that the judgment will be made according to what persons acting in good faith and in the same position as the contracting parties consider reasonable. In deciding what is reasonable, one should take into account the nature and purpose (goal) of the contract, the circumstances of the case, usages and practice of trade or profession. Since Croatia is a contracting state to the CISG, according to Art. 141 of the Constitution of the Republic of Croatia (OG Nos. 56/90, 135/97, 8/98 (consolidated text), 113/00, 124/00 (consolidated text), 28/01, 41/01 (consolidated text), 55/01 (correction), 76/10, 85/10 (consolidated text) and 5/14), the CISG forms part of the domestic legal order and it has primacy over national laws and regulations. Consequently, even in cases where the CISG is not applicable, the Croatian judges could use it as a source of law and follow the mentioned criterion.

had in the same circumstances.[2] Within this process, they apply a teleological method of interpretation based on all the circumstances before, at the time of and after the conclusion of the contract, which in the case at hand would include the negotiation stage, the reasons for inserting Clause 8(g) into the contract, arguments on the meaning of 'vegetables', etc.

At the same time, the objective criteria, such as basic principles of the law of obligations together with the mentioned COA provisions on the application of trade usages and mutually developed practices, would most likely play an important role in determining the contracting parties' agreement. In establishing the 'reasonable' intent, the Croatian judge would inter alia pay special heed to one of the basic principles of the law of obligations – 'načelo savjesnosti i poštenja' [principle of conscientiousness and honesty],[3] as well as the other principles that set limits on freedom of contract.[4] In relationships between traders, these basic principles also include the obligation to act with due care or, in terms of the COA, 'pažnja dobrog stručnjaka' [due care of a good professional]. Due care of a good professional means a raised level of care and conduct 'according to rules of profession and usages' in performing obligations arising out of professional activity (Art. 10(2) of the COA). Thus, in obligations between the traders,[5] the criterion of reasonableness would be even more accentuated by the obligation to act with a raised level of care and according to rules of profession and usages.[6] Consequently, the Croatian judges would have to establish which meaning of 'vegetables', the ordinary or technical one,

---

2 Pursuant to legal theory, this so-called *objective individual ratio* should overcome the so-called *objective general ratio*, the latter involving the interpretation of the contracting provisions in a way in which they are understood by majority of participants in the legal transactions according to the principle of conscientiousness and honesty. The latter approach was accepted in the court practice of the former Yugoslavia. See Blagojević and Krulj, *Komentar zakona o obligacionim odnosima*, p. 273; Perović and Stojanović, *Komentar zakona o obligacionim odnosima*, p. 346. However, the recent Croatian case law makes a distinction in the application of this criterion in commercial (B2B) and consumer (B2C) contracts, see VTSRH, 43 Pž-6632/2017-10 of 14 June 2018.

3 See USRH, U-III-5262/2010 of 6 June 2014, 4.1: 'Observing this principle entails evaluation of consciousness [and honesty] of each participant to a certain legal relationship. Every other action would be contrary to the principles of the rule of law and of legal certainty as the highest values of the constitutional order.'

4 Such as the principle of equality of the parties to the relationship, see County Court in Osijek, P-788/2014-14 of 1 April 2015, 26.

5 According to Art. 1 of the Companies Act (OG Nos. 111/93, 34/99, 52/00, 118/03, 107/07, 146/08, 137/09, 125/11, 152/11 (consolidated), 111/12, 68/13 and 110/15), unless otherwise provided by this Act, the trader is a legal or a natural person who independently and continuously performs an economic activity with the aim of making profit through the production and trade in goods or provision of services on the market, not including individual farmers and including persons pursuing free professions when they are considered traders within the meaning of special regulations governing their profession.

6 See the case before Administrative Court in Zagreb, UsI-3391/13-9 of 9 October 2014, requiring lawyers to act with an increased level of due professional care.

corresponds to rules of profession and usages between the traders. In order to do so, the courts would certainly consider Art. 12 of the COA on the application of trade usages and mutually developed practices. Since Imperial and Botanical Fruits have not agreed on the application of trade usage and there is no mutually developed practice between them, Art. 12(1) of the COA does not apply.[7] Nor does Clause 8(g) contain an explicit agreement on application of trade usage or a reference to the 'ordinary' understanding which would indicate that the contracting parties intended the trade usages to apply.[8] However, in accordance with standards in international contract law, Art. 12(2) of the COA introduces an objective approach to application of trade usages: in obligations between traders, trade usages which are applied regularly by traders in identical relations apply in all cases, unless the parties excluded their application explicitly or implicitly.[9] Moreover, according to Art. 12(3) of the COA, if these preconditions are fulfilled, trade usages and mutually developed practices between the parties are applicable even if they are contrary to dispositive rules. According to this objective criterion, it is not necessary that the contracting parties are aware or ought to have been aware of trade usages. However, the obligation of awareness could arise due to the fact that these traders are experts dealing in a special field of business. This obligation may again arise as a corollary to the obligation to act with a raised level of care 'according to rules of profession and usages' in performing obligations arising out of professional activity (Art. 10(2) of the COA). Therefore, it can be concluded that the Croatian courts would attach relative weights to the technical or ordinary meaning of the 'vegetables' and this will depend on the 'reasonable' intent of the contracting parties, which the courts would establish pursuant to the above-mentioned basic principles of the law of obligations. The courts would finally accept the meaning of 'vegetables' which would both correspond to the rules of profession and usages and be in accordance with the principle of conscientiousness and honesty, as well as other basic principles of the law of obligations.

Question 2: Expertise

In the case that Imperial had many decades of experience in the food retail industry and its director had an academic background in botanical studies, the courts would still come to the same result in their interpretation of the respective

---

7 Art. 12(1) of the COA corresponds to Art. 9(1) of the CISG, Art. 1.8(1) of the UNIDROIT Principles and Art. 1:105 of the PECL.

8 See VTSRH, Pž-2843/04 of 13 February 2007, where the court, referring to Art. 99(2) of the former COA (now Art. 319(2) of the COA), held that the parties have agreed on the application of the Special Practices in Construction by stipulating the application of general contractual conditions and conditions of performance.

9 This objective criterion for application of trade usage corresponds to standards in international contract law, e.g. in Art. 9(2) of the CISG, Art. 1.8(2) of the UNIDROIT Principles and Art. 1:105(2) of the PECL. The old COA of 1978 accepted only the subjective criterion.

contract term. Since the sole application of the subjective criterion would lead to more than one possible solution, the judge's decision on the meaning of the disputed term 'vegetables' would depend on the objective criteria prescribed by the law and could be influenced neither by Imperial's experience in the food retail industry, nor by its director's academic background in botanical studies. As already mentioned, the courts would establish the 'reasonable' intent of the contract parties by taking into account the understanding and meaning of the term 'vegetables' as determined by the rules of profession and usages applicable in that profession. In establishing the common intent of the contracting parties through the criteria of reasonableness, the court would take account of the balance between the rights and obligations of both parties by observing the basic principles of the law of obligations, especially the principle of conscientiousness and honesty that is incorporated in the criteria of reasonableness. Whether the meaning of the term 'vegetables' would correspond to the meaning of the disputed term arising from Imperial's experience in the food retail industry or to the meaning arising from its director's academic background in botanical studies, it is up to the judge to decide, by investigating the usual meaning of the term accepted in the rules of profession and usages.[10]

3. ENGLAND AND WALES

Question 1: Technical and Ordinary Meaning

The starting point for an English court will always be the common or ordinary meaning, because the court starts from the assumption that that is what the parties would have meant by the words. The courts will, however, supplant the ordinary meaning with any other meaning that the parties apparently intended, whether a private meaning (sometimes referred to as a private dictionary) agreed between them or evolved through a course of dealing, or a more generally adopted technical or other meaning used in their trade, club or any other community of which the parties are members.

Whether it will do so in a particular case depends upon whether, in all the circumstances, a reasonable observer would understand the parties to have intended the private or technical meaning rather than the ordinary meaning.

---

10 See Art. 13 of the Convention relating to a Uniform Law on the Formation of Contracts for the International Sale of Goods of 1964, where para. 1 defines 'usage' as any practice or method of dealing which reasonable persons in the same situation as the parties usually consider to be applicable to the formation of their contract. Para. 2 provides that when expressions, provisions or forms of contract commonly used in commercial practice are employed, they shall be interpreted according to the meaning usually given to them in the trade concerned. See also the corresponding provision in Art. 9 of the Convention relating to a Uniform Law on the International Sale of Goods. See Zubović, 'Primjena trgovačkih običaja', pp. 307 et seq.

This will, in the present case, depend in large part upon whether 'vegetables' has a technical meaning in the food retail industry generally. This would have to be sufficiently well established that all members of that industry would, without more, understand any use of the word within the industry to be in that sense. Otherwise, the ordinary meaning would prevail.[11] (Of course, there may be a universal technical meaning assumed among botanists in a botanical context, but Imperial Real Estate is not a botanical company and the contract is not made in a purely botanical context.) The relative weight attached to the technical and ordinary meanings depends upon the relative prominence they would have to the reasonable person when considering what the parties appear to have intended in all the circumstances.

Question 2: Expertise

Imperial Real Estate's decades of experience in the food retail industry and academic background are irrelevant unless known to Botanical Fruits. Only background known to both parties (and that both parties know the other parties know)[12] is relevant to the question of construction.[13]

Assuming that the experience and academic background of the director were known to both parties in this way, they *may* be relevant to the question of the proper interpretation of the clause, although not determinative. The experience in the industry may make it more likely that Imperial would be understood by the reasonable person to know about and intend the customary industry meaning. The academic background of Imperial's sole director may similarly affect whether the reasonable person would understand Imperial to be aware of and intend the technical meaning. In other words, both are relevant only insofar as they inform the answer to the basic legal test of what the reasonable person would have understood the parties to have intended by the term 'vegetables'.

A final factor, which may weigh against the decades of experience or academic background, is the fact that third parties who are not botanists (e.g. assignees, banks, other employees of Imperial) might be intended to read and understand the lease.[14]

---

11 This is because unless there is such a notorious technical meaning, although aware of both meanings, Botanical Fruits would not reasonably have understood Imperial Real Estate to intend the botanical meaning; and whether or not aware of the botanical meaning, Imperial Real Estate would not reasonably understand Botanical Fruits to assume that the botanical meaning would be the shared meaning.

12 *Codelfa Construction Prop Ltd v State Rail Authority of New South Wales* (1982) 149 CLR 337 (High Court of Australia) per Brennan J at 401.

13 It would not be reasonable for Botanical Fruits to think that Imperial Real Estate would understand the botanical meaning unless it knew that Imperial Real Estate had specialist botanical knowledge. It would not be reasonable for Imperial Real Estate to think that Botanical Fruits would intend the botanical meaning unless it knew that Botanical Fruits knew that Imperial Real Estate had specialist botanical knowledge.

14 See further the discussion of Case 6 below.

4. FINLAND

Question 1: Technical and Ordinary Meaning

The clause in dispute forbids the selling of vegetables. Under Finnish law, the basis for the interpretation is the common or ordinary meaning of the expressions used in the contract.[15] The common or ordinary meaning can be overruled if the expressions have specific meanings in a certain line of business. If both parties are aware of the specific meaning, the expression is interpreted to have that meaning. However, if one party is unaware of the specific meaning of a term, the more knowledgeable party has a duty to inform the other party in order to make the specific meaning applicable.[16]

In this case, Imperial Real Estate is not an expert in the field of botanical studies, and it is therefore not required to be aware of the botanical definition of 'vegetables'. Therefore, the meaning of 'vegetables' in Clause 8(g) of the contract should be interpreted to include additionally aubergines, tomatoes and cucumbers.

Question 2: Expertise

If Imperial Real Estate had many decades of experience in the food retail industry and its director had an academic background, Imperial is deemed to be an expert in the field of food retail. If the term 'vegetables' is used in its technical meaning in that field of business, then the technical meaning is to be applied. The fact that the director who had an academic background in botanical studies was drafting the contract indicates that Imperial would have been aware of the technical meaning. Therefore, Clause 8(g) should be interpreted in its technical meaning in this scenario.[17]

5. FRANCE

Question 1: Technical and Ordinary Meaning

Under Art. 1188 Cciv (formerly Art. 1156), the meaning of Clause 8(g) will be determined by reference to the common intention of the parties. Given the circumstances, the judge is likely to inquire about different points. First, he

15 See e.g. Annola, 'Tavallisuussäännön asema sopimustulkinnassa'; Aho, *Varallisuusoikeudellisen oikeustoimen tulkinnasta*, p. 255; Hemmo, *Sopimusoikeus I*, p. 650; and Pönkä, 'Tavoitteellisten tulkintasääntöjen merkityksestä liikesopimusten tulkinnassa', p. 932. See also the Finnish Supreme Court's decision 2018:37.

16 Hemmo, *Sopimusoikeus I*, pp. 608–610. See also the Finnish Supreme Court's decision KKO 1994:108.

17 Hemmo, *Sopimusoikeus I*, p. 610 and Pönkä, 'Tavoitteellisten tulkintasääntöjen merkityksestä liikesopimusten tulkinnassa', p. 929.

would ask the parties whether the purpose of the clause (namely 'striving for the biggest possible variety of products sold' in the shopping mall) was discussed during the negotiations that led to its insertion into the contract. Second, he would investigate whether Imperial and the vegetable vendor have adopted the ordinary meaning of the term 'vegetable' in their interpretation of their contract.

If Imperial's purpose was discussed between the parties during the negotiations and justified the inclusion of the clause in the contract, the court is more likely to consider that Botanical Fruits were expected to perform its contractual obligations in good faith pursuant to Art. 1104 Cciv (formerly Art. 1134 (3)). Good faith could for example require Botanical Fruits to check with Imperial or with the vegetable vendor which of the ordinary or technical meaning had been adopted between them. If Botanical Fruits does not perform its contractual obligations in good faith, it may be held liable by the court, which could lead to the payment of damages to Imperial.

If Imperial's purpose was not discussed between the parties during the negotiations, the court would have tended to refer to former Art. 1159 Cciv before the reform. According to this rule, ambiguous terms were to be interpreted in conformity with relevant usages. This required an analysis of whether a usage could be inferred from the practice developed in other shopping malls. Then this usage would have been interpreted as corresponding to the implied common intention of the parties.[18] The rule was removed from the Code by the 2016 reform, but could still inspire some judges under the cover of Art. 1188 (2) Cciv if they consider that a reasonable person would have reasoned in such a way.

Question 2: Expertise

Even if Imperial had a long experience in the food retail industry and if its director had an academic background in botanical studies, the reasoning of the court would most likely still be quite similar to the steps followed. Indeed, if the botanical competence of Imperial's director is to play a role in the interpretation of the contract, it will become apparent when the court inquires about the pre-contractual communications between the parties during the negotiations and/or in Imperial's pre-existing contractual relations with the vegetable vendor to whom he already rents a space in his shopping mall. If it appears that the technical meaning of the term 'vegetable' was not mentioned and/or not agreed upon and that the ordinary meaning of the term has been used for the performance of Imperial's contract with the vegetable vendor, then the court is likely to rule in favour of the ordinary meaning of the term irrespective of Imperial's and its director's backgrounds. The fact that the contract between Imperial and Botanical Fruits should also be interpreted in the light of the rules

18 J. Boré, 'Un centennaire: le contrôle par la Cour de cassation de la dénaturation des actes', *RTDCiv* (1972), no. 117.

and objectives governing the functioning of the mall as a whole would point in favour of such an interpretation as well.[19]

6. GERMANY

Question 1: Technical and Ordinary Meaning

From the German perspective, the agreement between Imperial Real Estate and Botanical Fruits is likely considered a 'Pachtvertrag' [lease contract] under §581 BGB. There are two provisions to be applied for the purpose of interpretation under German law, §133 and §157 BGB. §133 BGB provides the general rule on interpreting declarations of intent and focuses on the natural intention of the parties.[20] In contrast, §157 BGB, which states a general rule on the interpretation of contracts, refers to the normative, and therefore objective, meaning of a declaration.[21] There is a scholarly dispute about the relation of these provisions, but in practice both are applied by German courts for interpretation since there is no practical way to differentiate between them.[22] §157 BGB, in fact, states, that contracts should be interpreted with respect to the 'Treu und Glaube' [good faith principle] and 'Verkehrssitten' [local usages].

Since German law gives precedence to the subjective approach,[23] as a first step the real, natural intention of the parties has to be discovered. There are four classical methods of contract interpretation which have to be used in this case to establish the weight of a technical or ordinary meaning of a term in the light of the real intention of the parties. Those methods suggest that a term may be interpreted: (1) literally; (2) in light of the history of the contract; (3) systematically; and by (4) the purpose and objective of the contract.[24]

As a starting point of analysis, the literal interpretation applies to determine the explanatory value of a term or a clause. As the wording of a contract may be rather ambiguous, since parties usually do not use notions in their technical sense, the margin of possible results of interpretation is often rather broad.[25]

---

19 This aspect is made particularly clear in the new Art. 1189 Cciv. This article states indeed that where several contracts contribute to the same economic undertaking, they should be interpreted in the light of that undertaking.

20 J. Ellenberger, '§133' in O. Palandt (ed.), *Palandt Bürgerliches Gesetzbuch mit Nebengesetzen – Kommentar*, m.n. 1.

21 M. Wolf, '§157 BGB' in H.-T. Soergel, *Bürgerliches Gesetzbuch mit Einführungsgesetz und Nebengesetzen*, vol. II, m.n. 10.

22 BGH, 03.05.1994, *NJW-RR* 1994, 1008.

23 A. Lüderitz, *Auslegung von Rechtsgeschäften*, p. 309.

24 J. Busche, '§133 BGB' in K. Rebmann and F.J. Säcker (eds.), *Münchener Kommentar zum Bürgerlichen Gesetzbuch*, m.n. 6, 7.

25 Ibid., m.n. 7: literal interpretation supports every interpretative result which may be based on the wording.

Additionally, some authors advocate that terms must not be interpreted in a literal way only, commonly referred to as 'Verbot der Buchstabendeutung' [prohibition of literal interpretation].[26] Literal interpretation, therefore, could lead to any interpretative result which may be based on the wording.[27] Where the wording supports several meanings of a term, other methods mentioned become decisive.[28] As the parties' common intention prevails anyway, the wording of the contract is not an absolute limit to contract interpretation, as long as some minimal basis of a certain interpretation may be found in the text ('Trittstufentheorie' [footstep theory]).[29]

Habitual language use serves as the starting point for literal interpretation.[30] In particular, German courts use the habitual language approach quite extensively.[31] Therefore, in the case at hand it is necessary to establish whether aubergines, tomatoes and cucumbers may be defined as vegetables or fruits in habitual language usage. In the case of food, German law provides specific food terminology which purports to control labelling and advertisement on food. However, the effects on contract interpretation are not entirely clear. The official guidelines from the German Federal Ministry for Food, Agriculture and Consumer Protection, which have their basis in European food law, define aubergines, tomatoes and cucumbers as vegetables in the prevailing public understanding.[32] Consequently, this would lead to the classification of these items as vegetables.

As a second step of literal interpretation, the language use of the specific communication sphere in which the contract was concluded (e.g. a certain branch or market) that deviates from the habitual language use is taken into account.[33] In the case at hand, Imperial Real Estate and Botanical Fruits concluded a lease contract. For this kind of contract, no specific language use deviating from the habitual use has been established. In particular, botanical expertise is of no importance for that type of contract and knowledge of specific food terminology is not typically used in shopping mall lease relationships.

---

26 Ibid., m.n. 54.

27 Ibid., m.n. 7.

28 BGH, 10.02.1960, *NJW* 1960, 959.

29 BGH, 09.04.1981, *NJW* 1981, 1736.

30 OLG Schleswig, 30.08.2018, *BeckRS* 2018, 24758, see also M. Wolf, '§157 BGB' in H.-T. Soergel, *Bürgerliches Gesetzbuch mit Einführungsgesetz und Nebengesetzen*, vol. II, m.n. 32; OLG München, 05.04.1995, *NJW-RR* 1996, 239.

31 Ibid.

32 http://www.bmelv.de/SharedDocs/Downloads/Ernaehrung/Lebensmittelbuch/Leitsaetze Gemueseerzeugnisse.pdf?__blob=publicationFile.

33 BGH, 23.11.1994, *NJW-RR* 1995, 364.

Furthermore, individual characteristics in the language use may affect the literal interpretation, if the addressee is aware of these individual characteristics.[34] In the case at hand, there are no individual characteristics of language use. In fact, it is important to mention that a German court would perhaps also ask for local characteristics in the case at hand if indicated by the facts.[35]

Another aspect in this case is the interpretation in light of the history of the conclusion of the contract. Some authors advocate that the historical interpretation may just confirm the result of the literal and systematic interpretation.[36] Others emphasise that the interpretation in light of the history of the contract conclusion is as effective as the other methods.[37] To detect the common real intention of the parties, i.e. for the subjective interpretation, the history of the conclusion of the contract may serve as a rather important argument anyway.

Such historical interpretation shifts the risks of ambiguities under Clause 8(g) to the landlord in the case at hand. The restriction to the products to be offered by the tenant became part of the contract on the initiative of Imperial Real Estate and should be analysed as unilaterally proposed by the landlord. This may raise a kind of *contra proferentem* argument once again (see answers to Case 1).

Systematic arguments in interpreting the contract may be drawn from other parts of the contract, *inter alia* from a preamble (cf. Case 1) or other clauses within the contract, which could include, for example, terms on hygienic standards or opening hours. Additionally, the use of technical botanical standards or food law terminology in other parts of the contract may give hints to a certain meaning of the notion 'vegetables'. However, no such additional hints are indicated.

Finally, the content of the contract, especially the meaning of the notion 'vegetables', is to be determined by looking at the purpose of the contract. The purpose and the history of a contract are in a way connected, because one may find out about the purpose of the contract by exploring the history of a contract.[38] In finding out about the purpose of the contract, one has to

[34] J. Ellenberger, '§133' in O. Palandt (ed.), *Palandt Bürgerliches Gesetzbuch mit Nebengesetzen – Kommentar*, m.n. 14; cf. OLG Düsseldorf, 13.12.2017, *NZBau* 2018, 242, applying the German general rules on §§133, 157 BGB for interpreting tender documents.

[35] BGH, 24.03.2004, *NJW* 2004, 2230.

[36] BGH, 07.07.1960, VIII ZR 215/59, BGHZ 33, 321.

[37] BVerfG, 17.05.1960, BVerfGE 11, 126.

[38] W. Hefermehl, 'Anhang §133 BGB' in H.-T. Soergel, *Bürgerliches Gesetzbuch mit Einführungsgesetz und Nebengesetzen*, vol. II, m.n. 7.

consider the terms of the contract as a whole.[39] The purpose of Clause 8(g) is to establish the biggest possible variety of products which can be sold in the shopping mall. A broad interpretation of the term 'vegetables' would be in line with this purpose, because it leads to a more varied range of products in the shopping mall. However, that may be different in the case of juices, where mixtures of fruits and vegetables may enhance the overall number of products.

As a result, using the classical methods of contract interpretation a court applying German law would probably come to the conclusion that in cases like the one at hand the term 'vegetables' is not to be understood in its technical botanical sense.[40]

Furthermore, under §157 BGB, contracts should be interpreted with respect to 'Treu und Glaube' [good faith principle] and 'Verkehrssitten' [local usages]. In this case, from 'Treu und Glaube' it follows that if there are any difficulties of interpretation after the formation of the contract, one has to focus on the 'Vertrauensschutz' [protection of legitimate expectations].[41] One has to establish the usual sense of the term having regard to the concrete circumstances of the contract formation.[42] In fact, both parties legitimately may rely on this usual sense. Since there is no specific language use or commercial usages for conducting a 'Pachtvertrag' [lease contract] (see above), Imperial Real Estate may rely on the usual sense of 'vegetables' on the basis of the objective approach.

Question 2: Expertise

Imperial Real Estate's experience in the food retail industry and the botanical background of its director could lead to a different interpretation: the general approach of habitual language certainly remains untouched by that fact.[43] Also, the ability of Imperial Real Estate and its director does not contribute to the exercise of establishing a sector-specific meaning of the term 'vegetables'.[44] However, it may lead to a significant change in the individual characteristics of language use. For such an individual understanding of the term 'vegetables',

---

39 K. Larenz, *Methodenlehre der Rechtswissenschaft*, p. 319.

40 It is worth mentioning that Botanical Fruits may have a right to avoid the contract for mistake about the content of the contract (Inhaltsirrtum) according to §119 (1) first alternative BGB. This pre-supposes that Botanical Fruits can prove that it genuinely understood the term 'vegetables' in its technical botanical meaning. However, in the case of avoidance, Botanical Fruits has to pay damages for the reliance loss suffered by Imperial.

41 M. Wolf, '§157 BGB' in H.-T. Soergel, *Bürgerliches Gesetzbuch mit Einführungsgesetz und Nebengesetzen*, vol. II, m.n. 57.

42 Ibid.

43 J. Ellenberger, '§133' in O. Palandt (ed.), *Palandt Bürgerliches Gesetzbuch mit Nebengesetzen – Kommentar*, m.n. 14.

44 M. Wolf, '§157 BGB' in H.-T. Soergel, *Bürgerliches Gesetzbuch mit Einführungsgesetz und Nebengesetzen*, vol. II, m.n. 63.

it is important to consider whether the business partner can understand the term technically.[45] As the experience of Imperial Real Estate in the food retail industry enables it to understand the technical meaning of the term 'vegetables', this may raise the question as to why it did not proceed with a further enquiry on the meaning of the clause. Therefore, its special knowledge may serve as an argument again to shift the risk of misunderstanding. The typical counter-argument would be that the ability of Imperial Real Estate to understand the technical meaning of 'vegetables' does not change the legitimate expectations of Botanical Fruits[46] as to the meaning of a contract term in a field where technical botanical notions are unusual.

7. GREECE

Question 1: Technical and Ordinary Meaning

In the case at hand, resorting to the subjective criterion alone (Art. 173 CC) cannot deliver any results; therefore, the deciding judge will have to resort to the objective interpretation of Clause 8(g). The objective criterion relies upon the concepts of 'καλή πίστη' [good faith] and any applicable 'συναλλακτικά ήθη' [trade customs]:[47] for the present case, no applicable trade custom can be discerned. The court will seek to concretise the concept of 'καλή πίστη' by examining a number of parameters, both subjective and objective, such as eventual transactional usages and previous business relations between the parties, etc., but also the common language usage in Greece or the specific area where the food court is situated with regard to the products in question. In Greek everyday language usage, aubergines, tomatoes and cucumbers are usually characterised as vegetables rather than fruits. Consequently, it seems plausible to suggest that, in the absence of other relevant circumstances and taking stock of all surrounding circumstances, the ordinary meaning will weigh in the balance more heavily.

Question 2: Expertise

The normative meaning of Clause 8(g) and the outcome of its objective assessment are likely to be different from the answer to Question 1, if Imperial,

45 B. Biehl, 'Grundsätze der Vertragsauslegung', p. 195.

46 J. Ellenberger, '§133' in O. Palandt (ed.), *Palandt Bürgerliches Gesetzbuch mit Nebengesetzen – Kommentar*, m.n. 14.

47 For the relation of trade customs to the general standard of good faith under Art. 200 CC and the role the former play in the concretisation of the standard of good faith in each particular case, see Case 9.

namely the party that imposed the controversial term, had lengthy experience in the food retail industry and its director had an academic background in botanical studies; in any case, the specific importance of each parameter may not be determined *a priori*.[48]

For a different outcome, it is necessary that those two factors indeed affect Imperial's understanding of the term 'vegetables', for example if the director was actively involved in drafting the relevant clause and/or concluding the contract with Botanical Fruits, or if the long experience in food retail necessarily involves a profound knowledge of the scientific classifications of the various food categories. If such instances are at hand, a court would consider them in conjunction with the ordinary meaning and prevailing use of the term with respect to aubergines, tomatoes and cucumbers in everyday life and it would probably examine whether Imperial could and should have anticipated that the divergence between the ordinary and technical meanings may not necessarily be known to Botanical Fruits.

Conversely, the court would investigate whether Botanical Fruits, had it been aware of the distinction, could have reasonably expected that its contractual counterparty would be aware of the technical content of the term suggested in the agreement. As mentioned above, the objective criterion for the interpretation of contracts is not implemented by reference to any average person, but by reference to what the specific parties could and ought to have understood from their agreement; the courts, when applying this criterion, also rely upon the duty of each contractual party to formulate the terms of the agreement in a manner understandable for the counterparty.[49]

Therefore, if the specific knowledge of Imperial has somehow been reflected in the process of concluding the lease agreement, the court will probably interpret Clause 8(g) in the light of its technical sense; legal doctrine suggests that, when interpreting a legally relevant declaration of intent, particular circumstances of the parties to an agreement that are likely to affect the outcome of that interpretation and whether they were known to the other party must be considered by the deciding judge, equally in the context of the objective criterion (Art. 200 CC).[50]

---

48 Stathopoulos, *Civil Code*, vol. 1^{B}, Arts. 173 and 200 no. 119.

49 Filios, *General Principles*, §243: the person making a declaration of intent is under a duty to formulate it in a manner comprehensible for his counterparty, while the latter bears the burden of its due interpretation; Ladas, *General Principles*, §34 no. 22; see also Karassis, *General Principles*, §§ Γ 286, 292.

50 See Stathopoulos, 'On the method of interpretation', p. 35 n. 57 and pp. 47–50.

8. ITALY

Question 1: Technical and Ordinary Meaning

Assuming that the term 'vegetables' has two possible alternative meanings (a technical and an ordinary meaning), the relevant rule for the solution of the case appears to be, in the first instance, Art. 1369 c.c.[51] According to prevailing opinion, when applying Art. 1369, the adjudicator will examine the 'cause' of the contract in order to ascertain which interpretation of the term 'vegetables' is more consistent with the purpose and structure of the specific economic transaction agreed upon by the parties.

It can be supposed that Imperial Real Estate will find it easier to persuade a judge that the specific features of the lease require that the scope of the restraint imposed on Botanical Fruits should be interpreted according to the 'commercial' meaning of the term (vegetables) rather than to its technical meaning, which does not appear to be connected in any way to the economic purpose (the cause) of the transaction.

This conclusion is strengthened if one looks at Art. 1366, which refers to the notion of 'buona fede' [good faith] as a general rule for the interpretation of contracts.[52]

In the present case, in light of all the circumstances, reliance on the commercial, ordinary meaning of the term 'vegetables' appears to be far more reasonable, and good faith would then prevent parties from asserting the prevalence of the technical meaning. It would be hard for Botanical Fruits to rebut the connection between the clear economic purpose of Clause 8(g) and the reasonableness of the reliance on an interpretation of its scope as referring to commercial products rather than to botanical notions.

Question 2: Expertise

The specific academic or commercial background of Imperial's director would hardly make a difference. It could be used to demonstrate that the parties had a common intention that resolves the assumed ambiguity of the term 'vegetables'. In this connection, the relevant rule would be Art. 1362, which points out the need for the search for the common intention of the parties. It seems unlikely that consideration of the director's background or of Imperial's commercial experience could lead to an interpretation which contrasts with the above-mentioned considerations on the economic purpose of the transaction.

---

51 Art. 1369 c.c.: 'Expressions which may have different meanings, in case of doubt, must be understood according to the nature and to the object of the contract'; see above Case 1.

52 See above Case 1.

Nevertheless, according to a well-acknowledged scholarly opinion,[53] the principle of 'buona fede' [good faith] may lead to the prevalence of the less reasonable meaning (apparently in this case the botanical meaning), if one party has induced the other to rely on that meaning.

9. NETHERLANDS

Question 1: Technical and Ordinary Meaning

Where an expression used in the contract has both an ordinary and a technical meaning, the court would have to establish what meaning each party could reasonably attribute to the expression used and what meaning each party could reasonably expect the other to give the expression, in light of all the relevant facts and circumstances assessed in light of the standards of 'redelijkheid en billijkheid' [reasonableness and fairness].[54] For this purpose, the court may take the nature, background and knowledge of the parties involved into account as relevant background.[55] In its *Haviltex* decision, the Court explicitly refers to the societal position of the parties as being a relevant factor for the interpretation of the contract.[56]

Where a party lacks experience in a particular sector or industry, it may not reasonably be expected of him that he be aware of the technical meaning attached to certain expressions used in the contract. Indeed, it could be reasonable for that party to understand the contractual expression in accordance with ordinary usage. An important factor in this context will be the nature of the contracting party and the nature of the contract. If we assume that Imperial Real Estate is not actively involved in the food retail industry but simply the owner of a small food court who lets spaces to various vendors and that the contract is a lease contract and does not directly relate to the food retail industry, then it would be reasonable for Imperial Real Estate to rely on the ordinary meaning of 'vegetables' to include aubergines, tomatoes and cucumbers. Furthermore, if we assume that Botanical Fruits is aware or could reasonably be aware of such inexperience and unfamiliarity with technical or industry jargon, then it would not be reasonable for Botanical Fruits to rely on the technical meaning being attributed to the contractual expression. In such circumstances, the court would likely interpret the expression in accordance with its ordinary meaning. In that case, it would not be reasonable for Botanical Fruits to expect Imperial

53 Trimarchi, *Istituzioni*, p. 167.

54 Hoge Raad 13 March 1981, *NJ* 1981, 635 (Ermes/Haviltex) and Hoge Raad 20 February 2004, *NJ* 2005, 493 (DSM-Chemie/Fox).

55 Tjittes, 'Uitleg van schriftelijke contracten', p. 45.

56 Hoge Raad 13 March 1981, *NJ* 1981, 635 (Ermes/Haviltex).

Real Estate to appreciate the botanical meaning of 'vegetables'. Consequently, Clause 8(g) would probably be interpreted to include aubergines, tomatoes and cucumbers.

Where one party possesses certain expertise, such expertise will often put him in a position that he can anticipate the potential for a misunderstanding on the part of the other party with respect to the meaning to be attributed to the terms of the contract. In such a situation, there may be a duty of care on the knowledgeable party to take reasonable measures to ensure that the other party is not labouring under a misunderstanding and to clearly inform the other party of its own understanding with respect to the meaning to be attributed to the contractual expression, if he wishes to rely on that specific meaning.[57] Already in the pre-contractual stage, the parties are in a legal relationship governed by the principle of 'redelijkheid en billijkheid' [reasonableness and fairness] which requires them to be guided in their conduct by the legitimate interests of the other party.[58] A court could find it contrary to the requirements of 'redelijkheid en billijkheid' to allow one party to rely on a technical meaning if he failed to inform the other party of such technical meaning.

Conversely, where the experienced party could not reasonably be expected to have been aware of its counterpart's lack of experience, it may have reasonably relied on a shared background, in which case it would be reasonable to expect that they shared a common understanding of the contractual expression in line with the technical meaning. The nature of the contract will be a relevant factor in this context.

If both parties are familiar with, or in light of the circumstances reasonably can be expected to be familiar with, the technical meaning of the expression used in the contract and the nature and the purpose of the contract indicates that the technical meaning is intended, the court may conclude that it can be reasonably expected of both parties that they attached the technical meaning to the expression and that they each relied on the other party to share that technical meaning.

Question 2: Expertise

When deciding what meaning the parties could reasonably attach to the expressions used and which they could reasonably expect the other to give the expression, the court may take the nature, background and knowledge of the parties involved into account as relevant background.[59] Imperial Real Estate's decades of experience in the food retail industry, and its director's

57 Hoge Raad 15 November 1957, *NJ* 1958, 670 (Baris/Riezenkamp); Tjittes, *Uitleg van schriftelijke contracten*, p. 45; Bakker, 'Uitleg van commerciële contracten'.

58 See Hoge Raad 15 November 1957, *NJ* 1958, 670 (Baris/Riezenkamp); Asser/Sieburgh, *Algemene leer der overeenkomsten*, 6-III, no. 392.

59 Tjittes, *Uitleg van schriftelijke contracten*, p. 45.

academic background in botanical studies, will influence whether it can reasonably rely on attributing an ordinary meaning to the word 'vegetables'. These factors would be taken into account as relevant circumstances for the purpose of establishing which meaning the respective parties could reasonably attach to the contractual expression. In such a case, the court would likely find it to be unreasonable for Imperial Real Estate to rely on the ordinary meaning and expect Botanical Fruits to also do so, since it is aware that the term carries a specific, botanical meaning that Botanical Fruits would be familiar with.

10. POLAND

Question 1: Technical and Ordinary Meaning

The starting point for establishing the parties' common intention is to look at the sense of the term coming from the rules of language (the literal interpretation).[60] Priority is given to regional rules and the rules of society or of the professional environment that the parties share[61] before the common rules of the Polish language. Aside from the regional meaning of a word, the technical meaning is also seen as particularly relevant for the interpretation of a contract, if it is used commonly in a given business environment.[62] The interpretation process is not, however, limited just to the meaning of the term, but the term should be interpreted within the context used.[63]

Moreover, when the Polish court is deciding which meaning of the contractual term used it should take into account, it is likely to consider a number of factors other than simply whether the term used should be interpreted based on its technical or ordinary meaning.[64] As explained in the Opening Remarks, interpretation in accordance with the parties' common intentions and the contract's purpose takes precedence over the term's literal meaning. In the

---

60 Judgment of SN of 14.06.2012, I CSK 485/11; Decree of SN of 17.10.2012, I CSK 119/12.

61 Judgment of SN of 17.06.2009, IV CSK 90/09; Judgment of SN of 14.06.2012, I CSK 485/11.

62 B. Kaczorowska, 'Wizja wykładni umów w projekcie księgi pierwszej kodeksu cywilnego', TPP 2/2011, pp. 19–20.

63 Decree of SN of 29.06.1995, III CZP 66/95; Judgment of SN of 03.09.1998, I CKN 815/97; Judgment of SN of 08.07.2004, IV CK 582/03; Judgment of SN of 08.10.2004, V CK 670/03; Judgment of SN of 05.10.2005, II CK 122/05; Judgment of SN of 17.06.2009, IV CSK 90/09; Judgment of SN of 09.02.2012, III CSK 179/11; Judgment of SN of 14.06.2012, I CSK 485/11; Judgment of SN of 18.11.2016, I CSK 802/15; Ł. Węgrzynowski, 'Sądowe ustalanie treści stosunku umownego', PPH 2007/5/44–49; B. Kaczorowska, 'Wizja wykładni umów w projekcie księgi pierwszej kodeksu cywilnego', TPP 2/2011, p. 23.

64 E.g. Judgment of SN of 03.09.1998, I CKN 815/97; Judgment of SN of 25.03.2004, II CK 116/03; Judgment of SN of 05.10.2005, II CK 122/05; Judgment of SN of 17.12.2008, I CSK 250/08; Judgment of SN of 09.02.2012, III CSK 179/11; Judgment of SN of 23.05.2013, I CSK 569/12; M. Romanowski, 'Szczegółowe reguły wykładni kontraktów w świetle zasad europejskiego prawa kontraktów a reguły wykładni umów w prawie polskim', PPH 2004/9/12–18.

event of discrepancies, the result of an interpretation based on the term's literal meaning, i.e. established taking into account the semantic rules of language, will give precedence to the result of a subjective interpretation, respecting the theory of the parties' will.[65]

Some voices in the legal literature claim that in contractual relations between professional parties, the main evidence of the parties' common intentions should be the literal meaning of the term used in the contract.[66] This view is supported by the claim that professional parties should be expected to formulate their contractual provisions with clarity and deliberation, and therefore it is the term's literal (or technical) meaning that should be seen as representative of their intentions. At the same time, others claim that the need to look beyond the term's meaning is especially relevant for terms used in commercial contracts, which are often governed by habits and certain rules of cooperation. With respect to these contracts, it is necessary to question anyone involved in order to examine the parties' purpose and objective in concluding the contract.[67] Therefore, the Polish court's role is to examine whether, taking into account the circumstances under which the contract was concluded and its purpose, the parties to the contract had intended to give a different meaning to the term used in the contract than could be assumed on the basis of its ordinary or technical meaning.[68]

For example, in the SN's judgment of 13 February 2002,[69] the court considered the interpretation of the term 'zadatek' [pre-given amount] used in the contract.[70] The parties also used another similar term in the contract: 'zaliczka' [pre-calculated amount].[71] There is a significant difference between these two terms from a legal point of view, since if the parties to a contract decide to set 'zadatek' in it, then in the event that one of the parties fails to perform a contractual obligation, the other party may terminate the contract and demand payment of twice of the amount of the 'zadatek'. The function of this is to compensate the other party in the event of non-performance, but also to motivate the first party to properly perform the contract. When the parties to a contract set 'zaliczka', that only gives an advantage to the seller or the service provider, who then receives that amount prior to the performance of his

65 B. Kaczorowska, 'Wizja wykładni umów w projekcie księgi pierwszej kodeksu cywilnego', TPP 2/2011, p. 16; M. Romanowski, 'Szczegółowe reguły wykładni kontraktów w świetle zasad europejskiego prawa kontraktów a reguły wykładni umów w prawie polskim', PPH 2004/9/12–18.

66 M. Romanowski, 'Ogólne reguły wykładni kontraktów w świetle zasad europejskiego prawa kontraktów a reguły wykładni umów w prawie polskim', PPH 2004/8.

67 Judgment of SN of 03.09.1998, I CKN 815/97; Judgment of SN of 05.10.2005, II CK 122/05.

68 Judgment of SN of 25.03.2004, II CK 116/03.

69 Judgment of SN of 13.02.2002, IV CKN 672/00.

70 This is often translated as 'caution money' or 'earnest money'.

71 This is often translated as 'advance payment' or 'down payment'. These payments are both paid in advance, rather than just 'calculated'.

contractual obligations. However, these two terms are becoming increasingly commonly used interchangeably in the Polish language The dispute arose as to whether the payment made in advance in this case was a 'zadatek' or a 'zaliczka', which would bring about different consequences if there were a breach of contractual obligations. The Supreme Court, in its interpretation of the term used by parties, focused on the function and purpose of these two terms, rather than on whether technical or ordinary meanings should prevail, stating that the interpretation process may not be 'devoid of any rules'.[72]

Since both Imperial and Botanical Fruits are professional parties, it may be expected that the Polish courts would interpret Clause 8(g) by referring to its literal meaning. A preference may then be given to the technical meaning of the word 'vegetables', if it were proven that, in this business environment, the technical meaning of this term is commonly used. However, either party could try to defend their claim by referring to the contract's purpose or objective as pointing to the parties' intentions to use this term's specific meaning.

Question 2: Expertise

As mentioned above, when the court tries to establish the common intentions of the parties and the meaning of the term used, it looks at the literal meaning of the term, while also taking into account the understanding of the term in the professional circles that the parties share.[73] Moreover, the situational context is also taken into account, which includes, but is not limited to, the prior experiences of parties and their status.[74] In this respect, if both parties could be seen as being experienced in the field and having knowledge of the technical meaning of the term, it is even more likely that the technical meaning would prevail over the ordinary meaning. As a result, the technical meaning of the term used in Clause 8(g) would be more likely to prevail over the common language meaning.

In contractual relations between professional parties, the literal or technical meaning of the term may have more significance than other evidence that the parties may want to present to illustrate their common intention as to the understanding of that term.[75] This view is supported by the claim that professional parties may be expected to use clarity and deliberation when formulating contractual provisions, and therefore it is the literal (or technical)

72 See also Judgment of SN of 30.01.2004, I CK 129/03.

73 Judgment of SN of 08.10.2004, V CK 670/03; Judgment of SN of 14.06.2012, I CSK 485/11.

74 Judgment of SN of 04.07.1975, III CRN 160/75; Judgment of SN of 05.10.2005, II CK 122/05; Judgment of SN of 17.06.2009, IV CSK 90/09; Judgment of SN of 14.06.2012, I CSK 485/11; Judgment of SN of 28.02.2013, III CSK 70/12; Judgment of SN of 10.05.2013, I CSK 74/13.

75 M. Romanowski, 'Ogólne reguły wykładni kontraktów w świetle zasad europejskiego prawa kontraktów a reguły wykładni umów w prawie polskim', PPH 2004/8.

meaning of the term that should be seen as representative of their intentions. It would be less likely, therefore, for Imperial to claim that the contractual purpose was to exclude 'vegetables' within the common language meaning, since they would be presumed to be familiar with and to use the technical meaning of this term.

11. PORTUGAL

Question 1: Technical and Ordinary Meaning

There is a hierarchy between the ordinary meaning and the technical meaning. Normally, the ordinary meaning prevails over the technical meaning. According to the Portuguese Civil Code (Art. 236.°/1), Clause 8(g) of the contract between Imperial Real Estate and Botanical Fruits should be interpreted in accordance with the meaning of a 'declaratário normal' [reasonable person], who receives the declaration in the context of the real situation. Here, one must take account of what that person could have understood based on the behaviour of the other contracting party, unless it was not reasonable for her to rely on it.

In this case, both the technical meaning and the ordinary meaning of the words used in the contract are relevant. According to the Portuguese system, the standard of the reasonable man that receives the declarations (Art. 236.°/1) points in favour of the ordinary meaning, because this standard is an abstract person and this person does not have special knowledge concerning the technical use of the words. Still, Portuguese courts do consider concrete situations in applying the standard of the 'declaratário normal'. For instance, RLx 15 February 1996, CJ XXI, 1, 123 considered relevant the fact that the parties in a concrete contract were both lawyers.[76] In this case, the technical meaning prevailed. But this decision must be recognised as an exception, because the standard of the 'declaratário normal' prevails over the concrete interpretation from the real person in the real situation of the addressee.

Question 2: Expertise

The answer to Question 1 might be different if one takes into account Imperial Real Estate's many decades of experience in the food retail industry and its director's academic experience in botanical studies. In this case, it would be possible to say that Imperial Real Estate knew the intention of Botanical Fruits according to Art. 236.°/2 CC.

In determining whether contract language is clear and definite, the court will give the words their ordinary and common meaning unless it is apparent that

[76] Menezes Cordeiro, *Tratado de Direito Civil Português*, p. 760.

the parties used the words in a special or technical sense. If it is apparent that the words were used in their technical sense, the court will consider how the words are used by persons in the business or profession in which the words are used in a technical sense and interpret the words in that sense unless it is apparent that the parties did not intend such an interpretation.

As said previously, the interpretation of contractual practice could be relevant in defending a certain interpretation. But in this case, the party that defends the technical sense must prove such practice. Technical words are to be interpreted as commonly understood by persons in the profession or business to which they relate, unless clearly used in a different sense.

12. SCOTLAND

Question 1: Technical and Ordinary Meaning

Clause 8(g) of the lease prevents Botanical Fruits from selling 'vegetables or vegetable products'. The natural and ordinary meaning of words has been described in Scots law as the 'obvious starting point'.[77] The court must look for the meaning which a person of ordinary common sense would attribute to the term.[78]

The court is likely to approach this question by asking whether a person of ordinary common sense would consider cucumbers and tomatoes to be vegetables. Only someone who had in mind a specialist botanical meaning would describe them as fruits. This approach would favour Imperial Real Estate and tend to suggest that Botanical Fruits is in breach of Clause 8(g).

The court could consult the Oxford English Dictionary. This describes aubergines as vegetables, and both tomatoes and cucumbers as fruits. Consultation of this dictionary would suggest that Botanical Fruits is in breach of the lease by selling cucumbers and tomatoes. McBryde, a leading author on contract law, has suggested that the court must go further than considering only a dictionary meaning of the words: the process is more sophisticated, because the parties may have used the words in a different way.[79]

It seems unlikely that the court would resolve the question purely by reference to a dictionary.

The Scottish court would not focus solely on a literal approach. Lord Hodge in the Supreme Court explained that interpretation:

> is not a literalist exercise focused solely on a parsing of the word of the particular clause … [T]he court must consider the contract as a whole and, depending on the

[77] McBryde, *Contract*, para. 8-10.
[78] *Glasgow Training Group (Motor Trade) Ltd v Lombard Continental plc* 1989 SC 30 at 37.
[79] McBryde, *Contract*, para. 8-05.

> nature, formality and quality of drafting of the contract, give more or less weight to elements of the wider context in reaching its view as to the objective meaning.[80]

Although there is a need to interpret the clause in its contractual context, i.e. in the context of the lease as a whole, we are not told of any other clauses of the lease which would help the court to interpret Clause 8(g).

Use of a contextual approach would involve making reference to the circumstances surrounding the parties at the moment of formation of the contract. The question is not what those circumstances conveyed to the parties themselves, but rather what they would have conveyed to reasonable parties in the position of the contracting parties. It is an objective and not a subjective question. A reasonable businessperson in the position of the contracting parties would probably share what has been described as the natural and ordinary meaning of this phrase, i.e. would consider each of the three species as vegetables, notwithstanding the dictionary meaning. A contextual approach would therefore also favour Imperial Real Estate and tend to suggest that Botanical Fruits was in breach of Clause 8(g).

The court may also make use of the 'commercially sensible construction'. This means that where two competing interpretations are available, the court is entitled to select the one which accords with commercial common sense.[81]

A company in the process of negotiating a lease will be aware that the landlord is likely to want to restrict the business which that company can carry on in the food court. Landlords require to have control over the range of businesses in the food court and will want to ensure that a good variety of outlets is available. A restriction such as that contained in this lease is common, and both parties are likely to have understood why the restriction was in place. A reasonable commercial party is likely to have understood the phrase 'vegetables or vegetable products' as including tomatoes, cucumbers and aubergines. To decide otherwise is to give emphasis to technical interpretations. It is suggested therefore that a commercially sensible construction would also result in an interpretation which favoured Imperial Real Estate and tended to suggest that Botanical Fruits is in breach of the lease.

Question 2: Expertise

The answer to this question would not differ if Imperial had many decades of experience in the food retail industry and its director had an academic background in botanical studies.

80 *Wood v Capita Insurance Services Ltd* [2017] UKSC 24; [2017] 2 WLR 1095 at para 10.

81 *Rainy Sky SA v Kookmin Bank* [2011] UKSC 50; [2011] 1 WLR 2900, per Lord Clarke at 2908E–G.

13. SOUTH AFRICA

Question 1: Technical and Ordinary Meaning

Evidence that words were used in a technical sense is always admissible, even if the contract appears to be unambiguous.[82] In determining whether the ordinary or technical meaning of the term 'vegetables' should prevail, a court will therefore consider whether the term, in the context of the contract as a whole and the relevant factual matrix, was used in its ordinary or its technical sense. Furthermore, a court will take into account the purpose of Clause 8(g) as well as the facts explaining this purpose insofar as these facts are known to both parties (see Case 1, Question 2).

Considerations which may support Imperial's contention that the word 'vegetables' was used in its ordinary sense and which would be relevant as part of the factual matrix are:[83] the fact that Imperial and Botanical Fruits are parties negotiating with equal bargaining power (rendering it unlikely that a court would be inclined to interpret the clause restrictively); the fact that attributing the ordinary meaning to the word 'vegetables' does not preclude Botanical Fruits from conducting its trade, but simply restricts it from selling certain kinds of products; and finally, that the existence of this type of restraint in the various vendors' lease contracts probably serves to attract potential vendors on the basis that new and already established vendors will compete equally to attract customers (which in turn ensures that there is a greater variety of products sold in the small food court).

Should the primary interpretative factors not yield a definitive meaning, a court may resort to secondary interpretative factors, like the fact that parties have a duty to negotiate in good faith and that one party should not obtain an unreasonable or unfair advantage over the other.[84] In general, South African law does not recognise an implicit obligation, read into every contract, that parties should act in good faith. Good faith, reasonableness and fairness serve as abstract values underlying the law of contract; they do not constitute independent rules

---

82 *Sassoon Confirming and Acceptance Co. (Pty) Ltd v Barclays National Bank Ltd* 1974 1 SA 641 (A) 646A–C; *List v Jungers* 1979 3 SA 106 (A) 118D–119B.

83 See *Bedford Square Properties (Pty) Ltd v Liberty Group Ltd* 2010 4 SA 99 (GSJ), confirmed on appeal in *Bedford Square Properties (Pty) Ltd v Erf 179 Bedford View (Pty) Ltd* 2011 5 SA 306 (SCA).

84 *South African Forestry Co. Ltd v York Timbers Ltd* 2005 3 SA 323 (SCA) para. 32; *Super Rent (Pty) Ltd v Bax Global (Pty) Ltd* 2006 3 SA 422 (W). In the absence of anything to the contrary, it is assumed that the hierarchy of different categories of factors which a court may consider when interpreting a contract remain the same, in spite of the fact that the category of primary interpretative factors is broader than it was under the traditional approach to interpretation. For other examples of secondary factors which a court may consider, see Van Huyssteen et al., *Contract*, 301–302; Bradfield, *Christie's Law of Contract*, 256–261.

which a court may use to intervene in contractual relationships.[85] In other words, these abstract values justify the development of specific contractual rules or doctrines and it is these (rather than the values which justified their development) upon which a party should rely in the first instance.[86] Practically, this means that if Imperial simply relied on an argument that Botanical Fruits' interpretation of 'vegetables' would allow it to act in bad faith and afford it an unfair advantage, such an argument would not persuade a court to adopt an equitable interpretation if the primary interpretative factors resulted in an interpretation which favoured Botanical Fruits. However, if the meaning of the word 'vegetables' remained unclear after a consideration of the factors discussed in the previous paragraph, a court could adopt an equitable interpretation and come to the conclusion that the duty to negotiate in good faith means that Botanical Fruits should have informed Imperial that the former's understanding of the word 'vegetables' deviated from the plain and ordinary meaning of that word, thus prompting the court to attribute the ordinary meaning to the word in the absence of such conduct.

Question 2: Expertise

If Botanical Fruits can prove that the director of Imperial, by virtue of his academic background, knew that Botanical Fruits was negotiating on the assumption that the word 'vegetables' was being used in a technical sense, and that he failed to draw Botanical Fruits' attention to this 'incorrect' meaning in order to induce it to conclude the lease, then a court may attribute the technical meaning to the term 'vegetables'. This conclusion would be based on the fact that a court will not allow a party to contradict a representation as to the meaning of a contractual provision when that representation induced the counterparty to conclude a contract. In such event, Botanical Fruits could raise the defence of 'estoppel' (that is, a defence which would preclude ('estop') Imperial from relying on the ordinary meaning of the word 'vegetables');[87] if successful, a court would give effect to Botanical Fruits' understanding of the word.[88] In the absence of

---

85 For a general discussion of the role of good faith in the South African law of contract, see Van Huyssteen et al., *Contract*, 310–318.

86 A typical example is found in the answer to Question 2.

87 In addition to meeting the general requirements of estoppel, Botanical Fruits would need to prove that the director of Imperial had a duty to speak – see Sonnekus, *Estoppel*, 160–180.

88 The availability of estoppel in this context is a good example of the role of good faith in South African law (see the discussion at Question 1): it is contrary to good faith for a party who has made a representation as to the meaning of a term in order to induce the conclusion of a contract subsequently to insist that an alternative meaning should be attributed to the words in question (Du Plessis, 'Good Faith', para. 5 4 3; *Sampson v Union and Rhodesia Wholesale Ltd (In Liquidation)* 1929 AD 479–480). Therefore, even though a South African court might not explicitly justify an interpretation which favours Botanical Fruits' meaning on the basis that Imperial's director has acted in bad faith, such reasoning is implicit in binding Imperial to the (mis)represented meaning of the word 'vegetables'.

such a (mis)representation, it is unlikely that the mere fact that Imperial has a long history in food retail or that its director has an academic background in botanical studies would make a difference to the answer to Question 1.

14. SPAIN

Question 1: Technical and Ordinary Meaning

As to which meaning (technical or ordinary) may be attributed to Clause 8(g), the principle of confidence may be applicable. The protection of *fides* or confidence means that the usual or common interpretation – the common language – must prevail. In other words, we must interpret the contract according to the common understanding of the language.[89]

Besides, Art. 57 CCom, regarding business contracts, states that these contracts must be implemented and fulfilled in 'buena fe' [good faith], pursuant to the terms under which they were made and drafted, without misinterpreting them through arbitrary constructions of the correct, proper and usual sense of the words said or written, or restriction of the effects naturally arising from the way in which the parties to the contract would have explained their will and contracted their obligations.[90]

Therefore, these terms (cucumbers, tomatoes and aubergines) must be interpreted in the usual sense of the words and the usual meaning is to understand cucumbers, tomatoes and aubergines as 'vegetables'. According to legal scholars, we must give a non-specialist interpretation: that of laymen, not of experts.[91]

Besides, if these elements were not included in the category of vegetables, there would be a restriction of the effects of the contract against Art. 1.286 CC (see Case 1), which contains an objective interpretative factor focused on the nature and purpose of the contract. This provision implies that deciding between the technical and the ordinary meaning of the word 'vegetables' depends on these two factors: the nature and purpose of the contract. The Tribunal Supremo [Supreme Court] has also grounded some decisions on that rule and has established that interpretation must be in accordance with the proper and ordinary meaning of the words in the trade/area of business the contract concerns, giving preference to the semantic meaning and not to any academic meaning. We should take into account that Imperial owns a small food court and was striving for the biggest possible variety of products, which was the reason for the inclusion of Clause 8(g). Spanish jurisprudence states that

---

89 Along with the confidence principle, legal security also plays an important role (Jordano Barea, *Comentario*, p. 510).

90 See STS 04.11.1994 (RJ 1994/8368) and STS 21.05.2010, ECLI:ES:TS:2010:2651.

91 Such as García Pita y Lastres, *Derecho mercantil*, p. 509.

words and expressions which may have different meanings must be interpreted in a logical and rational way.[92]

Lastly, the Proposal for a Modernisation of the Civil Code, not yet enacted, contains Art. 1.278.3°, which provides that the meaning which persons 'de similar condición' [of similar condition] would give in similar circumstances should apply.[93]

From the above, the likelihood is that the ordinary meaning would prevail.

Question 2: Expertise

If Imperial had many decades of experience in the food retail industry and the director had an academic background in botanical studies, the outcome might have been completely different, because the technical understanding of 'vegetables' would prevail.

If one of the parties had read the declaration in a way that the other party could not ignore, then the contract should be interpreted in accordance with that meaning. This is because Art. 1.278 CC claims that if one party intended the contract to have a particular meaning that the other party could not ignore, the contract is to be interpreted in the way intended by the first party. In my opinion, the 'buena fe' [good faith] principle is clearly involved in the answer to this question.

A good example in the Spanish CC of the relevance of the experience and specific knowledge of the parties may be found in the rules on sales law. Art. 1.484 CC on hidden defects or encumbrances of the thing sold takes into account the special technical knowledge of the buyer,[94] and thereby denies the remedy of termination of the contract, given that the buyer could be aware of such issues.

The most likely successful interpretation here would be in favour of Botanical Fruits because of Imperial's long business experience and the director's academic knowledge of the products. The term 'vegetables' will probably be understood in its technical meaning.

15. SWEDEN

Question 1: Technical and Ordinary Meaning

A Swedish court interpreting Clause 8(g) would be strongly inclined to attribute the so-called ordinary meaning to this provision.

---

92 STS 23.07.2013, ECLI:ES:TS:2013:4241; STS 01.03.2013, ECLI:ES:TS:2013:1010.

93 Vattier Fuenzalida, 'La interpretación del contrato, entre la intención de las partes y el criterio de una persona razonable'. This scholar underlines the close relation to CSIG (Art. 8), UNIDROIT (Art. 4.2), PECL (1:302) and DCFR (Art. II.-8:102)

94 STS 24.02.2006 (RJ 2006/1563).

The general aim of interpretation is to establish the common intention of the parties.[95] The horizon from which the meaning of the contract is to be assessed is, consequently, intersubjective.[96] Interpretation regularly proceeds on the assumption that the language employed by the parties conforms to a shared linguistic standard of some generality.[97] In the present case, the court would probably employ the standard of 'allmänt språkbruk' [common linguistic usage].[98] Where such a standard is applicable, any party who wants to deviate from it needs to make that sufficiently clear to the other party. He has a 'klargörandeplikt' [clarification duty], which flows from the general 'lojalitetsplikt' [loyalty duty] binding contracting parties vis-à-vis each other.[99] If Botanical Fruits wanted the technical, botanical meaning to have an impact on the understanding of Clause 8(g), it should have, following this line of reasoning, reacted when confronted with the wording of that provision. In the present case, there is really nothing – short of the name of the lessee – indicating that the technical meaning in question should be taken into consideration when interpreting the contract.[100] In particular, there is no connection between the technical language considered and 'affärssammanhanget' [the transaction context], i.e., by extension, the apparent *point* of stipulating that Botanical Fruits will abstain from selling vegetables and vegetable products, given the fact that the mall already includes a vegetable vendor, in conjunction with the fact that the mall is of limited size.[101]

Does the question of the weight of the technical terminology turn on a matter of fact or a matter of law? To be able to answer that question, one would need to resolve one of the most controversial issues of Swedish contract law theory. Traditionally, there was a distinction made between 'tolkning' [interpretation], which is a matter of fact, and 'utfyllning' [complementary construction], which is a matter of law.[102] This distinction had its roots in early 20th century realist

95 See NJA 2016 p. 689 for an explicit statement by the Supreme Court to this effect. See also e.g. NJA 2015 p. 741; Adlercreutz and Gorton, *Avtalsrätt II*, p. 42; Bernitz, *Standardavtalsrätt*, p. 78; Lehrberg, *Avtalstolkning*, p. 64 f.; Samuelsson, *Tolkningslärans gåta*, p. 186 ff.; cf. J. Ramberg and C. Ramberg, *Allmän avtalsrätt*, p. 148 f.

96 See e.g. Adlercreutz and Gorton, *Avtalsrätt II*, p. 54 ff.

97 See especially Vahlén, *Avtal och tolkning*, pp. 43 ff. and 270 f.

98 See e.g. NJA 1977 p. 160; NJA 1989 p. 346; NJA 1990 p. 24; NJA 2006 p. 53. See also Bernitz, *Standardavtalsrätt*, p. 81; Lehrberg, *Avtalstolkning*, p. 92; and Vahlén, *Avtal och tolkning*, pp. 43 and 191.

99 See e.g. NJA 1957 p. 69; NJA 1981 p. 323; NJA 1982 p. 244; NJA 2012 p. 3; NJA 2017 p. 203. See also Vahlén, *Avtal och tolkning*, p. 180.

100 In NJA 1921 p. 511, technical language prevailed. However, even though the technical language in question was firmly embedded in the commercial context at hand, the ruling has been considered somewhat harsh; see Lehrberg, *Avtalstolkning*, p. 97. Cf. NJA 1966 p. 313; NJA 1978 p. 628.

101 See NJA 1999 p. 35, where the circumstances were somewhat similar and 'affärssammanhanget' was decisive in the interpretation offered by the Supreme Court.

102 See Karlgren, *Kutym och rättsregel*, p. 37; Lassen, *Haandbog i Obligationsretten*, p. 372; Lehrberg, *Förutsättningsläran*, p. 120; Stang, *Innledning til formueretten*, p. 448; Ussing, *Aftaler*, p. 432 f.; Vahlén, *Avtal och tolkning*, p. 193; cf. NJA 1999 p. 629.

theory. During the course of the last one hundred years it came to lose much of its appeal, and its worth is now definitely in doubt.[103] Presently, it is not possible to say, with any confidence, that interpretation is a matter of fact, a matter of law, or a matter of something else.[104]

Question 2: Expertise

Even if Imperial had many decades of experience in the food retail industry, and its director an academic background in botanical studies, the answer to Question 1 would still be the same. The technical language will prevail only when it is reasonable to assume that both parties, given the state of facts at the time of conclusion of the contract, intended Clause 8(g) to be understood accordingly. The fact that the director of Imperial has a mastery of botanical terminology does not, as such, indicate that Clause 8(g) should be understood on botanical terms. His knowledge is relevant, however, insofar as it makes it more likely that he will realise that Botanical Fruits did understand the provision in Clause 8(g) in the technical sense (if indeed it did), and that way, the content of the contract *may* be affected. In Swedish law, the line here is drawn by means of the so-called 'dolusregeln' referred to in the Opening Remarks. According to this rule, a contracting party is bound to the other party's understanding of a contract term at the time of conclusion of the contract if he in fact was aware, or must have been aware, of that understanding. In principle, this rule makes the requirement of bad faith *a matter of fact*, to be distinguished from the *normative* question prompted by the requirement of 'ordinary' bad faith found in many other rules of Swedish private law (*dolus* distinguished from *culpa* by means of the fact/value dichotomy).[105] Now, it should be clear that, even though Botanical Fruits might have understood the terms 'vegetables' and 'vegetable products' in the technical, botanical sense (we do not know that for a fact, albeit there are strong indications) the court is not entitled to conclude that the director of Imperial actually was aware, or must have been aware, of that fact, simply because he was well acquainted with botanical terminology.

16. EDITORIAL COMPARATIVE OBSERVATIONS

Question 1: Technical and Ordinary Meaning

The reporters from Croatia, Germany and Greece emphasised the subjective analysis as the first step in interpreting the clause. Evidence of the importance

---

103 See e.g. the doubt expressed by the Supreme Court in NJA 2010 p. 416.

104 On this theme, see Samulesson, *Tolkning och utfyllning*.

105 See Adlercreutz and Gorton, *Avtalsrätt I*, p. 43 f.

of the objective analysis can be found in the emphasis by several of the reporters of reasonableness as a criterion. In Croatia, if the court is unable to find the actual common intention, it looks for the reasonable intention, taking into account all the relevant circumstances in accordance with the understanding of the reasonable person. The court in the Netherlands would look for the meaning each party could reasonably expect the other to give to the expression in light of all relevant facts and circumstances assessed in light of the standards of 'redelijkheid en billijkheid' [reasonableness and fairness]. The English reporter refers to what a reasonable observer would have understood the parties to mean. Finally, the Portuguese court would look to the meaning as understood by the reasonable man who receives the communication in the context of the real situation, taking into account what that person could understand from the behaviour of the other party, unless it was not reasonable for her to rely on it.

Of the systems, adherence to a literal interpretation was notable only in the Polish report. The Polish reporter explained that a literal interpretation is appropriate because 'one may expect clarity and deliberation from professional parties in formulating contractual provisions'.

In several countries, the court would apply the common or ordinary meaning rather than a technical, botanical meaning of the term 'vegetables'. This is the starting point in English law, where the court assumes that this is what the parties meant. It appears as one of several factors in Greek law relevant to the objective analysis. It is also a significant point of reference in German, Italian, Dutch, Scots and Swedish law. In certain systems, the prevalence of the common or ordinary meaning constitutes recognition of the fact that either the actual parties, or reasonable parties in the position of the parties, would not be aware of technical terms used in the food retail industry. This is true of Portugal because the court looks to the sense in which the clause would be understood by a reasonable man who receives the declaration in the context of the real situation, taking account of what that person could understand from the behaviour of the other party, unless it was not reasonable for her to rely on it. Such a reasonable person would not have specialist knowledge of a technical meaning. Dutch law looks rather at the specific parties, the reporter noting that because Imperial is not in food retail, and Botanical Fruits is aware of Imperial's inexperience in that field, the common or ordinary meaning prevails.

The common or ordinary meaning may give way to a different shared meaning. This may occur in Finland and arises in England and Wales because of the 'private dictionary' rule.

Although established trade usage has a role to play in several of the legal systems, the exact role differs from system to system. In Croatia, the court will apply a trade usage if that usage is applied regularly by traders in identical relations, unless it is excluded explicitly or implicitly. In England and Wales, if 'vegetables' has a technical meaning in the food retail industry generally, which is well established, and all members would understand the word to have this meaning, then it will prevail. In Finland, the common or ordinary meaning will not apply if the term has a special meaning in a certain line of business and both parties are aware of this special meaning. In France, because ambiguous terms are interpreted in accordance with relevant usages, the court is likely to analyse practices developed in other shopping malls. In Poland, a technical meaning is relevant if it is commonly used in a professional or business environment shared by the parties. Finally, in Spain the Tribunal Supremo [Supreme Court] has emphasised the proper and ordinary meaning of the words in the business or contractual trade.

For other reporters, whilst established trade usage can be relevant, it was not relevant on these facts. The Swedish reporter noted that the technical meaning is a botanical rather than a shared business or professional meaning, leading him to conclude that the technical meaning is not relevant. Other reporters concluded that, on the facts of this case, there is no relevant trade usage (the Croatian, German and Greek reports). The English report noted that a botanical meaning is not relevant in a trade context.

The purpose, either of the individual clause or of the contract as a whole, is relevant in several legal systems. In France, the court would ask whether the purpose of the clause was discussed during negotiations. The purpose and objective of the contract is the fourth and last method of interpretation in German law. For the Italian reporter, the relevance of purpose is bound up with the court's use of the cause of the contract. The court would identify the cause and ask which interpretation is more consistent with the purpose and structure of the specific economic transaction. The commercial meaning is more closely connected to the cause (economic purpose) than the technical meaning. In Poland, the court looks at the circumstances under which the contract was concluded and its purpose, and the common intention and contract purpose can take precedence over the literal meaning.

Good faith, although relevant to several reporters, also operates in different ways. In France, because Botanical Fruits must perform in good faith, it must check with Imperial which of the ordinary or technical meanings is intended. In Germany, it dictates that the legitimate expectations of the parties must be taken into account having regard to the concrete circumstances of the contract. In Italy, good faith, as a general rule for interpretation of contracts, can act to prevent parties from relying on a technical meaning, or dictate that a less reasonable meaning is the correct one in situations where a party has been induced to rely on a meaning. In Greece, the objective interpretation relies on good faith. The Dutch reporter suggested that good faith applied in the pre-contractual phase, preventing reliance on a technical meaning.

Question 2: Expertise

Whilst some reporters indicated that the different facts of Question 2 potentially led to a difference of approach to interpretation,[106] others concluded that they did not.[107]

For some of the legal systems in which the amended facts of Question 2 make a difference, knowledge of the technical meaning leads to a duty to act on the part of the contracting party possessing such knowledge. In Germany, the experience of the Imperial director leads him to understand the term differently. The court would ask why the director had not further enquired about the meaning Botanical Fruits attributed to the clause. The Greek reporter envisaged the court asking whether the Imperial director should have anticipated a discrepancy not known to Botanical Fruits. The Greek court could also look into whether Botanical Fruits, had it been aware of the distinction, could have reasonably expected that Imperial would be aware of the technical content of the term. For the Dutch reporter, a party who possesses expertise is expected to anticipate misunderstanding. There is a duty of care on him to take reasonable measures to ensure that the other party is not labouring under a misapprehension. The Imperial director's expertise may make it unreasonable for Imperial to rely on the ordinary meaning.

For other systems where the knowledge and experience of Imperial's director made a difference, it did not necessarily lead to a positive duty to act. In Portugal, for example, the many decades of experience in the food retail industry of Imperial, coupled with the academic experience of the director, could lead the court to conclude that the director was aware of Botanical Fruits' intention. Only the South African reporter suggested that estoppel was relevant on these facts, noting that Imperial could be prevented from relying on the ordinary meaning of the word 'vegetables'.

In the case of the legal systems for which the different facts were not relevant, in English and Scots law this is because only background information known to *both* parties is relevant. In interpreting the clause, the court asks what the reasonable person in the position of the parties at formation possessing such information would have understood the clause to mean.

In Finland, if one party is aware of a special meaning, he must inform the other party of that meaning before it can be determinative. In Greece, the court considers the issue of knowledge from the perspectives of both parties.

---

106 Germany, Greece, the Netherlands, Poland, Portugal, South Africa and Spain.
107 Croatia, England and Wales, France, Italy, Scotland and Sweden.

CASE 3: COCKTAIL PARTIES

Jill is the manager of the professional event organiser 'PartyMax', who will host exclusive cocktail parties in the harbour during the Annual Film Festival. For that purpose, she rents a luxury yacht for the duration of 14 days from John, acting as director of 'Afloat'. Jill and John agree in Clause 8 of the agreement that 'PartyMax shall have the opportunity to return the yacht after seven days of the agreement, in which case Afloat will refund PartyMax a sum applicable to the remaining period.' Jill pays the full rent of €140,000 upfront. Nine days after commencement of the rental period, Jill returns the yacht and requests that PartyMax receive a refund of the rental fee of €50,000 for the remaining five days. Afloat refuses and argues that Clause 8 means that PartyMax could exercise the option to return the yacht only within the first seven days of the agreement. Jill disagrees and contends that the clause means that PartyMax could return the yacht at any time as soon as seven days have passed. In support of its understanding of Clause 8 of the rental agreement, Jill refers to an email exchange that took place days before the conclusion of the agreement. In one email Jill writes: 'I do not know yet whether we will actually need the yacht in the second week. Will the contract allow me to end the rental agreement whenever I want?' In a reply, John writes: 'Don't worry about it. Under the rental agreement, you will be allowed to bring back the yacht at any time after the first week and be refunded.'

1 *[Email Communication] Assume that the language of Clause 8 is ambiguous and that the email communication between Jill and John sufficiently shows that John's understanding of Clause 8 was the same as Jill's. If in your legal system the email communication itself should not be considered to constitute an agreement or a modification to the agreement, what role, if any, may the emails between John and Jill play in the interpretation of Clause 8?*

2 *[Later Emails] What would your answer to Question 1 have been had the emails been written after rather than before the conclusion of the contract, for example at some time during the first week of the rental agreement?*

3 *[Handwritten Letters and Oral Comments] What would your answers to Questions 1 and 2 have been if the communication between John and Jill consisted not of emails but instead of handwritten letters sent by regular mail, or of orally made comments?*

1. KEY ISSUES

The case concerns a manager of a professional event organiser who rents a luxury yacht for the duration of a film festival. The dispute concerns the exact meaning of an option to break which is included within the contract.[1] Specifically, the parties are at odds on the point at which the option is exercisable. This case is designed to provoke discussion of the impact that communications between the contracting parties may have on the interpretation process. The communication which took place in the case, if it is treated as relevant, appears to support the manager's interpretation. The reporters are asked to consider the impact where this communication is embodied in an email. Two possibilities are to be discussed in this respect: where the email is sent *before* the conclusion of the contract; and *after* conclusion. Answers to the case should illustrate whether the legal system has a lenient or restrictive approach to the use of such communications. At one extreme, there may be nothing to prevent their use, and at the other, they may be ruled out or entirely prohibited in the interpretative process in the particular legal system. Finally, reporters were asked to consider two different possibilities, namely that the communication (a) is embodied in a handwritten letter, or (b) is oral rather than in writing of any sort. This should allow reporters to discuss whether specific types of communication are given a special status in the interpretative process, or whether all kinds of communication are treated equally in this respect.

2. CROATIA

Question 1: Email Communication

Driven by the primary goal of interpretation, the discovery of the common will of the contracting parties, in interpreting the true meaning of the ambiguous Clause 8, Croatian courts would use the rules and methods of interpretation, developed in legal scholarship and case law,[2] mentioned in the responses to previous cases. Interpretation of ambiguous contract clauses by taking into account the other clauses and the contract as a whole will not apply in this case due to the fact that an email communication, as here, does not constitute an agreement or a modification to the contract. Even though the interpretation usually concerns the will expressed in the contract itself, the motives, intentions and goals of the contract, and the circumstances under which it was concluded, are taken into account when they are helpful in understanding what was

1 This interpretation issue in this case is modelled on the one in *Partenreederei MS Karen Oltmann v Scarsdale Shipping Co Ltd ('The Karen Oltmann')* [1976] 2 Lloyd's Rep 708.

2 See Opening Remarks, n. 14.

actually meant in the contract.[3] The Croatian courts would thus explore all circumstances before and at the time of the conclusion of the contract, including an email exchange in the negotiation phase which sufficiently proves that John's and Jill's understanding of Clause 8 was the same. The email exchange in the negotiation phase would constitute important evidence concerning the will of the parties, because the parties' failure to achieve common agreement on the issue at this phase would influence the purpose and goal of the contract, and possibly even the contract conclusion.[4]

Question 2: Later Emails

If emails were written *after* the conclusion of the contract, the courts would use them for the purpose of interpreting the clause in question, most likely considering them as the parties' explanations of the ambiguous Clause 8. The emails could be used as evidence to support the contention that John's and Jill's understanding of Clause 8 was the same and prove their mutually agreed or common intention in accordance with Art. 319(2) of the COA. Although the main goal of interpretation is to establish what the intention of the parties was at the time of contracting, the courts would also take into account the relevant parties' conduct subsequent to the conclusion of the contract as a circumstance indicating the parties' common and actual intention at the time of the contract conclusion.[5] Court practice establishes the requirement of overall and exact evaluation of all circumstances relevant for the contractual relationship, including those occurring after the conclusion of the contract.[6]

Question 3: Handwritten Letters and Oral Comments

In order to explore the actual common intention of the parties, their motives and the goal of contracting (e.g. economic purpose of the contract), the Croatian courts would consider all forms in which the parties' will is expressed.[7]

3 Gorenc et al., *Komentar Zakona o obveznim odnosima*, p. 468; Blagojević and Krulj, *Komentar zakona o obligacionim odnosima*, p. 266.

4 Such an understanding is confirmed by the settled Croatian case law. See for example, VSRH, Revt 249/14-2 of 9 April 2015.

5 See Perović and Stojanović, *Komentar zakona o obligacionim odnosima*, p. 351.

6 Pursuant to the settled Croatian case law, all circumstances of the relevant case must be taken into account when determining the true and common will of contracting parties. See the ruling of the Supreme Court VSRH, Revr 997/2013-2 of 25 February 2015 confirming that the true aim of contract conclusion was not to guarantee a new position to the plaintiff but rather to enable the claimant to fulfil his duties under the pre-existing contract with the plaintiff, since the plaintiff was in prison at the time. See also VSRH, Revr 1558/2014-2 of 6 May 2015.

7 Under Art. 249(1) of the COA, a statement of will to enter into a contract may be expressed in words, customary signs or other conduct that may, beyond any doubt, lead to a conclusion on the existence and the contents of such assent and on the identity of the person making that statement. According to Art. 249(2), it may also be expressed using different means of communication and, according to Art. 249(3), it must be made freely and in a serious manner.

This means that the courts would also examine and take into consideration all forms of communication between the parties that represent their will and constitute an outward manifestation of their intent, including handwritten letters sent by regular mail, orally made comments as well as emails.[8]

3. ENGLAND AND WALES

Question 1: Email Communication

If the email exchange itself amounted to a binding contractual agreement, rather than a non-contractual agreement or discussion as to what would be agreed under the subsequent rental agreement, that prior agreement would be admissible in construing the later (rental) agreement[9] or may entail rectification of the later agreement to reflect a binding antecedent agreement.[10]

Otherwise, the emails amount to pre-contractual negotiations and are therefore inadmissible for the purposes of contractual construction (whether or not the clause is ambiguous) by reason of a rule of policy to that effect.[11] Although pre-contractual telexes were admitted in evidence in an English contractual dispute about an almost identical interpretation issue – as to the words 'after 12 months trading'[12] – this was later disapproved as far as the task of construction of the contract is concerned.[13] Moreover, to the extent that the emails are being used to prove the subjective understandings of John and Jill, they are for that additional reason inadmissible or of no weight, as subjective intentions are legally irrelevant to interpretation, which is an objective question.[14]

The emails are, however, admissible for the purpose of establishing an estoppel by convention or giving rise to rectification, and may do so in this case,

8 This is well established in Croatian case law. Already by 2003, the Electronic Commerce Act (OG No. 173/03, 67/08, 36/09 130/11 and 30/14) had prescribed that, in principle, a contract concluded by means of an email would not be considered invalid simply because of the form in which it was concluded. See Matić, 'Elektronički oblik govora i isprava – Novi oblik?', pp. 167 et seq.

9 Being earlier, the email exchange cannot amount to a modification of the later written rental agreement.

10 *FSHC Group Holdings Ltd v GLAS Trust Corp Ltd* [2019] EWCA Civ 1361, [2020] 1 All ER 505 (CA).

11 See point (3) in the Opening Remarks.

12 *Partenreederei MS Karen Oltmann v Scarsdale Shipping Co. Ltd (The Karen Oltmann)* [1976] 2 Lloyd's Rep 708 (Kerr J).

13 Lord Hoffmann in *Chartbrook v Persimmon Homes Ltd* [2009] 1 AC 1101 (HL) at paras. 46–47, confirming that to the extent that the telexes were admissible in *The Karen Oltmann* it could only have been for the purposes of rectification or estoppel.

14 See point (1) in the Opening Remarks, and Lord Hoffmann's third principle in *Investors Compensation Scheme v West Bromwich Building Society* [1998] 1 WLR 896. Also, *Monypenny v Monypenny* (1861) 11 ER 671 (HL).

where the parties' subjective understandings are the same and the emails may show an outward expression of accord such as is necessary for rectification.[15]

Question 2: Later Emails

Subjective understandings of the parties are irrelevant, whether before or after the contract was entered into, for the reasons given in the immediately preceding paragraph. Moreover, conduct subsequent to entering into the contract is also inadmissible when seeking to interpret a contract, not least because all it can show is the subjective understandings of the parties as to the meaning of the contract, which is itself inadmissible and irrelevant, and also because it could not have been taken into account by the parties when drafting the contract as it post-dated that process.[16]

Question 3: Handwritten Letters and Oral Comments

There is no general rule of contract law under which form determines the admissibility or binding nature of an agreement, or the admissibility of evidence proving the background to an agreement. (There are some statutory requirements of form applicable to certain contracts for real property or guarantees.[17]) Accordingly, it would make no difference if the communications were handwritten or oral, rather than emails.

4. FINLAND

Question 1: Email Communication

The objective of the interpretation of contracts is to determine the mutual intention of the parties at the time of contract.[18] The court interpreting the

---

15 See point (4) in the Opening Remarks, and ibid. For an example of an estoppel by convention or representation established by a pre-contractual misrepresentation as to the effect of a written contract, see *Curtis v Chemical Cleaning and Dyeing Co.* [1951] 1 KB 805 (CA). Alternatively, John's statement may amount to a misrepresentation that induced the contract and gave Jill the right to rescind it and seek restitution, or to seek damages under section 2(1) of the Misrepresentation Act 1967 or by the tort of negligent misstatement.

16 See Lord Hoffmann's third principle in *Investors Compensation Scheme*. See also *Full Metal Jacket Ltd v Gowlain Building Group Ltd* [2005] EWCA Civ 1809 (CA) per Arden LJ at paras. 15 and 17. However subsequent conduct can give rise to an estoppel by convention, the parties then being bound by the meaning they have led each other to believe they will adopt, providing the conduct shows a clear consensus as to the meaning of the agreement. The doctrine of rectification is, however, unavailable in relation to post-contractual conduct, dealing as it does with a contract that fails properly to record the true agreement of the parties at that time of its drafting. These two doctrines are discussed in point (4) in the Opening Remarks.

17 The Statute of Frauds 1677; the Law of Property Act 1925.

18 Hemmo, *Sopimusoikeus I*, p. 604; Saarnilehto, *Sopimusoikeuden perusteet*, p. 149; and Telaranta, *Sopimusoikeus*, p. 94.

contract will not look beyond the written contract unless there is an ambiguity in a contract provision. Contract provisions may be considered ambiguous if they can be understood in two or more reasonable ways.

In this case the language of Clause 8 of the rental agreement is ambiguous and hence the court needs other material to determine the mutual intention of John and Jill. In Finland, the court may take into account basically any evidence that indicates the initial intention of the contracting parties.[19] Often preliminary negotiations are relevant in resolving these kinds of disputes. As such, emails – now used as a modern way of communication – are very commonly accepted as evidence.[20] If the authenticity of the emails is not in question, the email exchange between John and Jill will most certainly play a decisive role in the interpretation of Clause 8.

Question 2: Later Emails

As mentioned above, the objective of the interpretation of contracts is to determine the mutual intention of the parties at the time of formation of the contract. If there is an ambiguity in a contract provision, the parties can also define their mutual intention after the conclusion of the contract.[21] In this case, John's understanding of Clause 8 is the same as Jill's. Hence, the email exchange between John and Jill can be accepted as evidence in the interpretation of Clause 8 even though the emails have been written and sent after the conclusion of the contract.

Question 3: Handwritten Letters and Oral Comments

If the communication between John and Jill consisted not of emails but, instead, of a handwritten letter sent by regular mail, the answer to Questions 1 and 2 would be the same. In Finland, the form in which such evidence is presented does not affect the outcome of the court's decision if the evidence is otherwise considered reliable. Finnish courts accept emails as equally reliable evidence as handwritten letters unless the authenticity of the emails can be reasonably questioned.

Oral communication can be accepted as evidence as well, although usually it is very hard – or even impossible – to establish what the contents of the oral comments between the parties were. Basically, the only way to prove the contents of oral communication is by presenting evidence like recordings. According to Chapter 17 Section 1 of the Finnish Code of Juridical Procedure (4/1734),

---

[19] See Pönkä, 'Tavoitteellisten tulkintasääntöjen merkityksestä liikesopimusten tulkinnassa', pp. 921–922. See also the Finnish Supreme Court's decision KKO 2001:34.

[20] Hemmo, *Sopimusoikeus I*, pp. 587–590. See also the Finnish Supreme Court's decision 2018:37.

[21] Hemmo, *Sopimusoikeus I*, pp. 595–597.

the party who refers to material such as oral communications needs to provide evidence to support his or her claim.

5. FRANCE

Question 1: Email Communication

The principle is that the meaning of Clause 8 should be determined by reference to the common intention of the parties in accordance with Art. 1188 Cciv (formerly Art. 1156). If we assume that the wording of Clause 8 is not a sufficiently clear expression of the common intention of the parties, the application of Art. 1188 Cciv to the case may justify further reference to emails exchanged between the parties before the conclusion of the contract,[22] since the French legal system is not bound by the letter of the contract.[23]

The exchange of emails will be taken into account by the judge to determine the elements of Afloat's offer that were essential in the eyes of PartyMax and decisive for their acceptance.[24] Jill's email identified an element that was important to the company she manages and expressed her clear intention to clarify Afloat's offer in case her company would need the yacht only for one week. John, acting as Afloat's director, provides a clear answer to Jill's request for clarification. His answer can be considered as an explanatory development to the written offer addressed to PartyMax. One may consider that Jill's message highlighted one of the decisive elements for the conclusion of the contract. Correlatively, Afloat cannot argue that John did not know of the significance of his answer to PartyMax. Not only did Afloat formally make clear that they committed themselves to reimburse the second week's costs if the yacht was not used during the corresponding period, but they were aware that the conclusion of the contract resulted from them making this commitment.

Beyond the strict question of the interpretation and following on from it, the judge would deny Afloat the possibility to refuse the reimbursement on the basis of Arts. 1103 and 1104 Cciv (formerly Art. 1134 (1) and (3)). Art. 1103 Cciv obliges contracting parties to respect the terms of their contract, while Art. 1104 Cciv imposes on them the duty to perform their contractual obligations in good faith, which obviously includes behaviour consistent with the contractual obligations as they result not only from the letter of the contract but also from all the circumstances that surround the conclusion of the contract and may enlighten its content and scope.

---

[22] Civ. 1, 18 February 1986, *Bull. civ.* (1986) no. 31; Com., 8 December 1987, *Bull. civ.* (1987) no. 262.

[23] All the more so, since no *entire agreement* clause has apparently been inserted in the contract between Afloat and PartyMax.

[24] Cf. e.g. CA Paris, 7 November 2014, *JurisData* no. 2014-031948.

Question 2: Later Emails

The solution would be essentially the same if the exchange of emails occurred not before but after the conclusion of the contract. Emails exchanged after the conclusion of the contract would be used to determine a common understanding of the terms of the contract, and thus confirm the common intention of the parties. As in the previous scenario, the emails exchanged would trigger the application of Art. 1104 Cciv in favour of PartyMax.

Question 3: Handwritten Letters and Oral Comments

Here, the question of the proof of the intention of the parties may be critical.[25] Under French law, this question is governed by a different set of rules depending on whether the contract is 'civil' or 'commercial'. In the present case, the contract is an 'acte de commerce' [commercial act] in the sense of Art. L. 110-1 Ccom. It was concluded by two 'commerçants' [traders] under Art. L. 121-1 Ccom, for the purposes of their business.[26] The contract between Afloat and PartyMax is therefore a commercial contract. Under Art. L. 110-3 Ccom, proof may be provided by any means, subject to appraisal by the lower courts. This allows the courts to take into account not only contractual documents as such, but also exchanges of emails, letters, faxes, text messages or witnesses.[27] Therefore, in these scenarios too, the solution would essentially be the same. Whether the parties have exchanged emails, handwritten letters or words orally is irrelevant. The court has to take into account all circumstances surrounding the conclusion of the contract and its performance that may reveal the common intention of the parties.

Two remarks may be added. First, courts of first instance and of appeal are entitled to assess the clarity of the contract and should interpret it only in the event of obscurity or of ambiguity resulting either from the contractual terms or from the circumstances surrounding the contract. Second, evidence appraisal is essentially a question of fact within the jurisdiction of lower courts. Their assessment is subject to the control of the Cour de cassation. However, the review carried out by the Cour de cassation is limited to legal questions. Lower courts' judgments may be overturned only if the Cour de cassation considers that the facts have been distorted ('dénaturation') and that the interpretation of the contract has been strained.[28] This control is particularly relevant for written documents, be they formally part of the contract or not – such as emails or

---

25 Com., 3 May 1984, *Bull. civ.* (1984) no. 145, where a seller could not prove against the letter of the written contract since no evidence had been provided of the alleged phone call during which the buyer would have accepted a price increase.

26 Com., 19 January 1993, *Bull. civ.* (1993) no. 21.

27 Civ. 3, 14 November 1973, *Bull. civ.* (1973) no. 582; Civ. 1, 26 January 2012, *Bull. civ.* (2012) no. 13.

28 Civ. 3, 14 November 1973, *Bull. civ.* (1973) no. 582.

handwritten letters.[29] However, it becomes more difficult in the case of oral exchanges, except when testimonies were collected in writing.[30] In other words, evidence will be all the more crucial when the communications between John and Jill consisted of orally made comments.

6. GERMANY

Question 1: Email Communication

From a German perspective the agreement that PartyMax and Afloat concluded would probably count as a 'Mietvertrag' [hire contract] under §535 BGB.[31] In that respect the email communication of the parties prior to the conclusion of the contract may be of significance.

German law does not exclude the relevance of the material which is not found in the four corners of the contractual deed in the context of interpretation. However, there is a rebuttable presumption that the deed containing the contract mirrors the contract completely and correctly: 'Vermutung der Vollständigkeit und Richtigkeit einer Urkunde'.[32] The circumstances around contract negotiations may, therefore, also carry weight in interpretation and serve as material which can be used in the interpretative exercise.[33] The history of the conclusion of the contract may contribute to the picture the judge develops as to the intentions of the parties and the objectives and purposes of the contract. Therefore, the presumption that the deed containing the contract mirrors the contract completely and correctly may be rebutted by reference to proven circumstances existing at the time of the conclusion of the contract. These circumstances include email conversations and explanations of the content of the contract given prior to its conclusion.

In the case at hand, the email communication between PartyMax and Afloat carries significant weight for the interpretation of Clause 8. The explanation given by John prior to the conclusion of the contract constitutes the basis of the common understanding of the clause by both parties when it was later agreed.

However, it is worth mentioning that in this case the email conversation seems silent as to the conversation regarding the price. Therefore, additional arguments would be necessary to show that PartyMax would not only have the

29 Civ. 1, 4 November 1968, *Bull. civ.* (1968) no. 262; Civ. 1, 18 February 1986, *Bull. civ.* (1986) no. 31.

30 Civ. 1, 6 January 1969, *Bull. civ.* (1969) no. 3; Civ. 2, 8 October 1975, *Bull. civ.* (1975) no. 243.

31 Under such a contract, parties may agree on the right to end the contract even if a fixed period of the hire is agreed.

32 BGH, 11.05.2017, *BeckRS* 2017, 126042; BGH, 07.05.2002, *NJW* 2002, 3164 (acquisition of property).

33 BGH, 10.07.1998, *NJW* 1998, 3268.

right to end its custody over the yacht prior to the fixed period of the rental agreement, but that the price also reduced respectively. Usually a German court would imply such an effect on the price; however, there is no certainty as to what an individual judge would find on that point.

Question 2: Later Emails

An email communication *after* the conclusion of a contract could lead to a different effect, because the explanation given by John no longer constitutes the content of Clause 8 based on which the parties have concluded a contract. In contrast to Question 1, a unilateral explanation after concluding the contract has no effect on the expressions within the contractual negotiations under §157 BGB. Such an explanation after the contract negotiations may, however, be of relevance in two ways. First, leaving aside whether the email operates to modify the original contract, parties under German law may agree on a certain interpretation of unclear clauses of the contract in a manner binding upon them. Alternatively, such communication usually indicates the original intention and understanding of both parties, which is relevant for interpretation under §133 BGB.[34]

In the case at hand, the email communication sufficiently shows that the understanding of Clause 8 by PartyMax and Afloat was the same. The categorical presumption, whereby the parties have no intention of modifying the contractual agreements after concluding the contract, but rather intend to act under that contract, supports this assumption.[35] As a result, the email communication after the conclusion of the contract shows the common intention of the parties, and therefore carries decisive weight for the interpretation of Clause 8 and also supports the interpretation of PartyMax.

Question 3: Handwritten Letters and Oral Comments

Under German law, the form of the relevant communication does not matter as long as the contractual deed itself meets the requirements on legal form for the contract. The reasons for that depend on how the effect of the communication is construed: as long as the acts of communication between the parties are only used as indications of the original intention of the parties, there are no requirements of form. This result follows from the general rule that means of proof are not restricted to the contractual deed itself. If the court comes to an agreement on the right of interpretation of the contract taken from the communication after the conclusion of the contract, the same result follows from the fact that such an agreement usually does not come under the form requirement.[36]

---

34 M. Wolf, '§157 BGB' in H.-T. Soergel, *Bürgerliches Gesetzbuch mit Einführungsgesetz und Nebengesetzen*, vol. II, m.n. 36.

35 BGH, 02.23.1987, *NJW* 1987, 2437.

36 Ibid.

It is worth mentioning, however, that a court is free when considering the evidence to attribute more weight to a deed than to a testimony if comprehensive reasons are given, cf. §286 ZPO 'Freie Beweiswürdigung' [free consideration of evidence]. The free consideration of evidence is only restricted by logic, the law of nature and empirical judgment. As an example, the credibility of a witness which is the object of the 'Freie Beweiswürdigung' can be narrowed by the logic of the testimony.[37]

7. GREECE

Question 1: Email Communication

In the case at hand, the email communication may be used by the court in order to discover the content of Clause 8 of the agreement between PartyMax and Afloat. This is a classic example of a case where the interpreter must turn to elements lying outside the text of the agreement, the so-called 'συγκείμενα' ['complements' or 'proximates'], such as the parties' interests, the purpose of the agreement, the surrounding circumstances, the negotiations prior to the conclusion of the agreement, etc.; this possibility has been affirmed unanimously by legal doctrine and case law, provided that the said 'συγκείμενα' can be factually correlated in some way with the respective agreement per se.[38] In such a case, the issue of evidence becomes crucial; nonetheless, one must draw a clear dividing line between interpretation and evidence: a juridical act may form the object of both processes, but in the first case the juridical act is investigated in its normative context and meaning as the 'law of the parties', while in the second case the juridical act is examined purely in its ontological dimension, namely as an empirically identifiable fact that must and can be proven by any means of proof available, such as documents, witnesses, etc. Therefore, any court will first look at the evidence, in order to determine what the object of interpretation will be.[39]

To begin with, the text of Clause 8 of the agreement between PartyMax and Afloat specifies the time when the yacht may be returned to Afloat prior to the

---

37 BGH, 14.10.2003, *NJW-RR* 2004, 425.

38 Karassis, *General Principles*, §§ Γ 271–277, 298; Stathopoulos, *Civil Code*, vol. 1[B], Arts. 173 and 200 nos. 91, 127; Ladas, *General Principles*, §34 nos. 23, 42; Georgiades, *General Principles*, §41 no. 25; see also Case 8. Case law has affirmed this possibility with regard to the interpretation of testaments (see e.g. AP 1054/1974, NoV 23 (1975), 627; AP 182/76, NoV 24 (1976), 711; AP 1146/2002, first published in Isocrates; CA Athens 3015/76, Arm 31 (1977), 356; CFI Thessaloniki 43407/2007, first published in Isocrates); since this is affirmed with regard to a juridical act that is subject to strict form requirements, it can be inferred *e maiori ad minus* that it should also be true with regard to other juridical acts as well.

39 Papanikolaou, *Methodology*, §449.

end of the agreement, but it says nothing about the time when the option to end the agreement earlier than agreed may be exercised. This is the actual bone of contention between PartyMax and Afloat, namely when the option should be exercised, not when the yacht is to be returned. Jill poses exactly this question in her email exchange with John and John responds to that. Therefore, even though the email communication is not part of the agreement, the court will take the email correspondence into account in an effort to understand what the parties agreed on (see Arts. 444–445 CPC, which, in response to a line of previous court decisions, were amended in 2011 in order to include explicitly emails as plausible means of proof).[40] Therefore, the email communication is a useful complement that helps determine the precise content of the agreement in question.

Nonetheless, another opinion relevant to the contours of contract interpretation and its scope could also be examined. If the email exchange between Jill and John is deemed not to address the issue of when the option to end the contract earlier may be exercised, then there is a loophole in the contract. In this case the simple interpretation (also called 'εξηγητική ερμηνεία' [exegetic interpretation]) of the contract no longer suffices in order to determine this point and the interpreter must resort to the so-called 'συμπληρωτική ερμηνεία' [complementary interpretation] of the agreement. Greek legal doctrine also bases this possibility upon Art. 200 CC and implements two criteria in order to hermeneutically close the contractual gaps, namely the hypothetical will of the parties, as this may be discerned in the agreement between them, and the criterion of good faith.

The interpretation as such, even when it is summoned to complete a term insufficiently expounded and explained by the parties, must always stay within the fine contours of the hypothetical will of the parties and the criterion of 'καλή πίστη' [good faith], as mentioned in relation to previous cases, without endeavouring to invent a 'just' solution.[41] When applying this double standard, the judge is subject to a serious restriction: he may not violate the parties' intent by finding a 'just solution' overriding the parties' agreement. If the judge wishes to rectify indeterminacies or amend injustices in the contract that eventually arose out of a subsequent substantial change in the circumstances surrounding the transaction, he may resort to Art. 288 (which prescribes that the debtor must fulfil his duties according to the principle of 'καλή πίστη' and taking into

---

40 See CA Athens 32/2011, DEE 17 (2011), 591; CFI Athens 6302/2004, Arm 59 (2005), 239; Hellenic Parliament, *Explanatory Report [Αιτιολογική Έκθεση] to law 3994/2011*, p. 11 (available at https://www.hellenicparliament.gr/UserFiles/2f026f42-950c-4efc-b950-340c4fb76a24/e-expol-eis.pdf).

41 For the concept of 'συμπληρωτική ερμηνεία' and its relation to 'εξηγητική ερμηνεία', see Stathopoulos, *Civil Code*, vol. 1^{B}, Arts. 173 and 200 nos. 184–212; Georgiades, *General Principles*, §42 nos. 1–6, 9; Balis, *General Principles*, §90; Ladas, *General Principles*, §34 nos. 54–60; also Papanikolaou, *Methodology*, §§512–535; Karassis, *General Principles*, §§ Γ 377–396.

account the 'συναλλακτικά ήθη' [trade customs]) or Art. 388 CC (which allows a court to adjust the duties of the parties under a contract in the event of an unforeseen change of circumstances). However, both of these options go beyond the scope of interpretation of an existing contract.[42]

The courts do not seem to have fully grasped the fine distinction between exegetic and complementary interpretation and they generally tend to identify unclear terms that only need interpretational clarification as 'gaps' in the agreement.[43]

Question 2: Later Emails

The answer here does not differ substantially from the answer to Question 1 if the email communication between Jill and John took place after the conclusion of the agreement. Assuming that no modification or renewal of the agreement is intended by the parties (which is in any case possible), the court will examine the email correspondence as a mere 'self-interpretation' of the contract, namely a clarification of its content on the basis of the conduct of the parties after its conclusion.[44] The email communication in question addresses the main issue that is being disputed by the parties. Consequently, the judge will interpret the agreement in the light of the emails, taking into account both textual (i.e. the text of the agreement) and factual elements (namely the conduct of the parties) in order to discover the 'self-interpretation' of the contract and discern its normative meaning.

Question 3: Handwritten Letters and Oral Comments

The answers to Questions 1 and 2 as to the method that the court will use to detect the will of the parties remain the same, regardless of whether the means of proof are emails, handwritten letters sent by post or oral comments; what changes is the mode of proof applicable under the Greek CPC. More specifically, the deciding judge may take into account any of the means of proof enumerated in Art. 339 CPC which can be proposed by the parties; of particular

42 This is the so-called 'διαπλαστική ερμηνεία' [transformatory interpretation]; Georgiades, *General Principles*, §42 nos. 7–8; cf. Stathopoulos, *Civil Code*, vol. 1^{B}, Arts. 173 and 200 nos. 199–203, 206.

43 See e.g. AP 1450/1995, EEN 64 (1997), 272; AP 250/1998, NoV 47 (1999), 772.

44 For the latter, see Papanikolaou, *Methodology*, §494; Ladas, *General Principles*, §34 no. 23; cf. Karassis, *General Principles*, §§ Γ 275–276. The latter author explicitly enumerates among the instances of 'συγκείμενα' the behaviour of the parties and the manner in which they execute the contract until the dispute on a certain issue arises (§ Γ 275); however, he goes on to mention that in principle only 'συγκείμενα' that were at hand at the moment when the declaration of intent became definite (namely in the case of a contract when the said declaration was communicated to its addressee; Art. 167 CC) can and should be taken into account (§ Γ 276). Cf. Karakostas, *Civil Code*, vol. II, Arts. 173, 200 no. 868, noting that there is no interpretation when the parties agree on the true meaning of words or phrases after conclusion of the contract.

interest in the case at hand are 'έγγραφα' [documents], 'ομολογία' [confession] and 'μάρτυρες' [witnesses]. Handwritten letters are the archetypal form of private documents accepted by the Greek CPC as proof, provided that they satisfy the requirements set out in the law (Arts. 432-465 CPC; see especially Art. 445 CPC), and when they contain declarations of intent of a juridical nature, they constitute a rebuttable presumption that the declaration was proffered by the drafter of the document and that its content is genuine and true.[45]

Orally made comments are also acceptable for the purposes of interpretation of the agreement in question, but they present the additional difficulty that they should be proven in some way before the court; confession of the contracting parties, either before the court or extra-judicially (Arts. 352–354 CPC), or individual testimony by witnesses (Arts. 393 et seq. CPC) may be of use in this respect as well, although restrictions apply based on the value of the agreement as determined by its subject matter, and proof by witnesses is generally not as effective as documentary evidence. To sum up, the judge will equally take into account the information provided and proven by the parties in this respect (with the caveat that proof by documents tends to be more convincing) in order to determine the actual will of the parties.

8. ITALY

Question 1: Email Communication

Written or oral communications between parties are relevant factors for the interpretation of the contract under Art. 1362 c.c. The rule of Art. 1362 requires the adjudicator to search for the common intention of the parties (para. 1) and it indicates the parties' overall conduct as a relevant tool for the analysis of the parties' will (para. 2).

Communications exchanged between the parties prior to the final agreement can therefore be used in the interpretation process, first, because they can be regarded as a means of reconstructing the actual intention of both parties (under the general rule of the first paragraph of Art. 1362), and second, because they are usually considered as part of the parties' overall conduct.[46]

---

45 Tentes, 'Art. 445', no. 801. Actually, the exchange of handwritten letters would be, from a procedural law point of view, much less problematic than the exchange of emails. After some initial hesitation by the Greek courts, first case law and, since 2011, also the legislator affirmed that emails also fall under the category of 'mechanical depictions', which, according to Art. 444 CPC, have the same power of proof as private documents; see CA Athens 32/2011, DEE 17 (2011), 591; SCFI Athens 1327/2001, DEE 7 (2001), 377 et seq.; SCFI Athens 1963/2004, *Dike* 36 (2005), 587; SCFI Athens 1932/2011, EPolD 4 (2011), 482.

46 Cf. Gentili, *Senso e consenso*, p. 535 ff.

In this case, communications between the parties appear to have a strong interpretive value because they can be regarded as bilateral conduct showing a common understanding by both parties as to the meaning they attached to the contractual clause.[47]

Question 2: Later Emails

According to Art. 1362, para. 2 c.c., the conduct of the parties and their reciprocal communications can be employed as interpretative factors even if they are subsequent to the conclusion of the contract.

However, if communications are prior to the conclusion of the contract, one of the parties might try to rebut the interpretative value of such communications by contending that they referred to pre-contractual understandings that have been displaced by the ultimate contractual agreement.[48]

Conversely, communications exchanged after the contract is concluded could have greater value because they would reveal a subsequent express acknowledgement of a certain meaning of the contractual text, on the part of the party (John) who would take advantage of a different meaning. Alternatively, communications exchanged after the contract could be considered to be a new agreement modifying the original contract and producing autonomous legal effects.[49]

Question 3: Handwritten Letters and Oral Comments

Under Art. 1362, a court would give to handwritten letters and oral communications (apart from problems of proof) the same relevance as the emails, because the meaning of a written text can also be explained by reference to external written or unwritten factors.

9. NETHERLANDS

Question 1: Email Communication

In line with the decisions of the Supreme Court,[50] the court will have to determine the meaning that each party could reasonably attach to the terms of

47 Both judicial decisions and scholarly writing emphasise that, in order to be relevant for the interpretation, the parties' behaviour should be bilateral. Unilateral conduct is regarded as a relevant factor against the agent: Sacco, *Contratto*, p. 1363 ff; Bianca, *Contratto*, p. 427; Roppo, *Contratto*, p. 447; Cass. 8 June 2018 no. 15035; Cass. 19 July 2012 no. 12535; Cass. 25 October 2006 no. 22899.

48 See Cass. 12 December 2005 no. 27338; Cass. 15 October 1976 no. 3480

49 See Cass. 23 May 2014 no. 11533; Cass. 4 August 2000 no. 10250; Sacco, *Contratto*, pp. 1365–1366.

50 Hoge Raad 13 March 1981, *NJ* 1981, 635 (Ermes/Haviltex); Hoge Raad 20 February 2004, *NJ* 2005, 493 (DSM-Chemie/Fox).

the contract and which each could reasonably expect the other to have given to the contract, in light of all the relevant facts and circumstances assessed in light of the standards of 'redelijkheid en billijkheid' [reasonableness and fairness].

In taking all the relevant circumstances into account, the court would look at the negotiation history and the conduct of the parties before the contract's formation, in order to discover the meaning the contracting parties could reasonably attach to the expressions used in the contract.[51] It is permitted under the law of the Netherlands to provide evidence of the common intentions of the parties at the time of the formation of the contract by providing evidence of facts or circumstances that took place prior to the conclusion of the contract.[52] Pre-contractual communications between the parties can shed light on why certain provisions have been incorporated into the contract, why a certain formulation has been adopted or rejected, as well as the parties' understanding of the contractual expressions and therefore the meaning they intended and expected to be attached to them. Such pre-contractual communication includes email exchanges.[53] Jill would be allowed to submit the email communication between her and John to support her submission that they shared a common understanding with respect to the meaning of Clause 8. In weighing the material provided, however, the court must keep in mind that these are preliminary communications leading up to the conclusion of the final contract and that such communications are often unilateral statements that do not necessarily reflect the position and interests of the parties in a balanced way.[54] However, in this case they reflect a common understanding.

That being said, if the contract is comprehensive and detailed and is the result of careful drafting following extensive negotiations with the aid of legal advisors, the court may in first instance give more weight to the text of the contract, in the sense that the court may provisionally attach a linguistic meaning to the contractual expression as a starting point for interpretation.[55] It is assumed that both parties to such contracts could reasonably rely on a textual interpretation. If the court has reached a provisional determination that the ordinary linguistic meaning should prevail (because of the detailed nature of the contract, the extensive negotiations that preceded its conclusion and the assistance and advice given by legal advisers), the court has to then determine whether the party who submits a different interpretation has established this sufficiently to

---

51 Asser/Sieburgh, *Algemene leer der overeenkomsten*, 6-III, no. 363; Tjittes, 'Uitleg van schriftelijke contracten', p. 9; Tjittes, *Commercieel Contractenrecht*, p. 316.

52 Tjittes, *Uitleg van schriftelijke contracten*, p. 38; Asser/Sieburgh, *Algemene leer der overeenkomsten*, 6-III, no. 363; Tanja-Van Den Broek, 'Een kwestie van uitleg', p. 431.

53 Tjittes, *Uitleg van schriftelijke contracten*, p. 38.

54 Ibid., p. 38; Valk, 'Kijk naar jezelf'.

55 Hoge Raad 19 January 2007, *NJ* 2007, 575 (Pont Meyer); Hoge Raad 29 June 2007, *NJ* 2007, 576; Hoge Raad 9 April 2010, *JOR* 2010, 179; Hoge Raad 5 April 2013, *NJ* 2013, 214 (Lundiform/Mexx).

be allowed to provide evidence of this alternative interpretation. Ultimately, the court must establish the meaning the parties in the given circumstances could each reasonably attribute to the provision and that which they in this respect could reasonably expect the other to attribute to the wording. In these circumstances, it would therefore be for Jill to assert that the contract should be interpreted differently from the ordinary linguistic meaning, in which case she would be given the opportunity to provide evidence that it was reasonable for her to attach a different meaning to Clause 8 and to expect that John would share that meaning. Such evidence could include pre-contractual communications between the parties.

Question 2: Later Emails

Dutch law allows evidence of relevant facts and circumstances that took place after the conclusion of the contract to be admitted to uncover the meaning the parties could reasonably have attributed to the contract terms at the time of conclusion of the contract.[56] It may be relevant for the interpretation of a contract term to review what the parties said to one another about the term after the conclusion of the contract in order to establish what can reasonably be inferred from such statements as to their understanding of the contractual expressions.[57] In the event that the email communications took place after the formation of the contract, for instance at some time during the first week of the rental agreement, this could be relevant information. It will be for the court to weigh the evidence to establish whether such post-contractual statements reveal that the parties shared a common understanding with respect to the meaning to be attributed to contract terms.

Question 3: Handwritten Letters and Oral Comments

Applying the *Haviltex* norm, the court must determine the meaning each party could reasonably attach to the terms of the contract and which each party could reasonably expect the other to have given to the contract, in light of *all* the relevant circumstances assessed in light of the standards of 'redelijkheid en billijkheid' [reasonableness and fairness]. To this end, the court may take into account evidence of statements made by the parties before the conclusion of the contract. Such pre-contractual communication includes handwritten letters or

---

56 Hoge Raad 20 May 1994, *NJ* 1994, 574 (Gasunie/Anloo); Hoge Raad 20 May 1988, *NJ* 1988, 781, (Smeets/Kuyper); Hoge Raad 27 November 1992, *NJ* 1993, 273 (Volvo/Braam); Hoge Raad 20 November 1998, *NJ* 1999, 684 (Mokster/Wijsmuller); Hoge Raad 10 December 2004, *NJ* 2005, 239 (Diosynth/Groot-Van Veen); Hoge Raad 12 October 2012, *NJ* 2012, 589; Hoge Raad 18 September 2015, *NJ* 2015, 382 (ISG/RBS); Tjittes, *Uitleg van schriftelijke contracten*, pp. 39 and 52; Asser/Sieburgh, *Algemene leer der overeenkomsten*, 6-III, no. 363; Tjong Tjin Tai, 'Bewijs van de (inhoud van de) overeenkomst', p. 699.

57 Tjittes, *Uitleg van schriftelijke contracten*, p. 52; Valk in Schelhaas/Valk, *Uitleg van rechtshandelingen*, p. 27 ff.

even drafts of the contract.[58] By providing the court with the pre-contractual documentation, the judge is able to form a picture of how the contract came about and consequently how it should be interpreted.[59] The court may also consider evidence of oral communication between the parties.[60] To the extent that witnesses are used to provide reliable evidence of these oral communications, the court will have to weigh such evidence in accordance with the relevant rules of procedure as laid down in the 'Wetboek van Rechtsvordering' [Code of Civil Procedure]. This remains the case even if the contract includes an entire agreement clause. The Supreme Court has clarified that an entire agreement clause is one of the relevant circumstances that can be taken into account.[61] The meaning to be attributed to such a clause is dependent on the circumstances of the case, including the formulation of the clause, the nature and content and the detail and comprehensiveness of the contract, the foreign origin of such a clause, as well as the way in which the clause was incorporated during the negotiations and became part of the contract. Thus, if the entire agreement clause is part of the general conditions and one of the parties was not aided by legal advisors, less weight should be attached to the clause.[62]

10. POLAND

Question 1: Email Communication

As mentioned in the Opening Remarks, Polish courts may take into account any evidence presented to them in order to establish the parties' common intention. In addition, any evidence from the pre-contractual negotiations is seen as a part of the situational context that needs to be considered in finding out what the parties' common intention was,[63] even though such evidence does not have a binding character.[64] Therefore, it is seen as important for the parties to thoroughly document the pre-contractual negotiation phase, also by archiving the correspondence between the parties.[65] Jill could, therefore, use the email

58 Tjittes, *Uitleg van schriftelijke contracten*, p. 38; Tjittes, *Commercieel Contractenrecht*, p. 317.

59 Tjittes, *Uitleg van schriftelijke contracten.*

60 Tjittes, *Uitleg van schriftelijke contracten*, p. 52.

61 See in particular, Hoge Raad, 5 April 2013, *NJ* 2013, 214, no. 3.5.3.

62 See A-G Timmerman in Hoge Raad, 5 April 2013, *NJ* 2013, 214, no. 3.13.

63 Judgment of SN of 21.11.1997, I CKN 825/97; Judgment of SN of 03.09.1998, I CKN 815/97; Judgment of SN of 05.10.2005, II CK 122/05; Judgment of SN of 17.12.2008, I CSK 250/08; Judgment of SN of 17.06.2009, IV CSK 90/09; Judgment of SN of 14.06.2012, I CSK 485/11; B. Kaczorowska, 'Wizja wykładni umów w projekcie księgi pierwszej kodeksu cywilnego', TPP 2/2011, pp. 19–20.

64 Judgment of SN of 04.07.1975, III CRN 160/75; Judgment of SN of 02.07.2004, II CK 271/04; Judgment of SN of 05.10.2005, II CK 122/05; Judgment of SN of 15.06.2007, V CSK 63/07; Judgment of SN of 17.06.2009, IV CSK 90/09; Judgment of SN of 10.05.2013, I CSK 74/13.

65 B. Kaczorowska, 'Wizja wykładni umów w projekcie księgi pierwszej kodeksu cywilnego', TPP 2/2011, p. 19.

communication with John to prove that her interpretation of Clause 8 was the one agreed between the parties.

Question 2: Later Emails

Polish courts have also recognised that the parties' conduct after concluding the contract, for example the way in which the contract is performed, may point towards establishing the parties' common intentions as to a contractual term's meaning that the parties gave it at the moment of concluding the contract.[66] It has been stated in the legal literature that the parties' actions after concluding the contract may reflect their intentions at the moment of concluding it, whether they reflect upon it through deliberate behaviour or the spontaneous effects of their acts. The analysis of the parties' conduct may give a different direction to the process of interpreting the contract.[67] Therefore, it is likely that the answer would remain the same.

Question 3: Handwritten Letters and Oral Comments

Any evidence may be taken into account by Polish courts in order to establish the parties' common intentions. This also includes oral testimony of the parties to the contract.[68] Pursuant to Art. 247 of the 'Kodeks Postępowania Cywilnego' [Code of the Civil Procedure], the parties are limited in using oral testimony against other evidence in writing (e.g. a contractual term). However, that limitation does not apply in the event that it is necessary to interpret the contractual terms, since then the evidence from the oral testimony is not against the evidence in writing, but about it.[69] Written letters would constitute part of

66 Judgment of SN of 17.02.1998, I PKN 532/97; Judgment of SN of 03.09.1998, I CKN 815/97; Judgment of SN of 08.10.2004, V CK 670/03; Judgment of SN of 05.10.2005, II CK 122/05; Judgment of SN of 15.06.2007, V CSK 63/07; Judgment of SN of 17.12.2008, I CSK 250/08; Judgment of SN of 17.06.2009, IV CSK 90/09; Judgment of SN of 14.06.2012, I CSK 485/11; Judgment of SN of 16.01.2013, II CSK 302/12; Judgment of SN of 28.02.2013, III CSK 70/12; Judgment of SN of 10.05.2013, I CSK 74/13; Judgment of SN of 13.01.2016, V CSK 277/15; Judgment of SN of 18.11.2016, I CSK 802/15; A. Musiała, Commentary to the Judgment of SN of 26.03.2008, I UK 282/07, Prz. Orz. 2009/2/103–110.

67 B. Kaczorowska, 'Wizja wykładni umów w projekcie księgi pierwszej kodeksu cywilnego', TPP 2/2011, pp. 19–20.

68 Decree of SN of 29.06.1995, III CZP 66/95; Judgment of SN of 21.11.1997, I CKN 825/97; Judgment of SN of 08.07.2004, IV CK 582/03; Judgment of SN of 08.10.2004, V CK 670/03; Judgment of SN of 05.10.2005, II CK 122/05; Judgment of SN of 15.06.2007, V CSK 63/07; Judgment of SN of 17.12.2008, I CSK 250/08; Judgment of SN of 17.06.2009, IV CSK 90/09; Judgment of SN of 13.06.2012, II CSK 608/11; Judgment of SN of 14.06.2012, I CSK 485/11; Judgment of SN of 21.03.2013, III CSK 223/12; Ł. Węgrzynowski, 'Sądowe ustalanie treści stosunku umownego', PPH 2007/5/44–49.

69 Decree of SN of 29.06.1995, III CZP 66/95; Judgment of SN of 21.11.1997, I CKN 825/97; Judgment of SN of 08.10.2004, V CK 670/03; Judgment of SN of 05.10.2005, II CK 122/05; Judgment of SN of 17.12.2008, I CSK 250/08; Judgment of SN of 17.06.2009, IV CSK 90/09; Judgment of SN of 14.06.2012, I CSK 485/11; Judgment of SN of 21.03.2013, III CSK 223/12; Ł. Węgrzynowski, 'Sądowe ustalanie treści stosunku umownego', PPH 2007/5/44–49.

the correspondence that the parties should archive as potential evidence in the future of their intentions.[70] The answers to Questions 1 and 2 would remain the same whether the parties' common intention were documented in email communications, handwritten letters or oral statements.

11. PORTUGAL

Question 1: Email Communication

The email can be used to prove that Afloat knew that the understanding of Clause 8 was the one argued by PartyMax. Under Portuguese law, if both parties know each other's real intention, the declaration should be interpreted according to the parties' intention (Art. 236.°/2 CC). The email can be used to prove the real intention of both parties. In addition, it would be considered against 'boa fé' [good faith] if after the formation of the contract John were to refuse to accept something that he had negotiated before.

If we assume that the contract has an omission, it would also be possible to apply Art. 238.°. This article determines that the contract must be completed with the real intention, and the email could be very useful to prove the real intention of the parties according to Art. 239.°.

'Boa fé' would also play a role under Art. 239.° CC. John's behaviour, acting as director of Afloat, would be considered 'exercício inadmissível de uma posição jurídica' [behaviour against good faith] (or *venire contra factum proprium*), which means defending an interpretation that does not correspond to the agreement in the formation of the contract.[71]

Although the lease of the luxury yacht need not be in writing, the parties did decide to put the contract into writing. In this case, Art 222.° CC could permit the use of the email communications that were sent at the formation of the contract to complete the rules of the contract or interpret it. Even if the parties have a final written agreement, prior oral or written negotiations or contemporaneous oral negotiations are admissible to add to, vary or contradict the written agreement. Very often, during the negotiations, the parties express their subjective intentions.

Question 2: Later Emails

The answer to Question 1 would be the same if the emails had been written after the formation of the contract because in this case the emails must be seen as a

---

70 B. Kaczorowska, 'Wizja wykładni umów w projekcie księgi pierwszej kodeksu cywilnego', TPP 2/2011, pp. 19–20.

71 For cases on good faith, see the decisions previously referred to: RLx 2 October 1997 (Eduardo Baptista), CJ XXII (1997) 4, 100–102 and RLx 22 January 1998 (Soares Curado), CJ XXIII (1998), 1, 89–93. See Menezes Cordeiro, *Tratado de Direito Civil Português*, p. 760.

declaration concerning the interpretation of Clause 8. In addition, these emails can bind the parties during the execution of the contract based on good faith. In fact, Art. 762.°/2 CC establishes that in the fulfilment of their obligations parties must behave according to good faith.

Even if the emails were changed after the formation of the contract, they can be used to prove that Afloat and PartyMax share the same interpretation of Clause 8. Portuguese courts emphasise the importance of all of the declarations between the parties before and after the formation of contract.[72] The emails could be used as proof to confirm the parties' real intention (Art. 236.°/2). But also, Art 222.°/2 CC determines that clauses agreed after the formation of the contract are valid if it can be shown that they correspond to the declarant's intention. In the Portuguese legal system, the lease of the yacht need not be in writing.

Question 3: Handwritten Letters and Oral Comments

For the same reasons as discussed in the previous answer, if the communications between John and Jill were to consist not of written emails but handwritten letters sent by regular mail or orally made comments, these kinds of communications can be considered clauses of the contract and would be also considered valid if they corresponded to the parties' intention according to Art. 222.°/2 CC.

In fact, these communications can be seen in the Portuguese legal system as clauses that are negotiated after the formation of the contract but that complete the regulation of the contract.

12. SCOTLAND

Question 1: Email Communication

If we assume that the language of Clause 8 is ambiguous, the Scottish courts would attach great weight to the terms of the email communications passing between Jill and John. The exchange of emails prior to the conclusion of the contract would form part of the 'surrounding circumstances': what the parties thought they were agreeing, what they said and did and how they conducted themselves before and at the formation of the contract. This material would be treated as part of the factual context to be taken into account.[73] That material would be construed in light of an objective test, i.e. the meaning that the email communications would convey to reasonable contracting parties in the position of the contracting parties, rather than in terms of what the contracting parties themselves subjectively understood those words to mean.

---

72 Decision from STJ 3 March 1998 (Fernando Fabião), CJ/Supremo VI (1998) 1, 102–103.

73 *Wood v Capita Insurance Services Ltd* [2017] UKSC 24; [2017] 2 WLR 1095 at para. 10.

If we apply that test, it is undoubtedly the case that reasonable contracting parties in the position of Jill and John would understand the emails to mean that Jill could return the yacht after the elapse of the first week of the contract. We do not have any other background material which would operate to contradict that interpretation and therefore it is likely to be sufficient to convince a Scottish court that Jill's position should be sustained. A final point to make is that Scots law would likely reach the same result if the natural and ordinary meaning of the clause was unambiguous and favoured John's argument: in such a case, the email would be treated as part of the context and would likely be sufficient to supersede the literal meaning of the words.

Question 2: Later Emails

If the email exchanges took place after the conclusion of the contract, that would place a wholly different complexion on the solution to this case. The email communications would be treated as the subsequent conduct of the contracting parties. Scots law has a general rule against the admissibility of evidence of the subsequent conduct of the parties as an aid to construction.[74] However, matters are slightly complicated by the fact that Scots law makes a distinction between evidence of (1) subsequent conduct and (2) subsequent conduct which can be taken into account as part of the surrounding circumstances when the contract was entered into.[75] If the email communications 'throw light upon the state of affairs or the knowledge [of the parties] before and at the time of the conclusion of the contract',[76] then it may be considered by the court as (2). Admittedly, it is a very difficult exercise to categorise the email exchange as (1) or (2), but it is suggested that it is more likely that the Scottish courts would treat it as (1) and therefore irrelevant. On that basis, the clause would remain ambiguous and the courts would apply other interpretative criteria in order to undertake their evaluation. It is submitted that the commercially sensible construction would not be particularly helpful since both Jill and John's interpretation of the clause (return and refund within the first seven days or return and refund after the first seven days) is equally commercially plausible. Therefore, the courts would seek to identify the usual market practice in the particular market for the hire of

---

[74] *Miller & Partners Ltd v Whitworth Street Estates (Manchester) Ltd* [1970] AC 583; *L. Schuler AG v Wickman Machine Tool Sales Ltd* [1974] AC 583; *Cameron (Scotland) Ltd v Melville Dundas Ltd* 2001 SCLR 691, 695–696 at paras. 27–31 per Lord Hamilton; *Westbury Estates Ltd v The Royal Bank of Scotland plc* 2006 SLT 1143, 1151 at para. 38 per Lord Reed; and *Ballast plc v Laurieston Properties Ltd (In Liquidation) and others* [2005] CSOH 16 at paras. 157–159 per Lady Paton.

[75] See *Cameron (Scotland) Ltd v Melville Dundas Ltd* 2001 SCLR 691, 695–696 at paras. 30–31 per Lord Hamilton and *Wincanton Group Ltd v Reid Furniture plc* [2008] CSOH; 2008 GWD 29-446 at para. 16 per Lord Glennie.

[76] *Wincanton Group Ltd v Reid Furniture plc* [2008] CSOH; 2008 GWD 29-446 at para. 16 per Lord Glennie. Writer's annotations are shown in square brackets.

luxury yachts. In light of that information, the courts would reach a conclusion on the most likely interpretation of the clause.

Question 3: Handwritten Letters and Oral Comments

Finally, if the communication between John and Jill was not in the form of an email but contained in a handwritten latter or was oral in nature, this would not alter the solution to question one. As Lord Hoffmann noted in *ICS*:

> Interpretation is the ascertainment of the meaning which the document would convey to a reasonable person having all the background knowledge which would reasonably have been available to the parties in the situation in which they were at the time of the contract ... Subject to the requirement that [background material] should have been reasonably available to the parties ... it includes absolutely anything which would have affected the way in which the language of the document would have been understood by a reasonable man.[77]

Turning to the effect of the handwritten letter or oral exchange on the answer to Question 2, once again, this would not make any difference: these background materials would be considered subsequent conduct of John and Jill, and are inadmissible.

13. SOUTH AFRICA

Question 1: Email Communication

It remains unclear to what extent prior negotiations are excluded from consideration during the interpretation process.[78] There is nothing inherent in the adoption of an objective approach that dictates that evidence of prior negotiations should be excluded;[79] in fact, reference to the 'background to

77 *Investors Compensation Scheme Ltd v West Bromwich Building Society* [1998] 1 WLR 896, 912–913.

78 Arguably, the abolition of the distinction between 'background' and 'surrounding' circumstances in *KPMG Chartered Accountants (SA) v Securefin Ltd* 2009 4 SA 399 (SCA) para. 39 could have meant that *all* evidence – whether it related to objective facts, or the parties' negotiations, or subsequent conduct – was admissible, even in the absence of ambiguity. There were cases which supported this conclusion – see *Grobler v Oosthuizen* 2009 5 SA 500 (SCA) paras. 13–14; *Mkhize v Umvoti Municipality* 2010 4 SA 509 (KZP) para. 17. However, *Van Aardt v Galway* 2012 2 SA 312 (SCA) appears to have removed the possibility of considering evidence of prior negotiations although, as suggested in the main text, that conclusion may have been based on the particular facts of the case. As yet, there is no answer to the question whether South African judges who emphasise that the purpose of interpretation is to determine the parties' common intention (see the Opening Remarks) would admit evidence of prior negotiations as a matter of course.

79 For academic support for this statement, see Bradfield, *Christie's Law of Contract*, pp. 254–255; Van Huyssteen et al., *Contract*, p. 304.

the preparation and production of the document'[80] as a factor that may be considered by a court appears to be broad enough to include evidence of prior negotiations. But *Van Aardt v Galway*[81] serves as authority for the blanket exclusion of this evidence, although it was evident from the facts of that case that the parties in any event did not discuss the meaning of the disputed term during their negotiations.[82] In that event, any evidence of what each party had thought was the meaning of the provision would have amounted to evidence of their individual unexpressed intentions, which has never been admissible as an aid to interpretation in South African law.[83] However, if one could argue that the correspondence between Jill and John establishes, as an objective fact, the origin and purpose of Clause 8, then it should form part of the factual matrix.

On the assumption that there is a blanket exclusion on prior negotiations for the purposes of interpretation, Jill can tender the evidence to support a claim that the contract should be rectified. 'Rectification' is an equitable remedy, designed to correct a document which is an inaccurate reflection of the parties' agreement.[84] To succeed with such a claim, there must be proof of a common intention which is not reflected accurately in the document, that such inaccuracy is the result of a mistake, and how the document should be corrected to give effect to the parties' common intention.[85] In order to determine whether a document should be rectified, a court may consider the parties' prior negotiations.[86] Furthermore, a mistake will be found to exist whenever there is a discrepancy (rather than an obvious error) between the parties' prior intention or agreement and the document recording that agreement.[87] In other words, to the extent that one could argue that the parties deliberately used the word 'after' and that as a result there is no mistake which can be rectified, this does not preclude rectification in South African law. Finally, it is not a requirement that both parties should be mistaken; it is sufficient if one party was mistaken and the other party was aware of that mistake but failed to draw the mistaken party's attention to it in order to secure an advantage.[88]

In the alternative, Jill could tender the evidence to show that Afloat should be estopped from relying on its interpretation of Clause 8.[89] Thus, in order for a

---

80 *Natal Joint Municipal Pension Fund v Endumeni Municipality* 2012 4 SA 593 (SCA) para. 18.
81 2012 2 SA 312 (SCA) para. 9.
82 *Ibid.*, para. 10.
83 See e.g. *Coopers & Lybrand v Bryant* 1995 3 SA 761 (A) 768D.
84 *Intercontinental Exports (Pty) Ltd v Fowles* 1999 2 All SA 304 (A) para. 11.
85 See Van Huyssteen et al., *Contract*, p. 174 and the cases cited there in nn. 201–202.
86 *Van Aardt v Galway* 2012 2 SA 312 (SCA) para. 9.
87 *Tesven CC v South African Bank of Athens* 2000 1 SA 268 (SCA) paras. 15–16.
88 I.e. a unilateral mistake caused by the other party's unconscionable conduct – *Benjamin v Gurewitz* 1973 1 SA 418 (A) 426A.
89 See Case 2, Question 2.

court to give effect to the meaning ascribed to Clause 8 in the correspondence, Jill would need to prove that the requirements of estoppel have been met.[90]

Question 2: Later Emails

In terms of the current approach, evidence of subsequent conduct is admissible to interpret a contractual provision, even in the absence of ambiguity.[91] However, different justifications have been offered for the admissibility of such evidence. Where both parties have implemented the agreement in the same way, supporters of a subjective approach to interpretation would admit such evidence because it 'may be probative of [the parties'] common intention at the time they made the contract'.[92] Proponents of an objective approach would also admit such evidence, because the parties' conduct 'provides clear evidence of how reasonable business people situated as they were and knowing what they knew, would construe the disputed provision'.[93] Presumably the assumption here is that evidence of a shared implementation of the provision points to the objective meaning of that provision at the time of contract conclusion.[94] To the extent that this (South African) objective approach appears to be inconsistent with other common law approaches, it should be pointed out that Lord Hoffman's exposition of the modern principles of interpretation in English law has been understood to exclude evidence of prior negotiations only.[95]

Question 3: Handwritten Letters and Oral Comments

There is no difference in principle between written (whether by email or hand) or oral communications: the question is whether the evidence forms part of the factual matrix and the nature of the evidence is immaterial for the purposes of determining admissibility.[96]

---

90 As to which, see Sonnekus, *Estoppel*, p. 67 ff. The relationship between good faith and estoppel was discussed in Case 2, Question. 2, n. 88.

91 The traditional approach to contractual interpretation also admitted evidence of the parties' subsequent conduct, but only when the meaning of a term remained ambiguous after a consideration of the so-called 'background' circumstances (*MTK Saagmeule (Pty) Ltd v Killyman Estates (Pty) Ltd* 1980 3 SA 1 (A) 12F–H).

92 *Unica Iron and Steel (Pty) Ltd v Mirchandani* 2016 2 SA 307 (SCA) para. 21.

93 *Comwezi Security Services (Pty) Ltd v Cape Empowerment Trust Ltd* (759/11) [2012] ZASCA 126 (21 September 2012) para. 15. The only exception to this rule is where the parties' subsequent implementation is inconsistent with any possible meaning of the language used, in which case a court may not rely on that conduct as an aid during the process of interpretation.

94 As suggested by Nicholls, 'My kingdom for a horse', p. 589.

95 Wallis, 'What's in a word?', p. 686.

96 Kerr, *Principles of Contract*, 411 nn. 225–226.

14. SPAIN

Question 1: Email Communication

First of all, an email can be accepted before the Spanish courts as evidence of the common intention of the parties according to the Ley de Enjuiciamiento Civil (LEC) ['Civil Procedure Act']. Under this Act, an email can be considered a private document, and these are regulated in Art. 326 LEC. According to this article, private documents will provide full evidence in proceedings where their authenticity is not contested by the party they may harm. If the authenticity of a private document is contested, the party that filed the document may seek an expert's authentication of handwriting or any other means of proof that may be useful and relevant for such a purpose. Where the authenticity of the document cannot be deduced or should there be no proof of its authenticity, the court shall assess it in accordance with the rules of 'sana crítica' [fair criticism].[97] More precisely, Art. 326, third paragraph LEC states that where the party having an interest in an electronic document's effects requests them or where the document's authenticity is challenged, the provisions set forth in Art. 3 of the Ley de la Firma Electrónica ['Electronic Signature Act'] shall apply.[98] This article refers to electronic data such as the IP address, the server where the document is stored and other identifying data.[99]

In response to the question, the emails between John and Jill may play an important role in the interpretation of Clause 8, firstly because this communication reveals the common and real intention of the parties (Art. 1.281 CC), and secondly because, as Art. 1.282 CC says, in order to judge the intention of the contracting parties, their acts at the time of and subsequent to the conclusion of the contract shall be mainly taken into account. Although this rule does not include previous acts, the use of the term 'mainly' allows acts before the contract is concluded to be taken into account as well.[100] Therefore, Art. 1.282 CC is a very relevant interpretation factor insofar as it applies to every preliminary, contemporary and subsequent act. The whole context in which the contract is concluded may be taken into account,[101] a logical interpretation[102] which Spanish scholars call historical interpretation.[103]

---

97 STS 05.04.2010, ECLI:ES:TS:2010:1794.

98 Paragraph added by Ley 59/2003 de 19 diciembre (BOE 304, 20.12).

99 See on this issue: Bennasar, *La validez del documento electrónico*; Baturones, *La prueba de documentos electrónicos*, pp. 155–170; Abel and Picó i Junoy, *La prueba electrónica*, pp. 199–200.

100 STS 16.06.2005 (RJ 2005\4280); STS 01.02.2002 (RJ 2002\2099); STS 20.03.2001 (RJ 2001\4743).

101 Lete Achirica, 'De la interpretación', p. 1412; Rodríguez Marín, 'De la interpretación', p. 2281.

102 Almagro Nosete, 'De la interpretación', p. 734.

103 Díez-Picazo, *Fundamentos*, p. 502.

The interpreter will seek to discover the real and common intention of both parties through a subjective interpretation (Arts. 1.281 and 1.282 CC),[104] also called the 'principio espiritualista' [spiritualist principle],[105] which means that the common intention prevails in the issue of interpretation of contracts.[106]

Consequently, the emails exchanged between Jill and John as part of the preliminary negotiation – the pre-contractual stage – show what their real and common intention actually was. The emails will be accepted according to the procedural law provisions (Art. 326 LEC), as explained above.

Question 2: Later Emails

Had the emails been written after the conclusion of the contract, for example at some time during the first week of the rental agreement, the answer would be even more clear because that situation is included explicitly in the aforementioned Art. 1.282 CC. Scholars consider that what happens during the period of performance especially reveals the common intention of the parties.[107]

Question 3: Handwritten Letters and Oral Comments

If the communication between Jill and John had consisted of handwritten letters sent by regular mail, then the legal solution would be the same because they are private documents which reveal the common intention of the parties, and the same procedural provisions apply.

Orally made comments, such as telephone calls or oral statements made in person, may be difficult to prove before a court.

Apart from that, in terms of the interpretation method, there is no difference, because Art. 1.282 is applicable to any act of the parties whatsoever (oral, written, etc.) and the rules on interpretation cannot make the parties say something that they did not say or write.[108]

15. SWEDEN

Question 1: Email Communication

The email correspondence between Jill and John will most likely play a decisive role when interpreting Clause 8 of the contract according to the principles of Swedish contract law.

---

104 STS 25.01.2008 (RJ 2008\224); STS 02.02.2006 (RJ 2006\822). The two articles can be seen as a unity (STS 26.10.1990 (RJ 1990\8052)), or Art. 1.282 CC as a complement to Art. 1.281 CC.

105 Cano Mata, 'La interpretación', p. 197.

106 STS 16.06.2005 (RJ 2005\4280). See also STS 23.12.2004 (RJ 2005\83); STS 20.12.2012, ECLI:ES:TS:2012:8867.

107 Díez-Picazo, *Fundamentos*, p. 502.

108 See STS 01.10.2019, ECLI:ES:TS:2019:3011.

As there are no formal constraints on what circumstances may be accorded weight by the interpreter – everything relevant should be considered[109] – there is no reason to dismiss the email communication in question out of hand.[110] True, this correspondence precedes the conclusion of the contract, and is in this sense preliminary, but this does not in itself make the data irrelevant – even though we should be cautious.[111] The court is free to ask itself what might be deduced from the email exchange when ascertaining the meaning of the contract. This correspondence is simply part of the matrix of facts on the basis of which the courts will construct their interpretation, in principle no different from any other relevant matter.

Question 2: Later Emails

Suppose the email exchange took place after the conclusion of the contract? In principle, and as far as legal formants are concerned, it does not matter *when* the exchange took place. If the exchange indeed shows that John's understanding of Clause 8 was the same as Jill's at the time of conclusion of the contract, *that would be it*, regardless. As previously stated, *whatever* sheds light on the understanding of the parties – i.e. on the common intention – is relevant. There really are no 'legal formants' signifying the absence of formal constraints in this regard, save the oft-cited passage in the preparatory works of the Contracts Act (1915:218) mentioned in the first paragraph of the Opening Remarks.

Perhaps it should be added that, in accordance with the Swedish law of evidence, anything is admissible as evidence, and the evidence is evaluated freely by the court. The principle of 'den fria bevisprövningen' [the free examination of evidence] means that everything that has been submitted during the hearing should be considered by the court, at the court's discretion.[112] The principle can be found in Chapter 35 Section 1 of the Code of Judicial Procedure (1942:740).

This means that, normally, the conduct of the parties after the conclusion of the contract may be taken as an indication of how the contract was understood at the time of conclusion.[113] Whether or not such conduct in the actual case will be considered informative as to the original intention of the parties is, of course, dependent upon the nature of the actions.

---

109 See the Opening Remarks, n. 235.

110 A classic case, in which the preliminaries proved decisive, is NJA 1964 p. 454.

111 On preliminaries and interpretation see Adlercreutz and Gorton, *Avtalsrätt* II, p. 71 ff.; Lehrberg, Avtalstolkning, p. 118 ff.; J. Ramberg and C. Ramberg, *Allmän avtalsrätt*, p. 164 f. Generally, the idea that preliminaries should be treated with caution has no real hold on Swedish contract law scholars. If anything, the *importance* of preliminaries is stressed (see, however, J. Ramberg and C. Ramberg, *Allmän avtalsrätt*, p. 165).

112 See Lindell, *Civilprocessen*, p. 459 f.

113 See the answer to the question on Case 4.

Question 3: Handwritten Letters and Oral Comments

The answers to Questions 1 and 2 would not be affected if the communication consisted of handwritten letters or orally made comments, rather than of an email exchange. In principle, the form of a 'rättshandling' [juridical act] does not matter.[114] What matters is the content conveyed, and the content is to be ascertained by means of interpretation. In practice, proving exactly what was said during an oral conversation might be difficult, but that is a different matter.

16. EDITORIAL COMPARATIVE OBSERVATIONS

All respondents indicated that the communications between Jill and John would be considered, regardless of whether these consist of emails, handwritten letters or oral comments, albeit that the latter is, as some respondents point out, in practice harder to prove.

However, the conditions under which these communications may play a role in the interpretation of Clause 8 diverge.

First, let us examine the role of communications between Jill and John that take place *before* the conclusion of the contract. For courts in Croatia, Finland, France, Greece, Italy, Germany, Poland, Spain and Sweden, the primary aim or purpose of contract interpretation is to uncover or establish the actual or real intentions of the contracting parties. Put differently, courts would seek to discover the meaning that both parties in actuality attributed to the language of the contract. Consequently, in these jurisdictions, the court will likely consider evidence of communications between the parties to uncover Jill and John's real intentions.

These emails, handwritten letters or oral comments seem to play a somewhat different role in the Netherlands and Portugal. There, evidence of the meaning that Jill and John factually attributed to Clause 8 is not enough. The respondent for the Netherlands points out that the ultimate objective of contract interpretation there is not to discover parties' actual intentions, but rather to construe the meaning that in the given circumstances they could have reasonably attributed to the contractual language and that they reasonably may have expected the other party to have attributed to it. Hence, here, emails, handwritten letters or oral comments from John may prove that he read the contract the same way as Jill did, but that will only help Jill if this means that she was entitled to reasonably infer from these that John indeed had the same interpretation as her.

114 Cf. the Contracts Act (1915:218) Section 1(3), which reminds the reader that there are some cases where the form does matter, at least so far as the formation of contracts is concerned – and this is an indirect way of stating the principal rule: no form is required.

One also finds the application of a measure of reasonableness in the Portuguese report, which says that in Portugal it is against the principle of 'boa fé' [good faith] for a contracting party to interpret the contract in a manner different than what was negotiated and agreed to in the formation of the contract. The French report denotes a similar approach, although the reporter points out that the application of good faith is not part of establishing the content of the contract itself, but the performance of the contract as interpreted. In contrast with these jurisdictions, the Greek report notes that contract interpretation is not based on considerations of reasonableness, since contract interpretation should not involve finding a 'just' solution.

Second, the role of communications between Jill and John *before* the conclusion of the contract is very limited in England and Wales, Scotland and South Africa. Courts in these jurisdictions would consider communications between contracting parties before the conclusion of the contract inadmissible as evidence of pre-contractual negotiations or the subjective intentions of the parties. Both here and in their respective Opening Remarks, these reports explain that contract interpretation serves a different purpose than in the other jurisdictions. It is not aimed to uncover the subjective intentions of the contracting parties, but instead to ascertain the meaning of the contractual language itself, that is, what a reasonable person in the context and circumstances in which the parties found themselves would have understood the contract to mean. Consequently, the emails, handwritten letters or oral comments from John would only be admissible, not when it serves to demonstrate that John actually shared the same intentions as Jill, but only that a reasonable man, in the same positions and with the same knowledge as John and Jill, would understand Clause 8 as Jill did. The respondents for both Scotland and South Africa emphasise that communications between Jill and John before closing the contract may even be relevant as 'surrounding circumstances' or the 'factual context'.

When we consider the role of emails, letters or verbal statements exchanged *after* Jill and John concluded the contract, the various jurisdictions diverge both variously and subtly. The respondent for England and Wales is most reserved, explaining that the parties would not have been able to have taken account of subsequent communications at the time they entered into the contract. All subsequent conduct could show is the subjective understanding of the parties, which evidence, as discussed, is inadmissible in England and Wales. Germany seems to have a similar attitude, at least as the point of departure. Notwithstanding that, its respondent notes that the parties may agree on the interpretation of certain unclear clauses of the contract in a manner binding upon them. The Croatian, Polish and Swedish reports indicate a similar liberal attitude.

Third, the Scottish report allows for the possibility of subsequent exchanges being relevant for establishing the factual matrix, yet its respondents doubt whether it would likely come to that. In this respect, the South African respondent is more optimistic, explaining that Lord Hoffman's principles of contract interpretation, as discussed in the Opening Remarks to the three common law systems, are generally understood in South Africa as precluding pre-contractual negotiations alone. Consequently, if the emails, letters or comments conveyed after entering into the contract indicate that both Jill and John implemented the contract consistently, these may be used in South Africa as evidence supporting an agreed interpretation of Clause 8. This approach applies when a judge considers the clause to be unambiguous, yet not if the parties' shared conduct contradicts the clear wording of the agreement. The Dutch and especially the Spanish and Italian reports observe similarly that the way Jill and John implement the contract, including expressions as to the meaning that each attribute to Clause 8, may help interpret this provision. The French courts take a similar stance. Additionally, the respondents for Finland, Greece, Portugal and Germany add that if in their communications after the conclusion of the contract both parties express that they attribute the same meaning to the contractual terms, then these expressions may even amount to a binding clarification or specification of the contractual terms. The Italian report points out that later communications may even amount to a new agreement modifying the previous one.

In sum, we have seen that in all jurisdictions, email communication, as well as handwritten letters or oral comments, from John could be considered in support of Jill's contention that John understood Clause 8 in the same fashion as she did. However, these communications may contribute to contract interpretation in different ways for different purposes, and consequently with various degrees of admissibility.

CASE 4: ANIMAL WASTE

Guy is the director of 'Meat 'n' Bones', a meat processing company. Bernard runs a professional animal farm. Guy and Bernard conclude a contract according to which Bernard will supply Guy every week with 5,000 kilos of meat products, described in Clause 14 as 'animal waste and animal carcasses intended for human consumption'. Both agree that six months after concluding the contract, Bernard will start making his weekly deliveries. Six months have passed, and Bernard has by now delivered his first shipment of 5,000 kilos of meat products. However, Meat 'n' Bones refuses to pay Bernard the full purchase price that they initially agreed on. Guy explains that between 2,000 and 2,500 kilos of the delivery consists of animal waste that is not *intended for human consumption, which he says is useless to the operations of Meat 'n' Bones. This, Guy maintains, is contrary to Clause 14, in which the qualification 'intended for human consumption' applies to both 'animal waste' and 'animal carcasses'. Bernard is baffled. He understands Clause 14 to mean that the qualification 'intended for human consumption'* only *applies to 'animal carcasses' and not also to 'animal waste'. To him, Clause 14, therefore, includes* all *animal waste: both waste intended for human consumption and waste that is not. Moreover, Bernard is able to show that immediately after the conclusion of their contract, Guy had contacted Bernard, informing the latter that he filed a request for a government permit to store and process animal waste not destined for human consumption at the Meat 'n' Bones plant, including animal protein, rendered fats and pet food. Additionally, Bernard can also present evidence showing that days before he delivered the first shipping, Guy's request was denied. The fact that Guy filed this request, Bernard argues, shows that Guy had the same understanding of Clause 14 as Bernard had.*

Assume that the language of Clause 14 is ambiguous. Also assume that the fact that Meat 'n' Bones filed and informed Guy of the request above shows that Guy shared Bernard's interpretation of Clause 14. What role may the fact that Meat 'n' Bones filed the request for this permit play in the interpretation of Clause 14?

1. KEY ISSUES

The case concerns a dispute between the director of a meat processing company and the owner of a farm. A contract of sale and supply has been entered into between the parties, and the dispute relates to the definition of what is to be supplied under that contract. The clause contains a phrase which comprises two nouns and a description, and no commas are used. It is therefore unclear whether the description applies to the latter noun only, or to both nouns.[1] The case is designed to allow reporters to assess the weight to be given to post-contractual conduct in the interpretative process. In the case, the director seeks to rely on his own behaviour (the request for a specific permit) in the interpretative process. He aims to use that conduct to prove a shared understanding of the disputed wording. The conduct is known to the other party: the director has told the farm owner about his behaviour. The reporters are also asked, in broad terms, about the role of the request for the permit in the interpretative process. This might lead reporters to focus on the points discussed above, namely the extent to which the conduct was known to both parties. It is also possible that reporters may consider whether a request for a permit is a public fact, knowledge of which is available more broadly, outside the immediate context of the communications between the contracting parties.

2. CROATIA

Under the assumption that the language of Clause 14 is ambiguous, the courts would explore the common intention of the contracting parties in order to interpret the true meaning of its words. In this process of balancing, the courts would try to determine the purpose of Clause 14. However, if the purpose of the clause is not sufficiently clear, as in the case at hand, the courts may construe the wording of Clause 14 taking account of the request for a permit to store and process animal waste not destined for human consumption. As in Case 3, the conduct of the parties subsequent to the conclusion of the contract and before its performance would be taken into account as a supporting criterion in the contract's interpretation.[2] The Croatian courts would most likely consider the filed request as an act demonstrating Guy's intention, which is directly linked to the contract in question. Moreover, assuming that Meat 'n' Bones filing and informing Bernard of the aforementioned request is conduct demonstrating that Guy's understanding of Clause 14 is the same as Bernard's, the request would play a key role in establishing the common intention of the contracting parties. Besides the subjective criterion, the request would also indicate an understanding of Clause 14 that is consistent with basic principles of the law of obligations,

---

1 The interpretation problem in this case takes its inspiration from the discrepancies between language versions of Art. 14A(2)(c) of Regulation (EEC) No. 543/69 of the Council of 25 March 1969 on the harmonisation of certain social legislation relating to road transport, which the Court of Justice of the European Union considered in Case 90/83 *Michael Paterson and others v W. Weddel & Company Limited and others*, ECLI:EU:C:1984:123.

2 See Opening Remarks, n. 14.

such as the 'načelo savjesnosti i poštenja' [principle of conscientiousness and honesty]. Therefore, it can be concluded that the Croatian courts would use the request filed by Meat 'n' Bones as an important circumstance in interpreting the true meaning of Clause 14 and as relevant for the purpose of establishing the contracting parties' common intention at the time of contracting.[3]

3. ENGLAND AND WALES

All conduct subsequent to the contract becoming binding is irrelevant to and inadmissible in construction of the contract,[4] and so Bernard's filing of a request after the conclusion of the contract is irrelevant. The meaning of the contract is fixed at the time it becomes binding, by reference to what a reasonable person in the parties' shoes would understand the contract to mean at that time.

However, subsequent conduct can be taken into account by judges in four ways. The first is illegitimate: although legally irrelevant to the question of interpretation, the conduct may nevertheless in fact persuade some judges to interpret an ambiguous contract in a particular way (as they find it difficult to put the conduct out of their mind when construing the contract). The second and third are legitimate: the subsequent conduct may amount to a binding variation of the contract or give rise to an estoppel. Where the issue is the meaning of express terms, it would be very rare for the court to conclude that the parties reached a binding agreement to vary the terms, since that would require the parties in the subsequent conduct not only to intend a particular meaning but also to acknowledge the original meaning and that they no longer want it to apply. However, estoppel (by convention, as discussed in the Opening Remarks, or by representation, an allied doctrine) can and will sometimes apply.

Estoppel is introduced in point (4) of the Opening Remarks. Although not technically a matter of interpretation, but operating outside it, it has a similar practical effect to the process of interpretation and must be considered

---

3 In interpreting contracts, the Croatian courts establish the parties' common intentions by examining the facts (VTSRH, Pž-7947/04 of 11 July 2007). However, as a ground for appeal or revision, judgments invoke the failure to apply or erroneous application of the COA provisions on contract interpretation (*errores in judicando, errores juris*). See VSRH, Rev 1108/07-2 of 30 December 2008; VSRH, Rev 103/08-2 of 23 December 2008; VSRH, Rev 755/04-2 of 22 April 2008; VSRH, Revr 80/06-2 of 9 January 2008; VSRH, Rev 86/07-2 of 19 June 2007; VTSRH, Pž-7102/03 of 19 September 2006; VSRH, Rev 698/06-2 of 26 July 2006; VSRH, Rev 985/03-2 of 9 March 2006; VSRH, Rev-1076/1999-2 of 3 July 2002; VSRH, Rev 309/1995-2 of 7 March 1996, etc. See also VSRH, Rev 3495/1994-2 of 18 October 1995, where the court established that the courts of lower instances failed to discuss the matter by applying Art. 99 of the COA because substantive law was not applied correctly, and due to such an erroneous application of the substantive law the facts decisive for ruling the claim (un)grounded were not fully established.

4 See Case 3, n. 16.

alongside it. For such an estoppel, it is necessary to show that the parties have established a conventional basis for operating the relevant clause of the contract or one party has represented that it will operate the clause in that way, they have regulated their subsequent dealings on that basis or the representee has relied, and it would unjust or unconscionable to allow them or the representor to renege on that conventional basis.[5]

Here, the fact that Guy filed the request for the permit only demonstrates that he acted on his subjective understanding of the contract. If both parties acted independently from the other on the basis of a mutual mistake which remained uncommunicated between them, then there would be no estoppel.[6] However, the fact that Guy told Bernard about the request (and Bernard did not express his surprise or confusion) will be important evidence that the request was an outward manifestation on which Bernard could reasonably expect Guy to rely.

Fourth, the subsequent conduct might be evidence of the subjective understanding of the parties prior to entry into the contract. Such a shared subjective consensus at the time of contracting, if also outwardly expressed in some way, may give rise to a rectification of the contract.[7]

4. FINLAND

The starting point in interpreting a contract is the common intention of the parties, even if this differs from the literal meaning of the words in the written documents. In Finland, the courts and tribunals can take into account any evidence that indicates the intention of the parties.[8] This also includes the parties' actions after the conclusion of the contract.[9] There are no written form requirements for this kind of contract under Finnish law or parol evidence rule in court proceedings.[10] In this case, Meat 'n' Bones filed a request for a permit to store and process animal waste not destined for human consumption and informed Guy of the request. This can be taken as evidence of Bernard's intention at the time of contracting.[11]

5 *Norwegian American Cruises A/S v Paul Mundy Ltd (The Vistafjord)* [1988] 2 Lloyd's Rep 343 (CA) per Bingham LJ at 352.
6 As in *K Lokumal & Sons (London) Ltd v Lotte Shipping Co. Pte Ltd (The August Leonhardt)* [1985] 2 Lloyd's Rep 28 (CA) at 34–35.
7 See point (4) in the Opening Remarks.
8 See Pönkä, 'Tavoitteellisten tulkintasääntöjen merkityksestä liikesopimusten tulkinnassa', pp. 921–922. See also the Finnish Supreme Court's decision KKO 2001:34.
9 See e.g. Pönkä, 'Tavoitteellisten tulkintasääntöjen merkityksestä liikesopimusten tulkinnassa', p. 923.
10 Hemmo, *Sopimusoikeus I*, p. 596.
11 Kozlowska-Rautiainen and Mäenpää, *Legal Effects of Entire Agreement Clauses*, p. 25.

5. FRANCE

Given the ambiguity of the contractual terms, the court will first look for evidence of the common intention of the parties in accordance with Art. 1188 Cciv (formerly Art. 1156). The only elements of proof mentioned are circumstantial and rely on the observation of Guy's behaviour after the conclusion of the contract. The French Civil Code does not directly address this kind of situation, neither in Art. 1188 nor in the series of objective rules of interpretation expressed in Arts. 1189–1191 (formerly Arts. 1157–1164).

If the contract between Guy and Bernard were to be analysed as a contract of sale, it would be worth mentioning that the Code also contains a rule of interpretation that is specific to this kind of contract. Art. 1602 Cciv prescribes that obscure and ambiguous contracts shall be interpreted against the seller. Despite the fact that this article is specific to sale contracts, it is settled case law that it only applies when all other rules of interpretation are irrelevant to the case at stake.[12] Before considering this article, the court will therefore contemplate whether there is any other way to determine the common intention of the parties.

In 1988,[13] the Cour de cassation decided that courts may take into account the behaviour adopted by contracting parties after the conclusion of their contract in order to determine their common intention. In their interpretation of Clause 14, the court will consequently take into consideration Guy's request for a government permit to store and process animal waste not destined for human consumption. They will also consider the facts that Guy informed Bernard of his request and that his claim on the interpretation of Clause 14 followed the government's denial of his request. In this case, the court is therefore likely to depart from the rule of Art. 1602 Cciv and rather to apply the rule of interpretation provided in the 1988 decision of the Cour de cassation. In other words, the court is likely to consider the fact that Guy contacted Bernard to inform him that he filed a request for the government permit as a sign that the common understanding of Clause 14 at the time of the conclusion of the contract was that 'intended for human consumption' only applies to 'animal carcasses'.

6. GERMANY

As discussed in response to Case 3, behaviour after concluding the contract has no effect on the expressions within the contractual negotiations themselves

12 Req., 12 January 1857, *DP* (1857), jurispr. 407; Civ., 12 April 1918, *DP* (1921), jurispr. 224; Civ. 1, 26 June 1990, no. 89-12.186.

13 Civ. 1, 13 December 1988, *Bull. civ.* (1988) no. 352.

under §157 BGB. However, it could suggest the actual will and meaning of the parties at the time of negotiation under §133 BGB.[14]

Therefore an established common intention of both parties after concluding the contract could influence the interpretation of Clause 14. In this way the content of the contract can be determined after the conclusion of the contract.

In this case, German courts would presume that the request provides evidence for the actual intention of the applicant Meat 'n' Bones. Whereas there is no contradiction of Meat 'n' Bones against this presumption, one can assume that the request shows the actual intention of Meat 'n' Bones and supports the interpretation of Bernard. As an example of contradiction, Meat 'n' Bones could allege that it made the request for its own use of waste disposal or that it used the request to avoid the risk of misunderstanding of the ambiguous Clause 14 within the contract.

However, there has to be a common actual intention of both parties at the time of the contract, so that there is an effect on the interpretation of Clause 14.[15] It is important to note that an identical understanding would be sufficient, even if it is not a common one, in the sense that the parties did communicate on it, as was the case under Case 3. This leads to the question whether Bernard's actual intention at the time of conclusion of the contract was the same as Meat 'n' Bones intention. In the case at hand one must assume that German courts, through their ability to exercise 'Freie Beweiswürdigung' [free consideration of evidence][16] under §286 ZPO, would presume that Bernard's actual intention at the time of the conclusion of the contract was the same as that of Meat 'n' Bones. Under §286 ZPO, German courts may decide cases after their own conviction,[17] and without contradiction from Meat 'n' Bones or Bernard they would presume an original common agreement and support Bernard's interpretation.

7. GREECE

To begin with, in this case Guy's conduct strongly indicates that Guy shared Bernard's interpretation of Clause 14, because otherwise he would have no reason to inform him that Meat 'n' Bones applied for a permit to store and process animal waste not intended for human consumption. If Guy had indeed understood Clause 14 to refer only to products intended for human consumption, his act of informing Bernard would have been aimless at the very least. Therefore, in this

---

14 M. Wolf, '§157 BGB' in H.-T. Soergel, *Bürgerliches Gesetzbuch mit Einführungsgesetz und Nebengesetzen*, vol. II, m.n. 36.

15 Ibid.

16 Cf. Case 3.

17 BGH, 04.07.2007, *NJW* 2007, 2921.

case the subjective criterion of Art. 173 CC would be sufficient, had it not come to a dispute between the parties.

Because a dispute did arise, resorting to the objective criterion of Art. 200 CC is inevitable. No trade custom pertinent to the case at hand can be found; therefore, one turns to the concept of 'καλή πίστη' [good faith] and its concretisation in the case at hand.[18] Regarded in isolation, Guy's petition is probably not relevant, because it may have related to products of Meat 'n' Bones other than those procured by Bernard. The fact that Guy communicated his application to Bernard can be deemed to form a 'συγκείμενο' [proximate],[19] a complement to the agreement (like the parties' negotiations) that can and should be taken into account for the purposes of its objective interpretation, namely what Guy should have expected Bernard to make of his declaration of intent. So that such 'συγκείμενα' are taken into consideration, they must have been at hand at the time when the contract was concluded, but subsequent events may also be considered, if the parties referred to those at the time of the conclusion of the contract.[20]

Even if this was not the case here, Guy's course of action can still be treated as a form of 'self-interpretation' of the contract with Bernard, i.e. as indicative of what the parties understand the agreement to mean:[21] the judge will examine Guy's conduct after the conclusion of the agreement in conjunction with his agreement with Bernard in order to shed light on the meaning of the latter.[22]

8. ITALY

Guy's application for the government permit is conduct subsequent to the conclusion of the contract. Such conduct may be relevant, under Art. 1362 c.c., in order to determine the common intention of the parties.

The prevailing judicial position holds that the ambiguity of the contractual clause is a necessary condition for the parties' conduct to be taken in account as an interpretation factor, because the second paragraph of Art. 1362 (referring to parties' conduct), it is argued, would be subordinated to the first criterion of the

---

18 See Case 1, Question 3.

19 See Case 3, Question 1.

20 Karassis, *General Principles*, § Γ 276; Ladas, *General Principles*, §34 no. 23 with further references.

21 See Papanikolaou, *Methodology*, §494; cf. Ladas, *General Principles*, §34 no. 23.

22 It must be noted that courts rarely, if at all, make such fine notional distinctions in their rulings. The courts will usually be restricted to wording that shows, for example, that they take into account the particular conduct in order to interpret the contract. Whether they do so in the sense of examining a 'συγκείμενο' or in the context of a 'self-interpretation' of the contract is usually addressed by doctrinal analysis.

literal meaning of the words (in para. 1). Conversely, according to most scholarly opinions, and to another stream of judicial precedents, the investigation of the common intention of the parties implies that both criteria (the literal meaning of the words and the parties' conduct) are on an equal footing, so that it would not be necessary to assume ambiguity of the contractual wording in order to proceed to the examination of parties' behaviour as an indication of their common intention.[23]

The unilateral character of the behaviour considered here should not be a problem, because such behaviour would be used as an interpretative factor against its author.

Since we assume that Guy's request is specifically connected to the contract and to the meaning that both parties attached to it,[24] such unilateral behaviour, subsequent to the contract, appears to be very relevant against Guy.

9. NETHERLANDS

In line with the decisions of the Supreme Court, the court will have to determine the meaning that each party could reasonably attach to the terms of the contract and which each could reasonably expect the other to have given to the contract, in light of all the relevant facts and circumstances assessed in accordance with the standards of 'redelijkheid en billijkheid' [reasonableness and fairness].[25] The relevant circumstances of the case will generally include the nature of the contract, the pre-contractual background and the conduct of the parties after the contract's formation.[26]

Dutch law allows evidence of facts and circumstances that took place after the conclusion of the contract to be admitted in order to uncover the intentions of the parties at the time of conclusion of the contract.[27] It is suggested that the parties' conduct after the conclusion of the contract in the performance of their obligations can provide insight into the way the parties have understood their

23 See Case 1, n. 56.

24 On the need for a link between the subsequent conduct of the parties and the disputed contract, see Cass. 25 September 2007 no. 19928.

25 Hoge Raad 13 March 1981, *NJ* 1981, 635 (Ermes/Haviltex); Hoge Raad, 20 February 2004, *NJ* 2005, 393 (DSM-Chemie/Fox).

26 Tjittes, 'Uitleg van schriftelijke contracten', p. 9; Asser/Sieburgh, *Algemene leer der overeenkomsten*, 6-III, no. 363; Tjittes, *Commercieel Contractenrecht*, pp. 316–317.

27 Hoge Raad 20 May 1994, *NJ* 1994, 574 (Gasunie/Anloo); Hoge Raad 20 May 1988, *NJ* 1988, 781 (Smeets/Kuyper); Hoge Raad 27 November 1992, *NJ* 1993, 273 (Volvo/Braam); Hoge Raad 20 November 1998, *NJ* 1999, 684 (Mokster/Wijsmuller); Hoge Raad 10 December 2004, *NJ* 2005, 239 (Diosynth/Groot-Van Veen); Hoge Raad 12 October 2012, *NJ* 2012, 589; Tjittes, *Uitleg van schriftelijke contracten*', p. 39; Asser/Sieburgh, *Algemene leer der overeenkomsten*, 6-III, no. 363; Tjong Tjin Tai, 'Bewijs van de (inhoud van de) overeenkomst', p. 699.

agreement or what they intended with it.[28] If a contracting party has acted in a certain way that supports the claim that he understood the term in a particular way, that could support a claim that the clause should be interpreted in a way that corresponds with such conduct.[29]

By requesting a permit to store and process animal waste not destined for human consumption at the Meat 'n' Bones plant, including animal protein, rendered fats and pet food, Guy could be seen to be making preparations for receiving deliveries of animal waste including waste not intended for human consumption. This evidence of his subsequent conduct could be used to establish that Guy shared Bernard's interpretation of Clause 14.

10. POLAND

The Opening Remarks explained that Polish courts may consider any evidence presented by the parties in order to establish the parties' common intentions. Therefore, Bernard could also present as proof the fact that Meat 'n' Bones filed the request for a government permit as corroborating his interpretation of Clause 14.

Polish law has traditionally recognised that interpretation rules could only be used to determine the content and the sense of the parties' declarations of intentions. The question whether a declaration of intentions was made should be determined only on the basis of pertinent rules of Polish civil law procedure. More recent case law questions that approach and argues in favour of also using interpretation rules to determine whether certain acts of the parties could be perceived as declarations of their intentions.[30] In this respect, the fact that Meat 'n' Bones filed for a specific permit would be examined by the Polish court and potentially perceived as confirmation of its intentions to process all sorts of animal waste, as the clause in the concluded contract could be understood.

Additionally, the fact that Meat 'n' Bones applied for the permit is likely to be perceived by a Polish court as a sign of the performance of the contract in accordance with the meaning given to it by the other party, Bernard.[31] The fact that Guy contacted Bernard to inform him that he had filed for the permit could be perceived by Polish courts as confirmation that the parties discussed

---

28 Asser/Sieburgh, *Algemene leer der overeenkomsten*, 6-III, no. 363; Valk in Schelhaas/Valk, *Uitleg van rechtshandelingen*, p. 27.

29 Tjong Tjin Tai, 'Bewijs van de (inhoud van de) overeenkomst'; also see Tjittes, *Commercieel Contractenrecht*, p. 318.

30 Judgment of SN of 22.06.2006, V CSK 70/06; Judgment of SN of 15.06.2007, V CSK 63/07; Judgment of SN of 17.06.2009, IV CSK 90/09; Judgment of SN of 18.11.2016, I CSK 802/15.

31 Judgment of SN of 15.06.2007, V CSK 63/07.

the application for such a permit and the consequences for their contract in the event it was not acquired.[32]

For example, in the SN judgment of 19 November 2002,[33] the parties applied to the local environment protection authorities for a permit for processing certain fuels. The fact that this permit was denied had to be taken into account by the lower courts in establishing the parties' common intentions as to the characteristics of the machine for processing the fuel that was supposed to be built on the basis of the contract. Since the refusal to grant the permit was already known to the parties at the moment of concluding the contract, it was seen as unlikely by the SN that the parties would decide to build a machine suitable only for processing fuel that they were specifically not permitted to process. The SN's assumption is that the parties had to act rationally and aim at achieving a result compatible with common sense and the interests of both parties.

A recent SN judgment of 5 February 2014[34] might, however, support Guy's interpretation of Clause 14. It instructs Polish courts to acknowledge that the lapse of time since the moment of concluding the contract might have led to an unexpected change in the parties' relationship and their economic interests. Such a change of circumstances could mean that the performance of the contract pursuant to the original intentions of the parties is no longer of economic significance for one of the parties, which should be considered by the Polish courts. This new directive applies when the parties' relationship was long-term, like in the case of Meat 'n' Bones' delivery orders. Guy could then claim that, due to not having been granted the permit, the delivery of animal waste not intended for human consumption has lost its economic value for him. However, under the circumstances of the scenario, this claim is unlikely to succeed. The award of the permit was uncertain at the moment of concluding the contract, and therefore Guy should have anticipated the possibility of the permit not being granted. On the other hand, in the pertinent SN judgment, the change in circumstances could not have been foreseen at the moment of concluding the contract.

11. PORTUGAL

The contract terms are ambiguous. Therefore, the parties' actions during the contract's duration become a critical factor in the interpretation of the contract. A party is not likely to prevail in its interpretation of ambiguous contract language where its conduct is inconsistent with its proffered interpretation. Hence, to determine the parties' likelihood of success in their claims or defences,

32 Judgment of SN of 25.03.2004, II CK 116/03.
33 Judgment of SN of 19.11.2002, IV CKN 1474/00.
34 Judgment of SN of 05.02.2014, V CSK 125/13.

it is important to conduct a thorough factual investigation of the parties' conduct during the contract's duration.

Clause 14 of the contract should be interpreted according to Art. 236.°/1 of the Portuguese Civil Code. Effectively, the relevant moment for interpretation in accordance with the objectivist model of interpretation is the moment the parties diverge concerning the interpretation. It is to this moment that the rules concerning interpretation of contract will be applied. Therefore, elements and circumstances external to the language of the contract can be relevant in supporting a certain interpretation. In fact, the knowledge that Bernard has concerning Guy's request would be relevant for the application of Art. 236.°/1 CC. Art. 236.°/1 refers to the behaviour of the author of the declaration and in this behaviour it is possible to include post-contractual conducts.

Another possibility is to use the concept of 'boa fé' [good faith] and consider that Guy could not defend his interpretation of Clause 14 because his conduct objectively discloses the fact that he shared Bernard's interpretation. It would be against 'boa fé' if he changed his interpretation after his request was denied. In this case there is a so-called *venire contra factum proprium*, or 'exercício de uma posição jurídica contrário à boa fé' [behaviour against good faith]. The 'exercício de posições jurídicas contrário à boa fé' is included in Art. 334.° CC, which concerns the whole area of 'abuso do direito' [abuse of a right], but which can also be used in the interpretation and integration of contracts according to Art. 239.° CC.

12. SCOTLAND

A Scottish court would begin by seeking to identify the 'natural and ordinary meaning' of the words, construed in the context of the contract as a whole.

The Scottish court would not, however, apply a solely literalist approach. The court would consider the disputed words in their contractual and wider factual context.[35] This allows the court to consider the circumstances surrounding conclusion of the contract. The question is not what those circumstances convey about the intentions of the actual contracting parties. Rather, the question is what those circumstances would convey to a reasonable businessperson in the position of the parties to the contract. As such, it is an objective approach. In Scots law, the timing of the request for a government permit is crucial. Only circumstances surrounding actual conclusion of the contract are relevant. Here, the permit is applied for after conclusion of the contract. This piece of evidence does not, therefore fall into the class of circumstances surrounding conclusion of the contract.

35 *Wood v Capita Insurance Services Ltd* [2017] UKSC 24; [2017] 2 WLR 1095, per Lord Hodge at para. 10.

This piece of evidence, i.e. the request for a permit, is likely to be classed as post-contractual conduct. Post-contractual conduct or circumstances since the contract has been made are, as a general rule, excluded from the interpretative exercise. As McBryde explains: 'The meaning of the contract does not change according to what the parties do or changes in commercial practice or other circumstances.'[36] It is true that the courts have not always adhered to this rule, and it is perhaps observed more in England than in Scotland. Where consistent conduct of the parties can be identified, that conduct may be admissible.[37] The application for a permit, as a one-off event by one of the contracting parties only, would not fall within this class. The request for a permit is not an admissible piece of evidence in the interpretative exercise.[38]

The court may make use of the commercially sensible construction in order to interpret this phrase. Drawing on the authority of *Rainy Sky*, the court would be entitled to select the interpretation which accords with commercial common sense.[39] In doing so, they would look at the particular market within which each party is operating. The court is likely to consider whether it would be normal in the specific trade for a company to trade only in meat products for human consumption, or in both products for human consumption and products which are not for human consumption. The former interpretation would work in Guy's favour, and the latter in Bernard's favour. Identification of the market is clearly a key issue.

To summarise, the request for a permit is not admissible in the interpretative process. The court is likely to use a commercially sensible construction to resolve this case. This would involve the identification of the particular market which the parties are working in. The court would ask itself what practices are usual in that particular market. Drawing on the nature of commercial practices in the market in question, the court would draw a conclusion on the most likely interpretation of the phrase.

13. SOUTH AFRICA

If a court concludes that the steps taken by Guy and communicated to Bernard after the conclusion of the contract constitutes evidence of subsequent conduct, then this evidence would be admissible to interpret Clause 14.

---

36 McBryde, *Contract*, para. 8-30.

37 Ibid., para. 8-31.

38 Post-formation conduct by the parties is not admissible evidence in the interpretative exercise in Scots law, see McBryde, *Contract*, para. 8-30.

39 *Rainy Sky SA v Kookmin Bank* [2011] UKSC 50; [2011] 1 WLR 2900, 2908E–G per Lord Clarke.

14. SPAIN

As has already been said in Cases 1 and 3, the historical interpretation factor of the contract (e.g. the way in which it was elaborated or the conduct of the parties) is relevant in order to identify the intention of the parties according to Art. 1.282 CC. This provision leads Spanish courts to search, in order to find the common intention of the parties, 'outside' the contract, towards the parties' acts either prior, contemporary or *subsequent to* the contract.

However, in the interpretation of this article Spanish courts always require that if a party claims a fact in the context of a dispute with the other party, this fact must be relevant and consist of a 'common act', or, where the fact was unilateral, that it must have been accepted or known appropriately by the other party.[40]

Here this is the case, because a post-contractual action such as filing the request shows plainly that both parties shared Bernard's interpretation, and that even though it was a unilateral act, it was known by the other party. This means that it has intentional value and it is not simply a unilateral act. It may be considered an expression of a common intention in Spanish law.

15. SWEDEN

If the fact that Guy filed a request for a government permit to store and process animal waste not intended for human consumption *shows* that Guy shared Bernard's interpretation of Clause 14, it is, in effect, demonstrated that the parties had a common intention with respect to this clause. The courts will interpret the provision accordingly. The common intention prevails.[41]

The fact that the request was filed after (immediately after, but still after) the time of contract formation is of no consequence as long as it is shown that both parties had a shared understanding of Clause 14 *when the contract was concluded*.[42] All relevant matters count.[43]

Typically, the conduct of the parties following the conclusion of the contract will be but one component in the matrix of facts constituting the material (objective side) on which the interpreter's report on the parties' intention (subjective side) will be based. But, in a case like this, where the evidence actually

40 Díez-Picazo, *Fundamentos*, p. 504. See STS 28.09.1995 (RJ 1995\6454); STS 13.02.1992 (RJ 1992\842).
41 See the Opening Remarks on 'den gemensamma partsviljans företräde'.
42 See e.g. NJA 1941 p. 563; cf. NJA 1957 p. 69. Cf. the Contracts Act Section 39. On events subsequent to the conclusion of the contract as interpretative data, see especially Lehrberg, *Avtalstolkning*, p. 133 ff.
43 'Förslag till lag om avtal (1914) p. 140'.

shows that there was, in fact, a specific shared understanding of the contract, the interpretative process is effectively brought to a halt.[44] There is really no need for interpretation.[45] In this sense, the case would turn on a point of fact.

16. EDITORIAL COMPARATIVE OBSERVATIONS

Respondents from the jurisdictions of England and Wales and Scotland are unequivocal in their answer to the question at hand: Guy's filing for the permit is irrelevant for the interpretation of Clause 14. Here, the objective of contract interpretation is the natural and ordinary meaning of the words of the contracts, as interpreted by a reasonable person in the shoes of the parties at the time of conclusion. Even though case law suggests that Scottish courts would consider a comparatively broader context of circumstances surrounding the closing of the contract, this does not include later behaviour of the parties.

Conversely, respondents for the other jurisdictions, including that of South Africa, indicate that Guy's conduct is most likely to play a significant factor in the interpretation of Clause 14. Most respondents explained that the objective of contract interpretation is to uncover the common intentions of the parties, including those reporting for Croatia, Finland, France, Germany, Greece, Italy, the Netherlands, Poland, Spain and Sweden. Hence, for this purpose, a wider range of circumstances may be deemed relevant. Still, reports indicate different reasons for allowing Guy's conduct to be a significant factor in interpreting Clause 14. For example, in the Polish jurisdiction, the underlying reasoning is that parties are expected to act rationally; hence, they do not behave contrary to their own intentions. Subsequent conduct may then retroactively reveal what the parties intended at the time of conclusion. Alternatively, in the Dutch jurisdiction, the objective of looking to conduct after entering into the contract might help establish which meaning the parties could reasonably expect to have attributed.

Several respondents explain why the fact that Guy's conduct was unilateral does not diminish its significance for the interpretation of the contract. Guy's request for a permit might offer proof of *his* intentions but by itself not a *shared* intention. The German report points out that establishing the parties' common intention is, therefore, a separate step. The Italian and the Portuguese reports point out that even if Guy's actions do not constitute a common intention, courts might consider it to interpret the contract against Guy. Hence, Guy's actions will be used to support Bernard's reading of Clause 14. From a different angle, both the Greek and Spanish report note that the fact that Bernard was informed of

---

[44] As is pointed out by Høgberg, *Kontraktstolkning*, p. 96. See e.g. NJA 1964 p. 454.

[45] See Samuelsson, *Tolkningslärans gåta*, p. 190.

Guy's request for a permit might reveal that the Bernard understood the term in the same way as Guy did if Bernard did not show surprise or confusion. In that case, Guy's unilateral act does amount to a demonstration of both parties' shared understanding of Clause 14.

For the apparent dissimilarity between the common law and civil jurisdictions, some subtle commonalities appear as well. First, the Croatian and Dutch reports write that, even when conduct after the conclusion of the contract plays a role in interpreting the contract, the interpretation still involves construing the parties' intentions at the time the contract was concluded. The respondents for the three common law jurisdictions highlight the same temporal aspect of contract interpretation.

Second, even if the primary objectives of interpretation in civil and common law systems diverge, i.e. seeking to uncover the common intention of the parties and the ordinary meaning of the contractual language respectively, Guy's actions may turn out to be a relevant interpretation factor in both legal cultures. On the one hand, the respondents for England and Wales point out that Guy's conduct, albeit not itself a relevant factor for the interpretation of the contract, could have a similar effect *on* the interpretation of Clause 14. If Bernard did not demonstrate any surprise or confusion as Guy informed him of the request for a permit, then the equitable defence of 'estoppel' might justify him reasonably to have expected Guy to operate under a common understanding of Clause 14. On the other hand, the Greek report writes that if a court would not consider Guy's subsequent actions to sufficiently establish Guy's intentions (the 'subjective criterion'), then that conduct may still play a role in the 'objective' interpretation of the contract. Guy's conduct could be considered here a form of 'self-interpretation', in which case Guy's conduct itself is presumed to provide or justify a certain interpretation of the contract.

CASE 5: SHOWER VALVES

'Engineering Solutions' enters into a contract with 'Bath & Shower', under which the former is to supply the latter for a period of five years with thermostatic shower valves as intermediate products. Bath & Shower treats these thermostatic shower valves and sells the end products to its customers. Both parties understand and do not dispute that intermediate products are products that are supplied not to be sold to consumers in their existing form, but rather to be combined with other products to form a final end product to be sold to consumers. Clause 6 of the contract stipulates: 'Throughout the duration of this Agreement, Engineering Solutions hereby undertakes not to sell or supply products to third parties within the territory in which Bath & Shower operates.' After a certain period, Bath & Shower finds out that after concluding the contract, Engineering Solutions has started supplying its thermostatic shower valves as intermediate products to several competitors of Bath & Shower. Bath & Shower accuses Engineering Solutions of acting contrary to Clause 6 of the contract and consequently holds Engineering Solutions in breach of contract and liable for damages. Engineering Solutions refutes the claim of Bath & Shower. It argues that the term 'products' in Clause 6 refers to end products of the sort that Bath & Shower sells to its customers, not intermediate products that Engineering Solution produces. Hence, Engineering Solutions concludes, Clause 6 merely precludes it from entering the market in which Bath & Shower operates. It does not preclude it from supplying or selling intermediate products to competitors of Bath & Shower. In defence of its understanding of Clause 6, Engineering Solutions refers to the General Conditions applicable to the contract. Clause IX of the General Conditions stipulates: 'The Supplier is not precluded from selling or supplying directly or indirectly to third parties the same or similar intermediate products that it supplies under the Contract to the Other Party.' Clause IX, therefore, Engineering Solutions argues, shows that Clause 6 of the contract cannot be made to mean that Engineering Solutions is precluded from selling or supplying intermediate products. Hence, it concludes, the word 'products' in Clause 6 should be interpreted to refer to end products.

1 *[The Role of General Conditions] Assume that the term 'products' in Clause 6 is ambiguous. What weight can be given to Clause IX of the General Conditions in the interpretation of Clause 6?*
2 *[The User of General Conditions] Would it make a difference if it was Engineering Solutions who drafted and used the General Conditions?*

1. KEY ISSUES

The case concerns a sale and supply contract between two companies. The products sold are described as 'intermediate' products, and the case refers to a shared understanding between the parties that this means that products are not to be sold directly to consumers, but rather are to be combined to make further composite products for onward sale to consumers. The contract contains a geographical restriction preventing the supplier from supplying 'products' to third parties. The ambiguity lies in the fact that 'products' is used with no qualifying adjective. The contract leaves unclear whether intermediate or end products are the subject of the geographical restriction. The case is designed to analyse the impact in the interpretative process of 'General Conditions'. The facts of the case envisage both an actual contract between the parties and separate General Conditions which may apply to that contract. Whereas the clause of the contract may be ambiguous, the General Conditions include a clause which is more accurately drafted and may remove the ambiguity. Reporters are asked, in addition, to comment on whether it makes a difference if the party seeking to rely on the General Conditions drafted those General Conditions. This is designed to allow reporters to discuss different variations of what has been called the *contra proferentem* rule in contract interpretation.

2. CROATIA

Question 1: The Role of General Conditions
In order to determine what weight to give to Clause IX of the General Conditions in the interpretation of Clause 6, in addition to the COA provisions on interpretation, the Croatian courts would have to apply the COA provisions concerning general terms and conditions. The general COA provisions on interpretation do not contain rules defining the correlation between general terms and conditions on the one hand, and special contractual clauses on the other. Such rules are laid down in Arts. 295–296 of the COA. According to Art. 295(2) of the COA, general terms and conditions complement individually negotiated clauses stipulated by the contracting parties, and are, in principle, equally binding. However, pursuant to Art. 295(3) of the COA, in the event of a conflict between general terms and conditions and individually negotiated clauses, the latter prevail. Following these legal provisions, the Croatian courts would give prevalence to Clause 6 as an individually negotiated clause. The established case law and legal scholarship interpret the statutory provision in Art. 295(3) of the COA as stating that clauses in general terms and conditions

are of an accessory nature to individually contracted ones.[1] It is generally accepted that, since general terms and conditions are proposed by one contracting party, parties can derogate from them by agreeing otherwise. However, these legal formants do not answer the question of what role, if any, Clause IX of the General Conditions could play in the interpretation of Clause 6.

Therefore, in the case at hand, the Croatian courts would have to establish, by way of interpretation, the relationship between two contractual clauses – Clause 6 of the contract and Clause IX of the General Conditions. In order to determine whether Clause IX of the General Conditions complements Clause 6 of the contract or is derogated from by Clause 6, it is first necessary to examine the meaning of the ambiguous term 'products'. According to interpretation rules and methods developed by the case law and legal theory, the Croatian courts would take all relevant circumstances of the case into account (e.g. negotiations, purpose of the contract, general conditions, etc.). They would observe all contractual clauses, i.e. the contract as a whole, as a means to achieve the contracting parties' interests and goals. Since the contract is concluded with regard to thermostatic shower valves as intermediate products, by using the interpretation method envisaged in Art. 319(2) of the COA, the courts might interpret the term 'products' by restricting it to the intermediate products which are the actual subject matter of the contract. Moreover, since the term 'products' could be understood as any article produced by Engineering Solutions, a different interpretation could be against the purpose of the contract because Engineering Solutions does not produce end products. If on these grounds the court were to establish that both clauses resolve the same question (i.e. intermediate products) in different ways, it would have to find not only that the specially stipulated purpose of the contract expressed in Clause 6 affects the meaning and scope of Clause IX of the General Conditions, but also that it affects its validity according to Art. 295 of the COA. Through the interpretation of a contract, the true common will of the parties should be established, and if they have reached a special agreement on a certain matter, this should prevail over the general terms and conditions. On the other hand, if the court were to interpret the ambiguous term as referring to end products, according to the above-mentioned interpretation rules, Clause IX would certainly affect the court's interpretation of Clause 6. This having been said, such an interpretation would not affect the validity of Clause IX of the General Conditions. Therefore, Clause IX of the General Conditions could affect the court's interpretation of Clause 6 in either way, whereas the validity of Clause IX of the General Conditions would depend on the meaning of the ambiguous term 'products'.

---

1 Petrić, 'Tumačenje općih uvjeta ugovora i njihov odnos s posebno ugovorenim klauzulama u hrvatskom i europskom pravu', 27.

Question 2: The User of General Conditions

If Engineering Solutions drafted and used the General Conditions, the Croatian courts would find that relevant only in the event that the provision of the General Conditions is ambiguous. The statutory provisions – in particular the one on interpretation of pre-formulated standard contracts contained in Art. 320(1) of the COA – provide the solution where a contract is concluded on the basis of previously printed content or where it was prepared and proposed by one contracting party. In such circumstances, the court has to interpret any unclear clause in favour of the other contracting party.[2] Therefore, the fact that one party drafted and used general terms and conditions may affect the courts' interpretation under the *contra proferentem* principle set out in Art. 320(1) of the COA, which does not apply to unambiguous clauses[3] and does not apply if the ambiguity has been effectively resolved by interpretation based on the general interpretation rules applicable to the case.[4] Given that in the case at hand Clause 6 was individually negotiated, it cannot be subject to interpretation under the *contra proferentem* principle. Because Art. 320 of the COA applies only where there is an ambiguous clause included in the contract on the basis of the draft made by one party in advance, it does not apply to Clause IX, which is unambiguous.[5] Thus, the interpretation would have to be carried out in combination with Art. 295 of the COA, according to which special contractual clauses prevail over clauses in the general terms and conditions. Therefore, the fact that Engineering Solutions drafted the General Conditions, including Clause IX thereof, would on its own have no bearing on the interpretation of Clause 6.

---

2 This is well-established practice in the Croatian case law. See VSRH, Revt 192/11 of 8 January 2014; VSRH, Revt 580/11 of 8 January 2013; and VSRH, Revt 107/12 of 18 September 2013.

3 See VSRH, Rev 153/13-2 of 3 May 2017: 'However, it needs to be accentuated that the provisions of Art. 319 para. 2 COA and of Art. 320 para. 1 COA are applicable only in the case when the contract contains ambiguous terms.' See also County Court in Varaždin, Gž 886/2016-2 of 5 September 2018; VSRH, Revr 611/2013-4 of 27 May 2015; County Court in Zagreb, Gž R-115/15-2 of 20 January 2015; VSRH, Revr 580/2011-2 of 8 January 2013; and County Court in Varaždin, Gž.2402/12-2 of 21 August 2012.

4 Croatian case law and legal scholarship confirm that Art. 320(1) of the COA has only subsidiary relevance in relation to the general rule on interpretation of the contracts. See for example, VSRH, Rev-x 528/10-2 of 22 September 2010 and VSRH, Rev 153/13-2 of 3 May 2017, confirming such a relation between Arts. 319 and 320 of the COA; Petrić, 'Tumačenje općih uvjeta ugovora i njihov odnos s posebno ugovorenim klauzulama u hrvatskom i europskom pravu', p. 32.

5 The same approach was taken in the case before the Administrative Court in Zagreb, UsI-3391/13-9 of 9 October 2014, denying the application of the *contra proferentem* rule to an unambiguous clause from a mobile operator's price list. For an attempt to misuse the *contra proferentem* rule, see the ruling of the Supreme Court, VSRH, Revr 664/2011-2 of 18 February 2012.

3. ENGLAND AND WALES

Question 1: The Role of General Conditions

The task of interpretation takes into account all available materials. Other contract terms are particularly important materials. They are given a lot of weight, in the sense that the court will see its central task as being to, where possible, interpret both clauses of the contract in such a way as to provide a coherent (i.e. not internally inconsistent) set of meanings, because this is what the parties can be assumed to have intended. Only if that is impossible, or impossible without reaching a solution that does not seem sensible or likely to have been intended, will the courts have to prefer one clause to another and merely ignore the clause not preferred (often concluding that a mistake has been made in the drafting).

Clause IX will therefore be important in construing Clause 6. The use of the words 'intermediate products' in Clause IX might be said to show that the parties will qualify the word 'products' where they wish to do so, or that 'products' in Clause 6 must refer to a different thing to 'intermediate products' in Clause IX (otherwise the same term might have been used). Clause IX may also support Engineering Solutions' case, because on Bath & Shower's preferred construction of Clause 6, there is an apparent conflict between Clause 6 (which forbids the selling of intermediate products within the territory) and Clause IX (which permits the sale of intermediate products to third parties generally).

Whether the clauses of the contract were individually negotiated or standard form clauses will be relevant,[6] as will the other General Conditions and the way they interact with other basic clauses of the contract (e.g. whether other General Conditions are apparently qualified by the basic clauses). Similarly, the apparent commercial purpose, partly derived from the context, will be important: would the parties be intending by Clause 6 to prevent Engineering Solutions competing as to end products with Bath & Shower, or to prevent Engineering Solutions supplying intermediate products to Bath & Shower's competitors? Whether or not Engineering Solutions supplies enough end products to mount significant competition to Bath & Shower would be one relevant factor in understanding the purpose of the clause.

Question 2: The User of General Conditions

Where one party contracts on another's standard terms, any ambiguity in those terms will usually be construed against the party whose standard terms they are. This is known as the '*contra proferentem*' rule, which entails that the person whose standard terms they are is the '*proferens*' (the proferrer of the terms) against whom they are to be construed. The *contra proferentem* rule is

6 See n. 8 below, and accompanying text.

not a decisive rule resolving all ambiguities; rather it is a factor to be weighed alongside all other relevant factors. In essence, it requires the courts to consider that, all other things being equal, if the *proferens* had wanted the ambiguity resolved in his favour he would have specified that result in the drafting. The law takes the view that it was up to him to make it clear.[7]

If Engineering Solutions was the drafter of the General Conditions, the *contra proferentem* rule would lend some weight to Bath & Shower's argument that if Clause IX was intended to override the main contract clauses, it would have said, 'Despite what is set out in the clauses of the main contract' or would be explicit that it applies 'anywhere in the world'.

It is difficult to be more specific as regards the weight to be attributed to the identity of the drafter of standard terms, but the effect of the *contra proferentem* rule should not be overstated, and it will often not be decisive, especially where both parties are commercial parties represented by lawyers.

Furthermore, greater weight must be attached to any terms which were individually negotiated (e.g. the main contract itself) than to standard clauses (the General Conditions) where there is a conflict.[8]

4. FINLAND

Question 1: The Role of General Conditions

Under Finnish law, the common intention of the parties at the time of contracting is the basis for the interpretation.[9] If the common intention can be found, it even surpasses the written documents of the contract. If the parties' intentions vary, interpretation focuses on whether the other party knew or ought to have known of the other party's intention. If the other party knew or ought to have known of the other party's intention, this intention has relevance in interpreting an unclear contractual term. One party's intention affects the interpretation more easily in cases where the intention is not in conflict with the wording of the contract.[10]

In this case, the intention of the parties was to ban the sale of intermediate products. Furthermore, since the General Conditions refer to intermediate products, the buyer ought to have known the seller's intention to refer to intermediate products.

---

7 Per Staughton LJ in *Youell v Bland Welch & Co. Ltd* [1992] 2 Lloyd's Rep 127 (CA) at 134.

8 E.g. Lord Bingham in *Homburg Houtimport BV v Agrosin Private Ltd (The Starsin)* [2004] 1 AC 715 (HL) at 737.

9 See Hemmo, *Sopimusoikeus I*, p. 604; Saarnilehto, *Sopimusoikeuden perusteet*, p. 149; and Telaranta, *Sopimusoikeus*, p. 94.

10 Hemmo, *Sopimusoikeus I*, pp. 625–630. See also the Finnish Supreme Court's decisions KKO 1998:64 and KKO 1990:124.

Question 2: The User of General Conditions

The so-called 'Epäselvyyssääntö' [unclarity rule] states that ambiguities caused by the drafter of the contract must be resolved against the drafter or the party employing him or her. 'Epäselvyyssääntö' finds its expression in the Finnish Consumer Protection Act, but the rule is not restricted to consumer contracts and can thus be applied to business-to-business contracts, and hence it applies in this case.[11] However, as the starting point is that the parties' intention surpasses the written form, 'epäselvyyssääntö' would not apply if the true intention differs from the written form.

5. FRANCE

Question 1: The Role of General Conditions

The case revolves around the interpretation of an ambiguous term of a contract in relation to the General Conditions applicable to that contract. In these circumstances, the court would typically distinguish between two scenarios. Either the two clauses are compatible, and they should be interpreted in the light of each other, or they are incompatible, and one should prevail over the other.

The court would first analyse both terms and try to reconcile them. The underlying assumption is that the parties selected both terms to govern their contractual relations. Their common intention ought to be consistent. So should the meaning of the two clauses. It is for the court to reveal this coherence. This path of interpretation is particularly likely to be followed if a clause of the contract expressly refers to the General Conditions as part of the contractual agreement and if the party against whom the General Conditions are invoked recognises that he has received a copy of them.[12] In the present case, however, Clauses 6 and IX appear to be concretely incompatible.

In order to assess whether Clauses 6 and IX are compatible, the court would consider the rationale behind both clauses and behind the contract.

Clause 6 prevents Engineering Solutions from 'supplying products to third parties' within the territory of operation of Bath & Shower for the duration of the contract. This clause seems to rely on the assumption that using Engineering Solutions' thermostatic shower valves in their end products confers a competitive advantage on Bath & Shower. The rationale behind Clause 6 would be to

11 Hemmo, *Sopimusoikeus I*, p. 638 and Pönkä, 'Tavoitteellisten tulkintasääntöjen merkityksestä liikesopimusten tulkinnassa', pp. 927–930. See also the Finnish Supreme Court's decision 2016:10.

12 Civ. 1, 10 April 1996, *Bull. civ.* (1996) no. 177; Civ. 1, 17 November 1998, *Bull. civ.* (1998) no. 316.

protect that advantage. The 'products' under Clause 6 would therefore be the thermostatic shower valves.

Clause IX allows Engineering Solutions to provide third parties with the same intermediate products as those delivered to Bath & Shower. The thermostatic shower valves supplied by Engineering Solutions are intermediate products within the meaning of Clause IX. According to the clause, the supplier should be allowed to supply them to third parties. Whereas Clause 6 protects the buyer, Clause IX protects the supplier.

Clause IX contradicts the very purpose of Clause 6. As an individually negotiated term, Clause 6 is considered a more accurate reflection of the common intention of the parties at the time of the conclusion of the contract. As part of the contract itself, it would also be analysed as an element defining the contractual balance reached by the parties through negotiation. The court would then prioritise the particular term over the general one. This solution, initially set out by case law,[13] has been laid down in Art. 1119 Cciv since the 2016 reform. In conclusion, the court would thus prioritise Clause 6 of the contract over Clause IX of the General Conditions.

Question 2: The User of General Conditions

If the General Conditions were drafted and used by Engineering Solutions, the same line of argumentation is likely to be followed by the court. It would also be conceivable that the court might use the *contra proferentem* rule of Art. 1190 Cciv (formerly Art. 1162) as a subsidiary means to justify the prevalence of Clause 6 of the contract over Clause IX of the General Conditions. This provision of the Civil Code prescribes that non-negotiable terms imposed by one party should be interpreted against them. In the present case, it could be used as a legal basis for Clause IX to be interpreted against Engineering Solutions and in favour of Bath & Shower. Insofar as Clause IX is held incompatible with Clause 6, the courts could use Art. 1190 Cciv to apply the clause that is the most favourable to Bath & Shower, namely Clause 6.[14]

In practice, the court might however choose to only mention Art. 1119 and/or Art. 1188 Cciv (formerly Art. 1156) insofar as, contrary to Clause IX, it is held to express the common intention of the parties.[15] The reference to these articles is sufficient to justify that Clause 6 shall prevail. The reference to Art. 1190 Cciv is subsidiary and should only be used when still 'in doubt' – according to the words of the article itself.

---

13 Civ. 1, 17 June 1986, *Bull. civ.* (1986) no. 166; Civ. 1, 9 February 1999, *Bull. civ.* (1999) no. 44. See also J. Mestre, 'De l'interprétation de clauses en conflit', *RTDCiv.* (1999) 836.

14 See e.g. CA Paris, 8 March 1988, *JurisData* no. 1988-021176.

15 See e.g. Req., 6 February 1945, *GP* (1945), 116; Civ., 29 January 1948, *D.* (1948), 554.

6. GERMANY

Question 1: The Role of General Conditions

Under Clause 6 the term 'products' is ambiguous and the question arises whether or not it excludes intermediate products. Moreover, it is necessary to establish whether Clause IX of the General Conditions carries weight for the interpretation of Clause 6. In this case, the term 'products' may be interpreted to refer to 'end products'.

As a starting point, there is a 'Vorrang der Individualabrede' [priority of individual agreements over general agreements] under §305b BGB.[16] Therefore, in the event of a contradiction between the standard terms underlying the contract and an individually agreed clause, the individual clause overrides the general conditions.[17] This, of course, only holds true if a close interpretation of both clauses leads to a result which is contradictory. Consequently, the individual agreement, Clause 6, would have to be interpreted first.

A particular problem in the case at hand follows from the use of the General Conditions as a means to interpret the individual clause. German law does not exclude the General Conditions as material for the interpretation of the individual agreement. To use the General Conditions as material for interpretation of the individual agreement may be of relevance for the interpretation of Clause 6 in two ways. First, as a reason to use the General Conditions as material for interpretation, there is the presumption that there is free access to any material for interpretation. Secondly, the individual agreement may follow as a reaction of the parties to the General Conditions.

A German court would interpret the term 'products' by assuming arguments for the interpretation of both parties. If the individual agreement, Clause 6, follows the General Conditions, this reaction of the parties would serve as an argument for the interpretation of Bath & Shower and the term 'products' would be interpreted to refer to intermediate products as well. As a counter-argument, one could argue that there is a rule that the contract is to be interpreted as a whole, including the General Conditions.[18] As a result, the term 'intermediate products' in the General Conditions could align with the interpretation of the term 'products' to refer to 'end products'. It therefore supports the interpretation of Engineering Solutions.[19]

---

16 BGH, 11.05.2017, *BeckRS* 2017, 126042; BGH, 01.22.1990, *NJW-RR* 1990, 613; OLG Hamm, 21.04.2016, *RdTW* 2017, 111.

17 BGH, 09.03.1995, *NJW* 1995, 1494.

18 M. Wolf, '§157 BGB' in H.-T. Soergel, *Bürgerliches Gesetzbuch mit Einführungsgesetz und Nebengesetzen*, vol. II, m.n. 29; M. Schmidt-Kessel, 'Art. 8 CISG' in P. Schlechtriem and I. Schwenzer (eds.), *Kommentar zum Einheitlichen UN-Kaufrecht – Das Übereinkommen der Vereinten Nationen über Verträge über den internationalen Warenkauf (CISG)*, m.n. 29.

19 However, the factual basis is not clear enough to predict the court's decision on the interpretation of Clause 6.

Assuming that the German courts would support an interpretation of Clause 6 in favour of Bath & Shower, the rule giving priority to individual agreements over general conditions would apply. Therefore, the interpretation of the individual agreement would override the General Conditions.[20]

Question 2: The User of General Conditions

Basically, there would be no different result on the applicable interpretation if the General Conditions were drafted and used by Engineering Solutions. Nevertheless the 'Unklarheitenregel' [ambiguity rule], which states that ambiguous contract terms proposed by one of the contract parties shall be interpreted to the detriment of that party, might give a different result.[21] This rule is laid down under §305c (2) BGB especially for standard terms and has to be applied to ambiguous terms that are part of the General Conditions. This rule could shift the risk of ambiguity to Engineering Solutions if they drafted the General Conditions. But since Clause IX of the General Conditions could not be considered ambiguous itself, the 'Unklarheitenregel' cannot be applied (cf. Case 1).[22]

Furthermore, the guideline to interpret the contract as a whole and the priority rule mentioned above are not influenced by which person drafted the General Conditions.

7. GREECE

Question 1: The Role of General Conditions

The issue at hand in this case is not the interpretation of the General Terms and Conditions (GTC) included in the agreement between Engineering Solutions and Bath & Shower, but the question whether those GTC can be used in order to clarify an unclear term in the contract between them; this further presupposes that the GTC have been 'incorporated' into the agreement, in the sense that the parties are fully aware of their existence and their applicability[23] and they also did not try to override them by making special arrangements in the agreement (no such inference can be made from the facts of the case). Assuming, therefore, that the text of the GTC as such is clear and explicit as to which products Engineering Solutions is allowed to sell to third-party suppliers and that

---

20 Finally, it is worth mentioning that the broad interpretation of Clause 6 including intermediate products may violate competition law. Therefore, this could also serve as an argument for interpretation in favour of Bath & Shower.

21 J. Busche, '§157 BGB' in K. Rebmann and F. J. Säcker (eds.), *Münchener Kommentar zum Bürgerlichen Gesetzbuch*, m.n. 8.

22 M. Wolf, '§157 BGB' in H.-T. Soergel, *Bürgerliches Gesetzbuch mit Einführungsgesetz und Nebengesetzen*, vol. II, m.n. 59.

23 See Papanikolaou, *Methodology*, §563.

Engineering Solutions and Bath & Shower did intend for the GTC in question to form part of their agreement, it all comes down to a systematic interpretation of the contract between them:[24] the court will proceed to a combined reading of Clause 6 and Clause IX in order to determine how the term 'products' is to be understood in the context of Clause 6.

Question 2: The User of General Conditions

For the purposes of a systematic interpretation of the agreement between Engineering Solutions and Bath & Shower, it does not seem to make a difference whether the GTC were drafted and used by the one party or the other.[25] In respect of GTC, Greek legal doctrine essentially applies the interpretation criteria of Arts. 173 and 200 CC as described in previous chapters,[26] albeit with certain adaptations. First of all, since the GTC are drafted with the purpose of being used in a number of contracts, they usually cannot form the object of specific negotiations between the parties, so that the subjective criterion of Art. 173 CC will be practically irrelevant and the objective interpretation of Art. 200 CC will come to the fore; in this context, the average person of the circle of addressees with which a company uses its GTC will be relevant, not necessarily the individualised circumstances of each specific party.[27] Further rules apply to B2C agreements, which are not covered by the scope of this case study and would also not apply to the case at hand.[28] The underlying *ratio* behind the protection of consumers, i.e. the wish to protect the usually 'weaker' counterparty of the person proposing the GTC, is not necessarily applicable to B2B contracts, since such a negotiation imbalance is not inevitably at hand between businesses.[29]

In this case, the meaning of Clause IX is on its face sufficiently clear and, therefore, can be used to discern the true meaning of another provision of the agreement in question through systematic interpretation, as long as the GTC were integrated in the agreement. The question whether the GTC in question

---

24 For the applicability, under Greek law, of the classic methods of statutory interpretation (also to contracts and other juridical acts), see Case 1, n. 44.

25 Cf. Stathopoulos, *Civil Code*, vol. 1^B, Arts. 173 and 200 no. 174, who regards the *contra proferentem* rule (i.e. a contractual term must be interpreted to the detriment of the party that formulated it) as an unwritten rule of general validity; however, this view seems to have found little resonance with Greek law and legal practice outside the context of B2C contracts.

26 Karassis, *General Principles*, § Γ 328.

27 Papanikolaou, *Methodology*, §570; Karassis, *General Principles*, § Γ 332. This is commonly affirmed in Greek legal doctrine, at least regarding GTC applicable in consumer contracts, but Greek courts do not seem to have addressed the issue.

28 Both legal doctrine and the Greek courts suggest, for instance, that the GTC in B2C contracts are to be interpreted restrictively and, in case of doubt, to the detriment of the person who drafted and used them (*contra proferentem* interpretation); see Papanikolaou, *Methodology*, §§570–575; Karassis, *General Principles*, §§ Γ 332–335; cf. CA Athens 7110/1979, NoV 27 (1979), 1650; CA Patras 64/1988, NoV 37 (1989), 103.

29 Papanikolaou, *Methodology*, §§564–565, 574; cf. Karassis, *General Principles*, § Γ 331.

are abusive and violate the balance of interests between the parties goes a step beyond their interpretation.[30]

8. ITALY

Question 1: The Role of General Conditions

Art. 1341 c.c. states that general conditions drafted by one party bind the other party if the other party knew the general conditions or should have known them by means of ordinary diligence.

The problem of the enforceability of general conditions against the adhering party lies outside the scope of the rules on interpretation of contracts. Assuming that the requirements of Art. 1341 are satisfied, general conditions are part of the contract and therefore bind both parties and are relevant for the interpretation of other contractual clauses under the principle of systematic interpretation of Art. 1363 c.c.

Question 2: The User of General Conditions

Art. 1370 c.c. deals with the interpretation of standard form contracts and provides the rule known as interpretation *contra proferentem* (or *contra stipulatorem*): 'Clauses contained in standard form contracts drafted by one party, in case of doubt, are interpreted to the advantage of the other party.'[31] The interpretation of general conditions depends essentially on which party has drafted and used them, because Art. 1370 makes it clear that 'in case of doubt' general conditions have to be interpreted against the drafting party.

At first sight, it appears that the rule fits the facts of the case because, by assumption, Clause 6 is ambiguous, so one must conclude that this ambiguity raises a doubt as to the meaning of the contract as a whole. Therefore, in principle, interpretation *contra proferentem* should apply. However, some uncertainties affect the actual applicability of Art. 1370 c.c. to the present case, considering the variety of opinions as to the scope of Art. 1370.

Scholars have expressed two different positions as to the role of Art. 1370 and its appropriate place within the hierarchy of the rules on interpretation of contracts.[32] One traditional position holds that standard form contracts should be interpreted according to the ordinary hierarchical interpretation process. All rules on subjective interpretation should then apply to a contract of adhesion because the primary function of the interpretation process should be, as in

---

30 Good faith would probably play a role in the context of either Art. 200 CC or Art. 281 CC (general principle of good faith); cf. for consumer contracts Papanikolaou, *Methodology*, §586 *in fine*.

31 See in general Astone, 'Dell'interpretazione del contratto (sub art. 1370)', p. 587 ff.

32 Ibid., p. 597 ff.

other cases, the investigation of the parties' common intention. The application of rules of objective interpretation, such as Art. 1370, would be possible only if the primary rules on subjective interpretation did not suffice to discover a clear contractual meaning that can be justified as consistent with the parties' intentions.[33]

Judicial decisions usually adopt this perspective.[34] This implies that a court will first try to interpret the contract according to the literal meaning of the words, to the parties' overall conduct (Art. 1362) and to a consideration of the overall contractual terms (Art. 1363). Only if the contractual meaning still remains unclear will the court resort to Art. 1370 as a rule of objective interpretation.

Following this position, in the present case, a court could hold that Clause IX of the General Conditions and Clause 6 of the contract do not in fact raise any doubt as to their legal meaning because rules of subjective interpretation suffice to determine an unambiguous meaning. This conclusion would exclude the application of Art. 1370.

Conversely, if doubts still remained as to the meaning of the word 'products' after the application of subjective rules, Art. 1370 would play a strong role in inducing the court to interpret Clause IX of the General Conditions against the drafting party.

Other scholars contend that the use of general conditions drafted by one party excludes a proper agreement and for this reason would be incompatible with the application of general rules aimed at the search for the common intention of the parties. Art. 1370, from this perspective, would be the main and virtually the only rule governing the interpretation of standard form contracts. General conditions, it is argued, should always be interpreted against the drafter, regardless of any rule of subjective interpretation, and the application of Art. 1370 would not be conditional upon any remaining doubt as to the subjective meaning of the words.[35] According to this latter position, the interpretation of Clause IX against the drafting party would be immediately permitted.

Even though judges follow the first position, so restricting the scope of Art. 1370, a factor that could favour Bath & Shower, assuming that the General Conditions are drafted by Engineering Solutions, is the standard of 'buona fede' [good faith] in Art. 1366. In fact, when the use of general conditions evidences a clear imbalance of bargaining power between the parties, some decisions use Art. 1366 in order to protect the adhering party.[36]

---

33 Patti, *Le condizioni generali*, p. 338; Bianca, *Contratto*, p. 348–349; Maiorca, *Contratti standard*, pp. 631–632.

34 Cass. 18 May 2017 no. 12487; Cass. 14 March 2013 no. 6482; Cass. 22 February 2008 no. 4600.

35 Chinè, *Contrattazione standardizzata*, pp. 556–660; Richter, *L'interpretazione*, p. 1034; Costanza, *Interpretazione*, p. 30; Azzaro, *Contratti non negoziati*, p. 271; Genovese, *Contratto standard*, p. 1020.

36 Cass. 5 June 1985, no. 3353; Bigliazzi Geri, *L'interpretazione*, p. 253 ff.

9. NETHERLANDS

Question 1: The Role of General Conditions

Assuming the General Conditions have become part of the contract concluded between Engineering Solutions and Bath & Shower, in the case of a conflict between a provision in the contract and the General Conditions that form part of that contract, the provision in the parties' agreement will generally prevail over standardised provisions in General Conditions.[37] The underlying rationale is that the provisions in the parties' agreement will have been the subject of individual negotiation with the particular features of the transaction in mind, whereas the General Conditions are standardised terms, drafted for a multitude of transactions by one party. The Supreme Court has made it clear, however, that this is not a hard and fast rule of interpretation, but simply one factor to be taken into account when interpreting a contract in accordance with the *Haviltex* norm.[38] The court remains free to regard the General Conditions as relevant factors and an aid to interpretation to establish the meaning the parties could reasonably attach to the wording of Clause 6.

Question 2: The User of General Conditions

If the General Conditions were drafted and used by Engineering Solutions, which is relying on them, an interpretation *contra proferentem* may be called for. Art. 6:238 (2) BW contains a provision requiring a *contra proferentem* interpretation; however, the scope of application is limited to consumer contracts.[39] In relation to commercial contracts, the *Haviltex* norm prevails and a *contra proferentem* interpretation is only one factor that can be taken into account in the interpretation of the contract in accordance with that norm.[40] It is certainly not a hard and fast rule. This factor is on equal footing with other factors to be taken into account and which the court may consider depending on the circumstances.[41] Whether a *contra proferentem* interpretation is justified will depend on the circumstances of the case, including the nature of the contract and whether the parties were for instance supported by legal advisors. Consequently, when invoking the General Conditions, the term may be interpreted against Engineering Solutions. As their drafter and user, Engineering Solutions is responsible for ensuring that the drafting clearly

---

37 Asser/Sieburgh, *Algemene leer der overeenkomsten*, 6-III, no. 376; Tjittes, 'Uitleg van schriftelijke contracten', p. 16; Tjittes, *Commercieel Contractenrecht*, p. 307.

38 Hoge Raad 13 June 2003, *NJ* 2003, 506 (Vos Logistics Veendam/Heipro).

39 The provision is the implementation of Art. 5 of Council Directive 93/13 of 5 April 1993 on unfair terms in consumer contracts, *OJ* L 95/93.

40 Hoge Raad 24 September 1993, *NJ* 1993, 760 (Brackel/UNAT); Hoge Raad 9 September 1994, *NJ* 1995, 285 (Trouwborst/Tollenaar & Wegener); Hoge Raad 12 January 1996, *NJ* 1996, 683 (Kroymans/Sun Alliance).

41 Hijma, 'Uitleg contra proferentem', p. 468.

indicates its intention that Clause IX of the General Conditions should prevail over or qualify Clause 6 of the main contract. That being said, consideration of all the relevant facts and circumstances of the case, assessed in light of the standards of 'redelijkheid en billijkheid' [reasonableness and fairness] could give rise to other arguments that might lead to an interpretation that favours Engineering Solutions, if it is reasonable for Engineering Solutions to have understood the wording in this way and it could reasonably expect, in light of those circumstances, that Bath & Shower understood the wording in this – for Engineering Solutions, more favourable – way as well.[42]

10. POLAND

Question 1: The Role of General Conditions

In Polish law, general conditions constitute an inherent part of the contract they apply to.[43] This means that these conditions will be interpreted by Polish courts just like other contractual provisions, using the rules on interpretation expressed in Art. 65 KC (see the Opening Remarks). Therefore, Clause IX will be considered by Polish courts as far as the circumstances of the case demand it, in light of its purpose and of the parties' common intentions rather than of the literal meaning of its terms. The meaning of Clause IX would be determined in light of and in relation to all the contractual provisions.[44]

For example, in the SN judgment 10 October 2000,[45] the court decided that the general conditions had to be interpreted just like any other contractual provision, which meant that they should be interpreted in light of their nature and function.

In the event of a conflict between a contractual term and a provision in the general conditions, priority in application and interpretation is given to the contractual term, since it has been individually negotiated between the parties, and therefore should better reflect their intentions.[46] This is based on Art. 385 para. 1 KC. However, since Clause 6 is ambiguous and needs interpretation, it is unlikely that it would be in conflict with Clause IX. Clause IX would rather be used to explain the parties' contractual intentions or the purpose of Clause 6.

---

42 Valk in Schelhaas/Valk, *Uitleg van rechtshandelingen*, p. 51.

43 E.g. Judgment of SN of 20.12.2012, IV CSK 257/12.

44 Decree of SN of 29.06.1995, III CZP 66/95; Judgment of SN of 21.11.1997, I CKN 825/97; Judgment of SN of 08.07.2004, IV CK 582/03; Judgment of SN of 05.10.2005, II CK 122/05; Judgment of SN of 17.06.2009, IV CSK 90/09; Judgment of SN of 20.12.2012, IV CSK 257/12; Ł. Węgrzynowski, 'Sądowe ustalanie treści stosunku umownego', PPH 2007/5/44–49; B. Kaczorowska, 'Wizja wykładni umów w projekcie księgi pierwszej kodeksu cywilnego', TPP 2/2011, p. 23; E. Rott-Pietrzyk, 'Interpretacja owiadczenia woli (uwagi na tle rozwiza projektu księgi I kodeksu cywilnego)', TPP 4/2010, pp. 54–55.

45 Judgment of SN of 10.10.2000, V CKN 97/00.

46 B. Kaczorowska, 'Wizja wykładni umów w projekcie księgi pierwszej kodeksu cywilnego', TPP 2/2011, p. 23.

Question 2: The User of General Conditions

Whether the fact that Engineering Solutions drafted the General Conditions could be taken into account by Polish courts if Clause IX itself was also ambiguous. Polish courts use the interpretation rule of '*in dubio contra proferentem*' [in the event of doubt, interpret against the interests of the party that requested or drafted the clause]. Pursuant to Art. 385 para. 2 KC, this rule protects consumers, but there are cases where the courts have applied it also to B2B contracts.[47] This rule establishes that the party who drafted and imposed a specific contractual provision on the other contractual party bears the risk of this provision being deemed ambiguous. Unless the ambiguity can be removed by using standard interpretation rules, the ambiguous term should be interpreted in favour of the party who did not draft it. This does not mean that the interests of the party drafting the standard contract terms are not protected, since the drafting position gave that party a certain advantage in the contractual relationship.[48] However, if Clause IX is not perceived as ambiguous, the fact that it was drafted by Engineering Solutions would not influence the answer to Question 1.

11. PORTUGAL

Question 1: The Role of General Conditions

In the Portuguese legal system, there is a certain order concerning the interpretative factors which ought to be considered. Negotiated clauses prevail over non-negotiated clauses. Negotiated clauses can be used to render non-negotiated clauses irrelevant or even completely invalid.[49]

Generally, terms which have been negotiated individually take precedence over those which have not. This rule expressly results in Portuguese legislation from 'cláusulas contratuais gerais' [general conditions].[50] (Arts. 10.° and 11.° Decreto-Lei n. 446/85, 25 October – the General Conditions Law).[51] An interpretation which renders the terms of the contract effective is to be

---

47 Judgment of SN of 08.10.2004, V CK 670/03; Judgment of SN of 05.10.2005, II CK 122/05; Judgment of SN of 17.06.2009, IV CSK 90/09; Judgment of SN of 21.02.2013, I CSK 408/12; Judgment of SN of 28.02.2013, III CSK 70/12; B. Kaczorowska, 'Wizja wykładni umów w projekcie księgi pierwszej kodeksu cywilnego', TPP 2/2011, p. 21; E. Rott-Pietrzyk, 'Interpretacja owiadczenia woli (uwagi na tle rozwiza projektu księgi I kodeksu cywilnego)', TPP 4/2010, p. 54.

48 B. Kaczorowska, 'Wizja wykładni umów w projekcie księgi pierwszej kodeksu cywilnego', TPP 2/2011, p. 21.

49 STJ 4 October 2007 (Pereira da Silva).

50 Art. 7.° Decreto-Lei n. 446/85, de 25 de outubro with amendments Decreto-lei n. 220/95, de 31 de agosto, Decreto-Lei n. 249/99, de 7 de julho, and Decret-Law no. 323/2001, de 17 de dezembro.

51 Pais de Vasconcelos, *Teoria Geral do Direito Civil*, p. 560.

preferred to one which would not. There is a 'princípio do aproveitamento do negócio jurídico' [principle of *favor negotii*] that results from a lot of articles of the Civil Code. The exclusivity clause will not have any effect if it was interpreted as referring to 'end products'. The priority of the scope of contract is one factor that can be included in the position of the 'declaratário normal' (reasonable person) that results from the application of Arts. 236.°/1 and 239.° CC. The importance of analysing all the behaviour of the parties or the good faith interpretation can also play a role in this context[52] due to the application of Arts. 236.°/1, 236.°/2 and 239.°.

Question 2: The User of General Conditions

It would not make a difference if the General Conditions were drafted and used by Engineering Solutions, because the negotiated Clause 6 prevails over Clause IX of the General Conditions pursuant to Art. 7.° Decreto-Lei n. 446/85, 25 October. Therefore, it is not relevant if the General Conditions were drafted and used by Engineering Solutions or by Bath & Shower.

12. SCOTLAND

Question 1: The Role of General Conditions

The role of General Conditions in interpreting Clause 6 would much depend on the status of the General Conditions. Were they referred to in the contract entered into between Engineering Solutions and Bath & Shower? The contract may stipulate that the agreement between the parties is subject to the General Conditions. A reference such as this within the contract between the parties would incorporate the General Conditions as actual contract terms.[53]

If, however, the contract between the two parties did not refer to the General Conditions, then the issue which arises is whether they are nevertheless additional contract terms. Previously the parole evidence rule prevented the parties from establishing that additional terms existed.

This rule has been expressed as follows in Scotland:

> Where parties have reduced the terms of their agreement to writing, the obligations they have undertaken must be ascertained from the terms of that writing without the aid of extrinsic evidence. Parole evidence that their real intention was other than that so expressed is inadmissible, either when offered as explanatory of the writing, or with the object of proving that the obligations there undertaken were not those by which they intended to be bound.[54]

---

52 Menezes Cordeiro, *Tratado de Direito Civil Português*, p. 716.

53 *Hunter v Livingstone Development Corp.* 1986 SC (HL) 31, and see McBryde, *Contract*, para. 7-03.

54 Gloag, *Contract*, pp. 365–366, and see also Walker, *The Law of Contract and Related Obligations in Scotland*, para 24.13.

The rule was partially repealed by the Contract (Scotland) Act 1997. In terms of section 1(1), if a contract appears to comprise all the express terms of a contract, it is presumed that the document does comprise all the express terms. The question for the court in this case would therefore be whether the contract as signed by the parties appears to comprise all the express terms of the agreement between the parties. This presumption may indeed apply if the contract contains no reference to the General Conditions. It would be up to Engineering Solutions to overturn this presumption, and both oral and documentary evidence could be used by them in order to prove that the General Conditions were, in fact, additional contract terms.[55]

Parties to a contract can use an 'entire agreement' clause.[56] There is no suggestion in the facts of this case that an entire agreement clause was used. Such clause would state, in effect, that the document contains the entire agreement between the parties. That would have prevented reference to other documents in order to establish that the contract contained additional terms.

If the General Conditions are not contract terms, the question which arises is the extent to which Engineering Solutions could use them as evidence to support their interpretation of the contract. Clearly Clause 6 is ambiguous. Using the contextual approach, the Scottish court would be able to consider the circumstances which surround formation of the contract in order to interpret the terms of that contract.[57] The court is likely to ask what role the General Conditions played at the point of formation of the contract. Was a copy given by Engineering Solutions to Bath & Shower at the point of formation? If yes, then the General Conditions may be admissible as part of the factual matrix of the contract. The date on which a copy was given to Bath & Shower would be significant. If this event occurred significantly before the moment of formation, they would be likely to be found inadmissible as prior communications.[58] If this event occurred significantly after formation, they would be likely to be found inadmissible as post-contractual conduct.[59] Only circumstances surrounding the moment of formation are admissible. Depending on the role the General Conditions played at the time of formation of the contract, they may indeed be admissible as evidence, which would favour Engineering Solutions' interpretation.

---

55 Contract (Scotland) Act 1997, s. 1(2).

56 Such clauses are expressly provided for in s. 1(3) of the Contract (Scotland) Act 1997 and are in wide use.

57 *Wood v Capita Insurance Services Ltd* [2017] UKSC 24; [2017] 2 WLR 1095, per Lord Hodge at para. 10.

58 *Inglis v Buttery* (1877) 5 R 58 per Lord Gifford at 59–60, approved by Lord Blackburn (1877) 5 R HL 87 at 102; *Prenn v Simmonds* [1971] 1 WLR 1381 per Lord Wilberforce at 1384.

59 McBryde, *Contract*, paras. 8-30–8-33.

Question 2: The User of General Conditions

The answer to the above would not change if it was Engineering Solutions who drafted and used the General Conditions.

13. SOUTH AFRICA

Question 1: The Role of General Conditions

On the assumption that the General Conditions are applicable to the contract (for example, because they have been incorporated by reference),[60] a court will attempt to construe the document as a whole within the broader factual context.[61] There is a canon of construction that more specific terms on a topic (Clause IX) govern those which are more generally formulated and which relate to the same topic (Clause 6), on the assumption that parties gave greater consideration to the detail in the more specific term.[62] However, this presupposes that the terms in the General Conditions are the product of the parties' negotiations, and not simply standard terms formulated by one of them. If the General Conditions consist simply of standard terms imposed by Engineering Solutions for example, while the contract between it and Bath & Shower was individually negotiated, then the meaning of Clause 6 would prevail, provided such meaning was clear.[63] However, since this does not appear to be the case on these facts, the meaning of Clause IX – as the more specific term – will be used to clarify the meaning of Clause 6.

Question 2: The User of General Conditions

In theory, which party drafted and used the conditions would only make a difference if a court could not establish the meaning of Clause 6, read together with Clause IX and using the accepted principles of contractual interpretation. In practice, there is a tendency to apply the rules discussed below from the outset, whenever a court is dealing with exemption clauses, standard terms and instances of unequal bargaining power.[64] If a set of facts does not fall within one of these exceptions, then the rules are applied as a last resort. They are regarded

60 See e.g. Kerr, *Principles of Contract*, p. 343 ff; *Consol Ltd t/a Consol Glass v Twee Jonge Gezellen (Pty) Ltd* 2005 6 SA 1 (SCA) para. 29; *B & E International (Pty) Ltd v Enviroserv Waste Management (Pty) Ltd* 2000 4 SA 152 (SE) 158D–F.

61 *Privest Employee Solutions (Pty) Ltd v Vital Distribution Solutions (Pty) Ltd* 2005 5 SA 276 (SCA) para. 23.

62 Ibid., para. 23.

63 *B & E International (Pty) Ltd v Enviroserv Waste Management (Pty) Ltd* 2000 4 SA 152 (SE) 159A–E.

64 See Stoop, 'Contractual exemption clauses', p. 504 and the cases cited there; Cornelius, *Interpretation*, pp. 182–183.

as tertiary interpretative factors:[65] they are not rules of interpretation, but amount to conclusions as to what the law says the terms should mean.[66]

The maxim '*verba chartarum fortius accipiuntur contra proferentem*' [words must be construed against those who use them], or the *contra proferentem* rule, states that in cases of doubt, a provision should be construed against the party who formulated it, because that party had the opportunity to make its meaning clear.[67] This rule applies even if the clause does not favour the drafter of the clause.[68]

Another rule, '*semper in obscuris quod minimum est sequimur*' [in cases of doubt, a burden should be construed as lightly as possible], referred to as the *quod minimum* rule, operates in favour of the promisor and against the promisee and provides that in cases of doubt, the promisor's obligation should be interpreted as narrowly as possible.[69] The various justifications offered for this rule are that the debtor should not be obliged to do more than he intended or that if a promisee alleges a promise in his favour, but cannot prove its full scope, the promisor should receive the benefit of the doubt.[70] Where the two rules point in different directions, the *contra proferentem* rule takes precedence over the *quod minimum* rule.[71]

Thus, if Engineering Solutions drafted the General Conditions, the *contra proferentem* rule would mean that the clause is construed against it, while the *quod minimum* rule requires that the burden on Engineering Solutions should be construed as lightly as possible. The two rules therefore conflict, and in such a case the *contra proferentem* rule would take precedence.

14. SPAIN

Question 1: The Role of General Conditions

Assuming the word 'products' is ambiguous, the relation between Clause 6 and Clause IX of the General Conditions is relevant for the scope of the LCGC (General Conditions Act).[72] Article 6 LCGC states in its first paragraph that where there is a contradiction between the general conditions and the particular

65 *Van der Westhuizen v Arnold* 2002 6 SA 453 (SCA) para. 38; *Consol Ltd t/a Consol Glass v Twee Jonge Gezellen (Pty) Ltd* 2005 6 SA 1 (SCA) para. 49; Van Huyssteen et al., *Contract*, p. 302; Bradfield, *Christie's Law of Contract*, p. 262.

66 *Kliptown Clothing Industries (Pty) Ltd v Marine and Trade Insurance Co. of SA Ltd* 1961 1 SA 103 (A) 107H.

67 *Cairns (Pty) Ltd v Playdon & Co., Ltd* 1948 3 SA 99 (A) 121.

68 *Oostelike Transvaal Ko-Operasie Bpk v Kruger* 1958 2 SA 329 (T) 331–332.

69 *Cairns (Pty) Ltd v Playdon & Co., Ltd* 1948 3 SA 99 (A) 121.

70 Roberts, *Wessels' Law of Contract*, vol. I, paras. 1960–1963.

71 *Cairns (Pty) Ltd v Playdon & Co., Ltd* 1948 3 SA 99 (A) 122–123.

72 This Act is applied to B2B contracts (Art. 2).

conditions specifically foreseen for this contract, the latter will prevail over the former, except when the general conditions turn out to be more beneficial for the adherent than the particular conditions. Spanish scholars call the first idea the 'regla de la prevalencia' [prevalence rule].[73]

The rationale of this rule is that the law assumes that parties always include a specific clause to better govern their interests. In this sense, it reflects the parties' will in a better way. Therefore, the court would give preference to Clause 6, which prohibits selling or supplying products to third parties within the territory in which Bath & Shower operates.

A specific clause such as Clause 6 only makes sense if it looks to deny Engineering Solutions the ability to sell and supply at least the same products supplied to Bath & Shower. So, the meaning of the term 'products' used in Clause 6 must include intermediate products.

In addition to this interpretation, Art. 1.284 CC enters into play, as this provision states that if any clause of the contract should admit several meanings, it must be understood to have the meaning most suitable for it to be effective. It is obvious that Clause 6 would not be effective if intermediate products had not been included.[74]

Question 2: The User of General Conditions

The identity of the drafter of the General Conditions is relevant in Spanish law because paragraph 2 of Art. 6 LCGC states that doubts about the interpretation of obscure general conditions will be solved in favour of the adherent. This legal rule contains the classic principle of *interpretatio in dubio contra proferentem o contra stipulatorem*.[75] It implies a sanction on the grounds of the 'buena fe' [good faith] principle in an objective sense, and it is only applicable to standard terms drafted by one party.

Furthermore, Art. 1.288 CC also expresses the traditional rule of objective interpretation based on the principle of *contra proferentem o contra stipulatorem*, saying that the interpretation of obscure clauses in the contract must not favour the party who caused the obscurity.

Consequently, the law makes the person who had the duty to speak clearly liable. If that person has not fulfilled this duty, he must endure the consequences according to the good faith principle and the reciprocal duty of honesty and loyalty in trade.[76] Therefore, it is not only the common intention that is

---

[73] See on the prevalence rule: Díez-Picazo, *Fundamentos*, p. 514; Díaz Alabart, 'Reglas de interpretación', pp. 202–208; Ferrer Riba, 'Reglas de interpretación', pp. 361–378; Alfaro, *Las condiciones generales*, pp. 298–311. See also STS 01.07.2019, ECLI:TS:2019:2181.

[74] See STS 22.10.2010, ECLI:ES:TS:2010:5326; STS 04.05.2016, ECLI:ES:TS:2016:1900

[75] See STS 03.10.2005 (RJ 2005\6909); STS 09.07.1999 (RJ 1999\4767).

[76] See on the *contra proferentem* rule, among many others: Alfaro, *Las condiciones generales*, pp. 318–323; Díaz Alabart, 'Reglas de interpretación', pp. 209–215; Salvador Coderch, 'Reglas de interpretación', pp. 384–389.

important, but also the confidence which arises from the declaration made by both parties. According to Art. 1.288 CC, the party who made an ambiguous declaration must endure the consequences because of the confidence principle.

In conclusion, Spanish courts take into account who drafted the General Conditions in order to always favour the party who did not. It is common to find this principle in consumer contracts.[77] The TS has applied it to insurance contracts,[78] transport contracts,[79] public works contracts and real estate contracts in particular.[80]

15. SWEDEN

Question 1: The Role of General Conditions

Again, the weight to be accorded *any* fact possibly relevant to the understanding of the contract is a function of the nature of that fact and its relation to the other circumstances of the case, i.e. something that can only be assessed, by the courts, by actually engaging in interpretation. In the present case, in order to gauge the weight of Clause IX of the General Conditions, the court will have to consider the wording of that clause, its relation to the wording of Clause 6 – bearing in mind that Clause IX is to be found among the General Conditions applicable to the contract – as well as any other relevant matters, such as, perhaps, the nature and purpose of the agreement.[81]

The problem facing the interpreting court in this case will, roughly, have the following form. In line with the rule of thumb indicating that the contract is to be regarded as a coherent whole,[82] the General Conditions can be presumed to express the parties' understanding of the nature of their agreement. Accordingly, the court will attempt to construct a reading of Clause 6 of the contract that is commensurable with Clause IX of the General Conditions. However, the court will not be willing to unduly strain the interpretation in order to achieve coherence. If Clause 6 of the contract is deemed to contradict the General

77 See STS 04.11.2019, ECLI:ES:TS:2019:3419; STS 11.10.2019, ECLI:ES:TS:2019:3138. It is basically the same rule as Art. 5 Directive 93/13 CEE (unfair terms), implemented in Spain for consumer contracts in Art. 80, second paragraph, of the Revised Text of the General Law for consumer protection.

78 STS 11.12.2007 (RJ 2007\8919); STS 20.07.2011, ECLI:ES:TS:2011:5535; STS 3.03.2014, ECLI:ES:TS:2014:1238; STS 04.11.2019, ECLI:ES:TS:2019:3419.

79 STS 03.10.2005 (RJ 2005\6909).

80 STS 28.01.1989 (RJ 1989/156). On art. 1.288 CC, see recently STS 15.01.2013, ECLI:ES:TS:2013:1153; STS 12.04.2013, ECLI:ES:TS:2013:1899; STS 01.07.2015, ECLI:ES:TS:2015:3152; STS 09.09.2015, ECLI:ES:TS:2015:3711; STS 04.05.2017, ECLI:ES:TS:2017:1858.

81 See the answer to Case 1, Question 3.

82 See the answer to Case 1, Question 1, n. 117.

Conditions, the individually negotiated term takes precedence[83] – in conformity with the general aim of the interpretative activity, i.e. to establish the common intention of the parties.[84] In this case, the matter of striking the right balance between the individually negotiated provision and the standardised terms is especially complex, considering that it is not at all clear what it would *mean* to give Clause IX of the General Conditions weight in the interpretation of Clause 6 of the contract. There are, at least, two possibilities: the parties might have intended to make an *exception* from Clause IX – that clause will then be taken, by the court, to state a general rule that is not applicable in the current context; or the parties might have, in agreeing on Clause 6, answered *a different question* from that dealt with in Clause IX, namely whether Engineering Solutions is permitted to sell or supply *end* products to third parties. The whole, formed by contract and General Conditions, will be coherent on *both* readings.

When dealing with issues of this kind – where it is not possible to settle with reference to the purpose of the contract or the commercial set-up, etc.[85] – the courts are likely to favour the reading that embodies the fairest distribution of risk between the parties, perhaps relying on the models of risk distribution provided by extant statutory provision containing default rules.[86]

Question 2: The User of General Conditions

If it was Engineering Solutions who drafted and used the General Conditions, that would make a difference. Interpretation is always, it has been said, on one level or another about allocating responsibility,[87] and, naturally, when interpreting standardised terms, it matters, in that respect, who drafted, supplied or used the terms in question. All the more so when the terms are vague.

Thus, when deciding what weight is to be accorded the General Conditions, the courts are likely to take the conditions under which these terms were incorporated into the agreement into account[88] – especially where, as in the present case, one of the parties is clearly responsible.[89] As a last resort, if the

83 See e.g. Bernitz, *Standardavtalsrätt*, p. 85, Vahlén, *Avtal och tolkning*, p. 200 (cf. p. 262).

84 See the answer to Case 2, Question 1, n. 96, and with respect to the interplay between individual and standardised terms see e.g. NJA 1964 p. 85, NJA 1964 p. 152, NJA 1980 p. 398, NJA 1990 p. 24 and NJA 2013 p. 271.

85 See above the answer to Case 1, Question 3, and the answer to Case 2, Question 1.

86 See e.g. NJA 2012 p. 597 and NJA 2013 p. 271.

87 In Swedish contract law debates, this notion was first introduced by Folke Schmidt in a pair of highly controversial papers; see Schmidt, 'Typfall, partsavsikt och partsculpa' and Schmidt, 'En culparegel vid avtalstolkning'.

88 See e.g. NJA 1998 p. 3, where the Supreme Court made explicit mention of the fact that the terms under consideration had been agreed upon by organisations representing the interests of both parties.

89 Cf. NJA 1980 p. 46, where the Supreme Court refers to the fact that standardised terms are typically carefully drafted, with due consideration of the interests of both parties. This fact forms a point of departure for the interpretation, according to the principles set down in NJA 2013 p. 271.

vagueness cannot be dealt with by means of interpretation in the stricter sense, the courts may resort to the 'oklarhetsregel' [unclarity rule], according to which ambiguous terms are to be interpreted against the party responsible for the unclarity.[90]

16. EDITORIAL COMPARATIVE OBSERVATIONS

Reporters for the lion's share of the jurisdictions have reached the same conclusion in this case as to the order of precedence to be applied between Clause 6 of the contract and Clause IX of the General Conditions: with the exception of Greece, Italy and Poland, the terms of Clause 6 will take priority over those contained in Clause IX. The juridical basis for this order of precedence varies between the jurisdictions: some national respondents attribute it to a rule that specific terms must take priority over general terms, for example in Germany, South Africa and Spain, whereas in other jurisdictions, the order is rooted in individually negotiated terms taking primacy over standard terms, for example in England and Wales, France, the Netherlands and Portugal. Most of the jurisdictions applying that order of precedence include a rule to the effect that if the meaning of the term in the specific clause remains ambiguous, as is the case here – since the word 'products' could reasonably mean 'intermediate' or 'end products' without any additional context – then it is permissible in law for the courts to have recourse to the general conditions as an interpretive aid, for example in Croatia, England and Wales, Germany, the Netherlands, Scotland, South Africa and Spain, with the additional requirement in the latter jurisdiction of Scotland that the general conditions must have been incorporated into the contract by reference, or constitute part of the factual matrix behind, or the circumstances surrounding, the formation of the contract.

As for the three jurisdictions of Greece, Italy and Poland who would not give primacy to Clause 6 over Clause IX of the General Condition, the respondents for these jurisdictions point out that the notion of systematic interpretation – i.e. that the contract must be construed as a whole – is so strong that prioritisation between them is to be rejected. However, the exact mechanics of the systematic interpretation of Clause 6 and Clause IX varies between these jurisdictions at a granular level. For example, in Greece, an objective interpretation will be

90 On this rule, see the Opening Remarks. On the distinction between interpretation in the stricter sense and application of 'hjälpregler' [help rules] such as 'oklarhetsregeln', see Lehrberg, *Avtalstolkning*, p. 169 ff.; cf. e.g. NJA 2017 p. 237.

applied, with the court enjoined to apply the standard of the average person of the circle of addressees. This can be contrasted with Italy, where the national respondent reports that a subjective interpretation of the parties' common intention will be adopted in preference to an objective interpretation. However, if no assistance is to be derived from the subjective approach, the Italian courts will be entitled to have regard to objective factors. Meanwhile, in Polish law, the national respondent noted that the courts will seek to establish the purpose of the contract as a means of interpretation, together with the shared common intention of the parties, which will be given priority over the literal meaning of the words in the contract and General Conditions.

What is of particular interest, however, is the role that the concept of good faith plays in examining the relationship between the two contracting parties. For example, good faith is adopted as an instrument in Italy to protect the weaker party to the transaction and can thus play a residual role in shaping the outcome of the interpretive exercise. Likewise, in Portugal, where good faith can be harnessed as a means of calling the behaviour of the contracting parties to account. As for Spain, it would appear that the role of good faith is indelibly linked to the *contra proferentem* maxim and its scope of application in this case.

Turning now to the position if Engineering Solutions had drafted and used the General Conditions, in the majority of the jurisdictions under review, this would be a relevant consideration, for example in Croatia, England and Wales, Finland, France, Italy, Poland, South Africa, Spain and Sweden. The exceptions are Germany, Greece, the Netherlands, Portugal and Scotland, where the role of Engineering Solutions in proposing or producing the General Conditions would be irrelevant. In the former jurisdictions, where the fact that Engineering Solutions produced the General Conditions would indeed be taken into account, it is not the case that the terms of Clause IX are excluded as an interpretive aid. Instead, the terms can be considered, but the *contra proferentem* rule will be adopted so that the preferred meaning adopted should be the one that works against the interests of Engineering Solutions, thereby lending greater support to Bath & Shower's preferred interpretation. In some of these jurisdictions, it is a prerequisite that the written term to be interpreted be considered ambiguous before the *contra proferentem* is applied, for example in Croatia, Finland, Poland, Spain and Sweden, whereas in others, the requirement for ambiguity as a gateway criterion to the application of the *contra proferentem* rule is less obvious. However, some jurisdictions do not fit into this general pattern above. For example, in South Africa, the *contra proferentem* maxim competes with the *semper in obscuris quod minimum est sequimur* [in cases of doubt, a burden should be construed as lightly as possible] canon of construction, with the former being likely to win out.

In conclusion, we can see that each of the jurisdictions adopt different approaches to whether a hierarchy is to be applied as regards the status of Clause 6 vis-à-vis Clause IX. As for the role of the *contra proferentem* canon of construction, there would appear to continue to be a place for it in most of the jurisdictions under review, but rarely as a single interpretive factor: other interpretive rules must point in its favour before it is prayed in aid to arrive at a preferred construction.

CASE 6: CALL CENTRE

'Print Master' is a large print and fax machine seller. It enters into a five-year outsource contract with 'Premium Phone Services' (PPS), which is operating a call centre. Under this agreement, PPS provides to Print Master inbound and outbound call centre services for the purpose of order taking and customer service. This contract also includes a so-called service level agreement, under which PPS is to execute frequent monitoring of the service quality provided by PPS's call centre agents to Print Master's customers. Clause 16(k) provides: 'Premium Phone Services will conduct bi-weekly randomly augmented service quality tests and send the results of these tests to Print Master within 24 hours.' One month after concluding the outsource contract but before either PPS or Print Master have undertaken any performance, PPS transfers its rights in the agreement to another call centre operator, 'Magnificall', in response to a downward turn in the market. A month after all parties involved validly documented the transfer and Magnificall started its call centre services, Print Master contacts Magnificall and protests that Print Master only received a report on Magnificall's quality tests twice in the last month. Magnificall dismisses the complaints and argues that under Clause 16(k) it is obliged to conduct quality tests and send these reports only once every two weeks. It refuses to conduct these tests more often since that would bring about considerable costs. Print Master contends that 'bi-weekly' means twice a week, not once every two weeks. The transfer agreement was silent on this matter. The issue also never came up between Print Master and PPS. In support of its reading of Clause 16(k), Print Master presents evidence at the formation of the outsource agreement, which shows that both Print Master and PPS agreed that that said quality tests would be conducted twice per week.

Assume that Clause 16(k) is ambiguous, and the evidence offered by Print Master indeed indicates without doubt that Print Master and PPS both intended Clause 16(k) to mean that said quality tests would be conducted twice per week. Also assume that such evidence is sufficient to satisfy your jurisdiction that there was a common understanding or intention arising between the parties and that the transfer of rights was legally valid. How much weight, if any, may be given to the meaning that Print Master and PPS attributed to Clause 16(k), considering the fact that PPS is no longer a party to the agreement and Magnificall did not take part in the negotiation, drafting and conclusion of this clause?

1. KEY ISSUES

The case concerns an outsourcing contract between a company and a call centre. It incorporates a service level agreement in terms of which the call centre must monitor the service quality it provides. After formation, the call centre transfers its rights under the agreement to a third party. The phrase 'bi-weekly', which relates to the call centre's obligation to report on the service quality, is ambiguous. The case is designed to allow reporters to analyse whether the existence of evidence dating from the formation of the contract can be used in a dispute on the interpretation which takes place later, at which time there has been a change in the relevant personnel. The dispute arises between one of the original contracting parties and a new party to whom the call centre has transferred its rights under the contract. Essentially, the case allows reporters to consider the way in which interpretative disputes change (if at all) where an original contracting party is no longer involved, having been replaced by a transferee. Arguably, this type of situation raises competing policy issues, some of which may be discussed by the courts. The use against a third party of evidence dating from formation is arguably unfair to that third party. He or she may not have had access to it, and may be unaware of it. On the other hand, the third party can protect him- or herself against this eventuality: he or she may raise this issue in negotiations with the transferor and seek an indemnity from the transferor to protect him- or herself should such evidence subsequently emerge in the context of a dispute.

2. CROATIA

According to the COA, a legal transaction whereby PPS transferred its contractual position to Magnificall is characterised as a transfer of contract. Therefore, the answer to the above question should be considered, first, within the context of the COA provisions on the transfer of contract,[1] and then, if necessary, by taking into consideration the COA provisions on contract interpretation.

The main legal effect of transfer of a contract is defined by Art. 127(1) of the COA:[2] a new party steps into the contract and becomes the contracting party,

1 In its Part 7, Chapter VI, under the title 'Contract's Transfer', the COA contains three provisions relevant for the case at hand: a provision laying down the conditions for the validity of the transfer of contract (Art. 127); a provision on the scope of the transferor's responsibility (Art. 128); and a provision on the objections by the other contracting party (Art. 129).

2 Art. 127(1) of the COA reads as follows: 'Each of the parties to a contract may, if the other party agrees, transfer the contract to a third person, whereby the latter becomes the holder of all the former's rights and obligations arising out of that contract'.

while on the other side, a transferor steps out of the contract. Applying said provision to the case at hand, Magnificall, a new contracting party, replaced PPS, the former party, to the outsource contract. By stepping into PPS's shoes, Magnificall took over PPS's entire contractual position, including both its rights and its obligations. The COA contains no provision on how the transfer of contract affects the content and the scope of transferred contractual rights and obligations. However, it can be inferred that the transfer of contract leads to a change of contractual position, but has no effect on the content and scope of transferred rights and obligations. Pursuant to Art. 127 of the COA, by taking over PPS's contractual position, Magnificall took over all of PPS's obligations, which Magnificall is now obliged to perform in the same way as PPS was.[3]

Consequently, if the common intention of PPS and Print Master was that service quality tests have to be done twice a week, then Magnificall's obligation is the same. The transfer of the outsource contract from PPS to Magnificall does not affect in any way the content and the scope of Magnificall's obligation towards Print Master, and consequently Magnificall's obligation towards Print Master must be the same as PPS's obligation. This conclusion may be supported by analogy with Art. 98 of the COA.[4] According to Art. 98(3) of the COA, the same obligation that existed between the previous debtor and the creditor will exist between the person assuming the debt and the creditor.[5] Applying the said provision by analogy to the case at hand, one can conclude that the content and scope of Magnificall's obligation to perform the test are to be determined by the content and scope of PPS's obligation prior to the transfer.

Therefore, under the assumption that it was the common intention of Print Master and PPS that Clause 16(k) meant that the service quality test would be conducted twice per week, and under the assumption that evidence of a common understanding or intention of the parties as to the formation of the outsource agreement showed that both Print Master and PPS agreed that said quality tests would be conducted twice per week, the court ought to conclude that Magnificall is also obliged to perform this obligation twice per week, in the same way that PPS was obliged to do. Even in the event that Magnificall reasonably relied on the ordinary meaning of the word 'bi-weekly', as something that occurs every two weeks, and not twice a week, it is suggested that the courts would not give priority to Magnificall's reasonable reliance over PPS's and Print Master's common understanding of Clause 16(k). In order to determine the content and scope of Magnificall's obligation in relation to Clause 16(k), a court should, according to Art. 319(2) of the COA, investigate the common

3 Gorenc et al., *Komentar Zakona o obveznim odnosima*, p. 183.

4 Art. 98 of the COA provides for the effects of the substitution of a debtor in the case of an assumption of debt.

5 Kačar, Radolović and Slakoper, *Zakon o obveznim odnosima s komentarom*, p. 126.

intention of the parties to a contract in the light of the contractual principles determined by the COA. It would be against the principle of conscientiousness and honesty (Art. 4 of the COA) to attribute any other meaning to the disputed words, if the circumstances of the case undoubtedly indicate the same understanding of the term, i.e. the common and actual intention of the contracting parties.

Another legal principle in the COA imposes upon a party to a contract the duty to perform his/her obligation with a certain degree of quality (Art. 10),[6] this standard of quality being higher if that party is a professional (Art. 10(2)). Therefore, being a professional, Magnificall had a duty to act with due professional care or to use the statutory wording 'pažnja dobrog stručnjaka' [due care of a good professional], including a duty to inform itself of the actual meaning of Clause 16(k). Prior to becoming a party to the outsource contract concluded between Print Master and PPS, Magnificall as a third party should have made sure that it understood the actual content of the contract, together with the actual content and scope of PPS's rights and obligations. Since we are told that the evidence of the common understanding and intention of Print Master and PPS satisfies the requirements of Croatian law, then, notwithstanding that PPS is no longer a party to the agreement and despite the fact that Magnificall did not take part in the negotiation, drafting and conclusion of Clause 16(k), the courts would take into consideration the meaning attributed to this clause by the original parties to the contract.

3. ENGLAND AND WALES

In English law, the rights under a contractual agreement can usually be transferred to a third party by a process called 'assignment', subject always to any term in the contract prohibiting or regulating such a transfer.

The court would be more likely to construe the contract strictly, without reference to the background material, if it were the type of contract the parties would expect to be transferred (or even if it provided for such an assignment in its terms). This is because the reasonable reader would know that the words of a contract must have one meaning throughout the life of the contract, whether pre- or post-transfer, and therefore even pre-transfer would interpret

[6] Art. 10 of the COA entitled 'Conduct in the Course of Performing Obligations and Exercising Rights' provides in para. 1 that in performing their obligations, the parties shall act with due care as required in a legal transaction relating to a relevant type of obligation ('pažnja dobrog gospodarstvenika, odnosno pažnja dobrog domaćina' [due care of a good businessman or due care of a good host]). See VSRH, Revt 249/14-2 of 9 April 2015, where the Supreme Court qualifies banks as highly specialised financial institutions, which should act as good and responsible businessmen.

the contract keeping in mind only the more limited background material a post-transfer reader would have access to.[7] The authorities show that this principle is applicable to public documents and standard form documents.[8] It probably also applies to documents that are expected to be assigned.[9]

If the five-year outsourcing contract was likely to be assigned, then the evidence of a common understanding would be given little or no weight unless the evidence was available (to a potential assignee).

The important feature here is not whether the contract was in fact assigned (as almost any contract can be) but rather whether the contract was at the time of contracting one that was not unlikely to be assigned (or otherwise construed by other people). The mere fact that PPS is, as events have transpired, no longer a party to the contract, and Magnificall did not take part in the negotiation, is not of itself of any weight, because if the five-year outsourcing contract was unlikely to be assigned (although in fact assigned) then it is up to the assignee to inquire as to any relevant background or take its chances,[10] i.e. private material that an assignee would not be expected to have access would still be given weight.

In any event, this particular background material may well be inadmissible as comprising pre-contractual negotiations, although that would not bar their use for rectification or estoppel.[11]

4. FINLAND

The objective of the interpretation of contracts is to determine the mutual intention of the parties at the time of contract.[12] In Case 6, both contracting parties, Print Master and PPS, have understood the term 'bi-weekly' so that PPS is obliged to conduct quality tests twice per week. This mutual understanding has not been questioned in the case.

PPS later transferred its rights in the agreement to Magnificall. In Finland, this kind of transfer of rights is governed by the Finnish Promissory Notes

7 Per Campbell JA in the Australian case of *Phoenix Commercial Enterprises Pty Ltd v City of Canada Bay Council* [2010] NSWCA 64 at para. 151.

8 See e.g. *Dairy Containers Ltd v Tasman Orient CV* [2005] 1 WLR 215 (PC) per Lord Bingham at para. 12; *Attorney-General for Belize v Belize Telecom Ltd* [2009] 1 WLR 1988 (PC) per Lord Hoffmann at para. 36.

9 *Phoenix Commercial Enterprises Pty Ltd v City of Canada Bay Council* [2010] NSWCA 64; *Re Sigma Finance Corp.* [2010] 1 All ER 571 (SC) at para. 37.

10 *Chartbrook v Persimmon Homes Ltd* [2009] 1 AC 1101 (HL) per Lord Hoffmann at para. 40.

11 See Case 3.

12 See Hemmo, *Sopimusoikeus I*, p. 604; Saarnilehto, *Sopimusoikeuden perusteet*, p. 149; and Telaranta, *Sopimusoikeus*, p. 94.

Act (622/1947). According to Section 27 of the Act the transferee (here Magnificall) has the same rights towards the other contracting party (here Print Master) as its predecessor (here PPS) had.[13] With regard to the term 'bi-weekly', this means that Magnificall is bound to the mutual understanding of the initial contracting parties (Print Master and PPS). The fact that Magnificall did not take part in the negotiation, drafting and conclusion of Clause 16(k) is in this case irrelevant.

5. FRANCE

In the present case, the legal transaction between Print Master, PPS and Magnificall may be characterised as a 'cession de contrat' [assignment of contract]. The legal regime of this transaction is still partly disputed. The question of whether the common intention of the original parties to an assigned contract can be invoked against the assignee has no clear-cut answer so far – neither in statutes nor in case law.

Different elements may be taken into account by French courts. A first element is the wording of the assignment contract. As per new Art. 1216 Cciv,[14] the assignment contract results from an agreement between the two parties to the assigned contract and the assignee. It determines the rights and obligations that are transferred to the assignee and sets the parameters of the assignment.[15] As the expression of the common intention of Print Master, PPS and Magnificall, the assignment contract may contain useful indications as to the meaning of the adjective 'bi-weekly.' If the assignment contract reveals a common understanding that 'bi-weekly' means 'once every two weeks', this meaning will prevail over any previous agreement between Print Master and PPS.

If the assignment contract does not provide any useful indication, the court will still try to determine the common intention of the parties to the assignment contract under Art. 1188 Cciv (formerly Art. 1156). This common intention may be established by reference to relevant circumstances at the time of the conclusion of the assignment contract. In this respect, the common intention of Print Master and PPS in the initial contract is a significant element, especially if the meaning attributed by Print Master and PPS to the clause was known to Magnificall. The financial conditions of the assignment

13 See also Kaisto and Lohi, *Johdatus varallisuusoikeuteen*, p. 173 and Norros, *Johdatus velvoiteoikeuteen*, pp. 139–141.

14 Before being introduced in the Code by the 2016 reform, the principle was set out by case law – see e.g. Com., 6 May 1997, *JurisData* no. 1997-002064 and 1997-002065.

15 Com., 9 June 1998, no. 96-13.181.

may be another relevant element to be considered by the court.[16] They can be analysed as a concrete reflection of the contractual balance reached between the parties. They provide some indirect insights into the parties' common intention at the time of the conclusion of the contract. The question here is whether the financial conditions are likely to have taken into account the financial charge resulting for Magnificall from the application of Clause 16(k) if 'bi-weekly' is to be construed as 'twice a week'. If the financial conditions of the transaction are exceptionally favourable to Magnificall, the courts might consider that these conditions intend to counterbalance the special charge resulting from the high frequency of the quality tests.

Before the reform, the court could have subsidiarily relied on Art. 1159 Cciv to construe Clause 16(k) in accordance with a usage that would favour either one interpretation or the other. However, in such a case, the Cour de cassation would have required the parties to have expressly agreed on the application of the usage to their contract, which is not mentioned here.[17] Since the reform, and in the absence of a determinable common intention of the parties, the court will refer to Art. 1188 (2) Cciv and consider how a reasonable person in the same situation would objectively interpret the contract.

6. GERMANY

After two months there was a transfer of rights as a 'Vertragsübernahme' [transfer of agreement] under the analogy of §398 BGB[18] between PPS and Magnificall. Under German law, 'Vertragsübernahme' [transfer of agreement] is not mentioned in the BGB itself; however, through development of law there is a presumption that such a transfer is possible.[19]

As a starting point, interpretation of contracts is based on the proven common intention of the parties and the proven consensus at the time of the formation of the contract.[20] It is worth noting that the contract that must be interpreted in the case at hand is the service contract between Print Master and PPS. Furthermore, it is the key characteristic of the 'Vertragsübernahme',

---

16 See P.-Y. Gautier, 'L'incertitude règne encore sur la transmissibilité passive des obligations: au sujet de l'obligation de remise en état à la charge du cessionnaire du bail', *RTDCiv.* (2003) 725.

17 Com., 17 May 1988, *Bull. civ.* (1988) no. 167.

18 R. Schulze, '§398 BGB' in R. Schulze, H. Dörner, I. Ebert, T. Hoeren, R. Kemper, I. Saenger, K. Schreiber, H. Schulte-Nölke and A. Staudinger, *Bürgerliches Gesetzbuch Handkommentar*, m.n. 27.

19 BGH, 05.03.2015, BGHZ 204, 231, R. Schulze, '§398 BGB' in R. Schulze, H. Dörner, I. Ebert, T. Hoeren, R. Kemper, I. Saenger, K. Schreiber, H. Schulte-Nölke and A. Staudinger, *Bürgerliches Gesetzbuch Handkommentar*, m.n. 27.

20 J. Busche, '§157 BGB' in K. Rebmann and F.J. Säcker (eds.), *Münchener Kommentar zum Bürgerlichen Gesetzbuch*, m.n. 2.

that the new party to the contract, Magnificall, enters the contract at its initial stage.[21] This demonstrates the main difference between 'Vertragsübernahme' and 'Neuabschluss' [renewal of a contract].

After a transfer of agreement, every detail of the initial contract is of significance for interpretation and the common intention of the original contracting parties is the decisive factor for the interpretation process.[22] In fact, the transfer of rights does not change the interpretation of the wording of the contract.[23]

The interpretation of Clause 16(k) in favour of Print Master may be based on the evidence of a common understanding or intention of the parties offered by Print Master as there is no restriction as to the means of proving the intentions of the parties when they concluded the original contract. This general rule also applies in both the case of assignment and the transfer of the whole agreement. If, however, there would not be any available evidence of a common understanding of the parties, one may apply the normative, objective interpretation with respect to the 'Treu und Glaube' [good faith principle] and 'Verkehrssitten' [custom of trade] (cf. Case 2).

It is worth mentioning, however, that under German law there is an exemption to the prevalence of the original meaning of the contract in the case of general conditions. In the event of a transfer of agreement, the general conditions of the original contract do not govern the new relationship unless the new party was aware of the content of the general conditions or negligently did not know.[24]

7. GREECE

In order to discover the meaning of Clause 16(k) and how exactly it affects Magnificall, one must firstly interpret Clause 16(k) in its original context, namely in the agreement between Print Master and PPS. Even though the text of the Clause 16(k) is ambiguous, the 'συγκείμενα' [proximates] consisting of the evidence of a common understanding or intention of the parties presented by Print Master show in a satisfactory manner that both parties had the same understanding of the term 'bi-weekly'. Therefore, the subjective criterion of

21 D. Klimke, *Die Vertragsübernahme*, p. 7.
22 Ibid., p. 9.
23 BGH, 10.05.1995, *NJW* 1995, 2290. This also applies in the case of an assignment. In particular, the assignment does not change the interpretation even if there is a different subjective understanding made by the successor; OLG Frankfurt, 02.20.1995, *NJW-RR* 1996, 172. There is an exception to this rule in the case of general conditions: general conditions apply after an assignment only if the assignor knew or negligently did not know of the general conditions.
24 OLG Frankfurt, 20.02.1995, *NJW-RR* 1996, 172.

Art. 173 CC is satisfied, and the term must be understood in the sense that the parties wished to attribute to it.

Therefore, the problem arises in the transfer agreement between PPS and Magnificall. Presumably Magnificall took over all rights and duties of PPS as against Print Master. When a contractual relationship is transferred in its entirety, the provisions of the Civil Code on 'εκχώρηση απαιτήσεων' [assignment of claims] (Arts. 455–470) and 'αναδοχή χρέους' [assumption of debt] (Arts. 471–479) are applicable.[25] According to Art. 472 CC, the person assuming a foreign debt (here: another's contractual obligations), i.e. the new debtor, has as against the creditor the same obligations as the old one. From the facts of the case, it is not clear whether PPS informed the transferee (i.e. Magnificall) about the precise extent of its duties towards Print Master; actually, since there is evidence of the fact that Print Master and PPS had a common understanding of the clause in question, one is allowed to assume that PPS neglected to inform Magnificall about such particularities of the agreement. It does not make a difference whether PPS is no longer a party to the agreement, nor the fact that Magnificall did not take part in the negotiations; based on the facts of the case, the court would most probably find that Magnificall did not conclude a new agreement with Print Master, but it stepped into the position of PPS in the framework of an existing contractual relationship.[26]

Therefore, Magnificall cannot invoke as against Print Master a different understanding of Clause 16(k) (Art. 472 CC), or, to be more precise, Magnificall must establish that the obligation to perform quality tests twice a week was not transferred to it by PPS. In order to do so, one must interpret the transfer agreement between PPS and Magnificall: there is no room here for the subjective criterion of Art. 173 CC, because the parties are obviously in disagreement as to the meaning of the term 'bi-weekly'. Therefore, one has to turn once again to the objective interpretation of Art. 200 CC. No trade custom can be inferred that makes a quality test twice a week imperative; therefore, the principle of good faith must be concretised without taking into account any such practices. Here two factors may be of importance: firstly, whether PPS offered access to the evidence of a common understanding or intention of the parties to Magnificall, in order to provide

---

25 For those legal institutions in Greek law, see Georgiades, *Ενοχικό Δίκαιο – Γενικό Μέρος [Law of Obligations – General Part]*, §42 nos. 1 et seq. (assignment of claims), §43 nos. 1 et seq. (assumption of debt); Stathopoulos, *Γενικό Ενοχικό Δίκαιο [General Part of the Law of Obligations]*, §27 nos. 1 et seq. (assignment of claims), §28 nos. 1 et seq. (assumption of debt).

26 Cf. SCFI Rodopi 27/2011, first published in NOMOS, for the transfer of a lease agreement to a new lessee.

a more comprehensive understanding of the duties and rights transferred to the latter; and secondly, the principle of self-responsibility[27] entails that each party ought to make his declaration of intent clear enough for his counterparty. In view of the ambiguity of the term 'bi-weekly', the court would most certainly take into account the meaning of Clause 16(k) in the original agreement between Print Master and PPS, but it would also look into the terms of the agreement between PPS and Magnificall in order to determine what duties exactly were taken over by the latter (unless otherwise stated in the transfer agreement between the old and the new contractual party, the latter has the same rights and duties as the former as against the remaining contractual party; for the duties, in particular, see Art. 472 CC[28]).

To sum up, the original interpretation of Clause 16(k) is still critical after Magnificall assumed the obligations of PPS, insofar as Magnificall cannot prove otherwise; unless Magnificall can show, for example, that it negotiated carve-outs as to which rights and duties of PPS it took over in respect of the agreement between PPS and Print Master, the fact alone that PPS is no longer party to the agreement and Magnificall did not negotiate the original term in question would probably not be of any help to Magnificall.

8. ITALY

The evidence presented by Print Master is relevant under Art. 1362 c.c. for the interpretation of the original contract between Print Master and PPS, because it reveals the common intention of the parties.

The assignee of the contract (Magnificall) assumes all the rights and obligations that lay upon the transferor under the original contract (Art. 1406 ff. c.c.).

The question whether the evidence presented by Print Master of a common understanding between the parties is relevant as to the interpretation of the contract once the contract has been transferred to another party is not answered by any express rule, nor has any reported judicial decision specifically addressed this issue.

---

27 See Opening Remarks, section 6.3.

28 See Stathopoulos, *Law of Obligations – GP*, §27 nos. 136, 140a-2: the author states that from a legal point of view, when a contractual position is transferred, it is not the position as a whole that is assigned, but rather that each right and each obligation of the assigning party under the contract is assigned or assumed respectively by the assignee through individual assignments of claims and assumptions of debt; however, he goes on to remark that the transfer of a contractual position as a whole, namely this bundle, is regarded in the transactions as a uniform economic value.

The problem raised by this case has been analysed by a limited number of scholarly writings.[29] According to those authors, the assignee would receive the contractual position as a whole, including its 'history', which involves previous interpretations given by the original parties and evidenced either by their overall conduct, including the manner of performance of the original contract, or otherwise referable to their common intention. This conclusion is mainly grounded on the rules on the assignment of contract (Arts. 1406 et seq. c.c.). Those rules, it is submitted, would protect the original contractual party (here Print Master) in relation to its new counterparty by affirming the 'continuity' of the contractual relationship. After the transfer of the contract, the assignee would be bound by the very same contractual rules that bound the original parties, according to their original will and to their subjective interpretation.

This scholarly opinion appears to be mainly justified by the view of the protection of the original contractual party (here Print Master) who consents to the assignment of the contract and hence receives a 'new counterparty' while relying on the original subjective interpretation of the contract.

It is likely that a court will give a certain relevance to the interpretation that the original parties attributed to Clause 16(k), insofar as evidence clearly shows a common understanding between original parties. A court would probably justify the relevance of the interpretation of the original parties against the new party (the assignee: Magnificall) on the ground of the rules on assignment of contracts, as a means of protection of the legitimate interests of the original contractual party (Print Master).

However, since in the present case performance of the contract has not commenced at the time of assignment and the evidence presented by Print Master refers to the formation of the agreement, a court would probably also consider whether the assignee, at the time of assignment, had the actual opportunity to know the common understanding of the original parties as to the meaning of the ambiguous clause. If the evidence presented by Print Master is merely private and if no other element available to the assignee supports the subjective interpretation of the original parties, the protection of the interests of the original party (Print Master) could yield to the consideration of the legitimate expectations of the assignee.[30]

A court could consequently disregard the subjective interpretation of original parties and resort to other factors of interpretation such as the 'natura

29 V. Pescatore, *Cessione del contratto e interpretazione*, p. 683; Albanese, *Cessione del contratto*, p. 136; Albanese, *La circolazione del contratto*, p. 15; Oppo, *Scritti giuridici*, p. 181.

30 According to a very influential author, when the contract affects the interests of third parties, the legally relevant 'intention' is the objective intention 'in accordance with the text', while the psychological (subjective) intention may be relevant only between original parties; see Sacco, *Contratto*, p. 1349 (not specifically referring to the transfer of contract).

o oggetto del contratto' [nature or purpose of the contract] of Art. 1369 or use the 'buona fede' [good faith] provisions of Art. 1366 to protect the possible reasonable reliance of the assignee on a certain contractual meaning.

9. NETHERLANDS

Contract interpretation under the *Haviltex* norm looks to discover the meaning each party could reasonably attach to the terms of the contract and which they each could reasonably have expected the other party to have given to the contract's terms.[31] The court will assess all the relevant facts and circumstances in light of the standards of 'redelijkheid en billijkheid' [reasonableness and fairness].[32] This approach inevitably looks to the original contracting parties who were involved in the formation of the contract. Nevertheless, it may be that third parties are affected by the contract, including the situation where a third party accedes to an already concluded contract or where the rights and obligations under a contract are transferred to another. This third party was not involved in the negotiation and drafting of the contract; nevertheless, it will be bound by it. In such a situation there may be a discrepancy between the understanding and intention of the original contracting parties and the third party. This is particularly problematic when interpretation involves intentions and factors that are not accessible to the third party from the text of the contract or accompanying documents.[33]

In the Netherlands, the position of third parties in the context of contract interpretation can be taken into account in a number of ways. In the first place, the Supreme Court has developed a separate norm for the interpretation of certain types of contracts that affect a large number of third parties, in particular collective employment contracts (the so-called CAO).[34] For the interpretation of such contracts, in principle, the wording read in light of the contractual text as a whole is determinative.[35] Application of this CAO norm requires more than simply grammatical interpretation; instead, a reasonable

31 Hoge Raad 13 March 1981, *NJ* 1981, 635 (Ermes/Haviltex).

32 Hoge Raad 20 February 2004, *NJ* 2005, 393 (DSM-Chemie/Fox).

33 See Tjittes, *Uitleg van schriftelijke contracten*, p. 59.

34 Hoge Raad 17 September 1993, *NJ* 1994, 173 (Gerritse/HAS) and Hoge Raad 24 September 1993, *NJ* 1994, 174 (Hol/EIM). See also Hoge Raad 31 May 2002, *NJ* 2003, 110 and Hoge Raad 28 June 2002, *NJ* 2003, 111. CAO is the abbreviation for 'Collectieve Arbeidsovereenkomst' [collective employment contract].

35 Hoge Raad 17 September 1993, *NJ* 1994, 173 (Gerritse/HAS): 'voor de uitleg van de bepalingen van een CAO, de bewoordingen daarvan, gelezen in het licht van de gehele tekst van die overeenkomst, in beginsel van doorslaggevende betekenis zijn.'

interpretation according to objective standards is called for.[36] Relevant factors identified for this purpose in the case law include the text of the contract, including the wording of the provisions and formulations used elsewhere in the contract, the system created within the contract, the scope of the contract, the plausibility of the legal consequences of one or other interpretation, the intention of the contracting party to the collective employment contract to the extent that they stem from the text and the explanatory text available to third parties, and other relevant information that is publicly available.[37]

The underlying rationale for this separate norm for collective employment contracts is that the parties to such agreements are not present during the negotiations and therefore lack the background information that could shed light on the nature of the rights and duties contained in the contract.[38] Even if an individual employer or employee was involved in the negotiations, the CAO norm will be applied to the interpretation of the contract, because in the interests of legal certainty, a collective employment contract should not be interpreted differently depending on the involvement of a particular party in its formation.[39] Information that one of the parties may have obtained because it was present during the negotiations and drafting of the collective employment contract can only be admitted if such information is publicly available.[40] Publicly available information is not restricted to the preamble and explanatory notes accompanying the contractual document. The Supreme Court has held, for instance, that an article published in the Dutch law journal *WPNR* by the drafters (the Dutch Association of Insurers) of the binding resolution on subrogation (Bindend Besluit Regres) could inform the interpretation to be given to a contract that was subject to the CAO norm.[41] The contractual relationship between Print Master and Magnificall does not fall within the category of contracts that are automatically subjected to an objective interpretation in accordance with the CAO norm.

In the second place, in its *DSM-Chemie/Fox* decision,[42] the Supreme Court indicated that the *Haviltex* norm can be applied objectively. The interpretation will depend on the text of the contract, the system created within the contract,

---

36 Hoge Raad 31 May 2002, *NJ* 2003, 110; Hoge Raad 28 June 2002, *NJ* 2003, 111. Also see Tjittes, 'Contractsuitleg', p. 121; Tjittes, 'Uitleg van schriftelijke contracten', p. 11.

37 Tjittes, 'Uitleg van schriftelijke contracten', p. 11; Wissink, 'Uitleg volgens Haviltex of de cao-norm? Over een vloeiende overgang en de noodzaak om toch te kiezen', p. 408; Asser/Sieburgh, *Algemene leer der overeenkomsten*, 6-III, no. 374.

38 Wissink, 'Uitleg volgens Haviltex of de cao-norm? Over een vloeiende overgang en de noodzaak om toch te kiezen', p. 407.

39 Tjittes, 'Uitleg van schriftelijke contracten', p. 11; Hoge Raad 26 May 2000, *NJ* 2000, 473.

40 Wissink, 'Uitleg volgens Haviltex of de cao-norm? Over een vloeiende overgang en de noodzaak om toch te kiezen', p. 408.

41 Hoge Raad 27 February 2004, *NJ* 2005, 498 (Royal Nederland Verzekeringsmaatschappij/K).

42 Hoge Raad 20 February 2004, *NJ* 2005, 493 (DSM-Chemie/Fox).

the scope of the contract, the plausibility of the legal consequences of one or other interpretation, and other relevant information that is available to the external party. The Court indicated that an objective application of the *Haviltex* norm will be called for when the intention of the contracting parties is not apparent from the written contract and accompanying documentation, it follows from the nature of the contract that it is meant to affect the legal position of third parties not involved in the formation of the contract, it is foreseeable for the contracting parties that the number of third parties is relatively large, and a uniform interpretation of the contract is desirable.[43] For instance, in the case of general conditions and standard contracts,[44] insurance policies,[45] third party clauses,[46] or a retirement fund regulation in the employer–employee relationship,[47] the *Haviltex* norm will be applied objectively. The original contract concluded between Prime Master and PPS is not intended to affect the legal position of a large number of third parties in uniform manner, and therefore the criteria for an objective application of the *Haviltex* norm laid down in *DSM-Chemie/Fox* are not met. The contract was concluded to regulate the legal relationship between Prime Master and PPS. Consequently, it will be subject to the ordinary *Haviltex* norm.

An ordinary application of the *Haviltex* norm would seem to be called for, in which case all the relevant facts and circumstances would inform the interpretation to be given to the terms of the contract. In the situation that a third party becomes party to an already existing contract, it becomes bound by the terms of the contract. In *Staalcom/Neher*,[48] the Supreme Court said that the responsibility lies with the third party to take the initiative to inform itself about the intentions, understandings and expectations of the original contracting parties. The new contracting party is consequently, in principle, bound to respect the existing agreement reached between the original parties. Interpretation of the contract will take place in accordance with the *Haviltex*

43 Ibid.; Hoge Raad 9 July 2004, *NJ* 2005, 496 (Hoevers/Van Dijk): 'naar zijn aard … bestemd is anderen dan contractanten te binden'. ['according to its nature … the contract is meant to bind others than the contracting parties']. Also see Tjittes, 'Uitleg van schriftelijke contracten', p. 12; Tjittes, *Uitleg van schriftelijke contracten*, p. 60; Wissink, 'Uitleg volgens Haviltex of de cao-norm? Over een vloeiende overgang en de noodzaak om toch te kiezen', p. 414; Hartlief, 'De uitleg van contracten. Haviltex revisited', p. 1080.

44 Hoge Raad 30 November 2001, *JOL* 2001, 709 and 710. Also see Hoge Raad 18 October 2002, *NJ* 2003, 503 and Hoge Raad 20 September 2002, *NJ* 2002, 610; Hoge Raad 23 December 2005, *RvdW* 2006, 17 (De Rooij/Van Olphen).

45 Hoge Raad 16 May 2008, *NJ* 2008, 824 (Chubb/Europoint); Hoge Raad 11 October 2002, *NJ* 2003, 416 (Aegon/Veeneman).

46 Hoge Raad 18 October 2002, *NJ* 2003, 503.

47 Hoge Raad 18 October 2002, *NJ* 2003, 258.

48 Hoge Raad, 15 April 1977, *NJ* 1978, 163 (Staalcom/Neher). Also see Veenstra, 'Uitleg van een collectieve regeling tot vergoeding van massaschade'.

norm, and the Supreme Court has held that the mere involvement of a party who was not involved in the negotiation and formation of the contract does not alter that.[49]

Consequently, evidence of the parties' understandings at the time of conclusion of the contract and subsequent conduct by the parties remains admissible to establish the meaning to be attributed to the contract terms. This means that even information that is not publicly available, but which shaped the understanding and expectations of Print Master and PPS would continue to influence the interpretation of the contract once Magnificall became involved. On that basis, in light of the background material at the formation of the outsource agreement, it would be reasonable for Print Master to attribute to Clause 16(k) the meaning that the quality tests would be conducted twice per week and also to expect PPS to share that understanding. That being said, *DSM-Chemie/Fox* does establish a sliding scale, and the relevant circumstances have to be considered in light of the standards of 'redelijkheid en billijkheid' [reasonableness and fairness] and the circumstances of this case may indicate that it would be unreasonable and unfair to subject Magnificall, who has become a party to this contract without having access to this information, to an interpretation that is not linguistically obvious. In that case, less weight would be given to the pre-contractual evidence if this has not been made available to Magnificall.

10. POLAND

Pursuant to Polish law (Arts. 509 et seq. of the KC), the fact that the transfer of rights was valid means that Magnificall obtained all the rights and obligations of PPS arising on a contractual basis. However, the content of the contract does not change with the change of the parties.[50] Therefore, the court would probably first establish the content of the contract between the initial parties thereto. Here, the moment when the parties' common intention is to be established is the moment when the original parties made the declaration of intentions (an *ex tunc* interpretation).[51]

Polish courts would need to first investigate the parties' common intentions since, as explained in the Opening Remarks, that is in accordance with the mixed method of interpretation. Only if the common intention cannot be

49 See Hoge Raad 20 September 2002, *NJ* 2002, 610 (ING/Mullers); Hoge Raad 18 October 2002, *RvdW* 2002, 164 and 166.

50 G. Bieniek et al., *Komentarz do Kodeksu cywilnego, Księga Trzecia Zobowiązania*, p. 546.

51 Z. Radwański, *Wykładnia oświadczeń woli składanych indywidualnym adresatom*, pp. 78–79, Z. Radwański, *System Prawa Prywatnego*, vol. 2, p. 59.

established will the court interpret the terms of the contract referring to the objective criteria.

Since Polish courts accept any evidence in order to establish the common intentions of parties, the background material is also admissible as evidence,[52] even if it does not constitute part of the contract, as long as it were proven that neither party objected to its content.[53] The SN underlined, however, that in certain circumstances the initial (pre-contractual) communications of the parties may become irrelevant as a result of concluding the contract.[54]

In this case, according to the pre-contractual materials, the initial parties to the contract understood Clause 16(k) as requiring that quality tests be conducted twice a week. As a result, the content of the contract established between the initial contractual parties would also be binding on Magnificall, even though it did not participate in negotiating and drafting the contract, and even though PPS is no longer a party to the agreement. Most probably, Polish courts would hold that Magnificall was supposed to investigate what the content of the legal relation was when it decided to become a part of it. The rule remains that a transfer of contractual rights and obligations to another person does not change the content of those rights and obligations. Upon being asked about this case, members of the Polish judiciary and academia suggested that it was the duty of the transferee to investigate the state of matters. The practising lawyers also pointed out the obligation on the part of the transferor to disclose the information. If evidence of the common understanding was privately or publically available, that could influence the burden of proof as to when the duty to investigate or the duty to disclose was sufficiently performed, but would not eliminate these duties.

11. PORTUGAL

In this case there is a transfer of rights and Magnificall did not take part in the negotiations. Normally, evidence of a common understanding or intention of the parties is relevant to prove their intentions. PPS is no longer a party to the contract, but the position of Magnificall must be the same as that of PPS due to the transmission of the position from PPS to Magnificall according to Art. 424.° CC.

The word 'bi-weekly' must be interpreted according to the rules present in Art. 236.° CC, i.e. in terms of a 'declaratário normal' [reasonable person] in

52 Judgment of SN of 31.01.1983, IV CR 380/82; Judgment of SN of 03.09.1998, I CKN 815/97.

53 Judgment of SN of 04.07.1975, III CRN 160/75; Judgment of SN of 02.07.2004, II CK 271/04; Judgment of SN of 05.10.2005, II CK 122/05; Judgment of SN of 17.12.2008, I CSK 250/08; Judgment of SN of 17.06.2009, IV CSK 90/09.

54 Judgment of SN of 15.08.1975, I CR 462/75.

the position of Magnificall. However, if PPS has a common understanding of Clause 16(k), this interpretation will also be relevant for Magnificall. Therefore, the evidence of a common understanding or intention of the parties can be used to prove Print Master's intention, even if this evidence is private. In the case of a transfer of rights, the position of Magnificall would be the same as that of PPS.[55]

If PPS shared the same interpretation as Print Master, it would be considered against 'boa fé' [good faith] in the context of the performance of the obligations in the contract that Magnificall could put forward an alternative interpretation and, once again, an 'abuso direito' [abuse of a right] in terms of Art. 334.° CC can be used to exclude Magnificall's interpretation.

The fact that Magnificall did not take part in the negotiations is not relevant, since in the case of a 'transmissão da posição contratual' (transmission of rights and duties) Magnificall will step into the place of PPS.

The principle of confidence is recognised in Portuguese law as a subprinciple of 'boa fé'.[56] According to that principle, the declaration of a party is understood in the sense that the addressee could in good faith attribute to it, and it would be considered against good faith that Magnificall defends an interpretation that was not the common understanding of Print Master and PPS, because Magnificall is now in the position of PPS.

12. SCOTLAND

Scots law has a general rule against the admissibility of evidence of prior negotiations of the parties as an aid to construction.[57] Therefore, on the face of that general rule, it would appear that the background material between Print Master and PPS about how they agreed they would perform their obligations under the contract is irrelevant. However, a distinction is made between evidence of (1) prior negotiations and (2) prior negotiations which can be taken into account as part of the surrounding circumstances when the contract was entered into. Prior negotiations can be considered part of the surrounding circumstances, and thus admissible. Things said and done in the process of negotiation may be part of the surrounding circumstances. The facts must be known to both parties and can cast light on the commercial purpose of the

---

55 See Da Mota Pinto, *Cessão da Posição Contratual*, p. 5.

56 See Menezes Cordeiro, *Da Boa Fé no Direito Civil*, p. 1234, and Da Frada, *Teoria da Confiança e Responsabilidade Civil*, p. 17.

57 See *Chartbrook Ltd v Persimmon Homes Ltd* [2009] UKHL 38; [2009] 1 AC 1101; *Luminar Lava Ignite Ltd v Mama Group plc and Mean Fiddler Holdings Ltd* [2010] CSIH 01; 2010 SC 310.

transaction or the meaning which the parties gave to the words in question.[58] Admittedly, as recognised by the Scottish Law Commission, there is a very difficult line to be drawn between the permissible and impermissible use of pre-contractual material.[59]

Although the matter is finely balanced, if we take the view that the background material passing between Print Master and PPS is not subjective in nature on the ground that it provides evidence of mutual agreement between the parties as to how Clause 16(k) would operate, then it indeed would be admissible as evidence. This evidence would tend to work in Print Master's favour.

Turning now to the position of Magnificall as an assignee, its argument runs that it is not bound by any construction reached on the strength of the background materials between Print Master and PPS at the inception of the contract. The policy consideration here is that assignees 'should be protected from secret meanings attached to contracts by the original contracting parties'.[60] However, speaking extra-judicially, Lord Bingham was dismissive of the position of assignees as presenting a practical problem.[61] Furthermore, Lord Bingham's sentiments were echoed by Lord Hoffmann in *Chartbrook Ltd v Persimmon Homes Ltd*:

> Ordinarily, however, a contract is treated as addressed to the parties alone and an assignee must either inquire as to any relevant background or take his chance on how that might affect the meaning a court will give to the document. The law has sometimes to compromise between protecting the interests of the contracting parties and those of third parties. But an extension of the admissible background will, at any rate in theory, increase the risk that a third party will find that the contract does not mean what he thought. How often this is likely to be a practical problem is hard to say.[62]

---

58 See *Luminar Lava Ignite Ltd v Mama Group plc and Mean Fiddler Holdings Ltd* [2010] CSIH 01; 2010 SC 310, 320 per Lord Hodge.

59 Scottish Law Commission, *Review of Contract Law: Discussion Paper on Interpretation of Contract* (Scot Law Com Discussion Paper 147, 2011), para. 5.19. Following a more recent consultation, the Scottish Law Commission decided not to recommend legislative change to the law governing interpretation of contract (*Report on Review of Contract Law: Formation, Interpretation, Remedies for Breach and Penalty Clauses* (Scot Law Com No. 252, 2018)). Reasons given include both mixed responses to their consultation, and two Supreme Court cases which have clarified the law: *Arnold v Britton* [2015] UKSC 36; [2015] AC 1619 and *Wood v Capita Insurance Services Ltd* [2017] UKSC 24; [2017] 2 WLR 1095 (see the Report, paras. 2.13–2.14).

60 Scottish Law Commission, *Review of Contract Law: Discussion Paper on Interpretation of Contract* (Scot Law Com Discussion Paper 147, 2011), para. 6.12. See also *National Bank of Sharjah v Dellborg* [1997] EWCA Civ 2070.

61 Lord Bingham, 'A New Thing Under the Sun? The Interpretation of Contract and the ICS Decision', p. 388.

62 [2009] UKHL 38; [2009] 1 AC 1101, 1120B–G at para. 40 per Lord Hoffmann.

To conclude, therefore, the Scottish courts are unlikely to treat the situation any differently given that PPS has assigned its rights under the agreement to Magnificall. The conclusion reached above, namely that the background material would be admissible, is unchanged.

13. SOUTH AFRICA

The effect of an assignment[63] is that the assignee steps into the shoes of the original debtor (in this case PPS), who in turn ceases to be a contracting party. The content of the original contract remains the same and Magnificall can acquire neither greater nor lesser rights and duties.[64] This construction of the effect of assignment means that a court will not treat Magnificall as a third party, but rather as a contracting party. Although there does not appear to be any case law on the question whether an assignee is bound by the meaning of the contract as understood by the original contracting parties, this conclusion has been reached by the then Appellate Division in the context of a cession, on the basis that the cessionary steps into the shoes of the cedent and cannot, as a general rule, acquire greater rights than the cedent.[65]

By analogy, Magnificall would probably be bound by the meaning of the terms of the original contract as understood by Print Master and PPS – the fact that it was not a party to the negotiation or drafting of Clause 16(k) would be irrelevant. In any event, a third party would be bound by the meaning of the contract as accepted by the original contracting parties, unless some reason exists to protect the third party's reliance on the apparent meaning of the contract.[66] One such reason may be that Print Master and PPS created the impression that 'bi-weekly' meant twice a month, and Magnificall could not test the correctness of this representation (for example, because the material recording the original parties' understanding was only privately available). In such a case, Magnificall could raise the defence of estoppel so that a court could give effect to its understanding of the word 'bi-weekly'.[67]

---

63 This term usually denotes a transfer of both rights and duties in South African law (*Simon v Air Operations of Europe AB* 1999 1 SA 217 (SCA) 228H–I). On the facts, it appears that the 'transfer of rights' from PPS to Magnificall actually involved a transfer of both rights and duties and therefore the term 'assignment' is used in this answer.

64 *Van Achterberg v Walters* 1950 3 SA 744 (T) 745H; Bhana and Nortje, 'Principles of Contract', p. 245.

65 *Sampson v Union and Rhodesia Wholesale Ltd (In Liquidation)* 1929 AD 468, 482–483.

66 *Aussenkehr Farms (Pty) Ltd v Trio Transport* 2002 4 SA 483 (SCA) paras. 25, 27. There are therefore no special rules governing the use of extrinsic evidence to interpret a contract when a third party is involved.

67 Ibid., para. 27. See also Case 2, Question 2 and Case 3.

In any event, the background material presented by Print Master to support its contention that 'bi-weekly' means twice a week, and not once every fortnight, may be excluded if evidence of prior negotiations is inadmissible as a matter of course (see Case 3, Question 1).

14. SPAIN

Given that Clause 16(k) is ambiguous, the interpreter should identify the common intention of the parties through Art. 1.282 CC.

The evidence of a common understanding or intention of the parties presented by Print Master sheds light on the actual meaning of the expression 'bi-weekly' used in that clause. As a result, this meaning should be accepted by Spanish courts according to the aforementioned Art. 1.282; despite the fact that it only considers acts at the time of and subsequent to the contract, scholars and jurisprudence also accept acts prior to the contract.[68] Besides, the word 'acts' is meant in a broad sense, including documents, notes and so on. The preliminary or pre-contractual negotiations (written or oral) also play an important role in discovering the common intention of both parties (see Case STS 01.02.2016 ECLI:ES:TS:2016:322 regarding contractual interpretation solved by integrating the contract with the pre-contractual information signed by the parties). Therefore, the whole demeanour of both parties is relevant in order to find the real and common intention of the parties.

Given that Clause 16(k) is ambiguous, this evidence of a common understanding or intention of the parties presented by Print Master should be considered as a reflection of the common intention of the parties, thus binding Magnificall, who enters into the contract in the same position as PPS had. Magnificall subrogates to PPS's position and must assume the same rights and obligations, unless something new had been negotiated between them, which is not the case here. It is irrelevant that evidence was publicly available in order to bind Magnificall.

Therefore, it does not matter that Magnificall did not take part in the negotiation, drafting and conclusion of the contract. It still must comply with the common intention of the parties, which was the existing intention at the formation and conclusion of the contract.[69]

In addition, Magnificall does not have to conduct quality tests daily, as PPS used to do, because this was part of its own company policy.

---

68 See STS 09.02.1981 (RJ 1981\533); STS 06.10.1989 (RJ 1989\9888); STS 03.09.2007 (RJ 2007\4709).

69 Díez-Picazo, *Fundamentos*, p. 498.

15. SWEDEN

When assessing the scope of Magnificall's obligation to conduct quality tests under the contract, the meaning attributed to Clause 16(k) by Print Master and PPS will, under Swedish law, be accorded decisive weight by the courts. There is very little room for doubt. This conclusion follows, firstly, from the fact that, according to the settled principle of 'den gemensamma partsviljans företräde' [prevalence of the common intention of the parties],[70] the contract is to be interpreted according to the common understanding of the parties at the time of the conclusion of the contract, if such an understanding can be established; and secondly, because a transfer of rights does not affect the content of the rights transferred – this general principle can be regarded as a consequence of privity of contract (contracts do not bind third parties, and so the contract entered into by PPS and Magnificall cannot have any detrimental effect on the legal position of Print Master) and follows *ex analogia* from the Promissory Notes Act (1936:81) Section 27, which states that, when a 'enkelt skuldebrev' [simple note] – i.e. a note that is not negotiable – is assigned to a new creditor, the creditor's right against the debtor is not improved by the assignment.[71]

Deciding on this issue is a matter of law, not a matter of fact, seeing as the conclusion is arrived at through the application of a legal principle enshrined in a statutory provision. And it is not, strictly speaking, a matter of contract interpretation (since we *know* what the parties intended, which is to say that the question of what meaning should be attributed to Clause 16(k) does not arise). To sum up, the fact that PPS is no longer a party to the agreement and Magnificall did not take part in the negotiation, drafting and conclusion of Clause 16(k) will not be considered relevant by the courts when determining the legal effects of that clause. If Magnificall wants to recover, the claim must be directed towards PPS.

16. EDITORIAL COMPARATIVE OBSERVATIONS

In this particular case, reporters for the majority of the jurisdictions indicated that the evidence offered by Print Master – that they and PPS had a common understanding or intention at the conclusion of their contract that Clause 16(k) meant that service quality tests would be conducted twice per week – would

---

70 See the Opening Remarks.

71 See Mellqvist and Persson, *Fordran och skuld*, p. 151, Rodhe, *Obligationsrätt*, p. 134 ff. and 739. Cf. NJA 1997 p. 866, where the Supreme Court held that a third party, acquiring rights through a transfer, was bound by an arbitration clause in the agreement between the original debtor and the original creditor.

indeed be taken into account by a court. This was the legal position in the case of Croatia, Finland, Germany, Greece, Poland, Portugal, Spain and Sweden. These jurisdictions could be contrasted with England and Wales and South Africa, however, where such evidence would be inadmissible. As jurisdictions grounded in the common law tradition, the classic interpretative rule that pre-contractual negotiations cannot be taken into account would be applied in England and Wales and South Africa. In both these jurisdictions, Print Master's evidence would be treated as pre-contractual negotiations and, as such, drenched in subjectivity. The embargo on the admissibility of prior negotiations would also apply in Scotland, but the reporters for Scotland did highlight a certain subtlety in the Scottish rules of interpretation which would likely persuade a court to have regard to Print Master's evidence. Here, a distinction would be drawn between evidence constituting 'prior negotiations' – which cannot be considered by the Scottish court – and 'background material' forming part of the factual matrix and circumstances surrounding the formation of the contract between Print Master and PPS. The reporters suggested that Print Master's evidence would likely fall within the latter category, in which case it would indeed be taken into account by a Scottish court.

Certain jurisdictions occupy a half-way house between the extreme positions of Croatia, Finland, Germany, Greece, Poland, Portugal, Spain and Sweden on the one hand, where Print Master's evidence would be considered, and England and Wales and South Africa, on the other hand, where it would not. For example, the reporters for France and Italy highlighted that the courts would likely look at Print Master's evidence, which would take precedence, but that this was subject to a proviso or condition. In the case of France, the proviso arguably constitutes a meta-legal formant, in the sense that certain economic policy factors would be considered by a French court. Here, the French court would not treat Print Master's evidence as conclusive of itself, but instead would investigate the financial impact of Print Master's preferred interpretation on the assignee Magnificall, including the balance of risk and reward in the contract between Print Master and Magnificall. As such, it is not guaranteed that Print Master would succeed in convincing the court of its favoured construction, particularly if the price agreed by Magnificall in terms of the assignment was not a good economic deal for it. Meanwhile, the applicable proviso in Italy is slightly more subtle. Here, the Italian courts would account for the failure of Print Master and PPS to perform the contract subsequent to its formation, by looking to the purpose of the contract, and interestingly, they would use good faith as a means of protecting the reasonable reliance of Magnificall.

In conclusion, we can see that each of the jurisdictions adopt different approaches as to whether Print Master's evidence of a common understanding or intention would be taken into account. But what is particularly notable by its absence is any rule which would provide special dispensation to

Magnificall simply because it is an assignee, i.e. there is no rule in any of the jurisdictions which has as its target the protection of assignees from hidden private constructions.

Other factors or rules that would play a part in the interpretative task of the court include whether the law imposes a legal duty on the assignee Magnificall to investigate the meaning afforded by Print Master and PPS to the contractual term 'bi-weekly', for example in Croatia and Poland. Moreover, in the case of the latter jurisdiction, Poland, it would be incumbent on PPS to disclose the interpretation of the contractual term 'bi-weekly' when it entered into an assignation with Magnificall. A similar position would be adopted in Greece, although the principle of 'self-responsibility' would be applied in order to reach such a result. As for good faith, this potentially plays a live role in Italy and Greece. As such, in each of these jurisdictions, i.e. Croatia, Poland, Italy and Greece, the fact that the 'meaning' attributed by Print Master and PPS to the contractual term was private, rather than public, in nature will be borne in mind by the court and may play a significant role in the interpretation that they eventually reach. This can be contrasted with jurisdictions such as Sweden, where it would be irrelevant whether Print Master and PPS's understanding of the meaning to be attributed to the clause was private or public in nature: in both cases of private or public understandings, Magnificall would be bound by Print Master's and PPS's private or public interpretation.

CASE 7: BISCUIT

'Hartley Ceramics' is a company which makes ceramics. 'Arkwright Homecare' is a retailer. Both are small companies, formed relatively recently. In December 2011, the managing director of Hartley Ceramics, Ian, entered into a contract with the then managing director of Arkwright Homecare, John, agreeing that Hartley Ceramics would supply Arkwright Homecare with 500 pieces of specialist ceramics. Clause 1 of the contract describes the pieces to be delivered as 'biscuit'. After the commencement of the contract, Ian was replaced by Barton, who is now the manager at Hartley. In early 2012, Hartley delivers the first consignment of pieces of ceramics at Arkwright Homecare's offices. However, John is surprised when he discovers that the pieces that Hartley delivered are fired but not glazed. He presents background material at the formation of the agreement, which shows that both he and Ian understood 'biscuit' to mean fired and glazed. John refuses to take delivery of the ceramic pieces but is nonetheless set on having the contract performed as he interprets it. Barton refutes John's claim. He argues that 'biscuit' is a well-known and established term in the ceramics industry, used to indicate that the pieces are fired but not glazed. Apparently, Barton continues, John and Ian both attributed the same but unconventional meaning to the term 'biscuit'. Therefore, Barton concludes, Hartley performed the contract properly and Arkwright should accept the delivery.

Assume that the term 'biscuit' does indeed normally mean fired but not glazed, and that Hartley Ceramics can provide sufficient evidence to prove that both Ian and John were negotiating on a shared but unusual understanding that 'biscuit' meant both fired and glazed. If the background material satisfies the requirements for it to be accepted by a court as evidence in your jurisdiction, what weight can be given to the fact that Ian and John were negotiating on a common but incorrect understanding of 'biscuit' in interpreting Clause 1 of the contract?

1. KEY ISSUES

This case continues a theme already seen in Case 6, namely whether the interpretative process changes in any way where a change of persona has taken place after formation of the contract. In Case 7, the managing director of one of the contracting parties has changed. Reporters are required to consider the relevance to the dispute of common understandings which existed at the point of formation. Again, the dispute involves a new person, not present at the point of formation. That new person is confronted with the possible use of evidence relating back in time to formation. In contrast to Case 6, in Case 7 the same companies are involved: the relevant change is a change of managing director in one company only. The dispute centres on the meaning of a technical term used in the ceramics industry: 'biscuit'. At the point of formation, the original directors shared a common, but *erroneous* and unconventional, understanding of 'biscuit'. The new managing director does not share that understanding, preferring the meaning which is established and well known in the industry in question. Background material exists, dating from the point of formation, which supports the original shared but erroneous meaning. Reporters are asked to consider what weight can be given to that evidence in the later dispute involving the new managing director. The issue shows broad similarities to a famous German case which may be known to those interested in contract interpretation. This is the *Haakjöringsköd* case, in which both contracting parties erroneously thought that 'haakjöringsköd' was the Norwegian word for whale meat, when it is, in fact, the Norwegian word for shark meat.[1] The similarity exists at a broad general level only: Case 7 is based on completely different facts and raises additional issues.

2. CROATIA

According to the general rules on the interpretation of contractual terms, contained in Art. 319(1) of the COA, contractual clauses apply as they read. Where contractual terms are clear, one cannot argue that the intention of the parties departs from the written terms. Interpretation of clear contractual terms would contradict the concept and the very purpose of the process of interpretation.[2] However, where the contractual term is unclear or is disputed, a court may depart from the ordinary (literal) meaning of the expressions used, and rely on the common intention of the parties (Art. 319(2) of the COA).[3] The background material at the formation of the contract shows that John's and Ian's intention was to understand Clause 1, and the term 'biscuit', as indicating that pieces of specialist ceramics had to be fired and glazed. This departs from the common understanding of the term in the ceramics industry, where it means that ceramics have to be fired but not glazed. If the term 'biscuit' is considered to constitute a trade usage, then according to the Art. 12(2) of

1 RG 8 June 1920, RGZ 99, 147.
2 Gorenc et al., *Komentar Zakona o obveznim odnosima*, p. 468.
3 Ibid., p. 469. See also VSRH, Revr 468/06-2 of 16 January 2008.

the COA, its meaning established by traders in the same type of relations is applicable between the contracting parties, unless the parties excluded its application explicitly or implicitly. Therefore, the question arises whether John and Ian have implicitly excluded the ordinary meaning of the term 'biscuit' adopted in this industry. Background material at the formation of the contract shows that John and Ian have reached an agreement on the meaning of the term 'biscuit' which was different from the established meaning of the same term in the ceramics industry. Since the starting point for contract interpretation is the contracting parties' common intention,[4] a court would give priority to Ian's and John's common understanding of the term 'biscuit' over the meaning established in the ceramics industry. Such an interpretation is based not only on the parties' explicit statements, but also on their conduct. Consequently, one can argue that they both implicitly excluded the ordinary meaning of the word 'biscuit' from the contract.

Moreover, it has to be emphasised that, according to Art. 319(2) of the COA, the true meaning of the term 'biscuit' has to be determined not only by investigating the common intentions of the parties, but also through its understanding in the context of the principles established by the COA. First, it would be contrary to the principle of good faith or, if the phrase 'načelo savjesnosti i poštenja' is literally translated, the 'principle of conscientiousness and honesty', in Art. 4 of the COA to uphold Barton's argument that both John and Ian attributed the same but unconventional meaning to the term 'biscuit'. This principle requires the contracting parties to make an effort in understanding the other party's statements in a way that the other party wanted them to be understood. Barton's insisting on an understanding of the term 'biscuit' that departs from Ian's and John's common and actual intention might be characterised as against the *bona fides* principle. Second, the common intention of the parties to a contract has to be examined in the light of another principle, the principle of due care, according to which parties have a duty to perform their obligations with a certain degree of quality, this standard being higher for professionals (Art. 10 of the COA). To give effect to Barton's defence would be contrary to the principle of due care because this would in fact exonerate Hartley Ceramics from its duty of due care. The duty of due care has to be exercised not only in the performance of the contract but also in the negotiation and conclusion of the contract.[5] Hartley Ceramics, a company producing ceramics, was in a better position than Arkwright Homecare, a retailer, to understand the true meaning of the term 'biscuit' and to make additional efforts, according to its duty of due care, to do everything in order to avoid, at the time the contract was concluded, agreement on such an

4 Gorenc et al., *Komentar Zakona o obveznim odnosima*, p. 469.

5 Kačer, Radolović and Slakoper, *Zakon o obveznim odnosima s komentarom*, p. 292.

unconventional meaning of the word 'biscuit' as in the case at hand. Since Hartley Ceramics failed to do so, the acceptance of Barton's defence would in fact exonerate it from its duty of due care.

Therefore, by applying the subjective criterion within the limits of the objective criterion according to Art. 319(2) of the COA, the Croatian court would probably rely on Ian's and John's common understanding of the term 'biscuit', irrespective of the fact that their incorrect understanding departs from the ordinary meaning in the ceramics industry. Such an approach seems to be accepted both in the Croatian court practice and legal theory, according to which faulty expressions cannot prejudice the meaning that the contract parties actually intended to achieve by virtue of a certain contractual clause (*falsa demonstratio non nocet*).[6] The purpose (intention) of the contract cannot fail to be achieved due to the deficiencies in the means (words).[7]

3. ENGLAND AND WALES

English law does not ask what the correct or dictionary meaning of words used is, but rather asks what the parties could reasonably be understood to mean by their contract. Nevertheless, the court will presume that parties intend the usual (e.g. dictionary, or trade) meaning of any word.[8] Such a presumption will be rebutted in this case if Hartley is able to show that it and Arkwright contracted on the basis of a private shared meaning of 'biscuit', or (as English law calls it) a 'private dictionary'. English law admits evidence that parties habitually used words in an unconventional sense to support the case that they meant the words to be used in that sense, much like a trade usage or custom may show that a larger group uses a word in a particular sense.[9] The principle can only be used where the parties are using the word in an unconventional sense, and not to distinguish between two alternative conventional senses of a word.[10]

Accordingly, the court would ask whether Ian and John's common but incorrect understanding of 'biscuit' amounted to habitual use of the word in an unconventional sense. If their incorrect understanding of 'biscuit' was reached

6 Cigoj, *Komentar obligacijskih razmerij*, p. 345.

7 Perović and Stojanović, *Komentar zakona o obligacionim odnosima*, p. 345.

8 *Hold & Co. v Collyear* (1881) 16 Ch D 718 (Fry J) at 720.

9 *Chartbrook Ltd v Persimmon Homes Ltd* [2009] AC 1101 (HL) at para. 45 per Lord Hoffmann.

10 Ibid., explaining *Partenreederei MS Karen Oltmann v Scarsdale Shipping Co. Ltd (The Karen Oltmann)* [1976] 2 Lloyd's Rep 708 (Kerr J). In the latter situation, the court can employ rectification or estoppel by convention but not the private dictionary principle (which is part of the rules of ordinary construction): *Chartbrook*, ibid., at paras. 46–47.

independently and never tested between them (i.e. they never used the word in a way in which the difference between their meaning and the ordinary meaning would be apparent) then the private dictionary principle would probably not apply even though subjectively both Ian and John intended the same meaning – there had been no establishment of a private dictionary through usage. But if the lack of glazing in biscuit ceramics was adverted to by them, then the word was used between them in an unconventional sense (as in Case 6). In that case, the private dictionary meaning would probably take precedence, unless the court reached the view that a reasonable person in the parties' position would not understand them to intend any unconventional sense, for example if they knew that Ian was shortly to leave Hartley and that the supply contract was to be examined by third parties (such as banks) in a situation in which the detail of the products supplied would be important (and would have to be apparent solely from the words used in the contract).[11]

4. FINLAND

In the interpretation of contracts, words are to be interpreted according to their ordinary and common meaning.[12] Technical terms, on the other hand, are to be interpreted according to their technical meaning, unless it is apparent that the parties did not intend such an interpretation. However, due to the principle of freedom of contract, the parties can give words – also technical terms – whatever meaning they want.[13]

The objective of the interpretation of contracts is to determine the mutual intention of the parties at the time of contracting.[14] In this case, Ian and John, as the representatives of the contracting parties, were both of the understanding that the term 'biscuit' meant fired and glazed. The fact that the meaning of 'biscuit' is normally understood differently in the ceramics industry is

---

11 See further the discussion of Case 6.

12 See Annola, 'Tavallisuussäännön asema sopimustulkinnassa'; Aho, *Varallisuusoikeudellisen oikeustoimen tulkinnasta*, p. 255; Hemmo, *Sopimusoikeus I*, p. 650; and Pönkä, 'Tavoitteellisten tulkintasääntöjen merkityksestä liikesopimusten tulkinnassa', p. 932. See also the Finnish Supreme Court's decision 2018:37.

13 Hemmo, *Sopimusoikeus I*, pp. 607–620; KM 1990:20 pp. 22–23; Saarnilehto, *Sopimusoikeuden perusteet*, p. 153; and Telaranta, *Sopimusoikeus*, pp. 102–103. See also decision KKO 1996:7 in which the Finnish Supreme Court expressed that terms may be interpreted contrary to their ordinary and common meaning if it is evident that this is the intention of the contracting parties.

14 See Annola, 'Tavallisuussäännön asema sopimustulkinnassa'; Aho, *Varallisuusoikeudellisen oikeustoimen tulkinnasta*, p. 255; Hemmo, *Sopimusoikeus I*, p. 650; and Pönkä, 'Tavoitteellisten tulkintasääntöjen merkityksestä liikesopimusten tulkinnassa', p. 932. See also the Finnish Supreme Court's decision 2018:37.

irrelevant in determining the intention of the parties because, as mentioned, the parties may use technical terms in whichever manner they please. Ian's and John's mutual understanding of the term 'biscuit' will most certainly play a decisive role in the interpretation of Clause 1.

5. FRANCE

Judicial interpretation requires contractual ambiguity. The contract was concluded in 2011 between the representatives of the two parties according to a meaning of the term 'biscuit' that is unusual but was shared by the two representatives. At the time of the performance of the contract, the representative of the supplier has changed. The new representative, Barton, invokes the usual technical meaning of the disputed term in the ceramics industry.

Since the contract was concluded before 1 October 2016, its interpretation is governed by the old provisions of the Civil Code. Under Art. 1156 Cciv, the court will first look for the common intention of the parties. Under French law, pre-contractual negotiations may be used to prove the common intention of the parties. Hartley Ceramics and Arkwright Homecare are the two parties to the contract. During the pre-contractual negotiation and at the conclusion of the contract, the two companies were lawfully represented respectively by Ian and by John. As far as John can prove that he shared with Ian the understanding that 'biscuit' refers to fired and glazed pieces, this meaning of the term 'biscuit' can be identified as the common intention and understanding of the parties to the contract. As such, it prevails over the usual technical meaning invoked by Barton. The fact that this meaning is unusual is irrelevant.[15] Hartley Ceramics is party to the contract concluded by Ian and bound by its terms as they were understood at the time of its conclusion. The fact that Hartley Ceramics' representative has changed in the meantime is also irrelevant to the interpretation of the contract and cannot justify a change in the meaning of the term 'biscuit' at the time of the performance. As stated by Art. 1134 Cciv, the contract is the 'law of the parties' and shall be performed in good faith, which requires performance by Hartley Ceramics in a way that complies with the meaning of 'biscuit' that was agreed upon between Ian and John at the time of the conclusion of the contract.

---

15 On multiple occasions, the Cour de cassation has ruled that in the case of common error of the parties, the contract must be interpreted according to the genuine common intention of the parties as it has been clearly – even if erroneously – expressed by them: Civ., 25 August 1856, *S.* (1857), 37; Civ. 3, 15 February 1972, *RTDCiv.* (1972), 616; Civ. 1, 7 February 1989, *Bull. civ.* (1989) no. 63.

6. GERMANY

When concluding the contract Hartley Ceramics was 'vertreten durch' [represented by] Ian under §164 BGB and John represented Arkwright Homecare. After the conclusion of the contract, Ian was replaced by Barton.

From a German perspective, such a change of the agent does not affect the interpretation of a clause within the contract. In fact, the interpretation of a contract clause depends on the circumstances at the time of the conclusion of the contract.[16] As to intention and its defects, as a rule the intention of the agent actually acting is determinative: see §166 (1) BGB.

However, the case assumes that the common understanding of John and Ian of the term 'biscuit' differs from a usual or normal understanding, which says that 'biscuit' normally means fired but not glazed. Under German law, in this kind of case the rule of '*falsa demonstratio non nocet*' [false description does not vitiate] applies. Therefore, the common understanding proven prevails over the usual or natural meaning of the wording of the contract. Since the famous decision of the Reichsgericht in the case of 'Haakjöringsköd', in which both parties mixed up the Norwegian expression for shark meat, it has been accepted by the courts that this kind of mistake of both parties does not affect the interpretation.[17] This rule shows again how important the subjective approach to interpretation under German law is. There may be exceptions, where the parties deliberately use the wrong terms to mislead public authorities[18] (see §117 BGB on sham transactions) or where the *falsa demonstratio* rule conflicts with a formal requirement.[19]

In the case at hand, Hartley Ceramics can provide sufficient evidence to prove that both Ian and John were negotiating on an objectively incorrect but common understanding that 'biscuit' meant both fired and glazed. This background material could satisfy the requirements in order to be accepted by German courts. As a result, the common understanding of 'biscuit' of Ian and John could prevail over the usual or natural meaning of the wording of the contract.[20] Neither the agency itself nor the change of the agent affects this result.

---

16 M. Wolf, '§157 BGB' in H.-T. Soergel, *Bürgerliches Gesetzbuch mit Einführungsgesetz und Nebengesetzen*, vol. II, m.n. 51.

17 Reichsgericht, 08.06.1920, *RGZ* 99, 147, 148; see also for the application of this rule in a recent decision: BGH, 29.01.2015, BGHZ 204, 83.

18 This may be the factual background of Reichsgericht, 06.08.1920, *RGZ* 99, 147, which however was not argued in court.

19 Cf. R. Singer '§133 BGB' in N. Habermann (ed.), *J. von Staudingers Kommentar zum Bürgerlichen Gesetzbuch*, vol. I, m.n. 14, 36.

20 J. Busche, '§157 BGB' in K. Rebmann and F.J. Säcker (eds.), *Münchener Kommentar zum Bürgerlichen Gesetzbuch*, m.n. 51.

7. GREECE

In the case at hand, the intention and knowledge of the parties are decisive, pursuant to the subjective criterion of Art. 173 CC. Insofar as the intention of the parties and their understanding of the contractual terms coincides, it is irrelevant whether they both made false language usage when formulating their declarations of intent, as long as they were under the same false impression (*falsa demonstratio non nocet*).[21] Art. 173 CC already prescribes that, when interpreting a declaration of intent, the true intent of the parties is to be given precedence, regardless of the meaning of the wording used. When interpreting a contract, one must begin with the subjective criterion of interpretation and, when this suffices in order to reach a satisfactory interpretation that is commonly accepted by the parties, the objective criterion of Art. 200 CC is superfluous.[22]

In this case, the court would begin by examining what exactly became the object of the agreement between Hartley and Arkwright. It would also look to see if the persons who concluded the agreement, namely John and Ian, were indeed representing their respective companies, thus binding them. The facts offer no guidance as to the corporate form of Hartley and Arkwright; nonetheless, the rules on both personal and capital-based commercial companies in Greek law generally bind those companies to the acts of their representing organs, and even when those organs act beyond the scope of the powers attributed to them by the law or the founding agreement of the company (e.g. its articles of incorporation or its partnership agreement).[23] Therefore, the court, taking into account the agreement together with the background material confirming the common but erroneous understanding of the parties at the time of conclusion of the contract will most probably give precedence to this understanding of the term 'biscuit' by Ian and John over its established meaning, because in the context of interpretation of contracts the (common) will of the parties prevails as the result of the rule of private autonomy.[24]

---

21 Georgiades, *General Principles*, §41 no. 17; Filios, *General Principles*, §243 Δ.; Ladas, *General Principles*, §34 no. 29; Stathopoulos, *Civil Code*, vol. 1^{B}, Arts. 173 and 200 nos. 52, 82.

22 See Papanikolaou, *Methodology*, §§505–506; cf. Karassis, *General Principles*, §§ Γ 289–291, 295–296.

23 See Arts. 756, 759 CC on companies under the CC; Art. 86 Law 4548/2018 on stock corporations (GGI A' 104/13 June 2018); Art. 18 Law 3190/1955 on limited liability companies (GGI A' 91/1955), as amended.

24 Papanikolaou, *Methodology*, §506; Ladas, *General Principles*, §34 no. 29.

8. ITALY

This case raises a problem of conflict between the common intention of the parties and the objective and established meaning of the term in the business sector concerned.

The background material presented by John is relevant under Art. 1362 c.c. because it evidences the common intention of the (original) parties. Barton's contention as to the objective and established meaning of the term 'biscuit' in the ceramics industry is relevant under the same Art. 1362, para. 1, insofar as it refers to the literal meaning of the term, which is addressed by this article as the first relevant interpretation factor.

In principle, according to the literal wording of Art. 1362 c.c.,[25] the common intention of the parties should prevail, even though it is not exactly consistent with the proper usual meaning of the contractual text.

However, the majority (so far) of judicial precedents adopt a peculiar interpretation of Art. 1362 and of the relationship between the literal text of the contract and other possible factors (such as the background material presented by Hartley Ceramics) evidencing the common intention of the parties. According to this position, if the literal meaning of the contractual text is clear and unambiguous, it is deemed sufficient to express the parties' intention and, therefore, no further analysis aimed at the search for a different intention would be allowed. This approach, which in fact equates a 'clear' literal meaning with common intention, is summarised with the (unconvincing) maxim *in claris non fit interpretatio* [clear text does not need any interpretation].[26]

Assuming that the literal meaning of the term 'biscuit' is clear and uncontroversial (as Barton submits), if the court follows this traditional approach one would suppose that the case would be harder for Hartley Ceramics. However, it can be realistically expected that the evidence provided by Hartley Ceramics would be a relevant factor which may convince a judge to assign to the term the 'incorrect' subjective meaning shared by the parties. It is reasonable to suppose that in order to overcome the common literal meaning of the term 'biscuit', Hartley Ceramics will need to provide quite persuasive evidence showing that both parties had clearly attributed to the clause a peculiar meaning to convince the judge that the ordinary meaning of the contractual text in fact diverges from the parties' common intention. In addition, the court would probably feel compelled to specifically justify its decision by assuming some hypothetical ambiguity of the term or by emphasising the conclusiveness of the evidence provided by Hartley Ceramics and the

25 See Case 1.
26 See Case 1 n. 56.

consequent evident divergence between the contractual text and common intention.

A minority of judicial decisions and almost all scholars argue, more consistently with the text of Art. 1362, that the literal meaning should never be a primary factor for the interpretation and that the court should always consider it in connection with other subjective factors showing the common intention of the parties.[27] According to this position, the evidence provided by Hartley Ceramics would more easily lead to the prevalence of the subjective 'incorrect' meaning.

9. NETHERLANDS

The *Haviltex* norm explicitly states that the literal meaning of a word used in a contract is not determinative of the word's interpretation.[28] A contract is to be interpreted according to the meaning that each party could reasonably attribute to the terms of the contract and which each party could reasonably have expected the other to have attributed to it. Although the reference to reasonable expectations does not make it apparent, contract interpretation in the Netherlands is in the first place aimed at discovering the actual common intention or understanding of the parties.[29] A subjective interpretation founded on the shared common intention of the parties prevails over an interpretation based on (primarily) objective factors.

This starting point is not affected by the Supreme Court's decision in *DSM-Chemie/Fox*,[30] in which it was said that the interpretation of a written contract will each time depend on all the facts and circumstances of the individual case, assessed in accordance with the standards of 'redelijkheid en billijkheid' [reasonableness and fairness]. The purpose of the Supreme Court's consideration in that case was to reconcile two apparently contradictory interpretation norms (the CAO and *Haviltex* norms) by explaining that both norms must be positioned on a sliding scale of subjective and objective approaches to interpretation and that they have a common foundation – the relevant facts and circumstances and 'redelijkheid en billijkheid' [reasonableness and fairness].[31] The reference to 'redelijkheid en billijkheid' is not meant to objectify the interpretation process to undercut the relevance of the parties' actual, subjective intentions. If a shared common understanding

27 See Case 1 fn. 55.
28 Hoge Raad 13 March 1981, *NJ* 1981, 635 (Ermes/Haviltex).
29 Tjittes, *Uitleg van schriftelijke contracten*, p. 11.
30 Hoge Raad 20 February 2004, *NJ* 2005, 493 (DSM-Chemie/Fox).
31 Tjittes, *Uitleg van schriftelijke contracten*, p. 12; Asser/Sieburgh, *Algemene leer der overeenkomsten*, 6-III, no. 362.

can be established, it is reasonable and fair that the clause be interpreted in accordance with it. In that case, the actual common intention of the parties is a decisive factor in the interpretation of the contract in accordance with 'redelijkheid en billijkheid' [reasonableness and fairness].[32]

Although the primary objective of interpretation is to establish the actual common intention of the parties, this does not involve delving into the inner minds of the parties, which would in any case be impossible. This is what makes references to intention somewhat misleading, since it involves a psychological phenomenon that cannot be objectively verified. The focus is on finding the common intention of the parties as manifested in their statements and conduct.[33] The proof of the parties' common intention will depend on accessible circumstances, which may also include more objective factors such as the nature of the contract, the negotiation history, and the conduct of the parties before and after the conclusion of the contract.[34]

Consequently, if a contracting party can provide evidence of a common intention or understanding with respect to the meaning to be attributed to a particular contractual expression, the court will prefer an interpretation that accords with that common intention as opposed to an interpretation based on other, more objective, factors.[35]

The background information from the formation of the contract showing that both John and Ian understood 'biscuit' to mean fired and glazed is admissible to show that the parties shared a common understanding with respect to the meaning to be attributed to 'biscuit' in their contract. This evidence shows that it is reasonable for Ian to understand 'biscuit' as meaning fired and glazed and it was reasonable for him to expect John to also understand 'biscuit' to mean the same thing.

10. POLAND

The background materials would be accepted before Polish courts as evidence to prove the content of the contract (see further comments to Case 6).

According to the SN,[36] the real intentions of the parties should be taken into account in the first place, in order to establish the real content of the declaration of intent. The SN has clearly declared[37] that Art. 65 para. 2 of the KC allows a situation where the real meaning of the contract, established

32 Tjittes, *Uitleg van schriftelijke contracten*, p. 12; Tjittes, *Commercieel Contractenrecht*, p. 263.
33 Tjittes, *Uitleg van schriftelijke contracten.*
34 Ibid.
35 Ibid., pp. 11–12.
36 Judgment of SN of 29.06.1995, III CZP 66/95.
37 Judgment of SN of 17.06.2009, IV CSK 90/09.

using the interpretation directives indicated by this provision, will be different from the 'clear' meaning, established on the basis of language rules. The process of interpretation may end in establishing the 'clear' meaning only when the meaning of the contract is 'clear' after applying subsequent rules of interpretation – in other words, the interpretation process should not be reduced to a literal interpretation of the contract.[38] It means that, at present, Polish courts act according to the rule of *falsa demonstratio non nocet*.[39] Polish legal writing refers to the classic German textbook example here: the parties concluded a contract of sale for 'Haakjöringsköd', which in Norwegian means 'shark', but both parties understood as 'whale'.[40]

Applying this rule, the SN stated,[41] for example, that if a declaration includes a word that has a meaning defined in a legal act (for example 'rent'), then this meaning should be binding on the parties, unless it follows from the context that it was supposed to have another meaning for the parties.[42] In another case, the SN declared that Art. 65 of the KC does not impose such an interpretation of the declarations of the parties, which would attribute to the expression 'right of withdrawal' used by the parties the meaning that this expression has in legal language, i.e. 'uprawnienie prawnokształtujące' [entitlement that creates legal effect].

The *clara non sunt interpretanda* rule was abolished by the SN in one of its judgments,[43] where the SN referred to the criticism of this rule in legal writing. Legal writing convincingly claims that Art. 65 of the KC does not limit the application of the interpretation rules only to 'unclear' contract terms. Art. 65 allows for a situation when the proper (real) sense of the legal act, considering the context of the declaration of intentions of the parties thereto, will be different from its 'clear' meaning according to the language rules.

In conclusion, if Ian and John were negotiating on a common but incorrect understanding of the term 'biscuit', then that understanding is binding when interpreting Clause 1 of the contract.

11. PORTUGAL

If both parties use the term 'biscuit' when sharing an unconventional understanding of this term, this situation is called *falsa demonstratio non nocet*. If both parties share the same interpretation, even if the term used was

38 Z. Radwański, *System Prawa Prywatnego*, vol. 2, p. 54.

39 Ibid., p. 53; F. Zoll, A. Rachwał and U. Ernst, *Prawo cywilne, Część ogólna*, p. 112.

40 Z. Radwański, *System Prawa Prywatnego*, vol. 2, p. 53, F. Zoll, A. Rachwał and U. Ernst, *Prawo cywilne, Część ogólna*, p. 112.

41 Judgment of SN of 25.03.2004, II CK 116/03.

42 Judgment of SN of 15.11.1968, III CZP 104/68.

43 Judgment of SN of 07.12.2000, II CKN 351/00.

not correct, this use is relevant under Art. 236.°/2 CC. According to Art. 236.°/2 CC, the declaration should be interpreted by giving it the meaning that both parties share. Hence, in this case, the real intention is relevant, assuming that both parties knew the other party's real intention.

The director of Hartley has been replaced. According to the Portuguese system, the party to the contract is still Hartley, not the manager. The interpretation of Ian therefore binds Hartley, the corporation, and also Barton with his interpretation of the term 'biscuit'. It would be considered against good faith were Barton to impose his own interpretation of the word 'biscuit' despite the fact that this is the correct use of the term. These elements are the result of the application of Arts. 236.°/2 and 334.° CC.

One of the characteristics of contract interpretation in the Portuguese system is the focus on the subjective intent of the parties, the presence of *falsa demonstratio non nocet* [an erroneous designation does not impair]. The court will accordingly uphold the subjective intentions if the parties to the agreement express a certain intention, but the subjective intentions of the parties differ.[44]

12. SCOTLAND

The issue which arises is whether the term 'biscuit' is a term in ordinary usage or whether it is will be classed by the court as a 'technical term'. A leading author, Gloag, confirmed that it is possible to lead evidence of foreign or technical terms.[45] It seems likely that Barton would seek to lead expert evidence as to the meaning of 'biscuit' in the ceramics industry in support of its interpretation.

The more significant issue in the case is, however, whether the parties both used the word 'biscuit' in a particular way. As McBryde explains: 'if the parties are agreed that their expression had a special meaning, that "X" really meant "Y", the court should not impose the meaning "X"'.[46] This issue was considered

44 In a decision from the Portuguese courts RLx 7 March 1996 (Silva Salazar), CJ XXI (1996) 2, 74–77, it was said that the *falsa demonstratio non nocet* rule is destined to give satisfaction to the real intention of the parties. Both parties used the words intending it to bear a different meaning from the correct meaning. In this case it is not enough to have knowledge of the meaning that the other party gives to the expression. There must also be an agreement between both parties concerning this alternative meaning. In another decision, STJ 13 November 2003 (not published) (criticised by Menezes Cordeiro, *Tratado de Direito Civil*, p. 738), the court decided that the agreement between the parties concerning the meaning that one party had adopted was not needed and the contract was interpreted according to the real intention regardless of the agreement of the other party. Menezes Cordeiro, *Tratado de Direito Civil Português*, p. 738.

45 Gloag, *Contract*, p. 365.

46 Interestingly, he gives no case as authority for this point, quoting only another textbook, Walker and Walker, *Evidence*, edited by M. Ross and J. Chalmers (2nd edn, 2000), para. 27.19.3.

in detail in the Scottish Law Commission Report on Interpretation in Private Law.[47] This report cites a Scottish case in which it was clear, through extrinsic evidence held to be admissible, that the parties to the contract had used the term 'Whitsunday' in an unusual sense to mean 26 May, and that meaning was held to prevail.[48] The report also notes[49] an English case in which there was a contractual option to redeliver a chartered vessel 'after 12 months trading'. The parties were in dispute as to whether this meant at any time after the expiry of the 12-month period or rather on the expiry of the 12-month period. Pre-contractual telexes were led as evidence which suggested that the parties had used the expression to mean 'on the expiry of 12 months'. Kerr J found the evidence of the pre-contractual telexes to be admissible. He considered that such evidence would allow the court to identify which of two possible meanings was the one which was used by the parties.[50]

The Bill produced by the Scottish Law Commission in 1997 (which was not enacted) incorporated a rule on this point. This envisaged that the special meaning would be given effect if every other party at the time of contracting knew or could reasonably have been assumed to know that it was being used in that sense.[51]

Extrinsic evidence would be required in order to establish the special shared meaning of 'biscuit'. The English and Scottish cases referred to above suggest that, as a general rule, extrinsic evidence is admissible for this purpose. It seems highly likely that a Scottish court would find the extrinsic evidence in this case to be admissible. The question describes this material as 'background material at the formation of the contract.' This type of information is likely to be admissible as part of the factual matrix, using a contextual approach.[52] The date of the evidence would be crucial. If it was dated too far in advance of the date of formation, it would be classed as prior communings and thus inadmissible.[53] Equally, if it was dated too far after the date of formation, it would be classed as post-formation conduct and thus inadmissible.[54] Provided it is coextensive with formation, it will be admissible.

---

47 At paras. 3.3–3.21. See also the more recent Discussion Paper on Interpretation of Contract (D.P. No. 147), February 2011, paras 7.16–7.17.

48 *Hunter v Barron's Trs* (1886) 13 R. 883 and see also *Houldsworth v Gordon Cumming* 1910 SC (HL) 49, where a party offered to sell 'the estate of Dallas'. This phrase was interpreted in accordance with the court's idea of the special meaning agreed by the parties, i.e. the estate marked on an identified plan as the estate of Dallas and not another estate going by that name.

49 Para. 3.5.

50 *The Karen Oltmann* [1976] 2 Lloyd's Rep 708 at 713.

51 Clause 3(1)(2).

52 *Wood v Capita Insurance Services Ltd* [2017] UKSC 24; [2017] 2 WLR 1095 at para. 10.

53 *Inglis v Buttery* (1877) 5 R 58 per Lord Gifford at 59–60, approved by Lord Blackburn 5 R HL 87 at 102; *Prenn v Simmonds* [1971] 1 WLR 1381 per Lord Wilberforce at 1384.

54 McBryde, *Contract*, paras. 8-30–8-33.

13. SOUTH AFRICA

In terms of the traditional approach to interpretation, evidence that the parties have attributed their own, unconventional meaning to a word was always admissible, even in the absence of ambiguity.[55] If this exception continues to apply under the current approach to interpretation, then the meaning which John and Ian attributed to the word would be decisive.

On the assumption that the exception does not apply, it is possible that a court would accept the argument that the evidence establishes the meaning which the parties have attributed to a particular word as an objective fact, and as such, should be taken into account as part of the factual matrix.[56]

If this second argument does not succeed (because, for example, the background material presented by John forms part of the prior negotiations and the rule excluding such evidence is absolute), then the only way in which effect could be given to the parties' incorrect understanding of the term 'biscuit' would be to seek rectification of the agreement.[57]

14. SPAIN

Assuming that the term 'biscuit' does indeed normally mean fired but not glazed and that Hartley Ceramics can provide sufficient evidence to prove that both Ian (former director of Hartley Ceramics) and John (Arkwright Homecare's director) were negotiating on a common but incorrect understanding that 'biscuit' means both fired and glazed, Art. 1.281 CC combined with Art. 1.282 CC will be the first and most important rules to be applied (see Case 3).

According to Spanish legal doctrine, Art. 1.281 CC asks the interpreter to reconstruct the common thought and intention of both parties at the time of conclusion of the contract (historical interpretation).

Article 1.282 CC provides that the background material can be used as evidence of the common understanding of the word 'biscuit'. Such material can be taken into account according to legal doctrine and jurisprudence, which interprets 'acts' in a broad sense, including those prior to the conclusion of the contract (see Cases 3 and 6). In consequence, if this material offers evidence that the meaning assumed by both parties at the time of the conclusion of the contract was the same, this common and evident intention

---

55 *Richter v Bloemfontein Town Council* 1922 AD 57 70; *Rand Rietfontein Estates Ltd v Cohn* 1937 AD 317 327; Bradfield, *Christie's Law of Contract*, p. 250.

56 This argument is made by Santow J in *Spunwill Pty Ltd v BAB Pty Ltd* (1994) 36 NSWLR 290 309–310. See also McLauchlan, 'Common Assumptions', p. 237.

57 See Case 3, Question 1.

must prevail. This arises from Art. 1.281, the second paragraph of which says that where the words seem contrary to the evident intention of the contracting parties, the latter shall prevail over the former. In consequence, the Supreme Court states in STS 04.11.2016 (ECLI:ES:TS:2016:4717) that the search for the real intention of the parties must be the guiding principle. The literal interpretation has an instrumental character, and is the starting point of the interpretative phenomenon, but the intention represents the basis of the contract which is actually the criterion of contractual interpretation.

In addition, equally relevant is the fact that both companies are small companies which were set up relatively recently. Therefore, the interpreter may conclude that they did not yet know the technical meaning at the time of the conclusion of the contract.

For commercial contracts, Art. 57 CCom says even more clearly that contracts must be fulfilled in good faith, pursuant to the terms under which they were made and drafted.[58] There should be no restriction of their effects against the way in which both parties have expressed their will (see Case 2).

Spanish courts will accept the common understanding of the word 'biscuit', even if it was incorrect.

As for the succession in the management of Hartley Ceramics, Barton enters after the conclusion of the contract made between Ian and John, so he must assume the contract as carried out by Ian, the former director, regardless of the fact that he was incorrect in his usage of the term 'biscuit'. We reiterate the point that this 'wrong' meaning was shared by the other party and that it made up the common intention of the contract.

15. SWEDEN

The courts will, without hesitation, conclude that Clause 1 is to be read in accordance with the understanding shared by Ian and John at the time of conclusion of the contract. The fact that the parties were, in one sense, mistaken, is, in other words, immaterial.[59] This follows from 'den gemensamma

---

58 See STS 21.05.2010, ECLI:ES:TS:2010:2651; STS 04.11.1994 (RJ 1994\8368).

59 Section 32(1) of the Contracts Act offers some support for this conclusion. The provision contains the Swedish rule on 'förklaringsmisstag' [declarative mistake]. According to this rule, where a legal subject makes a mistake when declaring his legal intentions, resulting in a discrepancy between the actual content of the declaration and the meaning that the subject intended to convey, the declaring party is bound to his declaration, interpreted objectively, unless the receiving party was in 'ond tro' [bad faith] – i.e. knew or should have known – of the mistake. It should follow that, if both parties are mistaken, objectively speaking, albeit they both knew what was intended, they should not be considered bound to their joint declaration interpreted objectively. That they, in this situation, rather should be bound to what they jointly intended might, be said to follow *ex analogia* from Section 6(2) of the Contracts Act; see Lehrberg, *Avtalstolkning*, p. 41 ff.

partsviljans företräde' [prevalence of the common intention of the parties].[60] In the textbooks, it is customary, in the present context, where a mistake has been made by both parties jointly, to refer to the old Roman maxim *falsa demonstratio non nocet.*[61] It matters not how well established or how widespread the conventional understanding is. The conventional understanding will have to yield if the parties in reality shared a different interpretation, simply because the aim of the interpretative process is to establish what *they* meant.[62] The courts would really not find anything to discuss in this case.[63]

The fact that Ian later was replaced by Barton has no impact on the content of the contract.[64] The content is dependent on the intentions of the parties at the time of conclusion of the contract. Subsequent events are of relevance when interpreting the contract only insofar as they show what the parties intended at that time.[65]

16. EDITORIAL COMPARATIVE OBSERVATIONS

The reporters for all the jurisdictions reached the same conclusion on the relevance of the fact that both Ian and John were negotiating on a common but incorrect understanding of 'biscuit' in interpreting Clause 1 of the contract. The court is likely to give effect to the common intention of the parties. In all jurisdictions, the court will give effect to that meaning because at the time of concluding the contract, both Hartley and Arkwright (through John and Ian) attributed to the word 'biscuit' a particular, though erroneous, meaning.

Some jurisdictions reach this solution by the application of civil code provisions. This includes Croatia, France, Greece, Italy, Poland, Portugal and

60 See the Opening Remarks.

61 See e.g. Adlercreutz and Gorton, *Avtalsrätt II*, p. 58; Karlgren, *Avtalsrättsliga spörsmål*, p. 50 f.; Lehrberg, *Avtalstolkning*, p. 43; J. Ramberg and C. Ramberg, *Allmän avtalsrätt*, p. 131 f.; Vahlén, *Avtal och tolkning*, p. 97; Vahlén, *Formkravet vid fastighetsköp*, p. 84.

62 See the answer to Case 2, Question 1, at n. 95.

63 How the relation between the objective and the subjective elements of interpretation is to be understood is, though, the subject of much debate in Swedish contract law *theory*. Out of tradition – realist heritage and all – there is a strong tendency to favour the objective side. Critics have claimed that some moderation is called for, considering that interpretation remains subjectively oriented, i.e. striving for ascertaining the common intention of the parties, where possible. See e.g. Grönfors, *Avtalsgrundande rättsfakta*, p. 18 ff., 27; Grönfors, *Tolkning av fraktavtal*; Høgberg, *Kontraktstolkning*, p. 99 ff.; Lehrberg, 'Anm av Grönfors, Avtalsgrundande rättsfakta'; J. Ramberg, *Avtalsautonomi och den dispositiva rätten*; Samuelsson, *Tolkningslärans gåta*, p. 186 ff.; Samuelsson, *Tolkning och utfyllning*, pp. 63 ff., 425 ff.

64 See e.g. NJA 2011 p. 316.

65 See e.g. NJA 2007 p. 962; NJA 2012 p. 1095.

Spain. Others referred to precedents or legal cases which would guide the court towards this result. This would include England and Wales, Germany, the Netherlands, Scotland, South Africa and Sweden. In these cases, precedents are used perhaps because interpretation falls outside the civil code (Germany and the Netherlands) or because the jurisdiction is not codified (England and Wales, Scotland and South Africa). Poland makes use of both codal provisions and precedents.

In Finland, the law is embodied in 'legal literature and practice'. In Sweden, the operative rules can be found in the principle of 'den gemensamma partsviljans företräder', translated as the principle of the prevalence of the common intention.

In Germany, Greece, Poland, Portugal and Sweden, the reporters suggested that the Latin maxim *falsa demonstratio non nocet* would be relevant to the outcome of this case. This can be translated as meaning that a false description will not injure or vitiate, provided the thing or person has once been sufficiently described.

In France, Portugal and Spain, good faith has an impact. In Portugal, for example, it would be against good faith for Barton to impose an interpretation which differs from the original usage of the term 'biscuit'.

As to the reason for giving weight to the parties' attribution of an incorrect meaning to contractual terminology, we see a split between, on the one hand, the legal systems in which the aim of the interpretative exercise is to reach the true, subjective common intention of the parties, and, on the other, those in which a more objective aim is pursued. The majority of the legal systems fall into the former category.[66] This can be seen vividly in the Polish report, where the reporter notes that, according to the SN (Supreme Court), 'the real intentions of the parties should be taken into account in the first place, in order to establish the real content of the declaration of intentions.' So too in the Greek report the reporter notes that 'the intention and knowledge of the parties are decisive, pursuant to the subjective criterion of Art. 173 CC.' Thus the court departs from what would otherwise be the objective meaning of the contractual wording where the parties have a shared but erroneous subjective understanding of those words and phrases.

In England and Wales, Scotland and South Africa, the aim is to find out what the contract would mean to a reasonable person in the position of the contracting parties. South Africa is perhaps the most emphatic, with its rejection of the point that identifying the subjective common intention is the goal of the interpretative exercise.

Where the aim of the interpretative exercise in a particular legal system is to give effect to the shared subjective intention of the parties, it is not

66 Croatia, Finland, France, Germany, Greece, Italy, Netherlands, Poland, Portugal, Spain and Sweden.

surprising that the court in this case reaches the conclusion that the shared but erroneous understanding of a technical term is upheld by the courts. But where the interpretative method involves asking what the words would mean to a reasonable person in the position of the contracting parties at the time of formation, as is the case in England and Wales, Scotland and South Africa, an outcome upholding the shared but erroneous subjective understanding of a technical term appears anomalous. These legal systems, uncharacteristically, in this case uphold the shared subjective intention of the parties.

English law applies a presumption in this area: the court will presume that the parties intend the popular meaning of any word. This presumption may be rebutted if the parties can show that they are contracting on the basis of a private shared meaning. This is known in England and Wales and Scotland as the 'private dictionary rule'. Thus, a subjective outcome can be reached in a jurisdiction which has, at its basis, an objective interpretative approach.

Almost all the legal systems indicated that the court would take into account the fact that Ian and John shared an incorrect meaning of the word 'biscuit' in reaching the conclusion that this meaning would be upheld. Background material that supports this fact, however, is used in different ways and for different purposes.

One could say that Croatian, English, Finnish, German, Italian and Scots law apply a more 'mechanistic' approach, which shows greater adherence to the literal, natural, normal, or technical meaning of the word 'biscuit' as a first stage. Background evidence is brought in as a second stage to depart from the impression created at the first stage. This can be contrasted with legal systems which take a more holistic or unified approach, with less evidence of a prior adherence to the literal meaning. In these systems, the background evidence plays a more central role in the interpretative exercise. It is not relegated to a second stage.

Some legal systems would, as a first step, apply the 'normal' meaning of the word 'biscuit'. Background material can be used in order to depart from that normal meaning. This is the case in English law, where a presumption is applied that parties intend the popular meaning of the word. Background material is used to overturn, or rebut, that presumption.

In German law, this is part of the application of the Latin maxim *falsa demonstratio non nocet*,[67] exemplified by the 'Haakjöringsköd' case.[68] Thus in German law the 'common understanding proven prevails over the usual or natural meaning of the wording of the contract.'

Other legal systems identify the first step as the application of the 'technical', rather than the 'natural' or 'normal', meaning of the word. In Finland,

67 As already noted, this maxim is also referred to in the national reports from Germany, Greece, Poland, Portugal and Sweden.

68 Also referred to in the Polish report.

background material is used in order to prove that the parties did not intend the technical meaning. In Scots law, evidence is admissible in order to assist the court in the understanding of a foreign or technical term. As is the case in Finnish law, however, in Scots law the technical meaning of 'biscuit' would not be applied if the parties were able to establish a special, shared meaning of the term. Such evidence is admissible.

Croatia and Italy seem to emphasise a literal approach in particular, in contrast to the other legal systems.

CASE 8: CRATES OF BEER

'Goldwater' operates a beer brewery and 'Carryon' operates a road haulage company. The two companies enter into a contract in January 2012 in terms of which Carryon agrees to transport Goldwater's beer to a wholesale depot located 50 kilometres away. Clause 8 of the contract governs the collection of the beer by Carryon. It provides: 'Goldwater will make the beer available to Carryon at the brewery premises located at [details of the address].' In February, Carryon's driver arrives at the brewery and finds that the crates of beer that he is to collect are located on the fourth floor of the brewery. He will be unable, without assistance, to move the crates to the ground floor and load them on to the haulage vehicle. When he asks for assistance, he is told that none is available due to redundancies at the brewery. Carryon's driver leaves the brewery without collecting the beer. Carryon refuses to perform, arguing that Goldwater should have made the crates available at the front entrance of the brewery. Goldwater disagrees. It made the beer available at its premises, as was agreed in Clause 8 of the contract. It, therefore, raises an action against Carryon for breach of contract. Carryon disagrees with Goldwater's reading of Clause 8. It argues that Goldwater and Carryon have an ongoing business relationship and that under every previous contract between them, Goldwater consistently made the crates of beer available at the front entrance of the brewery. Clause 8, Carryon concludes, must be understood in the light of these facts.

Assume that the previous contracts between Goldwater and Carryon were identical in all significant respects. Also assume that the contract does not specify on which floor the crates are to be collected and that there is no local trade custom relevant to the matter at hand. To what extent may the manner of performance of the previous contracts between Carryon and Goldwater be given weight in the interpretation of Clause 8 of the 2010 contract?

1. KEY ISSUES

This is a case in which the dispute relates to the mechanics of delivery of goods under a contract between a manufacturer of goods and a road haulage company. The parties have differing interpretations of the terms of the contract governing the location at which the goods should have been made available to the haulage company for collection and onward delivery. The road haulage company seeks to make use of a previous and consistent course of dealing between the parties to support its interpretation of the disputed clause of the contract. The case makes clear that no local custom governs the issue. In this way, reporters are encouraged to focus on the relevance and importance of a previous course of dealing in the interpretative exercise.

2. CROATIA

Under assumptions that the previous contracts between Goldwater and Carryon were identical in all significant respects, that the contract does not specify on which floor the crates are to be collected, and that there is no local trade custom relevant to the matter at hand, the manner of performance of the previous contracts concluded between Carryon and Goldwater should be taken into account in the interpretation of Clause 8 of the 2012 contract.

According to Art. 319(2) of the COA, in interpreting a disputable contract clause the courts have to investigate the common intention of the parties to a contract (subjective criterion), and the clause must be understood in accordance with the principles of the law on obligations established by the COA (objective criterion). In the case at hand, the Croatian courts would use the manner of performance of the previous contracts as an objective criterion setting the parameters for establishing the common intention of Goldwater and Carryon. In doing so, the courts would observe the principle of due care (Art. 10 of the COA) in conjunction with the provision on usages and practices (Art. 12 of the COA). Pursuant to Art. 10(2) of the COA, in performing obligations relating to their professional activities, the parties must act with increased care in accordance with professional rules and usages. This is also applicable to the practices established between them. Also, in interpreting Clause 8, the Croatian courts would consider Art. 12(1) of the COA, which provides that any trade usages agreed upon by the contracting parties-traders, as well as *mutually developed practices* between the contracting parties-traders, shall apply to obligations between them. These statutory provisions enable the courts to use the prior course of dealing between Goldwater and Carryon as a ground for determining their common intention in order to interpret disputed clauses. According to these provisions, each party has a duty to act according to an established practice, which in order to be binding has to be consistent and repeated. It is not disputable that Goldwater and Carryon have an ongoing business relationship. Within this business relationship they have established a specific *modus operandi*, namely, Goldwater have always made the crates of beer available at the front entrance of the brewery. Therefore, Carryon, when concluding a new contract with Goldwater in January 2012, had reasonable expectations that the same *modus operandi* would be followed in the performance of the new contract. If Goldwater wanted to put an end to such a practice it had a duty to inform Carryon thereof. The duty to communicate stems from the principle of a duty to cooperate, which is provided for in Art. 5 of the COA. Moreover, the principle of a duty of due care also imposes on a contracting party a negative obligation. According to Art. 10(3) of the COA, in exercising their rights, parties to a contract must refrain from any action that may hinder the other party's performance. Consequently, Goldwater had a duty of due care to follow previously established practice. Moreover, Goldwater had to avoid any changes to its *modus operandi* in performing the new contract, unless it informed Carryon of the modifications related to the performance. Furthermore, any such deviation from the mutually developed practice arising between the parties would also be considered a breach of the 'načelo savjesnosti i poštenja' [principle of conscientiousness and honesty] laid down in Art. 4 of the COA.

In addition to setting the parameters and enabling the courts to interpret the parties' common intention, the above-mentioned provisions united under the objective criterion serve also to enhance the most important principle of contract law – the principle of preserving a contract. Interpretation *in favorem contracti* is the paramount criterion the courts have to observe in interpreting disputed clauses. Hence, in interpreting the contract or its clauses, the courts have a duty to aim at preserving the contract and its clauses rather than depriving them of their legal effects. This leads to the conclusion that the Croatian courts would interpret Clause 8 in line with the previously established practice between Goldwater and Carryon also because this would be *in favorem contracti*.

3. ENGLAND AND WALES

Evidence of usage between parties is admissible to show what parties meant by a term. This is essentially the same as the private dictionary principle discussed in Case 7. However, that may well not resolve the dispute between Carryon and Goldwater, as the fact Goldwater previously made the crates of beer available at the front entrance of the brewery does not mean that the parties necessarily treated Goldwater as contractually obliged so to do. It may have just been something Goldwater did to help Carryon, but that the parties never treated Goldwater as being obliged to, and it has been said that for a usage to imply part of an obligation into a contract it must be established as a practice having *binding* effect.[1] But ultimately the question remains one as to what a reasonable person in the parties' positions would understand Goldwater and Carryon to be required to do: given the past practice, when parties entered

[1] *Cunliffe-Owen v Teather & Greenwood* [1967] 1 WLR 1421 (Ungoed-Thomas J) at 1438.

into subsequent contracts, such as the 2012 contract, would they reasonably have understood Carryon to be obliged to do any more than attend at the front entrance of the brewery? Practical factors known to both parties may well point to this conclusion: for example, if a road hauler would usually use only a single driver and a single driver would be unable to carry the crates far (e.g. because the crates can only be moved for anything more than a small distance with a forklift truck), or if the driver would have no way of safely entering and manoeuvring the crates through the brewery (e.g. while brewing is ongoing). If the reasonable person would not understand Goldwater to be *obliged* to deliver the beer to the front entrance, then the contract will not require that, and there is no general principle of good faith in English law that can supplant the terms of the contract to nevertheless require this of Goldwater.

4. FINLAND

As has been emphasised above, the objective of the interpretation of contracts is to determine the mutual intention of the parties at the time of contract.[2] It is usually reasonable to assume that if a certain contract clause has been customarily understood by the contract parties in a certain way, the interpretation remains the same in new similar contracts with the same clause. There are only few Finnish Supreme Court decisions touching upon the relevance of the parties' earlier contractual practice in the interpretation of certain new legal acts; more discussion is found in the legal literature. In the legal literature, it is considered to be obvious that the previous contractual practice of the parties can be taken into account as one possible interpretation argument.[3] This necessitates, however, that the compared contracts are sufficiently similar in their contents and purpose. The more uniform the previous material is, the more relevant it becomes when interpreting the new legal act.[4] Thus it must be taken into account whether the expressions or the other behaviour of the contracting parties includes features which can be intended to mean divergent conditions of the contract. In addition, the interval between contracts cannot be too long.[5] It can also be taken into account that in contracts where the contents and purpose are uniform, it is possible to deviate completely from the previous regulations and the expressions of the legal act between the parties.[6]

---

2 See Hemmo, *Sopimusoikeus I*, p. 604; Saarnilehto, *Sopimusoikeuden perusteet*, p. 149; and Telaranta, *Sopimusoikeus*, p. 94.

3 Aho, *Varallisuusoikeudellisen oikeustoimen tulkinnasta*, p. 220; Hemmo, *Sopimusoikeus I*, p. 591; and Telaranta, *Sopimusoikeus*, p. 107.

4 Aho, *Varallisuusoikeudellisen oikeustoimen tulkinnasta*, p. 220.

5 Hemmo, *Sopimusoikeus I*, p. 591.

6 Aho, *Varallisuusoikeudellisen oikeustoimen tulkinnasta*, pp. 220–221.

However, there exists one Finnish Supreme Court decision (KKO 1976 II 44) which clearly shows the significance of previous contractual practice in the interpretation of the contract. In this case, A, a professional seller of motorboats and equipment, had sold a used outboard motor of brand X to B. A had given a 'sailing season guarantee' for the motor. The sales contract had later been terminated, and A had sold B another motor of brand Y. A had not given B any guarantee for the motor. However, the Supreme Court held that A was responsible for the durability of motor Y in the same way as he had been responsible for motor X, because he had not notified B of the essential change to the contract terms.

5. FRANCE

In a contract concluded in 2012 between Goldwater, a beer brewery, and Carryon, a road haulage company, Clause 8 provides that 'Goldwater will make the beer available to Carryon at the brewery premises located at …'. The ambiguity of the clause results from the fact that it fails to mention where exactly in Goldwater's premises the beer is to be made available.

Since the contract was concluded before 1 October 2016, its interpretation is governed by the old provisions of the Civil Code. Pursuant to Art. 1156, French courts search for the common intention of the parties. From this perspective, they may take into account not only the behaviour of the parties both before and after the conclusion of the contract,[7] but also previous contractual relations between the parties[8] or even with third parties.[9] In the present case, the court would take into account the fact that Goldwater always made the crates available at the front entrance of its premises for the previous contracts. As a consequence, Carryon developed the habit of sending the driver alone to take care of the collection of the brewer's beer. Without prior warning, the transporter could not be expected to anticipate a change in Goldwater's interpretation of the contract.

The court may also consider Art. 1134 (3) Cciv, according to which contracts shall be performed in good faith. A duty of collaboration between the parties may indeed be derived from this article and may justify that the parties do not render the performance of their co-contracting party more difficult.[10] This duty to collaborate would be all the more likely to be recognised given

7 Civ. 1, 7 May 1956, *Bull. civ.* (1956) no. 179; Com., 22 March 2005, no. 02-15.357.

8 Soc., 21 February 1957, *Bull. civ.* (1957) no. 205; CA Poitiers, 20 February 1991, *D.* (1991), 315.

9 Civ. 1, 24 January 1967, *Bull. civ.* (1967) no. 33.

10 Civ. 3, 17 July 1992, *Bull. civ.* (1992) no. 254; Civ. 1, 16 April 1996, *JurisData* no. 1996-001680; CA Paris, 27 April 1998, *JurisData* no. 1998-020939.

that Goldwater has previously consistently brought the crates to the front door, which could rightfully induce Carryon's expectation that it would still be the case for future contracts.

6. GERMANY

The question in the case at hand is whether a manner of performance of previous contracts in an ongoing business relationship between Carryon and Goldwater is to be taken into account in the interpretation of Clause 8 of the 2012 contract.

A custom established between the parties is usually not in itself binding on the parties, but serves as a key element of the interpretation of contracts concluded between them.[11] Therefore, the development of the ongoing business relationship of the parties, such as an established custom, serves as an important and often decisive argument for the interpretation of clauses like Clause 8.[12] Additionally, arguments based on a custom may also help to fill gaps of the contract by 'ergänzende Vertragsauslegung' [supplementary interpretation] or implication of terms.

In particular, such a custom may be used to explain the wording of a term like Clause 8. The custom then serves as an argument for what is usually understood by the parties when using these words.[13] In the case at hand, all previous contracts were identical in all significant aspects, such as the place of collection of the beer in front of the entrance of the brewery. Although there is no binding trade custom relevant in the sense of §346 'Handelsgesetzbuch' [HGB], Goldwater and Carryon implemented a 'Verkehrssitte' [custom of trade] under §157 BGB by always performing in the same way during their ongoing business relationship.[14] A 'Verkehrssitte' may only apply in the interpretation process, if it is in line with 'Treu und Glauben' [the good faith principle].[15] The 'Verkehrssitte' does not show the individual intentions of the parties but helps to interpret the declarations and to detect their usual meaning in an objective way.[16] Furthermore, German law recognises a supplementary

---

11 BGH, 29.01.2003, *NJW-RR* 2003, 926: the development of the ongoing business relationship is a key element of the interpretation. In contrast to that, a custom between the parties in an employment contract may become binding on the parties, see C. Picker, *Die betriebliche Übung*.

12 J. Busche, '§133 BGB' in K. Rebmann and F.J. Säcker (eds.), *Münchener Kommentar zum Bürgerlichen Gesetzbuch*, m.n. 54.

13 Ibid., m.n. 21.

14 Ibid., m.n. 21.

15 M. Wolf, '§157 BGB' in H.-T. Soergel, *Bürgerliches Gesetzbuch mit Einführungsgesetz und Nebengesetzen*, vol. II, m.n. 63.

16 BGH, 01.12.1965, *NJW* 1966, 502.

'Verkehrssitte' under §§242, 157 BGB, which not only helps in interpreting the terms of a contract but also supplements the contract.[17] In fact, the 'Verkehrssitte' gives substance to 'Treu und Glauben' and contributes to legal certainty.[18]

It is worth mentioning that without a rule in the contract, Goldwater would even have to stow the goods under §412(1) HGB. §412(1) HGB provides that this is the case if there is no local trade custom and no contractual custom to the contrary.

7. GREECE

In the case at hand, there is a disagreement between Goldwater and Carryon as to the place where the goods to be transported are to be made available to the carrier. Therefore, the subjective criterion of Art. 173 CC cannot lead to any satisfactory result and the objective criterion of Art. 200 CC is crucial.[19]

The objective criterion relies upon the 'καλή πίστη' [good faith] and the 'συναλλακτικά ήθη' [trade customs]. Trade customs relevant to the issue at hand do not exist. However, the manner of performance of the previous contracts can be decisive in determining the precise content of 'καλή πίστη' in the case at hand. It was mentioned above that elements outside the text of the agreement, the so-called 'συγκείμενα' [proximates],[20] may be used in order to determine what the parties should and could have been reasonably expected to understand in the specific context of the agreement. The court examines not only the text of the agreement, but also the surrounding circumstances,[21]

---

17 Ibid.

18 M. Wolf, '§157 BGB' in H.-T. Soergel, Bürgerliches Gesetzbuch mit Einführungsgesetz und Nebengesetzen, vol. II, m.n. 76.

19 According to Art. 173 CC, when interpreting a declaration of intent, the true will of the parties is crucial, regardless of the wording used. This subjective criterion can be implemented only when the opposite intentions of the parties concur; if any kind of disagreement arises, the interpretation must proceed to the next level, the objective criterion, whereby what is examined is not what the parties understood, but what they could and ought to have understood. Therefore, the subjective criterion essentially prescribes the prevalence of the meaning over the wording, when interpreting declarations of will, and its – admittedly narrow – field of application consists in favouring the shared understanding of the parties, including when the phrasing of the agreement is misleading for an external observer; see Case 7.

20 Papanikolaou, *Methodology*, §496; Ladas, *General Principles*, §34 no. 23; Karassis, *General Principles*, §§ Γ 274-7.

21 Greek legal doctrine resorts to linguistics with regard to the interpretation of a legal text and suggests that any text ('κείμενο') should be interpreted in relation to its context ('περικείμενο'), which in its turn essentially includes the insinuations ('συμφραζόμενα'), namely meanings that can be derived from the text, although they are not explicitly mentioned there, and the complements ('συγκείμενα' or 'παρομαρτούσες συνθήκες'); see Karassis, *General Principles*, §§ Γ 289–291.

such as the conduct of the parties during the conclusion of the agreement, their profession, their usual course of action in their affairs, the economic purpose of the agreement, etc.; the previous conduct of the contracting parties in their transactions or other relations is also treated in legal doctrine as a leading example of 'συγκείμενα' that may affect the outcome of the interpretation.[22] The 'συγκείμενα' are treated in a different manner depending on whether a declaration of intent that must be addressed to another person is interpreted subjectively or objectively: in the first case, those external elements must be positively known both by the person declaring his intent and his counterparty; in the second case, it suffices if both parties can merely detect their existence and their potential influence on the meaning of the contract between them.[23]

In the case at hand, the court will most probably take into account the manner of performance under the established contractual practice between the parties: since Goldwater had always made the crates of beer available to Carryon at the front entrance of its headquarters under all previous contracts between them, there is an established course of commercial conduct between the parties and this manner of performance of the previous contracts constitutes a complement to their agreement, which the court will most probably wish to examine in order to discern the precise meaning of the term currently disputed. Such previous conduct of the parties would most probably weigh in as an interpretation factor and determine how the latest agreement is to be interpreted and performed.

8. ITALY

Scholars usually mention the manner of performance of previous contracts between the same parties as a typically relevant factor for the interpretation of contracts under Art. 1362, second paragraph c.c., which refers to the overall behaviour of the parties as a tool for ascertaining their common intention.[24] Some reported cases do in fact refer to the performance of previous analogous contracts between the same parties and give it considerable weight.[25]

According to the usual pattern of the decisions on this matter, a court dealing with this case would, at first, consider whether it can proceed to the examination of the parties' behaviour as a relevant factor for the interpretation of the contract.

---

22 Karassis, *General Principles*, § Γ 275; Ladas, *General Principles*, §34 no. 23.

23 Karassis, *General Principles*, § Γ 277.

24 Roppo, *Contratto*, p. 448; Sacco, *Contratto*, p. 1364; Bianca, *Contratto*, p. 428; Oppo, *Profili*, p. 85.

25 Cass. 5 August 2002, no. 11707; Cass. 16 March 1981 no. 1516.

The answer would depend on what position the court holds on the relationship between the first and the second paragraphs of Art. 1362. The rule contained in the first paragraph points at the search for the common intention as the general aim of the interpretation process and refers to the literal meaning of the words as the first relevant factor. The rule of the second paragraph instructs the adjudicator to consider the overall behaviour of the parties in order to ascertain their common intention.

As already noted,[26] some judicial precedents (apparently the majority) regard the second paragraph of Art. 1362 as subordinated to the first one and so require that the literal meaning of the words be ambiguous for the judge to be allowed to examine the parties' behaviour and to apply other extra-literal interpretation factors. According to this position, if the contractual wording were deemed clear, no further analysis would be allowed.

On the contrary, other judicial decisions and almost all scholars argue, more consistently with the text of Art. 1362, that the literal meaning and the parties' conduct lie on an equal footing and that both are relevant tools for determining the meaning of the contract according to the will of the parties.

Assuming that the court concludes that the second paragraph of Art. 1362 is applicable to the present case, the behaviour here considered appears to satisfy the requirements for it to be a strong interpretative factor, because it involves both parties, it shows an established course of dealings between them, and it refers to the very same contractual performance.

Some scholars, in this connection, argue that when a party intends to modify the usual course of performance of analogous contracts within an ongoing business relationship, that party has the burden of warning the other party before the conclusion of the contract.[27] The rule of Art. 1366 c.c. (interpretation according to 'buona fede' [good faith]) is likely to strengthen this conclusion, because it protects reasonable reliance of one party on a given contractual meaning when such reliance has been induced by the other party.

In conclusion, the way in which previous identical contracts between the same parties were performed appears to be a highly relevant factor, especially if it can be proved that the parties have an established business relationship. It is likely that in such a situation a court would hold that Goldwater has a duty to disclose before the conclusion of the contract that Carryon would be required to change the usual manner of performance. Absent such disclosure, the scope of the obligation upon Carryon would be determined based on the manner of performance of previous contracts.

---

26 See above Case 1, n. 56; Case 7.

27 Bianca, *Contratto*, p. 428.

9. NETHERLANDS

Clause 8 of the 2012 contract is to be interpreted by establishing the meaning each party could reasonably attribute to the clause and the meaning they each could reasonably have expected the other to have attributed to it, taking into account the relevant facts and circumstances assessed in light of the standards of 'redelijkheid en billijkheid' [reasonableness and fairness].[28]

Where the parties have dealt with each other before, and thus have established practices with respect to how the contracts between them are performed, such previous dealings and practices will be relevant for the interpretation of a contract, since they can shed light on the meaning to be given to the same terms and concepts in a subsequent contract.[29] The previous dealings and practices established between the parties will shape the parties' intentions, understandings and expectations with respect to a new contract concluded between them. If the parties are aware of the earlier contract and do not reveal an intention to diverge from it in the new contract, then an interpretation of the terms in the later contract in line with the earlier contract seems apparent, since they constitute relevant circumstances.[30]

If Goldwater had made the crates of beer available at the front entrance of the premises under the previous contracts, then it would be reasonable for Carryon to understand Clause 8 in the contract to mean that the crates of beer would also be made available at the front entrance under the 2012 contract; moreover, it could reasonably expect Goldwater to attribute this meaning to Clause 8 as well, since this practice had been established by Goldwater. Furthermore, in line with the requirement that the contract be interpreted in accordance with the requirements of 'redelijkheid en billijkheid' [reasonableness and fairness], the court would likely regard it to be unreasonable and unfair to allow Goldwater to rely on an interpretation of the term that deviates from a practice it has established.

10. POLAND

Art. 65 para. 1 of the KC requires a statement of intent to be interpreted as required by, among other things, the circumstances in which it was made (known as situational context).[31] These circumstances are seen as separate from

28 Hoge Raad 13 March 1981, *NJ* 1981, 635 (Ermes/Haviltex); Hoge Raad 20 February 2004, *NJ* 2005, 493 (DSM-Chemie/Fox).

29 Tjittes, *Uitleg van schriftelijke contracten*, p. 35; Tjittes, *Commercieel Contractenrecht*, p. 310.

30 Tjittes, *Uitleg van schriftelijke contracten*, p. 35.

31 Judgment of SN of 17.06.2009, IV CSK 90/09.

the declaration itself.[32] According to the author of this rule,[33] Longchamps de Berier, the circumstances in which the statements of intent are made do not constitute a self-standing source of knowing the parties' will, but are only a background against which the content of the statement should be considered. Further, if from a statement of intent, in the context of the accompanying circumstances, there appears the intent of another content that would arise on the basis of the statement alone, then the statement of intent should be explained as it follows from the accompanying circumstances. However, it is not possible to accept an explanation that could not be constructed on the basis of the wording of the statement or would contradict the statement.[34]

The parties' past common experiences and previously concluded contracts are recognised as one of the elements of the situational context.[35] Against this background, Polish courts have universally accepted that the previous performance of contracts existing between the parties should be taken into account when establishing the content of a later contract.

Already in 1975,[36] the SN stated that, when evaluating the common intention of the parties according to Art. 65 para. 2 of the KC, the court should take into account the content agreed by the parties, which is to be found in the contract itself and outside of it (e.g. in negotiations). Additionally, if the parties were previously engaged in the same legal relations, one should also take into account the meaning they gave to the ambiguous expressions used in the contract in the previous legal relations between them.

In another case,[37] the SN clearly indicated that the interpretation of a contractual clause that gives rise to controversies as to its meaning, because its meaning is unclear, cannot be based solely on the linguistic method – i.e. on an analysis of the language of a particular part of the contract, but it is necessary to investigate the parties' intentions and aims, as well as the factual context in which the contract was agreed on and concluded. It cannot be done without interrogating the directly interested parties and eventually also taking into account other circumstances like (important in the case of business relations) the rules and customs concerning cooperation – between the contractual parties, as well as in relation to other parties. In addition, as indicated many times in case law, the aim of a contract should not be established solely on the basis of the wording of the contract, especially if this is unclear or ambiguous,

32 Z. Radwański, *Wykładnia oświadczeń woli składanych indywidualnym adresatom*, p. 97.
33 Ibid.
34 Longchamps de Berier, *Zobowiązania*, p. 145.
35 Z. Radwański, *System Prawa Prywatnego*, vol. 2, p. 69.
36 Judgment of SN of 04.07.1975, III CRN 160/75.
37 Judgment of SN of 03.09.1998, I CKN 815/97.

but other elements should also be taken into consideration, for example negotiations.

In conclusion, the fact that the parties to the contract have developed a custom between them (i.e. making the crates available at the front entrance of the brewery) should be taken into account when interpreting Clause 8 of the contract of 2012.

11. PORTUGAL

In this case, the important question is whether the previous contracts and, in particular, the way they were performed can influence the interpretation of Clause 8. According to Art. 236.°/1 of the Portuguese Civil Code, Clause 8 should be interpreted in accordance with the meaning given to it by a 'destinatário normal', i.e. what a reasonable man who receives the declaration in the context of the real situation could understand from the behaviour of the other party to the contract.

Previous circumstances and dealings are relevant to prove that Carryon had negotiated with Goldwater and counted on a performance similar to the other contracts. In this case, there is a continued contractual relationship, and this is an aspect that is relevant in the 'posição do real declaratário' [real situation]. The expression 'posição do real declaratário' points to a concrete standard in which extrinsic elements outside the contract can be relevant for the interpretation of Clause 8.

As already stated in relation to Case 1, the Portuguese Civil Code does not specifically address the issue of extrinsic evidence. However, Art. 236.°/1 CC states that all relevant circumstances of the case, including the negotiations, previous dealings, any practices the parties have established between themselves, usages and subsequent conduct of the parties can be taken into consideration when assessing the intent of the parties.

In a continued relationship, 'boa fé' [good faith] is also a behavioural standard that frames the parties' behaviours. In fact, it could be considered to be against 'boa fé' if Goldwater completely changed the place of performance and its conditions without any modification of the text of Clause 8. Clause 8 must be interpreted by giving relevance to previous dealings according to Art. 236.°/1 CC.

It would be possible to argue that there is an 'abuso de direito' [behaviour against good faith] and also that, in the negotiation of the contract, Goldwater did not fulfil its information duties (*culpa in contrahendo*, see Art. 227.° CC). In fact, the 'tutela da confiança' [principle of confidence] can play a special role in the interpretation of Clause 8 due to the application of Art. 236.°/1 CC, which cannot be applied in a sense that involves the violation of legitimate expectations.

12. SCOTLAND

Scots law applies an objective and contextual approach to the ascertainment of the meaning of the words used by the contracting parties.[38] If the parties have previous or concurrent dealings with each other in which a practice well known to each other is established, that practice will be afforded great weight in the interpretation of Clause 8. The established practice will form part of the circumstances surrounding the contract and provide evidence of how the parties have conducted their affairs in the past.[39] The parties will be deemed to have been aware of that established practice since it has been a regular feature in the way they have conducted themselves prior to the conclusion of the contract. For that reason, the course of dealing between Goldwater and Carryon would be given significant weight in the court's decision on interpretation.

If the court considered that the contract was truly ambiguous on this point, and that there were two possible constructions, it is likely to prefer the construction which is consistent with commercial common sense and to reject the other.[40] The court would have to be convinced, however, that there are two possible constructions. The Supreme Court recently warned that the parties must not invent drafting infelicities in order to be able to have recourse to commercial common sense.[41]

A Scottish court may also make use of the doctrine of 'course of dealing', which incorporates into a contract conditions which otherwise would not form part of the contract.[42] There must be a previous course of consistent dealing in which the terms of the contracts and the goods in question were consistent.[43] The parties also require to have knowledge of the conditions.[44] Each party must also, by words or conduct, have led the other party to believe that they assented to the conditions.[45] If Carryon is able to comply with these requirements and is able to prove that a course of dealing exists, that course of dealing would, in effect, become part of the contract between Carryon and Goldwater. This being the case, the court would be obliged to give effect to what

---

38 *Wood v Capita Insurance Services Ltd* [2017] UKSC 24; [2017] 2 WLR 1095, per Lord Hodge at para. 10.

39 McBryde, *Contract*, para. 8–23.

40 *Rainy Sky v Kookmin Bank* [2011] UKSC 50; [2011] 1 WLR 2900 per Lord Clarke at para. 21; *Wood v Capita Insurance Services Ltd* [2017] UKSC 24; [2017] 2 WLR 1095 at para. 10.

41 [2015] UKSC 36; [2015] AC 1619; Connal, 'Has the Rainy Sky Dried up? Arnold v Britton and commercial interpretation'.

42 See, for example, *Wood & Co. v G & J Burns* (1893) 20 R 602; *Rutherford & Son v Miln & Co.* 1941 SC 125.

43 *McCutcheon v David MacBrayne Ltd* 1964 SC (HL) 28, per Lord Devlin at 41.

44 McBryde, *Contract*, para. 7–29.

45 Ibid., para. 7–31.

is a contractual term, namely that Goldwater would be obliged to make the crates available at the front entrance of the brewery.

13. SOUTH AFRICA

In *Mcoyi v Inkatha Freedom Party*[46] it was stated that the way in which the terms of a political party's constitution have been implemented in the past is relevant to the interpretation of those terms. By analogy, the same rule ought to apply when a court is interpreting a contract which contains the same terms as previous contracts between the parties, the performance of which indicates a consistent interpretation of those terms.[47] The evidence of the prior course of dealing would form part of the 'background to the preparation and production of the document'[48] and assist in determining how a reasonable person in the position of the parties would interpret the provision.

As pointed out in Case 2, Question 1, it would not be sufficient for Carryon to argue that its interpretation of Clause 8 should be adopted simply on the basis that Goldwater has breached a duty to act in good faith by deviating from a shared understanding of the meaning of that clause in the past. A court would only adopt an equitable interpretation of the clause on the basis that the parties have a duty to negotiate in good faith, if the primary interpretative factors discussed in the Introduction did not yield a result. In that case, a court would presumably rely on such a duty to hold that Goldwater should have informed Carryon that it no longer subscribed to the same understanding of the clause and that, in the absence of such information, an equitable interpretation of Clause 8 is one which would favour Carryon's interpretation.

Alternatively, but to the same effect, Carryon could estop Goldwater from relying on its interpretation of Clause 8 because the parties' previous course of dealings placed a duty on Goldwater to inform Carryon of its changed understanding of the clause.[49]

14. SPAIN

The controversial expression 'to make available at the brewery premises' included in Clause 8 may be interpreted in the light of Art. 1.282 CC, which

---

46 2011 4 SA 298 (KZP) para. 43.

47 The rules relating to the admissibility of evidence for the purposes of interpretation apply irrespective of the nature of the document to be interpreted (whether statute, patent or contract). See *KPMG Chartered Accountants (SA) v Securefin Ltd* 2009 4 SA 399 (SCA) para. 39.

48 *Natal Joint Municipal Pension Fund v Endumeni Municipality* 2012 4 SA 593 (SCA) para. 18.

49 On the existence of a duty to speak in this context, see Sonnekus, *Estoppel*, pp. 172–175.

claims that the acts of both parties are essential in order to identify their common intention – not only the acts at the time of and subsequent to the conclusion of the contract, but also those prior to it. Spanish law gives importance to whatever has happened prior to the conclusion of the contract. According to legal doctrine and judicial decisions, the common intention of the parties may also be revealed from previous acts and the word 'actos' [acts] used in Art. 1.282 CC is intended to be broadly understood by scholars and judges, and as including documents and oral statements.[50]

In this case, 'Goldwater' and 'Carryon' have an ongoing business relationship and under those contracts (every single contract), Goldwater always made the crates of beer available at the front entrance of the brewery. If the present contract has the same economic function as the others previously concluded, the manner of their former performance must be relevant. This ongoing trading relationship helps identify the common intention of the parties regarding how to collect the crates of beer at the brewery premises.

In the scientific literature, Díez-Picazo[51] considers the previous contracts between the parties as a relevant interpretation factor from a broad interpretation of Art. 1282 CC. Moreover, other scholars[52] hold the opinion that the regular relationship between the parties creates a 'costumbre particular' [particular custom] which may be used as a decisive interpretation element to discover the common intention of the parties. Therefore, they have relevance and significance because both parties have established a way of performing which reveals their contractual purpose. Therefore, the way the crates used to be loaded in the past would constitute a 'práctica' [practice] and to deviate from it would be considered a breach of 'buena fe' [good faith].

This consideration will be explicit in Art. 1.279, third paragraph, of the above-mentioned Proposal for the Modernisation, published in 2009 but not yet enacted, which claims that in order to interpret a contract we must take into account the interpretation given by the parties to similar clauses and the practices established between them. In addition, Art. 1.278, second paragraph, of this Proposal states that if one of the parties had understood the contract, or one part of it, in a way that the other, at the moment of the conclusion of the contract, could not ignore, the contract will be understood in this way.

From the above, it is clear that Carryon's driver understood the contract according to the current practice that the other party could not ignore. The manner of former performance of previous contracts between the parties is determinant in the task of interpretation.

---

50 See STS 09.02.1981 (RJ 1981\533); STS 06.10.1989 (RJ 1989\9888); STS 03.09.2007 (RJ 2007\4709); STS 08.05.2012, ECLI:ES:TS:2012:4177 on the interpretative effectiveness of the previous behaviour of the parties.

51 Díez-Picazo, *Fundamentos*, p. 502.

52 Such as López y López, *Comentarios*, p. 33; or Jordano Barea, 'De la interpretación', p. 51.

15. SWEDEN

The manner of performance of the previous contracts between Carryon and Goldwater will be accorded weight in the interpretation of Clause 8 to *the extent that is appropriate* given the stability and length of their business relationship and all other matters deemed relevant by the courts. If the pattern developed between the parties – the 'partsbruk' [parties' practice] – is stable enough, i.e. if that pattern has engendered an understanding that Carryon is entitled to rely on, it will be decisive in the interpretation of Clause 8.[53] This is the standard test used by the courts to establish the content of individual 'viljeförklaringar' [will declarations],[54] and it is in congruence with the 'tillitsprincipen' [trust principle] – i.e. the fundamental principle of Swedish contract law embedded in the Contracts Act Section 32 (1) (the principle follows *e contrario* from this provision), according to which a party receiving a 'viljeförklaring' from another party is entitled to rely on the impression conveyed by the 'viljeförklaring', objectively interpreted, as long as the declaring party did not intend the 'viljeförklaring' to mean something else and the receiving party was not in 'ond tro' [bad faith] regarding that fact.[55]

Assuming that this same wording has been used by the parties throughout the relationship, and on the assumption that Goldwater has performed in identical fashion on every occasion, the courts will be inclined to conclude that Clause 8 will have to be construed in accordance with the norm thus established. In order to reach a different conclusion, an alternative meaning must be attributed to the behaviour of Goldwater. The first possibility to be considered in circumstances like these is that the manner of performance could be understood as an act of, or, rather, a series of acts of, *good will*. If what Goldwater has done, rightly understood, is to grant Carryon 'kulans' [leniency] – i.e. a concession not giving rise to any obligation – then, conversely, Goldwater is not entitled to rely on that behaviour.[56] However, in order to establish that this is, indeed, a case of 'kulans', the interpreting court would first have to arrive at the conclusion that Clause 8 and the corresponding provisions in the previous contracts do not in fact, when interpreted correctly, require that Goldwater performs in the manner in question. In other words, the court must be able to establish the standard in relation to which there is 'kulans'.

---

53 See e.g. NJA 1933 p. 260, NJA 1948 p. 620, NJA 1949 p. 87; NJA 2018 p. 171. On the role of 'partsbruk' in interpretation see e.g. Adlercreutz and Gorton, *Avtalsrätt II*, p. 73 ff., Lehrberg, *Avtalstolkning*, p. 122 ff.; J. Ramberg and C. Ramberg, *Allmän avtalsrätt*, p. 165.

54 See e.g. the answer to Case 1, Question 2.

55 See Förslag till lag om avtal (1914) p. 140.

56 Cf. e.g. NJA 1967 p. 143. On the problem of 'kulans' in interpretation, see Adlercreutz and Gorton, *Avtalsrätt II*, p. 101 ff.; Karlgren, *Passivitet*, p. 11 f.; Lehrberg, *Avtalstolkning*, p. 135 ff.; J. Ramberg and C. Ramberg, *Allmän avtalsrätt*, p. 166.

16. EDITORIAL COMPARATIVE OBSERVATIONS

All reporters confirmed that the manner of performance of the previous contracts would be taken into account in the interpretative process. The level of importance of this information ranges from 'relevant' (Finland, the Netherlands, Portugal and South Africa), through 'highly relevant' (Italy), to 'potentially decisive' (Sweden), 'often decisive' (Germany), 'decisive' (Spain and Greece) or of 'great weight' (Scotland).

In all the legal systems, use of this information arises as part of an objective stage of the interpretative process. This is obviously the case in legal systems such as England and Wales, Scotland and South Africa, where there is no attempt to identify the common intention, subjectively analysed. But even in those systems where the interpretative process begins by seeking to identify the subjective common intention, there is recognition that the subjective approach is impossible on these facts, and that objective factors must come to the fore.[57]

The manner of performance of previous contracts is specifically referred to in the codal provisions of the Croatian, Portuguese and Spanish civil codes as a factor which a court may take into account. Art. 12(1) of the Croatian COA, for example, provides that any trade usages agreed upon by the contracting parties-traders, as well as *mutually developed practices* between the contracting parties-traders, shall apply to obligations between them. For both codified and non-codified legal systems, it is relevant as part of the context, for example as the surrounding or background circumstances in Scotland and South Africa, or as the situational context in Poland. It can become a contractual or particular (rather than a trade) custom in Germany, Poland and Spain.

A theme which emerged from several of the reports was the protection of Carryon's reasonable or legitimate expectation that the manner of performance would be the same in the 2012 contract as it had been in the previous contracts. The Netherlands reporter commented that 'the previous dealings and practices established between the parties will shape the parties' intentions, understanding and expectations with respect to a new contract between them', and the Croatian that 'Carryon, when concluding a new contract in 2012 with Goldwater, had reasonable expectations that the same *modus operandi* would be followed in the performance of the new contract.' The Portuguese report referred to the creation of 'legitimate expectations'. The French and Finnish reports referred to Carryon's expectations without describing them as either reasonable

57 See, for example, the Greek report, and the references to Arts. 173 and 200 CC. The German report indicates that custom serves as an argument for what is usually understood by the parties when using these words, clearly an objective analysis.

or legitimate, the latter indicating that Carryon would assume it was the same this time.

Some of the reports sought to locate the protection of reasonable expectations in a specific part of the overall interpretative process. For the Greek reporter, the previous conduct of the contracting parties is treated in legal doctrine as a leading example of 'συγκείμενα', or elements outside the text of the agreement, which may be used in order to determine what the parties should and could have been reasonably expected to understand in the specific context of the agreement.

In Croatia, Finland, France, Italy, the Netherlands, Portugal and South Africa, Goldwater is subject to a duty to communicate to Carryon the fact that the 2012 contract would be performed in a different way from the previous contracts between the parties. These legal systems differed on the source of this duty. In Croatia it is part of the duty to cooperate. In France it arises from a general duty of good faith, understood as a duty to collaborate, and in South Africa as part of the 'fall-back' duty to negotiate in good faith.

Good faith may be relevant because it protects Carryon's reasonable reliance on a given contractual meaning, especially if induced by Goldwater (Italy), or sets a norm of reasonable behaviour (the Netherlands) or behavioural standards (Portugal). In Croatia, any deviation from the mutually developed practice arising between the parties would be considered a breach of the duty of conscientiousness and honesty, one of the basic principles of interpretation and highly significant in this context. In Croatia, a duty of care obliges the parties to refrain from any action that hinders the other's performance. Goldwater's conduct potentially infringes such a negative duty. Good faith is also relevant in France, Germany, Spain and, more surprisingly, in the mixed legal system of South Africa. It is available to the court there as a 'fall-back' where the primary interpretative factors have been applied and yet have failed to achieve a result.

Controls or limitations are, in some legal systems, placed on the court's ability to use this information. It seems highly likely that all legal systems would require the previous manner of performance to be 'consistent' and 'repeated'.[58] In Finland, the historic contracts must be similar in contents and purpose, and there must not be too significant a time-lapse between the contracts. In Italy, the established course of dealing must refer to the very same contractual performance. And in Spain, the existing contract must perform the same economic function as the other ones in the past.

Certain of the reporters suggested that this information might not be relevant if it did not constitute a legal obligation. The reporter for England and

58 These words are used in the Croatian report.

Wales indicated that if Goldwater were not contractually obliged to make the crates available on the ground floor, this practice would not be legally relevant in the interpretation of the 2012 contract. For a usage to imply part of an obligation into a contract, it must be established as having binding effect. The Swedish reporter explained the doctrine known as 'kulans', which he translated as leniency. Goldwater's previous acts, making the crates available on the ground floor, might be a concession or type of goodwill not giving rise to any legal obligation. If this constitutes 'kulans', Carryon is not able to rely on it in the context of the 2012 contract.

CASE 9: CRYSTAL VASES

'Murray' is a company that manufactures crystal vases. It has entered into a contract with 'OnTrack', an operator of cargo transportation by container freight trains. Clause 4 of their contract provides that Murray will be responsible for delivering its goods to 'Distribution Warehouse 10, at the local freight train station.' Murray delivers a consignment of goods to Distribution Warehouse 10. OnTrack refuses to ship them, however, explaining that delivery at a freight train terminal means delivery up to the actual container terminal. There the goods will be loaded into the appropriate containers. In fact, Murray delivered the goods to the entrance of the Distribution Warehouse, which is at least 800 metres away from the actual container terminal. The nature of the goods in question makes carriage of them, even over short distances, a complex task. Murray disputes OnTrack's view. It argues that Clause 4 of the contract is very clear on the issue of where the goods were to be delivered. It raises an action against OnTrack for breach of contract. OnTrack contests this action. It argues that Clause 4 must be read in light of the fact that it is a local custom of trade that goods are delivered up to the container terminal.

Assume that there is indeed, as OnTrack argues, a local custom of trade that goods are delivered by the manufacturers to the container terminal. How much weight is the court likely to give to this local custom of trade in interpreting Clause 4?

1. KEY ISSUES

This case maintains the focus on transport contracts which was seen in Case 8. The context is again the sale of goods, and the dispute concerns the interpretation of contractual clauses governing the way in which goods are to be delivered by the manufacturer to the cargo transportation company. The parties have differing interpretations of the terms of the contract which govern the location where goods are to be placed before collection by the cargo transportation company. This time there is a local custom of trade that goods should be delivered to a certain location. If the custom applies, it could potentially resolve the dispute, making clear exactly where the goods ought to have been placed for collection. The case is designed, therefore, to allow reporters fully to discuss the role of a custom of trade in the interpretative process.

2. CROATIA

The question here is whether Clause 4 stipulating the delivery of the crystal vases to 'Distribution Warehouse 10, at the local freight train station' for the purpose of transport may be read in accordance with the local trade custom requiring the crystal vases to be delivered by the manufacturers to the container terminal which is 800 metres away.

In interpreting disputed contractual clauses, the common intention of the parties should be explored and considered rather than the literal meaning of certain expressions used and the disputed clause must be construed in accordance with the principles of the law of obligations established by the COA (Art. 319(2)). Thus, the Croatian courts would explore the common intention of Murray and OnTrack within the context of the principles of the law of obligations relying on the objective criterion. The objective criterion includes Art. 10(2) of the COA on due care, which requires traders to observe rules of profession and usages. In this regard, Art. 12 of the COA provides the basis for the application of trade usages/customs, developed within a certain professional branch, to all legal relationships falling within the scope of that branch.[1] Trade usages are applicable to a certain commercial contract if the parties to it have agreed on their application (subjective theory), as well as if they are applied regularly by traders in the same type of contracts and the parties have not excluded their application (objective theory). Trade usages/customs also include local usages applicable in a certain branch or profession, as well as usages in a certain locality (food court, fair, harbour, city, region, stock exchange).[2] Thus, the local custom in a specific branch has a bearing upon the parties' rights and obligations[3] and traders are expected to observe the custom at the place of performance of the obligation, even if they are not familiar with it. The rationale behind the objective approach in Art. 12(2) of the COA is the understanding that contracting parties do not have to agree explicitly on a specific conduct for it to be binding upon them, if such conduct is generally accepted and established as usual conduct in business practice. However, trade customs/usages cannot apply against the will of the contracting parties, and even if the prerequisites for their application are fulfilled, they will not apply if the parties excluded

---

1 The Croatian Chamber of Economy issues certificates to confirm the existence and content of business (trade) usages in the territory of Republic of Croatia.

2 Barbić, 'Primjena običaja u hrvatskom trgovačkom pravu', p. 76.

3 See e.g. VSRH, Rev-1596/01-2 of 14 November 2001, where the court accepted the custom under which in the case of forwarding the goods the storekeeper has a duty to load the goods into the truck and list the individual articles and their weight according to the labels received by the committee which weighed the goods, and concluded that the custom was not requiring the storekeeper personally to weigh the goods.

their application explicitly or implicitly, for instance by contractually agreeing otherwise.[4] Hence, there is a need for interpretation of Clause 4, in relation to other contractual clauses and the contract as a whole, in order to determine whether the contracting parties intended to exclude the application of the local custom. If this was not their common intention, the Croatian court would interpret Clause 4 in the light of the customs effective in the locality where the contract is to be performed.[5] Furthermore, the court would interpret Murray's and OnTrack's common intention in accordance with other principles of the law of obligations. Possibly, Murray's deviation from the applicable local custom of trade could in the view of the court represent a violation not only of the principle of due care (Art. 10 of the COA) and of rules on trade customs/usages (Art. 12 of the COA), but also of the principle of conscientiousness and honesty (Art. 4 of the COA).

3. ENGLAND AND WALES

The weight given to the custom in resolving this case depends upon the strength and content of the local custom of trade that goods are delivered to the container terminal, and the nature and layout of the relevant freight train station.

The following two possibilities might usefully be considered. First, there may be several container terminals at the freight train station, or several delivery points at the one container terminal, with one terminal or one delivery point at the terminal corresponding to Distribution Warehouse 10. The custom may be that parties specify which distribution warehouse, yet delivery is always to the container terminal corresponding to that warehouse, not to the warehouse itself. If this is the situation, then the proof of the custom may well be conclusive, as it explains or amplifies what the contractual wording 'Distribution Warehouse 10, at the local freight train station' means without denuding the express wording of any effect. It may well be reasonable for the parties to understand the custom, if sufficiently notorious and universal as to go without saying, to apply in this way.

Second, and in contrast, there may be a single delivery point at a single container terminal, at which it is customary to deliver, even for all different warehouses. If this is the case, then applying the local custom would give the express words 'Distribution Warehouse 10' no useful function in the contract and would have the effect as if they were deleted altogether: if that is what the parties meant, surely they would not have said Distribution Warehouse 10. In those circumstances, the custom is actually inconsistent with the express

4 VSRH, II Rev 165/00-2 of 7 April 2004; VSRH, Rev 745/1990-2 of 19 September 1990.

5 Perović, *Obligaciono pravo*, p. 372.

words used, and would only be given effect if a court could conclude that the parties would reasonably understand that their expressly chosen words had no meaning or were a mistake or that it is customary (and provides some useful information) to give the warehouse number even though delivery is to the container terminal. The court would attach weight to the contrary possibility that, despite and in variance of the custom, in this particular case Murray was intended to deliver the goods at Distribution Warehouse 10.[6]

4. FINLAND

The principles concerning the interpretation of contracts under Finnish law are generally quite liberal and informal in the sense that many different viewpoints and arguments can be taken into account. The outcome of an interpretation dispute is rarely determined by a single argument.[7] However, the clear wording of a contract document is a fact that is usually difficult to override by reference to another source of interpretation such as contract drafts or commercial usage.[8] That is so especially in situations where the disputed clause is in a document drafted by – or at least read and accepted by – both parties, in other words, not in standard terms drafted solely by one of the parties.[9]

So, if we indeed assume that the wording of the disputed clause is unambiguous as such, the court would most likely decide the dispute according to the wording of the clause. The outcome of the dispute could only be otherwise if OnTrack, the party referring to the custom of trade, could seriously bring into question the *bona fides* of Murray, the party referring to the wording. That could be the case if, for example, OnTrack could indicate that it had been mistaken over the place of delivery and this mistake had been caused by or was at least clearly observable to Murray.

The substance of *bona fides* of the contracting party was discussed in the Finnish Supreme Court's decision 1990:99. In this case A and B had entered

6 Similarly, in *In re an arbitration between L Sutro & Co. and Heilbut Symons & Co.* [1917] 2 KB 348 (CA), an international sale of goods contract expressly provided for sale of goods to be shipped by sea to New York, and accordingly it was a breach of contract to supply goods offloaded on the western coast of the US and taken across the US by rail, despite a trade custom (that arose due to wartime difficulties) of doing exactly this. Per Swinfen-Eady J at 357: 'Where a method of conveyance and route, namely, a sea route, are specified, it is immaterial that there may co-exist some other usual mode of conveyance and route' and '[a]ny such usage, if found, would be inconsistent with the terms of the written contract, and repugnant to them'.

7 Aho, *Varalllisuusoikeudellisen oikeustoimen tulkinnasta*, pp. 133–134.

8 Pönkä, 'Tavoitteellisten tulkintasääntöjen merkityksestä liikesopimusten tulkinnassa', p. 922.

9 Hemmo, *Sopimusoikeus I*, pp. 584–585 and Saarnilehto, 'Epäselvä ehto', p. 9. See also Finnish Supreme Court's decision KKO 2008:53, para. 8, where the court briefly notes that the starting point in interpretation of a contract is the wording thereof.

into contract for the delivery of an installation-ready house. A claimed that the agreed price also included the construction of the house. However, the evidence presented in the case showed that the subject of the contract had only, as B had comprehended, been the delivery of building materials. There was no evidence that B would or should have understood that when concluding the contract, A had been of the belief that the construction of the house was also included in the price. Thus, the contract was considered to be established in substance of B's understanding.

Another problem for OnTrack is that there are certain additional requirements for the applicability of commercial usage in a single dispute. Firstly, the courts typically demand relatively convincing evidence of the existence of the usage and contents of it.[10] For example, the Finnish Supreme Court held in its decision KKO 1984 II 119 that the existence of commercial usage in a certain field of commerce had not been sufficiently proven by the fact that entrepreneurs in this field generally use certain clauses in their contract forms.

Secondly, in legal literature it has been regarded that even though the existence and contents of commercial usage had been convincingly proven, the usage is normally considered to be binding only between the entrepreneurs of that field. In other words, an entrepreneur cannot usually invoke commercial usage of its own field against consumers or entrepreneurs of other fields, unless they are for some reason aware of the usage.[11]

As an example of a case where commercial usage was deemed to be binding to the contracting parties, one can raise Finnish Supreme Court's decision KKO 2002:38. The circumstances of this case were, however, rather exceptional. It concerned a contract between a trotting race organiser and an owner of a trotter. The general competition rules confirmed by the Finnish trotting association were considered to become a part of the participation agreement between the parties even though neither of them had expressly referred to the rules. That was because the trotting association governed all trotting competition activity in Finland, and the competition rules confirmed by it were thus applied in virtually every trotting competition. As a professional in the branch, B could not have been unaware of this and was therefore deemed to be bound by the rules.

The description of Case 9 leaves open the question whether Murray was or should have been aware of the usage OnTrack invokes. Even though the answer was positive, it would be questionable whether the usage would be regarded as overriding the fairly clear wording of the clause. The decision would probably depend on whether Murray had actually noticed the contradiction between the clause and the usage, and if it did whether the mistake of OnTrack was

10 Hemmo, *Sopimusoikeus I*, p. 159.
11 Ibid. and Telaranta, *Sopimusoikeus*, p. 105.

observable to it. If Murray did not actually notice the contradiction, the mistake of OnTrack would not probably have turned out to be sufficiently evident so that noticing it could be reasonably expected of Murray. Merely the fact that Murray *could* have noticed the contradiction had it read the contract carefully would not probably suffice, because OnTrack could similarly have noticed the error.

5. FRANCE

Clause 4, the clause under scrutiny, provides that the manufacturer is responsible for delivering the goods to 'Distribution Warehouse 10, at the local freight train station'. Murray, the manufacturer, interprets the clause as an obligation to deliver to Distribution Warehouse 10 and leaves the goods at the entrance of the warehouse. OnTrack, the transporter, relies on a local custom of trade to require that the goods be delivered directly to the container terminal of the distribution warehouse (some 800 meters after the entrance).

Since the 2016 reform, the court would likely consider that the decision to be taken is not about the interpretation of the contract but rather about the determination of the modalities of its performance.[12] Under Art. 1194 Cciv (formerly Art. 1135), the parties are bound not only by the obligations expressed in their contract but also by those deriving from the contract on the basis of equity (reasonableness, fairness), usages or law. As a consequence, if the court considers that the local custom of trade invoked by OnTrack exists and is legally binding,[13] then they will take it into account even if the parties did not agree on its application beforehand.[14]

6. GERMANY

Local usage under German law may first serve as an argument for interpretation of contracts and second complement the contract by implying terms under §346 HGB. In particular, a local usage or custom which is followed for

12 See e.g. Ph. Simler in *JCl. Civil Code*, Art. 1188 à 1192, Fasc. 10, no. 55.

13 Civ. 1, 15 June 1994, *JurisData* no. 1994-001240; contrast Civ. 1, 26 November 1981. *Bull. civ.* (1981) no. 356 where the invocation of the usage was unsuccessful since it was considered not legally binding.

14 Before the reform, the court would have referred to the old Arts. 1159–1160 Cciv that have now been discarded. Unlike Art. 1194 Cciv (formerly Art. 1135), these rules were considered as mere guidelines supporting the judicial interpretation of contracts. As such they could not serve as legal basis for an appeal before the Cour de cassation except if combined with Art. 1135 Cciv (for an example of such a combination, see Civ. 1, 15 June 1994, *JurisData* no. 1994-001240).

some period of time[15] may serve as an argument in the interpretative process if the local usage concerns the field of activity of the parties (cf. Case 8).[16] It is worth mentioning that the parties may also agree on a clause which differs from the local usage.[17]

The relevance of local usage depends upon the remaining content of the contract. Firstly, it may serve as an argument in interpreting the wording ('delivery to Distribution Warehouse 10, at the local freight train station') if the wording is not entirely clear.[18] This however is not the case with the usage at hand: the fact that goods are usually delivered to the container terminal does not explain the wording in the case at hand. Usage may also serve as a basis for gap-filling in 'ergänzende Vertragsauslegung' [supplementary interpretation].[19] Therefore, what the parties would have intended, if they had foreseen this conflict and had been guided by the 'Verkehrssitte' [custom of trade] and 'Treu und Glaube' [the good faith principle], is decisive.[20]

In this case, there may be no common hypothetical intention of the parties to establish, since Murray, which knew that the nature of the goods in question makes the carriage a complex task, may not have intended to agree on delivering the goods to the actual container terminal. Therefore the 'ergänzende Vertragsauslegung' does not help in the case at hand either, because it is not clear if the usage would also apply in the case where a place of delivery clause had been agreed.

Furthermore, German law recognises a supplementary 'Verkehrssitte' under §§242, 157 BGB, which not only helps in interpreting the terms of a contract but also supplements the contract.[21] In fact, the 'Verkehrssitte' gives substance to 'Treu und Glauben' and contributes to legal certainty.[22]

In the case at hand there is a proven local 'Verkehrssitte', which supports OnTrack's opinion. A custom of trade has to be applied, notwithstanding that one party was not aware of it.[23] Furthermore, the custom of trade supplements the contract without requiring a hypothetical common intention.[24]

---

15 BGH, 30.03.1990, *NJW* 1990, 1724.

16 BGH, 30.09.2009, *NJW* 2010, 1136.

17 H. Wendtland, '§157 BGB' in H.G. Bamberger and H. Roth (eds.), *Beck'scher Onlinekommentar*, m.n. 24.

18 Ibid., m.n. 23.

19 J. Busche, '§157 BGB' in K. Rebmann and F.J. Säcker (eds.), *Münchener Kommentar zum Bürgerlichen Gesetzbuch*, m.n. 20, 26.

20 W. Flume, *Allgemeiner Teil des Bürgerlichen Rechts, Das Rechtsgeschäft*, vol. II, p. 322; see e.g. BGH, 11.10.2017, *NJW* 2018, 296.

21 M. Wolf, '§157 BGB' in H.-T. Soergel, *Bürgerliches Gesetzbuch mit Einführungsgesetz und Nebengesetzen*, vol. II, m.n. 69.

22 Ibid., m.n. 76.

23 Ibid., m.n. 72.

24 W. Flume, *Allgemeiner Teil des Bürgerlichen Rechts, Das Rechtsgeschäft*, vol. II, p. 322.

As a result, the custom of trade in the case at hand does not serve as an argument for the interpretation of the wording of Clause 4, but supplements the contract in an objective, normative way and, therefore, supports OnTrack's arguments.[25]

7. GREECE

In the case at hand, Murray and OnTrack are in disagreement as to the precise place where the consignment of goods is to be delivered to the freighter, because they understand Clause 4 in different ways. Therefore, the objective criterion of Art. 200 CC shall apply.

Art. 200 CC relies mainly upon the concept of 'καλή πίστη' [good faith] and it explicitly mentions the 'συναλλακτικά ήθη' [trade customs] as a pertinent standard for determining the applicable content of good faith in the specific contractual context. Legal doctrine holds that trade customs are not an independent criterion within the systematic of Art. 200 CC, but just a means of concretising the standard of 'καλή πίστη' applicable in each case.[26] The explicit reference to trade customs in the law underscores their importance for shaping the applicable standard of good faith in each case where a contract has to be interpreted objectively. Trade customs are permanent practices, namely courses of action which are usual either with regard to a specific category of transactions or within a specific professional circle or in a specific place.[27]

Regarding their normative content, trade customs are practices which are factually observed, but they do not constitute customary law, because they are not characterised by the element of the so-called *opinio necessitatis*; in other words, the parties observe them of their own free will and usage, not because they consider them to be binding in the sense of a legal rule. Nonetheless, through the reference made to them in Art. 200 CC (as well as Art. 288 CC on the proper execution of obligations), they are elevated to the status of a secondary rule of law.[28]

---

25 However, it has to be remarked that under German law an argument could be derived from §412 HGB again: without the clause the sender would be obliged to stow, therefore one could argue that the contract should be interpreted in a manner which will reduce the shippers position as little as possible. Finally, it is worth mentioning that the usual case would be a case of the goods being damaged during stowing with the consequential question on whose behalf the goods are stowed.

26 See e.g. Stathopoulos, *Civil Code*, vol. 1^B, Arts. 173 and 200 no. 115; Ladas, *General Principles*, §34 no. 24; Balis, *General Principles*, §88.

27 Papanikolaou, *Methodology*, §501; Ladas, *General Principles*, §34 no. 24; Stathopoulos, *Civil Code*, vol. 1^B, Arts. 173 and 200 nos. 113–116; Balis, *General Principles*, §§4, 88; cf. AP 678/1996, EEN 65 (1998), 38.

28 Stathopoulos, *Civil Code*, vol. 1^B, Arts. 173 and 200 nos. 113, 118; Papanikolaou, *Methodology*, §502.

Trade customs may not prevail when their application has been explicitly excluded by the parties[29] or when they contradict good faith.[30] It is important to note that trade customs, when they have not been precluded as described above, develop an autonomous interpretative force, in the sense that they may be taken into account for the purposes of interpretation of a contract even irrespective of whether the parties indeed were or ought to have been aware of them.[31]

In view of the prominent position that trade customs have in legal interpretation under Greek law, the court is very likely to take such a trade custom on the place of delivery of goods to be transported into account, when hearing the dispute between Murray and OnTrack with regard to the interpretation of Clause 4. Provided that the requisites mentioned above are at hand and a trade custom is indeed in place, the custom does not contradict the principle of 'καλή πίστη' and it has not been precluded by the parties, OnTrack may successfully invoke it, even if Murray was completely unaware of it.

8. ITALY

Under Art. 1368 c.c.,[32] local trade customs are a relevant factor for contract interpretation. As this rule employs external factors, unrelated to the specific contract to be interpreted, it is plainly considered a rule of objective interpretation.

According to the established position of scholars and courts, in order to apply trade usages as an interpretation factor it is necessary that contractual clauses be affected by some 'ambiguity', namely a remaining uncertainty that the rules of subjective interpretation have not solved. The few reported judicial decisions on Art. 1368 have always stated that it is merely a 'subsidiary' rule the relevance of which is conditional upon a persisting uncertainty as to the actual will of the parties. Therefore, Art. 1368 would not be employed by a court where the parties' intention can be ascertained through the application of rules of subjective interpretation which would be applied first.[33]

---

29 Stathopoulos, *Civil Code*, vol. 1^{B}, Arts. 173 and 200 no. 114 *in fine*; Karassis, *General Principles*, § Γ 288.

30 CA Athens 2449/1960, EEN 28 (1961), 225; Papanikolaou, *Methodology*, §503; Stathopoulos, *Civil Code*, vol. 1^{B}, Arts. 173 and 200 no. 117.

31 Karassis, *General Principles*, § Γ 288; Stathopoulos, *Civil Code*, vol. 1^{B}, Arts. 173 and 200 no. 113; Papanikolaou, *Methodology*, §503.

32 Art. 1368 c.c.: 'Ambiguous clauses are interpreted according to usual practices of the place where the contract was made. In contracts where one party is a firm, ambiguous clauses are interpreted according to usual practices of the place where the firm has its seat'.

33 Cass. 30 April 2012 no. 6601; Cass. 14 June 1991 no. 6752; Cass. 23 December 1986 no. 7864.

In other words, as scholars put it, usages concur to determine the contractual meaning regardless of whether parties knew or willed them, but usages cannot prevail over a contrary common intention of the parties.[34]

The court would therefore consider first the literal meaning of the words in light of all relevant rules of subjective interpretation, in order to assess whether it is possible to determine a subjective meaning of Clause 4. If the court concludes that the clause unambiguously provides that the goods are to be delivered at the entrance of the distribution warehouse, then the court will not give weight to local customs of trade to assign to the clause a different meaning.

Should the court conclude that the clause still remains ambiguous after the application of rules of subjective interpretation, OnTrack's contention as to the existence of a local custom of trade requiring goods to be delivered up to the container terminal would be given a considerable weight in determining the legally relevant meaning of Clause 4.

9. NETHERLANDS

Following the *Haviltex* norm,[35] a contract is to be interpreted according to the meaning each party could reasonably have attributed to its terms and which they each could reasonably have expected the other to have attributed to them. To this end, the court should have regard to a wide variety of relevant facts and circumstances, which will include patterns of behaviour existing within a particular contracting community, trade usages and customs, as well as other relevant facts and circumstances surrounding the contractual relation assessed in light of the standards of 'redelijkheid en billijkheid' [reasonableness and fairness].[36] Consideration can therefore be given to what is customary throughout the country, in a particular place or in a particular sector or industry within which the contract is concluded for the purpose of interpreting the terms in the contract.[37] Art. 6:248(1) BW further recognises

34 Roppo, *Contratto*, pp. 452–453; Sacco, *Contratto*, p. 1374 ff.; but, for a comprehensive and critical explanation of the current relevance of Art. 1368 and of its relationship with other interpretation factors, see Astone, 'Dell'interpretazione del contratto (sub art.1368)', p. 564 ff. (esp. pp. 577–578).

35 Hoge Raad 13 March 1981, *NJ* 1981, 635 (Ermes/Haviltex).

36 Hoge Raad 20 February 2004, *NJ* 2005, 493 (DSM-Chemie/Fox).

37 Hoge Raad 26 October 2001, C99/312 HR, *JOR* 2001, 275, concerning the interpretation of 'agent' in accordance with usage in the shipping industry; Hoge Raad 17 February 2006, *NJ* 2006, 378 (Royal & Sun Alliance/Universal Pictures), concerning the interpretation of 'accident' in an insurance policy in accordance with practices in the insurance exchange; also Hoge Raad 16 May 2008, *NJ* 2008, 284 (Chubb/Europoint). See Rechtbank Arnhem

that 'gewoonte' [custom] may be relevant to establishing the content of the contract in the sense that the duties arising under the contract may stem from 'gewoonte' [custom].

Where a party lacks experience in a particular contracting community, such as a sector, industry or locality, it may not reasonably be expected of him that he be aware of a customary meaning attached to certain expressions used in the contract. Indeed, it could be reasonable for that party to understand the contractual expression in accordance with common linguistic usage. In contrast, where both contracting parties are active within a certain contracting community, it is reasonable for them to rely on a meaning that accords with the common usage in that contracting community and to expect the other to share that meaning. It should be noted, however, that the customary meaning is merely one of the factors that can be taken into account for the purpose of interpreting the contract; it is not decisive. The court may still take other relevant circumstances into account in order to uncover what meaning each party could reasonably have attributed to the contract term and what meaning they could reasonably expect the other party to have understood.[38]

If we assume that Murray does not regularly conclude contracts for the transportation of its products in containers by rail, and is therefore unfamiliar with the local custom of trade, then it would be reasonable for Murray to rely on the ordinary meaning of the wording used in Clause 4. Furthermore, if we assume that OnTrack is aware or could reasonably be aware of such lack of familiarity with the local custom of trade, then it would not be reasonable for OnTrack to rely on the customary meaning given to Clause 4 without having informed Murray thereof. In such cases, the court could interpret the expression in accordance with its ordinary meaning. In that case, it would not be reasonable for OnTrack to expect Murray to deliver right up to the actual container terminal. Conversely, if Murray regularly concludes these types of contracts and is familiar with the local custom of trade, or reasonably could not have been unaware of it, then OnTrack could reasonably expect Murray to share its customary understanding of the wording in Clause 4 and it would be unreasonable for Murray to rely on the ordinary meaning of the wording in Clause 4.

---

24 January 1918, W 10316 concerning the interpretation of clause in the coffee trade; Hoge Raad 20 May 1949, *NJ* 1950, 72, Hoge Raad 15 November 1968, *NJ* 1969, 1 and Gerechtshof Amsterdam 18 December 1970, *NJ* 1971, 212 concerning the interpretation of a clause in an insurance policy. Asser/Sieburgh, *Algemene leer der overeenkomsten*, 6-III, no. 376; Tanja-Van Den Broek, 'Een kwestie van uitleg', p. 431; Tjittes, *Uitleg van schriftelijke contracten*, p. 43; Tjittes, *Commercieel Contractenrecht*, p. 314.

38 Hoge Raad 17 February 2006, *NJ* 2006, 378 (Royal & Sun Alliance/Universal Pictures).

10. POLAND

When interpreting the content of Clause 4, Polish courts would take into account the local custom of trade in accordance with Art. 65 para. 1 of the KC, as explained in the Opening Remarks. According to Radwański,[39] customs are the reflection of certain established social practices (experience) and do not play a normative function. The scope of customs may differ from universal to professional or regional. Customs have to be proven in civil proceedings in the same way as other facts.[40]

In case law, there is a visible tendency to see an established custom as a part of the circumstances in which a statement of intent was made. It is indicated that, when interpreting the contract, the court should take into account the situational context, which follows from Art. 65 para. 1[41] (see further comments to Case 8). The SN[42] specified that the interpretation of a contractual clause that gives rise to controversies as to its meaning, because its meaning is unclear, cannot be based solely on the linguistic method. Instead, it is necessary to investigate the parties' intentions and aims, as well as the factual context in which the contract was agreed on and concluded. This includes, for example, the rules and customs concerning cooperation, both between the contractual parties, as well as in relation to other parties, which is particularly important in business relations (see further comments to Case 8). In any case, the business status of the parties must be taken into account.[43]

Legal writing explains further[44] that customs established in certain environments or professional circles, if they attribute specific meaning to particular expressions or behaviours, should be considered when interpreting a contract (see further comments to Case 2). However, the SN recently suggested that the manner of conducting business dealings by one of the contractual parties could indicate the existence of an established custom,[45] which has been contested among legal scholars.[46] Namely, in order to recognise an established custom, a numerous group of individuals in a given environment or a professional circle should use a particular practice for an extended period of time. The practice of one individual could indicate an established custom only if that individual monopolised the market. Therefore, a manner of conducting business dealings by one of the contractual

39 Z. Radwański, *System Prawa Prywatnego*, vol. 2, p. 65.
40 Ibid.
41 Judgment of SN of 17.06.2009, IV CSK 90/09.
42 Judgment of SN of 3.09.1998, I CKN 815/97.
43 Judgment of SN of 17.06.2009, IV CSK 90/09.
44 M. Safjan in *Kodeks cywilny, Komentarz do art. 1-449^{10}*, vol. 1, p. 215.
45 Judgment of SN of 18.11.2016, I CSK 802/15.
46 P. Sobolewski, 'Komentarz do art. 65 KC', point 32.

parties could indicate at most how that party interpreted a given contractual provision.[47]

The SN[48] also established that an unclear contractual clause that refers to the character of a 'służebność' [servitude] should be interpreted according to the common custom (practice), i.e. specifically in the case of a person acquiring part of an immovable property, a 'służebność gruntowa' [land servitude] is established, and not a 'służebność osobista' [personal servitude].

In the given case, if Clause 4 was perceived as unclear, a Polish court would take the local custom into consideration when determining its meaning. This local custom could differently reflect on the parties' contractual intentions.

11. PORTUGAL

In the Portuguese system, Art. 3.° CC states that usages and trade customs can be relevant if they are not against good faith and if the law admits them. In the interpretation of contract field, there is no reference to custom in Art. 236.° CC. Here, too, the standard concerning 'a posição do real declaratário' [the real circumstances of the person who receives the declaration] permits that customs can also be relevant in the context of interpretation if they have a role in the interpretation and integration of contract.

The problem is that the custom is local and there is not a uniform industry-wide trade custom. Therefore, it may be doubtful whether custom can provide any sort of consistent normative framework for deciding disputes between the parties. Nonetheless, a local custom can be used to justify an interpretation of Clause 4 as a tacit clause if it is considered reasonable. Moreover, the 'princípio de boa fé' [principle of good faith] can be used to justify a certain interpretation of Clause 4 that takes into account the local custom. In this case, the Portuguese system has one rule (Art. 762.°/2 CC) concerning the execution of contract that imposes that the parties must subject themselves to 'boa fé' in the performance of their duties arising from the contract.

12. SCOTLAND

Whilst it is possible to prove a custom of trade that words in a contract have a special trade meaning, this is only possible provided that that meaning does not

47 Ibid.
48 Judgment of SN of 29.12.1967, III CRN 59/67.

contradict the express terms of the contract.[49] Words that have either a legal meaning or a well-established ordinary meaning may be 'so well understood that the Court will not admit the possibility that they have been used in an exceptional sense.'[50] It is only in cases of ambiguity that proof will be allowed that words have, by a custom of trade known to both parties, a special meaning.[51] This approach has allowed a Scottish court, for example, to decide that 'a thousand rabbits' in a lease of a rabbit warren meant 1,200.[52]

It seems likely that a Scottish court would consider that Clause 4 was not ambiguous: it quite clearly indicates that the goods are to be delivered to Distribution Warehouse 10. The court is likely to find that evidence of the trade custom is inadmissible because it contradicts the express (and unambiguous) terms of the contract.

In principle, the Scottish court can make use of the commercially sensible construction in order to consider a custom of trade.[53] In this case, however, because Clause 4 is unambiguous, use of the commercially sensible construction is ruled out.[54]

Custom of trade is more often discussed in an implication rather than an interpretation context. Custom of trade in the implication context is very difficult to prove: '[i]t is essential that it should be certain, that it should be uniform, that it should be reasonable and that it should be notorious'.[55] It makes no difference that one of the parties is ignorant of the custom: the court is entitled notwithstanding this ignorance to find that the custom of trade exists.[56] The custom may be confined to a certain geographical area or confined to certain trades or professions.[57]

In conclusion, because Clause 4 is not ambiguous, the Scottish court could not refer to a custom of trade in the interpretation context. Although it is possible for terms to be implied into a contract on the basis of custom of trade, the standard of proof is very high. OnTrack may nevertheless be able to prove that the relevant custom exists. If so, the contract will contain an implied term which will govern the place of delivery.

---

49 Gloag, *Contract*, p. 382; McBryde, *Contract*, para. 9–60.
50 Gloag, *Contract*, p. 382.
51 Ibid.
52 *Smith v Wilson* (1832) 3 B & Ad 728.
53 McBryde, *Contract*, para. 9–60.
54 *Arnold v Britton* [2015] UKSC 36; [2015] AC 1619.
55 McBryde, *Contract*, para. 9–60, relying on *'Strathlorne' Steamship Co. v Baird & Sons* 1916 SC (HL) 134.
56 McBryde, *Contract*, para. 9–60, relying on *Constan Industries of Australia Pty Ltd v Norwich Winterthur (Australia) Ltd* [1985–86] 160 CLR 226.
57 McBryde, *Contract*, para. 9–60, relying on *William Morton & Co. v Muir Bros & Co.* 1907 SC 1211; *Bruce v Smith* (1890) 17 R 1000.

13. SOUTH AFRICA

Evidence of a trade usage is always admissible and, once proved to exist, will alter the apparent meaning of the clause.[58] However, before a court will consider the interpretation of Clause 4 in terms of the local custom, OnTrack must prove that there is a recognised custom that manufacturers are required to deliver their goods to the actual container terminal.[59] The existence of a trade usage is a question of fact.[60] OnTrack is required to show that the custom is universally and uniformly observed within the particular trade concerned; long-established, notorious, reasonable and certain; and that it does not conflict with the law or the clear provisions of the contract.[61] In order to satisfy these requirements, the evidence relating to the existence of the custom must be clear, consistent and convincing. Furthermore, OnTrack is required to prove that the alleged custom has in fact been acted upon on previous occasions (which necessitates the calling of witnesses), otherwise the allegation that there is such a custom amounts to mere opinion and is of little weight.[62]

If OnTrack is successful in meeting these requirements, then a court will interpret Clause 4 in terms of the relevant custom, unless there is an express or tacit term in the contract which excludes it. Arguably, this particular custom is not excluded by Clause 4 because the latter merely specifies the general location of the delivery; it does not state exactly where in Distribution Warehouse 10 the goods should be offloaded. Furthermore, the fact that Murray may be unaware of the custom is irrelevant; once a custom or trade usage is proved to exist, parties are deemed to be aware of it by virtue of their participation in the relevant market.[63]

14. SPAIN

This case deals with the weight given to a local custom of trade when interpreting an ambiguous contractual clause.

---

58 *Joubert Bros v Abrahamson* 1920 CPD 103 107; Hosten (rev. Knobel), 'Custom and Usage', para. 395; Cornelius, *Interpretation*, p. 175; Roberts, *Wessels' Law of Contract*, vol. I, para. 1854.

59 *Golden Cape Fruits (Pty) Ltd v Fotoplate (Pty) Ltd* 1973 2 SA 642 (C) 646A.

60 *Bertelsmann v Per* 1996 2 SA 375 (T) 382I–383A.

61 These requirements are summarised in *Crook v Pedersen Ltd* 1927 WLD 62 71; *Golden Cape Fruits (Pty) Ltd v Fotoplate (Pty) Ltd* 1973 2 SA 642 (C) 645H, and are discussed in detail in Bradfield, *Christie's Law of Contract*, pp. 190–196.

62 *Golden Cape Fruits (Pty) Ltd v Fotoplate (Pty) Ltd* 1973 2 SA 642 (C) 646H; *Crook v Pedersen Ltd* 1927 WLD 62 70.

63 *Crook v Pedersen Ltd* 1927 WLD 62 69; Sharrock, 'Principles of the Law of Contract', p. 553.

According to Art. 1.287 CC, the uses or customs of the country have to be taken into account to interpret any ambiguities in contracts, standing in for the omission of clauses which are usually set forth therein. In addition, scholars emphasise the importance of the customs of trade when it comes to the interpretation of contracts, especially business contracts.[64] Customs also have an integration function in Spanish contract law (Art. 1.287 *in fine* and Art. 1.258 CC) whenever a lacuna needs to be filled.

Such customs must be a matter of evidence before the courts[65] and for this it is important to know that despite the use of the term 'país' [country] in Art. 1.287 CC, legal doctrine gives the meaning of 'local' custom of trade.[66] However, 'local' can have different meanings: the place where the contract was concluded or the place of performance or the place of the common residence of the parties or where the goods are located. It is a controversial issue which Spanish legal scholars have tried to analyse by analogy with rules of international private law, such as Art. 10.5 CC.[67] The Proposal for a Modernisation, not enacted yet, solves this question with its reference to the 'usos de los negocios' [use of trade] without any local reference (Art. 1.279, para. 4).

Scholars such as De Castro also consider that the use of trade is not applicable in cases where neither party was aware of it or where, despite being aware of it, both parties had decided to exclude it. In any event, this rule is an objective interpretation factor and it is used to clarify ambiguous clauses. The principle of 'buena fe' [good faith] could be applied because of its overarching nature and of its scope, which applies not only to interpretation but also to contractual performance. Therefore, insofar as Murray has deviated from the local custom, Spanish courts may consider it a breach of contract.

From the above, local custom must be applied, as OnTrack argues, and the goods should have been delivered by the manufacturers to the container terminal.

15. SWEDEN

In order to determine the weight of the local custom of trade in interpreting Clause 4 of the contract, the courts will have to consider the relation obtaining between the wording of the individual norm, i.e. Clause 4, interpreted in the

---

64 STS 04.10.1982 (RJ 1982\5537); STS 03.12.1990 (RJ 1990\9538); STS 24.06.1995 (RJ 1995\4984); STS 03.05.2011, ECLI:ES:TS:2011:2665.

65 STS 22.09.1989 (RJ 1989\6347); STS 16.10.1998 (RJ 1998\7564).

66 STS 01.07.2013, ECLI:ES:TS:2013:3868.

67 López y López, *Comentarios*, p. 1417; Jordano Barea, 'De la interpretación', p. 517.

light of all relevant circumstances, and the content of the general norm, i.e. the local custom.

To elaborate, it is without question that a local custom of trade very well might be relevant when assessing the content of the contract by means of interpretation[68] – there are, as stated previously, no formal constraints in this regard[69] – but the question of *what* relevance, to be precise, can only ever be answered case by case, taking the individual circumstances at hand into consideration.[70] A general norm, such as a local custom of trade – the same applies to every single objective norm, be it ordinary language, rationality (economical or not), 'sakens naur' [the nature of things], custom, at any level, the practice of the parties or whatever – only takes hold where the interpretive data does not allow the interpreter to construct an understanding that is singular to the specific agreement interpreted.[71] And even then, the general norm applies *on the assumption* that it represents the individual understanding of the parties. The courts will assume that the parties are, for instance, rational. And, of course, this manoeuvre is only justified where both parties actually are subject to the norm under consideration. For instance, in the present case the courts must establish whether Murray and OnTrack are part of the trade community in which the custom in question is observed.[72] What is more, interpretation is rarely *simply* about resolving the tension between general norm and individual understanding. There is rather, typically, a complex interplay between the singular and the general – the courts make use of, or refer to, the general norms in order to arrive at an individual understanding.[73]

Thus, in order to assess how much weight the court is likely to give to the local custom of trade in interpreting Clause 4, it is necessary to go into the specifics of the case. It is constitutive of the interpretive problem which the court faces in this case that Clause 4 is, prima facie, unambiguous. Murray has indeed, as specified, delivered to Distribution Warehouse 10. The question is if the circumstances will allow the court to construct a reading going against the grain of the wording. Sustaining such a reading – having regard to matters typically accorded weight in the interpretative practice of Swedish courts – is (1) the nature of the goods, i.e. the complexity of carrying them; (2) the fact that Murray has, in spite of this complexity, undertaken to carry the goods, in

68 See e.g. NJA 1989 p. 269 and NJA 1996 p. 400.
69 See the answer to Case 1, Question 1, at n. 120.
70 On the role of custom in interpretation see generally Karlgren, *Kutym och rättsregel*, p. 29 ff.
71 See Adlercreutz, *Om avtalstolkning*, p. 581; Adlercreutz and Gorton, *Avtalsrätt II*, p. 39 f., 73 f., Samuelsson, *Tolkningslärans gåta*, p. 178 ff.; Vahlén, *Avtal och tolkning*, p. 248 f.; cf. Grönfors, *Tolkning av fraktavtal*, p. 29 ff., 81 ff.
72 Cf. NJA 1921 p. 511.
73 See e.g. NJA 1981 p. 323; NJA 1998 p. 3; NJA 2015 p. 110.

accordance with Clause 4 (implying that they will have devised a means of dealing with the complexity involved, which is relevant assuming that it is possible to employ those means in order to cover the final distance up to the actual terminal); and (3) the local custom of trade, which, in this case, is congruent with what the court most likely will consider to be an economically sound allocation of risk, namely to let Murray be responsible for carrying the goods all the way up to the container terminal.[74] (The court is not allowed to accord any importance to the geographical conditions on site – specifically the distance between entrance and terminal – unless it is shown that they were known to both parties at the time of conclusion.[75]) Will this suffice? Only the court can decide; which is to say that the interpretive judgment is not precluded by any kind of legal standard. The decision will be a decision on, among other things, the weight of the local custom concerned.

16. EDITORIAL COMPARATIVE OBSERVATIONS

All the reporters indicated that the local trade or custom could potentially be taken into account. Certain reporters identified the rationale behind the use of custom. In Sweden there is an assumption that usages correspond to the most probable implicit intention of the parties. In both Poland and Portugal, its role is not normative. In Poland it is a reflection of established social practices.

In each of the systems, the local custom would be used as part of an objective stage of the overall approach to interpretation. Certain systems, such as the Greek and Italian, apply a subjective approach to interpretation as a first step.[76] In those systems, custom was resorted to only when the subjective approach had failed to provide a solution. In most of the systems, custom is part of an objective approach, for example as part of the situational context in Poland or the real circumstances of the person who receives the contractual declaration in Portugal.

Custom or trade usage is specifically referred to in the legislative provisions of Croatia, France, Italy, Germany, Greece, Poland, Portugal and Spain. In common law or mixed legal systems (England and Wales, Scotland and South Africa), the use of custom in interpretation has been established in case law. In the other systems, custom is applied as a matter of principle rather than because of specific legislation.

74 Cf. NJA 2012 p. 597.

75 See the answer to Case 2, Question 1.

76 In the French system too custom is only resorted to if the ambiguity in the contract cannot be dispelled by searching for the common intention of the parties.

A divergence of approach exists in relation to whether an ambiguity must exist in the disputed clause before the court can make use of a local custom. The reporters from France, Germany, Italy, Poland, Scotland and Spain suggested that local custom could only be used to interpret the contract if it contained an ambiguity. The Finnish reporter doubted whether the custom would make a difference in the resolution of the case, however. The Finnish and Scottish reporters indicated that the custom would not override the fairly clear wording of Clause 4. The South African reporter, by contrast, indicated that evidence of custom was 'always admissible', and the Swedish reporter indicated that, notwithstanding the fact that the clause was not ambiguous, custom could be used by the court.

A high degree of similarity emerged in relation to the criteria which must apply before a practice could be recognised as a relevant custom and therefore used by a court. For most systems, the key question is whether both contracting parties operate in the locality and sphere of business in which the custom applies.[77] Only if this is the case can the court make use of the custom.

Most legal systems require the custom to have been observed with some regularity.[78] This requirement appears to be more pronounced in Greece ('permanent practices') and South Africa ('long-established'). England and Wales, Scotland and South Africa apply the criterion of notoriety, i.e. that the custom is sufficiently notorious to go without saying. Whilst all the legal systems recognise that a local, rather than a national, custom could be relevant, the reporter from Spain noted controversy over the exact meaning of 'local', given that it could mean the location of conclusion or performance of the contract, the common residence of the parties or where the goods are located.

Several reporters tackled whether the contracting parties must actually be aware of a custom before that custom could be used by the courts in the context of their dispute. The majority of reporters came to the conclusion that they did not require to be so aware.[79] The reporter from the Netherlands noted a reasonableness requirement, i.e. that the custom could be applied to a party unaware of the custom if that party could reasonably have been aware of it. This position perhaps reflects the rationale for the usage of custom as explained by the reporter from Sweden, i.e. the assumption that the custom

77 Croatia, England and Wales, Finland, Germany, Greece, Netherlands, Poland, Scotland, South Africa, Spain and Sweden.

78 Croatia and Germany.

79 Croatia, Italy, Germany (in the exercise of supplementing rather than interpreting the terms under §§242 and 157 BGB), Greece, Netherlands, South Africa and Spain.

corresponds to the most probable implicit intention of the parties. Seven of the reporters noted the contracting parties' ability expressly to exclude a specific custom.[80]

In several legal systems, good faith was identified as playing a role in the use of custom in interpretation of the contract[81] or indeed in supplementing the contract terms.[82] In Portugal, the principle of good faith justifies an interpretation that takes into account local custom. In Greece, trade customs are not an independent criterion, but rather a criterion that helps to concretise the standard of good faith required in each case. In Greece, a custom would be excluded if it contradicted good faith. And in Croatia, Murray's conduct in deviating from the applicable local custom could represent the violation of the principle of conscientiousness and honesty.

No clear pattern emerged from the reports on the importance the court would be likely to give to evidence of custom in interpreting the disputed Clause 4. The Swedish reporter, for example, noted that the answer largely depended upon the court's analysis of the facts. Whilst in the Netherlands custom is only *one* of the factors to be taken into account, in Italy the courts would give to the custom 'considerable weight', and in Greece, the court is 'very likely to take such a trade custom … into account'. The reporters from Finland and South Africa noted strict evidentiary requirements. In Finland, 'relatively convincing evidence' of the existence and content of the custom is required. In South Africa, '[e]vidence must be clear, consistent and convincing'.

80 Croatia, Italy, Germany, Greece, Scotland, South Africa and Spain.
81 Croatia, Greece, Portugal and Spain.
82 Germany.

CASE 10: THE MACHINE

'Bingham' is a company specialising in the development of industrial machinery to help businesses become more economically efficient. Bingham enters into a contract with 'Peel' in terms of which Bingham develops a custom-made machine that rationalises Peel's production of copper wire which it sells to the construction industry. Clause 2 provides that, in return, Peel is due to pay a purchase price consisting of both a modest initial sum for the development of the machine and an additional 35% of the profits made by Peel by using the device over the next five years. Bingham and Peel have agreed to use a method by which they calculate the 35% of the profit – there is no dispute on this point. After Peel has paid the initial sum and Bingham has manufactured and delivered the machinery, time passes, and Bingham hears nothing from Peel. Bingham contacts Peel on several occasions throughout the next year. The answer from Peel is always the same: Peel has chosen not to use the machine. Therefore, Peel reasons, there is no profit from which to calculate Peel's payment of 35% to Bingham. Bingham is very unhappy about this, having calculated the overall profit from the transaction assuming the use of the machine by Peel. In fact, as matters stand, Bingham contends, this will be a losing contract. Bingham further argues that, even though there is no clause in the contract which binds Peel to make use of the machine, Peel must be understood to have, in effect, taken it upon itself to pay more than merely the initial sum. To this end, Bingham had instructed an independent accountant to produce a report which estimates the amount of profit which would have been earned had the machine been used. In addition, Bingham continues, because Peel made the promise to pay 35%, Bingham was justified in expecting Peel to actually use the machine. Finally, Bingham concludes, it is simply not fair to interpret Clause 2 as Peel advocates.

Assume that the contract is a valid contract; that there is no local trade custom relevant to the matter at hand; no prior course of dealing between the parties; and that no evidence of any communication regarding the use of the machine. Without providing an interpretation of Clause 2 yourself, explain the factors the courts may be willing to attach weight to the interpretation of Clause 2, including the relative weight attached to each.

1. KEY ISSUES

The case concerns a contract to supply a machine which, if used, would allow the user to complete its industrial process more efficiently.[1] In terms of the contract, there is both a purchase price and, additionally, a formula to be applied to profits made using the machine. This is to allow the supplier of the machine to share in the profits gained with the machine. The contract does not, however, include an obligation on the user to *actually use* the machine. In fact, the machine is not used, and no profits are made to which the formula could be applied: the supplier is paid nothing by way of profit-share. The case makes clear that no custom of trade nor previous course of dealing between the parties applies. Nor has there been any communication between the parties concerning the use of the machine. Case 10 is different from the previous cases, in that it presents an open question. This case is not designed with any single aim in mind. Arguably, there is a gap in the contract. This being the case, reporters may discuss national attitudes to supplementation or implication. Reporters are asked, therefore, to address any relevant interpretation factors the courts in their respective jurisdiction might attach weight to in the interpretation of the disputed clause. In this way, this case offers reporters the opportunity to discuss any legal rules or doctrines which they may not consider a matter of interpretation strictly speaking, but nonetheless observe to be relevant for resolving the interpretation issue in question.

2. CROATIA

This case concerns a contract whereby Bingham has created a custom-made machine and has allowed Peel to use it in return for a payment. Payment consists of two parts: a fixed initial part of a modest amount and a variable part calculated as 35% of the profit. The question posed is whether in the absence of a clause in the contract binding Peel to use the machine, Peel has the obligation to pay more than merely the initial sum.

Under the assumptions that this is a valid contract, that there is no local trade custom relevant to the matter at hand nor a prior course of dealing between the parties, and that there is no evidence of any communication regarding the use of the machine, the Croatian courts would have to explore the common intention of the parties by means of additional interpretation methods and rules respecting the basic principles of the law on obligations. These different

1 This case was loosely inspired by the Scottish case *North American and Continental Sales Inc v Bepi (Electronics) Ltd* 1982 SLT 47. The facts of Case 10 differ from this case, as do the legal issues raised.

interpretation rules developed by court practice and legal theory include inter alia the determination of the purpose of the contract by applying the teleological method of interpretation. The ambiguous contract terms must be interpreted in a way that enables the realisation of its purpose which the contracting parties intended to achieve by concluding the contract. Consequently, the Croatian courts would primarily explore whether in concluding the contract Bingham and Peel had the same purpose in mind. Based on the circumstances of the case at hand, the courts could conclude that their common intention was the development of a custom-made machine that would rationalise *production* of copper wire, which implies the *use* of the machine.[2] Therefore, the courts would most likely interpret the part of Clause 2 concerning the payment for the use of the machine over the next five years in the light of the established common purpose of the contracting parties. In exploring the contracting parties' common intention, the court would have to rely on the basic principles of the law of obligations. Accordingly, the interpretation of their common intention would have to be in line with the above-mentioned principle of conscientiousness and honesty (Art. 4 of the COA) and the principle of due professional care (Art. 10(2) of the COA), but also some other principles such as the 'zabrana prouzročenja štete' [prohibition of causing damage] and 'dužnost ispunjenja obveze' [duty to perform an obligation]. Pursuant to Art. 8 of the COA, each party is obliged to refrain from an act which may cause damage to the other party, while, according to Art. 9 of the COA, each party to a contract is obliged to perform its obligations and is liable for its performance/ defective performance/non-performance. Consequently, the Croatian courts would interpret Clause 2 in a way that corresponds to these basic principles of the law of obligations and would establish its meaning accordingly. By virtue of interpretation, the courts would fill the gap in the contracting parties' statements.

3. ENGLAND AND WALES

The most important interpretative factor is the words used and their meaning. Here, significant weight will be attached to the fact that there is no express clause in the contract which binds Peel to make use of the machine. Such a clause could easily have been drafted if intended, although it may (depending upon the circumstances) have been so obvious as to go without

2 Having in mind precisely cases such as the one at hand, legal scholarship has advised the right holders to contract for the minimum amount of periodic royalties (plus the percentage) which are independent of the production, sale or profits from the use of the licensed subject matter. Such a clause has an indirect effect of forcing the acquirer to use the licensed subject-matter. See Mutabžija, 'Klauzule plaćanja kod ugovora o licenciji', pp. 12–13.

saying and so be implied. Further, there is a clause providing that Peel is to pay a sum for using the machine. The precise wording of this clause may be important as an indication that the parties did or did not understand that Peel had to make use of the machine.

The next important factor is the commerciality of the deal. If both parties would have understood the contract to be a heavily losing one for Bingham if Peel did not use the machine, that weighs in favour of Peel being obliged so to do, but only if and to the extent that Bingham would have been obviously unlikely to take the commercial risk of Peel not using the machine: commercial parties do take risks all the time, and in this case Bingham is provided with some upfront payment in the pricing model. Moreover, if Peel decides not to use the machine, then it has wasted its initial sum, which provides an economic incentive for Bingham to use it and reduces the risk Peel takes by the contract even without an obligation on Bingham to use the machine. But the courts will only imply an obligation to use the machine if it is necessary for business efficacy or so obvious that it must have been intended that it goes without saying.[3]

Fairness or otherwise is, strictly speaking, irrelevant, as there is no general duty of good faith in English law.[4] That said, the courts will sometimes imply a fetter on a party's discretion so as to prevent it acting in bad faith, capriciously or irrationally, where the reasonable observer would understand such a fetter to apply. This may apply to a bank's discretion to set an interest rate,[5] or an employer's right to choose the amount of an employee's bonus.[6] More relevantly to this case, it may also apply to a publisher's decision as to how many copies it will publish when fulfilling its obligation to publish a book (each copy of which obliges the publisher to pay the claimant royalties).[7] Whether it applies to the instant case, and specifically Bingham's apparently free choice as to whether to employ the machine developed by Peel, depends upon what it would be reasonable for the parties to understand the contract to have provided.

4. FINLAND

In Finnish contract law there are several legal principles and doctrines that must be taken into account when solving this case. Perhaps the most important

---

3 *Marks & Spencer plc v BNP Paribas Securities Services Trust Co (Jersey) Ltd* [2016] AC 742.
4 See point (7) in the Opening Remarks.
5 *Paragon Finance plc v Nash* [2001] EWCA Civ 1466; [2002] 1 WLR 685 (CA).
6 *Cantor Fitzgerald International v Horkulak* [2008] EWCA Civ 1287 (CA).
7 *Abrahams v Reiach (Herbert) Ltd* [1922] 1 KB 477 (CA) per Scrutton LJ. Although in that case, unlike the present case, there was an express obligation to publish.

principle here is that a contract should be interpreted as an entirety, taking into account its objectives, background and context.[8] This principle can be illustrated with the Finnish Supreme Court's decision KKO 2010:69. In this case, A and B had made cooperation agreements in 1987 and in 1989 that could, under the contract, be ended by notice only if there was a valid reason, such as if the business was unprofitable or the purpose of the contract was not achieved. Later C, who had taken over B's business, ended the contracts by notice in April 2004. The ground for notice was reorganisation of the business due to changes in the markets.

The meaning of the contract, the possibility of changes in circumstances and the contract parties' opportunity to negotiate the reorganisation of the business were taken into account when interpreting the terms of the contract. The court held that C did not have a valid reason to cancel open-ended contracts.

Correspondingly, in the facts of this case it would be insufficient to narrow the analysis only to the disputed clause concerning the fee. On the contrary, the starting point of interpretation should be the question of how the parties have understood the purpose and nature of the contract. One must ask whether Bingham has voluntarily taken the risk of Peel not using the machine and, further, the risk of the contract being unprofitable.

However, it may well be that one cannot detect any mutual objective shared by the parties. In other words, the parties have understood the objectives of the contract differently. In that case, it must be asked which of the parties have been, or at least should have been, aware of the dissensus. One general principle in the Finnish law of property is the principle of 'vilpittömän mielen suoja' [protection of sincere mind].[9] According to that principle, one must protect a party who has acted in good faith. In a situation where a contracting party has noticed that the other party has understood some clause in a different way than he understands it himself, but the other party does not notice this dissensus, protection of good faith supports the solution that the clause should be interpreted in favour of the party in *bona fides*.

If it turns out that both parties have been in *bona fides* in the dissensus, this may lead to the question whether the contract should be considered void. It could be argued that since there has really never been any mutual understanding of the essential terms of the contract, the alleged contract has never come into existence. This solution, however, would be quite impractical, because the parties have already for some time acted as though the contract had existed. Bingham has fulfilled its obligations according to the contract, or at least most of them. At this point one could consider the principle of 'pätevyyssääntö'

8 Hemmo, *Sopimusoikeus I*, p. 584 and Saarnilehto and Annola, 'Sopimuksen tulkinta', p. 448. See accordingly also the Finnish Supreme Court's decisions KKO 2003:26 and 2010:69.

9 Tuomisto, *Varallisuusoikeus*, pp. 100–101.

[validity rule], whereby one should prefer interpretative alternatives that leave the contract valid. However, it has been pointed out that the 'pätevyyssääntö' must not be applied so expansively that it would water down the effects of rules concerning the invalidity of contract, which still serve an important function in contract law.[10]

If the mutual intention of the parties cannot be traced following the above-mentioned interpretation principles, or if it does not even exist, rules of 'tavoitteellinen tulkinta' [target-oriented interpretation] may become applicable. The rules of 'tavoitteellinen tulkinta' form a heterogeneous set of interpretation rules that share the common feature that they do not necessarily aim to find out the real mutual intention of the parties, but rather to distribute the risk of ambiguity in a reasonable way.[11] When applying the principles of 'tavoitteellinen tulkinta', the eventual interpretation of the contract does not get its content only from the intent of the parties but is also affected by rules reflecting legal policy.[12] The rules of 'tavoitteellinen tulkinta' have been called 'pakkotulkintanormi'[13] [coercive interpretation norms], meaning that due to the need to somehow solve the interpretation question in the end ('ratkaisupakko' [duress to decide]), the interpreter must have some tools even in a case where the common intent of the parties cannot be reliably found out.

The most important of these interpretation rules is the 'epäselvyyssääntö' [unclarity rule], whereby an unclear contract should be interpreted in favour of the party who has not drafted the contract.[14] The 'epäselvyyssääntö' is particularly important in contracts between a business and a consumer. In these situations, the significance of the 'epäselvyyssääntö' has been consolidated by incorporating it into the Finnish Consumer Protection Act (38/1978) Chapter 4 Section 3. In legal literature it has even been asked whether the significance of the 'epäselvyyssääntö' has been overemphasised in some cases.[15] The description of the present case does not indicate whether the contract has been drafted by the parties together or by one party solely. If, however, it turns out that one of the parties is responsible for the drafting, this might well become a relevant factor in the court's decision.

One more rule of the 'tavoitteellinen tulkinta' deserves to be mentioned here: the 'minimisääntö' [minimum rule]. According to 'minimisääntö', a contract

---

10 Hemmo, *Sopimusoikeus I*, pp. 652–653.

11 Ibid., p. 632.

12 Ibid., p. 634.

13 Aho, *Varallisuusoikeudellisen oikeustoimen tulkinnasta*, p. 236.

14 See generally Hemmo, *Sopimusoikeus I*, pp. 638–640 and Saarnilehto and Annola, 'Sopimuksen tulkinta', pp. 452–453. The Finnish Supreme Court has referred to 'epäselvyyssääntö' in numerous decisions. See e.g. decisions KKO 1978 II 126, 1993:127, 2002:65, 2009:13, 2010:69, 2011:13 and 2016:10.

15 Norros, 'Onko ei-kielletty aina sallittua auton osamaksuostajalle?', pp. 854–865, criticising Finnish Supreme Court's decision KKO 2009:13.

should be interpreted in favour of the obliged party. In other words, the scope and content of contractual obligations should be interpreted restrictively rather than expansively.[16] When considering this case, one could refer to the 'minisääntö', arguing that since Peel has not explicitly committed to use the machine, this interpretation cannot be derived from the unclear contract. However, the court would probably not give too much weight to this argument. In legal literature it has been pointed out that the 'minimisääntö' easily leads to coincidental results if it is applied to a mutually binding contract. It has been suggested that the 'minimisääntö' should be given weight mainly in the interpretation of unilateral commitments.[17]

5. FRANCE

Pursuant to their contract, Bingham has delivered a custom-made machine to Peel. According to Clause 2 of the contract, the price to be paid by Peel consists of an initial amount of money that has been paid for the development of the machine and an additional 35% of the profits generated by the use of the machine by Peel over the following five years. However, Peel argues that it does not have to pay anything more to Bingham, since it chose not to use the machine.

As a matter of principle, French courts would again interpret Clause 2 by reference to the common intention of the parties. The wording of the litigated term seems to be quite clear and unambiguous, which does not leave much room for interpretation.

Nonetheless, the courts could consider relying on Art. 1104 Cciv (formerly Art. 1134 (3)), which requires the parties to perform their contract in good faith. One could indeed argue that the wording of Clause 2 relied on the shared assumption that Peel would use the machine for at least five years after the delivery. Peel's decision not to use it would thus amount to a manifestation of bad faith for which Peel could be held liable.[18]

Other provisions of the French Civil Code could potentially be considered, although less convincingly. To begin with, under Art. 1304-2 Cciv (formerly Arts. 1170 and 1174), a condition the fulfilment of which depends exclusively on the will of the debtor is null and void, except if the other party has already performed their own obligations in full knowledge and understanding of the situation. Leaving the choice to the debtor as to whether they want to

---

16 Annola, *Varallisuusoikeus*, p. 449; Hemmo, *Sopimusoikeus I*, pp. 647–648; and Pönkä, 'Tavoitteellisten tulkintasääntöjen merkityksestä liikesopimusten tulkinnassa', pp. 930–932.

17 Hemmo, *Sopimusoikeus I*, pp. 648–649.

18 Y. Picod in *JCl. Civil Code*, Art. 1134 et 1135, Fasc. unique (unrevised).

perform their obligation would indeed deprive the obligation of its binding force as a contractual obligation. In the present case, Clause 2 could be analysed as setting the obligation for Peel to pay Bingham 35% of the profits generated by the custom-made machine under the implicit condition that Peel uses the machine.[19] In this analysis, the condition would be under the control of the sole debtor and therefore would be null under Art. 1304-2 Cciv (formerly Art. 1174). However, such a solution would in practice not provide much relief to Bingham.[20]

Besides, Art. 1304-3 Cciv (formerly Art. 1178) provides that such conditions shall be held as fulfilled if the debtor of the obligation has prevented its fulfilment. Peel could be considered to have deliberately prevented the fulfilment of the condition by choosing not to use the machine.[21] As a consequence the condition could be held as fulfilled and Bingham could be entitled to 35% of what would have been the likely profits generated by the use of the custom-made machine. Still, such a solution is not quite straightforward, given the difficulty of assessing such 'likely profits.'

Eventually, another possibility would be for the court to decide to rescind the contract for non-performance of some of Peel's obligations by Peel if the court were to consider that Peel was expected to use the machine for at least five years.[22] Nevertheless, on account of the custom-made nature of the machine, such an option might not be the most helpful to Bingham either.

6. GERMANY

From a German perspective, Bingham and Peel probably concluded a 'Werkvertrag' [contract to produce the machine as a specific result] under §631 BGB. This qualification is not changed by the calculation of the remuneration based on the profits gained by Peel. There is no specific rule in the German codification for the situation at hand, that a debtor of a price calculated based on profits does not cooperate in pursuing profits at all.

It is unclear how a German court would decide if the decision were to be based on interpretation. It could use interpretation by referring to the behaviour of the parties[23] and thereby conclude that there is a duty or an onus to use the machine. The relevance of what was discussed between the parties before the

19 Cf. Soc., 25 November 1971, *Bull. civ.* (1971) no. 688.

20 Com., 19 January 2010, *JurisData* no. 2010-051288.

21 Cf. Civ. 1, 2 June 1993, *Bull. civ.* (1993) no. 198.

22 For a precedent, see Civ. 1, 25 April 1968, *Bull. civ.* (1968) no. 122.

23 J. Busche, '§133 BGB' in K. Rebmann and F.J. Säcker (eds.), *Münchener Kommentar zum Bürgerlichen Gesetzbuch*, m.n. 54.

conclusion of the contract[24] is obvious in that context. In the case at hand, Peel and Bingham have agreed on the payment of an initial sum and to use a method by which they calculate the 35% of the profit from using the machine over the next five years. That is why a German court could decide that using the machine was part of the contractual basis for the price agreement.

However, German courts would usually apply legal rules rather than interpret the contract: under general contract law, non-cooperative behaviour which prevents the price claim becoming due may make the price payable at law by applying §162 BGB or §326 (2) BGB.

Under §162 BGB, the use of the machine is assumed to be a condition under §158 BGB for the payment of 35%. §162 BGB says that if the fulfilment of a condition is prevented by the party to whose disadvantage it would be and this prevention would be against good faith and fair dealing, the condition is deemed to have been fulfilled. Peel's behaviour of not making use of the machine would probably be assumed to be in bad faith. As a result, Peel's obligation would become due.

§326 (2) BGB follows the same basic reasoning, providing that if the creditor is solely or predominantly responsible for the circumstance making the debtor's performance impossible, the debtor becomes or remains entitled to the price, which may then be reduced in some respects. One could argue in the case at hand that Peel's behaviour leads to an application of this rule (directly or by way of analogy) because Peel thereby prevents the success of Bingham's performance.[25]

7. GREECE

The interpretation scheme applicable with regard to juridical acts in Greek law is more or less uniform and consists in the combination of the subjective and the objective criterion (Arts. 173 and 200 CC respectively), appropriately adapted to the particularities of each case (e.g. whether a unilateral juridical act or a contract is in play, etc.). In this case, the subjective interpretation apparently can offer no conclusive results; the understanding of the parties with regard to Clause 2 is essentially different. Therefore, Clause 2 must be examined in the light of the objective criterion of Art. 200 CC, i.e. what the parties could and should have understood taking into account all pertinent circumstances. We also take for granted that there is no relevant previous conduct between the parties, no communication between them concerning the use of the machine and no relevant local trade custom; therefore, the court will have

24 BGH, 10.10.1989, *NJW* 1990, 441; BGH, 13.03.2003, *NJW* 2003, 2235.

25 It is worth mentioning that in addition to that a price claim may follow from §32 UrhG.

to turn to other 'συγκείμενα' [proximates] of the contractual relationship in question in order to sufficiently flesh out the applicable standard of 'καλή πίστη' [good faith] under Art. 200 CC. Bingham puts forward a number of arguments to help the court discern the normative meaning of the agreement between Bingham and Peel. At the end of the day, the question to what extent the court will rely upon the one or the other argument depends upon their relevant strength and the degree to which the relevant allegations are proven.[26]

Regarding the relative weight attached to each interpretative factor, there are no general rules and the wording almost universally used by the Greek courts when applying the criteria of Arts. 173 and 200 CC does not offer any leads for the classification of the relevant factors by importance. Greek courts almost invariably state in their decisions involving contract interpretation that they reached their judgment 'after applying the criteria of Arts. 173 and 200 CC';[27] the fine distinctions and methodological observations mentioned above have been elaborated basically by legal doctrine. Returning to the rule of Art. 200 CC, in particular, this is essentially nothing more than a general clause which has to be concretised each time on the basis of the facts at hand. Legal doctrine affirms that the various elements of evaluation contained in the general clause of Art. 200 CC are actually volatile elements in the sense that Wilburg attributed to the term (*bewegliches System*) and their relative strength cannot be predetermined, except for the relative prevalence of good faith over trade customs; regardless of whether the various elements of Art. 200 CC arise out of the text or the context of the agreement, each and every one of them can be equally useful in discerning the normative meaning of the agreement.[28]

In view of the above, the court is likely to take all arguments put forward by Bingham into account, in order to discover the normative meaning of Clause 2; in other words, it will examine all those arguments and their combined effect on the interpretation of the clause in question. Since the concretisation

---

26 See Stathopoulos, *Civil Code*, vol. 1^B, Arts. 173 and 200 no. 119, 173–183, who notes certain unwritten interpretation rules, such as the principle of *contra proferentem* (i.e. the interpretation to the detriment of the person formulating a term), the *favor contractus* and the *benigna interpretatio* (both favouring the interpretation option that safeguards the agreement or the unilateral legal act), the prevalence of the usage of the *locus contractus*, etc.; nonetheless, even these principles do not offer a structured scheme for classifying the interpretation factors by importance, but rather constitute fragmentary rules to be applied *in concreto*.

27 See e.g. AP 183/2011, first published in NOMOS; AP 3/2011, first published in NOMOS; AP 804/1980, NoV 29 (1981), 72; CA Athens 1922/2012, ChrID 13 (2013), 193; CA Athens 4108/2012, first published in NOMOS; Stathopoulos, *Civil Code*, vol. 1^B, Arts. 173 and 200 no. 22; Balis, *General Principles*, §88.

28 Papanikolaou, *Methodology*, §503; cf. Stathopoulos, *Civil Code*, Vol. 1^B, Arts. 173 and 200 nos. 22, 100–119, 173–183; Karassis, *General Principles*, § Γ 275.

of the general clause of Art. 200 CC leads the court to treat the 'συγκείμενα' of the contract as a group of volatile elements, it is hard to determine, based on court practice, what importance exactly would be attributed to each one of Bingham's arguments.

Notwithstanding the above, it seems plausible to suggest that the first and the fourth argument (namely the fact that this is a losing contract for Bingham and the unfairness that this entails) would be taken more seriously into consideration by the court. The court would then possibly turn to the relative value of the work dedicated by Bingham to the development of the machine in relation to the initial fee paid upfront and the proportionality of the business risk assumed; if the initial fee is substantially lower than the value of the resources invested by Bingham in the development of the machine and this was or ought to have been known to Peel, it could be inferred on the basis of dealing in 'καλή πίστη' that the payment arrangement is suggestive of a duty for Peel to at least make use of the machine over a certain period of time, in order to properly remunerate Bingham (or provide further payment irrespective of its profits, which, however, would most probably supersede the mere interpretation of the agreement; see immediately below for the relationship of Art. 200 CC to Art. 288 CC).

The second argument put forward by Bingham, i.e. that Peel ought to have understood that it has to pay more, is at the end of the day a claim that Bingham will seek to confirm through Art. 200 CC. The admission by Bingham that no clause binding Peel to use the machine was included in the contract could perhaps play an important role. In respect of the independent accountant's report, the importance that the court would place on it depends, at the end of the day, on its verifiability; more likely, this would be of use after having affirmed, on the basis of the combined analysis of all surrounding circumstances, an obligation by Peel to make use of the machine and in order to determine the amount owed to Bingham, but not whether there is such an obligation in the first place.

Finally, the court would most probably apply the same approach with regard to the third argument by Bingham: the court will have to weigh the possible inferences of the 35% clause affirming an obligation by Peel to make use of the machine against Bingham's admission that no clause stipulating such an obligation for Peel was included in the contract. In this respect, it is useful to note that the arguments put forward by Bingham about Peel's contractual practice may lead the court to an apparently similar, but in its essence different, working method: Art. 288 CC provides that the debtor of each obligation must fulfil his or her duties in accordance with 'καλή πίστη' [good faith], also taking into account the 'συναλλακτικά ήθη' [trade customs]. At first glance, this provision is tautological with Art. 200 CC, since the same criteria apply for both (namely 'καλή πίστη' and 'συναλλακτικά ήθη'). However, the application of Art. 288 CC goes a step beyond the interpretation of a contract: it regulates the manner in which a contract should be executed, after its meaning has become clear. And it is possible that the judge may decide that the parties are under a duty to perform in a different manner than the agreement between them, in order to satisfy the requirement of 'καλή πίστη' in business transactions.[29] However, if the judge reaches such a conclusion and bases it upon Art. 288 CC, this is no longer an interpretation of a contract, but a supplementation or an adaptation, on the basis of overriding legal principles (essentially for reasons of fairness in business transactions), of what the court found to be the contractual agreement. It must be noted that the provisions of Arts. 200 and 288 CC, in spite of the difference in their subject matter, are treated as complementary and, therefore, are at times invoked together by the courts.[30] When this is the case, it is not always easy to determine whether the deciding judge proceeded to the interpretation of the contract under Art. 200 CC or its adaptation under Art. 288 CC.

8. ITALY

If the case has to be treated within the framework of the rules on contract interpretation, several rules would potentially be relevant.

First of all, Art. 1362, first paragraph, c.c., as already seen, provides that the court should pay reasonable attention to the literal meaning of the words used by the parties. This preliminary examination of the wording of Clause 2 may lead a court to find that Peel is under no legal obligation to use the programme and that, in the event of non-use, the only contractual obligation that lies upon Peel is to pay the small initial sum.

If the court holds that the expressions used by the parties in framing Clause 2 are sufficiently clear and that no margin of doubt affects their legal meaning, the court could be satisfied with such literal interpretation, which places upon Bingham all the risks as to the profitability of the contract. This conclusion could be suited to a court willing to adopt the current prevailing judicial approach whereby, when the wording of the contract is clear and an examination of its literal meaning does not leave any remaining ambiguity, such wording should be deemed sufficient to express the parties' intention and

---

29 See AP 669/2011, NoV 60 (2012), 329 (for the application of Art. 288 on lease agreements); CA Athens 1903/2012, DEE 18 (2012), 952 (for insurance contracts).

30 See AP (plenum) 32/1998, EEN 65 (1998), 605; AP 554/1993, EllDni 34 (1994), 1094; Stathopoulos, *Civil Code*, vol. 1^{B}, Arts. 173 and 200 nos. 193–194, noting that a strict distinction between the two provisions and their application is not always feasible and, possibly, also not necessary; Stathopoulos, 'Art. 288' in Georgiades and Stathopoulos (eds.), *Αστικός Κώδιξ: ερμηνεία κατ' άρθρο – νομολογία – βιβλιογραφία, Τόμος Δεύτερος: Γενικό Ενοχικό [Astikos Kodex: Commentary by Article – Case Law – Bibliography, Volume II: General Part of the Law of Obligations]*, no. 37.

the judge must then abide by such literal meaning because the other rules on contract interpretation would not be relevant.[31]

However, while examining the literal meaning of the words, the court is required to investigate the contract as a whole, because, according to Art. 1363, each contractual clause must be interpreted through other clauses and the literal meaning must be determined pursuant to a global consideration of all contractual provisions. Therefore, such a comprehensive consideration of the contract as a whole might lead the court to conclude that other contractual clauses, though not imposing any express obligation upon Peel, nevertheless support the idea that Peel should be subjected to some further obligation besides the payment of the small initial sum. Should this be the case, given the ambiguity of the literal meaning of the contract that would result from a global consideration of its clauses, the court would probably resort to other interpretive factors in order to pursue an 'objective' interpretation.

Art. 1369, generally regarded as a rule of objective interpretation, provides that ambiguous clauses must be interpreted according to the nature and object of the contract.[32] Therefore, in this case, the court should try to determine whether the interpretation of the contract as imposing only a limited obligation upon Peel is not consistent with the overall economic purpose of the contract and with the structure and content of all obligations arising from it. A court should then examine the way in which the contract distributes risks, costs and benefits between the parties, in order to determine the objective economic structure and purpose of the specific contract. This examination should allow the court to decide whether the economic risk as to the actual future utility of the machine to the buyer should be placed entirely upon the developer or on both parties. Both solutions are possible.

A comprehensive account of the purpose and object of the contract could lead the court to conclude that it is consistent with the overall balance of contractual obligations that the developer bear the risk of the non-use of the machine by the buyer. This would be the case if the court found that the contract amounts to a transaction which has an aleatory character for the developer of the machine. If so, the structure of contractual obligations would imply that the prospective profits to the developer depend upon the actual utility of the machine to the intended user. This conclusion could make sense, as a possible 'economic purpose' of the contract, because it could be consistent with a contractual structure purporting to align the parties' interests so that the developer has the best incentives to provide a useful product to the buyer. In this situation, the non-use of the machine would be one of the possible outcomes of the intended transaction and it would be governed by Clause 2, which would

---

31 See above Case 1, n. 56; Case 7; Case 8.

32 See above Case 1.

leave Peel free to disregard the result of Bingham's efforts without bearing any further cost.

On the other hand, a comprehensive consideration of the nature and object of the contract could lead the court to conclude that the overall balance of contractual effects should not be construed as imposing the risk of non-use of the machine on the developer alone. In this case a court would strive to find some contractual basis to impose on Peel some further obligations aimed at a reasonable satisfaction of Bingham's interests. It is very likely that a court willing to impose this sort of obligation upon Peel would resort to the good faith interpretation of Art. 1366. Most scholars and courts usually construe this rule as a tool for protecting the party who has relied on the meaning which appeared the most reasonable considering all the circumstances.

Therefore, one possible effect of the good faith interpretation is that Bingham be entitled to some sort of compensation if it were fair and reasonable that Bingham understood the meaning of the relevant contractual clauses as entailing some sort of further obligation upon Peel and Peel somehow led Bingham to believe so. However, if the court finds that the literal meaning of Clause 2 in light of an overall consideration of the contract as a whole is not ambiguous and that it does not impose any further obligation upon Peel, it is quite unlikely that the good faith principle alone would suffice to overcome such a clear contractual text. Usually, Art. 1366 is not intended as a rule allowing courts to modify the economic balance set down by the parties or to enforce principles of 'contractual justice'.[33]

Nevertheless, some scholars argue for a more relevant function of good faith in the interpretation process. According to their arguments, the duty to interpret in accordance with good faith would not be subjected to the constraints of the hierarchy principle and Art. 1366 should always be applied, irrespective of any ambiguity or doubt as to the subjective meaning of the contract. Good faith interpretation, it has been submitted, would either allow courts to adapt the contractual provisions to unexpected circumstances,[34] or to construe the contract in accordance with fundamental legal principles (especially constitutional principles, such as solidarity),[35] or to choose, amongst possible objective meanings, the one that better fits parties' needs.[36] If a court followed those views, it might either conclude that the non-use of the machine by Peel is an unexpected circumstance, or that some fundamental (constitutional) principles require that Bingham be protected against an unexpected or unfair

33 See e.g. Cass. 16 February 2001 no. 2293.

34 Bessone, *Adempimento e rischio contrattuale*.

35 Bigliazzi Geri, *Note*, who acknowledges that Art. 1366 has a 'corrective' function.

36 Costanza, *Profili*; see also Scognamiglio, *Interpretazione*, p. 364, who argues that good faith interpretation can help the judge to imply terms according to the nature of the economic transaction.

loss, or that one of the possible objective meanings of the contract is that it imposes on Peel some obligation aimed at the protection of Bingham's interests and that this meaning is better suited to Bingham's legitimate expectations. A court willing to adopt this approach might find that the contract presents an unexpected or unfair imbalance that can be cured through good faith interpretation.[37]

A last resort for the protection of Bingham's interests could be found in Art. 1371, which provides the last rule on contract interpretation, stating that: 'If, notwithstanding the application of the rules provided for by this chapter, the contract still remains unclear, it must be interpreted in such a way as to impose the least possible burden on the obliged party, if the contract is gratuitous; in such a way as to strike an equitable balance between the interests of the parties, if the contract is onerous.' This rule can be applied only in exceptional cases where the contractual meaning cannot be determined through the application of any interpretation factor and yet the contract cannot be deemed void for lack of certainty.[38] In this case, Art. 1371 could possibly allow the court to strike an equitable balance between contracting parties' interests and to grant some compensation to Bingham.

In general, if the circumstances do not allow the court to justify its decision as a mere subjective or objective explanation of the content of the contract, a legal argumentation aimed at the protection of Bingham's legitimate interests would probably resort to the 'integrazione del contratto' [implication of terms] pursuant to Arts. 1374 and 1375 c.c.[39]

To apply Art. 1374,[40] the court should assume that the contract does not regulate the case of non-use of the machine and so there is a 'lacuna' [gap] that needs to be filled by an external source. The law could supplement the will of the parties by providing some statutory rule (usually taken from the code regulation of 'nominated' contracts) which fits the specific issue left unregulated by the parties. 'Equità' [Equity] would fill the contractual gap with a rule tailored to the inner legal and economic balance that the contract itself expresses.[41]

In the present case, if the court is convinced that the absence of a contractual provision regulating the obligations upon Peel in the event of non-use of the machine amounts to a gap (and not to a deliberate choice of

37 See e.g. Cass. 5 March 2009 no. 5348.

38 Gentili and Astone, 'Dell'interpretazione del contratto (sub art. 1371)', p. 633.

39 On the distinction between interpretation and 'integrazione del contratto' [implication of terms] see Rodotà, *Le fonti di integrazione del contratto*, pp. 93 ff.; Bigliazzi Geri, *L'interpretazione del contratto*, p. 25 ff.; Gentili, *Senso e consenso*, p. 461 ff.

40 Art. 1374: 'The contract obliges the parties not only to the effects they have expressly agreed upon but also to those further effects that result from law, usages or equity'.

41 On Art. 1374 in connection with problems of interpretation of contracts, see also Cian, *Forma solenne e interpretazione*, pp. 204–207; for a comprehensive account of the role of good faith and equity in contracts see M. Barcellona, *Clausole generali*.

the parties), the court would first look for a suitable rule providing some sort of obligation upon Peel within the code regulation of 'nominated contracts'.

If no nominated contract regulation or any other legal rule is deemed applicable to the case, since we assume that there is no relevant trade custom, the court would resort to 'equità' in order to decide whether the economic balance of the specific transaction requires any implication of terms providing some additional obligation upon Peel.

Alternatively, a court could apply the duty of 'buona fede' [good faith] in the performance of contracts (Art. 1375 c.c.)[42] and conclude that Peel's behaviour infringing the duty of good faith amounts to breach of contract. The conceptual framework for the application of 'buona fede' in the performance of contract would be slightly different, because it does not necessarily presuppose a specific gap in the contractual regulation, but it would rather require the court to assess, in the light of all relevant circumstances, whether or not non-use of the machine by Peel or its refusal to pay an additional sum is in fact consistent with the overall economic and legal purpose of the contractual terms.[43]

The courts usually derive a more general principle of 'buona fede' from Arts. 1337 (which provides that in the pre-contractual stage parties must act according to good faith), 1366 and 1375.[44] Such a general principle of good faith is usually conceived as implying a duty of 'solidarity' and cooperation between the parties and has sometimes also been connected to the prohibition of abuse of rights.[45] The courts apply the general duty of good faith to police abusive conduct in the performance of contracts, in cases where it can be argued that one party, though formally abiding by the contract, is in fact frustrating the legitimate contractual expectations of the other party. The idea of a general principle of 'buona fede' and the (assumedly) underlying notion of 'solidarity' have gained widespread acceptance by the courts and scholars, and could hypothetically play a role in inducing a court to treat Peel's behaviour as an abuse of its contractual rights amounting in fact to a breach of contract.

9. NETHERLANDS

In line with the Supreme Court's decisions in *Haviltex*[46] and *DSM-Chemie/Fox*,[47] the court must establish the meaning the respective parties could

42 Art. 1375: 'The contract must be performed according to good faith'.
43 See e.g. for a similar application of the duty of good faith in the performance of contracts Cass. 20 April 1994 no. 3775.
44 See recently Cass. 29 January 2018 no. 2057 and compare Cass. 20 April 1994 no. 3775.
45 See Cass. 18 September 2009 no. 20106.
46 Hoge Raad 13 March 1981, *NJ* 1981, 635 (Ermes/Haviltex).
47 Hoge Raad 20 February 2004, *NJ* 2005, 493 (DSM-Chemie/Fox).

reasonably attach to the terms of the contract and the meaning they each could reasonably expect the other to give to them, in light of all the relevant facts and circumstances assessed in light of the standards of 'redelijkheid en billijkheid' [reasonableness and fairness].

To determine the meaning each party could reasonably attach to the expressions used in the contract, the court can have regard to a wide variety of relevant facts and circumstances, including the terms and structure of the contract, its nature and purpose, the negotiation and drafting history, the parties' statements and conduct, the parties' conduct after the conclusion of the contract, the nature of the contracting parties, trade usages, and other relevant facts and circumstances surrounding the contractual relationship.[48]

In the contract between Bingham and Peel, the court would likely consider a large range of circumstances, including in particular the purpose of the contract, the nature of the contracting parties and the requirements of 'redelijkheid and billijkheid' [reasonableness and fairness]. The purpose of the contract would be an important factor in identifying what the parties could reasonably expect from each other.[49] An interpretation that gives effect to the commercial purpose of the contract would be preferred over one that renders the contract futile.[50] In this case, the purpose of the contract was to improve Peel's economic efficiency with the help of the new machine developed by Bingham; this was also reflected in the arrangement on the price. It is likely that the more efficient Peel becomes through the use of the new machine, the greater the profits to be earned, and therefore Bingham's remuneration would be commensurate to the achievement of the efficiency objective.

In its *Vodafone/ETC* decision,[51] the Supreme Court emphasised, recalling its *Haviltex* decision, that the content of the parties' agreement cannot be based on a purely literal reading of the contract. The rights and obligations of the parties not only stem from what they have explicitly agreed upon, but also from 'redelijkheid en billijkheid' [reasonableness and fairness], which governs the legal relationship between the parties. When establishing what is required under the contract and how it should be performed, the parties must take the justified interests of the other party into account and conduct themselves towards each other in accordance with the 'eisen van de redelijkheid en billijkheid' [requirements of reasonableness and fairness].[52]

---

48 Tjittes, *Uitleg van schriftelijke contracten*, pp. 32 ff.; Tjittes, *Commercieel Contractenrecht*, pp. 301 ff.

49 Hoge Raad 17 September 2004, *NJ* 2005, 169 (Wessanen/Nutricia); Tjittes, *Uitleg van schriftelijke contracten*, p. 37; Tjittes, *Commercieel Contractenrecht*, p. 312.

50 Tjittes, *Uitleg van schriftelijke contracten*, p. 38; Asser/Sieburgh, *Algemene leer der overeenkomsten*, 6-III, no. 376.

51 Hoge Raad 19 October 2007, *NJ* 2007, 565 (Vodafone/ETC).

52 Hoge Raad 15 November 1957, *NJ* 1958, 670 (Baris/Riezenkamp); also see Art. 6:2 BW.

In light of the nature and scope of the contract, and in particular the nature of the price agreement between the parties, the court would likely find that Peel ought to have understood that by not using the machine Bingham would not be entitled to receive its percentage of the profits and therefore would not be able to recoup its costs. Although the contract does not contain an obligation requiring Peel to actually use the machine once delivered by Bingham, Peel is required to take Bingham's justified interests into account, and in refusing to use the machine the court could find that Peel did not do so, consequently putting Bingham at an unfair disadvantage which would be contrary to the requirements of 'redelijkheid en billijkheid' [reasonableness and fairness]. In that case, although it is unlikely that the court would impose an obligation on Peel to actually use the machine, it could require Peel to compensate Bingham for the loss it has suffered to the extent that can be reliably calculated. There is discussion in doctrine, however, whether this would result from a normative interpretation of the contract in line with the requirements of 'redelijkheid en billijkheid' [reasonableness and fairness] or on the basis of the 'aanvullende werking van de redelijkheid en billijkheid' [supplementary function of reasonableness and fairness] found in Art. 6:248(1) BW.[53]

At the same time, the court would consider the social and economic position of the parties, the (power) relationship between them, and their conduct and expertise. If the contract is comprehensive and detailed, and the product of careful drafting following extensive negotiations between Bingham and Peel with the aid of legal advisors, the court could give more weight to the 'taalkundige betekenis' [linguistic meaning].[54] The court would weigh Bingham's experience with respect to the development of industrial machinery with the purpose of helping businesses to become more economically efficient and establishing an appropriate pricing regime that serves its own economic interests. If it is assumed that the contract was concluded following extensive negotiations and was drafted carefully with the assistance of legal advisors, the court could consider whether Bingham should bear the risk of not incorporating a specific provision detailing at least the minimum level of use to be made of the machine, by attributing a textual meaning to the contract.

---

53 See for instance the discussion between Grosheide and Drion, 'Enerzijds, anderzijds'. On normative interpretation, see Van Dunne, *Verbintenissenrecht. Deel 1. Contractenrecht*. On the supplementary function, see Kornet, *Contract Interpretation and Gap Filling: Comparative and Theoretical Perspectives*; Asser/Sieburgh, *Algemene leer der overeenkomsten*, 6-III.

54 Hoge Raad 19 January 2007, *NJ* 2007, 575 (Pont Meyer); Hoge Raad 5 April 2013, *NJ* 2013, 214 (Lundiform/Mexx).

10. POLAND

As mentioned in the Opening Remarks, a Polish court interpreting Clause 2 would take into account primarily the parties' common intention, which is to be established at the moment of making the statement of intent (this interpretative factor is explained in the comments on Case 1), and the purpose of the contract. Both of these interpretive factors have equal standing under Polish law.

The purpose of the contract is not identical to the content of the contract; however, doctrine claims that sometimes it is impossible to clearly distinguish between these two interpretive factors.[55] Radwański defines the purpose of the contract as the state of things (affairs) that is to be achieved as a result of performing the contract. The purpose of the contract has an individual character,[56] which means that it is established by the parties to a given contract, and in this sense it is common to them.[57] While this purpose may be stated in the text of the contract, it may also follow from the accompanying circumstances.[58] According to the SN, the purpose of the contract established by the parties always has priority over the usual purpose of a contract of the same type.[59] A hidden aim that one of the parties wants to achieve cannot be established as a purpose of a legal act.[60] However, at the same time, the purpose of the contract does not have to be intended by both parties.[61]

According to Radwański,[62] the obligation expressed in Art. 65 para. 2 of the KC to investigate the purpose of the contract does not mean that it has to be established in every case. If the investigation does not give any valid or useful results, the purpose of the contract should not be considered in the interpretation process.

While Polish courts should give the same weighting to the parties' common intention and to the purpose of the contract, using the interpretive factor of establishing the contract's purpose is perceived as the less certain rule of interpretation.[63] Still, the majority opinion is that the purpose of the

55 T. Zieliński, 'Nieważność czynności sprzecznych z ustawą', *RPEiS* 1967, no. 2, p. 77, as referred to in Z. Radwański, *System Prawa Prywatnego*, vol. 2, p. 71.

56 Z. Radwański, *System Prawa Prywatnego*, vol. 2, p. 72.

57 Differently: S. Buczkowski, 'Umowy o roboty budowlano – montażowe. Wybrane zagadnienia prawne'.

58 Decree of SN of 06.02.1984, III PZP 8/84; Judgment of SN of 22.01.1996, IV CR 35/85; Judgment of SN of 21.02.1977, IV CR 2/77; Judgment of SN of 31.01.1983, IV CR 380/82.

59 Judgment of SN of 09.12.1975, III CRN 307/75.

60 Judgment of SN of 19.12.1972, III CZP 57/71.

61 Z. Radwański, *System Prawa Prywatnego*, vol. 2, p. 74.

62 Ibid.

63 Z. Radwański, *Wykładnia oświadczeń woli składanych indywidualnym adresatom*, p. 115.

contract may prevail over the literal wording of the contract, and therefore it may be expected that also when interpreting Clause 2 it would be used on equal terms as the other directives on interpretation.[64]

11. PORTUGAL

As there is no prior course of dealing between Bingham and Peel, and there is no evidence of any communication regarding the use of the machine, the Portuguese courts could apply Art. 237.° CC. This article states that in the case of doubt, in contracts between parties negotiating at arm's length, the meaning most onerous to the party setting the terms prevails, while in onerous contracts the meaning that results in a more balanced contract prevails.

Portuguese courts hold that in contractual interpretation, a fair interpretation must prevail.[65] If the initial sum that was paid in this case is considered rather modest, the fair interpretation would impose that the clause be interpreted with the meaning that a small percentage of the profits should be given to Bingham.

If there are no external or internal factors that can help to establish a certain interpretation, integrative factors can also have some relevance, for example those referred to in Art. 239.° CC. This article gives as integrative elements 'a vontade que as partes teriam e previssem o ponto omisso' [the intention that the parts would have had if they had foreseen the omission in the contract] or 'boa fé' [good faith]. 'Boa fé' is the decisive factor because if the intention the parties would have is against good faith, good faith must prevail. 'Boa fé' in this case does not necessarily determine that Peel must use the machine. More likely, it only requires a fair interpretation of Clause 2 in the sense of compensating for a lack of equality in the bargaining positions of the parties.

12. SCOTLAND

First of all, the Scottish courts would subject the words to scrutiny in order to determine their natural and ordinary meaning.[66] There is nothing in the wording of the contract which obliges Peel to continue to use the machine

64 Ibid.

65 Menezes Cordeiro, *Tratado de Direito Civil Português*, p. 742. See on this point the following cases: STJ 23 January 1996 (Martins da Costa), CJ/Supremo IV (1996) 1, 56–59; RLx 15 February 1996 (Almeida Valadas), CJ XXI (1996), 1, 121–124; and STJ 13 February 2003 (Oliveira Barros), SJ/Supremo VIII (2003), 1, 97–101.

66 *City Wall Properties (Scotland) Ltd v Pearl Assurance plc* [2003] CSOH 211; 2004 SC 214; *Middlebank Ltd v University of Dundee* [2006] CSOH 202; *Macdonald Estates plc v Regenesis*

once it has been developed and, taken literally, the words are sufficiently clear to the effect that Peel must pay 35% of the profits generated by using the programme over the subsequent five years. If Peel decides not to use the machine, a literal construction points towards Peel's argument that it has no duty to make any additional payment to Bingham.

However, the Scottish courts would not look at the literal interpretation in isolation, but would, rather, apply a contextual approach, considering the factual matrix.[67] This would allow the court to make reference to the circumstances surrounding the conclusion of the contract and the parties' background knowledge. We are told that we have no evidence of any communications passing between the parties with regard to the use of the machine and we have no information about their informal understandings and what they were (or were not) aware of when they concluded the contract. Hence, it is unlikely that the Scottish courts would derive any assistance from the interpretative tools of the surrounding circumstances and the parties' background knowledge.

The Scottish courts are also able to make use of the 'commercially sensible construction'.[68] The court would enquire whether an objective reasonable businessperson would believe it commercially sensible for Bingham and Peel to enter into a contract whereby there is the possibility that Peel could avoid the payment of an additional fee by refusing to use the machine it has paid for. On the one hand, it is difficult to see how it would make commercial common sense for Bingham to enter into such a contract. On the other hand, one might argue that it is only fair that Peel should not be obliged to make further payments to Bingham in respect of a machine that it has decided is not suitable for its requirements. Therefore, recourse to the commercially sensible construction would not be useful in this context. Indeed, the courts have stated that they must exercise caution 'against excessive confidence that [their] view as to what might be commercially sensible necessarily coincides with the views of those actually involved in commercial contracts'.[69]

The Scottish case of *North American and Continental Sales Inc v Bepi (Electronics) Ltd*[70] raised the same issue of principle. Party A had developed a system which claimed to be capable of reducing wastage in printed circuit board manufacture. Party A granted to party B an exclusive licence to market

---

(2005) Dunfermline Ltd [2007] CSOH 123; 2007 SLT 791; *Autolink Concessionaires (M6) plc v Amey Construction Ltd* [2009] CSIH 14; 2009 GWD 9-146.

67 *Wood v Capita Insurance Services Ltd* [2017] UKSC 24; [2017] 2 WLR 1095 per Lord Hodge at para. 10.

68 See, most recently, *Rainy Sky SA v Kookmin Bank* [2011] UKSC 50; [2011] 1 WLR 2900 and *Arnold v Britton* [2015] UKSC 36; [2015] AC 1619.

69 *Credential Bath Street Ltd v Venture Investment Placement Ltd* [2007] CSOH 208; 2008 GWD 9-168, para. 24.

70 1982 SLT 47.

software in the UK. Party A was paid through royalties on sales by party B. Party B did not use the system, and so there were no royalties and, as a result, no payment made to party B. The court implied a term into the contract binding party B to use the system.

If the present case came before a Scottish court, it seems highly likely that the court would consider *North American and Continental Sales Inc v Bepi (Electronics) Ltd* to be a case which is in point. *North American* was decided at Outer House level and, as a result, would not bind a higher court (the Inner House of the Court of Session or the UK Supreme Court). The court is likely to apply the current approach to implication of terms in fact, to be found in *Marks & Spencer plc v BNP Paribas Securities Services Trust Co (Jersey) Ltd.*[71] Two tests are applied by the court in order to determine whether a term should be implied. The first is known as the 'business efficacy' test, in terms of which the court will imply a term if it is necessary to make the contract workable.[72] The second is the 'officious bystander' test: this imagines that an officious bystander suggests a term to the contracting parties, and they respond to the effect that such a term is so obvious that it goes without saying.[73] If this would be the case, then a term will be implied. It is important to stress that terms are not easily implied, and both tests are difficult to overcome.[74] The court is likely to apply the tests for implied terms in order to resolve this case.

13. SOUTH AFRICA

As its point of departure, a South African court would consider the primary interpretative factors discussed in the Introduction. The language of Clause 2 does not favour Bingham's interpretation: Peel may have promised to pay 35% of the profits made by using the machine, thereby creating the expectation that it would use it, but an expectation does not, without more, translate into an obligation.[75] Although a court would consider the language of the provision within the context of the contract itself and the broader factual matrix, there is insufficient information to determine whether this evidence

---

71 [2015] UKSC 72; [2016] AC 742, esp. at paras 21–23; and see Cabrelli, 'Implying terms in law: Belize no more?'.

72 *The Moorcock* (1889) 14 PD 64, per Bowen LJ at 68.

73 *Reigate v Union Manufacturing Co* [1918] 1 KB 592, per Scrutton LJ at 605; *Shirlaw v Southern Foundries (1926) Ltd* [1939] 2 KB 206, per MacKinnon LJ at 227.

74 As illustrated by the recent decision of Lord Doherty in *Mayfly Containers Ltd (In Liquidation) v Monuments Containers Ltd* [2018] CSOH 115, 2018 GWD 40-486.

75 *Bresgi v Lazersohn* 1939 AD 445 454; *Foodtown Incorporated (Pty) Ltd v Florenca* 1974 1 SA 635 (A) 639F–G. As mentioned previously, it would also not suffice to argue that Peel has breached a duty to act in good faith by not using the machine, because South African law does not automatically imply such a duty into every contract.

would persuade a court to adopt either Peel or Bingham's interpretation. Finally, while a commercially sensible interpretation of the clause would assume that a reasonable businessperson in Bingham's position would not conclude a contract which is a losing one, it is equally possible that a commercially sensible construction would dictate that a party like Peel should not be obliged to pay for a machine which it has decided not to use. Therefore, it is unlikely that a court would adopt Bingham's interpretation solely upon a consideration of these factors.

It is also unclear whether a consideration of secondary interpretative factors, like an equitable construction based on the notion that the parties have negotiated in good faith, would favour Bingham's argument. This is due to the fact that what constitutes an equitable interpretation of Clause 2 on the facts is not immediately apparent.

Therefore, in order to succeed with its argument that Peel was obliged to use the machine, Bingham would have to prove that there was a tacit term to the effect that Peel would use the machine. The existence of a tacit term is a question of fact.[76]

It has been said that a 'tacit term', as opposed to an 'implied term' (a term which is automatically read into a contract of a particular type by operation of law[77]), is one which is based on the parties' actual though unexpressed consensus (they actually thought about a term, but did not bother to express it) or on an imputed consensus (the parties did not in fact think about a term, but had the situation requiring the term been pointed out to them, would have consented to include the particular term in their contract).[78] In both cases, a court will use the test(s) set out in *Reigate v Union Manufacturing Co. (Ramsbottom) Ltd*[79] in order to determine whether such a tacit term exists. To paraphrase, a tacit term will only be found to exist if 'it is necessary in the business sense to give efficacy to the contract';[80] according to the court, this means that if an impartial bystander had asked the parties during negotiations what would happen in a situation which they had not foreseen, and their response to the question is that they did not provide for it in their contract because the answer is self-evident, the parties are taken to have intended (or are presumed to have intended in cases where they have not thought about the situation at all) to include a tacit term in their contract.[81]

---

76 *Transnet Ltd v Rubenstein* 2006 1 SA 591 (SCA) para. 30; *Wilkens NO v Voges* 1994 3 SA 130 (A) 136I–137A.

77 *Alfred McAlpine & Son (Pty) Ltd v Transvaal Provincial Administration* 1974 3 SA 506 (A) 531D–E.

78 Ibid., 531H–532A.

79 [1918] 1 KB 592.

80 Ibid., 605.

81 Ibid.

According to Kerr, this formulation does not imply two separate tests to determine the existence of a tacit term, the first based on 'business efficacy' and the second on the so-called 'officious bystander' test.[82] This opinion has some support in case law.[83] However, more recent cases have suggested that there are in fact two (or more) tests which may be used in determining whether a tacit term exists.[84] This suggests that a tacit term may be imported on the basis of one test but not the other.[85] These recent cases also suggest that there has been a shift in the way in which the 'officious bystander' test is now applied by the Supreme Court of Appeal. The term is no longer based on what the parties themselves would have said; it is now the so-called bystander who determines whether the term is so obvious that it goes without saying.[86] In other words, there has been a shift in recent case law from an ostensibly subjective approach (what the parties would have intended) to an objective approach (what a reasonable person in the position of the parties would have said).[87] Kerr criticises this new approach, because it allows a court to disregard the parties' intention or presumed intention and to make a contract for them on the basis of what it considers to be reasonable.[88]

The (new) objective nature of the enquiry has been accompanied by a simultaneous limitation of the type of evidence which may be considered in determining whether a tacit term exists. When the approach was still subjective, all evidence could be considered, including evidence of prior negotiations and subsequent conduct.[89] According to some academic commentators, this is related to the fact that the incorporation of a tacit term had nothing to do with the process of interpretation, which is focused on determining the meaning of express terms.[90] However, the current approach of

---

82 Kerr, *Principles of Contract*, pp. 367–370; Kerr, 'Implied provisions in contracts', p. 196.

83 *Wilkens NO v Voges* 1994 3 SA 130 (A) 137A–C; *Consol Ltd t/a Consol Glass v Twee Jonge Gezellen (Pty) Ltd* 2005 6 SA 1 (SCA) para. 50.

84 *Seven Eleven Corporation of SA (Pty) Ltd v Cancun Trading No 150 C.C.* 2005 5 SA 186 (SCA) para. 34; *Van Aardt v Galway* 2012 2 SA 312 (SCA) para. 25 n. 20, referring to *Attorney General of Belize v Belize Telecom Ltd* [2009] 2 All ER 1127 (PC) paras. 21–27 with approval.

85 This seems to be the effect of concluding that there is more than one test in English law – see the discussion in Lewison, *Interpretation of Contracts*, pp. 321–322 and the cases cited there.

86 *Seven Eleven Corporation of SA (Pty) Ltd v Cancun Trading No 150 C.C.* 2005 5 SA 186 (SCA) para. 34.

87 Cornelius, 'The unexpressed terms of a contract', p. 502; Kerr, 'Implied provisions in contracts', p. 199 ff.

88 Kerr, 'Implied provisions in contracts', p. 204.

89 See e.g. Kerr, *Principles of Contract*, p. 367; *Dutch Reformed Church Council v Crocker* 1953 4 SA 53 (C) 62H; and, more recently, *Botha v Coopers & Lybrand* 2002 5 SA 347 (SCA) paras. 26–27.

90 Maxwell, 'Interpretation of contracts', p. 277; Kerr, *Principles of Contract*, p. 367. The distinction between the incorporation of tacit terms and the process of interpretation is also

the Supreme Court of Appeal is to exclude evidence of previous negotiations (although probably not of subsequent conduct) from an investigation into the existence of a tacit term;[91] the implication is that it views the process as part of the interpretation of the contract.

In proving the existence of a tacit term to the effect that Peel would use the machine, Bingham may refer to the fact that without such a term, the contract will be a losing one. In calculating the quantum of damages, there is an assumption that parties will at least break even after their respective performances.[92] This assumption may also play a role in determining whether the tacit term is necessary to give business efficacy to the contract, although, as suggested in the discussion of the primary interpretative factors, such a consideration is not likely to be decisive. Another factor which a court may take into account is that the machine is custom-made; Bingham will not be able to recover its losses by making the machine available to another company.

However, a court will not incorporate a tacit term into a contract if it conflicts with the express terms of that contract, because parties cannot agree on two conflicting provisions simultaneously.[93] In the past, it was also said that a court would not easily conclude that there was a tacit term in the contract because it was neither entitled to make a contract for the parties nor in the position to read a term into the contract simply on the basis that it would have been reasonable or convenient to include that term.[94] Finally, and probably most importantly, a court would only read a tacit term into a contract if it was satisfied that the bystander's question would have evoked a prompt and unanimous response from both parties. If one of the parties were to have asked for more time to consider its response, a tacit term would not be read into the contract.[95] Therefore, if a court concluded that Peel would have had to consider the implications of a duty to use the machine, irrespective of the circumstances, then it would be unlikely that it would infer that there was a tacit term to this effect.

It is worth mentioning that it is unclear to what extent the new approach to tacit terms would require a reformulation or abandonment of these traditional factors.

---

referred to in *Consol Ltd t/a Consol Glass v Twee Jonge Gezellen (Pty) Ltd* 2005 6 SA 1 (SCA) para. 49.

91 *Van Aardt v Galway* 2012 2 SA 312(SCA) para. 12.

92 *Trichardt v Van der Linde* 1916 TPD 148 153; Lubbe and Murray, *Farlam and Hathaway*, p. 605 n. 6.

93 *Pan American World Airways Incorporated v SA Fire and Accident Insurance Co. Ltd* 1965 3 SA 150 (A) 175; Kerr, *Principles of Contract*, p. 366.

94 *City of Cape Town (CMC Administration) v Bourbon-Leftley and Another NNO* 2006 3 SA 488 (SCA) para. 19.

95 *Botha v Coopers & Lybrand* 2002 5 SA 347 (SCA) para. 24.

14. SPAIN

The question requires saying which factors the Spanish courts would adopt in order to attach weight in the interpretation of Clause 2. The first factor is Art. 1.284 CC, because this provision says that where any clause of the contract admits several meanings, it must be understood to have the meaning most suitable for it to be effective.[96] Therefore, Clause 2 actually does not bind Peel to make use of the machine and the company can use it or not, but the second option would make the contract ineffective. In consequence, every useless interpretation shall be rejected.[97]

The second factor is Art. 1286, because according to this provision if contractual terms may have different meanings, they will be understood as the meaning which is most in accordance with the nature and subject matter of the agreement. There is no doubt that the contract would make no sense for Bingham if Peel does not use the machine. The contract loses its economic function for one of the parties. Bingham would not have entered into the contract if there were to be hardly any economic compensation. This agreement only possesses contractual meaning for both parties if Peel uses the machine.

Therefore, to give an effective meaning to the contract, Peel should use the machine. Otherwise, an onerous contract such as this one would become an almost gratuitous contract, which seems to be far from the common intention of the parties. Finally, the 'buena fe' [good faith] principle plays an important role[98] in the sense that Peel should use the machine to be honest in legal trade, giving effectiveness to the agreement, because the deal requires using the machine in order to obtain profits to be shared with Bingham. The contract would lose almost the entire sense and utility for Bingham in the event of non-use. The social-economic function of the contract would disappear. Spanish Law calls this purpose 'causa' [economic and social purpose] and Bingham would be entitled to terminate the contract in the event of non-use of the machine by Peel.

15. SWEDEN

Most likely, Swedish courts will not consider this to be a matter of interpretation at all. The problem lies, one could say, too deep within the implicit dimension

---

96 STS 22.10.2010, ECLI:ES:TS:2010:5326; STS 04.05.2016, ECLI:ES:TS:2016:1900.

97 The maintenance of contract principle (based on Art. 1.284) may be found explicitly in the following judicial decisions: STS 22.04.2013, ECLI:ES:TS:2014:2246; STS (Plenary session) 15.01.2013, ECLI:ES:TS:2013:1153; STS 29.01.2015, ECLI:ES:TS:2015:835. This last judicial decision quotes the PECL and Vienna Convention.

98 On the good faith principle in contractual interpretation: STS 30.01.2003 (RJ 2003\2024); STS 30.01.2017, ECLI:ES:TS:2017:328.

of the agreement. As has been pointed out previously, the style of Swedish contract law thinking is *realistic*.[99] In interpretation, this realist tendency is manifested in the conviction that there should be something palpable – something *real* – to interpret, in order for there to be interpretation at all.[100] To engage in interpretation where there is no factual basis is to commit the principal vice, namely to turn to fictitious legal reasoning, concealing the legal judgment in 'tolkningens täckmantel' [the shroud of interpretation], which is not a technical term, but a revealing and oft-used phrase.[101]

The crux of the problem in the present case is that the answer required necessitates a decision on a point which the parties clearly did not consider. The difficulty is accentuated by the fact that the court must, unless it wants to reject Bingham's claim altogether, which might seem overly formalistic, deliver an answer in quantitative terms – a fixed figure – that can only be arrived at through considerations of what is fair and reasonable.[102] To say, under such circumstances, that the answer follows from the contract, properly interpreted, is too much of a stretch.[103]

Most likely, a Swedish court will prefer to construe the problem in this case as a matter of 'motivvillfarelse' [error of motive], to be dealt with by means of 'utfyllning' [complementary construction], rather than 'tolkning' [interpretation],[104] i.e. by supplying a legal norm to fill the gap in the contract. A 'motivvillfarelse' is, by definition, a mistake of *fact* (say *x* on the assumption that *y* is the case, while, in fact, *z* is true), as opposed to a 'förklaringsmisstag' [declarative mistake], which is a mistake regarding *the content of the contract* (say *x* while intending to say *y*).[105] Cases of 'motivvillfarelse' fall outside of the scope of 'avtalstolkningsläran' [the doctrine of interpretation of contracts].[106] They are dealt with according to the rules of 'förutsättningsläran' [the doctrine

99 See the answer to Case 2, Question 1, at n. 100 and Case 4, n. 42. Interested non-Swedish-speaking scholars may find the essay on Swedish contract law by Jan Hellner in the *Festschrift* for Atiyah helpful; see Hellner, *Scandinavian Legal Realism in the Law of Contract.*

100 Sometimes this tendency is followed even when the result seems to flout common sense; the decision in NJA 2013 p. 1190 could be offered as an example.

101 A somewhat recent example would be NJA 2017 p. 113, where the Supreme Court recommended using the general provision on unfair terms (Section 36 of the Contracts Act) when dealing with exemption clauses in consumer relations, rather than traditional methods, including restrictive interpretation.

102 Cf. NJA 1992 p. 439, where the Supreme Court held it to be 'natural' to interpret a contract that made no mention of the duration of the contractual relation to mean that the contract was valid indefinitely.

103 Cf. NJA 1991 p. 319, where, under somewhat similar circumstances, the level of compensation was set in the contract.

104 On this distinction see the answer to Case 2, Question 1, at n. 101.

105 On this distinction see the illustrative case NJA 1949 p. 134. See also Adlercreutz and Gorton, *Avtalsrätt I*, p. 272 f. and, especially, Lehrberg, *Förutsättningsläran*, p. 108 ff. On the rule applicable in cases of 'förklaringsmisstag' see the answer to the question on Case 7, n. 59.

106 See however J. Ramberg and C. Ramberg, *Allmän avtalsrätt*, p. 198 ff.

of tacit assumptions], which is a separate body of rules that rests on case law and scholarly writing.[107] 'Förutsättningsläran' stipulates that a 'felaktig förutsättning' [faulty assumption] that is 'väsentlig' [essential], 'synbar' [apparent] as well as 'relevant' [relevant] renders the 'rättshandling' [juridical act] based on the assumption in question 'overksam' [inefffective].

If 'förutsättningsläran' is found applicable, any terms of the contract that are based on the faulty assumption will be considered to be without effect.[108] In order to gain access to a positive legal consequence, the courts will need to resort to 'individuell utfyllning' [individual complementary construction], which is the process of filling a gap in a contract with an individual, tailor-made solution or norm,[109] *or* to 'jämka' [adjust] the content of the contract by making use of Section 36 of the Contracts Act (1915:218), which contains the general clause on unfair terms in Swedish contract law.[110]

Either way, all relevant circumstances should be considered, and, either way, reference might be made to the general principle of contract law holding that the seller of goods or services is entitled to a fair price when the contract is silent on the matter (see Section 45 of the Sale of Goods Act (1990:931)). That is not to say that, quite simply, Bingham will be entitled to a fair price, set by market standards. The solution will have to do justice to the specific problem at hand.

The question will be if Bingham has the right to further compensation for its services, in a situation where (1) the contract is silent, (2) which is an effect of the fact that Bingham, and possibly Peel as well, negotiated under the faulty assumption that Peel would actually use the machine, and (3) even if Peel did not share that assumption, it could not have been unaware of the fact that Bingham did enter the contract under it; (4) what is more, it was Peel's behaviour that falsified the assumption. Simply put, Peel took advantage of a lacuna in the contract text. Or so it would seem. But the contract was, perhaps, badly drafted. Should, for instance, Clause 2 be taken to mean that Peel was obligated to use the machine for five years, even if, say, a better option presented itself? Hardly.

The question of the price to be paid by the buyer is poorly regulated in this contract. Deciding the case is ultimately about allocating the risks

---

107 See e.g. NJA 1949 p. 134, NJA 1981 p. 269, and NJA 1985 p. 178; cf. NJA 1996 p. 410 and Lehrberg, *Förutsättningsläran*.

108 See Lehrberg, *Förutsättningsläran*, p. 564 ff.

109 On 'individuell utfyllning' see Adlercreutz and Gorton, *Avtalsrätt II*, p. 29 ff.

110 In the present context, reference might be made to the early cases NJA 1979 p. 483, NJA 1979 p. 666, and NJA 1984 p. 229, where the Supreme Court had to deal with the question to what extent Section 36 is applicable in business-to-business relations. It is clear, from the wording of the provision and from these cases, that Section 36 is indeed applicable, in principle, but that it is necessary to show restraint out of respect for freedom of contract.

associated with this deficiency. And the advantage of having recourse to 'individuell utfyllning' or 'jämkning' [adjustment] is that the risk may be evenly distributed between the parties or distributed in whatever way the court finds appropriate.[111] *What* distribution the court will prefer and *how much weight* the court will attach to the factors in play is not possible to ascertain beforehand.

16. EDITORIAL COMPARATIVE OBSERVATIONS

Very few of the national reporters indicated that their legal systems would unequivocally compel Peel to use, or not use, the machine, as the case may be. For example, only in Croatia and Spain would the contractual rules of interpretation be applied to force Peel to use the machine, thus entitling Bingham to be paid 35% of the profits generated by Peel. In both of Croatia and Spain, this result would be rooted in the teleological method of interpretation, i.e. that the purpose of the contract was the production of copper wire, which assumes the ongoing use of the machine. Conversely, the national reporters for Scotland were clear to the effect that the rules of contractual interpretation would indicate that Peel was not bound to use the machine, regardless of whether a literal or contextual construction was adopted by the courts.

In the case of many other jurisdictions, the national reporters suggested that the courts would be likely or very likely to adopt the rules of contractual interpretation, on balance, to compel Peel either to use the machine or to pay damages for a failure to do so, for example in Finland, France, Germany, the Netherlands (subject to the caveat discussed below in this paragraph), Poland and Portugal. This was often for a range of different reasons, entailing the application of diverse interpretive principles, whether in isolation, as a mixture, or sometimes in combination with each other. For instance, in Finland, France, Germany, Portugal and Spain, the principle of good faith would likely be harnessed by a court in order to find in favour of Bingham's preferred construction. This would be grounded in the notion that good faith as an interpretative factor would require Peel to use the machine on the basis that: (1) its failure to do so would constitute the manifestation of bad faith (France and Germany); (2) its failure to do so would constitute the breach of a duty imposed on Peel where it has checked whether Bingham has understood the clause in a different way than it understands it itself, and it has discovered that to be the case (Finland); or (3) a fair interpretation ought to be reached (Portugal). Turning away from the concept of good faith, the national reporters for jurisdictions such as France and Germany pointed to the role that 'performance impossibility' would play in rendering it likely that a court

---

111 Cf. e.g. NJA 2017 p. 113.

would hold Peel to use the machine. The notion of 'performance impossibility' is a reference to the relevance that a court would attach to the fact that Peel's actions have directly prevented the full performance of the obligations anticipated in the contract, i.e. that the machine would be used and that a payment would be made to Bingham as a result thereof. Meanwhile, in Poland, an examination of the purpose of the contract would likely cause a Polish court to hold that Peel must use the machine and pay 35% of the profits generated to Bingham. As for the Netherlands, like the Polish courts, the purpose, nature and structure of the contract – the contractual objective being the production of an industrial piece of machinery by Bingham with the purpose of assisting Peel in becoming more economically efficient – would likely result in a court finding that Peel be compelled to use the machine, failing which Peel would be bound to pay compensation to Bingham if it refused, or was unable to do so. However, this would be subject to the overall caveat that the social and economic context of the parties would be taken into account, as well as serious consideration given to whether the contract was carefully drafted following extensive negotiations between Bingham and Peel with the aid of their legal advisors: in such a case, the national reporter for the Netherlands was sceptical that Bingham's preferred construction would be accepted by the courts, on the ground that Bingham ought to, and could, have inserted a positive obligation on Peel to use the machine, but did not do so.

In certain jurisdictions, the national reporters were of the view that the result of the application of the rules of contractual interpretation would furnish an unclear result: this was the case in England and Wales, Greece, Italy and South Africa. In Greece, the national reporter indicated that he was unable to express an opinion as to how the Greek courts would balance the following competing interpretive principles to reach a result, namely: (1) the relative value of the work devoted by Bingham to the development of the machine in relation to the initial fee paid upfront and the proportionality of the business risk assumed, i.e. the lower the initial fee paid by Peel, then the more likely Peel is under a duty to use the machine; (2) the failure of Bingham to impose a positive obligation on Peel to use the machine; and (3) good faith. The position in Italy is similar, where the following principles of interpretation would have to be put in the balance, namely: (1) the clear effect of the literal interpretation, i.e. that no obligation has been placed on Peel to use the machine; (2) the systematic interpretation of construing the contract as a whole, which would indicate that Peel should be subjected to some further obligation; and (3) good faith.

In certain jurisdictions, what is particularly noteworthy is that techniques in the law of contract, other than the law of contractual interpretation, would be put to use to resolve the dispute. For example, Scotland is mentioned above as a jurisdiction where the rules of contractual interpretation would indicate that Peel is not legally bound to use the machine if it does not wish to do so.

However, the law of 'implied terms-in-fact' could operate to compel Peel to do so, on the basis that there is a clear gap in the contract that must be plugged. The law of South Africa is similar, although this process is referred to as applying a 'tacit term', rather than an 'implied term-in-fact'. Sweden follows a similar path, where the law of 'complementary construction' could function to fill the gap in the contract, albeit that the Swedish national reporter was sceptical that the Swedish courts would go as far as to adopt this technique to compel Peel to use the machine.

One final observation concerns the extent to which meta-legal formants of an economic and social nature would be resorted to by the courts in this final case to resolve the dispute between Bingham and Peel. Reference has already been made to the law in the Netherlands and the significance attached to the social and economic background of the parties, including their bargaining strength, as factors to be considered. The position in Greek law would be similar, where the degree of investment in the machine made by Bingham would be a relevant factor. Likewise in Swedish law, where the courts would account for the allocation and balance of the economic risks struck by the parties in the contract. Spanish law would also enquire whether the contract would lose its economic function and sense if Bingham's construction were not adopted. Furthermore, English law would put great importance on the commerciality of the deal, for example whether the parties would have expected the contract to be a losing one if Peel did not use the machine. Scots law and South African law would adopt a similar approach, although the national reporters for both of these jurisdictions doubted whether much assistance could be derived from having recourse to the commercial context in this final case.

PART III
GENERAL CONCLUSIONS

CONCLUSIONS

Jaap BAAIJ, David CABRELLI and Laura MACGREGOR

This book sought to inform practitioners, scholars and students alike. In a world in which jurisdictions are no longer isolated normative orderings, and where both traders and consumers engage in contractual relationships beyond national borders daily, obtaining a better understanding of local judicial practices of interpreting contracts is indispensable. After all, as pointed out at the outset of this book and in the chapter by Remus Valsan on the law and economics of contract interpretation, contracts are necessarily incomplete, and few breach of contract disputes do not involve at least a disagreement as to the nature of the performance that the contract requires of the parties.

This volume's comprehensive comparative study advances our understanding of contract interpretation in European private law in three respects: it enriches the conventional conceptual framework for the methods of contract interpretation; it challenges the presumptive dichotomy of common and civil law jurisdictions; and it provides a finer-grained analysis of the role of standards of 'good faith' in contract interpretation. Below, we will explain and offer examples of the ways in which this volume realises these three innovations. We will conclude with observing to what extent there can be said to exist a 'common core' of contract interpretation in European private law.

1. ENRICHING THE CONCEPTUAL FRAMEWORK: DISTINGUISHING AIMS AND MODALITIES OF INTERPRETATION

Legal scholarship often distinguishes the methods of interpretation employed in different jurisdictions in terms of a single spectrum ranging from the textual to the more contextual. However, the national reports and comparative analyses presented in this volume call for a finer-grained theoretical framework. Indeed, a two-dimensional matrix recognising both the aims and modalities of interpretation methods is capable of revealing more nuanced differences and similarities between jurisdictions.

First, the aim of judicial contract interpretation involves what a court seeks to uncover; the means of interpretation involves how that aim is to be achieved. The national reporters' Opening Remarks show that we may distinguish three aims. The first involves the meaning of the contractual terms that the actual parties factually intended ('actual intentions'). The second aim is to uncover the meaning a reasonable individual in the position of the actual parties would attribute to the contractual terms ('reasonable meaning'). Third, we make out the aim of establishing the meaning that principles of good faith, fairness or 'justness' dictate that one party was entitled to expect the other party to attribute to the contractual terms ('fair meaning').

Second, the national reports allow us to derive at least two types of modalities or *means* of interpretation. In the first modality, the interpretation method is looking to *subjective* markers of contracting, that is to say, expression of intentions throughout the *process* of contracting. The other modality is characterised by the focus on *objective* markers of contracting or the empirically observable features of the *outcome* of that process, in particular the words of the contract.

When plotted into a two-dimensional matrix, the distinction between aims and modalities of interpretation would look something like this:

Figure 1. Matrix Methods of Contract Interpretation

Aim/Modality	Actual Intentions	Reasonable Meaning	Fair Meaning
Subjective/Process			
Objective/Outcome			

One might expect that courts in jurisdictions that place greater weight on the actual intentions of the contracting parties (aim) would tend to look to subjective markers of the contracting process (modality), while courts underscoring reasonable meaning (aim) would prefer objective markers of the outcome of that process (modality). If that turns out to be correct, using a two-dimensional matrix rather than a single spectrum offers little methodological value. However, the national reports demonstrate that interpretation methods are not as straightforward as it might seem. Two examples bear this complexity out.

First, in a significant number of jurisdictions under review, courts would seek to uncover the actual intentions of the contracting parties by primarily examining subjective markers of the contracting process. These include Croatia and Poland. Courts in other jurisdictions, however, seek to uncover the parties' common intentions by first examining the ordinary meaning of the contractual language, hence the most prominent objective marker of the eventual outcome of the contract process. These include Germany, Greece, Finland and Sweden. Similarly, in South Africa, courts may aim to ascertain the reasonable meaning, but are open to admitting extrinsic evidence of the circumstantial context of the contracting process to this end. The national reports offer an example in respect to Case 7. This case was designed to encourage analysis of the parties' shared but erroneous understanding of an expression. Each national reporter suggested that a court would give weight to the parties' shared but erroneous understanding. Diversity exists in the way courts approach this issue, i.e. through provisions of a code or precedents. Even in legal systems which characterise the modality of the interpretative approach as essentially objective, a shared subjective but erroneous understanding can be highly relevant.

Second, aims and modalities within jurisdictions do not rule each other out. For one, the Netherlands and Portugal represent jurisdictions emphasising the aim of establishing the 'fair meaning' of contracts. Courts in these jurisdictions determine this meaning by looking to both subjective and objective markers of contracting, that is to say, the parties' statements during the negotiation process as well as the ultimate meaning of the contractual terms. In this respect, various jurisdictions present a hierarchy in interpretation aims. In some jurisdictions, courts first aim to uncover the actual intentions and only when this quest is without results turn to other aims. Courts in Italy, Croatia and Germany tend to switch secondarily to establishing the *reasonable* meaning, while Greek courts would turn to the *fair* meaning of the contractual terms when the actual intentions cannot be established satisfactorily.

2. NUANCING THE COMMON LAW VERSUS CIVIL LAW DICHOTOMY

The book further asks us to reconsider the presumptive dichotomy of common law and civil law in contract interpretation. Comparative legal studies frequently travel the well-beaten path of the common law versus civil law dichotomy. A comparative analysis might indeed expose stark differences between the two legal cultures. In fact, this volume has revealed quite a number of those divergences. For example, the rule that pre-contractual material is inadmissible in the process of interpretation is one that the English and Welsh and South African courts (as well as the Scottish courts in a weaker form) continue to apply. This is in stark contrast to civilian jurisdictions, where such pre-contractual documents will be considered either as a matter of course or on the satisfaction of conditions. Moreover, what is striking about Case 1 is the extent to which civilian jurisdictions such as Finland, France, Germany, Portugal, Spain and Sweden will have recourse to academic writings as a key factor in interpretation. This can be contrasted with the common law and mixed jurisdictions, where the value of legal scholarship is limited to an explanatory role, rather than as a source of the relevant rules (see the South African report for Case 10).

However, a comparatist is wise to avoid the popular cultural opposition between common and civil law jurisdictions as a matter of paradigmatic presumption. By keeping an open mind, subtle cross-cultural similarities and delicate intra-cultural variations may defy expectations. This volume offers four examples to support this proposition.

First, in most civil law jurisdictions reviewed in this volume, the civil code is the primary source guiding the interpretation of contracts. In the Netherlands, however, despite its long-standing and sophisticated civil code, the methods of contract interpretation are developed through case law primarily. In this respect, this civil law jurisdiction is similar to the common law jurisdiction of England and Wales, and the jurisdictions which have experienced significant influence from the common law, the so-called mixed jurisdictions of Scotland and South Africa. Clearly, the Netherlands is here an outlier among civil law jurisdictions. Nevertheless, this example cautions the comparatist against assuming the primacy of civil codes in civil law jurisdictions. Moreover, Case 7 shows that the type of legal source of itself does not say anything about which interpretation method is used. All the legal systems gave significant weight to a shared but erroneous understanding of a particular phrase held by the contracting parties. Some of the legal systems achieved this through specific code provisions, whereas in others it was achieved through the application of case law as binding precedent. The results of this case seem to suggest that whether or not a legal system is codified is not particularly significant in the interpretative context: the same outcomes can be achieved in both codified and non-codified systems.

Second, the nature of the interpretation question in South Africa is similar to, for example, the Netherlands, Italy and Spain. In these jurisdictions, the process of interpretation is one of both of fact and of law. The judicial interpretation of a contract is factual to the extent that the meaning attributed to the document is excluded from review by the highest courts. However, the lower court's reasoning of the chosen interpretation methods is not excluded from review on appeal. This example demonstrates that certain features of the English, Welsh or even Scottish jurisdictions are not necessarily inherent to the common law generally. Hence, differences between the common law in Great Britain and civil law in continental Europe are not as fundamental as they might appear to be at face value. The illustration discussed here, therefore, also proves the value of including a non-European jurisdiction influenced by the common law (South Africa).

Third, South African courts are more open than the Scottish courts to admitting evidence of the parties' statements after concluding the contract, thus bearing a greater resemblance to several civil law jurisdictions, such as the Dutch, Spanish and Italian ones. Similarly, in Case 9 every national reporter suggested that a custom of trade would be relevant in the interpretative exercise. Looking at the way in which custom was used (regardless of the stage at which it became relevant), we find a similarity between the systems. Many of the legal systems identified the same factors which required to be proved in order to identify a legally relevant custom: presence in the locality in question; regular observance in the trade; and notoriety. The degree of weight to be given to custom differed, although most reports suggest a high degree of weight. This similarity in method may obscure differences in aim, however. In Italy and Greece, the court would seek, as a first step, to apply a subjective interpretation. Only if that exercise failed would there be a reference to custom in a second objective stage. Thus, one could say that the aim of the interpretative process was essentially subjective. This can be contrasted with all the other systems where custom was used as a route to an overall objective approach.

Lastly, mixed systems cannot be placed in either of the civilian or common law traditions: they have experienced influence from both. Certain questions concerning mixed legal systems, raised in the Introduction, can be considered in the light of the answers in the Scottish and South African national reports. Is there evidence that each system has followed a 'dominant' tradition? As stated in the Introduction, it has been said that mixed legal systems in the commercial law area assimilate entirely over time with the common law.

Taking Scotland first of all, despite the fact that, in the field of interpretation of contract, UK Supreme Court decisions are binding on the Scottish courts, the Scottish national report discussed examples of 'rebellion' by the Scottish judges. One such example is the Scottish courts having greater recourse to the 'commercially sensible construction', in a manner which conflicts with binding Supreme Court authority. English influence on South Africa is, in comparison to Scotland, less recent and has experienced more overt resistance. The inclusion of only four English cases in the South African report suggests that the influence of English law there is now minimal. The references to good faith in the South African report also set that legal system aside from the common law tradition.

These mixed legal systems appear to have forged their own approach to interpretation of contract. Assimilation with the common law has not been total in either system. Whether the approaches to interpretation in these countries are 'hybrid' approaches of the common law and the civil law traditions is a question which could only be answered after more intensive research. The relevance of good faith to interpretation in South Africa raises this intriguing possibility.

3. THE ROLE OF GOOD FAITH

The third intended contribution of this book is to offer a comprehensive analysis of the role of standards of 'good faith' in contract interpretation. In the common law/civil law dichotomy referred to above, good faith is seen as characteristic of civilian systems and not of common law systems. Debates about the common law/civil law dichotomy have tended to overemphasise differences, however. The English law of contract, for example, often deploys the concepts of 'reasonableness' to achieve similar ends. Moreover, of course, the English courts have recently been developing an implied term of good faith applying in so-called 'relational' contracts. It is no longer true, it seems, to think of good faith as a fault line which splits the two traditions.

Moving specifically to interpretation and this project, national reporters from civilian systems have referred to 'good faith'. Good faith is, however, also referred to in the national report for South Africa, a mixed legal system. In that legal system, it can be used as a fall-back where the primary interpretative factors have failed to achieve a result.

The particular focus on *method* in this project allows us to compare these approaches. Ultimately, it allows us to ask whether the presence of good faith in the civilian systems is as significant a difference as some would have us believe.

In the national reports from the civilian countries, we see good faith being used as a norm which sets a standard of reasonable behaviour, or which shapes the legitimate or reasonable expectations of the contracting parties. It is reasonable, for example, to expect one's contracting party to adhere to the manner in which contracts have been performed in the past, where a course of dealing exists (Case 8). Good faith is here playing a very similar role to reasonableness in English and Scots law. 'Reasonableness' is an important concept in the context of interpretation in the law of England and Wales and of Scotland. As a starting position, the court asks what the disputed words would mean to a reasonable person in the position of the contracting parties. The 'touchstone' in English law is the reasonable person in the position of the contracting parties. It is the expectations and understandings of that reasonable person which are relevant to the process of interpretation. It is therefore not surprising that the English and Scottish courts also find a consistent course of dealing to be highly relevant to the interpretation of a later contract. These outcomes tend to suggest that the differences between the two traditions may be more theoretical than practical.

The full picture is, however, more complex. The national reports have highlighted some roles for good faith in civilian systems which are not seen in common law and mixed legal systems. An example is the use by the courts in civilian systems of good faith in order to 'check', or 'police', contractual behaviour. It was relatively common in the civilian national reports to see good faith characterised as a positive duty, imposing, for example, duties of conscientiousness and honesty. One excellent example is Case 10, where the notion of good faith would be used to compel the acquirer of a custom-made machine to use it on the ground that (i) this would be a fair interpretation or (ii) its failure to do so would constitute the manifestation of bad faith or a breach of a duty imposed on it. By contrast, the legal systems significantly influenced by the common law would not intervene here, except perhaps to imply a term if the contract could be considered truly unworkable without one.

Finally, various reports present good faith, not complementary to or in conflict with principles of contractual autonomy, but as intrinsic to it. For example, certain reports identified reliance as a key factor, and good faith as a way in which such reliance can be protected. One illustration is Italian law in the context of Cases 1 and 6. In the former case, where a contracting party A has released an information brochure at the time the contract with contracting party B is formed, Italian law would deploy good faith to prevent party B from adopting an interpretation that is inconsistent with the terms of that document. Additionally, the Polish reporters explain that in their jurisdiction, the binding character of a contract rests on good faith, as there is a principle that one is bound by the trust or reliance the promisor induces in the promisee.

4. A COMMON CORE?

As this book is part of the Common Core of European Private Law Project, there is no way of avoiding the following questions: does a common core of contractual interpretation in European private law exist, and what does this core consist of? Before addressing these questions, it is worth repeating that each and every comparative analysis necessarily implies a common core. As elaborated in the chapter by Jaap Baaij on this book's methodology, no comparison – in fact, no act of communication – is even imaginable without bringing about a foundation of 'sameness'. Any difference, no matter how radical, is unavoidably a difference relative to what the objects of comparison have in common. This is not a 'bug' of comparative law, but rather an inescapable 'feature', a constitutive element of human communication and knowledge.

This implicit foundation of sameness does not mean that a comparative common core of juridical practices in contractual interpretation is a given. On the contrary, the inescapable sameness enables the comparatist to ascertain in the first place whether there is such a comparative common core or whether none is to be found. In fact, as explained in more detail in the exploratory chapters, the editors are confident that the factual method that the Common Core Project observes, and the methods of translation introduced for this book in particular, are capable of determining reliably a common core of contractual interpretation – if there is one.

The editors would suggest that the national reports reveal that a common core, to the extent that there is one, is not precluded by rigid divisions between the common law and the civil law, between a subjective and an objective approach, or between a literal and a contextual approach. The approach of each legal system is, rather, a nuanced one. Reference to factual concepts, for example custom of trade or course of dealing, is justified within both subjective and objective approaches. The editors set out to uncover these subtle distinctions while encouraging readers to form their own conclusions from the material laid out in this book.

Perhaps the common core one could infer from the answers provided by the national reports is that every legal system strives to reach a compromise between staying true to the actual intentions of the parties, assessing what a reasonable person would understand from the contract drafting, and preventing outcomes that are unfair or unjust. Each court draws on the material available to it in order to reach this compromise. From this vantage point, the differences between the jurisdictions appear to consist of ideas of what a common intention and reasonableness amounts to and what are the appropriate methods by which these could best be ascertained. Here, the jurisdictions reveal a variety of conceptual, doctrinal and pragmatic resemblances and distinctions.

At the same time, the book may be instructive for those seeking to strengthen a common core on the subject of the interpretation of contracts in European private law. In the future, a common core may be achieved through EU legislation, as was the aim of the Proposal for a Common European Sales Law, or through scholarly soft law instruments such as the Principles of European Contract Law and the Draft Common Frame of Reference, which were discussed in the chapter by Lorna Richardson on the attempts by the EU legislator to regulate contract interpretation. Even if any harmonisation instrument could come to pass, the nuanced distinctions between the judicial methods of resolving interpretation issues in the various jurisdictions suggest that a single set of general formalised rules might not be enough. After all, in keeping with the legal philosophies of Rudolf Schlesinger and Rodolfo Sacco, positive legal rules are only one of an assortment of possible legal and meta-legal formants, and the degree to which they inform judicial practices may differ from one jurisdiction to the next.

Irrespective of the reader's reason for looking into the judicial interpretation of contracts, the editors hope that this book will provide a valuable source of information and insight and help gain a deeper understanding of one of the central subjects of contract law.

REFERENCES

Aa Mota Pinto C.A., *Cessão da Posição Contratual* (Coimbra: Almedina, 2003)
Abel Lluch X. and Picó i Junoy J., *La prueba electrónica* (Barcelona: Esade/Bosch, 2011)
Adlercreutz A. and Gorton L., 'Om avtalstolkning', *SvJT* (1990) 578 ff.
——, *Avtalsrätt I* (13th edn, Lund: Juristförlaget i Lund, 2010)
——, *Avtalsrätt II* (6th edn, Lund: Juristförlaget i Lund, 2010)
Águila-Real J., *Las condiciones generales de la contratación* (Madrid: Civitas, 1991)
Aho M.L., *Varallisuusoikeudellisen oikeustoimen tulkinnasta* (Helsinki: W. Söderström Osakeyhtiö, 1968)
Ainsworth J., 'Lost in Translation? Linguistic Diversity and the Elusive Quest for Plain Meaning in the Law' in Cheng L., Sin K.-K. and Wagner A. (eds.), *The Ashgate Handbook of Legal Translation* (Farnham: Ashgate, 2014)
Albanese A., 'La circolazione del contratto tra autonomia privata e simmetria informativa', *Rivista di diritto civile* (2011) 15
——, *Cessione del contratto* (Bologna: Zanichelli, 2008)
Almagro Nosete J., 'De la interpretación de los contratos' in Sierra Gil De La Cuesta I., *Comentario del Código civil* (vol. 6, 2nd edn, Barcelona: Bosch, 2006)
——, 'La interpretación contractual', Madrid: *Diario La Ley*, no. 7769 (2012) 1–2
Alpa G., 'Unità del negozio e principi di ermeneutica contrattuale', *Giurisprudenza italiana*, (1973) I, 1, 1507
——, *L'Interpretazione del contratto* (Milan: Giuffrè, 1983)
Annola V., 'Tavallisuussäännön asema sopimustulkinnassa', *Oikeustieto* (2016) 19–21
Asser/Sieburgh C., *Mr. C. Asser's handleiding tot de beoefening van het Nederlands burgerlijk recht. verbintenissenrecht. Algemene leer der overeenkomsten*, 6-III (Deventer: Kluwer, 2018)
Astone F., 'Dell'interpretazione del contratto. Art. 1363–1370' in Navarretta E. and Orestano A. (eds.), *Dei contratti in generale. Artt. 1350–1386, Commentario del codice civile diretto a E. Gabrielli* (Turin: UTET, 2011)
Ayres I., 'Default Rules for Incomplete Contracts' in Newman P. (ed.), *The New Palgrave Dictionary of Economics and the Law* (vol. I, New York: Stockton Press, 1998)
——, 'Ya-Huh: There Are and Should be Penalty Defaults' (2006) 33 *Florida State University Law Review* 589
Ayres I. and Gertner R., 'Filling Gaps in Incomplete Contracts: An Economic Theory of Default Rules' (1989) 99 *Yale Law Journal* 87
Azzaro A.M., *I contratti non negoziati* (Naples: ESI, 2000)
Baaij C.J.W., 'Confronting the Conjecture of Cultural Incommensurability in Comparative Law' (2014) 25(2) *King's Law Journal* 287
——, 'Legal Translation and the "Contamination" of Comparative Legal Research' in Glanert S. (ed.), *Comparative Law: Engaging Translation* (New York: Routledge, 2014)
——, *Legal Integration and Language Diversity* (Oxford: Oxford University Press, 2018)

Badawi A.B., 'Interpretive Preferences and the Limits of the New Formalism' (2009) 6 *Berkeley Business Law Journal* 1
——, 'The Attributes of Transactions and Interpretive Preferences: The Limits and Borders of Contractual Formalism', Bepress Working Paper (2007), available at http://works.bepress.com/adam.bbadawi/3
Baird D. and Morrison E., 'Serial Entrepreneurs and Small Business Bankruptcies' (2005) 105 *Columbia Law Review* 2310
Bakker P.S., 'Uitleg van commerciële contracten', *WPNR* (2011) 6890–6891
Balis G.A., *Γενικαί Αρχαί του Αστικού Δικαίου* [*General Principles of Civil Law*] (8th edn, Athens: P. Sakkoulas Publishers, 1961)
Bamberger H.-G. and Roth H. (eds.), *Beck'scher Onlinekommentar BGB*, commentary (48th edn, Munich: C.H. Beck Verlag, 2018)
Barak A., *Purposive Interpretation in Law* (Princeton, NJ: Princeton University Press, 2011)
Barbić J., 'Primjena običaja u hrvatskom trgovačkom pravu' (2005) 43 *Hrvatska akademija znanosti i umjetnosti* 47
Barcellona M., *Clausole generali e giustizia contrattuale* (Turin: Giappichelli, 2006)
Baretić M., 'Načelo savjesnosti i poštenja u obveznom pravu' (2003) 24 *Zbornik Pravnog fakulteta Sveučilišta u Rijeci* 571
Barnett R.E., 'A Consent Theory of Contract' (1986) 86 *Columbia Law Review* 269
——, 'The Sound of Silence: Default Rules and Contractual Consent' (1992) 78 *Virginia Law Review* 821
Bayern S., 'Contract Meta-Interpretation' (2016) 49 *The University of California, Davis Law Review* 1097
——, 'Rational Ignorance, Rational Closed-Mindedness, and Modern Economic Formalism in Contract Law' (2009) 97 *California Law Review* 943
Beale H. and Dugdale T., 'Contracts between Businessmen: Planning and use of Contractual Remedies' (1975) 2 *British Journal of Law and Society* 45
Beale H., Fauvarque-Cosson B., Rutgers J. and Vogenauer S., *Cases, Materials and Texts on Contract Law* (3rd edn, Oxford: Hart, 2019)
Beale H. (ed.), *Chitty on Contracts* (33rd edn, London: Thomson Reuters, 2018)
Bebchuk L. and Shavell S., 'Information and the Scope of Liability for Breach of Contract: The Rule of *Hadley v. Baxendale*' (1991) 7 *Journal of Law Economics and Organization* 284
Beck T., *Anwaltsstrategien bei der Vertragsgestaltung* (Stuttgart: R. Boorberg Verlag, 2007)
Bell G.J., *Principles of the Law of Scotland* (4th edn, Edinburgh: Thomas Clark Bookseller, 1839)
Below K.-H., *Bürgerliches Recht Allgemeiner Teil* (Wiesbaden: Gabler Verlag, 1960)
Ben-Shahar O., 'The Tentative Case against Flexibility in Commercial Law' (1999) 66 *University of Chicago Law Review* 781
Ben-Shahar O. and Porat A. (eds.), *Fault in American Contract Law* (Cambridge: Cambridge University Press, 2010)
Berg A., 'Thrashing through the Undergrowth' (2006) 122 *Law Quarterly Review* 354
Bernitz U., *Standardavtalsrätt* (7th edn, Stockholm: Norstedts Juridik, 2008)
Bernstein L., 'Merchant Law in a Merchant Court: Rethinking the Code's Search for Immanent Business Norms' (1996) 144 *University of Pennsylvania Law Review* 1765
——, 'Opting Out of the Legal System: Extralegal Contractual Relations in the Diamond Industry' (1992) 21 *Journal of Legal Studies* 115

——, 'Private Commercial Law in the Cotton Industry: Creating Co-operation through Rules, Norms and Institutions' (2001) 99 *Michigan Law Review* 1724

——, 'The Questionable Empirical Basis of Article 2's Incorporation Strategy: A Preliminary Study' (1999) 66 *University of Chicago Law Review* 710

Bessone M., *Adempimento e rischio contrattuale* (Milan: Giuffrè, 1969)

Betti E., *Teoria generale del negozio giuridico* (2nd revised edn, Naples: ESI, 1994)

Bhana D. and Nortje M., 'General principles of Contract' (2005) *Annual Survey of South African Law* 196

Bianca C.M., 'La nozione di buona fede quale regola di comportamento contrattuale', *Rivista di diritto civile* (1983) I, 205

——, *Diritto Civile 3. Il contratto* (Milan: Giuffrè, 2000)

Biehl B., 'Grundsätze der Vertragsauslegung', *Juristische Schulung* (2010) 195

Bieniek G., Ciepła H., Dmowski S., Gudowski J., Kołakowski K., Sychowicz M., Wiśniewski T. and Żuławska Cz., *Komentarz do Kodeksu cywilnego, Księga Trzecia Zobowiązania* (1st edn, Warsaw: Wydawnictwo Prawnicze, 1999)

Bigliazzi Geri L., 'L'interpretazione del contratto. Artt. 1362–1371 (ristampa con prefazione, note di aggiornamento e bibliografia a cura di V. Calderai)' in *Il codice civile, Commentario* (Milan: Giuffrè, 2013)

——, *Note in tema di interpretazione secondo buona fede: art. 1366 codice civile* (Pisa: Pacini, 1970)

Bingham, Lord 'A New Thing under the Sun? The Interpretation of Contracts and the ICS Decision' (2008) 12 *Edinburgh Law Review* 374

Blagojević B.T. and Krulj V., *Komentar zakona o obligacionim odnosima* (Beograd: Savremena administracija, 1980)

Bonamini T., *Premesse al contratto e clausole di stile* (Naples: ESI, 2017)

Boré J., 'Un centenaire: le contrôle par la Cour de cassation de la dénaturation des actes', *RTDCiv* (1972) 249

Bowers J.W., 'Murphy's Law and the Elementary Theory of Contract Interpretation: A Response to Schwartz and Scott' (2005) 57 *Rutgers Law Review* 587

Boyd White J., 'Law as Rhetoric, Rhetoric as Law: The Arts of Cultural and Communal Life' (1985) 52 *The University of Chicago Law Review* 684

——, 'Thinking About Our Language' (1987) 96 *Yale Law Journal* 1960

——, *Justice as Translation* (Chicago: University of Chicago Press, 1990)

Bradfield G.B., *Christie's Law of Contract in South Africa* (7th edn, Durban: LexisNexis, 2016) 225–263

Broseta Pont M. and Martínez Sanz F., *Manual de Derecho mercantil* (vol. II, 12th edn, Madrid: Tecnos, 2005)

Buczkowski S., 'Umowy o roboty budowlano – montażowe. Wybrane zagadnienia prawne', *Studia Prawnicze* (1964) no. 3, pp. 18–20

Burton S.J., 'A Lesson on Some Limits of Economic Analysis: Schwartz and Scott on Contract Interpretation' (2013) 88 *Indiana Law Journal* 339

Bussani M. and Mattei U., 'The Common Core Approach to European Private Law' (1997) 12 *Columbia Journal of European Law* 344

Cabrelli D., 'Implying terms in law: Belize no more?' (2016) 20(3) *Edinburgh Law Review* 338

Calderai V., *Interpretazione dei contratti e argomentazione giuridica* (Turin: Giappichelli, 2008)

Campbell D., 'The Relational Constitution of Contract and the Limits of "Economics": Kenneth Arrow on the Social Background of Markets' in Deakin S. and Michie J. (eds.), *Contracts, Co-operation and Competition: Studies in Economics, Management and Law* (Oxford: Oxford University Press, 1997)

—— (ed.), *The Relational Theory of Contract: Selected Works of Ian Macneil* (London: Sweet and Maxwell, 2001)

Cano Mata A., 'La *interpretación* de los contratos civiles', Madrid: *Anuario de Derecho Civil*, XXIV (1971) 193–206

Capilli G., *L'interpretazione del contratto secondo gli usi* (Naples: Jovene, 2017)

Capitant H., Terré F. and Lequette Y. (eds.), *Les grands arrêts de la jurisprudence civile* (vol. 2, Paris: Dalloz, 2015)

Capodanno M., *L'interpretazione del contratto* (Padua: CEDAM, 2006)

Carresi F., 'Dell'interpretazione del contratto (art. 1362–1371)' in *Commentario del codice civile Scialoja - Branca* (Bologna: Zanichelli, 1992)

——, 'Il contratto' in *Trattato di diritto civile e commerciale diretto da Cicu e Messineo e continuato da Mengoni*, XXI, 2 (Milan: Giuffrè, 1987)

——, 'L'interpretazione del contratto', *Rivista Trimestrale di diritto e procedura civile* (1963) I, 479

Cartwright J. and Hesselink M.W., 'Introduction' in Cartwright J. and Hesselink M.W. (eds.), *Precontractual Liability in European Private Law* (Cambridge: Cambridge University Press, 2008)

Casella M., *Il contratto e l'interpretazione* (Milan: Giuffrè, 1961)

Chantepie G. and Latina M., *Le nouveau droit des obligations - commentaire théorique et pratique dans l'ordre* (Paris: Dalloz, 2018)

Chantepie G., 'L'exigence de clarté dans la rédaction du contrat', *RDC* (2012) 989

Charny D., 'Hypothetical Bargains: The Normative Structure of Contract Interpretation' (1991) 89 *Michigan Law Review* 1815

——, 'Non-Legal Sanctions in Commercial Relationships' (1990) 104 *Harvard Law Review* 375

——, 'The New Formalism in Contract' (1999) 66 *University of Chicago Law Review* 842

Chénedé F., *Le nouveau droit des obligations et des contrat: consolidations, innovations, perspectives* (Paris: Dalloz, 2018)

Chinè G., 'Contrattazione standardizzata' in *Il contratto in generale*, XIII, 2, in Bessone M. (ed.), *Trattato di diritto privato* (Turin: Giappichelli, 2000)

Choi S.J., Gulati M. and Posner E.A., 'The Dynamics of Contract Evolution' (2013) 88 *New York University Law Review* 1

Cian G., *Forma solenne e interpretazione* (Padua: CEDAM, 1969)

Cigoj S., *Komentar obligacijskih razmerij* (Ljubljana: Časopisni zavod Uradni list SR Slovenije, 1984)

Clive E., 'European Initiatives (CFR) and Reform of Civil Law in New Member States: Differences between the Draft Common Frame of Reference and the Principles of European Contract Law' (2008) XIV *juridica international*

Cohen G.M., 'Implied Terms and Interpretation in Contract Law' in Bouckaert B. and De Geest, G. (eds.), *Encyclopedia of Law and Economics* (vol. III, Cheltenham: Edward Elgar, 2000)

——, 'The Negligence-Opportunism Tradeoff in Contract Law' (1992) 20 *Hofstra Law Review* 941

Collins H., *Regulating Contracts* (Oxford: Oxford University Press, 1999)

Connal C., 'Has the Rainy Sky Dried up? *Arnold v Britton* and commercial interpretation' (2016) 20(1) *Edinburgh Law Review* 71

Cooter R.D., 'Decentralized Law for a Complex Economy: The Structural Approach to Adjudicating the New Law Merchant' (1996) 144 *University of Pennsylvania Law Review* 1643

Córdova A., 'Reflexiones sobre la naturaleza de la interpretación jurídica: entre Betti y Gadamer', Madrid: *Revista Crítica de Derecho Inmobiliario* (1995) 2133–2151

Cornelius S., 'The unexpressed terms of a contract' (2006) 17 *Stellenbosch Law Review* 494

——, *Principles of the interpretation of contracts in South Africa* (Durban: LexisNexis Butterworths, 2002)

Costanza M., 'Interpretazione dei negozi di diritto privato' in *Digesto delle discipline privatistiche, Sezione civile*, X, 25 (Turin: UTET, 1993)

——, *Profili dell'interpretazione del contratto secondo buona fede* (Milan: Giuffrè, 1989)

Cuffaro V., 'L'interpretazione del contratto' in Lipari N. (ed.), *Trattato di diritto privato europeo*, III (Padua: CEDAM, 2003)

Cunningham L., 'Toward a Prudential and Credibility-Centered Parol Evidence Rule' (2000) 68 *University of Cincinnati Law Review* 269

D'Auria M., *L'interpretazione del contratto nel diritto privato europeo* (Milan: Giuffrè, 2012)

Da Frada C., *Teoria da Confiança e Responsabilidade Civil* (Coimbra: Almedina, 2007)

Davidson D., 'Belief and the Basis of Meaning' (1974) 27(3/4) *Synthese* 309

——, 'On the Very Idea of a Conceptual Scheme' (1974) 47 *Proceedings and Address of the American Philosophical Association* 5

Davis K., 'Licensing Lies: Merger Clauses, the Parol Evidence Rule and Pre-contractual Misrepresentations' (1999) 33 *Valparaiso University Law Review* 485

De Almeida F., *Texto e Enunciado na Teoria do Negócio Jurídico* (Coimbra: Almedina, 1992)

De Castro y Bravo F., *El Derecho civil de España* (vol. II, Cizur Menor: Thomson-Civitas, 1952; reprinted 2008)

——, *El negocio jurídico* (Madrid: Civitas, 1971; reprinted 1997)

De Geest G. (ed.), *Encyclopedia of Law and Economics* (vol. III, Cheltenham: Edward Elgar, 2000)

Díaz Alabart S., 'Reglas de interpretación' in Bercovitz Rodríguez-Cano R. (coord.), *Comentarios a la Ley de condiciones generales de la contratación* (Cizur Menor: Aranzadi, 1999)

Díaz Jiménez M.C., '*Interpretatio contra stipulatorem* y principio de interpretación más favorable al consumidor', Madrid: *Actualidad Civil*, 14 (1994) 315–328

Díez García H. and Gutiérrez Santiago P., 'Interpretación e integración del contrato' in Bercovitz Rodríguez-Cano R. (dir.), *Tratado de contratos* (book I, Valencia: Tirant lo Blanch, 2009)

Díez-Picazo L., *Fundamentos del Derecho Civil Patrimonial* (vol. I, 6th edn, Cizur Menor: Thomson-Civitas, 2007)

Doucouliagos C., 'A Note on the Evolution of Homo Economicus' (1994) 28 *Journal of Economic Issues* 877

Du Plessis J., 'Giving practical effect to good faith in the Law of Contract' (2018) 29 *Stellenbosch Law Review* 379

Dupichot J., 'Pour un retour aux textes : défense et illustration du « petit guide-âne » des articles 1156 à 1164 du Code civil' in *Etudes offertes à Jacques FLOUR* (Paris: Répertoire du Notariat Defrénois, 1979)
Elías Baturones J.J., *La prueba de documentos electrónicos en los Tribunales de Justicia* (Valencia: Tirant lo Blanch, 2008)
Fabre-Magnan M., *Droit des obligations – 1. Contrat et engagement unilatéral* (Paris: PUF, 2016)
Farnsworth E., '"Meaning' in the Law of Contracts' (1967) 76 *Yale Law Journal* 939
Fauvarque-Cosson B., 'L'interprétation du contrat: observations comparatives', *RDC* (2007) 481
Fauvarque-Cosson B. and Mazeaud D., *Principes Directuers du Droit Européen du Contrat* (Paris: Association Henri Capitant, 2008)
—— (eds.), *European Contract Law. Materials for a Common Frame of Reference: Terminology, Guiding Principles, Model Rules*, (Munich: Sellier, 2008)
Fauvarque-Cosson B., Mazeaud D. and Tenenbaum A., *Terminologie Contractuelle Commune. Projet de Cadre Commun de Référence* (Paris: Association Henri Capitant, 2008)
Ferrer Riba J., 'Reglas de interpretación' in Menéndez A. (dir.), *Comentarios a la Ley sobre condiciones generales de la contratación* (Madrid: Civitas, 2002)
Filios P.C., *Γενικές Αρχές Αστικού Δικαίου* [*General Principles of Civil Law*] (3rd edn, Athens: Ant. N. Sakkoulas Publishers, 2009)
Fish S., *Doing What Comes Naturally: Change, Rhetoric, and the Practice of Theory in Literary and Legal Studies* (Durham, NC: Duke University Press, 1989)
Flour J., Aubert J.-L. and Savaux E., *Les obligations, 1. L'acte juridique* (Paris: Sirey, 2014)
Flume W., *Allgemeiner Teil des Bürgerlichen Rechts, Das Rechtsgeschäft* (vol. II, 4th edn, Berlin: Springer Verlag, 1992)
Fohlin P., *Avtalstolkning* (Uppsala: Iustus, 1989)
Gadamer H.-G., *Truth and Method*, trans. Weinsheimer J. and Marshall D.G. (3rd edn, London: Continuum, 1975/2004)
García-Pita y Lastres J.L., *Derecho mercantil de obligaciones. Parte General* (Barcelona: Marcial Pons, 2003)
Gautier P.-Y., 'L'incertitude règne encore sur la transmissibilité passive des obligations: au sujet de l'obligation de remise en état à la charge du cessionnaire du bail', *RTDCiv* (2003) 725
Gava J. and Grene J., 'Do We need a Hybrid Law of Contract? Why Hugh Collins Is Wrong and Why It Matters' (2004) 63 *Cambridge Law Journal* 605
Genovese A., 'Contratto standard e comune intenzione delle parti', *Obbligazioni e contratti* (2007) 1020
——, *L'interpretazione del contratto standard* (Milan: Giuffrè, 2008)
Gentili A., *Senso e consenso. Storia, teoria e tecnica dell'intepretazione dei contratti* (Turin: Giappichelli, 2015)
Gentili A. and Astone F., 'Dell'interpretazione del contratto. Art. 1371' in Navarretta E. and Orestano A. (eds.), *Dei contratti in generale. Artt. 1350–1386, Commentario del codice civile diretto a E. Gabrielli* (Turin: UTET, 2011)
Georgiades A.S., *Ενοχικό Δίκαιο – Γενικό Μέρος* [*Law of Obligations – General Part*] (2nd edn, Athens: P.N. Sakkoulas Publishers, 2015)

——, *Γενικές Αρχές Αστικού Δικαίου* [*General Principles of Civil Law*] (5th edn, Athens: P.N. Sakkoulas Publishers, 2019)
Georgiades A.S. and Stathopoulos M. (eds.). *Αστικός Κώδιξ: ερμηνεία κατ' άρθρο – νομολογία – βιβλιογραφία. Τόμος II: Γενικό Ενοχικό* [*Astikos Kodex: Commentary by article – case law – bibliography. Volume II: General Part of the Law of Obligations*] (Athens: P. Sakkoulas Bros. Publishers, 1979)
——, *Αστικός Κώδιξ: ερμηνεία κατ' άρθρο – νομολογία – βιβλιογραφία. Τόμος I^B: Γενικές Αρχές* [*Astikos Kodex: Commentary by article – case law – bibliography. Volume I^B: General Principles*] (2nd edn, Athens: P. N. Sakkoulas Publishers, 2016)
Ghestin J., Jamin Ch. and Billiau M., *Traité de droit civil – Les effets du contrat* (Paris: LGDJ, 2001)
Gilson R., Sabel C. and Scott R.E., 'Text and Context: Contract Interpretation as Contract Design' (2014) 100 *Cornell Law Review* 23
Giorgi G., *Teoria delle obbligazioni nel diritto moderno italiano* (Florence: Cammelli, 1876)
Gloag W.M., *Contract* (2nd edn, Edinburgh: W. Green & Son Ltd., 1929)
Goetz C. and Scott R.E., 'The Limits of Expanded Choice: An Analysis of the Interactions between Express and Implied Contract Terms' (1985) 73 *California Law Review* 26
Gorenc V. et al., *Komentar Zakona o obveznim odnosima* (Zagreb: Narodne novine, 2014)
Grassetti C., 'Interpretazione dei negozi giuridici "inter vivos", (Diritto civile)' in *Novissimo digesto italiano*, VIII (Turin: UTET, 1962)
——, *L'interpretazione del negozio giuridico con particolare riguardo ai contratti* (Padua: CEDAM, 1938) (reprint 1983)
Grey C., 'The New Formalism', Stanford Law School, Public Law and Legal Series Working Paper No. 4 (1999), available at http://ssrn.com/abstract=200732
Grimaldi C., 'Paradoxes autour de l'interprétation des contrats', *RDC* (2008) 207
Grönfors K., *Avtalsgrundande rättsfakta* (Stockholm: Nerenius & Santérus, 1993)
——, *Tolkning av fraktavtal* (Gothenburg: Jure, 1989)
Grosheide F.W., 'Lees maar, er staat wat er staat', *Contracteren* (2000) 100–107
——, 'Lees maar, er staat wat er staat', *WPNR* (2001) 6428, 5–13
Grosheide F.W. and Drion C.E., 'Enerzijds, anderzijds', *Contracteren* (2008) 30–32
Großfeld B., *Core Questions of Comparative Law*, trans. Grosswald Curran V. (Durham, NC: Carolina Academic Press, 2005)
Habermann N., Jickeli J., Singer R., Stieper M. and Knothe, H.-G. (eds.), *J. von Staudingers Kommentar zum Bürgerlichen Gesetzbuch*, commentary, (vol. I, 14th edn, Munich/Berlin: Sellier/De Gruyter Verlag, 2012)
Hadfield G.K., 'Judicial Competence and the Interpretation of Incomplete Contracts' (1994) 23 *Journal of Legal Studies* 159
Hart O. and Moore J., 'Agreeing Now to Agree Later: Contracts that Rule Out but do not Rule In', NBER Working Paper No. 10397 (2004), available at http://www.nber.org/papers/w10397
——, 'Contracts as Reference Points' (2008) 123 *The Quarterly Journal of Economics* 1
——, 'Foundations of Incomplete Contracts' (1999) 66 *Review of Economic Studies* 115
Hart O. and Holmstrom B., 'The Theory of Contracts' in Bewley T. (ed.), *Advances in Economic Theory* (Cambridge: Cambridge University Press, 1987)
Hartlief T., 'De Uitleg van Contracten. *Haviltex* Revisited', *Tijdschrift voor Privaatrecht* (2004) 41, 1065–1084

Hellenic Parliament, *Explanatory Report [Αιτιολογική Έκθεση] to law 3994/2011*, available at https://www.hellenicparliament.gr/UserFiles/2f026f42-950c-4efc-b950-340c4fb76a24/e-expol-eis.pdf (Athens)

Hellner J., 'Scandinavian Legal Realism in the Law of Contract' in Cane P. and Stapleton J. (eds.), *Essays for Patrick Atiyah* (Oxford: Clarendon Press, 1991)

——, 'The parol evidence rule och tolkning av skriftliga avtal i svensk rätt' in *Festskrift till Bertil Bengtsson* (Stockholm: Nerenius & Santérus, 1993)

——, 'Tolkning av standardavtal', *Jussens venner* (1994) 266

Hemmo M., *Sopimusoikeus I* (new 2nd edn, Helsinki: Talentum, 2003)

Herberger M., Martinek M., Rüßmann H. and Weth S., *juris PraxisKommentar-BGB* (vol. II, 7th edn, Heidelberg: Hüthig Jehle Rehm Verlag)

Hijma J., 'Uitleg contra proferentem' in Hartlief T. and Stolker C.J.J.M. (eds.), *Contractvrijheid* (Deventer: Kluwer, 1999)

Hoffman L., 'The intolerable wrestle with words and meanings' (1997) 114 *South African Law Journal* 656

Høgberg A.P., *Kontraktstolkning. Særlig om tolkningsstiler ved fortolkning av skriftlige kontrakter* (Oslo: Universitetsforlaget, 2006)

Hörster H.E., *A Parte Geral do Código Civil Português* (Coimbra: Almedina, 2009)

Hosten W.J. (rev. Knobel M.) 'Custom and Usage' in Joubert W.A. and Faris J.A. (eds.), *The Law of South Africa* (vol. V(2), 2nd edn, Durban: LexisNexis Butterworths, 2004)

Hutchison D., 'Nature and basis of Contract' in Hutchison D. and Pretorius C. (eds.), *The Law of Contract in South Africa* (3rd edn, Cape Town: Oxford University Press, South Africa, 2017)

Irti N., *Testo e contesto. Una rilettura dell'art. 1362 del codice civile* (Padua: CEDAM, 1996)

——, 'La sintassi delle clausole (note intorno all'art. 1363 c.c.)', *Rivista trimestrale di diritto e procedura civile* (1989) 421

——, 'Principi e problemi di interpretazione contrattuale', *Rivista trimestrale di diritto e procedura civile* (1999) 1143

—— (ed.), *L'interpretazione del contratto nella dottrina italiana* (Padua: CEDAM, 2000)

Jaume Bennasar A., *La validez del documento electrónico y su eficacia en sede procesal* (Valladolid: Lex Nova, 2010)

Jensen M.C. and Meckling W.H., 'Theory of the Firm: Managerial Behavior, Agency Costs and Ownership Structure' (1976) 3 *Journal of Financial Economics* 305

Johnson J., 'Strategic Bargaining and the Economic Theory of Contract Default Rules' (1990) 100 *Yale Law Journal* 615

Jordano Barea J.B., 'De la interpretación de los contratos' in Paz-Ares C., Díez-Picazo L., Bercovitz R. and Salvador Coderch P. (dirs.), *Comentario del Código civil* (book II, Madrid: Ministerio de Justicia, 1991)

Joseph J.E., 'Indeterminacy, Translation and the Law' in Morris M. (ed.), *Translation and the Law* (Philadelphia: Benjamins, 1995)

JurisClasseur Civil Code (Paris: LexisNexis – online commentaries of the French civil code)

Kačer A., Radolović A. and Slakoper Z., *Zakon o obveznim odnosima s komentarom* (Zagreb: Poslovni zbornik d.o.o., 2006)

Kaczorowska B., 'Wizja wykładni umów w projekcie księgi pierwszej kodeksu cywilnego', Transformacje Prawa Prywatnego 2/2011, pp. 9–32

Kahn Ph., 'L'interprétation des contrats internationaux', *JDI* (1981), reproduced in *Un siècle d'étude du droit international - Choix d'articles parus au Clunet (1874–2000)* (Paris: Litec, 2006)
Kaisto J. and Lohi T., *Johdatus varallisuusoikeuteen* (Helsinki: Talentum, 2008)
Kaplow L., 'Rules versus Standards: An Economic Analysis' (1992) 42 *Duke Law Journal* 55
Karakostas I.K., *Αστικός Κώδικας: Ερμηνεία - Σχόλια - Νομολογία, Τόμος Δεύτερος: Γενικές Αρχές (άρθρα 127–286)* [*Astikos Kodikas: Commentary - Gloss - Case law, Volume II: General Principles (articles 127–286)*] (Athens: Nomiki Vivliothiki Publishers, 2005)
Karassis M.D., *Γενικές Αρχές του Αστικού Δικαίου - Δικαιοπραξία* [*General Principles of Civil Law - Juridical Act*] (vol. I, Athens/Komotini: Ant. N. Sakkoulas Publishers, 1996)
Karlgren H., *Avtalsrättsliga spörsmål* (2nd edn, Stockholm: Norstedt, 1954)
——, *Kutym och rättsregel* (Stockholm: Norstedt, 1960)
——, *Passivitet* (Stockholm: Norstedt, 1965)
Katz A.W., 'Contract Theory - Who Needs It?' (2014) 81 *University of Chicago Law Review* 2043
——, 'The Economics of Form and Substance in Contract Interpretation' (2004) 104 *Columbia Law Review* 496
——, 'Your Terms or Mine? The Duty to Read the Fine Print in Contracts' (1990) 21 *Rand Journal of Economics* 518
Kerameus K.D., Kondylis D.G. and Nikas N.T., *Ερμηνεία του Κώδικα Πολιτικής Δικονομίας I: 1–590* [*Commentary of the Code of Civil Procedure I: 1–590*] (vol. I (2 vols.), Athens/Thessaloniki/Komotini: Sakkoulas Publishers/Ant. Sakkoulas Publishers/Dikaio & Oikonomia-P.N. Sakkoulas Publishers, 2000)
Kerr A.J., 'Implied provisions in contracts: is there to be a new role for the hypothetical bystander? Conflicting Supreme Court of Appeal decisions' (2006) 123 *South African Law Journal* 195
——, *The principles of the Law of Contract* (6th edn, Durban: Butterworths, 2002)
Klimke D., *Die Vertragsübernahme* (Tübingen: Mohr Siebeck Verlag, 2010)
Köhler H., *BGB Allgemeiner Teil* (39th edn, Munich: C.H. Beck Verlag, 2015)
Kornet N., *Contract Interpretation and Gap Filling: Comparative and Theoretical Perspectives* (Ius Commune Europeaum no. 60, Antwerp/Oxford: Intersentia, 2006)
Kostritsky J.P., 'Plain Meaning vs. Broad Interpretation: How the Risk of Opportunism Defeats a Unitary Default Rule for Interpretation' (2008) 96 *Kentucky Law Journal* 43
Kozlowska-Rautiainen D. and Mäenpää K., 'Legal Effects of the Entire Agreement Clauses', *Business Law Forum* (2012)
Kraus J.S., 'Philosophy of Contract Law' in Coleman J. et al. (eds.), *The Oxford Handbook of Jurisprudence and Philosophy of Law* (Oxford: Oxford University Press, 2004)
Kraus J.S. and Scott R.E., 'Contract Design and the Structure of Contractual Intent' (2009) 84 *New York University Law Review* 1023
Kraus J.S. and Walt S., 'In Defense of the Incorporation Strategy' in Kraus J. and Walt S., (eds.), *The Jurisprudential Foundations of Corporate and Commercial Law* (Cambridge: Cambridge University Press, 2000)
Ladas P.B., *General Principles of Civil Law* [*Γενικές Αρχές Αστικού Δκαίου*] (vol. II, Athens/Thessaloniki: Sakkoulas Publishers, 2009)
Lamy Droit du Contrat, Etude no. 331 (Rueil-Malmaison: Wolters Kluwer France - Les Editions Lamy - online commentaries of the French law of contract)

Lando O. and Beale H. (eds.), *Principles of European Contract Law: Part I and II* (The Hague/London/Boston: Kluwer Law International, 2000)
Lando O., Clive E., Prüm A. and Zimmermann R. (eds.), *Principles of European Contract Law: Part III* (The Hague/London/Boston: Kluwer Law International, 2003)
Larenz K. and Canaris C.-W., *Methodenlehre der Rechtswissenschaft* (4th edn, Berlin: Springer Verlag, 2014)
Larenz K., Wolf M. and Neuner J., *Allgemeiner Teil des Bürgerlichen Rechts: Ein Lehrbuch* (10th edn, Munich: C.H. Beck Verlag, 2012)
Lassen J., *Haandbog i Obligationsretten. Almindelig Del* (3rd edn, Copenhagen: G E C Gads Forlag, 1917–1920)
Le Tourneau Ph. (ed.), *Droit de la responsabilité et des contrats* (Paris: Dalloz, 2017)
Legrand P., '"Il n'y a pas de hors-texte": Intimations of Jacques Derrida as Comparatist-at-Law' in Goodrich P., Hoffmann F., Rosenfeld M. and Vismann C. (eds.), *Derrida and Legal Philosophy* (London: Palgrave Macmillan, 2008)
——, 'Econocentrism' (2009) 59(2) *University of Toronto Law Journal* 215
——, 'Issues in the Translatability of Law' in Bermann S. and Wood M. (eds.), *Nation, Language, and the Ethics of Translation* (Princeton, NJ: Princeton University Press, 2005)
——, 'The Same and the Different' in Legrand P. and Munday R. (eds.), *Comparative Legal Studies: Traditions and Transitions* (Cambridge: Cambridge University Press, 2003)
——, 'Word/World (of Primordial Issues for Comparative Legal Studies)' in Madsen M.R., Kjær A.L., Krunke H. and Petersen H. (eds.), *Paradoxes of European Legal Integration* (Aldershot: Ashgate, 2008)
Lehrberg B., 'Anm av Grönfors, Avtalsgrundande rättsfakta', *SvJT* (1996) 461 ff.
——, *Avtalstolkning* (5th edn, Uppsala: Iusté, 2009)
——, *Förutsättningsläran* (Uppsala: Iustus, 1989)
Lete Achirica J., 'De la interpretación de los contratos' in Domínguez Luelmo A., *Comentarios al Código civil* (Valladolid: Lex Nova, 2010)
Lewison K., *The Interpretation of Contracts* (6th edn: London: Sweet & Maxwell, 2015)
Lindell B., *Civilprocessen* (2nd edn, Uppsala: Iustus, 2003)
Llewellyn K.N., *The Bramble Bush: The Classic Lectures on the Law and Law School* (Oxford: Oxford University Press, 2008)
Longchamps de Berier R., *Zobowiązania* (3rd edn, Poznań: Księga, 1948)
López y López A.M., 'De la interpretación de los contratos' in Albaladejo M. (dir.), *Comentarios al Código civil y Compilaciones Forales* (book XVII, vol. 2, Edersa, 1981)
——, 'De la interpretación de los contratos' in Cañizares Laso A. et al. (dirs.), *Código Civil comentado* (vol. III, Madrid: Civitas-Thomson Reuters, 2011)
Lubbe G. and Murray C., *Farlam & Hathaway Contract: cases, materials and commentary* (3rd edn, Cape Town: Juta & Co. Ltd, 1988)
Lüderitz A., *Auslegung von Rechtsgeschäften* (Heidelberg: C.F. Müller Verlag, 1966)
MacCormick N., *Institutions of Law: An Essay in Legal Theory* (Oxford: Oxford University Press, 2006)
——, *Rhetoric and the Rule of Law: A Theory of Legal Reasoning* (Oxford: Oxford University Press, 2005)
Macgregor L., 'Crossing the Line between Business Common Sense and Perceived Fairness in Contractual Interpretation' (2015) 19(3) *Edinburgh Law Review* 378

MacQueen H., 'Good Faith in the Scots Law of Contract: An Undisclosed Principle?' in Forte A.D.M., *Good Faith in Contract and Property Law* (Oxford: Hart Publishing, 1999)
Maiorca S., 'Contratti standard' in *Novissimo Digesto Italiano, Appendice*, II (Turin: UTET, 1981)
Malaurie Ph., Aynès L. and Stoffel-Munck Ph., *Les obligations* (Paris: LGDJ, 2018)
Malinvaud Ph., Fenouillet D. and Mekki M., *Droit des obligations* (Paris: LexisNexis, 2017)
Maskin E. and Tirole J., 'Unforeseen Contingencies and Incomplete Contracts' (1999) 66 *The Review of Economic Studies* 83
Matić T., 'Elektronički oblik govora i isprava – Novi oblik?' (2006) 56 *Zbornik Zbornik Pravnog fakulteta Sveučilišta u Zagrebu* 165
Maxwell C., 'Interpretation of contracts' in Hutchison D. and Pretorius C. (eds.), *The Law of Contract in South Africa* (3rd edn, Cape Town: Oxford University Press, South Africa, 2017)
Mazeaud D., 'Droit des contrats: réforme à l'horizon !', *D.* (2014) 291
McBryde W.W., *The Law of Contract in Scotland* (3rd edn, Edinburgh: W. Green & Son Ltd., 2007)
McLauchlan D.W., 'Common assumptions and contract interpretation' (1997) 113 *Law Quarterly Review* 237
McMeel G., *The Construction of Contracts: Interpretation, Implication and Rectification* (2nd edn, Oxford: Oxford University Press, 2011)
——, *The Construction of Contracts* (3rd edn: Oxford: Oxford University Press, 2017)
Medicus D., *Allgemeiner Teil des BGB* (10th edn, Heidelberg: C.F. Müller Verlag, 2010)
Mellqvist M. and Persson I., *Fordran och skuld* (8th edn, Uppsala: Iustus, 2007)
Mendes C., *Teoria Geral do Direito Civil* (Lison: AAFDL, 1995)
Menezes Cordeiro A., 'A interpretação contratual anglo-saxónica', *Direito*, Ano 141, III, (2009)
——, *Da Boa Fé no Direito Civil* (4th reprint, Coimbra: Almedina, 2001)
——, *Tratado de Direito Civil Português*, II, Parte Geral (4th edn, Coimbra: Almedina, 2014)
Mestre J., 'De l'interprétation de clauses en conflit', *RTDCiv.* (1999) 836
Miller G., 'Bargaining on the Red-eye: New Light on Contract Theory', New York University Law and Economics Working Papers (2008), available at http://lsr.nellco.org/cgi/viewcontent.cgi?article=1135&context=nyu_lewp
Miquel J., 'La interpretación de los contratos. Vinculación entre teoría y práctica', Barcelona: *Revista Jurídica de Cataluña* (1981) 789–803
Mišćenić E., 'Croatian Case "Franak": Effective or 'Defective' Protection of Consumer Rights?' (2016) V *Harmonius Journal of Legal and Social Studies in South East Europe* 184
——, 'Legal Translation vs. Legal Certainty in EU Law' in Mišćenić E. and Raccah A. (eds.), *Legal Risks in EU Law: Interdisciplinary Studies on Legal Risk Management and Better Regulation in Europe* (Bern: Springer, 2016)
——, 'Uniform Interpretation of Article 4(2) of UCT Directive in the Context of Consumer Credit Agreements: Is it possible?' (2018) 3 *Revue du droit de l'Union européenne* 127
Mitchell C., *Interpretation of Contracts* (London: Routledge, 2007)

Monterde García J.C., 'Orígenes y aplicación jurídica del aforismo latino *in claris non fit interpretatio*', Madrid: *Diario La Ley*, no. 6310 (2005) 1–40

Moreno-Torres Herrera M.L., 'Arras, opción de compra e interpretación del contrato', Madrid: *Diario La Ley*, no. 7821 (2012) 1–17

Morgan J., *Great Debates in Contract Law* (2nd edn, London: Palgrave Macmillan, 2015)

Motos Guirao M., 'La interpretación del contrato mercantil y el artículo 59 del Código de comercio', Barcelona: *Revista Jurídica de Cataluña*, vol. LXXII (1955) 34–47

Muris T.J., 'Opportunistic Behavior and the Law of Contracts' (1981) 65 *Minnesota Law Review* 521

Murray J., 'Contract Theories and the Rise of Neoformalism' (2002) 71 *Fordham Law* Review 869

Musiała A., Glosa do wyroku Sądu Najwyższego z dnia 26 marca 2008 r., sygn. akt I, UK 282/07, Gdańskie Studia Prawnicze no 2, 2009, pp. 103–109

Musielak H.-J. and Voit W. (eds.), *Zivilprozessordnung mit Gerichtsverfassungsgesetz – Kommentar*, commentary (12th edn, Munich: Franz Vahlen Verlag, 2014)

Mutabžija J., 'Klauzule plaćanja kod ugovora o licenciji' (2005) 14 *Pravo i porezi* 7

Myburgh F., 'Thomas Kuhn's *Structure of Scientific Revolutions*, paradigm shifts, and crises: analysing recent changes in the approach to contractual interpretation in South African law' (2017) 134 *South African Law Journal* 514

Nicholls D., 'My kingdom for a horse: the meaning of words' (2005) 121 *Law Quarterly Review* 577

Noldeke G. and Schmidt K., 'Option Contracts and Renegotiation: A Solution to the Hold-up Problem' (1995) 26 *The Rand Journal of Economics* 163

Norros O., 'Onko ei-kielletty aina sallittua auton osamaksuostajalle?', *Lakimies* (2009) 854–865

——, *Johdatus velvoiteoikeuteen* (Helsinki: Forum Iuris 2010)

Oppo G., *Profili dell'interpretazione oggettiva del negozio giuridico* (Bologna: Zanichelli, 1943 (also in Oppo G., *Obbligazioni e negozio giuridico, Scritti Giuridici,* III (Padua: CEDAM, 1992)

Örücü A.E., 'Methodology of Comparative Law' in Smits J.M. (ed.), *Elgar Encyclopedia of Comparative Law* (2nd edn, Cheltenham: Edward Elgar, 2012)

Orücü E. et al. (eds.), *Studies in Legal Systems: Mixed and Mixing* (The Hague: Kluwer Law International, 1996)

Pacchioni G., *Dei contratti in generale* (Padua: CEDAM, 1939)

Pacifici Mazzoni E., *Istituzioni di diritto civile italiano* (Florenca: Cammelli, 1927)

Pagador López J., *Condiciones generales y cláusulas contractuales predispuestas* (Barcelona: Marcial Pons, 1999)

Pais de Vasconcelos P., *Contratos Atípicos* (2nd edn, Coimbra: Almedina, 2009)

——, *Teoria Geral do Direito Civil* (6th edn, Coimbra: Almedina, 2010)

Palandt O. (ed.), *Palandt Bürgerliches Gesetzbuch mit Nebengesetzen – Kommentar*, commentary (77th edn, Munich: C.H. Beck Verlag, 2018)

Papanikolaou P.A., *Μεθοδολογία του Ιδιωτικού Δικαίου και Ερμηνεία των Δικαιοπραξιών* [*Private Law Methodology and Interpretation of Juridical Acts*] (Athens: Ant. N. Sakkoulas Publishers, 2000)

Papantoniou N.S., *Η καλή πίστις εις το αστικόν δίκαιον* [*Good faith in civil law*] (Athens: Ant. N. Sakkoulas Publishers, 1957)
Patterson D., *Law and Truth* (Oxford: Oxford University Press, 1996)
Patterson E., 'The Interpretation and Construction of Contracts' (1964) 64 *Columbia Law Review* 833
Patti S., 'Le condizioni generali di contratto e i contratti col consumatore' in Rescigno P. and Gabrielli E. (eds.), *Trattato dei contratti* (Turin: UTET, 1999)
Perović S., *Obligaciono pravo* (Beograd: Novi dani, 1981)
Perović S. and Stojanović D., *Komentar zakona o obligacionim odnosima* (Novi Sad: Pravni fakultet Kragujevac i Kulturni centar Gornji Milanovac, 1980)
Pescatore V., 'Cessione del contratto e interpretazione', *Rivista trimestrale di diritto e procedura civile* (1999) 583
Petrić S., 'Koncept nepoštenih ugovornih odredbi s posebnim osvrtom na potrošačke ugovore' in Tomljenović V., Petrić S. and Mišćenić E. *Nepoštene ugovorne odredbe: europski standardi i hrvatska provedba* (Rijeka: Pravni fakultet Sveučilišta u Rijeci, 2013)
——, 'Tumačenje općih uvjeta ugovora i njihov odnos s posebno ugovorenim klauzulama u hrvatskom i europskom pravu' (2001) 12 *Hrvatska pravna revija* 26
Phillipson R., *English-Only Europe? Challenging Language Policy* (New York: Routledge, 2003)
Picker C., *Die betriebliche Übung* (Tübingen: Mohr Siebeck Verlag, 2011)
Pönkä V., 'Tavoitteellisten tulkintasääntöjen merkityksestä liikesopimusten tulkinnassa', *Defensor Legis* (2013) 919–939
Posner E.A., 'A Theory of Contract Law under Conditions of Radical Judicial Error' (2000) 94 *Northwestern University Law Review* 749
——, 'Economic Analysis of Contract Law after Three Decades: Success or Failure?' (2003) 112 *Yale Law Journal* 829
——, 'Law, Economics, and Inefficient Norms' (1996) 144 *University of Pennsylvania Law Review* 1697
——, 'The Parol Evidence Rule, the Plain Meaning Rule, and the Principles of Contractual Interpretation' (1998) 146 *University of Pennsylvania Law Review* 533
Posner R.A., 'Let Us Never Blame a Contract Breaker' in Ben-Shahar O. and Porat A. (eds.), *Fault in American Contract Law* (Cambridge: Cambridge University Press, 2010)
——, 'The Law and Economics of Contract Interpretation' (2005) 83 *Texas Law Review* 1581
——, *The Problems of Jurisprudence* (Harvard University Press, 1990)
Pringsheim F., '*Animus* in Roman Law' (1933) 49 *Law Quarterly Review* 43
Prütting H. and Gehrlein M. (eds.), *ZPO Kommentar*, commentary (8th edn, Cologne: Luchterhand Verlag (Wolters Kluwer), 2016)
Radwański Z., *System prawa prywatnego, Prawo Cywilne. Część Ogólna* (vol. 2, 1st edn, Warsaw: CH Beck, 2002)
——, *Wykładnia oświadczeń woli składanych indywidualnym adresatom* (1st edn, Wrocław: Ossolineum, 1992)
Ramberg J., 'Avtalsautonomi och den dispositiva rätten' in *Festskrift till Anders Agell* (Uppsala: Iustus, 1994)
——, 'Avtalstolkningsmetoder' in *Festskrift till Gösta Walin* (Stockholm: Norstedts Juridik, 2002)

Ramberg J. and Ramberg C., *Allmän avtalsrätt* (8th edn, Stockholm: Norstedts Juridik, 2010)
Rebmann K., Säcker F.-J., Rixecker R., Oetker H. and Limperg B. (eds.), *Münchener Kommentar zum Bürgerlichen Gesetzbuch,* commentary (8th edn, Munich: C.H. Beck Verlag, 2018)
Rehbinder E., *Vertragsgestaltung* (2nd edn, Cologne: Luchterhand Verlag (Wolters Kluwer), 1993)
Rei M.R., *Da interpretação da declaração negocial no Direito Civil Português* (PhD thesis, Lisboa: Universidade de Lisboa, Faculdade de Direito, 2010)
Reid E. and Blackie J., *Personal Bar* (Edinburgh: W. Green, 2006)
Reid K. and Zimmermann R. (eds.), *A History of Private Law in Scotland* (2000)
Reimann M. and Zimmermann R. (eds.), *Oxford Handbook of Comparative Law* (2nd edn, Oxford: Oxford University Press, 2019)
Répertoire de droit civil (Paris: Dalloz – online commentaries of French civil law)
Richard de la Tour J., 'Les principes, les directives et les clauses relatives à l'interprétation', *RDC* (2016) 392
Richardson L., 'Commercial common sense in contractual interpretation: further views from the Inner House' (2017) 21(3) *Edinburgh Law Review* 423
——, 'Commercial common sense revisited: further developments in contract interpretation and commercial leasing' (2016) 20(3) *Edinburgh Law Review* 342
Riesenhuber K., *Europäisches Vertragsrecht* (2nd edn, Berlin: De Gruyter Verlag, 2006)
Rizzo V., *Interpretazione del contratto e relatività delle sue regole* (Naples: Edizioni scientifiche italiane, 1985)
Roberts A.A., *Wessels' Law of Contract* (vol. I, 2nd edn, Durban: Butterworths & Co. (Africa) Ltd, 1951)
Rodhe K., *Obligationsrätt* (Stockholm: Norstedts Juridik, 1956)
Rodotà S., *Le fonti di integrazione del contratto* (Milan: Giuffrè, 1969)
Rodríguez Marín C., 'De la interpretación de los contratos' in Pasquau Liaño M. (dir.), *Jurisprudencia civil comentada. Código civil* (book II, Granada: Comares, 2000)
Romanowski M., 'Ogólne reguły wykładni kontraktów w świetle zasad europejskiego prawa kontraktów a reguły wykładni umów w prawie polskim', Przegląd Prawa Handlowego 2004/8, pp. 11–18
——, 'Szczegółowe reguły wykładni kontraktów w świetle zasad europejskiego prawa kontraktów a reguły wykładni umów w prawie polskim', Przegląd Prawa Handlowego 2004/9, pp. 12–18
Roppo V., 'Il Contratto' in Iudica G. and Zatti P. (eds.), *Trattato di diritto privato* (Milan: Giuffrè, 2011)
Rott-Pietrzyk E., 'Interpretacja oświadczenia woli (uwagi na tle rozwiązań projektu księgi I kodeksu cywilnego)', Transformacje Prawa Prywatnego 4/2010, pp. 45–59
Saarnilehto A., 'Epäselvä ehto', *Oikeustieto* (2012) 9–10
——, *Sopimusoikeuden perusteet* (new 7th edn, Helsinki: Talentum, 2009)
Saarnilehto A. and Annola V., 'Sopimuksen tulkinta' in Saarnilehto A. (editor-in-chief), *Varallisuusoikeus* (2nd edn, Helsinki: SanomaPro, 2012)
Sacco R., 'L'interpretazione' in Sacco R. and De Nova G., *Il contratto* (Turin: UTET, 2016)

——, 'Legal Formants: A Dynamic Approach to Comparative Law (Installment I of II)' (1991) 39(1) *The American Journal of Comparative Law* 1

——, 'Legal Formants: A Dynamic Approach to Comparative Law (Installment II of II)' (1991) 39(2) *The American Journal of Comparative Law* 343

Safjan M., in Pietrzykowski K. (ed.), *Kodeks cywilny, Komentarz do art. 1-449*[10] (vol. 1, 9th edn, Warsaw: CH Beck, 2018)

Salvador Coderch P. and Ruiz García J.A., 'Reglas de interpretación' in Menéndez A. (dir.), *Comentarios a la Ley sobre condiciones generales de la contratación* (Madrid: Civitas, 2002)

Samuelsson J., *Tolkning och utfyllning. Undersökningar kring ett förmögenhetsrättsteoretiskt tema* (Uppsala: Iustus, 2008)

——, *Tolkningslärans gåta* (Uppsala: Iustus, 2011)

Sánchez Calero F., *Instituciones de Derecho Mercantil* (27th edn, Madrid: McGraw Hill, 2004)

Santos Junior E., *Sobre a Teoria da Interpretação dos negócios jurídicos* (Lisboa: Associação Académica da Faculdade de Direito de Lisboa, 1988)

Schauer F., 'Formalism' (1988) 97 *Yale Law Journal* 509

——, Playing by the Rules: A Philosophical Examination of Rule-Based Decision-Making in Law and in Life (Oxford: Oxford University Press, 1991)

Schelhaas H.N., 'Pacta sunt servanda bij commerciële contractanten. Over redelijkheid en billijkheid en objectieve uitleg bij handelscontracten', *Nederlands Tijdschrift voor Burgerlijk Recht* (2008) 150–160

Schelhaas H.N. and Valk W.L., *Uitleg van rechtshandelingen*, Preadviezen 2016 Vereniging voor Burgerlijk Recht (Zutphen: Uitgeverij Paris, 2016))

Schlechtriem P. and Schwenzer I. (eds.), *Kommentar zum Einheitlichen UN-Kaufrecht – Das Übereinkommen der Vereinten Nationen über Verträge über den internationalen Warenkauf (CISG),* commentary (6th edn, Munich: C.H. Beck Verlag, 2013)

Schlechtriem P. and Witz C., *Convention de Vienne sur les contrats de vente internationale de marchandises* (Paris: Dalloz, 2008)

Schlesinger R.B. (ed.), *Formation of Contracts: A Study of the Common Core of Legal Systems* (Dobbs Ferry, NY: Oceana, 1968)

Schmidt F., 'En culparegel vid avtalstolkning', *SvJT* (1960) 420 ff.

——, 'Typfall, partsavsikt och partsculpa', *SvJT* (1959) 497 ff.

Schmidt-Kessel M., 'Implied Terms – auf der Suche nach dem Funktionsäquivalent' in *Zeitschrift für vergleichende Rechtswissenschaft* (1996) 101

Schmittat K.-O., *Einführung in die Vertragsgestaltung* (4th edn, Munich: C.H. Beck Verlag, 2015)

Schroth P.W., 'Legal Translation' (1986) 34 *American Journal of Comparative Law* 47

Schulze R., Dörner H., Ebert I., Hoeren T., Kemper R. Saenger I., Schreiber K., Schulte-Nölke H. and Staudinger A., *Bürgerliches Gesetzbuch Handkommentar,* commentary (9th edn, Baden-Baden: Nomos Verlag, 2017)

Schwartz A. and Scott R.E., 'Contract Interpretation Redux' (2010) 119 *Yale Law Journal* 926

——, 'Contract Theory and the Limits of Contract Law' (2003) 113 *Yale Law Journal* 541

——, 'The Common Law of Contract and the Default Rule Project' (2016) 102 *Virginia Law Review* 1523

Schwartz A. and Watson J., 'Conceptualizing Contractual Interpretation' (2013) 42 *The Journal of Legal Studies* 1
Scognamiglio C., *Interpretazione del contratto e interessi dei contraenti* (Padua: CEDAM 1992)
Scott R.E., 'Text versus Context: The Failure of the Unitary Law of Contract Interpretation' in Buckley F.H. (ed.), *The American Illness: Essays on the Rule of Law* (New Haven, CT: Yale University Press, 2013)
——, 'The Case for Formalism in Relational Contract' (2000) 94 *Northwestern University Law Review* 847
——, 'The Death of Contract Law' (2004) 54 *University of Toronto Law Journal* 370
Scott R.E. and Triantis G.G., 'Anticipating Litigation in Contract Design' (2006) 115 *Yale Law Journal* 814
Scottish Law Commission, *Report on Interpretation in Private Law* (Scot Law Com No. 160, 1997)
——, *Report on Review of Contract Law: Formation, Interpretation, Remedies for Breach and Penalty Clauses* (Scot Law Com No. 252, 2018)
——, *Review of Contract Law: Discussion Paper on Interpretation of Contract* (Scot Law Com Discussion Paper 147, 2011)
Serrano Fernández M., *Estudio de Derecho comparado sobre la interpretación de los contratos* (Valencia: Tirant lo Blanch, 2005)
Sharrock R., 'The general principles of the Law of Contract' (2009) *Annual Survey of South African Law* 510
Shavell S., 'Damage Measures for Breach of Contract' (1980) 11 *Bell Journal of Economics* 466
Simon H.A., 'Theories of Bounded Rationality' in McGuire C.B. and Radner R. (eds.), *Decision and Organization* (Amsterdam: North-Holland, 1972)
Smits J. (ed.), *Elgar Encyclopaedia of Comparative Law* (2nd edn, Cheltenham: Edward Elgar, 2012)
Sobolewski P., 'Komentarz do art. 65 KC' in Osajda K. (ed.), *Kodeks cywilny. Komentarz* (21st edn, Warsaw: Legalis, 2019)
Soergel T., *Bürgerliches Gesetzbuch mit Einführungsgesetz und Nebengesetzen*, commentary (vol. II, 13th edn, Stuttgart: Kohlhammer Verlag, 2000)
Sonnekus J.C., *The Law of Estoppel in South Africa* (3rd edn, Durban: LexisNexis, 2012)
Stang F., *Innledning til formueretten* (3rd edn, Oslo: Aschehoug, 1935)
Stathopoulos M.P., 'Περί της μεθόδου ερμηνείας της δηλώσεως βουλήσεως' [On the method of interpretation of the declaration of intent] (1969) 25 *Neon Dikeon* 1 (Athens: reprint, unnamed publisher)
——, *Γενικό Ενοχικό Δίκαιο* [*General Part of the Law of Obligations*] (5th edn, Athens/Thessaloniki: Sakkoulas Publishers, 2018)
Stein P., 'The Two Schools of Jurists in the Early Roman Principate' (1972) 31 *Cambridge Law Review* 8
Stella Richter G., 'L'interpretazione dei contratti del consumatore', *Rivista trimestrale di diritto e procedura civile* (1997) 1034
Steyn J., 'Does Formalism Hold Sway in England' (1996) 49 *Current Legal Problems* 43
——, 'The Intractable Problem of the Interpretation of Legal Texts' (2003) 25 *Sydney Law Review* 5

Stone M., 'Formalism' in Coleman J. et al. (eds.), *The Oxford Handbook of Jurisprudence and Philosophy of Law* (Oxford: Oxford University Press, 2004)

Stoop P.N., 'The current status of the enforceability of contractual exemption clauses for the exclusion of liability in the South African Law of Contract' (2008) 20 *South African Mercantile Law Journal* 496

Sunstein C., 'Must Formalism Be Defended Empirically?' (1999) 66 *University of Chicago Law Review* 636

——, *Legal Reasoning and Political Conflict* (Oxford, Oxford University Press, 1998)

Tanja-van den Broek T.H., 'Een kwestie van uitleg', *WPNR* (2002) 6493, 430–436

Telaranta K.A., *Sopimusoikeus* (Helsinki: Lakimiesliiton kustannus, 1990)

Terré F., Simler Ph. and Lequette Y., *F. ChF. tt, Droit civil : les obligations* (Paris: Dalloz, 2018)

Testu F.-X., *Contrats d'affaires* (Paris: Dalloz, 2010)

Tirole J., 'Incomplete Contracts: Where Do We Stand?' (1999) 67 *Econometrica* 741

Tjittes R.J., 'Contractsuitleg', *RM Themis* (2003) 121–122

——, 'Uitleg van schriftelijke contracten', *RM Themis* (2005) 2–29

——, *Commercieel contractenrecht* (The Hague: Boom Juridisch, 2018)

——, *Uitleg van schriftelijke contracten* (Nijmegen: Ars Aequi Libri, 2009)

Tjong Tjin Tai T.F.E., 'Bewijs van de (inhoud van de) overeenkomst', *Nederlands Juristenblad* (2008) 699

Tomljenović V., Petrić S. and Mišćenić E., *Nepoštene ugovorne odredbe: europski standardi i hrvatska provedba* (Rijeka: Pravni fakultet Sveučilišta u Rijeci, 2013)

Trebilcock M.J., *The Limits of Freedom of Contract* (Cambridge, MA: Harvard University Press, 1997) 55

Triantis G.G., 'The Efficiency of Vague Contract Terms: A Response to the Schwartz-Scott Theory of U.CC. Article 2' (2002) 62 *Louisiana Law Review* 1065

Trimarchi P., *Istituzioni di diritto privato* (Milan: Giuffrè, 2016)

Tuomisto J., 'Julkisuusperiaate ja vilpittömän mielen suoja' in Saarnilehto A. (editor-in-chief), *Varallisuusoikeus* (2nd edn, Helsinki: SanomaPro, 2012)

Turco C., 'Note in tema di ermeneutica contrattuale e principio di buona fede', *Rivista critica di diritto privato* (1991) 305

Ulmer P., Brandner E. and Hensen H.-D., *AGB-Recht* (11th edn, Cologne: Dr. Otto Schmidt Verlag, 2011)

Uría R., Menéndez A. et al., *Curso de Derecho mercantil* (vol. II, 2nd edn, Cizur Menor: Thomson-Civitas, 2007)

Ussing H., *Aftaler paa Formuerettens Omraade* (3rd edn, Copenhagen: Gad, 1950)

Vahlén L., 'Bidrag till avtalstolkningens systematik', *JFT* (1964) 380 ff.

——, *Avtal och tolkning* (Stockholm: Norstedt, 1960)

——, *Formkravet vid fastighetsköp. Särskilt dess inverkan på regler om förutsättningar och fel* (Stockholm: Norstedt, 1951)

Valk W.L., 'Kijk naar jezelf', *Contracteren* (2002) 57

Van Dunne J.M., *Verbintenissenrecht. Deel 1. Contractenrecht* (5th edn, The Hague: Kluwer, 2004)

Van Huyssteen L.F., Lubbe G.F. and Reinecke M.F.B., *Contract: general principles* (5th edn, Cape Town: Juta and Co. Ltd, 2016)

Van Zeben C.J., Du Pon J.W. and Olthof M.M., *Parlementaire Geschiedenis van het nieuwe Burgerlijk Wetboek* (1981), Boek 3, Boek 5, Boek 6

Vattier Fuenzalida C., 'La interpretación del contrato, entre la intención de las partes y el criterio de una persona razonable', Madrid: *Actualidad Civil*, 14 (2010) 1–40

Veenstra H., 'Uitleg van een collectieve regeling tot vergoeding van massaschade', *Nederlands Tijdschrift voor Burgerlijk Recht* (2007) 2–8

Venuti L., *The Translator's Invisibility: A History of Translation* (2nd edn, London: Routledge, 1995/2008)

Vermeule A., 'Three Strategies of Interpretation' (2005) 42 *San Diego Law Review* 607

Viglione F., *Metodi e modelli di interpretazione del contratto. Prospettive di un dialogo tra common law e civil law* (Turin: Giappichelli, 2011)

Vogenauer, S., *The Drafting of the CESL: An Assessment and Suggestions for Improvement* (15 October 2012), available at http://www.europarl.europa.eu/RegData/etudes/note/join/2012/462475/IPOL-JURI_NT(2012)462475_EN.pdf

von Bar C., Clive E. and Schulte-Nölke H. (eds.), *Principles, Definitions and Model Rules of European Private Law, Draft Common Frame of Reference (DCFR)*, Interim Outline Edition (Munich: Sellier, 2008)

——, *Principles, Definitions and Model Rules of European Private Law, Draft Common Frame of Reference (DCFR)*, Full Edition (Munich: Sellier, 2009)

von Savigny F.K., *System des Heutige Romanes Rechts* (vol. 3, 1840)

Walker D.M., *The Law of Contract and Related Obligations in Scotland* (3rd edn, London: T & T Clark, 1995)

Wallis M., 'What's in a word? Interpretation through the eyes of ordinary readers' (2010) 127 *South African Law Journal* 673

Węgrzynowski Ł., 'Sądowe ustalanie treści stosunku umownego', Przegląd Prawa Handlowego 2007/5, pp. 44–49

Whitford W., 'Relational Contracts and the New Formalism' (2004) *Wisconsin Law Review* 631

Wicker G., Racine J.B., Sautonie-Laguionie L. and Bujoli F. (eds.), *Principes Contractuels Commun. Projet de Cadre Commun de Référence* (Paris: Association Henri Capitant, 2008)

Wigmore J.H., *Wigmore on Evidence* (vol. 9, 9th edn, Boston: Little, Brown and Company, 1981)

Wilhelmsson T., *Vakiosopimus ja kohtuuttomat sopimusehdot* (new 3rd edn, Helsinki: Talentum, 2008)

Williamson O.E., *Antitrust Economics: Mergers, Contracting, and Strategic Behaviour* (New York: Basil Blackwell, 1987)

——, *The Economic Institutions of Capitalism* (New York: Free Press, 1985)

——, 'Transaction Cost Economics: The Governance of Contractual Relations' (1979) 22 *Journal of Law and Economics* 233

Windscheid B., *Lehrbuch des Pandektenrechts* (vol. I, 6th edn, 1887)

Wissink M.H., 'Chapter 5: Interpretation. Art. 5:101–5:107' in Busch D. et al. (eds.), *The Principles of European Contract Law and Dutch Law. A Commentary* (Nijmegen: Ars Aequi Libri; The Hague/London/New York: Kluwer Law International, 2002)

——, 'Uitleg volgens *Haviltex* of de CAO-norm? Over een vloeiende overgang en de noodzaak om toch te kiezen', *WPNR* (2004) 6579, 407–15

Wolter A., *Prawo cywilne, Zarys części ogólnej* (8th edn, Warsaw: Państwowe Wydawnictwo Naukowe, 1986)

Woodward W., 'Neoformalism in a Real World of Forms' (2001) *Wisconsin Law Review* 971
Ziccardi F., 'Interpretazione (Interpretazione del negozio giuridico)' in *Enciclopedia giuridica Treccani*, XVII (Rome, 1978)
——, *Le norme interpretative speciali* (Milan: Giuffrè, 1972)
Zimmermann R., *The Law of Obligations: Roman Foundations of the Civilian Tradition* (Oxford: Clarendon Press, 1990)
Zimmermann R., Visser D. and Reid K. (eds.), *Mixed Legal Systems in Comparative Perspective: Property and Obligations in Scotland and South Africa* (Oxford: Oxford University Press, 2004)
Zoll F., Rachwał A. and U. Ernst., *Prawo cywilne, Część ogólna* (1st edn, Warsaw: LexisNexis, 2011)
Zubović A., 'Primjena trgovačkih običaja' (2006) 27 *Zbornik Pravnog fakulteta Sveučilišta u Rijeci* 307
Zweigert K. and Kötz H., *An Introduction to Comparative Law*, trans. T. Weir (3rd edn. Oxford: Oxford University Press, 1998)

APPENDIX I

The Editorial Instructions for the National Reporters

1. INTRODUCTION

Thank you for agreeing to write a national report for the Common Core of European Private Law study on the Interpretation of Commercial Contracts. We are delighted to be working with you in this unique, international research project. To allow for a substantial, consistent and comprehensive comparative legal analysis, it is vital that all national reports have the same focus, address the same issues and do so in the same manner. That is why we kindly ask you to carefully study and closely follow the instructions in this document. These instructions include both general *Common Core* standards and guidelines specifically for the Interpretation of Commercial Contracts project. They cover both the answering of the questionnaire and formatting issues.

The following documents should be treated as forming integral parts of these instructions:

- 'The Approach:' an explanation of the overall approach of the Common Core of European Private Law, by the Project's editors, Ugo Mattei and Mauro Bussani. Please pay particular attention to the sections on 'Method – The Cornell Project' and 'Method – Legal Formants';
- 'Instructions about how to answer the questionnaires': Appendix to 'The Approach' covering general Common Core standards for national reports. Take particular account of the distinctions of 'operative rules', 'descriptive formants' and 'meta-legal formants'.

2. THE APPROACH

2.1. THE GENERAL 'COMMON CORE-APPROACH'

The method of the Common Core of European Private Law is 'factual'; what is compared are not doctrinal systems but, rather, the most likely outcome, the so-called operative rules, that would be applied in specific hypothetical cases in the various legal systems. This analysis is informed not merely by legal rules, but by any element in the legal system that may determine or influence the legal outcome, hence by any relevant 'legal formant'. Moreover, the Common Core approach makes use of questionnaires. These contain hypothetical problems, based on which the most likely solutions in the respective national legal systems are compared.

2.2. THE SPECIFIC APPROACH OF THE INTERPRETATION STUDY

When applied to the comparative study of the Interpretation of Contracts, the general Common Core approach entails the following. What is compared are the *ways* in which contracts are interpreted, rather than the meanings that would be attributed to the language of the contracts. In other words, the objects of comparison are the 'interpretation factors', the factors that a court may find relevant in deciding how to interpret a contract. The possible *content* of a contractual clause is therefore not compared; you do not need to report *what* a certain contractual clause would mean or ought to mean in your legal system.

Consequently, in their national reports the respondents aim to predict which interpretation method the court would most likely apply if presented with the problem in question. This prediction is based on any of the possible relevant 'legal formants', from legal rules and case law, to settled practice and prevailing schools of thought in academic literature.

2.3. THE SCOPE OF THE INTERPRETATION STUDY

The national reports should not be extended to address matters beyond the scope of the study. The scope of this study is limited to written, commercial agreements, between professionals 'at arm's length'. The study does not include the interpretation of unilateral private legal documents, such as wills or deeds. Also excluded from the study are oral agreements and specific types of agreements such as consumer, labour and arbitration agreements, and agreements for the transfer of real property.

Further, the term 'interpretation' must be understood broadly. It does not merely involve the methods of ascertaining, for example, the actual linguistic meaning or the actual intentions of parties, but also what, according to the national legal system, the contract *should* be understood to mean, or what the parties *should* have intended.

3. GUIDELINES FOR ANSWERING THE QUESTIONNAIRE

In addition, please address at least the following aspects concerning all questions of the questionnaire:

(i) You are asked to start your report with Opening Remarks, being a general introduction for your jurisdiction, of no more than 800 words.

Here you can discuss more general matters that you consider important for all or most cases, or any other items relating to contract interpretation that you think the reader should know about your legal system in advance.

(ii) In your legal system, is there a certain order or hierarchy in which the discussed interpretation factors ought to be considered?

(iii) Legal formants:
Please integrate the answers to the following question into your legal analysis:
- What are the legal formants from which you derive your answer? For example, please explicate in the text or in footnotes if your answer is based on particular legislative rules (including domestic, European and international); rules of evidence or other procedural rules; doctrine or scholarly writing; 'unwritten law' or legal principles; maxims or canons of interpretation; a general interpretation practice applied by (lower) courts; or any other relevant legal or extra-legal formants.
- Do the various legal formants give rise to the same answer, or do they point in different directions? If applicable, acknowledge and do not eliminate possible conflicts between relevant legal formants.
- Moreover, do not attempt to reconcile or hide diverging opinions in the relevant literature.
- What is the rationale or origin of the legal formants on which your answer rests?
- Have there been significant (recent) developments regarding the subject matter in question?

(iv) With respect to legal formants involving doctrinal considerations:
- Indicate in each case the nature of interpretation in question. For example, is the interpretation method at hand aimed at finding the intent of the parties; the linguistic meaning of the contract at hand; the 'reasonable' construction of the agreement; or any other objective?
- In your legal system, is the question at hand considered a question of law or rather a question of fact?
- Does the question in your legal system fall within the scope of the law of contractual interpretation, another subject of contract law, or a different field of law altogether?

(v) Important style notes:
- Your report should not include comparisons with other national legal systems of international or European instruments such as the PECL, DCFR, and so on. Any elements that you find to be characteristic of your legal system should be explained without legal comparative analyses. On the other hand, if you think particular comparative legal findings

are relevant to the project, please share these with the volume editors in a separate communication.

- Do not present your observations as if you are a judge making a legal decision. That is, do not use sentences such as 'Article X of the Civil Code determines that in this case … etc.' The Common Core approach entails that reporters operate as observers who estimate how a question would likely be answered in his/her legal system. Hence, legal rules are only signposts or indicators – 'legal formants' – for such an answer (e.g. 'Article X is likely to serve as an argument for … etc.').
- Do not add facts to the case, as to avoid incomparability with other reports. However, if you feel that your answer to the question clearer when contrasted with alternative facts, phrase this point in hypotheticals (e.g. 'This would not have been the case if …').
- The following items should not be addressed in the body of the text but instead in footnotes or the Opening Remarks:
  - information about your legal system that does not affect your answer to the question at hand but which you nonetheless find to be informative to the reader in this context;
  - issues that may relate to the question but do not involve the actual interpretation of the contract;
  - notifications to the readers whenever the facts of the cases and the focus of the question does not agree comfortably with your legal system, for example when the assumptions of the case or question would appear to be odd assumptions in the context of your legal system.

(vi) Quality

Lastly, we ask you to take the utmost care in making your observations. First, for the reader, you will be the 'spokesperson' of your legal system. Legal scholars, practicing lawyers and students will consult your national report to gain knowledge on contractual interpretation in your legal system. Second, the overall comparative analyses and conclusions of the book are entirely dependent on the accuracy and sophistication of each single national report. Therefore, we would welcome you to invite colleagues in your legal system to read and critique your report prior to submission.

4. FORMATTING GUIDELINES

4.1. UK STYLE

For the drafting of your report, please adhere to the following guidelines.

4.2. LANGUAGE AND QUOTATION GUIDELINES FOR DOMESTIC LEGAL TERMS

- For the purposes of both formatting and comparative analysis, it is vital that in all national reports legal terms or legal phrases referring to domestic legal concepts or legal institutions are placed within single inverted commas (' ...'). This applies to all national reports, regardless of whether the language of your legal system is English or not.
- If the language of your legal system is not English, legal terms or words naming domestic legal concepts or legal institutions should be written in the language of your legal system. For example, do not use terms such as 'good faith' unless, of course, the actual English words 'good faith' are used in your legal system (e.g. the English, Scottish and South African systems).
- Place the domestic legal term in its original language inside inverted commas. The term should be followed directly (in the body of the text, not in footnotes) by an English translation, placed in square brackets ([...]). This English translation should be as literal as possible, even when it makes the translation look odd. An explanation or description of the domestic concept should follow in the following sentences (not in footnotes), in the English language. Both the literal translation and subsequent explanation should under all circumstances avoid referencing to English or other foreign legal concepts or institutions that you may consider to be equivalent or near equivalent. The reason is that otherwise, the report would contain a perhaps implicit comparative legal analysis, which would affect the overall comparative legal analysis carried out by the editors. Further, the explanation should be in layman's terms, that is, without further domestic legal terminology.

  Example: 'This problem is solved with reference to the concept of 'aanvullende werking van de redelijkheid en billijkheid' [the complementary effect of reasonableness and fairness]. This concept entails that ... etc.'

- Although a literal translation between square brackets will not be necessary if the language of the national legal system is English, further description or explanation should still be provided, in the text directly after the use of the term.

  Example: 'Reference is often made to the 'four corner rule.' This rule entails that ... etc.'

- Quotations from, for example, court judgements, authoritative texts, textbooks, etc., are better avoided, especially quotes that exceed a single sentence. However, if you feel that it is nonetheless vital to use a quotation, please phrase the quote in the body of the text using the original language of your jurisdiction, and subsequently provide a translation of the quote in the footnote when the original language is not English. Here, too, the translation should be as literal as possible, without using any legal terms that you deem equivalent in the English language. As with using domestic legal terms, explain the significance of the quotation in the body of the text. Please explain in layman's terms, that is, while avoiding further domestic legal terminology as much as possible.

4.3. REFERENCE SYSTEM AND BIBLIOGRAPHY

Please list at the beginning of your national report, tables of all relevant legislative sources and legal cases that you have used in the answers to all cases. Next, provide a list of abbreviations used in your report. Subsequently, include the aforementioned Opening Remarks of no more than 800 words. At the end of the full national report, please include a bibliography with all the sources cited throughout the text of all cases, and in all notes, as well as any other important titles that you think should be included. Lastly, use footnotes rather than endnotes. Number the notes in an unbroken sequence per case, not throughout the whole report.

4.4. WORD COUNT AND LAYOUT

In light of the maximum number of words requested by the publisher, the full national report should consist of approximately 8,800 words. This includes the Opening Remarks (max. 800 words) and footnotes, but excludes tables of statutes and cases, list of abbreviations and bibliography. This word limit means that your answers need to be concise and to the point. However, whenever appropriate, you can decide to elaborate upon points in your answers to some of the questions and be brief in answers to other questions, as long as ultimately the total word count of the full report will be approximately 8,800 words. If by answering one question you need to address the same issue that you already discussed in your answer to a question under a previous case, you may refer back to that answer, as long as it does not take away from clarity and precision.

Please use Times New Roman as your font (size 12pt) and save your file in Word format only. Give your document the following title: 'InterpretationContracts_NationalReport_[name legal system]'. The file need only be sent electronically, as an attachment to an e-mail to the volume editors.

If you have any questions relating to formatting or about how to answer the questionnaire, do not hesitate to contact the volume editors.

Good luck and thank you!

Jaap Baaij
David Cabrelli
Laura Macgregor

APPENDIX II

The Questionnaire

CASE 1: JEWELLERS KING

'Premier' is the owner of numerous retail units in a local shopping centre. At present, it leases two units to two jewellers. It decides to lease a third unit for 15 years to 'Jewellers King', a company also operating a retail jewellery sales business. Clause 12(d) of the lease contract with Jewellers King provides: 'With regard to any of its retail units, Premier shall not lease any such unit – other than Jewellers King's unit and two other units only – for a use entailing the retail sale of jewellery.' Within 19 months of entering into the lease contract, Premier grants a lease of one of its other retail units to a fourth jeweller. Jewellers King is infuriated. It argues that Clause 12(d) prohibits Premier from granting another lease at the shopping centre to a jeweller. Premier is surprised. It argues that the phrase 'two other units only' refers to two units in addition to the three units that it is already leasing to Jewellers King and the two other jewellers. In effect, it concludes, under Clause 12(d) it is therefore permitted to let up to a total of five jewellery retail units. Jewellers King disagrees. It argues that the phrase 'two other units only' is a reference to the two units that were *already* let to jewellers. Hence, since Jewellers King was the third jeweller to lease one of Premier's retail units, the total number of three jewellery retail units had been reached. Premier was thus prohibited from leasing any more retail units to other jewellers. Premier stands firm. In order to support its reading of Clause 12(d), it refers to the fifth recital of the preamble of the lease contract, which reads: 'Whereas Premier intends to let no more than a total of five units at the shopping centre for the purposes of the retail sale of jewellery'. Therefore, Premier argues, Clause 12(d) cannot be interpreted as having the effect that it is in breach of the lease contract by letting a fourth retail unit to a jeweller.

1 [Preamble] Assume that the language of Clause 12(d) is ambiguous. What role, if any, may the preamble play in corroborating Premier's interpretation of Clause 12(d)? Would it make a difference if it involved not a preamble but another Clause in the contract?
2 [Information Brochure] Would your answer be different if Premier had not referred to the preamble but rather to Premier's information brochure with similar text?

3 [The Contract's Purpose] Assume that neither the preamble nor an information brochure had mentioned anything relating to the purpose of Clause 12(d) of the lease contract. What role, if any, may Premier's reliance on the purpose or objective of Clause 12(d) of the lease contract, being that it was restricted to letting five units at the shopping centre, still have played in the interpretation of Clause 12(d)?

CASE 2: BOTANICAL FRUITS

'Imperial Real Estate' owns a small food court and lets spaces to various vendors. It enters into a lease agreement with 'Botanical Fruits', a store which sells fruits and fruit juices. The mall already includes a vegetable vendor. Because Imperial strives for the biggest possible variety of products sold in its small shopping mall, the director of Imperial requires that Clause 8 of the lease contract reads: 'Botanical Fruits will abstain from selling: … (g) any vegetables or vegetable products.' Botanical Fruits accepts. Soon after Botanical Fruits opens business, Imperial discovers that Botanical Fruits is selling aubergines, tomatoes and cucumbers, as well as juices containing these products, in large quantities. After warning Botanical Fruits numerous times that, under Clause 8(g) of the lease contract, the latter is to cease selling aubergines, tomatoes and cucumbers immediately, Imperial holds Botanical Fruits in breach of its obligations and terminates the lease contract. Botanical Fruits disagrees that it breached its contractual obligations and contests the termination of the contract. As Botanical Fruits tried to tell Imperial recently, botanically speaking, cucumbers are ripened ovaries of a flowering plant, and botanical experts therefore classify aubergines, tomatoes and cucumbers as fruits. Imperial had heard Botanical Fruits' arguments before but found them simply preposterous. In ordinary, common language for everyday purposes, Imperial contends, aubergines, tomatoes and cucumbers are considered vegetables.

1 [Technical and Ordinary Meaning] Assume that both Imperial and Botanical Fruits are correct; the technical, botanical meaning of 'vegetables' excludes aubergines, tomatoes and cucumbers, and the common or ordinary meaning of 'vegetables' includes these items. What relative weight will be attached to both the technical or ordinary meaning play in the interpretation of Clause 8(g)?

2 [Expertise] Would your answer to Question 1 be different if Imperial had many decades of experience in the food retail industry, and its director had an academic background in botanical studies?

CASE 3: COCKTAIL PARTIES

Jill is the manager of the professional event organiser 'PartyMax', who will host exclusive cocktail parties in the harbour during the Annual Film Festival. For that purpose, she rents a luxury yacht for the duration of 14 days from John, acting as director of 'Afloat'. Jill and John agree in Clause 8 of the agreement that 'PartyMax shall have the opportunity to return the yacht after seven days of the agreement, in which case Afloat will refund PartyMax a sum applicable to the remaining period.' Jill pays the full rent of €140,000 upfront. Nine days after commencement of the rental period, Jill returns the yacht and requests that PartyMax receive a refund of the rental fee of €50,000 for the remaining five days. Afloat refuses and argues that Clause 8 means that PartyMax could exercise the option to return the yacht only within the first seven days of the agreement. Jill disagrees and contends that the clause means that PartyMax could return the yacht at any time as soon as seven days have passed. In support of its understanding of Clause 8 of the rental agreement, Jill refers to an email exchange that took place days before the conclusion of the agreement. In one email Jill writes: 'I do not know yet whether we will actually need the yacht in the second week. Will the contract allow me to end the rental agreement whenever I want?' In a reply, John writes: 'Don't worry about it. Under the rental agreement, you will be allowed to bring back the yacht at any time after the first week and be refunded.'

1 [Email Communication] Assume that the language of Clause 8 is ambiguous and that the email communication between Jill and John sufficiently shows that John's understanding of Clause 8 was the same as Jill's. If in your legal system the email communication itself should not be considered to constitute an agreement or a modification to the agreement, what role, if any, may the emails between John and Jill play in the interpretation of Clause 8?
2 [Later Emails] What would your answer to Question 1 have been had the emails been written after rather than before the conclusion of the contract, for example at some time during the first week of the rental agreement?
3 [Handwritten Letters and Oral Comments] What would your answers to Questions 1 and 2 have been if the communication between John and Jill consisted not of emails but instead of handwritten letters sent by regular mail, or of orally made comments?

CASE 4: ANIMAL WASTE

Guy is the director of 'Meat 'n' Bones', a meat processing company. Bernard runs a professional animal farm. Guy and Bernard conclude a contract according to which Bernard will supply Guy every week with 5,000 kilos of meat products, described in Clause 14 as 'animal waste and animal carcasses intended for human consumption'. Both agree that six months after concluding the contract, Bernard will start making his weekly deliveries. Six months have passed, and Bernard has by now delivered his first shipment of 5,000 kilos of meat products. However, Meat 'n' Bones refuses to pay Bernard the full purchase price that they initially agreed on. Guy explains that between 2,000 and 2,500 kilos of the delivery consists of animal waste that is *not* intended for human consumption, which he says is useless to the operations of Meat 'n' Bones. This, Guy maintains, is contrary to Clause 14, in which the qualification 'intended for human consumption' applies to both 'animal waste' and 'animal carcasses'. Bernard is baffled. He understands Clause 14 to mean that the qualification 'intended for human consumption' *only* applies to 'animal carcasses' and not also to 'animal waste'. To him, Clause 14, therefore, includes *all* animal waste: both waste intended for human consumption and waste that is not. Moreover, Bernard is able to show that immediately after the conclusion of their contract, Guy had contacted Bernard, informing the latter that he filed a request for a government permit to store and process animal waste not destined for human consumption at the Meat 'n' Bones plant, including animal protein, rendered fats and pet food. Additionally, Bernard can also present evidence showing that days before he delivered the first shipping, Guy's request was denied. The fact that Guy filed this request, Bernard argues, shows that Guy had the same understanding of Clause 14 as Bernard had.

Assume that the language of Clause 14 is ambiguous. Also assume that the fact that Meat 'n' Bones filed and informed Guy of the request above shows that Guy shared Bernard's interpretation of Clause 14. What role may the fact that Meat 'n' Bones filed the request for this permit play in the interpretation of Clause 14?

CASE 5: SHOWER VALVES

'Engineering Solutions' enters into a contract with 'Bath & Shower', under which the former is to supply the latter for a period of five years with thermostatic shower valves as intermediate products. Bath & Shower treats these thermostatic shower valves and sells the end products to its customers. Both parties understand and do not dispute that intermediate products are products that are supplied not to be sold to consumers in their existing form, but rather to be combined with other products to form a final end product to be sold to consumers. Clause 6 of the contract stipulates: 'Throughout the duration of this Agreement, Engineering Solutions hereby undertakes not to sell or supply products to third parties within the territory in which Bath & Shower operates.' After a certain period, Bath & Shower finds out that after concluding the contract, Engineering Solutions has started supplying its thermostatic shower valves as intermediate products to several competitors of Bath & Shower. Bath & Shower accuses Engineering Solutions of acting contrary to Clause 6 of the contract and consequently holds Engineering Solutions in breach of contract and liable for damages. Engineering Solutions refutes the claim of Bath & Shower. It argues that the term 'products' in Clause 6 refers to end products of the sort that Bath & Shower sells to its customers, not intermediate products that Engineering Solution produces. Hence, Engineering Solutions concludes, Clause 6 merely precludes it from entering the market in which Bath & Shower operates. It does not preclude it from supplying or selling intermediate products to competitors of Bath & Shower. In defence of its understanding of Clause 6, Engineering Solutions refers to the General Conditions applicable to the contract. Clause IX of the General Conditions stipulates: 'The Supplier is not precluded from selling or supplying directly or indirectly to third parties the same or similar intermediate products that it supplies under the Contract to the Other Party.' Clause IX, therefore, Engineering Solutions argues, shows that Clause 6 of the contract cannot be made to mean that Engineering Solutions is precluded from selling or supplying intermediate products. Hence, it concludes, the word 'products' in Clause 6 should be interpreted to refer to end products.

1 [The Role of General Conditions] Assume that the term 'products' in Clause 6 is ambiguous. What weight can be given to Clause IX of the General Conditions in the interpretation of Clause 6?
2 [The User of General Conditions] Would it make a difference if it was Engineering Solutions who drafted and used the General Conditions?

CASE 6: CALL CENTRE

'Print Master' is a large print and fax machine seller. It enters into a five-year outsource contract with 'Premium Phone Services' (PPS), which is operating a call centre. Under this agreement, PPS provides to Print Master inbound and outbound call centre services for the purpose of order taking and customer service. This contract also includes a so-called service level agreement, under which PPS is to execute frequent monitoring of the service quality provided by PPS's call centre agents to Print Master's customers. Clause 16(k) provides: 'Premium Phone Services will conduct bi-weekly randomly augmented service quality tests and send the results of these tests to Print Master within 24 hours.'

One month after concluding the outsource contract but before either PPS or Print Master have undertaken any performance, PPS transfers its rights in the agreement to another call centre operator, 'Magnificall', in response to a downward turn in the market. A month after all parties involved validly documented the transfer and Magnificall started its call centre services, Print Master contacts Magnificall and protests that Print Master only received a report on Magnificall's quality tests twice in the last month. Magnificall dismisses the complaints and argues that under Clause 16(k) it is obliged to conduct quality tests and send these reports only once every two weeks. It refuses to conduct these tests more often since that would bring about considerable costs. Print Master contends that 'bi-weekly' means twice a week, not once every two weeks. The transfer agreement was silent on this matter. The issue also never came up between Print Master and PPS. In support of its reading of Clause 16(k), Print Master presents evidence at the formation of the outsource agreement, which shows that both Print Master and PPS agreed that that said quality tests would be conducted twice per week.

Assume that Clause 16(k) is ambiguous, and the evidence offered by Print Master indeed indicates without doubt that Print Master and PPS both intended Clause 16(k) to mean that said quality tests would be conducted twice per week. Also assume that such evidence is sufficient to satisfy your jurisdiction that there was a common understanding or intention arising between the parties and that the transfer of rights was legally valid. How much weight, if any, may be given to the meaning that Print Master and PPS attributed to Clause 16(k), considering the fact that PPS is no longer a party to the agreement and Magnificall did not take part in the negotiation, drafting and conclusion of this clause?

CASE 7: BISCUIT

'Hartley Ceramics' is a company which makes ceramics. 'Arkwright Homecare' is a retailer. Both are small companies, formed relatively recently. In December 2011, the managing director of Hartley Ceramics, Ian, entered into a contract with the then managing director of Arkwright Homecare, John, agreeing that Hartley Ceramics would supply Arkwright Homecare with 500 pieces of specialist ceramics. Clause 1 of the contract describes the pieces to be delivered as 'biscuit'. After the commencement of the contract, Ian was replaced by Barton, who is now the manager at Hartley. In early 2012, Hartley delivers the first consignment of pieces of ceramics at Arkwright Homecare's offices. However, John is surprised when he discovers that the pieces that Hartley delivered are fired but not glazed. He presents background material at the formation of the agreement, which shows that both he and Ian understood 'biscuit' to mean fired and glazed. John refuses to take delivery of the ceramic pieces but is nonetheless set on having the contract performed as he interprets it. Barton refutes John's claim. He argues that 'biscuit' is a well-known and established term in the ceramics industry, used to indicate that the pieces are fired but not glazed. Apparently, Barton continues, John and Ian both attributed the same but unconventional meaning to the term 'biscuit'. Therefore, Barton concludes, Hartley performed the contract properly and Arkwright should accept the delivery.

Assume that the term 'biscuit' does indeed normally mean fired but not glazed, and that Hartley Ceramics can provide sufficient evidence to prove that both Ian and John were negotiating on a shared but unusual understanding that 'biscuit' meant both fired and glazed. If the background material satisfies the requirements for it to be accepted by a court as evidence in your jurisdiction, what weight can be given to the fact that Ian and John were negotiating on a common but incorrect understanding of 'biscuit' in interpreting Clause 1 of the contract?

CASE 8: CRATES OF BEER

'Goldwater' operates a beer brewery and 'Carryon' operates a road haulage company. The two companies enter into a contract in January 2012 in terms of which Carryon agrees to transport Goldwater's beer to a wholesale depot located 50 kilometres away. Clause 8 of the contract governs the collection of the beer by Carryon. It provides: 'Goldwater will make the beer available to Carryon at the brewery premises located at [details of the address].' In February, Carryon's driver arrives at the brewery and finds that the crates of beer that he is to collect are located on the fourth floor of the brewery. He will be unable, without assistance, to move the crates to the ground floor and load them on to the haulage vehicle. When he asks for assistance, he is told that none is available due to redundancies at the brewery. Carryon's driver leaves the brewery without collecting the beer. Carryon refuses to perform, arguing that Goldwater should have made the crates available at the front entrance of the brewery. Goldwater disagrees. It made the beer available at its premises, as was agreed in Clause 8 of the contract. It, therefore, raises an action against Carryon for breach of contract. Carryon disagrees with Goldwater's reading of Clause 8. It argues that Goldwater and Carryon have an ongoing business relationship and that under every previous contract between them, Goldwater consistently made the crates of beer available at the front entrance of the brewery. Clause 8, Carryon concludes, must be understood in the light of these facts.

Assume that the previous contracts between Goldwater and Carryon were identical in all significant respects. Also assume that the contract does not specify on which floor the crates are to be collected and that there is no local trade custom relevant to the matter at hand. To what extent may the manner of performance of the previous contracts between Carryon and Goldwater be given weight in the interpretation of Clause 8 of the 2010 contract?

CASE 9: CRYSTAL VASES

'Murray' is a company that manufactures crystal vases. It has entered into a contract with 'OnTrack', an operator of cargo transportation by container freight trains. Clause 4 of their contract provides that Murray will be responsible for delivering its goods to 'Distribution Warehouse 10, at the local freight train station.' Murray delivers a consignment of goods to Distribution Warehouse 10. OnTrack refuses to ship them, however, explaining that delivery at a freight train terminal means delivery up to the actual container terminal. There the goods will be loaded into the appropriate containers. In fact, Murray delivered the goods to the entrance of the Distribution Warehouse, which is at least 800 metres away from the actual container terminal. The nature of the goods in question makes carriage of them, even over short distances, a complex task. Murray disputes OnTrack's view. It argues that Clause 4 of the contract is very clear on the issue of where the goods were to be delivered. It raises an action against OnTrack for breach of contract. OnTrack contests this action. It argues that Clause 4 must be read in light of the fact that it is a local custom of trade that goods are delivered up to the container terminal.

Assume that there is indeed, as OnTrack argues, a local custom of trade that goods are delivered by the manufacturers to the container terminal. How much weight is the court likely to give to this local custom of trade in interpreting Clause 4?

CASE 10: THE MACHINE

'Bingham' is a company specialising in the development of industrial machinery to help businesses become more economically efficient. Bingham enters into a contract with 'Peel' in terms of which Bingham develops a custom-made machine that rationalises Peel's production of copper wire which it sells to the construction industry. Clause 2 provides that, in return, Peel is due to pay a purchase price consisting of both a modest initial sum for the development of the machine and an additional 35% of the profits made by Peel by using the device over the next five years. Bingham and Peel have agreed to use a method by which they calculate the 35% of the profit – there is no dispute on this point.

After Peel has paid the initial sum and Bingham has manufactured and delivered the machinery, time passes, and Bingham hears nothing from Peel. Bingham contacts Peel on several occasions throughout the next year. The answer from Peel is always the same: Peel has chosen not to use the machine. Therefore, Peel reasons, there is no profit from which to calculate Peel's payment of 35% to Bingham. Bingham is very unhappy about this, having calculated the overall profit from the transaction assuming the use of the machine by Peel. In fact, as matters stand, Bingham contends, this will be a losing contract. Bingham further argues that, even though there is no clause in the contract which binds Peel to make use of the machine, Peel must be understood to have, in effect, taken it upon itself to pay more than merely the initial sum. To this end, Bingham had instructed an independent accountant to produce a report which estimates the amount of profit which would have been earned had the machine been used. In addition, Bingham continues, because Peel made the promise to pay 35%, Bingham was justified in expecting Peel to actually use the machine. Finally, Bingham concludes, it is simply not fair to interpret Clause 2 as Peel advocates.

Assume that the contract is a valid contract; that there is no local trade custom relevant to the matter at hand; no prior course of dealing between the parties; and that no evidence of any communication regarding the use of the machine. Without providing an interpretation of Clause 2 yourself, explain the factors the courts may be willing to attach weight to the interpretation of Clause 2, including the relative weight attached to each.

INDEX

D

E

www.ingramcontent.com/pod-product-compliance
Ingram Content Group UK Ltd.
Pitfield, Milton Keynes, MK11 3LW, UK
UKHW051918100926
8556IPUK00021B/1246

9 781780 689593